DANISH STUDIO C
1950 – 2010
IN DESIGNMUSEUM DANMARK

Bodil Busk Laursen

Catalogue of the collection in
DESIGNMUSEUM DANMARK 2017

PREFACE		5
INTRODUCTION	Danish ceramics at the beginning of the 20th century	10
	The classical period of Danish studio ceramics 1950 – 1980	14
	New trends and developments 1980 – 2010	17
	Danish studio ceramics in an international context	27
CATALOGUE	About this catalogue: Danish Studio Ceramics 1950 – 2010	32
	Key to structure of catalogue entries	42
	List of names of ceramicists and artists	44
	Biographical summaries and catalogue of works	47
APPENDICES	The 'Lark' table service	346
	Glossary of terms used in ceramics	352
	Ceramic exhibitions in Designmuseum Danmark 1950 – 2010	354
	Select bibliography	357

PREFACE

Millennia have gone by since the first pots were made in Denmark. The rich resources of clay in the country have been used by people since the Stone Age and have resulted in products that range from building materials to products for household use and to sculptural artworks. The plasticity of clay, with its many potential uses, has inspired a continual process of developing shapes, forms of expression, craft techniques and technology.

Danish Studio Ceramics 1950-2010 is the prosaic title of this catalogue of Designmuseum Danmark's collection of unique ceramic works from the 60-year period covering the post-war years and leading up to the present. The catalogue describes 632 works by 133 ceramicists and artists, and in doing so gives an overview of the diversity and high quality of Danish ceramics. This process documents and throws into relief the paradigm shift which has taken place since the 1980s when handmade functional ceramic articles for domestic use began to be overtaken by free sculptural forms of expression, and at the same time the centre of gravity in this field began to move from a nationally-rooted central basis towards extended interaction with the international ceramic scene.

The aim of this catalogue of Danish Studio Ceramics 1950 – 2010 is to provide a nuanced depiction of a remarkable epoch in the history of Danish ceramics, as represented in Designmuseum Danmark's collections, which have not previously been documented in a comprehensive form and which have only been exhibited on a limited scale.

In the years of growing prosperity after the end of the 2nd World War, numerous solo studio workshops were set up, all over Denmark, by professionally trained ceramicists. They were able to set production rapidly in motion, with the aid of improved technical equipment and a stimulating demand for good functional products for domestic use. Much of this functional ceramic ware was visually interesting and artistically rewarding, but from the end of the 1970s onwards it was increasingly priced out of the market by inexpensive mass imports of ceramic household products from overseas. It was normal practice, however, for independent studio ceramicists to work on creating unique objects alongside their functional ceramic products, and gradually these became a major focus, in step with the growth of competition and the artistic/conceptual trends of the time. The years from 1980 to the present form a rich and still ongoing period in Danish ceramics, in which ceramicists and artists have continued to create experimental works, with a wide variety of starting-points and approaches, which highlight the importance of clay as a material in a creative process.

Designmuseum Danmark, in its acquisitions processes, has placed its focus on unique works made by studio ceramicists, and these are the subject of this catalogue. This has the consequence that certain important ceramic artists attached to the porcelain factories and other ceramic workshops in Denmark are not represented in the catalogue, even in cases where their works are to be found in the museum's collection. But from the biographical summaries in the catalogue it is evident that there has been a close and strong relationship between the factories and the studio ceramicists, many of whom have spent longer or shorter periods working in the factories, in an environment of close professional and skilled cooperation with the staff there. The development-history of the museum's collection of studio ceramics is one of the central issues of the present catalogue. It can be shown that three-quarters of the works concerned were acquired within four years of being made. This is particularly the case of works acquired in the last three decades, possibly as a result of the passion for contemporary ceramics evinced by both museum director Kristian Jakobsen and myself.

Acquisitions for the collection have often been made possible by grants from foundations and private persons. One of the museum's most generous patrons throughout its history has been *Ny Carlsbergfondet*, the New Carlsberg Foundation, established by brewer Carl Jacobsen, who was also a driving force in the setting up of the Danish Kunstindustrimuseum (now Designmuseum Danmark) in 1890. In 2002 the New Carlsberg Foundation celebrated its 100-year's jubilee, and with customary generosity it donated, in that context, an impressive sum for the publication of a series of catalogues of the museum's collections in a number of central areas. That series has now reached its conclusion with this present ninth volume. The major donation was initiated in my time as director of the museum (1995-2010), and I attach great importance to thanking the New Carlsberg Foundation's board members, then and now, for their continued support for this comprehensive project.

Among other foundations of great significance to the museum and to Danish ceramics in general, special thanks are due to Annie & Otto Johs. Detlefs' Foundation, which in 2005 set up the Ceramics Prize and its travel bursary, awarded annually until 2013 in the museum and from 2016 onwards at CLAY Museum of Ceramic Art Denmark.

In connection with the preparation of this catalogue I have benefited from the friendly and unstinting support of museum director Anne-Louise Sommer, to whom I am very grateful. The same applies to the willing help I have received from chief accountant Poul-Erik Mortensen and director's secretary Henriette Falkenberg Andreasen.

The fixed point in my work over several years has been Designmuseum Danmark's Library, a deeply professional, busy and cheerful oasis, and my second home. There I have been spoiled by being met with great courtesy and good advice by the head of the library, Lars Dybdahl, who has read and commented on sections of the catalogue. And exceptional helpfulness has been forthcoming from the librarians Anja Lollesgaard, Nils Frederiksen and Sara Fruelund, as well as library assistant Peter Querling Jacobsen, whom I cannot thank enough for all they have meant to me and my work. Anja Lollesgaard has also contributed with proof-reading and Nils Frederiksen with the preparation of the list of reference publications in the select bibliography.

Through the years many willing and knowledgeable people have contributed to the work on Danish Studio Ceramics 1950-2010. It has been a work in progress for a long time, and it has only been after my retirement from the museum that I have been able to devote myself fully to it. But before that major efforts had been made, by several colleagues, on the collection of data and the information about the ceramicists and artists and their works that is now included in the catalogue. I would like to thank Julie Skov Nicolaisen, and in particular the museum's former registrar, Charlotte Malte, who undertook the basic collection and coordination of the material, and with whom I have had through the years an inspiring dialogue about Danish ceramics. In connection with the completion of research and editing of biographical data and descriptions of works, Christine Rosenlund, was employed as academic assistant, and I would like to thank her warmly for her important and highly qualified contribution. Registrar Peniila Laviolette is also owed thanks for her unfailing helpfulness with finding works and information.

Two load-bearing elements in the present catalogue are the photographic material it contains, and the graphic layout of text and photographs. The latter has been entrusted to the graphic artist Jeanne Philip, as has been the case for all the volumes in this series. She has carried out this major task with great success, together with the various authors, and she has upheld the general principles for the series with fine aesthetic sensibility for the very diverse objects involved. Cooperation with Jeanne Philip has been a genuine pleasure, and it is thanks to her that it has been possible to create a clear identity for the series as a whole. Similarly, there has been a splendid and fruitful cooperation with photographer Pernille Klemp; through the years she has taken almost two thousand new photographs of objects in the museum's collections for publication in the nine volumes of the series of catalogues. In her long career Pernille Klemp has developed a particular sensitivity for photographing three-dimensional objects, and this has been used not least to the advantage of the almost 700 works in this catalogue. The translator of the catalogue for its English version, Joan F. Davidson, has faithfully interpreted my text; this has been a rewarding process, for which I am extremely grateful.

The practising ceramicists themselves were among the most useful sources for Danish Studio ceramics 1950–2010. The survey conducted in 2007-08 to obtain information about the techniques and materials used for their individual works resulted in replies providing crucial information to supplement and enrich the existing registration; that information is now embedded in this catalogue and has been an invaluable contribution to it.

I am deeply grateful for this help and for the many follow-up conversations and meetings with a wide circle of ceramicists; this has provided the essential inspiration for my work through the years on this subject. I would also like to express special thanks to the ceramicist Peder Rasmussen, whose knowledge and humour have been for me a source of instruction and confirmation of my love for the wonderful and diverse world of ceramics.

Ever since Designmuseum Danmark was founded, ceramics has been an area with high priority in the museum's collecting processes, and several generations of the museum's academic staff have engaged intensively with both Danish and international ceramics. This is true of the former directors Emil Hannover, Erik Lassen and Kristian Jakobsen. In my own time I took great pleasure in working with museum curators Vibeke Woldbye and Jørgen Schou-Christensen. In the preparation of this catalogue Jørgen Schou-Christensen has generously contributed his expertise and knowledge, gained through many years of working in the museum and with Danish applied art.

In the final stages of work on the catalogue many good friends and family members have provided invaluable help and support. They have unselfishly used time on proof-reading, and given editorial advice and encouragement to the project in general. I would like to express my thanks in particular to Mogens Bencard, Thora Fisker, Helle Lassen, Aino Kann Rasmussen and Susanne Thestrup Truelsen.

Bodil Busk Laursen
Copenhagen, Spring 2017

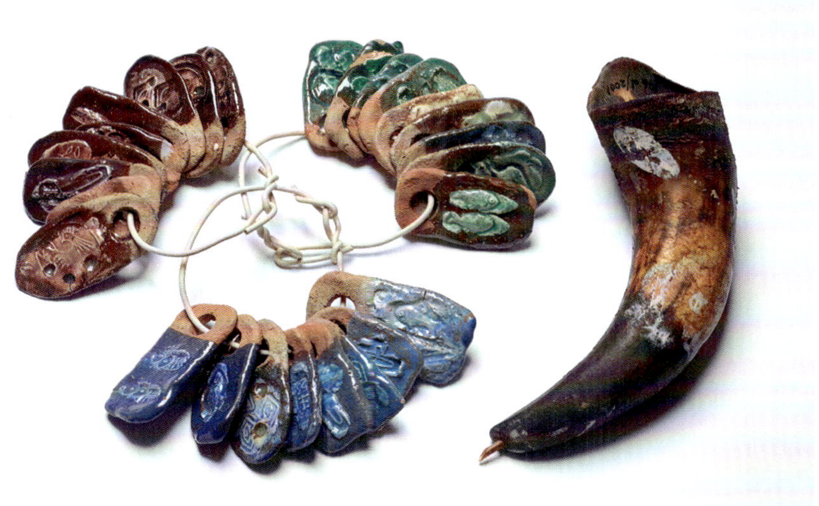

Glaze samples and painting-horn made and used by ceramicist Lisa Enqvist (1914-1989)
Mus.no. 196a-d/2001
Foto: Pernille Klemp.

INTRODUCTION

Danish ceramics at the beginning of the 20th century

It was in connection with the Nordic Exhibition of Industry, Agriculture and Art, held in Copenhagen in 1888, that Danish ceramics began its modern breakthrough. The exhibition was a landmark, both for the development of applied art enterprises in general, and more particularly for the experimental ceramic art that was carried forward at that time by a small group of painters and sculptors who combined forces in the *'Dekorationsforeningen'* (the Decorative Art Association), formed for the purpose of participating in the 1888 exhibition. The World Exhibitions in Paris in 1878, 1889 and 1900 provided an opportune setting in which ceramics could win intensive attention, not least because the rich ceramic culture and motif-world of Japan had come to the fore in the displays and was being incorporated as a source of inspiration in the development of the new *Art Nouveau* style. There were also displays of masterly Japanese-inspired stoneware by French ceramicists, with fantastic glazes, inspired by nature, of a kind never before seen; these works were purchased by European museums of decorative art and by others in the art world who were fascinated by them, including the Danish artists Niels Hansen Jacobsen (1861-1941) and J. F. Willumsen (1863-1958), who both lived in Paris for a number of years in the 1890s. It was in Paris that Willumsen met Paul Gauguin (1848-1903), who created a number of innovatively modelled sculptures in stoneware in the period from the mid 1880s to 1889; they were fired in the workshop belonging to the ceramicist Ernst Chaplet (1835-1909). Designmuseum Danmark (originally the Kunstindustrimuseum) owns seven of these works, five of them previously owned by Gauguin's Danish wife, Mette Gauguin, and later donated to the museum by *Ny Carlsbergfondet* (the New Carlsberg Foundation). These important works by Gauguin opened the way for clay to be attributed new significance as an artistic medium; from the 1940s onwards they have been exhibited in the museum together with several examples of contemporary French stoneware, and have thus been accessible as objects of study for specialists and the public in general.[1]

The 1888 exhibition in Copenhagen was a triumphant success for the Royal Copenhagen Porcelain Manufactory[2] with its blue Japanese-inspired under-glaze painted ware, by the factory's great artistic innovator, architect Arnold Krog (1856-1931). Bing & Grøndahl's Porcelain Factory had acquired talented input from artist and theatre-director Pietro Krohn (1840-1905), whose *Hejrestel* (Heron service), created for this exhibition, became internationally known and was acquired by several European museums of applied art. The ceramic firm Kähler Keramik also attracted considerable attention on account of the lustre glazing by Herman A. Kähler (1846-1917). In 1885 Arnold Krog and Pietro Krohn were appointed artistic directors of their respective factories, and they laid down the basis for new artistic lines in the factories' production, which continued to win acclaim at the successive World Exhibitions in Paris in 1889, Chicago in 1893 and in Paris again in 1900 and 1925. In 1893 Pietro Krohn became the first director (1893-1906) of the Danish Kunstindustrimuseum and his forward-looking, perceptive personality, along with his enthusiastic commitment to communication with the public, provided for the museum the best imaginable beginnings.[3]

The 1888 exhibition was also of great significance for the Danish Kunstindustrimuseum, in that part of the profit from the exhibition was set aside for a building-fund for the new museum – a development that had been under discussion in the Danish Association for Industry from as early as 1851. It was only when a fund was set up by Brewer Carl Jacobsen (1842-1914), of Ny Carlsberg Brewery, for the purchase of objects for such a museum, that the plans began to become realistic. The Danish Kunstindustrimuseum was established in 1890 by the Association for Industry and Carl Jacobsen, and it opened in 1894 in a building constructed for the purpose on City Hall Square in the centre of Copenhagen.

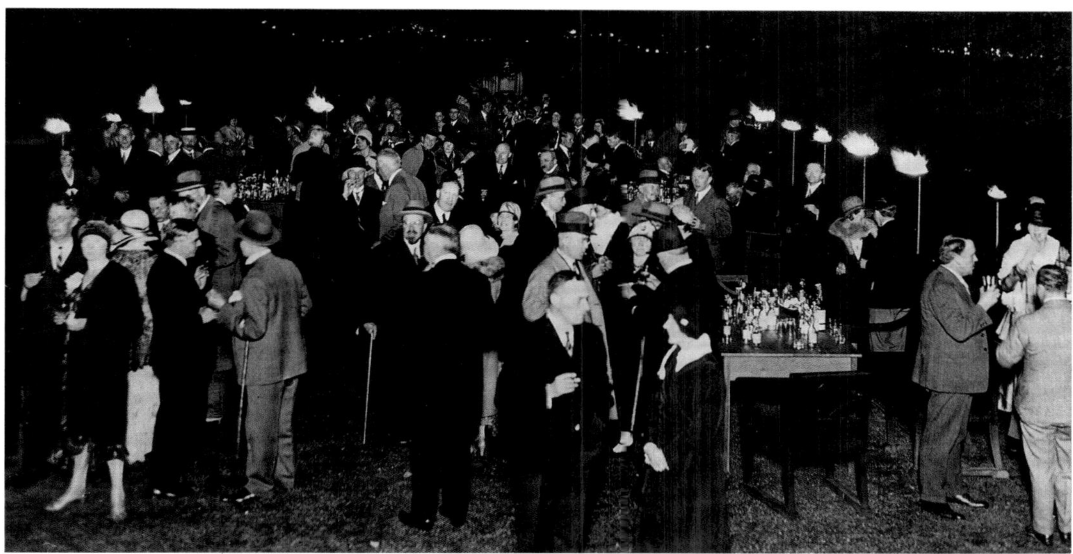

Inauguration of Kunsthåndværkerskolen (the School of Arts and Crafts) in the garden of the Kunstindustrimuseum (now Designmuseum Danmark) in 1930. Photo in the Arkiv for Dansk Design, Designmuseum Danmark's Library.

In association with the newly established Kunstindustrimuseum various craft schools were set up, and when the museum moved to its present buildings in Bredgade, Copenhagen, in 1925, a workshop was included for the museum's ceramics class; in 1927 there were 21 students enrolled in the day-time school for ceramics and 29 in the evening class. When the School of Arts and Crafts *(Kunsthåndværkerskolen)* was set up in 1930, the existing craft classes were incorporated into it; it was there that the first studio ceramicists were taught, and many of them went on to establish relatively short-lived shared workshops in the 1930s and 40s. In this pioneering generation one can see the actual beginnings of studio ceramics in Denmark, based in principle on solo workshops.[4]

In the great Nordic Exhibition of 1888, which was almost on the scale of a World Exhibition, the image of Danish ceramics presented was layered and complex, covering new experimental ceramic art outside the products of the two porcelain factories and the other ceramic firms. The collection of work by The Decorative Art Association*(Dekorationsforeningen)* had been produced in the premises of the potter J. Wallmann, in Utterslev near Copenhagen, but the works were designed, decorated and modelled by the painters who made up the group. Karl Madsen (1855-1938), the art critic and later director of the Danish National Gallery, was the ideologue, while the architect Thorvald Bindesbøll (1842-1908) was the artistic moving force within the group; in as early as 1883 he had made his first attempts with Italian-inspired slip-treated and lead-glazed earthenware and sgraffito decoration, and had developed this in subsequent years in a fruitful collaboration with his circle of artist friends.[5] With its participation in the Nordic Exhibition of 1888 the Decorative Art Association sought to reach out to the public with their freely modelled and decorated ceramic works, which were far-removed from traditional pottery wares. Later these works, some with national-romantic motifs, came to be referred to as art ceramics – or more accurately as 'ceramic works made by fine-artists'. Many of the Decorative Art Association's works were rapidly acquired by the Kunstindustrimuseum and subsequently ceramic works by painters or sculptors have formed an acquisition-category throughout the 20th century. As it turned out, participation in the 1888 exhibition proved to be a great disappointment for the Decorative Art Association, since it resulted in relentlessly strong criticism and failure of understanding of the originality of the works. The time was not ripe for appreciation of the new ceramics. Nothing was sold and the Association was dissolved by the beginning of the 1890s, when its members went their separate ways in pursuit of their individual artistic goals, mainly outside the area of ceramics. But Thorvald Bindesbøll continued working with ceramics, from 1891 until 1906, and developed his original abstract motifs and free strong brush-treatment on the large plates and jugs that today can be found in museums and private collections in Denmark and beyond. Even though Bindesbøll's works are not included in the present catalogue because of its chronological boundaries, it is essential to refer to him because his significant ceramic body of work constitutes a portal to 20th century Danish ceramics and is still a source of inspiration. Through his work he became a form of catalyst for some of the contemporary ideological debates arising from social and aesthetic considerations – e.g. the conflict between industrialisation's alienation of the individual and the richer human values embodied in craftsmanship. The moral aspects of these issues first came to the fore in England, because of its early industrialisation process, and there they were formulated through the Arts & Crafts movement. The movement's ideas – with its

Ceramic works and drawings by Thorvald Bindesbøll (1846-1908) in the exhibition "Anna didn't come home that night". The exhibition was created by Robert Wilson for DesignMuseum Danmark in the year 2000. Photo Pernille Klemp.

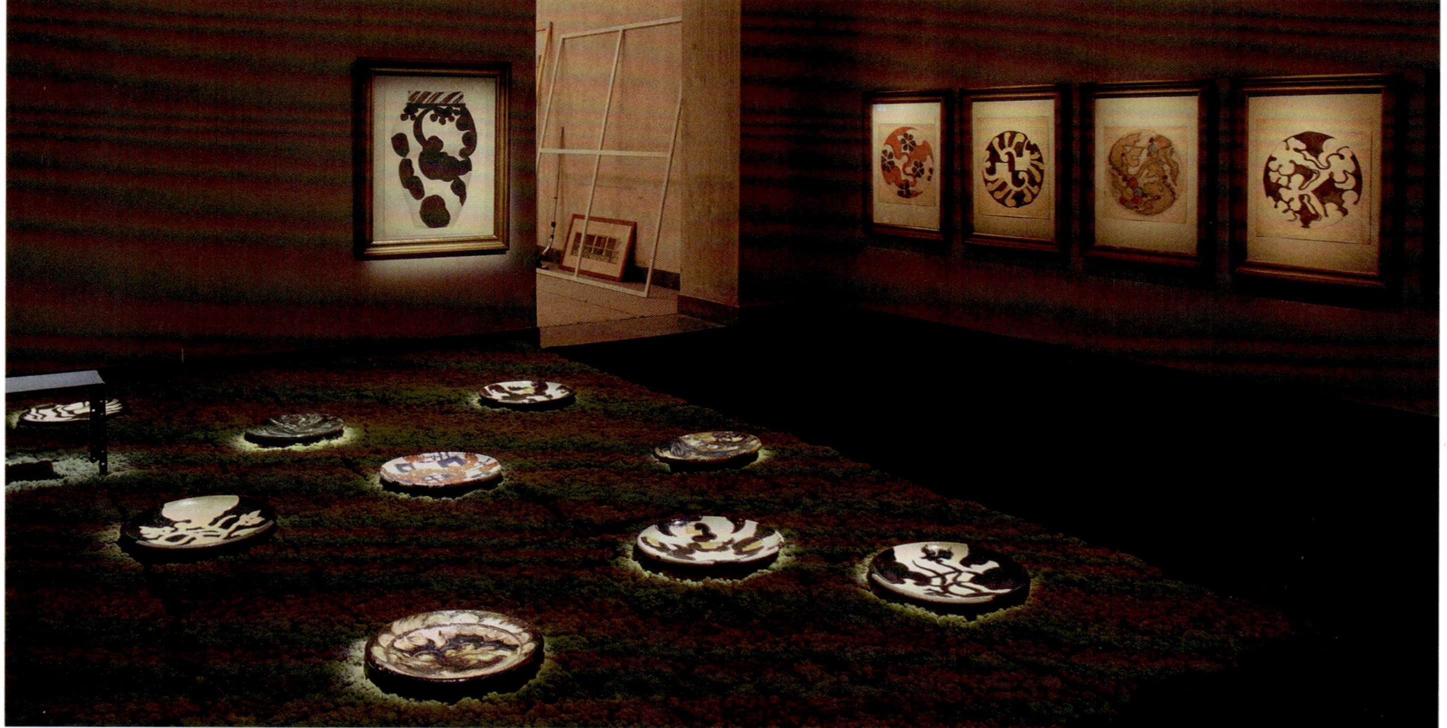

Utopian programme for combining the highest quality of art and craftwork in pursuit of an ideology of beauty in architecture, applied art, crafts and fine art – won widespread support in creative artistic circles in Europe and the USA. Bindesbøll did not take part in this debate as a writer or commentator, but he put into practice the ideals of the Arts & Crafts movement about cooperation between artist and craftsman. The background to the development of Bindesbøll's strikingly modern and original ornamentation can be traced in the museum's huge collection of his drawings, which show that he mastered historic styles and adopted for his own purposes a large treasury of motifs and of knowledge about decorative applications from many parts of the world, not least from Japanese art. From a present-day perspective it can be difficult to imagine that Bindesbøll's ceramics were viewed with great scepticism in his lifetime. He sold virtually nothing and gave his works away to artists and friends.

Thorvald Bindesbøll set new standards for Danish applied art and craftwork. The museum possesses major examples of his works in a variety of areas, including in particular ceramics, furniture, silver and graphics, and it has devoted four major special exhibitions to his work – in 1898, 1909, 1926 and finally 1996, when the museum contributed to the celebration of Copenhagen as European City of Culture with the exhibition and publication *'Thorvald Bindesbøll – en dansk pioner'*.[6] Long after his death in 1908 Bindesbøll's international reputation has lived on and also grown, e.g. through the Council of Europe's exhibition *'The Sources of the XXth Century'*, held in Paris in 1960, where his modernity was brought home to the international art world and his achievements were set in the framework of art history together with the ceramic works of other major artists from the avant-garde of the 20th century.[7]

Use of stoneware as an artistic material was inspired by Japanese and French ceramics; among the many artists that spent time in Paris were some Danes who were attracted by this material, such as the sculptor Niels Hansen Jacobsen, for whom glazes held a particular fascination, also after his return to Denmark, where he built the house and workshop in Vejen, in Jutland, which later became Vejen Kunstmuseum, and houses *inter alia* the main collection of the artist's stoneware. The painter J. F. Willumsen, who lived in Paris around 1890-94, worked for a number of years with both earthenware and stoneware. He became artistic director at Bing & Grøndahl in 1897-1901, with the objective of creating a success for the factory at the World Exhibition in Paris in 1900. Willumsen achieved results, in that a number of symbolistic and sculptural works were created under his leadership, and the artistic lines he laid down became a guiding principle for the factory throughout the following decade. Willumsen's ceramic art is well represented in the museum's collection, with e.g. the major work *Familievasen* (The Family Vase) from 1891.[8]

From the beginning of the 20th century both the Royal Porcelain factory and Bing & Grøndahl developed distinguished forms of stoneware products. But several other practitioners soon emerged, as described in an article from 1960 by the art historian Merete Bodelsen (1907-86), entitled *Tradition og Stilskifte i Dansk Stentøj* (Tradition and changes of style in Danish stoneware). The author mentions three categories of production of Danish stoneware, with different contexts, at that time: the porcelain factories; the new generation of studio ceramicists who had studied at Kunsthåndværkerskolen from the 1940s onwards; and the ceramic firm of Saxbo (1931-68), where the firm's owner and chemical engineer Nathalie Krebs (1895-1978) developed a production of finely-shaped smooth stoneware, glazed with her own perfect Chinese-inspired glazes.[9]

Denmark continued to take part in the World Exhibitions throughout the first half of the 20th century, and then in the triennials in Milan in the 1950s and 60s. At the major World Exhibition in Paris in 1925 the artists from the porcelain factories in particular, including Axel Salto, Fanny Garde and Jean Gauguin, received very appreciative attention, and the same applied to Kähler Keramik.

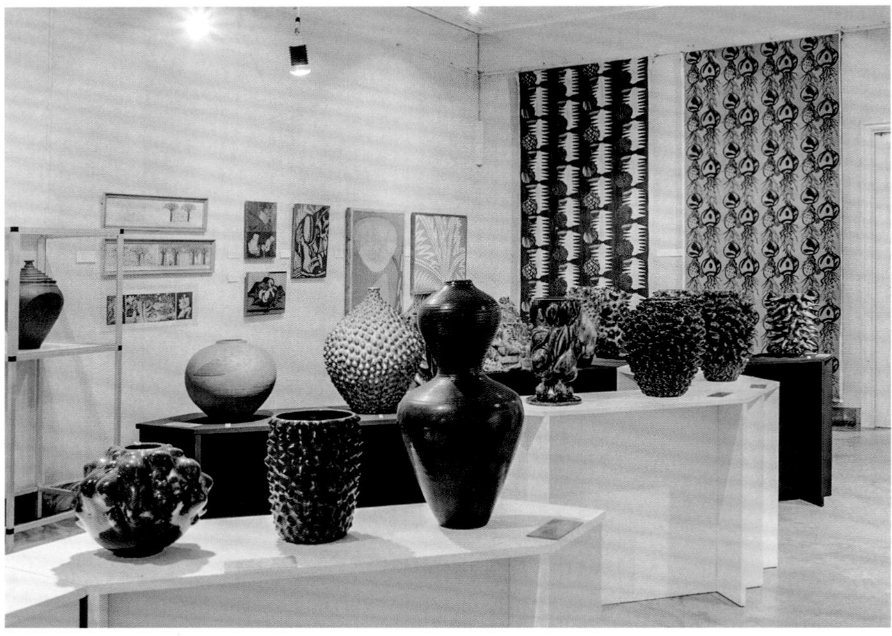

Photo from the exhibition "Det brændende nu" (Burning Moment) about the artist and ceramicist Axel Salto (1889-1961). The exhibition was curated by Lars Dybdahl, Librarian and Head of Research, Designmuseum Danmark 1989. Photo Ole Woldbye.

The classical period of Danish studio ceramics 1950 – 1980

'The brother disciplines of art craftwork and applied art, taken together, are one of the forms of cultural expression of a country and a period of time'. This was the opening sentence of a review by Christian Poulsen, himself one of the 20th century's major Danish ceramicists, of the 1956 annual exhibition held by the National Association of Danish Craftwork; Poulsen analyses both functional ceramics and *'decorative ceramics'.*[10] The review is interesting, because in addition to writing about the works of several of the exhibiting ceramicists, Poulsen discusses more generally the prevailing conditions for ceramic practitioners in workshops and factories, and identifies problems in the unresolved relationship between ceramic art, craft, and machines, and between unique creations and serial production. Poulsen looks at these unresolved relationships as a consequence of the development of democratic society, in which *'all citizens have the economic means to satisfy not only the need for good functional objects in the home, but also the motivation to own things that are not objects for practical use in a narrow sense – servants in our physical environment – but have the function of breaking holes in the walls of materialism to reach through to dreams and poetry.'* With regard to functional ceramics Poulsen highlights the *'technical civilisation'* of the production of the two Danish porcelain factories, describing it as e.g. representing the cleansed forms of modernism and as succeeding in eliminating spiritless style-imitations of earlier epochs. Concerning studio ceramics, he concludes that there is *'no reason to promote production based on ordinary earthenware'*, a statement that also relates to his evaluation of porcelain and stoneware as the materials best suited to objects for everyday use, on the strength of *'their durability, their widest possible range of use and the vitality of their textural effects.'*

As for *'decorative ceramics'*, Poulsen writes that some ceramicists express the view that it is meaningless to make a functional object for domestic use as a unique ceramic work, with a relatively high price. Poulsen does not share that point of view.

According to his definition it is the artistic work itself that embodies an intention, *'a striving that can be perceived in a little ceramic bowl when it has a quality that can create, across all national boundaries, a feeling of connectedness, of pleasure and a sense of significance in existence that goes beyond materialism, of understanding and of pride in being human.'* Reverting to the beginning of his review, Poulsen writes: *'To be able to make a material come alive, to be able to create tension between form, colour, picture or ornament and us is art. If the term 'art' in the phrases* 'art craftwork' *and* 'applied art' *is to have meaning it must refer to art as a discernible presence within the work.'* As will be apparent from the works in the present catalogue, Christian Poulsen's views on the universal significance of ceramics and on the preconditions for ceramics of quality are in accordance with those upheld by the museum.

Christian Poulsen's article touches on several other issues that have been raised throughout the 20th century, including the ever-increasing expectations in terms of scenographic contexts for exhibitions and the consequent economic demands placed on the exhibitors. This was a problem that already affected the first studio ceramicists in connection with their participation in the annual exhibitions by Danish Crafts Association in the 1940s, and continued later in those arranged by the National Association of Danish Craftwork, for which the participants had to pay a certain amount and themselves carry the loss if the works exhibited were damaged. Christian Poulsen had a solo exhibition in the museum in 1964 for which he arranged his works on raw gas-concrete blocks – a modern and low-cost solution.

Information about the socio-economic conditions experienced by the many studio ceramicists in the first decades after the Second World War is sadly lacking. Generally speaking there are no records on important matters concerning production and selling methods. Was this carried on through standing cooperation on these matters between studios, or were these tasks dealt with on an individual basis? One fixed anchor for a number of the studios between 1931 and 1981 was their relationship with the association *Den Permanente*, which became an important sales organisation for Danish craftworkers and for applied art enterprises. Den Permanente's commercial display was reserved for its members, numbering on average 125, who were admitted to this democratic association on the basis of assessment by an adjudication committee. The initiative-taker was Kay Bojesen (1886-1958), himself a talented and internationally known designer and producer with considerable persuasive abilities, but from the start members experienced conflicts of interest between idealist attitudes and commercial motivations, and these, together with bad economic results, finally led to the association being dissolved and abolished in 1981.[11]

Den Permanente was the main international display window for Danish craftsmanship and applied art, placing its major focus on a range of goods that lived up to the criteria that functionalism set up for the design of objects for domestic use. Den Permanente's export department arranged large sales drives, including some in the USA, and tourists in Denmark, as well as all others with an interest in contemporary crafts and design, undertook pilgrimages to this 'Mecca' in the centre of Copenhagen, which had a reputation that still lives on both nationally and internationally. The significance of Den Permanente for one individual studio ceramicist is described in an article by Helle Allpass from around 1970, in which she vividly describes her relief at being able to deliver a large part of what she produced there and in that way escape from the burdensome work of selling. The honourable status conferred by membership of Den Permanente also helped to promote sales to the many craft shops around Denmark.[12]

The growth of public interest in arts and crafts during the period of increased prosperity in the 1960s was to the advantage of studio ceramicists, but demand for handmade functional ceramics also carried with it an in-built risk, in the form of the many spiritless copies of sought-after high quality products.

The combination of increasing imports of cheap mass-produced domestic wares and dwindling quality in some areas of Danish ceramic products led to a falling off of demand during the 1970s, aggravated by the oil crisis and general developments in society after the booming days of the 60s. This was also a contributing factor to another development: several of the next generation of studio ceramicists with 'artistic morality' (Christian Poulsen's expression) stopped making functional ceramic products and instead focused on art ceramics, devoting themselves to creating unique pieces.

New times and attitudes were announcing themselves, heralded for example by a landmark exhibition at Den Permanente in 1972 which came into being as a collaborative project by nine ceramicists: Hans Munck Andersen, Birgitte and Hans Börjeson, Marie Hjorth, Bodil and Richard Manz, Ursula Munch Petersen, Gerd Hiort Petersen and Anne Marie Trolle. The title of this critical and innovative exhibition was *'At være keramiker'* (Being a ceramicist) and its aim was *inter alia* to discuss the justification for being a ceramicist in relation to contemporary economic and social issues.[13]

This was the period when stoneware was the prime material of choice for studio ceramicists making serial products for domestic use, and this was fostered in particular by Richard Kjærgaard's teaching at Kunsthåndværkerskolen from the mid 1950s. But as early as the 1940s Christian Poulsen and Richard Kjærgaard himself had experimented with stoneware, before it became, from the 1960s onwards, an essential material for production of both unique works and functional ceramics. Both the major porcelain factories began developing their use of stoneware around 1900, as did the smaller prominent ceramic enterprises L. Hjorth and Kähler Keramik.

It was not until around 1970 that porcelain began to be used in studio workshops. In the 1970s early experiments were made, by both Bodil and Richard Manz and Birgitte and Hans Börjeson, with production of porcelain paste, and they succeeded relatively fast in producing both functional objects and unique works in porcelain, thanks to the new small electric and gas kilns that made it possible to fire at sufficiently high temperatures in small workshops. As early as 1977 the museum held a very extensive exhibition entitled *'Variation i porcelæn'* by Bodil and Richard Manz, with serial versions of functional products and unique works in the high-quality porcelain that they developed after spending a period of time in a workshop in Japan in 1975. A selection of fine objects from that exhibition is to be found in the museum's collection.

The 'in-between generation' of studio ceramicists who were born in the 1940s and studied in the 60s made their mark in earnest from the beginning of the 70s. Studio ceramics developed through experiments with materials and methods that led to new design ideas and new types of work. Clay as a material in a creative process became a convincing presence from the 1980s. This is reflected in the Kunstindustrimuseum's acquisitions of studio ceramics, which were relatively sparse in the 1960s and 70s, but increased considerably in the following decades. The 'in-between generation' of studio ceramicists, numbering some 50 or so, make up the largest group of those included in the present catalogue. At the same time several of the catalogue's earlier generation of studio ceramicists were continuing their work, some of them – like Gertrud Vasegaard, Gutte Eriksen, Lisbet Munch-Petersen, Richard Kjærgaard and Gudrun Meedom Bæch – until after the turn of the millennium.

New trends and developments 1980 – 2010

The period 1980-2010 can be seen as the beginning of a new era in which ceramics as an art form took a role in an international context and on market conditions.

Through this period a new energy came to characterize the field of ceramics, expressed both in the works themselves and in the organisation of the processes involved. New trends resulted in the bringing into existence, within Denmark and internationally, of various forms of cooperation around diverse directions and goals within ceramics. The will to engage with the world was evident in the creation of exhibition groups and the setting up of exhibition platforms for new ceramics. The large range of ceramicists and the development of new approaches to ceramics can clearly be seen in the museum's many acquisitions from 1980 and throughout the two following decades: 195 pieces in the 1980s, 163 in the 1990s and 185 from 2000-10. The present catalogue's biographical summaries and photographs of works provide an opportunity to study the period's many diverse tendencies and directions, while taken as a whole they present a lively depiction of parallel currents in artistic development. The biographies contain information of a more general nature as well as descriptions of the work of the individual concerned, including collaboration with others, affiliation with groups, education, and collegiate connections.

The features of the developments in this period are sketched out in the following section, which describes a selection of the initiatives and activities that carried the new ceramics forward. These activities are particularly related to persons who have been connected with the museum through exhibitions and acquisitions and who are thus integrated into the range of studio ceramics that are present in the museum's collection.
A recurring problem through this period has been the need for exhibition platforms for contemporary studio ceramics, a need that has grown in step with the larger number of ceramicists who have made a name for themselves since the 1980s. The large number of practitioners and the explosive development of unique works led in the 90s to the establishment of ceramic galleries in Copenhagen and Kolding - *Galleri Nørby* (1992-2007) and *Galleri Pagter* (1997-) respectively, both as private initiatives. While Galleri Pagter has concurrently shown other art besides ceramics, Galleri Nørby was a gallery purely for ceramics, founded and for many years run by Ingrid Nørby. The gallery's focus was on studio ceramics, with practitioners from the whole country and from several generations, and the gallery became a centre and gathering-place for Danish ceramicists during a 15-year period, in which 125 exhibitions were shown, involving 125 ceramicists, 63 of whom are represented in the museum's collection. Among other initiatives for exhibition-platforms in this period, mention can be made of *Udstillingssted for Ny Keramik* (described below) 1996-2000, *Drud & Køppe Gallery/ Køppe Gallery 2006-08, Ann Linnemann Studie Galleri* 2008- , and most recently *Copenhagen Ceramics* 2012-14.

As was the case for young Danish furniture designers in the 1980s and 90s, when the established great names within furniture design overshadowed the chances young talented designers had to break through to producers with new projects, in the field of ceramics a similar tendency can be seen; it was to an overwhelming degree the established ceramicists that were invited to exhibit in the more official Danish and international contexts. The frustrations experienced by the younger ceramicists in the final decades of the 20th century were clearly expressed in an exhibition in 1993 entitled *'Keramikkens Underskov – aktuel keramik af yngre keramikere', (The undergrowth of ceramics– current ceramics by young ceramicists)* which was held in Copenhagen and Aarhus. The exhibition was arranged by two young ceramicists, Turi Heisselberg Pedersen and Jan Helmark. In the preface to the catalogue of the exhibition they formulated its origins 'as a reaction to a series of major ceramic exhibitions in 1991 which all concerned known and experienced people, now living or deceased'.[14] The exhibition's battle cry 'Set ceramics free!' was expanded on in the catalogue by Turi Heisselberg Pedersen, beginning with a summary of the well-known history of Danish ceramics, from the early great figures such as Bindesbøll, Hammershøi, Willumsen, Hansen Jacobsen and Salto, and going on to name the significant studio ceramicists from the first half

Front cover of the catalogue of the exhibition "Keramikkens underskov" (The undergrowth of ceramics) arranged by a group of young ceramicists. The exhibition was shown in Copenhagen and Aarhus in 1993.

Photo Jens Peter Engedal. Layuot: Jens Ole Markussen.

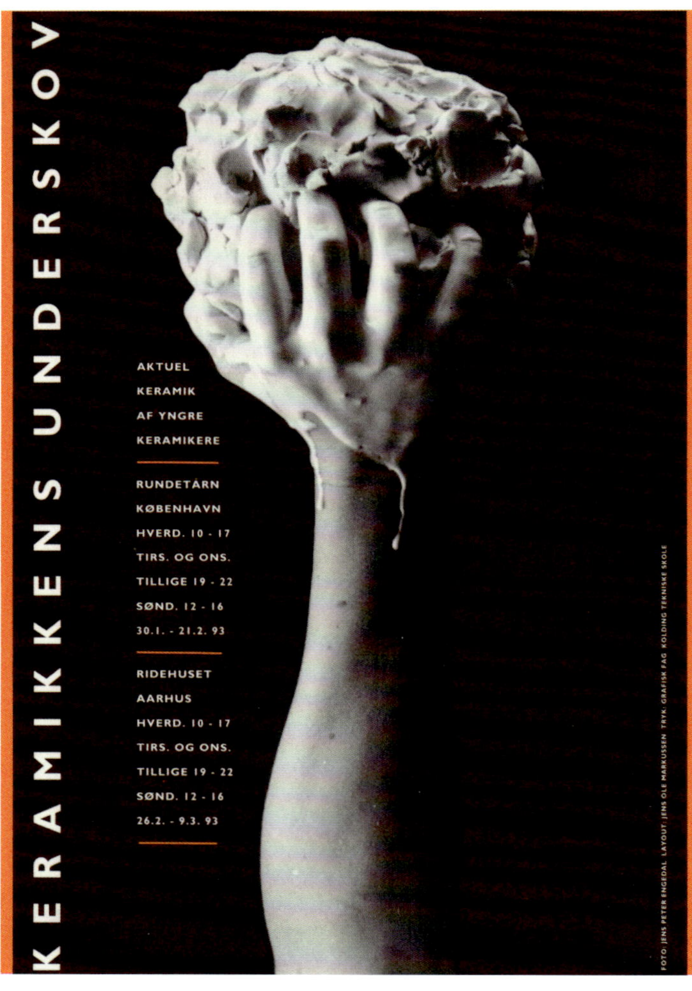

of the 20th century, culminating in the Danish Design ideology of the 1950s and 60s. She challenges everyone to take the contemporary context and look with new eyes at ceramics as a material and as a skill, and to come to grips with a debate about the relationship between art and craftsmanship, about things in a world where there are all too many things, about the dangers of overconsumption in relation to the environment, and about the perilous sliding away from art and intuition towards a focus on sales and packaging. The exhibition *'Keramikkens Underskov'* marked out a clear goal of being in dialogue with the surrounding world and of opening eyes to the potential importance of ceramics. It is thought-provoking that these aims echo several of the same issues raised in the 1972 exhibition *'At være keramiker'*, mentioned earlier, which like *'Keramikkens Underskov'* was arranged by a group of young ceramicists, critical of society, who had a new agenda for the field of ceramics (see p. 16). Conditions for young practitioners in ceramics had not improved in the 21 intervening years, and the exhibitors' appeal to the rest of the world to take ceramics seriously was just as topical as the need to find an identity for applied art. *'Keramikkens underskov'* brought together 34 ceramicists, ten of whom are represented in the museum's collection (Lone Skov Madsen, Steen Ipsen, Barbro Åberg, Martin Bodilsen Kaldahl, Morten Løbner Espersen, Anne Tophøj, Bente Skjøttgaard, Vibeke Rytter, Esther Elisabeth Pedersen, Mogens Davidsen).

But more than ten years before *'Keramikkens underskov'* there were Danish ceramicists from the established 'in-between generation' who had wanted to articulate new and different attitudes to ceramics and who had taken matters into their own hands, with high ambitions and potential impact. The group *Multi Mud* was formed in 1980 by Karen Bennicke, Heidi Guthmann Birck, Aage Birck, Gunnar Palandar, Peder Rasmussen and Lene Regius, and represented a wide range of forms of expression as the actual departure-point for their programme. The group continued in existence until 1986 and is represented in the museum's collection; it produced several large and demanding exhibitions in Germany, Austria and Scandinavia. The peak achievement for *Multi Mud* was the celebrated exhibition in 1983 at the Ny Carlsberg Glyptotek, Copenhagen, where the group were given *carte blanche* to use the rooms there to create a dialogue between the Glyptotek's statues from antiquity and their own displayed ceramic sculptural works. The exhibition was partly documented in *Multi Mud*'s information report from the same year, which gives an impression of the group's significant and very diverse works as well as of the extensive preparatory work carried out on their motifs. The exhibition became a form of compass-reading of the artistic capability of ceramics to re-interpret the forms and picture-world of antiquity, delivered through the analytical and inspirational ideas of the exhibitors and their evident skilled craftsmanship. *Multi Mud* is one example among many of the use of group exhibitions to render visible current trends and themes, and to provide a staged setting for new ceramic works in a specially chosen context.

Since the 1980s many Danish studio ceramicists have become members of exhibition groups which periodically attract attention with presentations, in Denmark and further afield, of the group's current works. Usually the groups are composed of ceramicists of the same generation and with some extent of study experience in common, e.g. the Art and Craft Schools in Kolding, Aarhus, Copenhagen and most recently Bornholm. Among the oldest groups, whose members are all represented in the museum's collection, are *8 keramikere* (1987-96)[15] and *Keramiske Veje* (1985-)[16] geographically centred in Central Jutland and Copenhagen respectively. An example of a group formed after the turn of the millennium is *New Danish Ceramics* (2003-),[17] which is described here in more detail because the group held its first exhibition, in 2003, in the museum. In that context the group formulated a programme-statement which summarises the group's – and its generation's – approach to ceramic work and thus provides a general description of new ceramics seen from the perspective of prominent young ceramicists:

> *It is characteristic of this generation to have an approach to their work that borders on research. Systematic and in-depth experimentation is carried out with both method and expression. Their works are typically based on an overall concept. Or they use as their departure-point the framework of a specific space or situation. Often materials, techniques and forms are used with connotations, as references. Historic and contemporary styles can be combined in a post-modern way – a modernist, industrial form may be coupled with classic celadon glaze, or works similar to common pottery products may be reassembled in new forms and sprayed with monochrome industrial glazes. Regardless of individual artistic directions, ceramic materials and processes play a key role. Our forms of expression range from hushed minimalist, through fluidly organic to pop-like capricious. The group's works form an extension of the Danish ceramic tradition in the way that they concentrate on examination of the form, treatment and variations of the pot, the bowl and the dish, and their symbolic and functional nature.*[18]

Representatives of the same generation, in many cases also members of *New Danish Ceramics*, came together in 1996-2000 around the setting up of *Udstillingssted for Ny Keramik* (Exhibition venue for New Ceramics) in Kompagnistræde in the centre of Copenhagen. The ceramicists Turi Heisselberg Pedersen, Lone Skov Madsen and Mark Lauberg took the initiative for this venture, and ran it together until 1999, when the group was joined by Bente Skjøttgaard and Michael Geertsen. In these premises, which became not just an exhibition space but also a gathering place, 31 exhibitions were mounted within four years, mainly showing the work of Danish ceramicists. The exhibitions became an eye-opener and showcase displaying new ceramics to the rest of the world and an important 'laboratory' for stimulating experimentation with different materials and processes. They also provided the opportunity to develop new display ideas, involving original handling of spatial concepts, e.g. with objects and works on all horizontal and vertical surfaces, and with podiums and showcases banished. Several of the exhibitors displayed processes, e.g. *Deform* (Gitte Jungersen, Flemming

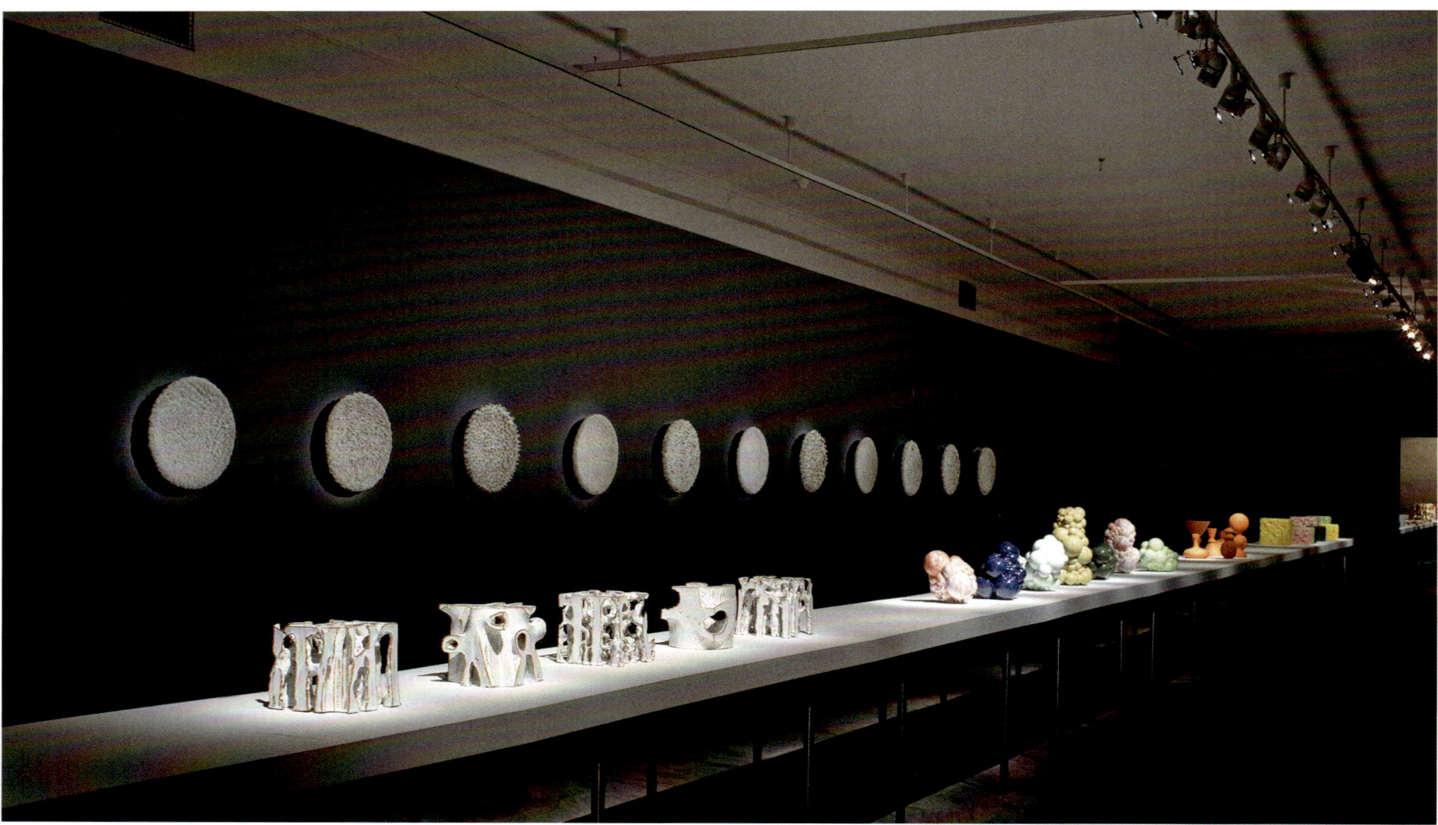

In the exhibition "New Danish Ceramics" a newly created group of young ceramicists displayed their works in Designmuseum Danmark in 2003.

Photo Anders Sune Berg

Tvede Hansen 1997), themes or series, e.g. 20.623 *Sorte Punktnedslag på Hvide Beholdere* (Lone Skov Madsen 1997) or provided narrative commentary in the form of references to functional ceramics, e.g. in *Kultiveret primitivitet – Fra hånden i munden* (Anne Tophøj 1997), *Tabletop* (Steen Ipsen, Michael Geertsen, Rigmor Als Jørgensen 1999), *Den dybe tallerken igen* (Turi Heisselberg Pedersen, Karin Schou 1997) and *Lertøj* (Ole Jensen 2000). As the titles indicate, poetry and humour were very much present in the exhibition rooms, which were physically on a small scale but intellectually tremendously lofty.[19]

There were other exhibition groupings among young ceramicists at various times, including *Junta* and *Keramik under jorden*, the latter set up in 2003 and consisting of 11 young ceramicists aiming to examine ceramics in the larger context including design and art. In the interests of 'setting ceramics free' the group consciously sought out alternative surroundings – in 2004 a bunker – for their exhibitions.[20]

The ceramic landscape expanded in many respects in the 1990s, again because of initiatives taken by persons among the ceramicists' own ranks, who succeeded in creating a new institution in Middelfart, on Funen. The Danish Ceramic Museum, CLAY, (previously Grimmerhus), a museum for contemporary Danish and international ceramics, has grown to be large and influential since it was established in 1994. The ceramicist Peter Tybjerg originally took the initiative to found the museum and was its first director and an early member of the international group of artists *Clay Today*, which in 1990 arranged a month-long international symposium at Tommerup Teglværk on Funen. The works from the symposium came to form the basis for the collection in the ceramic museum set up a few years later. Among the Danish participants in *Clay Today*, apart from Peter Tybjerg, were the ceramicists Nina Hole, Betty Engholm, Birgit Krogh and Niels Huang; *Clay Today* also stood behind the establishment in 1998 of Guldagergaard, the International Ceramic Research Centre in Skelskør, which for some years was run together with the ceramic museum. Guldagergaard offers young ceramicists from the whole world periods as artists-in-residence and assists established ceramicists with techniques and firing. *Clay Today* has beyond any doubt been important in Denmark in promoting material-based experimental developments in ceramics, built on strong international relations.[21] The museum's collection includes works by Nina Hole and Peter Tybjerg.

The increasing focus on ceramics also had a perceptible effect in the Danish museums, with 20th century ceramics as a particular acquisition field. In addition to the Kunstindustrimuseum, which between 1980 and 2010 held 62 ceramic exhibitions and acquired 358 ceramic works, the Trapholt Museum in Kolding, founded in 1988, was very active. An important initiative was Trapholt's hosting of the Danish Ceramics Triennial in the years 1994, 1997 and 2000, when the museum, in cooperation with a jury of practising ceramicists, invited around 50 Danish studio ceramicists to exhibit works. All are documented in the triennal catalogues.[22] Today Trapholt has a significant collection of studio ceramics, and the same is true of Vejen Kunstmuseum, whose director over the last twenty years, an art historian with specialist knowledge of ceramics, has built up a comprehensive collection of Danish applied art ceramics, studio ceramics and ceramic works by Danish artists who work primarily as painters.[23]

Even though the groups of ceramicists multiplied and played a significant role in the overall picture of ceramics at the time, individualisation among practising ceramicists also became increasingly pronounced in recent decades, as did pressures of competition among them. The fact of belonging to a defined group and participating in the group's exhibitions or in setting up exhibition venues cannot today form a substitute for developing one's own career. Solo exhibitions and one's own network with contacts to galleries, exhibition venues and museums are preconditions for a career.

The various applied art, craft and design courses in Copenhagen/Bornholm, Aarhus and Kolding have played an important role as the 'home port' of several vintages of extremely competent ceramicists who have subsequently been able to set up their own or shared studio workshops and careers, often with a range of products that includes both functional ceramics and unique works. Serial production as an approach to ceramics is built into the Danish tradition and is practised in the context of developing objects for practical use as limited series in the studio workshop, out-sourced or as designs for products to be pursued in another framework.

In recent decades the courses of study available in Copenhagen have undergone several structural changes, including establishment of a new research line as a feature of the programme to academicize the field of design and applied art. Throughout this process it has proved possible to maintain an overriding artistic /aesthetic dimension, with form as the central focus of tuition. How conditions for courses in ceramics will develop after 2016, when extensive savings from the political side will be imposed on the Design School of the Royal Academy of Fine Arts, is not yet clear at the present time, but the prospects give rise to concern. This is now the only institution in the country offering ceramic study, since the ceramic course at Design School Kolding was abolished in 2007, and teaching of the subject at Det Jyske Kunstakademi (Jutland Art Academy) ceased in around 1996.

Ceramic works by Danish painters and sculptors, 1950 – 2010

As a result of the museum's acquisition policy the collection contains examples of ceramic works made by Danish fine-artists – a group of works emerging from a historical basis rooted in the era when the museum was set up at the end of the 19th century with the inclusion of the Decorative Art Association's works; this gave rise to the designation "artists' ceramics" (see p. 11). By 1950 the collection had been supplemented with works by the sculptor Niels Hansen Jacobsen and the painter J. F. Willumsen, as well as with sculptural works by artists from the two main porcelain factories, including Axel Salto, Jais Nielsen, Knud Kyhn and Jean Gauguin. From that period there were also works by artists from Kähler Keramik, such as Herman H. C. Kähler, Karl Hansen Reistrup, L. A. Ring, Jens Thirslund and Svend Hammershøi.[24]

The museum's choices concerning works made between 1950 and 2010 by fine-artists require further discussion in some cases, since its acquisitions in this area did not have the same consistency and background as its choices in the area of studio ceramics. Here it has been more a question of a series of adhoc decisions made as opportunities arose to acquire works that reflected the museum's interest in following developments in the work of selected artists who have used sculptural and graphic elements in ceramic materials at points in time when there was a parallel new departure and seeking out of new approaches in methods taken into use in studio ceramics.

In the period around 1950 the museum acquired a recent work by a fine-artist outside the realm of applied art; this happened in connection with an enquiry from Asger Jorn to the museum about an exhibition in 1955. In the previous year Jorn and his family had stayed in Albissola, an Italian town well-known for its ceramics. In that year he had organised an international artists' congress there, for the purpose of promoting new creativity through ceramic experiments.[25] Jorn kept up his association with Albissola, and when he worked on his huge commissioned relief for Aarhus Statsgymnasium in 1959 he also chose to have it made there. The iconic photograph of Jorn sitting on a Vespa that is being pushed over heaps of clay, leaving tyre marks that were later incorporated into the relief, also comes from that time. The result of Jorn's approach to the museum was an exhibition held in 1955, and the museum acquired from it a sculpture by Jorn in the form of a mask, named *Monsieur Pancake*. The museum owns four works by Jorn, all of them from the early 1950s.

Jorn's approach to ceramics was a 'search for the un-aesthetic and for sculpture', aiming at liberating clay from 'perfect' functional ceramics and the decadent, lavishly decorated showpieces produced for example by the old European porcelain factories.[26] Others who shared his views included not just the other members of the Cobra-movement, but also artists such as Picasso, Miró, Fontana and Noguchi. Before the period he spent in Albissola, Jorn had been interested in ceramics. He moved in 1929 to the town of Silkeborg in central Jutland, in an area with a tradition for pottery, and there he met Erik Nyholm, a fish farmer; together they sought advice from local potters before Nyholm built his first kiln in 1950. Nyholm then developed an experimental ceramics production with a departure-point in the strongly artistic environment around Jorn and the other Cobra artists.

Erik Nyholm continued working with ceramics throughout his life and became, with his uninhibited approach to clay, one of Denmark's most influential ceramic artists; his strong and original works from the 1980s, often large dishes with abstract nature-inspired decoration, are well represented in the museum's collection. In connection with some of his large commissioned works Nyholm collaborated from the end of the 1980s with Tommerup Teglværk (Tommerup Keramiske Værksted) on Funen, which through the years has become the master workshop for art ceramics and an often-used partner in cooperative production of large sculptures and commissioned works for public sites and architectural projects in Denmark.[27]

In Designmuseum Danmark in 1955 the artist Asger Jorn (1914-1973) held the first exhibition in Denmark of his ceramic works from Albissola.

Photo in Arkiv for Dansk Design, Designmuseum Danmark s Library.

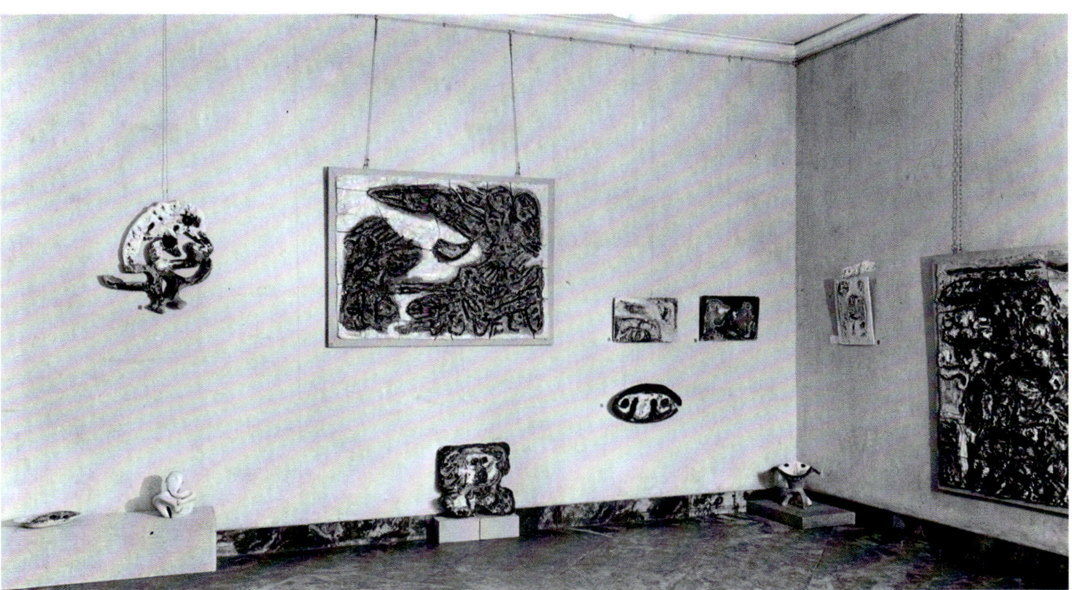

At the beginning of the 1980s the artists involved with the Eks-school, the experimental art school founded in Copenhagen in 1961, contributed to stirring up interest in experimenting with ceramic sculpture, and displayed their work in exhibitions such as that held in Horsens Kunstmuseum i 1985. In the 1980s the Kunstindustrimuseum acquired new works by Kirsten Christensen, Lene Adler Petersen, Bjørn Nørgaard, Peter Brandes and Niels Erik Gjerdevik, who have all continued to work with ceramics as a medium.

Five examples of Lene Adler Petersen's work are to be found in the museum's collection, all of them from the first half of the 1980s. Three of them are small sculptures and two are earthenware dishes from the series *Dishes for Dickens*. From the same period there is Bjørn Nørgaard's model in stoneware for a fountain, and a work from 1988 by Niels Erik Gjerdevik, *Danmarkskort* (Map of Denmark), which belongs to the group of neo-expressive sculptures.

Kirsten Christensen took a completely different approach to ceramic material, working from the beginning of the 1970s to develop a technique of scoring and brush-painting narrative motifs and progressions on thin clay plaques covered in slip and fired as stoneware; the museum's collection includes the work *Blå Grav* (Blue grave) from 1983 and two smaller works related to the issue of the relationship between art and art-craftwork.

The breadth of range in the collection was highlighted in connection with a retrospective exhibition in the museum in 1981 by Bjørn Wiinblad, when the museum had the opportunity to supplement its collection by adding works from the early phases of his development of pictorial and graphic expression.

In the 1990s two works by Peter Brandes that were made at Tommerup Keramiske Værksted were acquired; they consisted of a pot in glazed earthenware from 1991 and the sculpture *Hyrden* (The shepherd), one of many Biblical motifs in Brandes's extensive ceramic production. From a different motif-group, focusing on classical antiquity, seven other works were acquired, including a series of oval dishes with themes from the Odyssey.
Since the turn of the millennium the museum has acquired four works by fine-artists, including in 2002 a powerful green-black

glazed pot with bubble shapes by Bjørn Poulsen and from 2005 two works that both have a political /critical message, one of them by the artistic partnership of (Sofie) Hesselholdt & (Vibeke) Mejlvang, entitled *The Wall*, taking inspiration from the erection of the wall in the West Bank in Palestine, and the other, by Mette Vangsgaard, a tableau of a desolate island, extinguished and apocalyptic.

Designmuseum Danmark's collection of Danish ceramic works by painters and sculptors from after 1950 is not extensive, but it contains interesting testimony from that period, showing how the fine- artists have contributed to enriching ceramic culture and keeping clay alive in an exchange process with the experimental activities of the studio ceramicists.

The studio ceramicists and their experimental activities
The acquisition history of the museum's collection of Danish ceramics in the 20th century shows that the museum has to a remarkable degree felt itself untrammelled by any formal division between the genres of craft/applied art, art and design, and has not operated with firmly-fixed ideological preferences as to the diverse approaches to ceramic material. For the museum during the turbulent period 1980-2010 it was, as in earlier times, the quality of the works and the interest they aroused that mattered. These acquisition criteria were laid down at an early stage (see p.34), and are also applied to other areas of the museum's acquisitions.
For applied art as a whole, and not least for ceramicists, the period has been marked by continuing ambivalence in attitudes to the century-old hierarchical ranking of art and applied art/ design, or 'fine' art versus 'minor' art, which has plagued the identity of applied art for so long. Today, however, the lines of that discussion seem to be less sharply drawn, the boundaries are no longer so clear-cut and they are increasingly being broken down in different ways, while internally there is cross-disciplinary work being carried out within the diverse applied art fields. The post-modern extended concept of art can be inclusive, to a great degree, of a wider range of ceramic practice, whether one thinks of unique sculptural pieces by ceramicists or of ceramic works by artists. But the increased focus on creative art forms within ceramics does not seem, as has been claimed, to have eliminated functionally directed applied art as a specific artistically coloured area with its strong ideological and craft-related traditions for exploration of materials and development of design.[28]

In Denmark functional ceramic production has not died, but is continuing and developing in studio workshops and is being designed in cooperation with a variety of producers. Some of this activity has for instance led to the setting up of the Danske Keramikfabrik on Bornholm, a new ceramic production facility owned by 19 ceramicists and small firms, where handmade ceramic products are made to order, ensuring that production can take place in Denmark. This adds a new chapter to Bornholm's long and influential history as a ceramic centre, owing its origins to the island's rich deposits of various clays, along with the presence of the ceramics factory L. Hjorth, now over a hundred years old, as well as the many excellent studio ceramicists and the Royal Academy's School of Design on Bornholm.

The museum's collection contains works that are representative of many approaches to ceramic materials that have developed during the 20th century, and that are illustrative of changing international movements and trends in the Danish ceramics tradition. But there is a decisive difference between, on the one hand, the ceramicists' choice to work with clay coupled with basic studies in ceramics as the foundation of their production, and on the other hand the fine-artists' use of clay, which is often motivated by trying out the material as one of many in their range of methods. Danish ceramicists' basis of knowledge and skill in relation to their craft allows them to create works themselves through the whole process from idea to reality and this is still a fundamental characteristic of their work, enabling them through the depth of their knowledge about the material to produce both distinguished functional works and free artistic creations. It is not unusual for a studio ceramicist to work concurrently in parallel with functional forms and with sculptural ceramics, and the pot, dish and cylinder are still the basic forms that constitute the departure-point for spatial and abstract new interpretations, not just for Danish ceramicists but universally.[29] In the museum attention continues to be focused on contemporary ceramics and on acquisition of art-based unique works by Denmark's many influential ceramicists. And new ones keep arriving on the scene. In recent years the end-of-studies exhibitions at the Art Academy's School of Design on Bornholm, showing work by graduates of the Craft Programme's Glass and Ceramics courses, bear witness to an undimmed desire to explore and experiment with new and old materials, forms and processes and a context coloured by artistic readiness.

Overview and current status

Ceramic objects have been a feature of Danish life through the ages. Techniques for making them have developed over time. The potter and ceramicist have developed wonderful technical and artistic possibilities and devised new materials, methods and forms of expression. The production of functional objects as a basis for a solo enterprise or as a process directed towards prototypes for manufacturers has a long tradition in Danish culture, and that tradition still plays a role for Danish ceramicists who have studied at craft or design school and have attained the necessary theoretical and practical insight into the subject. Tradition is not a simple concept – it can stand in the way of innovation and cause stagnation, but it can also create a useful

Porcelain figures by ceramicist Louise Hindsgavl. From the exhibition "in reality…" held in Designmuseum Danmark in 2006 together with jewellery designer Mette Saabye. Photo Pernille Klemp.

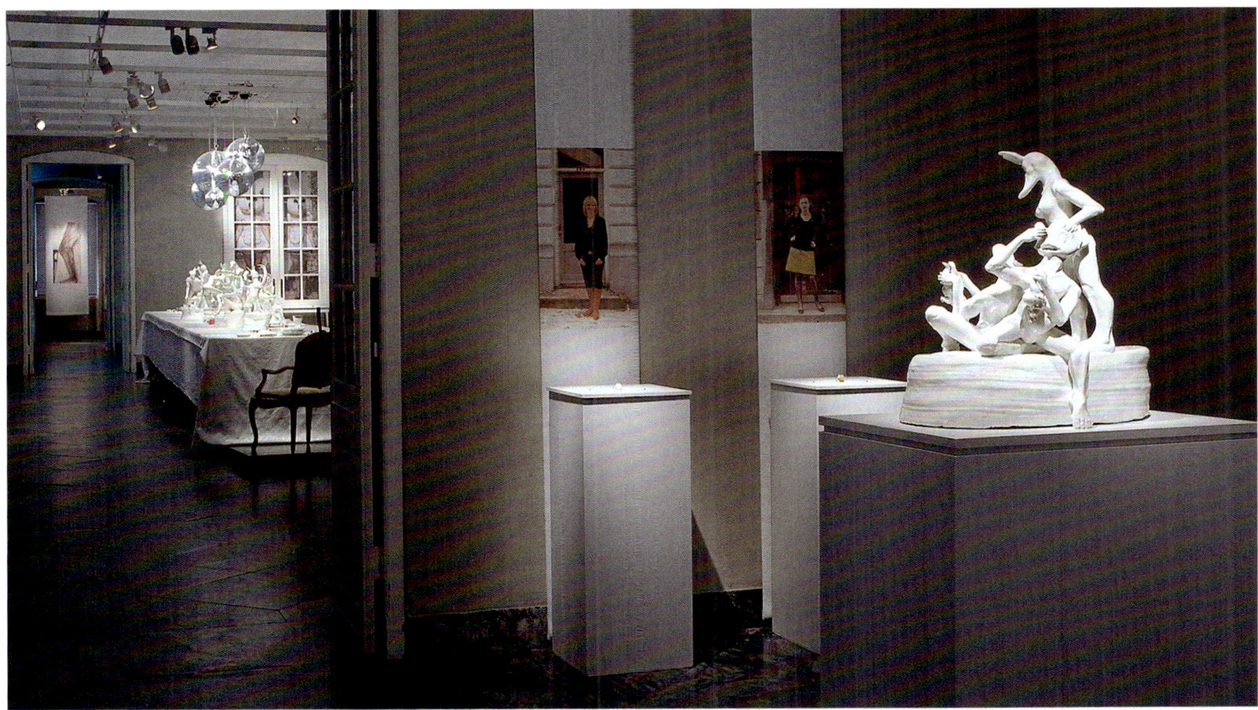

departure-point for reflection, rebellion and renewal. In Danish ceramics, tradition has fulfilled both roles; it has contributed to maintaining a strongly professional standard of craftsmanship and fundamental values related to design and function, and at the same time the weight of tradition has been strong and sufficiently broad-based to incite a generation's rebellion, frustration and action. With the 20th century's 'isms' as the background, and a working context of current international trends in craftsmanship, art and architecture, new technology, new materials and all the media-enabled visual culture, work is going on daily in the studio workshops around the country, with clay as the basic substance and within all genres.

This catalogue of *Danish Studio Ceramics 1950-2010*, which focuses on unique works from studio ceramicists, presents a large amount of material which can hopefully be used for further studies. Through the biographies of 134 ceramicists and artists and 632 works the collections in Designmuseum Danmark are documented throughout this diverse and interesting period when Danish studio ceramics enjoyed a flourishing heyday at a distinguished international level. In the 21st century most of the studio ceramicists are engaged in art-based ceramic undertakings that include commissioned work and many different types of projects, forms, structures and attitude-conveying content. Immersion in an experimental ceramic process and abstract design involving digital tools are elements in present-day ceramic practice that combine in a continual interaction with classical craft skills. In general this symbiosis between tradition and modernity seems to have become embedded in Danish ceramics in the course of the 20th century.

The museum's collecting process throughout the last century has followed the development of ceramics and since the 1980s has laid weight on the acquisition of works that have significance as new interpretations or as developing the conveying of meaning. At the same time the building up of the collection has taken place slowly and with due respect for aesthetic precepts that have been developed in the institution over more than 100 years. These precepts have rested on criteria of judgement linked to a perception of general 'Danish' qualities, for example in the statement the works embody about the ceramicists' fundamental interest in the materials, their respect for skilled craftsmanship and a strong sense of form.

If one considers the individuality and diversity that characterize present-day leading Danish ceramicists in relation to the sweeping globalisation of art trends and the influence of the art market, one might well ask whether today it is at all relevant to think in terms of the concept of Danish ceramics. At any rate one can state clearly that in Denmark there are ceramic works of high quality being made by ceramicists who live in this country and who persist in the will to experiment and thereby to keep clay alive in an artistic process.

Danish studio ceramics in an international context

From the end of the 19th century and right up to the present day, Danish ceramic works have been shown in many international exhibitions, and it is evident that evaluations from abroad have had a strong influence in the identification of the specific character of Danish ceramics, not least where studio ceramics from the second half of the 20th century are concerned. It is not possible to review all relevant exhibitions from this period, but here there are a few that should be mentioned as having had a particular influence on the general profile of Danish studio ceramics seen from abroad. The Kunstindustrimuseum has been involved in these exhibitions and the museum's own collection to some degree represents the same types of values.

After the Second World War a number of Nordic travelling exhibitions were organised to display Scandinavian Design, some arranged by craft organisations, but others by museums, e.g. *The Arts of Denmark*, shown at the Metropolitan Museum of Art in New York in 1960, and *200 Years of Royal Copenhagen* in collaboration with the Smithsonian Institution in 1974-1976. While Gertrud Vasegaard was working at Bing & Grøndahl she took part at the end of the 1950s in the 20th Ceramic International, and in that connection a work of hers was incorporated into the collections of the Everson Museum of Art, Syracuse, NY. With that work and others Gertrud Vasegaard was represented in the exhibition *O Pioneers! Women Ceramic Artists 1925-1960*, which took place in 2015 at the Alfred Ceramic Art Museum, Alfred University, New York. 22 ceramic artists from the USA and Europe were selected for that exhibition, and its purpose was to establish these leading ceramic artists in the art history of the 20th century.[30]

In 1981-82 the exhibition *Danish Ceramic Design*, curated by William Hull, then director of the Palmer Museum of Art, Pennsylvania, made a major impact. Hull had become strongly interested in Danish ceramics, and in the preceding decade he had made numerous journeys to Denmark, visiting some 100 ceramicists in all parts of the country, and working out plans for an exhibition of Danish ceramics to be held in his own museum and four other American museums. This intensive preparation resulted in the exhibition '*Danish Ceramic Design*', which presented 220 new works by 46 ceramicists, 34 of them included in this present catalogue. The exhibition did not include works by fine-artists.

In his preface to the exhibition catalogue William Hull set out clearly the purpose of the exhibition: 'The present exhibition is an overview of the potter's art in Denmark today. It might be referred to as a profile of the field, in that it is not an attempt to show the work of every potter, but was conceived to explore the range of activity and diversity to be found in container forms from country potters to the world-class potters of that kingdom, including commercially produced wares designed by studio potters, a term defining ceramic artists working in their own studios or workshops.'[31]

The pinpointing of the container or pot as a general metaphor for Danish ceramics was and is not unique in what is written about ceramics, but few people have followed this line so devotedly and appreciatively as William Hull, who saw in this a counter-element to the sculptural ceramics developed from the 1950s in the USA and later followed up in large parts of the western world. In his description of Danish ceramics Hull highlighted the importance of immersion in the form of the container as a form of access for the ceramicist to the sensitive treatment of design and decoration, glazing and material texture. Hull perceived particular properties, a special quality, in Danish ceramics that formed a counterbalance to broad international influence.

In the exhibition Hull collected an impressive cross-section of the Danish studio ceramicists of the time, representing both the older generation and the 'in-between' generation, and with study-background from the various colleges in the country as well as ceramicists associated with the porcelain factories and the smaller ceramic firms. The catalogue contains presentations of all the participants with Hull's informative descriptions, which testify to his thorough knowledge of their work.

In connection with the preparation of the exhibition Hull had been in contact with Dorris U. Kuyken-Schneider, the director, over many years, of the ceramic collections at the Boijmans Van Beuningen Museum in Rotterdam; she is a connoisseur of West European ceramics who created, in the years 1970-1995, a particularly fine collection of Danish ceramics, published in a catalogue encompassing identification of distinctive characteristics of Danish ceramics and providing insightful analyses of four Danish ceramicists, Gertrud Vasegaard, Gutte Eriksen, Alev Siesbye and Bodil Manz.[32] In addition to those four the collection in Rotterdam contains works by 41 Danish studio ceramicists, all from the 20th century (and all represented in Designmuseum Danmark's collection); the works are described in the publication together with a presentation of the most important ceramic factories: Bing & Grøndahl, Kähler Keramik, the Royal Porcelain Factory, L. Hjorth (Bornholm) and the Saxbo stoneware factory.

Dorris U. Kuyken-Schneider stated in the catalogue of the Danish works in the collection that the aim of the collection was to focus on the 'container' form, either on objects with a clear functional purpose or on works related to a storage function in the case of 'free' ceramics. At the same time the catalogue text stresses that Danish ceramics is concerned with much else besides 'the vessel theme'. Throughout her incisive analyses of the four selected ceramicists the author lays weight on what they have in common – that they all work both with functional ceramics and with unique works with a universal appeal that owes its origins to inspiration from other cultures, in particular China and Japan.

In 2002, twenty years after William Hull's exhibition of '*Danish Ceramic Design*', a new exhibition of Danish ceramics was arranged in the USA, once more as a result of an American initiative, and using the earlier exhibition as a reference point. The idea of presenting Danish ceramics to the American public came this time from Wendy Tarlow Kaplan, who was an experienced curator with close connections to Denmark, and Hope Barkan; both had a keen interest in ceramic art and both are collectors of modern ceramics. The preparations took place over several years and included almost 80 visits to studio ceramicists in all areas of Denmark, with focus on unique 'one-off' works. It was stressed by the curators that the exhibition would lay weight on continuity of form, i.e. 'the vessel theme', but would also show new trends in Danish ceramics. The exhibition was entitled *'From the Kilns of Denmark'* and opened in the American Craft Museum, New York, in 2002 and in four other American museums in 2003-04; it was then shown in the Danish House in Paris and in the building shared by the Nordic embassies in Berlin.

'From the Kilns of Denmark' displayed one or several works by 30 studio ceramicists, 11 of whom had also been included in '*Danish Ceramic Design*': Gertrud Vasegaard, Gutte Eriksen, Bodil Manz, Malene Müllertz, Bente Hansen, Gerd Hiort Petersen, Inger Rokkjær, Jane Reumert, Beate Andersen, Alev Siesbye and Gunhild Aaberg. The exhibition's 19 'new' ceramicists came mostly from the generation born in the 1960s and mainly educated at Kunsthåndværkerskolen: Morten Løbner Espersen, Michael Geertsen, Turi Heisselberg Pedersen, Steen Ipsen, Gitte Jungersen, Martin Bodilsen Kaldahl, Ann Linnemann, Better Lübbert, Lone Skov Madsen, Bente Skjøttgaard, Flemming Tvede Hansen, Hans Vangsø and Barbro Åberg. But there were also several 'new' names from the older 'in-between' generation, born in the 1940s, such as Aage Birck, Karen Bennicke, Sten Lykke Madsen, Peder Rasmussen and Nina Hole. The works in the exhibition were virtually all made directly for *'From the Kilns of Denmark'*, and all the ceramicists were represented by several works except for Gertrud Vasegaard, in whose case the museum

had lent one single very distinctive work (catalogue no. 2/1988). The intensive preparation carried out by the curators resulted in the presentation of a solidly comprehensive image of Danish ceramics around the turn of the millennium and was very well-received; several works were sold in the USA and some of the exhibiting ceramicists made useful contacts with galleries. A weighty English-language catalogue was produced for the exhibition, with a perceptive article by Gerd Bloxham Zettersten about Danish studio ceramics up to 2002, with analyses of the participating ceramicists' educational background, body of work and placing within the ceramic trends of the time.[33]

'*From the Kilns of Denmark*' can probably be seen as at least a temporary end to the large-scale ceramic exhibitions of Danish or other nationalities; they belong rather to the 20th century. In present-day globalised culture each ceramicist fights his own battle, and running through the present catalogue's biographical summaries will show very clearly that international status nowadays is more important than ever before for Danish ceramicists. They take part in a large range of international exhibition activities and are represented in galleries and at large art and craft fairs, e.g. Collect in London and New York, and SOFA in Chicago, Miami and New York. Danish ceramicists are in serious competition with both their compatriots and ceramicists from the rest of the world.

Notes nos. 1-33 refer to pp. 10-29

1 Bodelsen, Merete: *Gauguin's Ceramics in Danish Collections*, Copenhagen 1960; Zinck, Inge-Lise: *Keramiske værker af Paul Gauguin*, Kunstindustrimuseet 2010; Nielsen, T., 1999; Groom S., 2004

2 Subsequently referred to as the Royal Porcelain Factory; it became Royal Copenhagen from 1987 onwards

3 Gelfer-Jørgensen, M., Copenhagen 2014

4 Lisa Engqvist, Gutte Eriksen, Richard Kjærgaard, Finn Lynggaard, Gudrun Meedom Bæch, Lisbet Munch-Petersen, Christian Poulsen, Gertrud Vasegaard and Birthe Weggerby

5 The artists August Jerndorff, Otto Haslund, Niels Skovgaard, Joakim Skovgaard, Suzette Skovgaard, Elise Konstantin-Hansen and Theodor Philipsen; Brandes, P. (ed.). The ceramicist Thorvald Bindesbøll, Copenhagen 1997; Laursen, B.B. (ed.) Copenhagen 1996.

6 Laursen, B.B. (ed.), Copenhagen 1996

7 Groom, S., Tate Liverpool 2004

8 Rasmussen, P., 2016

9 Bodelsen, M., 1960; Lassen, E., 1968; Opie, J., 1989; Dybdahl, L., 1997; Lautrup-Larsen, L., 2007

10 Poulsen, C.: *Keramisk nytårsstatus*. Dansk Kunsthaandværk 29, 1956, pp. 190-98.

11 Sieck, F., 1981

12 Allpass, H.: *Hvordan er det for et lille værksted at være medlem af Den Permanente .../ What it's like for a small Workshop to be a member of the Permanent exhibition ...* Dansk Brugskunst, 42, 5-6, 1970-71, pp. 143-46

13 Nielsen, T., 2004, pp. 70-77

14 Heisselberg-Pedersen, T. and Jan Helmark (eds): *Keramikkens underskov*, Kolding 1993

15 Lis Ehrenreich, Anne Fløche, Ulla Hansen, Kim Holm, Inger Rokkjær (1934-2008), Kirsten Sloth, Inge Trautner, Hans Vangsø

16 Beate Andersen, Lisa Engqvist, Bente Hansen, Sten Lykke Madsen, Bodil Manz, Richard Manz, Malene Müllertz, Jane Reumert, Gunhild Aaberg

17 Morten Løbner Espersen, Michael Geertsen, Flemming Tvede Hansen, Steen Ipsen, Gitte Jungersen, Lone Skov Madsen, Turi Heisselberg Pedersen, Bente Skjøttgaard, Anne Tophøj

18 *New Danish Ceramics*, 2003

19 *Ny Keramik / New Ceramics, Udstillingssted for ny keramik*, 2002

20 Members of the group 2004: Jane Holmberg Andersen, Marianne Nielsen, Kristine Tillge Lund, Marianne Krumbach, Karin Blach Nielsen, Anders Ruhwald, Christin Johansson, Luise Hindsgavl, Signe Schjøth, Christian Buur Bangsgaard, Ane Møller Davidsen

21 Seisbøll, L., 1998

22 Andersen, Sven Jørn and Eva Bræmer (eds), Kolding 1994, 1997, 2000

23 Nielsen, T., 2009

24 Dannesboe, K., 1990

25 Lehmann-Brockhaus, U., 2007

26 de Waal, Edmund, in: *Lerets Magi*, p. 42

27 Seisbøll, L., 1998

28 Garth, Clark: *How envy killed the Crafts*, 2008. Damsbo, M. and Louise Birch Sørensen, 2011

29 de Waal, E., 2011

30 Shales, E., 2015

31 Hull, W., 1981

32 Keuken-Schneider, D.U., 1995

33 Bloxham Zettersten, G., 1990

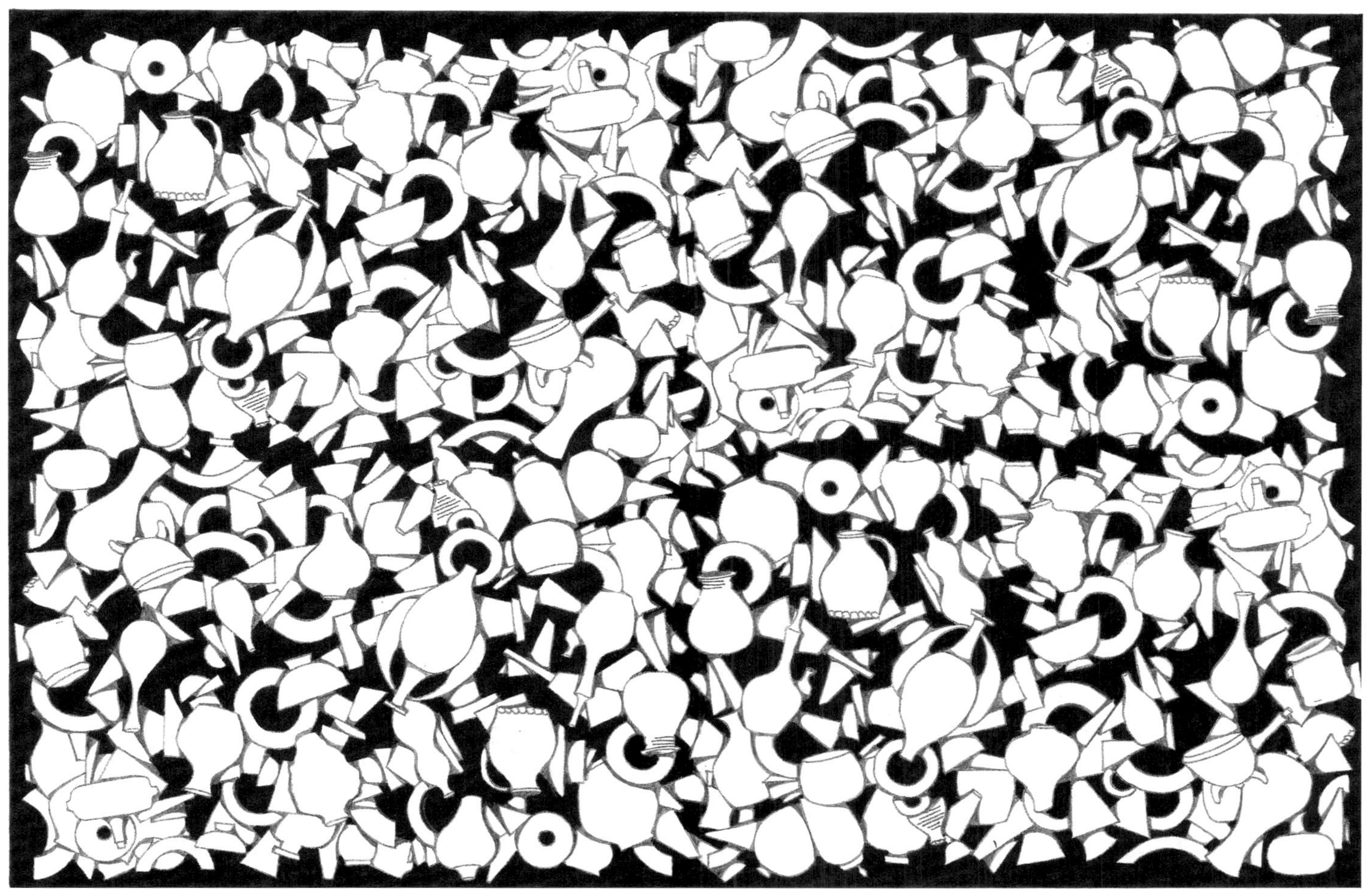

Sketch by the ceramicist Michael Geertsen. 2014

CATALOGUE

About this catalogue: Danish Studio Ceramics 1950 – 2010

Ever since the setting up of the Kunstindustrimuseum in 1890, ceramics has had an important place in the museum's acquisition activities, with the Danish ceramic collections, together with Danish furniture design and industrial design from the last 100 years, as high priority areas. These are the main collections in the representation of Danish design and craftsmanship, built up on an ongoing basis, in most cases through acquisition of contemporary works. The museum has contributed to making Danish culture from the second half of the 20th century internationally recognised for applied art and design through extensive exhibition activities and publications, along with forging close links with the leading craft practitioners, designers, artists, architects and applied art producers.

From the last decades of the 19th century a new chapter in Danish ceramics was heralded in, and it developed through the following century in a triad involving studio ceramics, ceramic works by painters and sculptors, and the country's manufacturers of applied art products. The openness and willingness of the firms involved to cooperate with studio ceramicists and artists has had a decisive influence on the character and quality of Danish ceramics. Through these cooperative links the factories' immense technical and craft-related knowledge and expertise have been channelled out into the ceramic studio workshop milieu.

The purpose of this catalogue of *Danish Studio Ceramics 1950-2010* is to contribute to documentation of a significant epoch in the history of Danish ceramics. That history is represented in the ceramic collection in Designmuseum Danmark, but has not previously been published in the form of a comprehensive overview, and exhibitions in the course of the years have only shown the works concerned on a limited scale. *Danish studio ceramics 1950-2010* forms a chapter within Danish ceramics – a period in which generally increasing prosperity in the decades after the Second World War created an economic basis for the many workshops that were set up throughout Denmark, with considerable help from new technical equipment and from the availability of professional education courses in Ceramics at Kunsthåndværkerskolen and the other educational institutions. The same period of just over half a century constituted both the heyday of traditional studio-workshop-based functional ceramics and also the break-away from the functional tradition towards 'free' creations using clay in sculptural and conceptual forms. The history of these developments is illustrated through the catalogue's 632 works and the biographies of the 133 ceramicists and fine-artists who have made them.

The character and contents of this catalogue

This catalogue aims to be a comprehensive catalogue of the museum's collection from the period in question. Such catalogues, common in the museum world, present a clearly defined area within a collection, e.g. a particular type of object, usually defined by material, and a period or a geographical area; the range of possible subjects is vast, but it is characteristic that all objects or works within the selected area should be included.

This type of catalogue thus not only provides information about the works themselves, but also offers insight into how the collection has been built up and what the museum's acquisition practice has been. One could say that it is a type of test for the museum, allowing the public to follow the choices that have been made over time: have the important works been collected, and is it the most influential practitioners that have been selected for attention? This must and shall of course be a matter for debate – in this case not least among ceramicists themselves and other interested professionals. Here it is important to stress that most of the works in this catalogue were acquired at the time they were made, which has made the museum an active player in the process of ongoing development. Only unique works made by a named ceramicist in a studio workshop are included in this catalogue. This has the consequence that the museum's other Danish ceramic collections from the period 1950 – 2010 are excluded. Unique studio ceramic works have been central in the museum's ceramic collecting and are therefore richly represented. With regard to the painters and sculptors included in the catalogue, their works in many cases were made in conjunction with professional established workshops.[34]

The priority given by the museum to unique works from studio workshops has meant that the large-scale production of series of functional ceramics that has been vital to the economy of the workshops has mostly not been collected, and is therefore not represented in the catalogue.

Another area excluded is that of the museum's important collections of works from the two large porcelain factories: the Royal Copenhagen Porcelain Manufactory/ Royal Porcelain Factory (1775-1987, known as Royal Copenhagen 1987-), and Bing & Grøndahl (1853-1987, incorporated into Royal Copenhagen in 1987). This means that the important porcelain services that were produced in the period covered, many of them in cooperation with studio ceramicists included in this catalogue, have to be left out, as do their many excellent sculptural works in stoneware, porcelain and faience.[35] Even though it is true of a number of ceramicists that they were involved in the factories' artistic workshops during shorter or longer periods, it is only in very few cases that works included here have the artist's signature and also the factory mark.[36] Finally, the boundaries set for the catalogue's contents also exclude a number of influential larger or smaller ceramic firms which have contributed significantly to delineating Danish ceramics over the last 100 years or so, and from which many works are to be found in the museum's collections.[37]

For the series of catalogues of its various collections that Designmuseum Danmark has published, it was decided at the start that the chosen subjects should each be covered within a single volume. The scale of works and ceramicists that are covered in this catalogue match that criterion. It was also important for the choice of the catalogue's subject that the material should be representative in relation to the main lines of development in the period in question. The catalogue is not 'THE book' about Danish ceramics in the 20th century, but a publication of material, a stepping-stone on the way to the major publication which Danish ceramics deserves, and to which the museum's collections can contribute by documenting important episodes of the story.

The growth of the collection

Contemporary ceramics, as already mentioned, has been a priority collecting area from the very start of the Kunstindustrimuseum's existence, but acquisitions have naturally been subject to several factors that have influenced their type and number. Three variables in particular can affect outcomes: access to works, whether they are older or contemporary, which the museum considers to be important for representation of Danish ceramics; the museum's limited economic resources; and finally lack of space.

Despite the museum's focus on ceramics, which reflects the importance of this area in Danish culture, it is only one of many collection-areas in applied arts and crafts, alongside furniture, textiles, glass, silver, industrial design, graphics, etc., and the museum has therefore not been able to adopt the function of specialist museum for one particular area. Developments in the arts and applied arts in the 1980s were based on different ideals, new types of work and an increasingly international orientation, which led many ceramicists and glass artists to want to have their 'own' museums. This resulted in the setting up in 1984 of the Glass Museum in Ebeltoft and in 1994 of the Grimmerhus Museum of Ceramics (CLAY) in Middelfart, which were both initially run by practitioners of their subjects.

From its first beginnings in the 1890s the Kunstindustrimuseum had the task, in collecting, of focusing on contemporary applied art in Denmark and abroad, so from the very beginning the acquisition of new art and craft works was a central concern. It is therefore potentially of interest to examine how the museum has administered this responsibility for contemporaneity in acquisitions and what principles have formed the basis for additions to the collections.

The museum's acquisitions policy in the first decades after it was set up are described in an article from 1916 with the title *Et Par Principper for Kunstindustrimuseets Erhvervelser af moderne danske Arbejder (A few principles relating to the Kunstindustrimuseum's acquisitions of modern Danish works)*, written by the museum's then director, Emil Hannover (1864-1923), who was an international authority in the field of ceramics. An extract is given here, since these principles in many respects have been used as guidelines for the museum until the present day:

> *... It may possibly be of some small use to clarify here a few of the principles according to which acquisitions of modern Danish (and also foreign) decorative works are undertaken by the museum. To begin with it has to be said that an object that is a candidate for inclusion in the museum must first and foremost correspond to the concept of art handicraft, by which we understand a piece of pre-eminent craft, which, whether it serves a practical purpose or a purely decorative one, achieves such a high standard of artistic quality that it has visibly been produced from artistic initiative.... That an object meets certain artistic standards is not however sufficient for it to secure admission to the museum's collections, to allow it there to have a function to fulfil. In addition to the artist and craftsman there is a third factor in the process when we consider the creation of a piece of craftsmanship. That is the material, with its beautiful characteristics which both the artist and the craftsman must awaken from their slumbers and put to use.... Only when there is the right balance in these relationships will an object carry the stamp of being a born entity, which is what we demand of something that is a candidate for inclusion in the museum. But our demands go further still. We require not just that the object is an entity, but also that it is out of the ordinary... To have significance it must be the expression of an original personality... For our acquisitions of modern works it is a conditio sine qua non, that they are products of distinctively artistic individuality, which also means that inevitably they will be typical as products of their time.*[38]

At the end of the article Hannover writes about taste, stating that when all is said and done, one should not take into account, in acquisition policy, considerations other than one's own *'purely personal taste'*, and that all *'judgements of taste that with some justification can be called qualified and positive, are very often taken instinctively fast, without having good reasons worked out, but in fact rest at the deepest level on tried and tested principles'.* Today museums are reluctant to speak of taste, which has elitist connotations and is not politically correct, but Hannover's words articulate well the process of weighing-up that takes place in making an individual acquisition; it should also be underlined, however, that the existing collections always form a sounding-board for evaluation of potential new purchases. There can be very different factors involved and many choices to be made; it may be between a ceramicist/artist with a strong position and an already weighty representation in the museum's collection, or on the other hand a young talent with a first work to be acquired. What will be the verdict of time, and in what future context will the chosen work be seen?

A review of the acquisitions that are included in the present catalogue clearly shows that the museum has taken the prescribed contemporaneity seriously, in that 3/4 of the studio ceramic works collected between 1950 and 2010 were acquired either in the year they were made (most often the case) or within four years. In other words, 428 of the catalogue's 632 works were acquired as new creations. Among the catalogue's 134 ceramicists and other artists there are 38 who are represented with one single work, while it is chiefly studio ceramicists from the earliest generation such as Gertrud Vasegaard, Lisbet Munch-Petersen, Christian Poulsen, Gutte Eriksen, Richard Kjærgaard, Lisa Engqvist, Bjørn Wiinblad and Gudrun Meedom Bæch, and from the following generation Ursula Munch-Petersen, Alev Siesbye, Bodil Manz, Richard Manz, Malene Müllertz, Bente Hansen, Jane Reumert, Myre Vasegaard and Sten Lykke Madsen who have more than ten works in the collection. Gertrud Vasegaard is far ahead with incomparably the richest representation, 39 works, of which 22 came into the collection as contemporary acquisitions while the others are chiefly donations from private persons received during the 1980s and 90s. The many donations testify to the widespread admiration for this distinguished ceramic artist among collectors and ceramics-enthusiasts. The same can be said about Gutte Eriksen, who is represented with the second highest number of works, 21, of which 12 were acquired by the museum near the time when they were made.

The Kunstindustrimuseum has never had fixed sums to spend on acquisitions in its operational budget, and it has therefore been dependent on contributions from external sources. A glance at this catalogue's information about acquisitions will show that many objects have been acquired as a result of donations from a number of foundations, which are named in each case. These non-profit-making foundations have a distinctive character and role in Denmark, and their extensive support for cultural causes is of immense benefit to the cultural institutions of the country in a great many ways, ranging from large building works to the purchase of individual items, e.g. of ceramic work. To eliminate misunderstanding it has to be stressed that all the works in the collection have been chosen by the museum, with a subsequent request for support sent to a foundation. The museum has a particularly close relationship to *Ny Carlsbergfondet* (the New Carlsberg Foundation), created in 1902 by the brewer and patron of the arts Carl Jacobsen (1842-1914), who was among those who took the initiative to set up the Kunstindustrimuseum in 1890. The foundation's generosity to the museum throughout the years has been an important factor in enabling the collections, in virtually all the fields and epochs covered, to maintain an appreciable standard of volume and quality, just as the financing of the series of catalogues that includes this present volume has been made possible by a significant grant from *Ny Carlsbergfondet.*

Among the major donors in connection with the collection of studio ceramics 1950-2010, 39 works were donated by *Ny Carlsbergfondet,* 42 by *Statens Kunstfond* (the Danish Arts Foundation) (museum inventory numbers beginning with D) and 87 were donated by *Selskabet Kunstindustrimuseets Venner* (now *Designmuseets Venner*) (the Association of Friends of the Museum). The Association of Friends was set up in 1910 and until the beginning of the 1980s its support was exclusively reserved for acquisitions of older applied art /craftworks. But in 1983 in a departure from the previous practice, the Friends donated an early work by Asger Jorn, from 1953 (catalogue no. 239). In the year 2000 it was decided that the Association of Friends would in future concentrate its support activities on acquisition of contemporary art/craft work, and this has meant that e.g. the collection of studio ceramics has since then been able to acquire many new works.[39] Another foundation, *Højesteretssagfører C.L. Davids Legat for Slægt og Venner* (Supreme Court Advocate C.L. David's Foundation for Family and Friends), deserves mention here, since that foundation in the first decade of the 21st century has donated grants for several large and important acquisitions, e.g. of works by Karen Bennicke, Aage Birck, Asger Jorn, Bodil Manz, Malene Müllertz, Peder Rasmussen, Alev Siesbye and Per Weiss.

If one takes an overview of the pace of acquisition of the catalogue's 632 works from 1950 to 2010 divided up by decade, there is a conspicuously large range, from 22 in the 1950s, 26 in the 1960s and 43 in the 1970s to 195 in the 1980s, 163 in the 1990s and 185 from 2000 to 2010. The fluctuations naturally call for explanations, but the main reason actually has to lie in the new

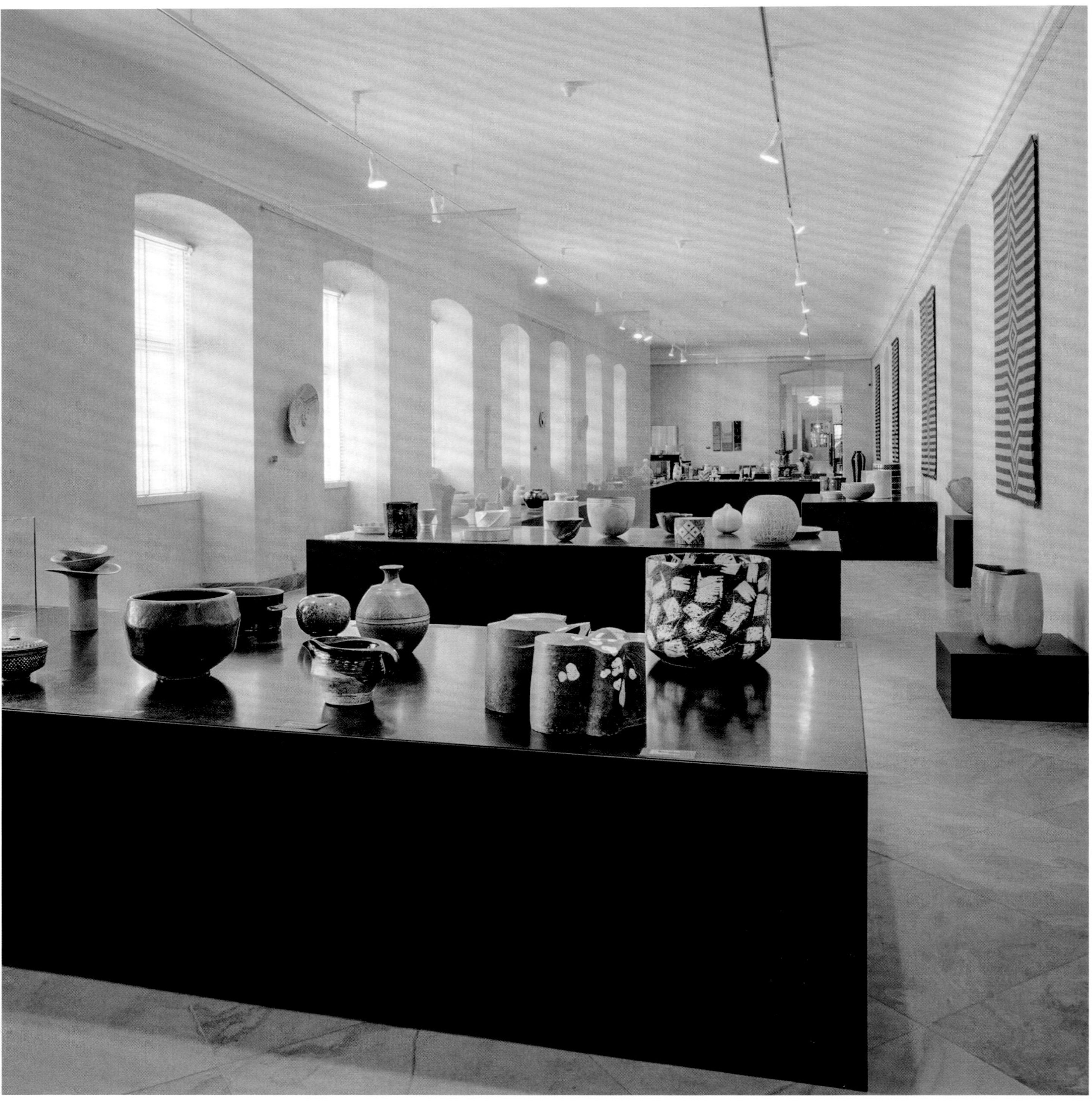

Photo from the exhibition "Danish Ceramics 1947-1997", the largest exhibition of Danish studio ceramics held in Designmuseum Danmark until now. The exhibition was organised in 1997 by Vibeke Woldbye, museum curator.

Photo Ole Woldbye.

and interesting development of Danish ceramics in that period. Many leading ceramicists from the 1980s onwards created a multitude of important pioneering works that held references to the international ceramics scene, in a break-away from the 'Danish tradition'. That tradition had been described in 1960 by the art historian Merete Bodelsen, a perceptive connoisseur of Danish ceramics, as a cultural tradition distinguished by continuity and a striving to create art of a timeless nature in harmony with the most noble traditions in ceramic craft.[40] In the introduction to the museum's major retrospective exhibition in 1997, '*Dansk Keramik 1947-1997*', museum curator Vibeke Woldbye (1932-2015) referred to Merete Bodelsen's description with the addition *'to that it must be added that Danish ceramics continuously takes its departure-point in the functional, or at any rate in a design-realm that owes its origins to functional applied art. And then there is the undefinable: respect for material, clarity, textural effect'.*[41] The quotations signal the value the museum placed on classical Danish ceramics at the threshold of a new era; already in 1993 some of the young ceramicists had shown their desire to break away from the earlier generations and had argued for a new and up-to-date view of ceramics and of its placing in the contemporary context, setting out their case in the convincing exhibition *'Keramikkens underskov'.* (see p. 18)

The requirement of contemporaneity in connection with acquisitions of applied art has been met not just through acquisitions but also in exhibition policy. In the period 1950-2010 the Kunstindustrimuseum held a total of 129 ceramic exhibitions (see list of exhibitions p. 354), an average of two a year, and in connection with those exhibitions it made 27 purchases. Of the 129 exhibitions held, only four showed ceramics from before 1900, while all the others had exhibits from the 20th and 21st centuries. In addition to the exhibitions on the list, ceramic works through the years have also been included in a large number of the museum's major thematic exhibitions, including currently in 2016/17 '*Learning from Japan*', with many historic and recent examples of Danish and Japanese studio ceramics and a focus on the continuing importance of Japan as a source of inspiration in Danish architecture and applied art, not least in the field of ceramics.[42]

On several occasions the Kunstindustrimuseum has presented large-scale selections of the studio ceramics collection; the two most important of these were the exhibitions *'Brændpunkter-Dansk Keramik 1890-1990'*[43] *and 'Dansk Keramik 1947-1997'.* The selection of works for *'Brændpunkter'* testifies to the museum's preferences among the major well-known ceramic artists from before 1950. The exhibition contained 148 works by 94 ceramicists (in the present catalogue 49 of the 94 are represented), beginning with works by Thorvald Bindesbøll and Niels Hansen Jacobsen, and then others by Patrick Nordström (1870-1929), the founder of the stoneware tradition at the Royal Porcelain Factory, and from the same factory the two influential stoneware artists Jais Nielsen (1885-1961) and Axel Salto (1889-1961). From Bing & Grøndahl works were displayed by the architect and ceramicist Carl Petersen (1874-1923), who was inspired by Japanese and Chinese ceramics and decorative motifs to experiment independently in the early years of the 20th century and introduced trials of stoneware in the factory as artistic director in 1911-13. In the *'Brændpunkter'* exhibition several works from the 1930s by ceramicists associated with the ceramic firm of Saxbo (1929-68) under the direction of the chemical engineer Nathalie Krebs (1895-1978) were displayed. All of the above-mentioned stoneware artists had between three and five works in that exhibition, as did the early studio ceramicists Gutte Eriksen, Christian Poulsen and Gertrud Vasegaard, while the other ceramicists in the exhibition were represented by just one selected work.

In 1997 the museum held another major exhibition of selected works from the collection, with the title *'Dansk Keramik 1947-1997'*, featuring works by 66 ceramicists and artists, all of them included in the present catalogue except seven who were primarily connected with the factories. Among the artists exhibited were Peter Brandes, Niels Erik Gjerdevik, Asger Jorn, Erik Nyholm, Bjørn Nørgaard and Lene Adler Petersen. The ceramicists represented belonged chiefly to the generations born in the 1940s and 50s, and most of them had studied at Kunsthåndværkerskolen with Richard Kjærgaard as the charismatic head of the ceramics department and with stoneware as the material at the centre of their work. There were also representatives of earthenware in the exhibition – e.g. Gudrun Meedom Bæch, Lisa Engqvist, Inger Rokkjær and Anne-Lise Bruun Pedersen. The last two in particular used the raku technique, which had been cultivated from the 1960s by a group of ceramicists with studio workshops in Jutland and links to Det Jyske Kunstakademi and to the exhibition group *8 keramikere*. That group had several exhibitions in Denmark and abroad in the years around 1990, some in Galerie Besson in London.

At the same time as this exhibition was held in the museum, another exhibition of Danish ceramics from 1850-1997 was shown in the exhibition venue at Sophienholm, Lyngby, north of Copenhagen, curated by Lars Dybdahl, the museum's present Head of Library and Research; this grand exhibition included many historic and contemporary loans from the museum's collections, and conveyed a convincing account of 150 years of the country's applied art ceramics as well as unique art works from individual studio ceramicists and artists – a total of 407 works, of which 39 were new works made for the exhibition by a corresponding number of ceramicists.[44]

As is apparent from the list of the museum's ceramic exhibitions, they have to a large extent presented work by Danish ceramicists, but in the 1970s and 80s in particular several presentations of foreign ceramicists were arranged, including Ryozo Miki and Hiroaki Morino from Japan, David Leach and Glenys Barton from England, and Erik Ploen from Norway. Taking an overall view it seems that the connection to British design and ceramics has been dominant since the Second World War, but that this also applied earlier in that century, when functionalism had a strong grip in Danish culture and there was a pronounced interest in British design. In 1932 the museum held an extensive exhibition of *'Britisk Brugskunst'* (British applied art) arranged by the eminent architect and professor at the Architecture School of the Academy of Fine Arts, Steen Eiler Rasmussen (1898-1990), and at another exhibition in 1959 called *'British Design'* the museum purchased a work by Geoffrey Whiting.

The orientation towards English ceramics showed itself in the 1940s in admiration for Bernard Leach and his Japanese-inspired ceramics, which gained a widespread following through *A Potter's Book*, published for the first time in 1940 and subsequently in numerous reprints and new editions. The book had an enormous distribution and significance, chiefly in Britain, but it also became virtually a textbook for studio ceramicists in the early post-war period. Several Danish ceramicists found their way to St Ives in Cornwall and spent short or long periods there at Bernard Leach's studio, including Gutte Eriksen, Lisa Engqvist and Anne Kjærsgaard. In the opposite direction there were British 'studio potters' who were interested in Danish/Scandinavian ceramics in particular in the 1950s, when *Scandinavian Design* and *Danish Modern* had made an impact.[45] Other relationships arose through the years between Danish and British ceramicists; in 1992 the exhibition group *Keramiske Veje* invited Elisabeth Fritsch to participate in that year's exhibition. Fritsch was familiar with Danish ceramics because of the period she had spent as artist-in-residence at Bing & Grøndahl in 1972-73, when she had had her first solo exhibition here.

In the museum's very limited range of modern foreign ceramics the British collection is dominant, with more than 50 works acquired since the 1970s – by e.g. David Leach, Elisabeth Fritsch,

Richard Batterham, Janice Tchalenko, Walter Keeler, Ewen Henderson, Alison Britton, Colin Pearson, Nicholas Rena, Yasuda Takeshi and Edmund de Waal. A particular group of works from the 1970s by Hans Coper was donated in 2001 by Dorris and Fred U. Kuyken-Schneider as part of a major bequest to the benefit of the museum. The warm relations between the museum's ceramics curator Vibeke Woldbye and Dorris U. Kuyken-Schneider, for many years head of the department of modern ceramics at the Boijmans Van Beuningen Museum in Rotterdam, came to be of immense benefit to Danish ceramics, since this influential and perceptive Dutch connoisseur of contemporary ceramics acquired some 250 works by selected Danish ceramicists during the years 1970-1995.[46]

The connections between English and Danish ceramics intensified further in the later decades of the 20th century, when several Danes who had studied applied art took post-graduate courses in London at the Royal College of Art, formed gallery contacts and joined exhibition groups. One result of these connections was the large and interesting exhibition *'Britisk Keramik-British Ceramics.2000.dk'*, arranged and shown by Grimmerhus Museum of Ceramic Art (CLAY) in the year 2000 with the participation of 31 British ceramicists; one of the curators was Martin Bodilsen Kaldahl, who had taken an MA at the Royal College of Art in 1988-90. The exhibition was an important opportunity to experience the diversity of expression, materials and techniques in contemporary British ceramics and to discover similarities and differences between British 'studio potters' and Danish studio ceramicists.[47]

As yet another ramification of relations between Danish and British ceramicists, in 2007 the exhibition group *END* was formed, with Alison Britton, Richard Slee and Martin Smith from Britain, together with Marit Tingleff from Norway and Karen Bennicke, Martin Bodilsen Kaldahl and Peder Rasmussen from Denmark. The group held its first exhibition in the museum that year.[48]

Sources and bibliographical material

The live and primary sources for studio ceramics are of course the ceramicists and artists who live and work in locations all round Denmark in their inspiring and hospitable workshops and home environments. There traces can be found of the innumerable experiments that form the basis for their works and that have their place in the long historical sequence that has ensured the continued standard of quality of Danish ceramics in terms of choice of materials, craftsmanship and content.

Many of the ceramicists and artists in this catalogue have written informatively, in periodicals and other catalogues, about their approach to their work and their products, about inspiration and cooperation with colleagues and about being a ceramicist. There is a discernible openness and willingness to exchange useful knowledge about materials and methods, and there are connections running in all directions through the ceramic landscape. Full publications about present or past studio ceramicists, on the other hand, are few and far between – only a handful exist, and they have all been published after the year 2000.[49] Articles, reviews and exhibition catalogues, however, provide a web of information that can be used in conjunction with comments in reference works about education, factories and workshops.

The history of Danish studio ceramics from the decades around the middle of the 20th century is described in greatest detail by the art and architecture historian Gerd Bloxham Zettersten, in a fundamental study, from 1990, amplified in several subsequent articles in which she discusses and analyses important factors in the context of the early 'studio earthenware' from 1930-1960.[50] The starting point of the study, in 1930, coincides with the setting up of Kunsthåndværkerskolen in the Kunstindustrimuseum's Pavilion, beside the museum. The school was owned and run by 'Det tekniske Selskab' (The Technical Society) through its School Committee, with the museum represented on its board because the museum's craft school, set up in 1901, had been incorporated into the new school.[51] In the ceramics courses the students were taught drawing and brush techniques with particular weight on modelling and throwing clay; pottery as a craft in Denmark was thought to be a dying skill, so it was seen as particularly necessary to train students to ensure that there would be future ceramicists who would be able to throw their own shapes. The purpose of the school was unequivocally to train craft workers for industrial production. There was tuition in earthenware and earthenware techniques, but experiments with stoneware had already been carried out in the factories and in larger ceramic workshops such as Herman A. Kähler in Næstved and L. Hjorth in Rønne on Bornholm from as early as 1902. The school aimed at training craft workers to be of use in industrial firms, but in the 1950s many individual workshops for textiles, metalwork, woodwork and ceramics came into existence, and this generated extensive criticism from industrial producers, who saw those workshops as competitors.

In the 1930s and 40s, with a departure-point in earthenware, the first generation of important studio ceramicists was educated at Kunsthåndværkerskolen. That generation, through their teaching – lasting many years - of new generations of ceramicists, and as a result of their own ceramic activities, played an important role in the development of the field of ceramics in the decades after 1950. In the 1930s the first shared workshops were set up, but seldom lasted long, because of insufficient resources. Bloxham's study, which was in part based on interviews with a number of the main personages, covered 57 earthenware ceramicists, of whom 11 are represented with many works in the museum's collection, including Lisa Engqvist, Gutte Eriksen, Richard Kjærgaard, Finn Lynggaard, Gudrun Meedom Bæch, Lisbet Munch-Petersen, Christian Poulsen, Gertrud Vasegaard, Birte Weggerby and Bjørn Wiinblad.[52] In the course of the 1950s most of them went over to working with stoneware; a few, such as Lisa Engqvist, whose painterly and delicately-shaped works reflect the best of popular ceramics in many cultures, and Gutte Eriksen, who created an original oeuvre in hard-fired earthenware with roots in Japan and the Leach tradition, continued to work in earthenware throughout their lives. From this group of early great studio ceramicists, all strong and individualistic personalities representing different approaches to ceramics, lines can be traced forward to the present. But as Bloxham's study shows, right from the early days of studio ceramics in the 1930s and 40s there was a rich blossoming of ceramicists. With experience from applied art manufacturing, pottery workshops, technical schools, the Academy of Fine Arts and elsewhere they formed together an ample body of talent and energy to create the fertile environment in which the post-war Danish studio ceramics could grow.

In 2007-08 the Kunstindustrimuseum carried out an investigation with a survey that was sent out to all the ceramicists and artists in the present catalogue, asking them to provide details about the works that were in the museum's collection. Thanks to the participants' readiness to reply with technical and other information, often followed up with conversations, the museum's knowledge about the collection of studio ceramics has been extended and this new material has been an important source for the catalogue's descriptions of works and biographical summaries. This material will in future be accessible in Designmuseum Danmark's Library.

The main access-route to publications about Danish ceramics is *'Dansk Keramisk Bibliografi'*, compiled by Gunnar Jakobsen – a bibliographical work of 967 pages, published in 2014 (a revised and up-dated version of the original edition from 1998). This work contains references to publications on Danish ceramics from the 18th century and up to the present, with the main emphasis on the period 1880-2013.[53] The bibliography also covers biographical reference works, publications with lists of marks and signatures, workshops and factories, educational institutions, exhibition groups, ceramicist- and artist- families, exhibitions, shops and galleries, and many other subjects. The main section, which covers references to ceramicists, artists and designers, is a true treasury, since knowledge about this enormous gallery of persons otherwise consists of a complex web of references in periodicals, newspapers, exhibition catalogues, reviews, brochures, etc. The bibliography contains in the same volume a Danish, an English and a German text and has references to publications in Danish and other languages. This bibliography thus renders access to the study of Danish ceramics dramatically less burdensome, in addition to the fact that its clear division of subjects allows the reader to form an overview of the history of the field of Danish ceramics, the persons involved and the form of their involvement.

Designmuseum Danmark's Library is Denmark's professional library for applied art, craft and design, and since the museum was founded it has been an integrated part of the institution. The Library contains a comprehensive collection of Danish and international books and periodicals as well as the Archive of Danish Design and the Artist Archive. The latter is a large collection of original material about individual artists, craftworkers and designers, in the form of reviews, pamphlets, portraits, exhibition invitations, etc., that make up a vast source material e.g. for Danish studio ceramics.

Most importantly of all, it must be remembered that it is within Designmuseum Danmark's walls that the physical collection of these ceramic works lies – all 632 works, now catalogued and documented in print, and visually recorded in individual photographs in this volume.

Notes nos. 34-53 refer to pp. 32-41

34 Kähler Keramik, Næstved; NEES Fællesværksted, Holstebro (1980-84); L. Hjorth, Rønne; Tommerup Teglværk, Tommerup (1984-)

35 re Table-services: Gertrud Vasegaard, *Testel* 1955-57, Bing & Grøndahl. Table-services *Gemina and Gemma* 1959-62, *Capella* 1973-75, Royal Porcelain Factory. Bodil Manz, table-service *Facet* 1982-84, Bing & Grøndahl. Alev Siesbye, table-services *Sirius* and *Leda* and a series of bowls *Midnight*, 1990s, Royal Porcelain Factory

36 Sten Lykke Madsen and Ivan Weiss are included because of their independent artistic activities in the factories and the establishment of their own workshops after moving in 2004 from Royal Copenhagen's historic factory buildings in Smallegade, Frederiksberg, Copenhagen

37 Among others: Eslau (1944-2002), Herman A. Kähler (1839-1974), Palshus Stentøj (1949-1971) and Saxbo (1931-1968)

38 Hannover, E., 1916, pp. 133-136

39 Christensen, C., 2010

40 Bodelsen, M., 1960

41 Designmuseum Danmark, Exhibition Archive

42 Gelfer-Jørgensen, M., 2013

43 Dannesboe, K., (ed.), 1990

44 Dybdahl, L., 1997

45 Watson, O., 1990, p. 30; Opie, J., 1989

46 Keuken-Schneider, D., 1995

47 Seisbøll, L., 2000

48 Bodelsen Kaldahl, M., Betak Cleemann, J., Christiansen, M. (ed.), END exhibition catalogue, 2007

49 Gertrud Vasegaard: Jørgensen, H., 2011;
Bodil Manz: Bruun, N. and Bodil Busk Laursen (eds), 2009;
Ursula Munch-Petersen: Nielsen, T.: 2004;
Richard Manz: Manz, C. (ed.), 2015;
Jane Reumert: Dirckinck-Holmfeld, K. (ed.), 2003;
Alev Siesbye: Dostoglu and Alexandra de Cramer (ed.), 2016;
Bjørn Wiinblad: Olsen, L.H., 2016;
Karen Bennicke: Bennicke, K. (ed.), 2016

50 The term 'studio earthenware' is used synonymously with the present catalogue's 'studio ceramics'.
See: Bloxham Zettersten, G., 1990

51 Hannover, E., 1920; Gelfer-Jørgensen, M., 2014

52 Bloxham Zettersten, G., 1990

53 Jakobsen, G., Copenhagen 2014

Key to the structure of catalogue entries

This catalogue is organised alphabetically by surname of the ceramicists/artists included in it. It should be noted that the Danish characters 'æ', 'ø' and 'å' (the last-mentioned sometimes written 'aa') come at the **end** of the alphabet used in English. For technical reasons the entries in this catalogue necessarily follow the Danish alphabetical order, and readers may find it most convenient to use the list of names on p. 44 to find page numbers for any individual ceramicist's entry.

The individual entries in the catalogue follow a specific system:
Biographical data, including education, employment and the year of establishment of the artist's own studio workshop, with in many cases a reference to an internet website where detailed information about exhibitions, representation of works, prizes and awards, etc. may be found.

A general description of the individual ceramicist's work as a background to a brief account of the works by that artist that are to be found in the museum's collection. The number of works is of significance for the length of the description, in which weight is also given to the individual artist's importance within the field of ceramics more generally, for example through exhibition cooperatives, initiatives regarding exhibition locations, teaching at the design schools, and published works.

In some cases references are given to publications that have been of particular use in compiling these entries. Readers in search of further information are also referred to this catalogue's bibliographical list, which includes general comments, and above all to the major source of bibliographical knowledge about Danish ceramics and its practitioners, Gunnar Jakobsen's *Dansk keramisk bibliografi / Danish ceramics bibliography / Dänische keramische Bibliographie*, Copenhagen, 2014.

Information about the museum's works by the ceramicist/artist in question, including: category (e.g. pot, vase, sculpture), date, title (if given), materials, technique (firing temperatures in centigrade), measurements (in centimetres), maker's mark and acquisition (exhibition, gallery, directly from the ceramicist/artist, donation from foundation or from private person), with references to descriptions in the museum's publications. The works are listed chronologically, in accordance with the museum numbers; e.g. mus. no.150/1990, indicates that 150 is the object's number, while 1990 shows the year when the object was acquired and registered by the museum. A particular group of works has numbers beginning with D, which denotes an object deposited by *Statens Kunstfond*, the Danish Arts Foundation. Those objects are included last in the lists of works.

The chronological ordering of listing the works by the museum's inventory number has been chosen, rather than ordering by the date of the actual work (which is indicated alongside the title of the individual object), because the intention in the catalogue is to give weight to the building up of the museum's collection, showing for example when the works were acquired in relation to when they were made. This information is of relevance in providing insight into the museum's acquisition practice.

The catalogue's information on materials and techniques is based to a large extent on an investigation carried out by the museum in 2007/2008, involving questionnaires that were sent out to ceramicists/artists whose works were included in the museum's collection in the period 1950-2010. The many replies sent back constitute a significant body of information that was received by the museum with warm gratitude, and has been of great use in compiling the present catalogue.

Readers are also referred to the glossary (p. 352) for explanations of technical terms.

The ceramicists and artists included in this catalogue

The collections of Danish ceramics in the Kunstindustrimuseum (the Danish Museum of Art and Design, now Design Museum Danmark), from the birth of the museum in 1895 and up until the present day, consist of works by both ceramicists and fine-artists. Most of the ceramicists whose works are included in this catalogue were educated in the craft and design colleges in Copenhagen and Kolding or in Aarhus at the Det Jyske Kunstakademi (The Jutland Art Academy) and Aarhus Kunstakademi (Aarhus Art Academy), while a few of them trained as potters in one of the ceramic workshops/potteries or ceramic firms that were so numerous in Denmark in earlier days, and in which many of the others also spent shorter or longer periods. The fine-artists represented have completed studies at the Danish Art Academies, or have had at least sporadic association with them, in most cases with the Royal Danish Academy of Fine Arts. For most, in both groups, these forms of study have been supplemented over the years by periods spent in workshops and teaching posts in Danish institutions or abroad, and in both groups there are a few cases of autodidacts.

A feature that the 119 ceramicists in the catalogue have in common, with very few exceptions, is that they have developed an unbroken stream of ceramic activity involving establishing and maintaining their own studio workshops. They represent several 'generations' of ceramicists, beginning in around 1930 with the early major 'names' such as Lisbet Munch-Petersen, Gertrud Vasegaard, Christian Poulsen and Gutte Eriksen, who continued their individual production in the decades up to the millennium and even beyond, and who have had enormous influence on the development of Danish studio ceramics. Among the major artists and ceramic pioneers are Asger Jorn and Erik Nyholm, who are represented in the museum's collection with significant works. The generation that followed consists of a large and important group of 52 ceramicists and artists born in the first half of the 1940s and of 18 born in the 1950s. Together the works of these 70 individuals make up the basis of the museum's collection of studio ceramics from 1950 and up to the present; they were the leading figures in the international breakthrough of Danish ceramics in the later decades of the 20th century, and their works, which are among the most appreciated and sought-after on the international exhibition scene, are also represented in museums and private collections in many different parts of the world. As teachers and advisers many of them have played an important role for the next generation of ceramicists, born in the 1960s – a generation which is represented in the catalogue by 20 individuals. The smallest and youngest group in the catalogue consists of four ceramicists born in the 1970s.

The geographical location of the studio workshops

Just as there is a span of generations among the ceramicists in the catalogue, ranging over the whole period covered, there is also a wide geographical distribution of studio workshops over all areas of the country, with some 45 in and around Copenhagen, 30 in the rest of Sealand, 12 on Bornholm, 4 on Funen and 30 in Jutland. In all seven ceramicists have at present, or have had, workshops that they have established elsewhere in Europe or in the USA. This geographical distribution reflects to some degree proximity to the education centres in Copenhagen, Aarhus and Kolding respectively; it is also related, in very recent years, to the Glass and Ceramics Programme at the Design School on Bornholm, which holds a particular status because of the strong ceramic and artistic environment created in and around the ceramic firm of L. Hjorth.

List of names of ceramicists and artists

AHLMANN, PER ... 48
ALLPASS, HELLE ... 49
ANDERBERG, TOVE ... 50
ANDERSEN, BEATE ... 54
ANDERSEN, CLARA ... 56
ANDERSEN, HANS MUNCK ... 58
BENNICKE, KAREN ... 60
BERNARD, NELL ... 66
BERTELSEN, HANNE ... 67
BERTRAM, HELGE ... 68
BIRCK, HEIDI LUZIE GUTHMANN ... 71
BIRCK, AAGE ... 72
BLOCH, MERETHE ... 75
BLOCH, OLE ... 75
BRANDES, PETER ... 76
BROKSØ, TINE see CLAYDIES ... 97
BRUHN, INGER ... 80
BRUUN, CHRISTIAN ... 81
BRYNJOLF, JØRGEN ... 82
BÆCH, GUDRUN MEEDOM ... 82
BÆKHØJ, POUL ... 85
BÖRJESON, BIRGITTE ... 86
BÖRJESON, HANS ... 86
von BÜLOW, ANE KATRINE ... 89
BØRSTING, STEN ... 91
BAARSTRØM, GERD ... 92
CHRISTENSEN, KIRSTEN ... 93
CHRISTIANSEN, JESPER ... 96
CLAYDIES:
BROKSØ, TINE ... 97
KJÆLDGÅRD-LARSEN, KAREN ... 97
DAVIDSEN, MOGENS ... 98
DAVOLIO, SANDRA ... 99
EHRENREICH, LIS ... 100
ENGQVIST, LISA ... 101
ERIKSEN, GUTTE ... 108
ESPERSEN, MORTEN LØBNER ... 115
FISCHER-HANSEN, ELSE ... 118
FLØCHE, ANNE ... 120
GAIHEDE, JYTTE ... 122
GEERTSEN, MICHAEL ... 123
GJERDEVIK, NILS ERIK ... 125
GLOB, LOTTE ... 126
GOLDENBERG, LENNY ... 127
HANSEN, BENTE ... 128
HANSEN, FLEMMING TVEDE ... 135
HANSEN, JØRGEN ... 136
HARRISON, ANNE MARIE ... 138
HEIDE, DORTE SCHIERUP ... 139
HERLUFSDATTER, MARIANNE ... 141
HERMANSEN, INGE MARIE BULLER ... 141
HESSELHOLDT, SOFIE see
HESSELHOLDT & MEJLVANG:
HESSELHOLDT, SOFIE ... 143
MEJLVANG, VIBEKE ... 143
HINDSGAVL, LOUISE ... 144
HJORTH, MARIE ... 147
HJORTH, ULLA ... 148
HOLE, NINA ... 149
HOLM, KIM ... 152
HOUGAARD, KARIN ... 154
HØM, JULIE ... 154
IPSEN, STEEN ... 156
JENSEN, BERIT HEGGENHOUGEN ... 159
JENSEN, ELSE KAMP ... 160
JENSEN, OLE ... 161
JOCHIMSEN, JOBIM A. M. see SOUVENIX ... 291
JORN, ASGER ... 163
JUNGERSEN, GITTE ... 167
KALDAHL, MARTIN BODILSEN ... 168
KJÆLDGAARD-LARSEN, KAREN see CLAYDIES 97
KJÆRGAARD, RICHARD ... 170

KJÆRSGAARD, ANNE ... 176
KNUDSEN, PER BØRGLUM ... 177
KRISTENSEN, KNUD ... 178
KRISTENSEN, NINA MØLLER ... 179
KRISTIANSEN, BO ... 180
KRÜGER, ANDERS ... 183
KÄHLER, HERMAN JØRGEN ... 184
LINDBLAD, GRETHE ... 185
LINNEMANN, ANN ... 186
LÜBBERT, BETTER ... 188
LYNGGAARD, FINN ... 189
MADSEN, LONE SKOV ... 192
MADSEN, STEN LYKKE ... 194
MANZ, BODIL ... 198
MANZ, RICHARD ... 206
MAY, MARIANNE ... 212
MEJLVANG, VIBEKE see
HESSELHOLDT & MEJLVANG ... 143
MEYER, LILLER ... 213
MORTENSEN, IDA HOLM ... 213
MUNCH-PETERSEN, LISBET ... 214
MUNCH-PETERSEN, URSULA ... 219
MÜLLERTZ, MALENE ... 226
MØHL, FELIX ... 231
MØLLER, DORTHE ... 231
NYHOLM, ERIK ... 232
NØRGAARD, BJØRN ... 236
PACKNESS, JESPER ... 238
PEDERSEN, ANNE LISE BRUUN ... 239
PEDERSEN, ESTHER ELISABETH ... 241
PEDERSEN, TURI HEISSELBERG ... 242
PETERSEN, GERD HIORT ... 244
PETERSEN, LENE ADLER ... 248
POULSEN, BJØRN ... 251
POULSEN, CHRISTIAN ... 252
POULSEN, METTE AUGUSTINUS ... 256
POULSEN, TUE ... 257
RANSLET, ARNE ... 258
RASMUSSEN, PEDER 1 ... 258
RASMUSSEN, PEDER 2 ... 260
REGIUS, LENE ... 266
REIFF, ERIK ... 268
REUMERT, JANE ... 271
ROKKJÆR, INGER ... 276
RUHWALD, ANDERS ... 278
RYTTER, VIBEKE ... 280
SCHMIDT, VIBEKE FONNESBERG ... 281
SIESBYE, ALEV ... 282
BENTE SKJØTTGAARD ... 287
SLOTH, KIRSTEN ... 290
SOUVENIX:
JOCHIMSEN, JOBIM A.M ... 291
TOPHØJ, ANNE ... 291
STEPHENSEN, SNORRE LÆSSØE ... 293
SØRENSEN, JØRGEN HAUGEN ... 297
THING, INGER ... 298
THOMSEN, SYS ... 301
TOPHØJ, ANNE se SOUVENIX ... 291
TYBJERG, PETER ... 305
VANGSGAARD, METTE ... 306
VANGSØ, HANS ... 307
VASEGAARD, GERTRUD ... 309
VASEGAARD, MYRE ... 320
VEJLØ, CHARLOTTE ... 325
WEGGERBY, BIRTHE ... 326
WEISS, IVAN ... 328
WEISS, PER ... 331
WIINBLAD, BJØRN ... 334
ØRSTED, METTE MARIE ... 338
AABERG, GUNHILD ... 339
ÅBERG, BARBRO ... 343

BIOGRAPHICAL SUMMARIES AND CATALOGUE OF WORKS

AHLMANN, PER 1965 –

Ceramicist

1988-90	Tommerup Ceramic Workshop
1991-95	Designskolen Kolding, Jutland
1995-98	Shared workshop, Amager; 1998-2001 Viktoria, Copenhagen
2001-03	Designskolen Kolding, instructor
2003-	Own studio workshop, Tommerup, Funen www.perahlmann.dk

Fascination with clay as a material is a prime motivational force in the sculptural pieces created by Per Ahlmann (PA); he has a rare ability to give form to wet and soft clay, whether as modelled shapes that suggest insights into indefinable organic tissue or as more architecturally formed structures. The composite elements of the works are given

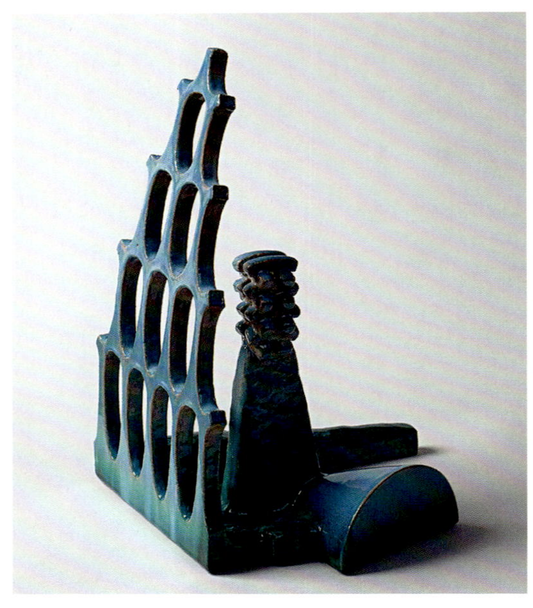

2. 122/2009

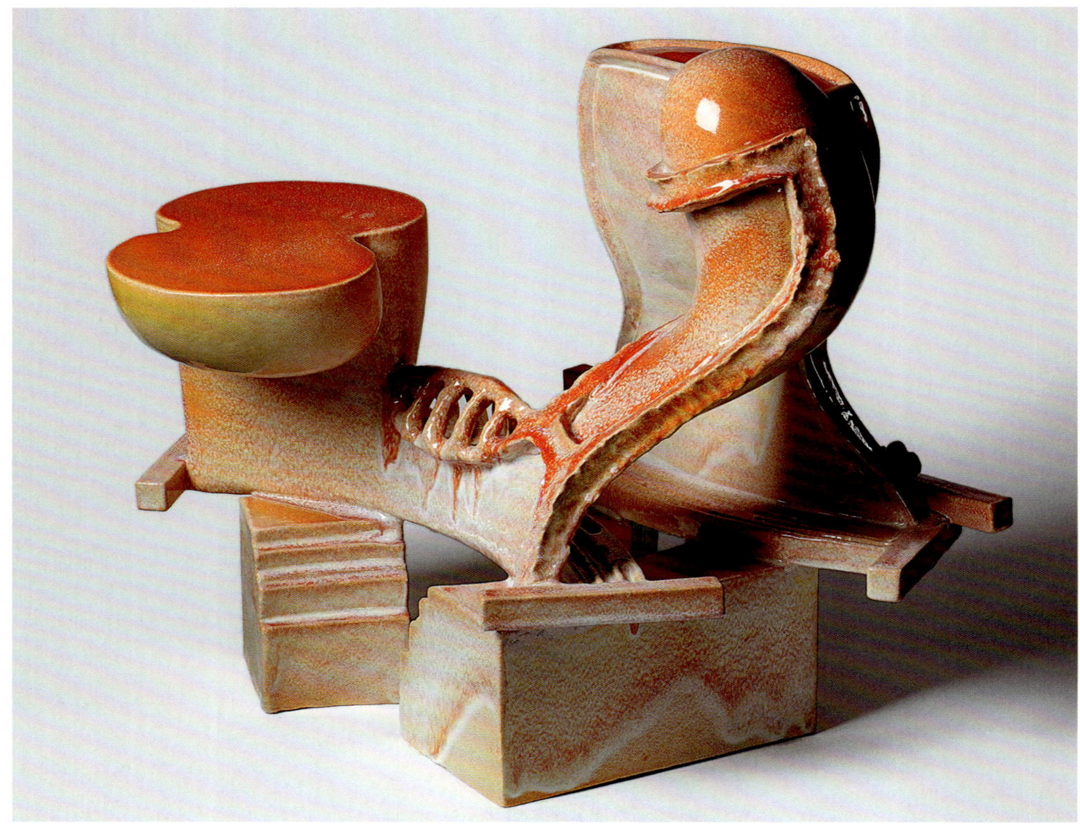

1. 237/2006

emphasis by the rich colour tones of the glaze, which span the whole spectrum and are often aggressive and provocative. *Babewell* **(1)**, a work which the museum acquired from PA's first solo exhibition in 2006 in Galleri Nørby, is conspicuous with its glossy salmon-coloured glaze, achieved using three firings. The colour underscores the main theme of the sculpture, taking inspiration from the sculptor Rudolf Tegner's *Danserindebrønd*, in Elsinore, depicting three young women dancing around the rim of a well. PA implies in this work a connecting line drawn from the erotic allure of the lightly clad dancers and their delicate movements to the more insistent and titillating fetish culture of the present.

The museum's other work, entitled *Tomorrow* **(2)** provides a contrast to *Babewell*, in that it has no soft shapes, and the blue colouring is cool and distant. Clearly delineated architectural forms characterize this vision of the future. In his exhibition in 2006 PA came to the fore as an important representative of abstract ceramic sculpture, and in 2007 he was awarded *Annie & Otto Johs. Detlefs'* Prize for Ceramics. Since then he has continued to explore this direction, with works that flow freely between the categories of sculpture, ceramic pieces and objects, and more recently, in his solo exhibition *Scalp* in Galleri Kant in 2014, he moved into new realms. Throughout all his ceramic works PA has been closely involved with Tommerup Ceramic Workshop. It was Esben Lyngsaa Madsen, the owner and director of the workshop, who originally encouraged him to take up ceramics. In 2003 PA established his own workshop in Tommerup.

1. Sculpture, 2006. *Babewell*
Stoneware, majolica- and cryolite-glazed; modelled, fired at 1040°.
H 45 x W 56 x D 39. Mark: none. Mus.no. 237/2006
ACQUISITION: *Per Ahlmann*, 2006, Galleri Nørby, Copenhagen. Donation from *Højesteretssagfører C. L. Davids Legat for Slægt og Venner*

2. Sculpture, 2006. *Tomorrow*
Earthenware, glazed; modelled, assembled pieces. H 35 x W 24 x D 23.5.
Mark: 'Ahlmann 06'. Mus.no. 122/2009
ACQUISITION: Donation from *Ny Carlsbergfondet*

ALLPASS, HELLE 1932 – 2000

Ceramicist

1951-56	Studied architecture at the Royal Danish Academy of Fine Arts
1956-57	Worked with ceramicist Thora Garde
1957-	Own studio workshop, Mørdrup, N Sealand

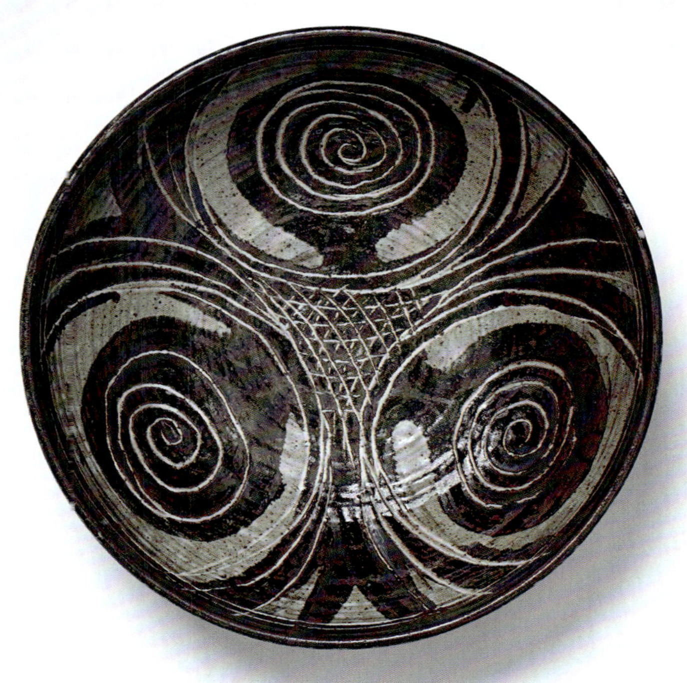

3. 48/1972

Helle Allpass (HA) belonged to the generation of ceramicists, in the postwar period, who combined producing a very extensive range of controlled-quality hand-thrown ceramics, mass-produced for domestic purposes, with creating well-defined unique works in robust stoneware. The museum's large thrown and glazed dish from 1972 **(3)** is a good example of the latter type of work; it is pleasingly shaped with a fine harmony in the choice of materials and expression. The workshop's products were widely distributed and in the 1960s and 70s they were sold through Den Permanente, in Copenhagen, where HA also had several solo exhibitions. HA was represented in a number of official international exhibitions of Danish applied art and design in the 1960s.

HA was the third generation in a family of ceramicists, and ran her own workshop for almost half a century. Her daughter, the ceramicist Ane Schollert, Copenhagen, is carrying the tradition into the fourth generation.

3. Dish, 1972

Stoneware, glazed; thrown, decorated. H 16 x Diam 56.6. Mark: none. Mus.no. 48/1972. ACQUISITION: Helle Allpass. Donation from *Kunstindustrimuseets 50-års Jubilæumslegat*

ANDERBERG, TOVE 1942 –

Ceramicist
Autodidact

1973	Studied Chemistry, Aarhus University
1974-	Own studio workshop, Uggerhalne, Vodskov, Jutland

Tove Anderberg (TA) provides her works with a special character both in terms of their idiom and the texture of their glaze. One perceives them as being created from within outwards, from an inner depth; they are organic, or even anthropomorphic, as is emphasized by the often delicate and subdued colours of the glazes, with their matte silky sheen and perfect totally-covering layer. Throughout over 40 years, from her workshop in northern Jutland TA has created an extensive *oeuvre* which has been exhibited both nationally and internationally and which has led to 12 commissioned works, most of them ceramic, but including some in bronze, textiles, etc.

7. 171/1984

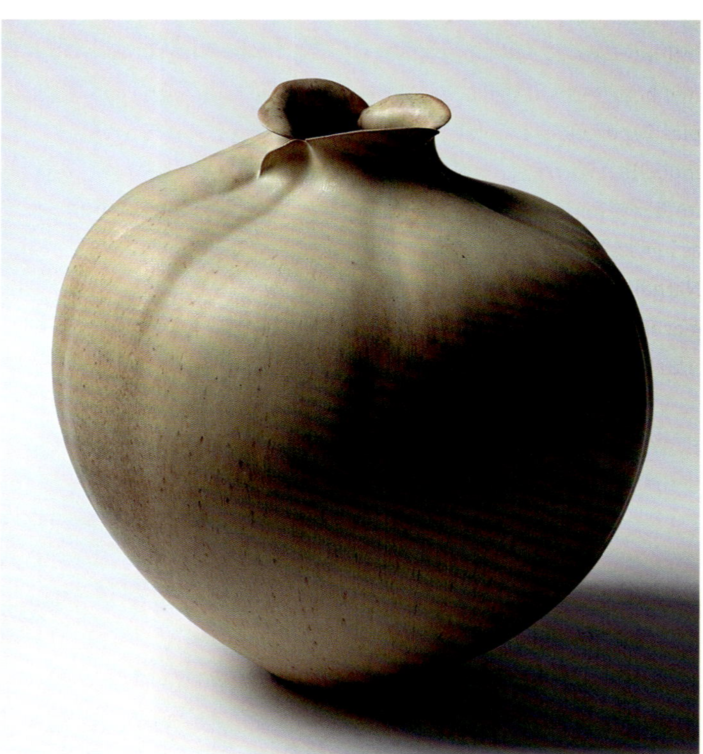

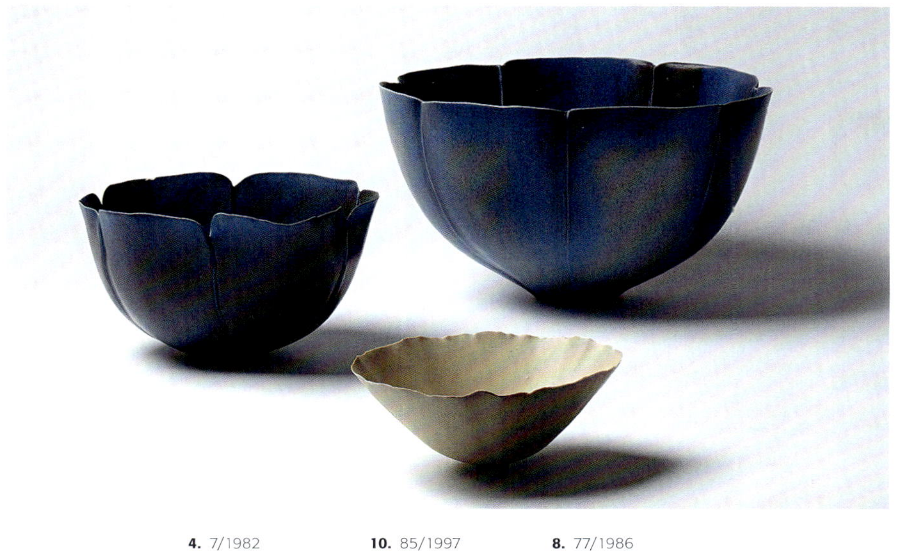

4. 7/1982 **10.** 85/1997 **8.** 77/1986

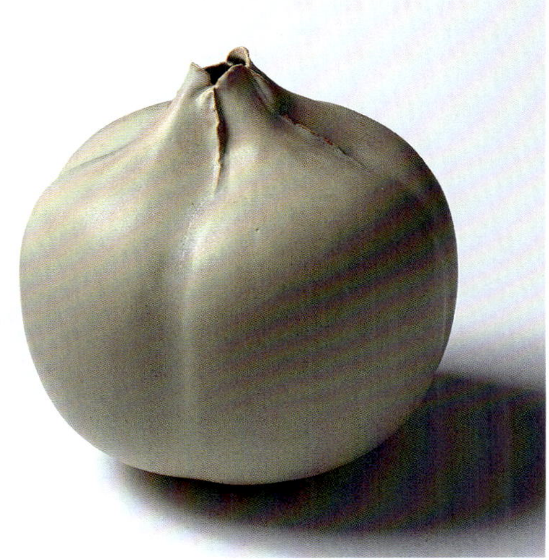

5. 8/1982

In common with other contemporary Danish ceramicists, TA began by producing articles for everyday use in thrown stoneware, but was influenced by a visit to England in the mid 1970s, during which she met both Bernard Leach and Lucie Rie, to convert to using the more plastic porcelain clay, and from that she developed to creating her modelled sculptural works. Another important source of inspiration for her work with glazes, to which she gave high priority from as early as her studies in Chemistry at Aarhus University, was the study of Nathalie Krebs's glazes for the Saxbo company. The perfection of these glazes was not merely adopted into TA 's work but further developed into her own personal expression, involving from an early stage the very luminous glazes that became characteristic of her works.
The museum's collection of TA's works comprises ten pieces, eight of them from the 1980s and the two most recent from around 2000. The principal object in the collection is a work that is almost 50 cm in height, entitled *Læber i rytme. Hommage à Ib Geertsen* **(11)**, from 2000. The leaves terminate at different heights, indicating rhythm, and the glaze is sprayed on with a layer of orange and six layers of yellow. The work testifies to TA's confident modelling of the large corpus and the sensual references to the human figure which are a frequent motif in her works.

Important inspiration also comes from impressions of the powerful and manifold forms of nature in TA's everyday surroundings. This emerges clearly in many of the works in the collection, which bear references ranging from stone, landscapes, shore and sea, flowers and fruit. The titles of her works often refer to inspiration from nature, e.g. *Sandbowl* **(4)**, *Seedbowl* **(5)**, *Fine feathers* **(7)**. The harmony of form and glaze finds convincing expression in the large open bowl *September yellow*, where the warm golden uranium glaze on the outer side brings out the leaf decoration and brings to mind autumn and the warmth of late summer **(9)**.

Since the 1970s TA has participated in many group exhibitions and has had several solo exhibitions, including a memorable one in Silkeborg Bad Kunstcentret in 2002. The most recent retrospective overview of TA's work was presented in Vendsyssel Kunstmuseum in 2012, in an exhibition celebrating her 70th birthday, which gathered more than 80 works in a comprehensive display of this very individualistic and distinguished ceramic body of work. See: Tove Anderberg. *Håndens/åndens værk*, Vendsyssel Kunstmuseum, 2012

4. Bowl, 1980. *Sandskål* (Sandbowl)

Stoneware, earthenware, tin-glazed; modelled, fired at 1260°. H 8.5 x Diam 19.5. Mark: 'Tove Anderberg' inscribed on base. Mus.no. 7/1982

ACQUISITION: *Keramiske arbejder*, 1980-82, Nordjyllands Kunstmuseum. Donation from *Ny Carlsbergfondet*

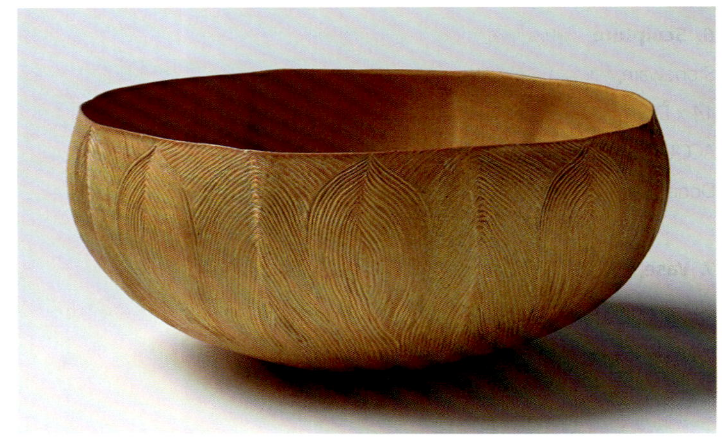

9. 128/1991

6. 37/1983

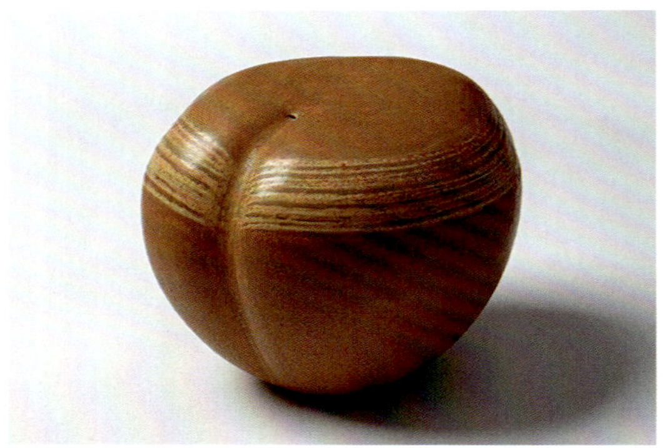

5. Vase, 1981. *Kimplante* (Seedling)

Stoneware, porcelain, tin-glazed; thrown, modelled, assembled, fired at 1260°. H 22.5 x Diam 21.5. Mark: 'Tove Anderberg' inscribed on base. Mus.no. 8/1982

ACQUISITION: *Keramiske arbejder*, 1980-82, Nordjyllands Kunstmuseum. Donation from *Ny Carlsbergfondet*

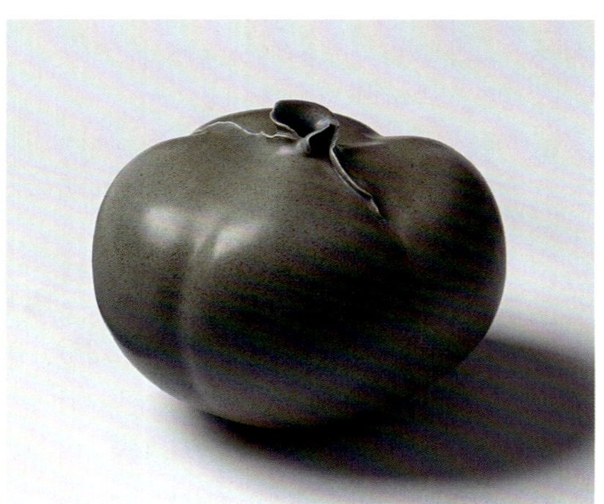

12. 418/2008

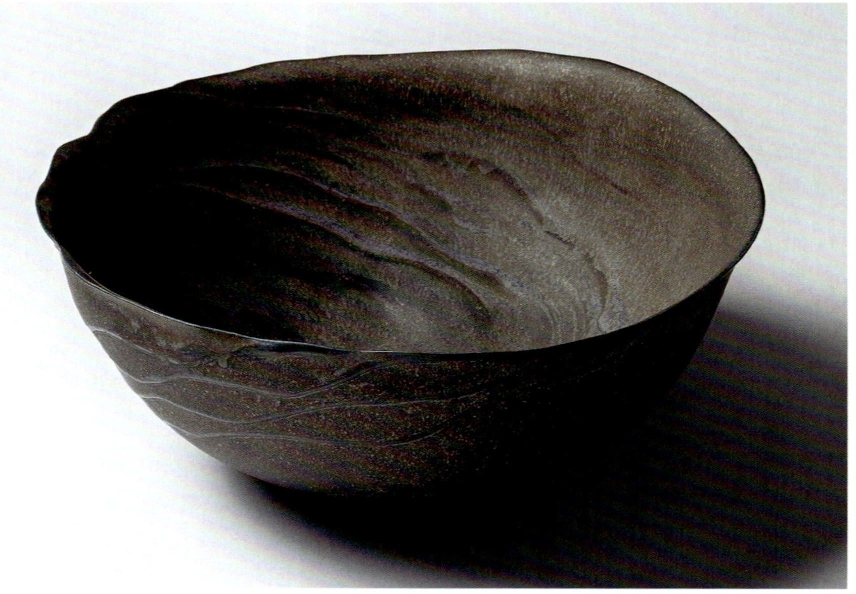

13. D 1586

6. Sculpture, 1982. *Sten* (Stone)
Stoneware, feldspar- and ochre-glazed; modelled, sprayed, fired at 1260°. H 14 x Diam 16. Mark: 'Tove Anderberg' inscribed on base. Mus.no. 37/1983
ACQUISITION: *Tove Anderberg and Grete Balle*, 1983, Galleri Stubtoft, Sorø. Donation from Benny *Dessaus Mindelegat*. See: *Brændpunkter*, 1990

7. Vase, 1984. *Fjerpragt* (Fine feathers)
Stoneware, porcelain, tin- and feldspar-glazed; modelled, fired at 1260°. H 38 x Diam 37. Mark: 'Tove Anderberg' inscribed on base. Mus.no. 171/1984
ACQUISITION: *Efterårsudstillingen,* 1984, Charlottenborg. Donation from *Finansieringsinstituttet for Industri og Håndværks Jubilæumslegat*. See: *Brændpunkter*, 1990

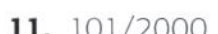
11. 101/2000

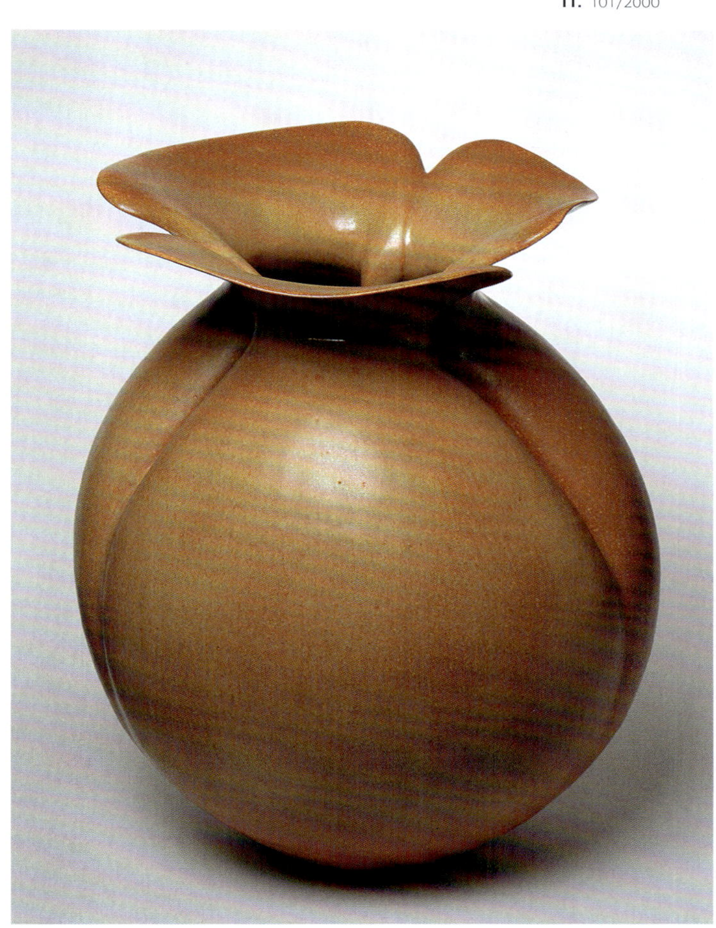

8. Bowl, 1985. *Kineserier* (Chinoiserie)
Stoneware, porcelain, feldspar-glazed; modelled, assembled, sprayed. H 21.5 x Diam 35. Mark: 'Tove Anderberg' inscribed on base. Mus.no. 77/1986
ACQUISITION: *Tove Anderberg*, 1985, Kunsthallen, Copenhagen. Donation from *Kunstindustrimuseets Venner*

9. Bowl, 1989/90. *September gul* (September yellow)
Stoneware, porcelain, uranium- and tin-glazed; thrown, cut decoration, fired at 1260°. H 14 x Diam 29. Mark: 'Tove Anderberg' inscribed on base. Mus.no 128/1991
ACQUISITION: *Krukken og dens modsætning*, 1990, Kunsthallen. Donation from *Kunstindustrimuseets Jubilæums- og Mindelegater*

10. Bowl, 1982. *Nattens blomst* (Flower of the night)
Stoneware, porcelain, tin-glazed; modelled, assembled, fired at 1260°. H 14 x Diam 25.5. Mark: 'Tove Anderberg' inscribed on base. Mus.no. 85/1997
ACQUISITION: *Tove Anderberg-Naturens poesi / nye keramiske arbejder, Kunstindustrimuseet,* 1983. Donation from *Ausa Regitze Tillys Legat*

11. Vase, 2000. *Læber i rytme – Hommage à Ib Geertsen*
(Lips in rhythm – Homage to Ib Geertsen)
Stoneware, porcelain, tin-glazed with ash; thrown, modelled, assembled, fired at 1260°. H 49 x Diam 40. Mark: 'Tove Anderberg' inscribed on base. Mus.no. 101/2000. ACQUISITION: Donation from *Ny Carlsbergfondet*

12. Vase, 1990s
Stoneware, glazed; thrown, modelled, assembled. H 15. Mark: 'Tove Anderberg' inscribed on base. Mus.no. 418/2008
ACQUISITION: Donation from the estate of Ambassador Niels Christian Tillisch, Copenhagen, 2008

13. Bowl, 1982. *Under overfladen* (Under the surface)
Stoneware, tin-glazed with ash; thrown, cut, modelled, fired at 1260°. H 13 x Diam 32. Mark: 'Tove Anderberg' inscribed on base. Mus.no. D 1586
ACQUISITION: Galleri Stubtoft, Sorø. On deposit from *Statens Kunstfond*, 1985

ANDERSEN, BEATE 1942 –

Ceramicist

1960-64 Kunsthåndværkerskolen

1964- Strandstræde Keramik, studio and shop shared with Jane Reumert and Gunhild Aaberg, Copenhagen
www.beate-andersen.dk

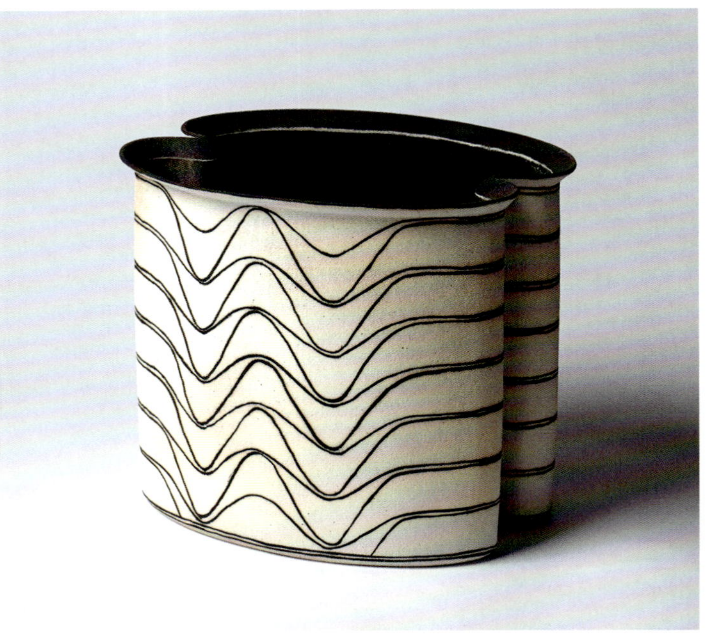

19. 216/1997

In the course of many journeys to Nepal, Tibet and India, Beate Andersen (BA) has studied and become fully engaged in the prolific world of patterns in those cultures, and this has enriched the development of the decoration she convincingly applies to her ceramic works. For BA the goal and purpose of work with ceramics is to achieve full integration of pattern and form. The mastery she has achieved through years of intense and spiritual absorption in ceramic decoration was recently displayed in the many works that were included in the 30-year anniversary exhibition held by *Keramiske Veje* at the exhibition venue Sophienholm in 2015.

BA studied at Kunsthåndværkerskolen with the charismatic ceramics teacher Richard Kjærgaard, and completed her studies in 1964 at the same time as Jane Reumert and Gunhild Aaberg. At the start of their careers it was an advantage to share the costs of setting up a workshop, so together they created the shared workshop community *Strandstræde Keramik*, which still exists as a studio workshop, gallery and shop in inner Copenhagen. It is remarkable that the three ceramicists, despite their shared workshop, have developed very differently with strongly divergent ceramic forms of expression.

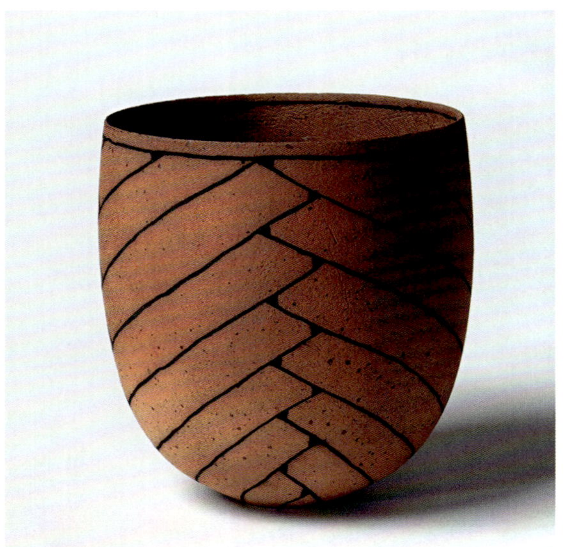

18. 12/1990

In parallel with other ceramicists of her generation, BA was influenced, in her choice of stoneware and classical basic shapes as the departure-point for her work, by the teaching at the college and the ideals embedded there concerning in particular the responsibility to produce good articles for domestic use at reasonable cost. The container, the dish, the jug and the bowl, in many different nuances, have shown themselves to offer perfect opportunities to achieve the harmony between decoration, materials and form that she has continued to seek and has succeeded in finding.

The seven works by BA in the museum's possession are evenly distributed over the 1970s, 80s and 90s. They are all thrown and reflect two categories of her creations: one consisting of stoneware and porcelain

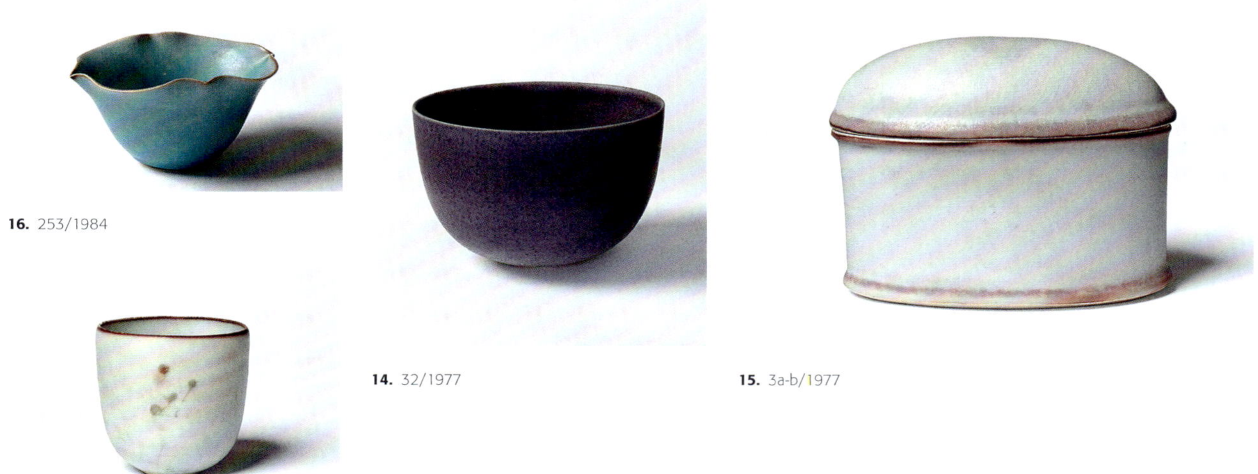

16. 253/1984

14. 32/1977

15. 3a-b/1977

17. 254/1984

glazed with barium glazes, which when fired with oxygen-access emerge with blue/green nuances **(14,16)**, and the other featuring dry glazes (usually reddish or ash grey) on stoneware, on which patterns with optic effects are built up with simple brush strokes of black oxide, before the object is fired at 1300° **(18-20)**. The age-old pursuit of playing with the geometric patterns of the Orient has found an excellent Danish proponent in BA.BA has exhibited regularly in Denmark and abroad throughout her career and is a member of the exhibition group *Keramiske Veje*. Her work is represented in several influential museums and in private collections.

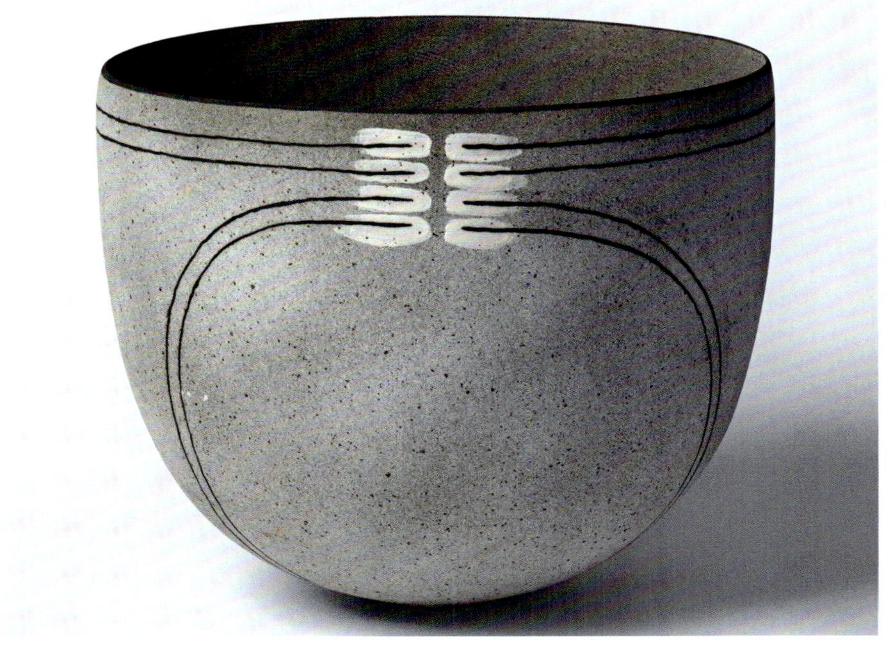

20. D 1235

14. Bowl, 1977

Porcelain, barium glazed; thrown, fired at 1280°. H 8.5 x Diam 13.5. Mark: 'BA' stamped on base. Mus.no. 32/1977. A cquisition: *Strandstræde keramik,* 1977, Kunstindustrimuseet. Donation from *Overretssagfører Odin Kaysers Legat*

15. Lidded pot, 1977

Porcelain, barium-glazed; cast, fired at 1280°. H 11 x Diam 13.5. Mark: 'BA' stamped on base. Mus.no. 3a-b/1977 ACQUISITION: *Strandstræde keramik,* 1977, Kunstindustrimuseet. Donation from *Overretssagfører Odin Kaysers Legat*

16. Bowl, 1982

Stoneware, barium-glazed; thrown, shaped, fired at 1280°. H 7 x Diam 12.5. Mark: 'B 82' painted on base. Mus.no. 253/1984 See: *Brændpunkter*, 1990. *Thomsen, S.,* 1983

17. Cup, 1981

Porcelain, barium-glazed; thrown, decorated. H 7 x Diam 7. Mark: 'B 81' painted on base. Mus.no. 254/1984. See: *Thomsen, S.,* 1983

18. Vase, 1989

Stoneware, dry- and iron-glazed; thrown, sprayed, brush-painted, fired at 1300°. H 17 x Diam 15. Mus.no. 12/1990 ACQUISITION: Strandstræde Keramik, Copenhagen. Donation from *Ny Carlsberg Museumslegat.* See: *Brændpunkter*, 1990

19. Vase, 1997

Stoneware, dry-glazed; modelled, cast, brush-painted, fired at 1300°. H 19.5 x W 18 x D 22.5. Mark: 'Beate 1997' painted on base. Mus.no. 216/1997 ACQUISITION: *Keramiske veje,* 2005, Den Frie

20. Bowl, 1990

Stoneware, dry-glazed; thrown, modelled, brush-painted, fired at 1300°. H 28 x Diam 32.5. Mark: 'Beate 1990' painted on base. Mus.no. D 1235 ACQUISITION: On deposit from *Statens Kunstfond*, 1995

ANDERSEN, CLARA 1944 –

Ceramicist

1966-68	Pottery apprentice
1968-71	Det Jyske Kunstakademi, ceramics
1971-2004	Own studio workshop, Aarhus
1982-88	Aarhus Kunstakademi, chemistry of glazes, instructor
1988-91	Designskolen in Kolding, Ceramics and Glass, principal instructor

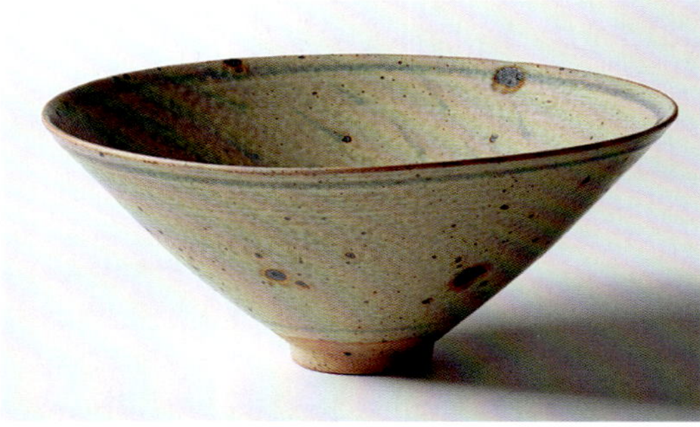

24. 293/1992

Clara Andersen was taught by Gudrun Meedom Bæch at Det Jyske Kunstakademi. She rapidly set up her own workshop and took part in adjudicated exhibitions both in Denmark and internationally. She took part in the first serious effort to present Danish ceramics in the USA – '*Danish Ceramic Design*' in 1982, arranged by William Hull; her work is also represented e.g. in the Boymans-van Beuningen Museum, Rotterdam, acquired for that museum by the Head of its Ceramics Department, Dorris U. Kuyken-Schneider, who is an expert connoisseur of Danish ceramics.

In the period around the mid 1980s, Clara Andersen developed what became known as the *Y-skåle* (Y-bowls) taking inspiration from Persia and the Far East. The thin-walled bowls are made of thrown earthenware or stoneware and usually glazed in warm monochrome shades. The works in the museum's collection are all examples of types of Y-bowls, and include a very fine large glazed bowl acquired at the exhibition '*Jysk Sommer*' held in the museum in 1989 **(22).**

Clara Andersen is a particularly well-educated and skilled ceramicist who has taught at several education centres. She has not been active since 2004, when she gave up her studio in Aarhus.

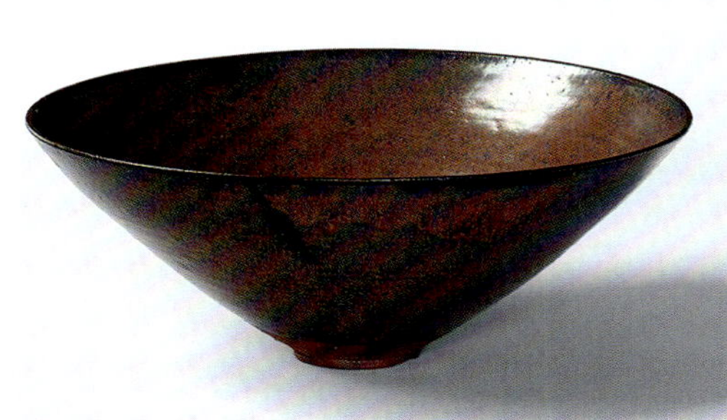

21. 162/1984

21. Bowl, 1984

Earthenware, borax-glazed with iron and ochre; thrown, fired at 1150°. H 9 x Diam 22.3. Mark: 'C' in a square stamped on the base. Mus.no. 162/1984

ACQUISITION: Clara Andersen. Donation from *Finansieringsinstituttet for Industri- og Håndværks Jubilæumslegat*. See: *Brændpunkter*, 1990

22. Bowl, 1986

Earthenware, lithium-glazed; thrown, fired at 1100°. H 16 x Diam 32.5. Mark: 'C' in a square stamped on the base. Mus.no. 158/1989

ACQUISITION: *Jysk sommer*, 1989, Kunstindustrimuseet. Donation from *Benny Dessaus Mindelegat*. See: Dybdahl, L., 1997

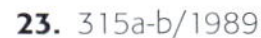

23. 315a-b/1989

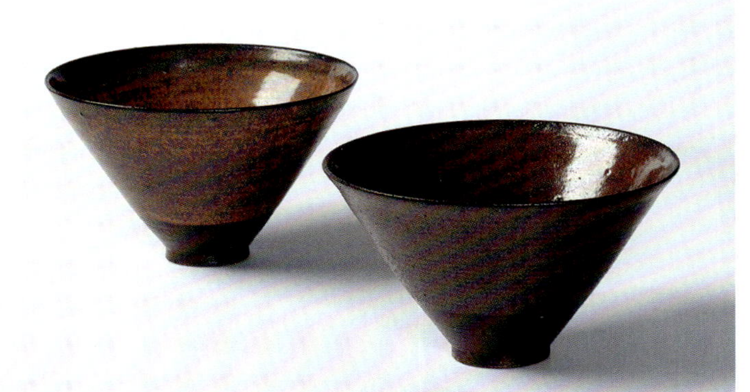

23. Two bowls, 1984

Earthenware of own composition, borax-glazed with iron and ochre; thrown, fired at 1150°. H 8.3, x Diam 14. Mark: a: 'C' in a square stamped on the base, 1984; b: '55 1984', C in a square. Mus.no. 315a-b/1989

ACQUISITION: *Månedens souvenir*, 1989, Kunstindustrimuseet's shop

24. Bowl, 1992

Stoneware, feldspar- and barium-glazed; hand-thrown, brush-painted, fired at 1260°. H 9.5 x Diam 22.4. Mark: Painted 'C' in a plaster stamp on base. Mus. no. 293/1992.

ACQUISITION: Clara Andersen, 1992, *Dalhoff Larsens Fond*. See: Dybdahl, L., 1997

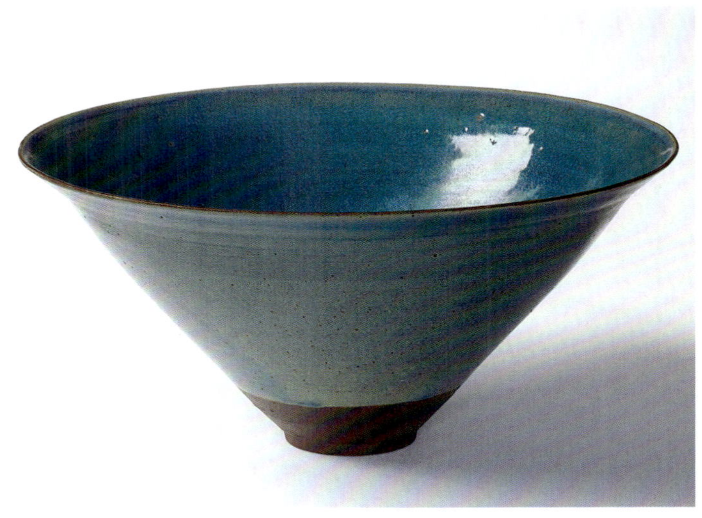

22. 158/1989

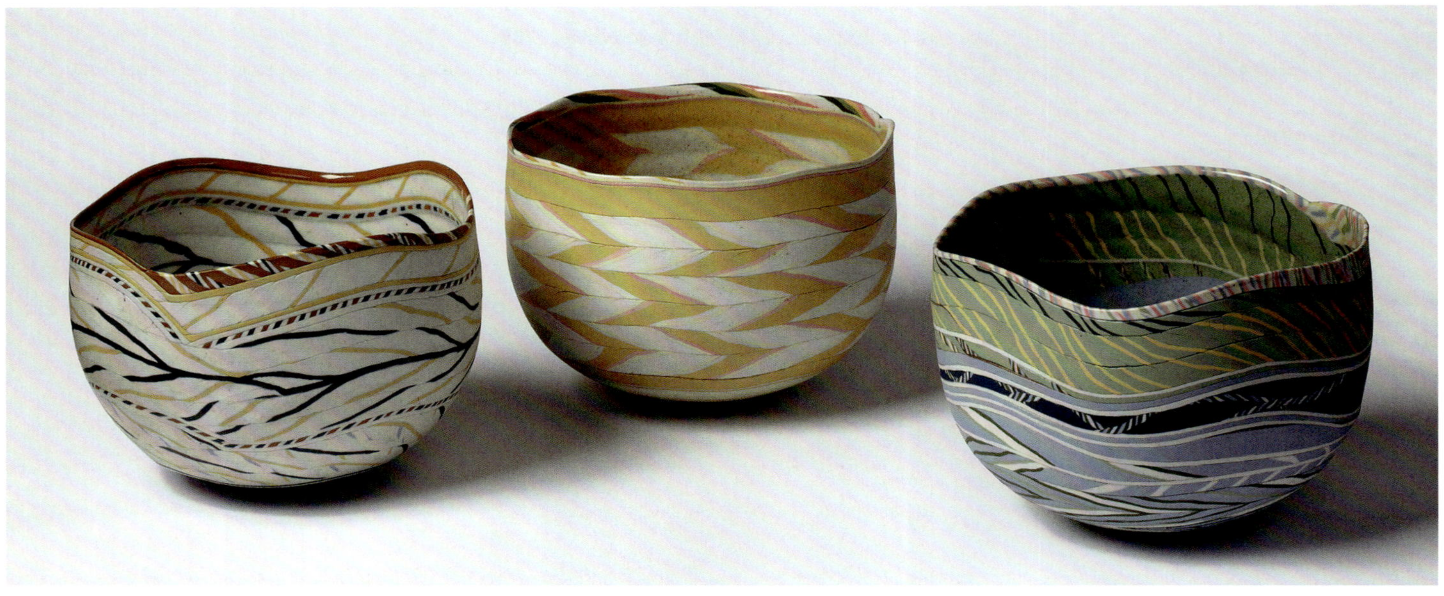

26. 71/1984 **27.** 64/1987 **28.** 65/1987

ANDERSEN, HANS MUNCK 1943 –

Ceramicist

1963-68	Kunsthåndværkerskolen
1968-71	The Royal Porcelain Factory, employed as artist
1972-73	The Royal Danish Academy of Fine Arts, Design
1973-	Shared workshop with Gerd Hiort Petersen, Bornholm
1984	The International Ceramics Studio, Kecskemét, Hungary
	www.gerdoghans.dk

After he had completed his studies at the Kunsthåndværkerskolen, Hans Munck Andersen (HMA) was employed at the Royal Porcelain Factory as an independent creative artist; there he met the ceramicist Gerd Hiort Petersen, whom he later married. In 1973 they moved to Bornholm, where they set up their home and studio workshop, which is still the basis for their ceramic work. This includes shared exhibition activities with good international contacts to museums, galleries and private collectors. In 2010 Danmarks Keramikmuseum (now CLAY) held an impressive retrospective exhibition; it convincingly presented their artistic partnership during the previous 40 years.

From the mid 1970s onwards HMA undertook journeys to Crete, focusing on the boldly coloured prehistoric pottery and Roman antique glass which he had previously seen in Germany; this inspired HMA to develop the personal and impressive technique he uses for his works in porcelain and for which he is still internationally famous, producing bowls that are admired as poetic, refined and effective in a manner beyond comprehension.

For the production of his works he uses coloured porcelain paste (*neriage*) with added metal oxide, which is rolled out in long thin strips in different colours. The strips are twisted together and pressed, in a complex pattern, using a sponge, into a damp plaster mould, which serves as a support for the building up of the bowl and maintains its humidity during the work. When the object has dried to the right degree the plaster mould is removed and the bowl is taken out; Before firing it is finished with a process of retouching the outer and inner sides and glazing the inner side with a clear shiny glaze. With this painstakingly-developed and time-consuming technique HMA composes endless variations of pattern- and colour-effects and creates a wide range of different expressions, as can be seen from the museum's

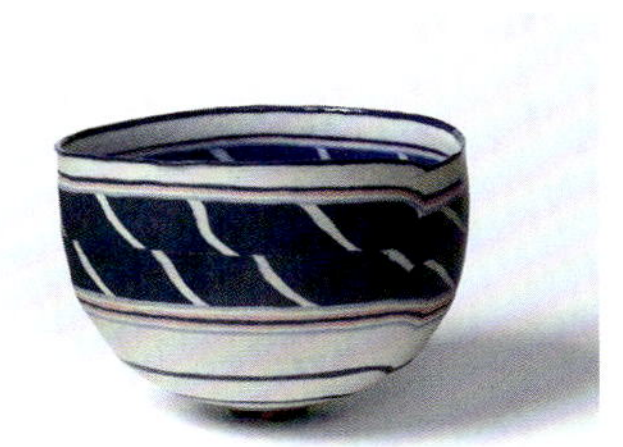

25. 65/1977

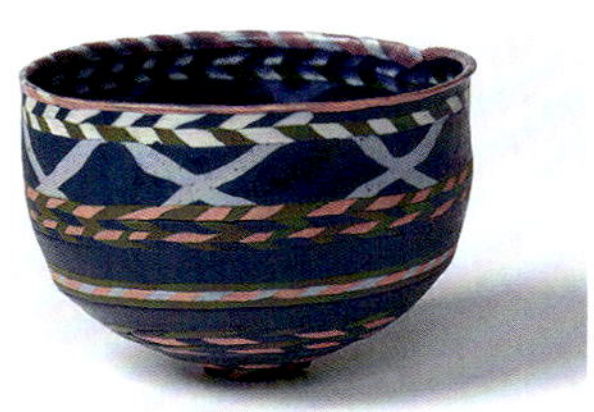

29. D 1545

six works from the years 1976-1986 **(25-30)**. In some cases HMA has worked with the silversmith Mogens Bjørn- Andersen (1911-2014) to incorporate silver thread into the bowls **(25,28)**.

Within the last ten-year period HMA has taken up work once more with sculptural forms; he experimented with them during his years at the Royal Porcelain Factory, when he began using coloured porcelain paste, e.g. in a Pop Art inspired portrait of the American civil rights campaigner Angela Davis. With his most recent porcelain sculptures, designed in some cases to hang on walls and in others as free-standing objects, HMA creates a world of curving forms or architectural elements which are assembled and glazed to perfection, so that the white porcelain paste becomes glossy and startlingly silky-soft to the touch. Few artists have managed to tease so many mysterious creations out of porcelain as HMA has done.

See: *Keramisk Stoflighed, Gerd Hiort Petersen & Hans Munck Andersen,* Danmarks Keramikmuseum, 2010

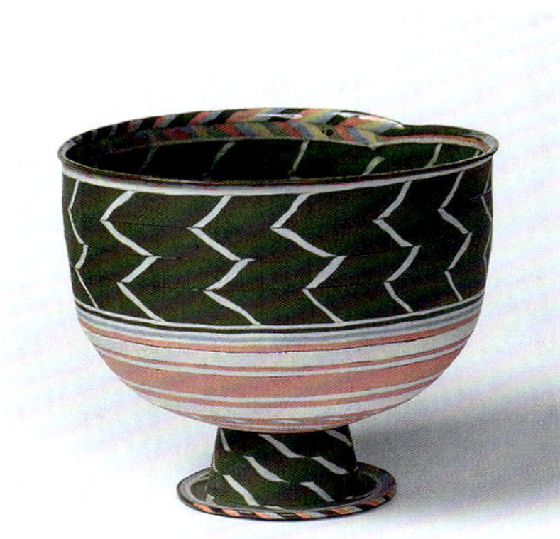

30. D 1546

25. Bowl, 1976

Pre-coloured porcelain (neriage), silver, clear feldspar glaze; pressed into a plaster mould, fired at 1300°. H 12 x Diam 16. Mark: none. Mus.no. 65/1977 ACQUISITION: *Danske Kunsthåndværkere*, 1977, Kunstindustrimuseet. Donation from *Overretssagfører Odin Kaysers Legat*. See: *Brændpunkter*, 1990. *Revere McFadden, D.,* 1982

26. Bowl, 1980. ***Efterår*** (Autumn)

Pre-coloured porcelain (neriage), feldspar-glazed; pressed into a plaster mould, reduction-fired at 1300°. H 16 x Diam 21. Mark: 'HMA, VII' on base. Mus.no. 71/1984. ACQUISITION: Jakob Feldballe, Gallerihuset, Kolding. Donation from *Finansieringsinstituttet for Industri og Håndværks Jubilæumslegat.* See: Dybdahl, L., 1997

27. Bowl, 1985. ***Oktogonal zigzag gul*** (Octagonal yellow zigzag)

Pre-coloured porcelain (neriage), feldspar-glazed; pressed into a plaster mould, reduction-fired at 1300°. H 16 x Diam 21. Mark: 'HMA, XII' on the base. Mus.no. 64/1987

ACQUISITION: *Gerd Hiorth Petersen og Hans Munck Andersen*, 1986, Galerie Nord, Frederikshavn. Donation from *Kunstindustrimuseets Venner*

28. Bowl, 1986. ***Dam*** (Pond)

Pre-coloured porcelain (neriage), silver, synthetic-ash-glazed; pressed into a plaster mould, reduction-fired at 1300°. H 16 x Diam 21. Mark: 'HMA, XIII' on base. Mus.no. 65/1987

ACQUISITION: *Keramik i Kolding*, 2005, Galleri Feldballe, Kolding

29. Bowl, 1978

Pre-coloured porcelain (neriage), glazed; pressed into a plaster mould, fired at 1300°. H 7. Mark: none. Mus. No. D1545

ACQUISITION: On deposit from *Statens Kunstfond*, 1982

30. Bowl, 1980

Pre-coloured porcelain, feldspar-glazed; pressed into a plaster mould, fired at 1300°. H 14.7. Mark: 'HMA VI' on base. Mus.no. D 1546

ACQUISITION: On deposit from *Statens Kunstfond*, 1982

BENNICKE, KAREN 1943 –

Ceramicist

1958-61	Abbednæs Pottemageri; Kurt Olsen; Enø Pottemageri; Karl Larsen
1961	Own studio workshop, Ring; later Rettestrup and Vordingborg
1972-74	Studio workshop shared with Peder Rasmussen, Copenhagen; 1974- Bregentved, Bennicke & Rasmussen Studio
1994-2002	Danmarks Designskole, instructor; 2005- external examiner
1996-97	Det Jyske Kunstakademi, instructor www.karenbennicke.dk

Karen Bennicke (KB) is one of Denmark's most radically experimental and uncompromising ceramic artists and has produced successive striking innovations in Danish ceramic sculpture over a period of more than 30 years, during which she has exhibited her work nationally and internationally and experienced that her work came to be represented in ceramic museums in the Nordic region and in the rest of world.

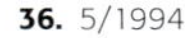

36. 5/1994

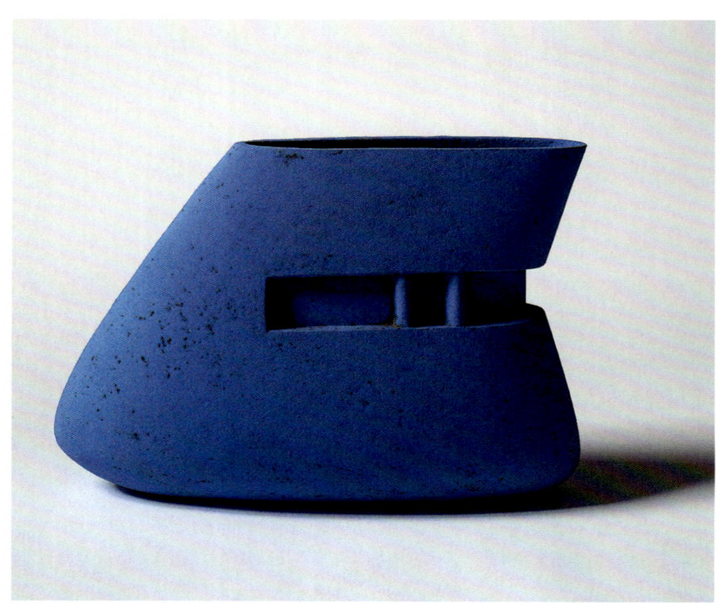

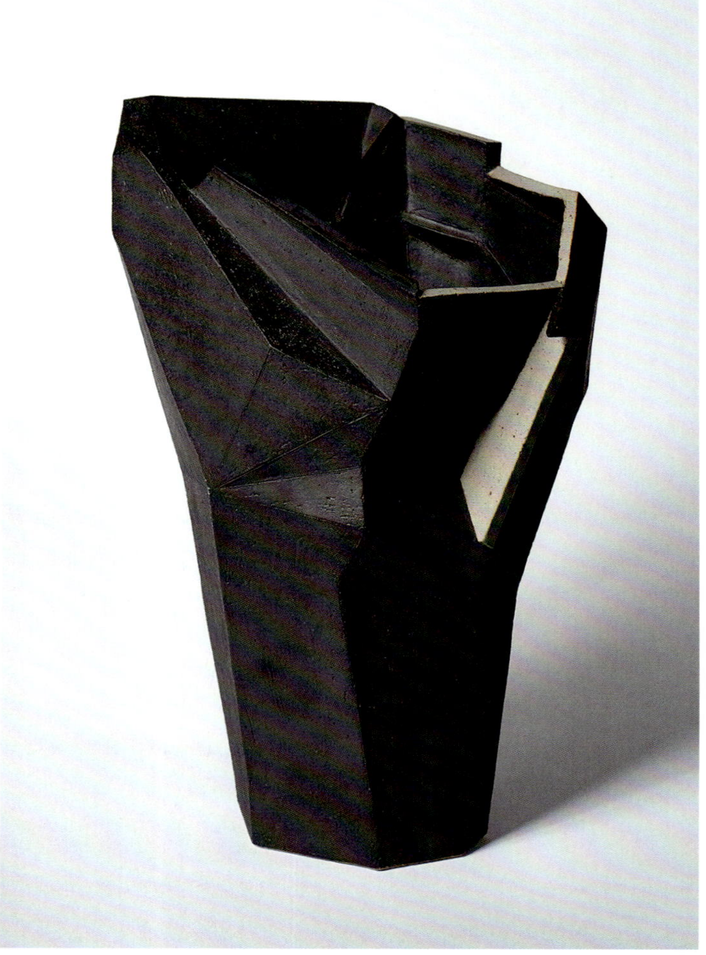

34. 44/1987

It is form, spatial challenges and content itself - the ideas and narratives – that provide the departure-point for her works. Often she chooses a theme for the exhibition towards which she is working and then analyses and explores it in a series of works. Inspiration can come from avant-garde pictorial art, utopian architectural models or conceptual art, but everyday objects may also slide in and become meaningful in the laboratory where KB's shapes and ideas are developed. Behind the material realisation of the works there is an exacting process of sketching and composition of models and patterns required for production of the specific ceramic sculpture.

KB did not study ceramics as an academic subject; she had become fascinated by clay when she was still a child, and embarked as soon as possible on practical training as a potter in various workshops. She set up her own studio workshop when she was 18; in 1972 she married the ceramicist Peder Rasmussen, with whom she has since shared a workshop combined with a gallery, from 1974 at Bregentved, on Sealand. In the early years she mainly made successive series of ceramic products for domestic use; these were sold by Den Permanente, but at the same time KB developed a desire to play down this activity in favour of untrammelled sculptural ceramic creations in stoneware. This led, *inter alia*, to the setting up in 1980 of the exhibition group *Multi Mud*, together with Peder Rasmussen, Heidi Guthmann Birck, Lene Regius, Aage Birck, and Gunnar Palander, which became a means of breakthrough for new post-modern trends in Danish ceramics. The group was the first of several provocative exhibition groups in Denmark and it continued in existence until 1985.

38. 370/2004

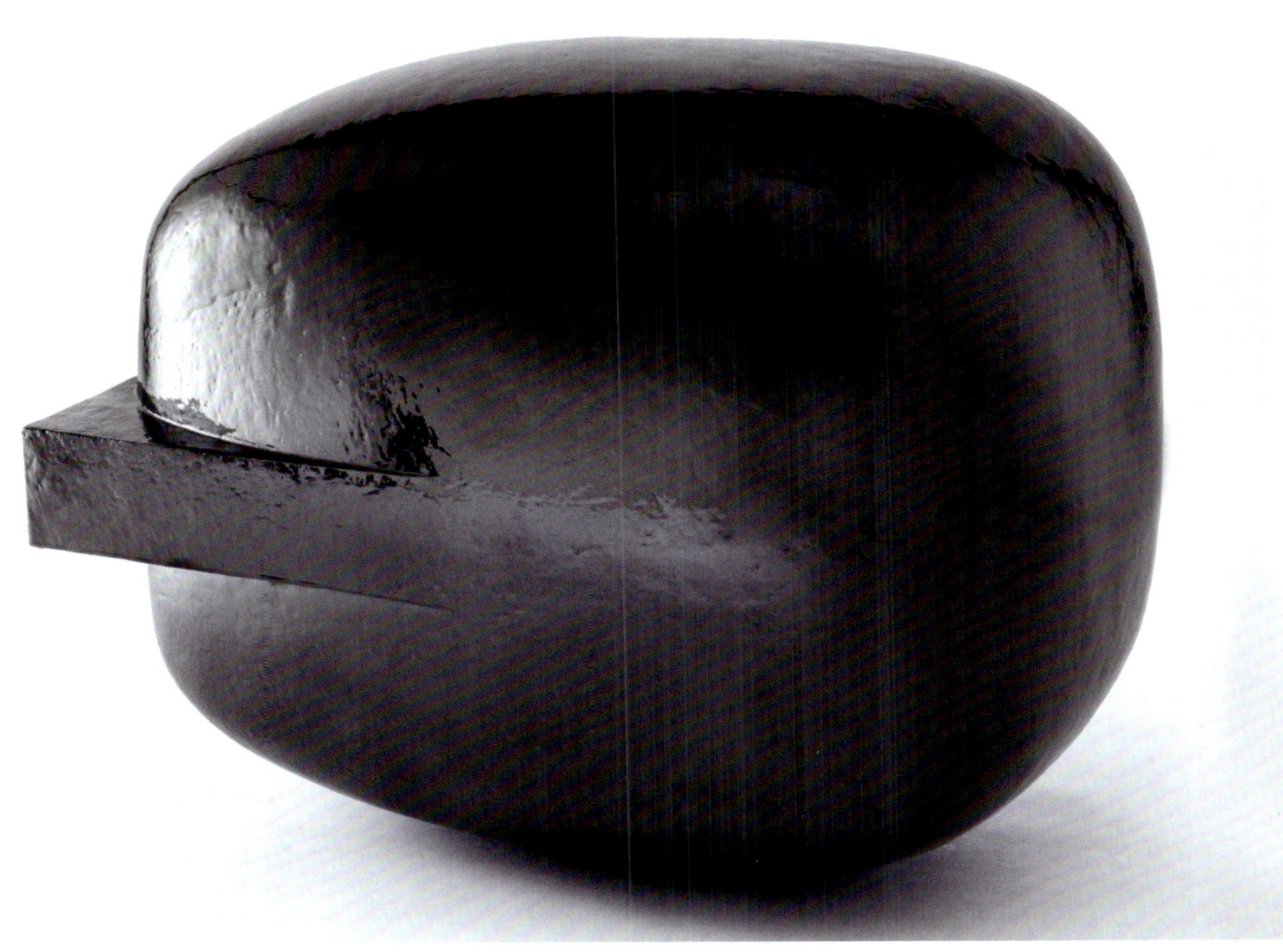

The museum's collection contains ten of KB's works from the period 1984-2005, and this makes it possible to follow some of the themes and processes that characterize her work. From the 1980s there are five works, all of them made in stoneware and slab technique. While on the one hand they reflect the traditional functional forms of jugs and vases, it is clear that it is not function that is the objective here, but rather an exploration of optical spatial conditions through the displacement of planes and the use of colours and geometric decoration to achieve illusionary effects **(31-35)**. This dissolution of volumes into facets and planes (casting a questioning spotlight onto our conception of reality) has been a recurring element in KB's work and in recent years has resulted in large and complex monochrome sculptures which are developed from a basis of thoroughly detailed studies of models, but at the same time are the culmination of a process which in itself may produce an unpredictable result. The process is both controlled and controlling.

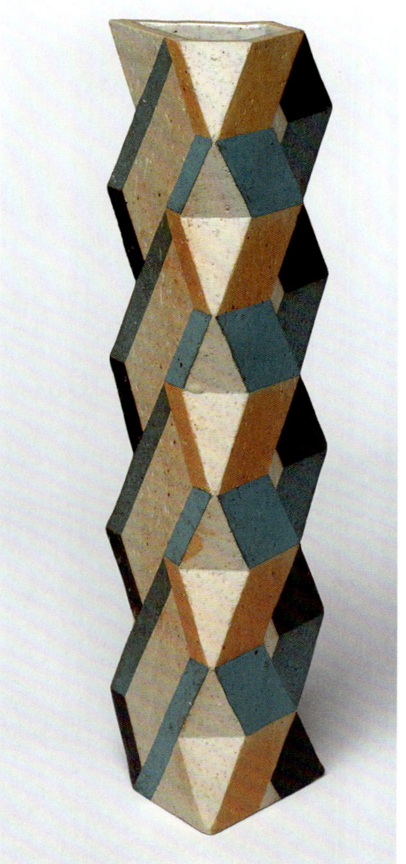

33. 83/1986

The museum has two works from the 1990s which bear witness to the range of KB's *oeuvre*. One of them, from 1993, has the title *Pram* (Barge) and is a modelled monochrome object in an organic idiom with a saturated matte blue colour **(36)**. The slab technique of the works from the 1980s is here replaced by modelling, as it is in the other work **(37)** purchased from the artist's solo exhibition in Galleri Nørby i 1998. That sculpture is a bold work, untraditional in form and technique (involving an angle grinder) and absolutely monumental; it embodies a revolt against 'correctness' in classical Danish ceramics and was acquired by the museum in that spirit.

Towards the end of the 1990s a new and important theme emerged: work with the form of the human head as a repetition of a basic sculptural motif. The exhibition '*Persona*' in 1999, at the *Udstillingssted for Ny Keramik*, Copenhagen, showed the rich potential of that theme through an extensive series of works in different ceramic materials – open/closed, reclining/standing – which, despite their common form provided through the variety of treatments many possibilities for interpretation and insight. This theme is represented in the museum's collection by a significant work, the sculpture *Liggende hovedform* (Reclining head shape) from 2001, a monumental abstract, perfect and closed form of monolithic character **(38)**. The sculpture was part of the major exhibition-presentation of Danish ceramics entitled '*From the Kilns of Denmark*', which was shown in the USA, Paris and Berlin in 2002-2004. From the same period there was an assignment for Folketinget, the Danish Parliament, consisting of a series of head shapes exhibited on pedestals in parallel with other portrait busts displayed in the Parliament building.

The architectural aspect is strongly present in much of KB's work and has created the departure-point for her probing of architecture's many spatial forms, as recently inspired by a young generation of architects through computer-animated projects. The breadth of range in KB's architectural experiments and her personal dedication to expression of these artistic strategies can be seen in two works in the museum's collection. The earlier of those, *Formscape* **(40)**, is from 2003 and presents assembled motion-filled elements in dynamic relations. The second work, from 2005, is entitled *City View* **(39)** and is an assembled relief built up out of a series of geometric volumes mostly in white and bluish tones, along with silver leaf, with alternating matte and glossy effects. It is part of the series of works with the title *ACTION-ARCHITECTONES* (referring to sculptures, named *ARCHITECTONES*, by the Russian avantgarde artist Kazimir Malevich) which KB displayed in an exhibition in New York in 2005.

Since 1980 KB has been a focal point in the avant-garde ceramic elite in Denmark, and through her teaching at Danmarks Designskole in the years 1994 to 2002 she has had strong influence on the development of contemporary ceramics. For her experimental work she received an award, *Annie & Otto Johs. Detlefs' Keramikpris*, in 2010. KB has also completed ten public commissioned works in Denmark and Sweden.

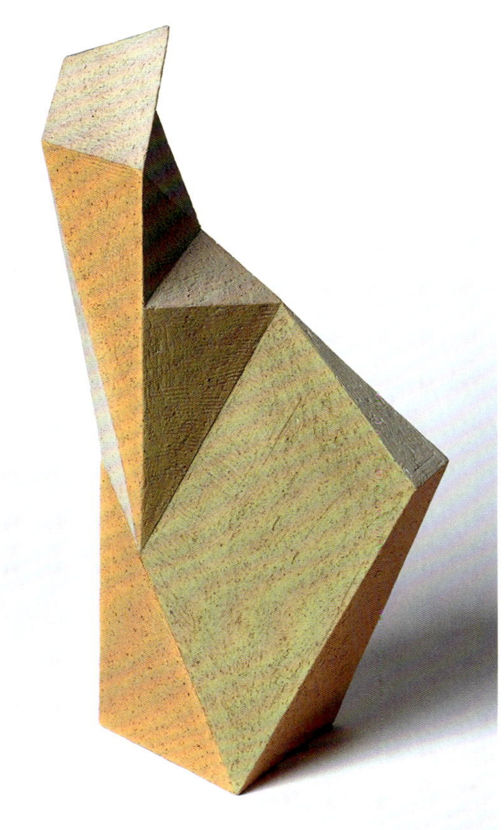

35. 176/1988

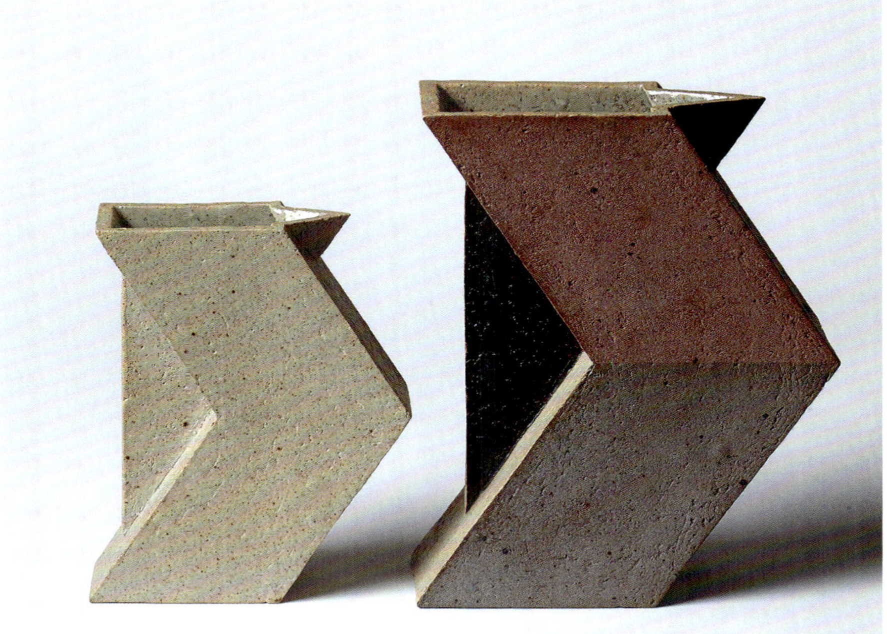

31. 152/1984

32. 153/1984

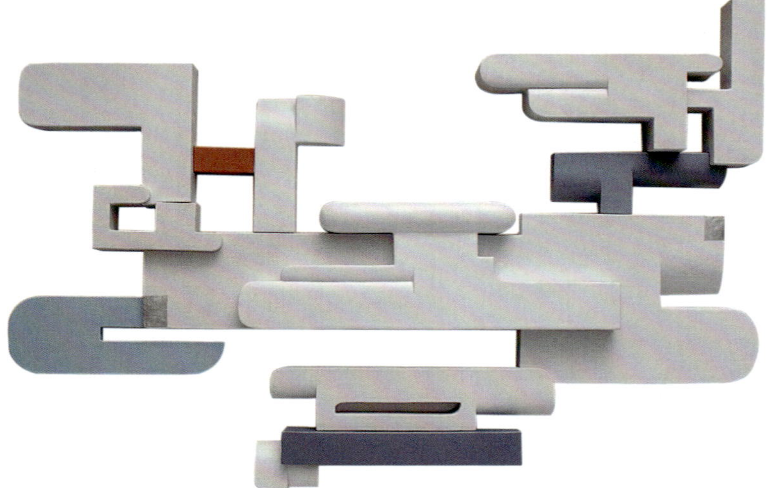

39. 103/2011

37. 51/1998

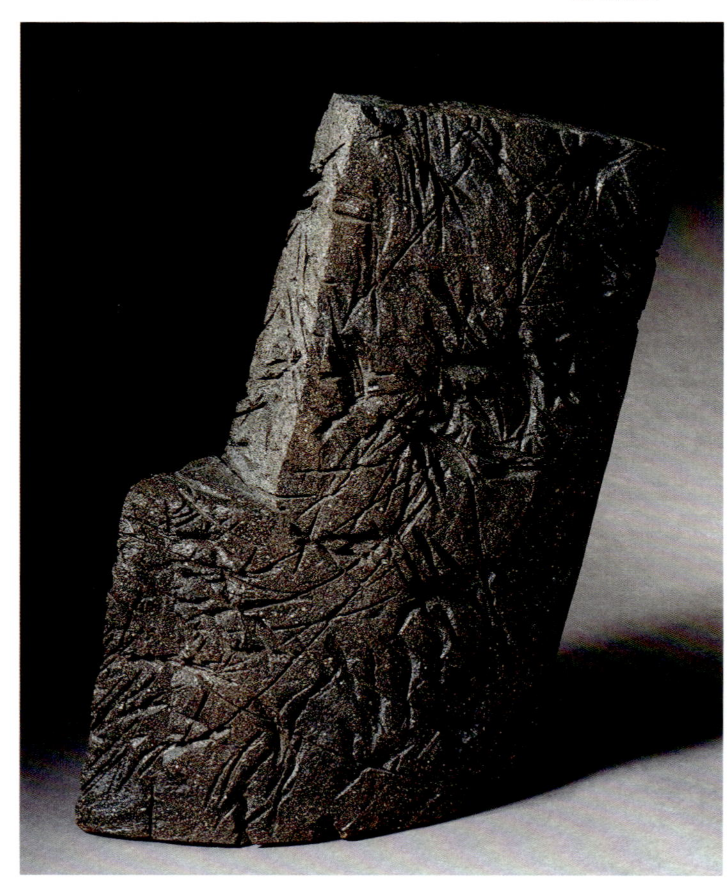

31. Jug, 1984

Stoneware, clear glazed; slab technique, fired at 1300°. H 15.8 x W 12.5. Mark: 'K.B. Denmark' painted on base. Mus.no. 152/1984

ACQUISITION: Karen Bennicke. Donation from *Finansieringsinstituttet for Industri og Håndværks Jubilæumslegat*. See: *Brændpunkter*, 1990

32. Jug, 1984

Stoneware, prepared stains; slab technique, fired at 1300°. H 20.7 x W 16.7. Mark: 'K.B. Denmark' painted on base. Mus.no. 153/1984

ACQUISITION: Karen Bennicke. *Donation from Finansieringsinstituttet for Industri og Håndværks Jubilæumslegat*. See: *Brændpunkter*, 1990

33. Vase, 1985

Stoneware, prepared stains; slab technique, fired at 1300°. H 30 x W 7.5. Mark: 'K.B. Denmark' painted on base. Mus.no. 83/1986

ACQUISITION: *Keramik – Karen Bennicke*, 1985, Galleri K, Copenhagen. Donation from *Kunstindustrimuseets Venner*. See: *Brændpunkter*, 1990

34. Vase, 1987

Stoneware, prepared stains; slab technique, fired at 1300°. H 35 x Diam 24. Mark: 'KB Denmark' painted on base. Mus.no. 44/1987

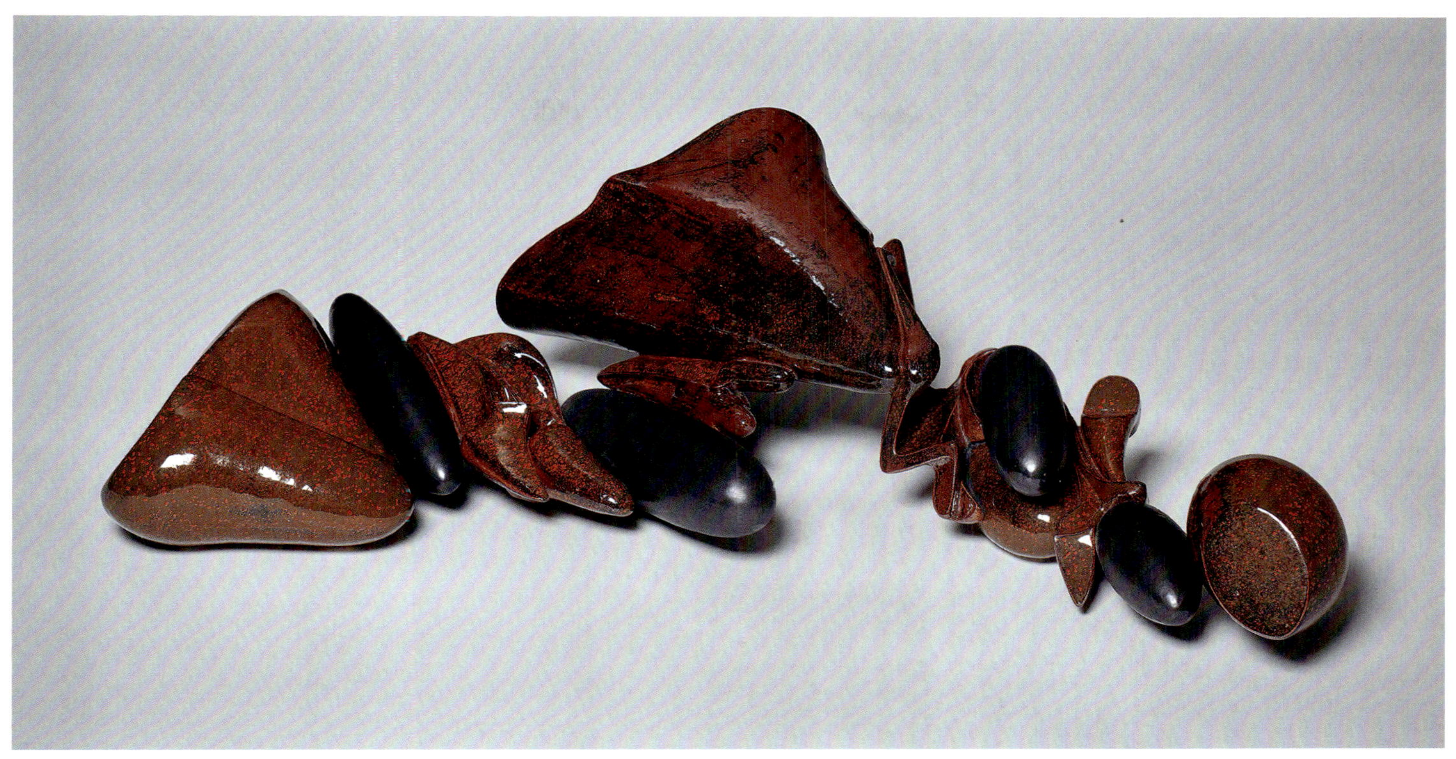

40. 47/2010

ACQUISITION: *Fem facetter – nyt dansk kunsthåndværk*, 1987, Kunstindustrimuseet. Donation from *Nationalbankens Jubilæumsfond*

35. Vase, 1987
Stoneware, prepared stains; slab technique, fired at 1300°. H 38,5. Mark: 'K.B. Denmark' painted on base. Mus.no. 176/1988. ACQUISITION: Karen Bennicke. Donation from *Kunstindustrimuseets 50-års Jubilæumslegat*

36. Object, 1993. *Pram* (Barge)
Stoneware, matte glaze; modelled, fired at 1100°. H 28.5 x W 41.5. Mark: 'KB 1993'on base. Mus.no. 5/1994. ACQUISITION: *Ler*, 1994, Trapholt

37. Sculpture, 1998
Earthenware, perlite; modelled, finished with angle grinder, hard-fired at 1000°. H 68 x W 62. Mark: 'K.B. 1998' painted on base. Mus.no. 51/1998 ACQUISITION: Galleri Nørby. Donation from *Kunstindustrimuseets Venner*

38. Object, 2001. *Liggende hovedform* (Reclining head shape)
Stoneware, oxide-glazed; modelled, fired as faience at 1020-1100°. H 64 x W 75 x D 62. Mark: none. Mus.no. 370/2004
ACQUISITION: Karen Bennicke. Donation from *C. L. Davids Legat for Slægt og Venner*. See: *From the Kilns of Denmark*, 2002

39. Sculpture/relief, 2005. *City View*
Stoneware, glazed, silver; modelled, fired at low temperature, mounted on a wooden panel. H 78 x L 119.5 (dimensions of panel). Mark: none. Mus.no. 103/2011. ACQUISITION: Karen Bennicke, *Action – Architectones*, Nancy Margolis Gallery, New York. See: *Laursen, B.B.*, 2005

40. Sculpture, 2003. *Formscape*
Stoneware, glazed; modelled, parts glued together, fired at 1260°. H 20 x L 80 x W 40. Mark: 'KB 03' painted on base. Mus.no. 47/2010. ACQUISITION: Donation from *Statens Kunstfond*

BERNARD, NELL 1935 – 1999

Ceramicist, sculptor, and graphic artist
Autodidact

1950-69	Lived in France
1963-	Own studio workshop, from 1969 in Egtved, Jutland

Nell Bernard (NB) uses ceramic material in her robust sculptures, taking inspiration both from nature and from building-like structures. Her background as an artist consisted of many years of association with the art milieu in Paris, extensive travelling and a period of living in Algeria. NB was the daughter of the sculptor Robert Jacobsen, and she married Bernard Ivon Léauté, who became Robert Jacobsen's assistant; this resulted in the couple going to live in Egtved, in Jutland, at the end of the 1960s, and NB set up her own workshop there.

The sculpture *Mærkelig Sol* (Strange Sun) **(41)** is from 1970 and was acquired by the museum in that year. The expressive work, with attached hollow spikes and running glazes in shades of lilac and orange, shows clear impressions of the artist's hands on the oval base.

41. Sculpture, 1970. *Mærkelig sol* (Strange Sun)
Stoneware, earthenware, partly glazed; modelled. H 40 x W 37. Mark: 'NB 70' inscribed on base. Mus.no. 68/1970
ACQUISITION: Donation from *Generalinde Kofoeds Legat*

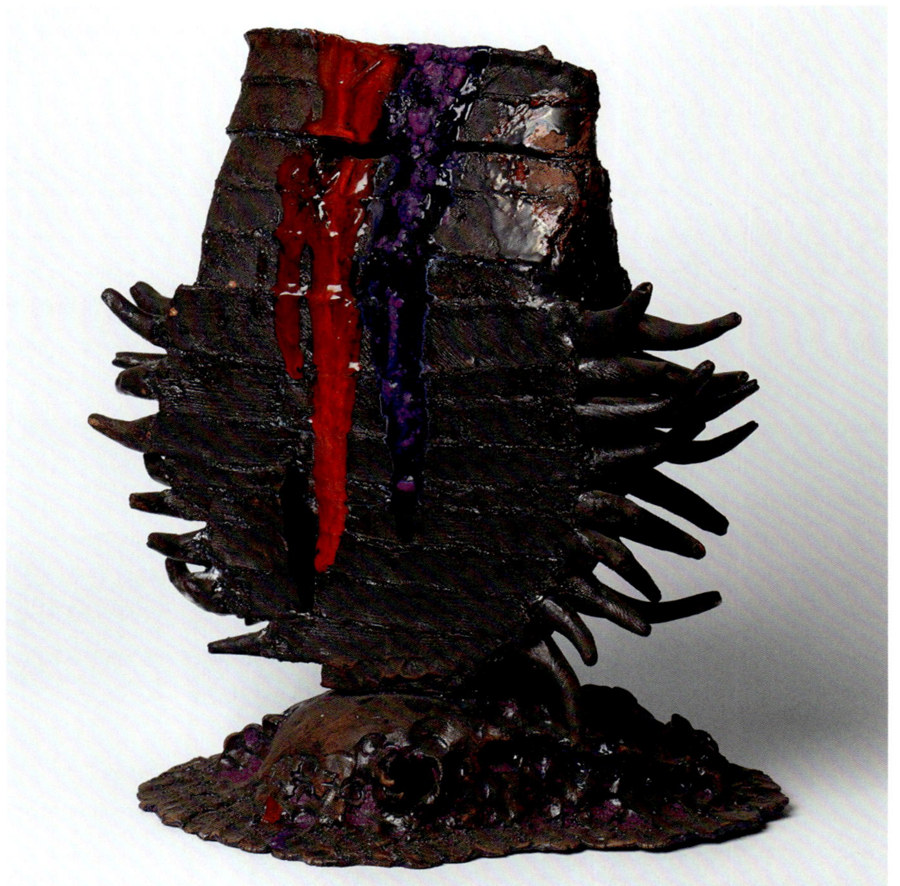

41. 68/1970

BERTELSEN, HANNE 1961 –

Ceramicist

1986-91 Danmarks Designskole

1991- Own studio workshop, Copenhagen
www.hannebertelsen.dk

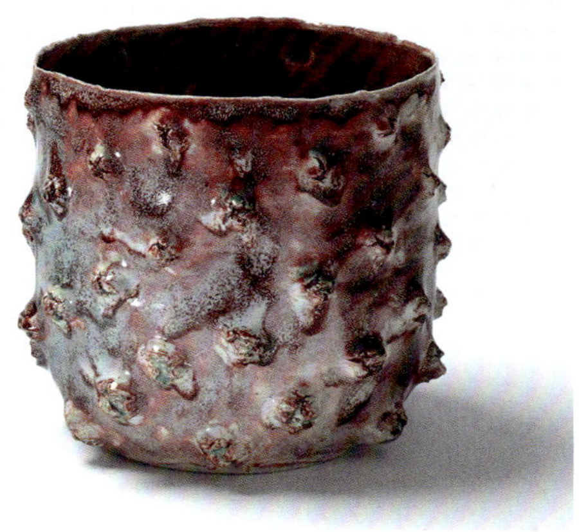

42. 98/2010

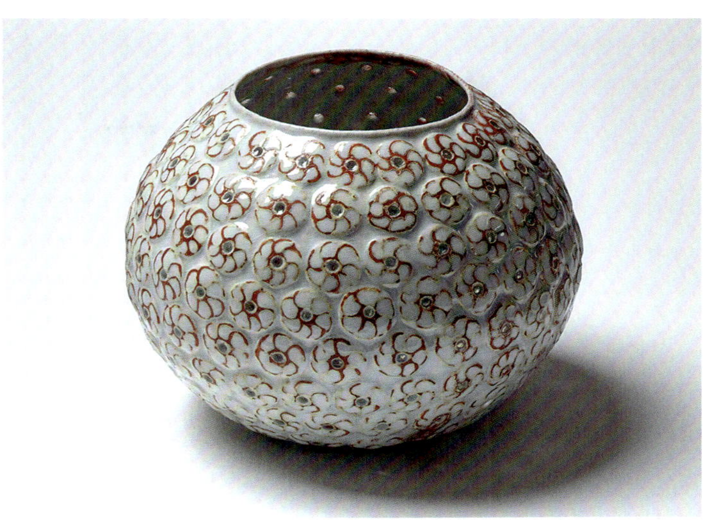

43. 99/2010

Hanne Bertelsen (HB) held a solo exhibition of her work at Galleri Pagter, Kolding, in 2008, and the museum acquired two pieces from it; both were executed in porcelain, but with different techniques – a significant indication of this artist's range in her very large production of both serially-produced ceramics for everyday use and unique works which she has been engaged in making since completing her studies at Danmarks Designskole. One of her works **(42)** is modelled in such a way that while the shape lends itself to the course of the oxblood glaze running down over the vase, it is also highlighted by it, while the other work **(43)**, with fine patterning in relief, is covered with a clear feldspar glaze.

HB is continuing the tradition of making functional objects in her own workshop/shop in Copenhagen in combination with selling through established museums, galleries and craft- and design- shops in Denmark and other Nordic countries. HB has regularly taken part in exhibitions in Denmark and abroad throughout many years.

42. Vase, 2008. *Porcelain med udbrud* (Porcelain with eruptions)
Porcelain, oxblood-glazed; thrown, modelled, reduction-fired at 1300°.
H 19 x Diam 18.5. Mark: 'HB' painted on base. Mus.no. 98/2010
ACQUISITION: Galleri Pagter, Kolding

43. Vase, 2008. *Boole – lysfanger* (Parabola – light-catcher)
Porcelain, clear feldspar-glazed; cast, modelled, slip, reduction-fired at 1300°.
H 17 x Diam 11. Mark: 'HB' painted on base. Mus.no. 99/2010
ACQUISITION: Galleri Pagter, Kolding

BERTRAM, HELGE 1919 – 1988

Painter

1936-39 Technical education in Building and Construction, Copenhagen

1939-46 Studied at the Royal Danish Academy of Fine Arts, School of Painting, School of Sculpture

1964-71 Royal Danish Academy of Fine Arts, School of Art Education, lecturer, head of department

1980-85 Royal Danish Academy of Fine Arts, School of Art Education, Rector

1971 Royal Danish Academy of Fine Arts, Professor

The significance of Helge Bertram (HB) in the ceramic field is associated with his lifelong uncompromising and methodical exploration of the many materials and media he used in his work in order to reach an understanding of the relationship between nature and art. One of HB's chief contributions was the establishment of 'Skolen for Kunstpædagogik' (Teacher-Training in Art Education), which he started, led and guided throughout almost 25 years. The departure-point for the school was to educate artists to become teachers of the new subject entitled 'Art and understanding of art' in upper school (gymnasium) classes, and in that context the teaching laid emphasis on an experimental approach.

Ceramics had a special place in the teaching that concerned studying historical/cultural forms of utensils, basic chemical and geological concepts, and exercises with dimensions, cutting out, dividing up and decorating clay surfaces. There was a series of experiments, carried out in collaboration with the Royal Academy's Colour-Technical Laboratory, with the aim of putting together a chemically and colouristically harmonious palette – i.e., a palette of colours which are colouristically compatible without conflicting with each other chemically; the experiments were described in a report with colour samples of the pigments produced.

HB had the opportunity to put the experimental approach to use in practice through his ceramic art work for a swimming hall in Holstebro, Jutland, commissioned from him by *Statens Kunstfond* in 1969. This ceramic work was intended for the walls of the hall, and HB became involved in the detailed planning. His idea was to colour the bricks for the building and the tiles as a single aesthetic entity, with references to atrium houses and pre-Christian Roman mosaics. He wanted motifs with the atmosphere of beaches and sea, and blue and green colours, as the departure-point for the total plan. The building's surfaces should be finished in different materials, some of which were to be specially produced while others were building materials that were normally available. A special feature was a large quantity of fluoride-glazed bricks, each one of them hand-dipped in the glaze, individually stacked in the furnace and fired with great difficulty at Trasbjerg Teglværk near Holstebro.

The many variations in pattern, the colour combinations and the integration of the materials into the architecture and purpose of the building make this work into a unified work of art – a *Gesamtkunstverk* – in which the artistic application succeeds in being one with the building.

As an offshoot of the decoration of the swimming hall, HB was given a further task in Holstebro, this time in connection with the pedestrian street system in the centre of the town. He created paving, street furnishings and a surprising piece of water art consisting of two large

51. 168/2005

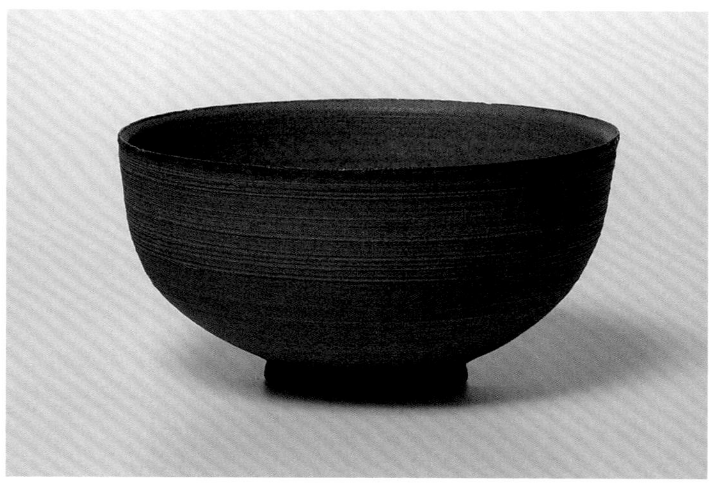

walls, situated on the walking axis in the middle of the street. Here again HB used glazed bricks and tiles combined with concrete slabs to form this interesting solution to the creation of different zones in the pedestrian street.

In 2005 the artist's widow, Elisabeth Bertram, offered the museum the opportunity to acquire samples of HB's ceramic experiments **(44-54)**, with records of ingredients and colour pigments used that document his research. This material has been included in the museum's collection, and it is to be hoped that it will be used by ceramicists for research purposes; at the same time it provides documentation for one of the major ceramic assignments in Denmark in the 20th century.

44. Bowl, glaze sample, 1954 (no photo)
Stoneware, glazed with cryolite with potassium content; fired at 1240°.
H 7 x Diam 14.8. Mark: none. Mus.no. 161/2005
ACQUISITION: Donation from Elisabeth Bertram, Copenhagen

45. Bowl, glaze sample, 1954 (no photo)
Stoneware, iron-oxide-, vanadium-oxide- and cryolite-glazed; fired at 1240°.
H 5 x Diam 14. Mark: none. Mus.no. 162/2005
ACQUISITION: Donation from Elisabeth Bertram, Copenhagen

46. Bowl, glaze sample, 1954 (no photo)
Stoneware, glazed; thrown within a mould (jiggering process), fired at 1240°.
H 10 x Diam 12. Mark: none. Mus.no. 163/2005
ACQUISITION: Donation from Elisabeth Bertram, Copenhagen

47. Bowl, glaze sample, 1954
Stoneware, iron-oxide-glazed, interior manganese- and cryolite-glazed;
fired at 1240°. H 6.8 x Diam 15.8. Mark: none. Mus.no. 164/2005
ACQUISITION: Donation from Elisabeth Bertram, Copenhagen

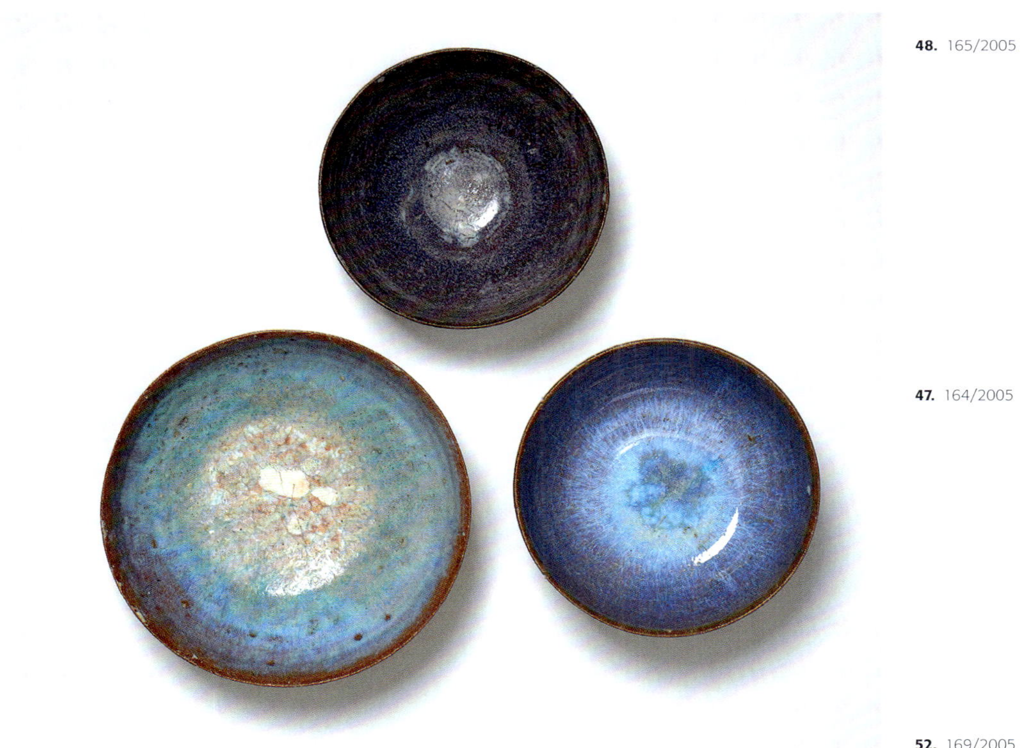

48. 165/2005

47. 164/2005

52. 169/2005

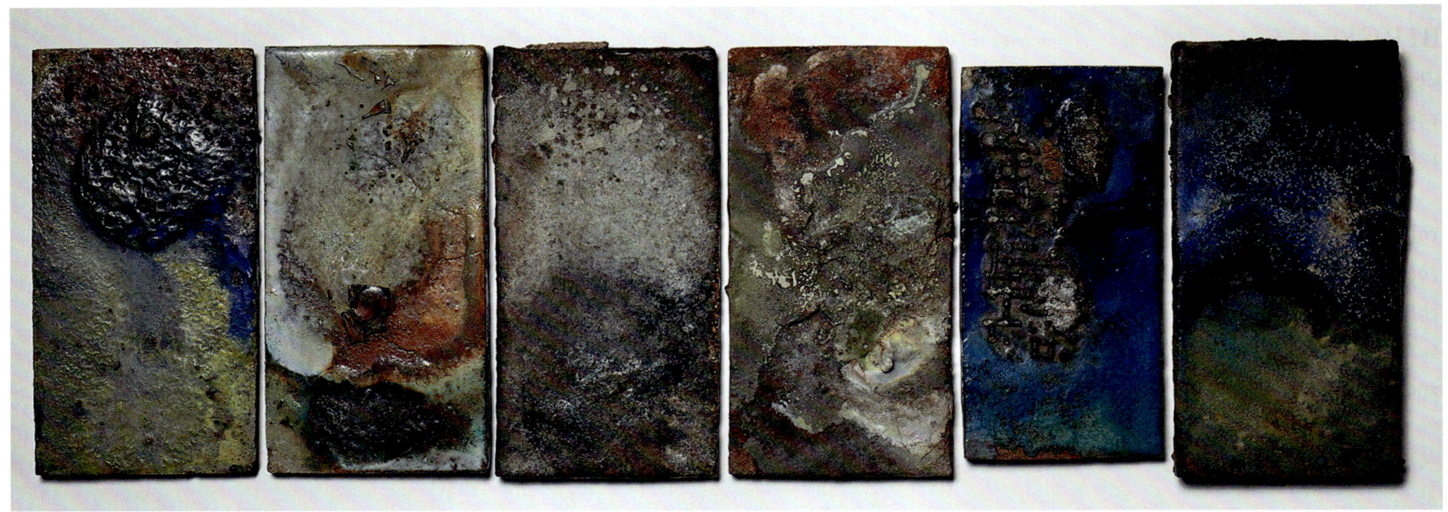

53. 170a-f/2005

48. Bowl, glaze sample, 1954

Stoneware, cryolite-glazed with vanadium; fired at 1240°. H 8.5 x Diam 16.5. Mark: none. Mus.no. 165/2005

ACQUISITION: Donation from Elisabeth Bertram, Copenhagen

49. Bowl, glaze sample, 1958-59 (no photo)

Stoneware, crystal formations inside at the bottom; fired at 1200°. H 6 x Diam 16.5. Mark: none. Mus.no. 166/2005

ACQUISITION: Donation from Elisabeth Bertram, Copenhagen

50. Bowl, glaze sample, 1958 (no photo)

Earthenware, cryolite-glazed with added copper-oxide and hematite; fired at 1040°. H 12.5 x Diam 14.5. Mark: none. Mus.no. 167/2005

ACQUISITION: Donation from Elisabeth Bertram, Copenhagen

51. Bowl, glaze sample, 1954

Stoneware, cobalt- and feldspar-glazed; thrown, fired at 1240°. H 17.2 x Diam 14. Mark: none. Mus.no. 168/2005

ACQUISITION: Donation from Elisabeth Bertram, Copenhagen

52. Bowl, glaze sample, 1955

Stoneware, cryolite-glazed with vanadium, crystal formations inside at the bottom; thrown, fired at 1240°. H 7 x Diam 19.8. Mark: Indecipherable signature. Mus.no. 169/2005

ACQUISITION: Donation from Elisabeth Bertram, Copenhagen

53. Six ceramic plaques, 1960-61

Stoneware; fired at 1150-1200°. W 24 x D 12 x H 2. Mark: none. Mus.no. 170a-f/2005

ACQUISITION: Donation from Elisabeth Bertram, Copenhagen

54. Tile, 1954 (no photo)

Stoneware, crushed granulate, cobalt; fired at 1240°. W 24.5 x D 19. Mark: none. Mus.no. 171/2005

ACQUISITION: Donation from Elisabeth Bertram, Copenhagen

BIRCK, HEIDI LUZIE GUTHMANN 1941 –

Ceramicist, sculptor

1959-62	Ceramics and sculpture, Munich, craft apprenticeship
1962	Handwerkskammer für Oberbayern, Munich, certificate of completion of apprenticeship
1963-64	Ceramicist with G. Liebenthron, Bremen
1964-65	Ceramicist with J. Tessier, Villenauxe, France
1965	Workshop, Keramik Studio, with Aage Birck, Copenhagen;
1986-	Haderslev, Jutland
1999	Retrospective exhibitions with Aage Birck, Danmarks Keramikmuseum-Grimmerhus
	www.heidiguthmannbirck.dk

The ceramic works created by Heidi Guthmann Birck (HGB) do not lend themselves to being described within the Danish ceramic tradition, but they have contributed to showing the diversity of the Danish ceramics scene in the last half century, during which she has had a workshop in Southern Jutland shared with her ceramicist husband Aage Birck, and has exhibited extensively in the Nordic region and the rest of Europe. HGB is represented in leading European museums and collections, and in recent years she has made large sculptures in bronze (*SHE-MAN*, 2013-14, OJD Fonden, Solrød; *LIVSTRAPPEN*, 2014-15, VUC Haderslev).

Inspiration for HGB's work comes from the desire to present the human form as an image of something of universal validity. Even though the sculptures most frequently take the human form as departure-point, they are not purely naturalistic, but narrate or exemplify the divisions or split states humans live with, in their minds and in relation to the surrounding world. These split states have been illustrated by the artist in various phases of her work, from the early wall reliefs from around 1980 to the portrait busts on pedestals in following years, exhibited for example in *Multi Mud*'s landmark exhibition at the Glyptotek in 1983, with inspiration from selected works from the museum's collection. Later themes have included depictions of fantasy beings in a mythological universe populated by chimeras and 'manimals'. From the end of the 1990s there are also detailed studies of dolls as a medium for exposing superficial appearances, naive innocence, as opposed to the concealed narratives that can be contained in playing with dolls. A major theme in this artist's work from recent years is represented by the moving sculptures of malformed children, based on examples in the medical-history collections in Berlin and Copenhagen. The works are all made in black-fired clay, painstakingly modelled and embodying a singular poetic beauty and objectivity which makes a deep impression. The confrontation with these deformities as works of art serves to open up a sensibility in the observer, who is left to question his own imprinted ideals about perfect human form and to feel an awakening recognition that the imperfect is an entirely valid part of life. (See: Guthmann Birck, Heidi , *deFORM abNorm – et forlig med den menneskelige diversitet.* In: 'Det uperfekte barn'. Steno Museet, Aarhus Universitetsforlag 2008, pp. 64-75). The museum's sculpture is from the year after the exhibition in the Glyptotek, and belongs to the series known as the double portraits, in this case with on one side a man/human and on the other a warrior/soldier **(55)**.

55. Sculpture, mounted on slate slab, 1984. *Soldat* (Soldier)
Stoneware, salt-glazed, slate slab; modelled, fired at 1285°. H 42.5 x W 48.5.
Mark: 'Heidi G Birck 84'. Mus.no. 123/1988.
ACQUISITION: *Heidi Guthmann Birck – Aage Birck. Unika i keramik*, 1988, Kunsthallen Nikolaj. Donation from *Kgl. Brand*

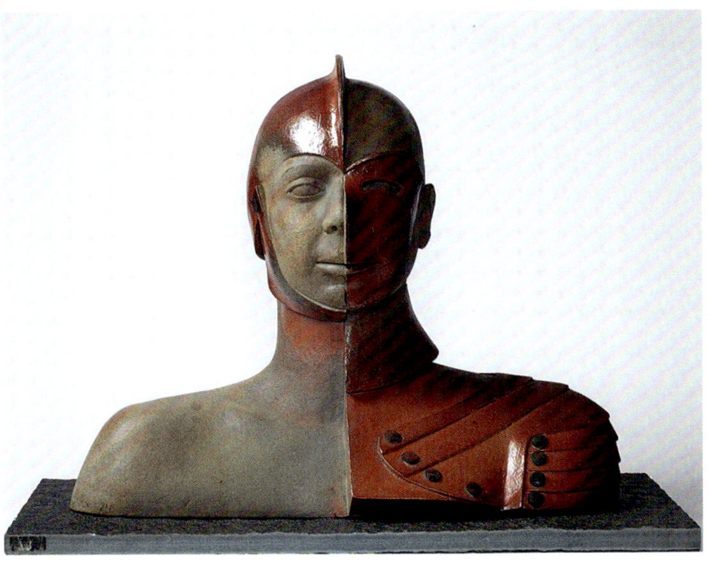

BIRCK, AAGE 1941 –

Ceramicist. Autodidact

1959-63	Hjørring Seminarium, qualified as teacher
1963-1970	Danmarks Lærerhøjskole, lecturer
1965-	Studio workshop shared with Heidi Guthmann Birck, Copenhagen
1970-	Ålkær, Southern Jutland
1986-	Haderslev, Jutland
1987-98	Kunsthåndværkerskolen in Kolding, course teacher
1999	Retrospective exhibition with Heidi Guthmann Birck, Danmarks Keramikmuseum- Grimmerhus
	www.aagebirck.dk

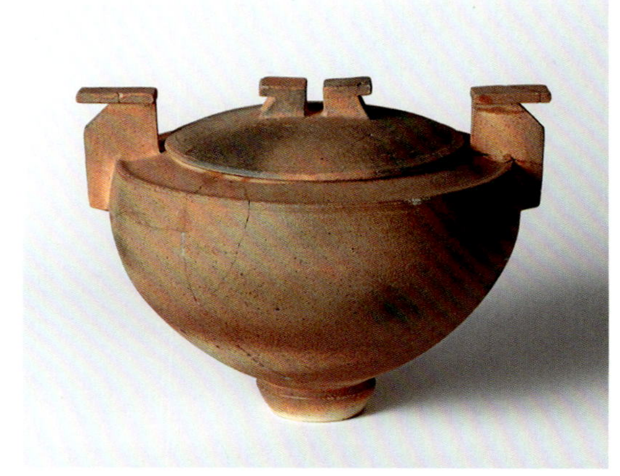

56. 121a-b/1988

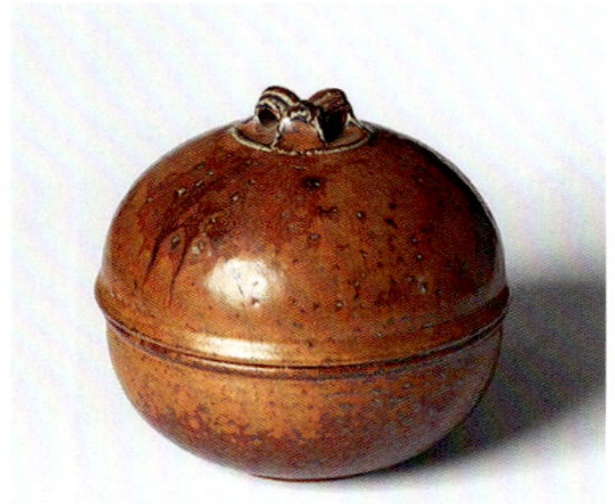

58. 128a-b/1992

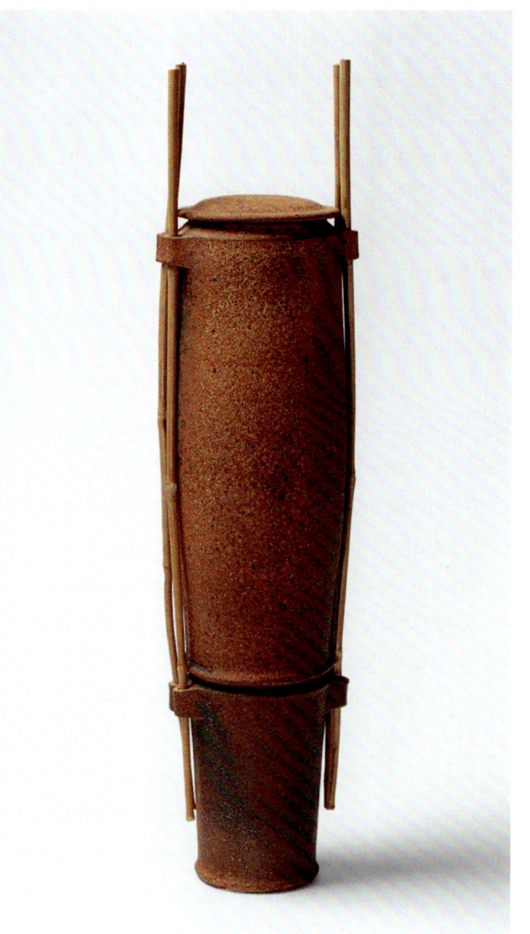

62. D 1673

In the period of almost fifty years during which he has worked as a ceramicist, Aage Birck (AaB) has achieved a rare degree of skill in technical aspects of the craft, and this has allowed him freedom to develop the artistic potential of his work. From the workshop shared with his wife and fellow ceramicist Heidi Guthmann Birck he has over the course of time produced an extensive series of works that reflect their individualistic ceramic production and have been shown at an impresssive number of exhibitions in Germany and in the Nordic region. The workshop has also had the capacity to carry through demanding ceramic assignments which have involved both artists supporting each other and at the same time making space for both to stand out individually as creators of the completed work.

The museum's collection contains seven works by AaB from the years 1982-2006, and this offers the possibility of experiencing the differing techniques and the development of form that characterize phases in his work. The earliest work, a thrown lidded pot from 1981-82, reduction-fired in a salt furnace with pre-coloured slips under a salt glaze, and glazed on the inside with a celadon glaze, was exhibited in *Multi Mud's* exhibition in Århus Kunstbygning in 1983 **(58)**. In the period 1980-85 both Heidi Guthmann Birck and AaB belonged to this epoch-making and rebellious exhibition group which distanced itself from the traditional canon of Danish ceramics.

From the 1980s there are works that reflect AaB's continuous probing of ceramic materials and processes, including development of types of clay, glazes and firings, incorporating new knowledge and inspiration from many cultures and epochs **(56-57)**. In a work from 1987 an early example can be seen of the use of supplementary materials – in this case bamboo **(62)**, which was to become an important and developmental element in the form of works to come. The lidded pot was included in the major retrospective exhibition for the couple in Kunsthallen Nikolaj in 1988, which displayed the convincing results of almost 25 years of focused work on ceramic development. Gradually AaB has worked towards a more sculptural approach, with emphasis on surfaces and ruptures and on the importance of the surfaces for the work with glazes. The museum owns a very fine piece from 1998 which illustrates this development towards minimalism and monumentalism **(59)**. In recent years AaB has developed several series of works in salt-glazed stoneware with integrated objects – e.g. tools, bones, wood and iron. These non-ceramic things, 'ready-mades', have evidently provided inspiration for unexpected constellations in which the container, which has been a recurrent basic form throughout the whole *oeuvre*, slides into the background to leave in the forefront a geometric and abstract idiom with contrast-filled, consistent and often humorous expressions.

In 2007 the museum acquired two objects in this category: *Rituelt kar* (Ritual Vessel) and *Rituel Økse* (Ritual Axe), both of muffle-fired sooty stoneware with added corroded iron elements – juxtapositions that carry associations with ritual mysticism and doom-laden visions **(60-61)**.

AaB has had great importance as the course-teacher in ceramics at Kolding Designskole for more than ten years, and in 1993 he was one of the initiators of Denmark's Museum of Ceramic Art, Grimmerhus (now CLAY). In 2009 AaB was awarded the prestigious European Westerwald Prize for salt-glazed stoneware.

56. Tureen, 1988

Stoneware, celadon-glazed, bamboo; sinter slip, reduction-fired at 1285°.
H 25 x W 33 x Diam 28.5. Mark: none. Mus.no. 121a-b/1988
ACQUISITION: *Heidi Guthmann Birck – Aage Birck. Unika i keramik*, 1988, Kunsthallen Nikolaj. Donation from *Kgl. Brand*

59. 124/1999

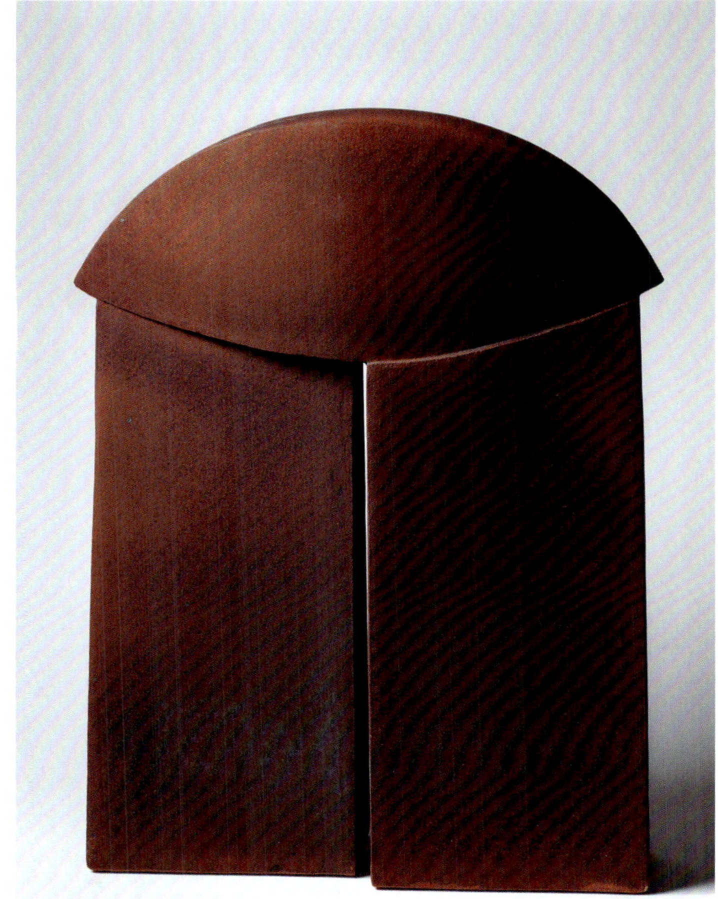

57. Lidded pot, 1985

Stoneware, zinc- and crystal- glazed; thrown, fired at 1285°, oxidized. H 16. Mark: 'Birck 85' inscribed on base. Mus.no. 122a-b/1988
ACQUISITION: Aage Birck. Donation from *Kgl. Brand*. See: *Brændpunkter,* 1990

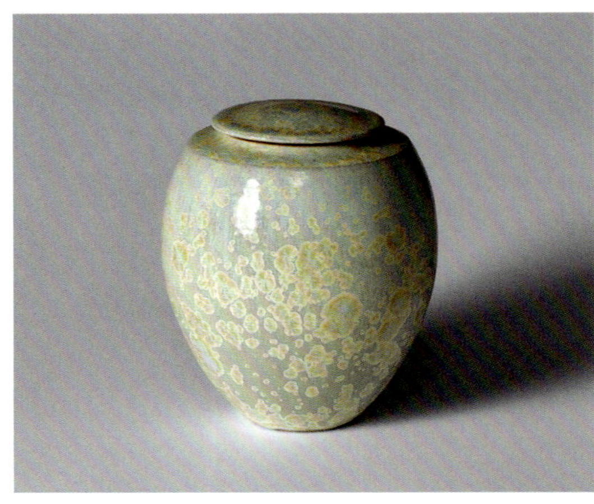

57. 122a-b/1988

58. Lidded pot, 1981-82

Stoneware, exterior salt-glazed, interior celadon-glazed; thrown, slip, reduction-fired in salt kiln at 1285°. H 21.5 x Diam 12.8. Mark: 'Birck' inscribed on base. Mus.no. 128a-b/1992
ACQUISITION: Aage Birck. *Multi Mud,* Århus Kunstbygning, 1983

60. 196/2006 **61.** 197/2006

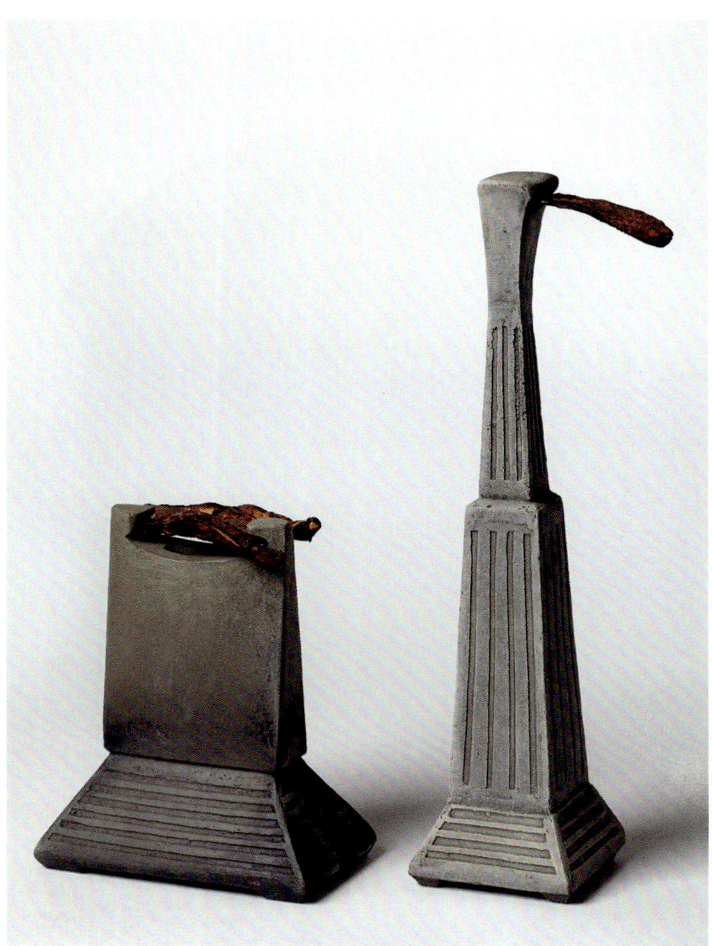

59. Sculpture, 1998

Stoneware; slab technique, sinter slip, fired at 1285°. H 50 x W 36 x D 14. Mark: 'Aage Birck 1998' inscribed on base. Mus.no. 124/1999
ACQUISITION: Aage Birck

60. Sculpture, 2006. ***Rituelt kar*** (Ritual vessel)

Stoneware, iron; modelled, muffle-fired. H 23.5 x W 18.5. Mark: none. Mus.no. 196/2006. ACQUISITION: *Ceramicisten Aage Birck*, 2006, Roskilde Kunstforening. Donation from *C. L. Davids Legat for Slægt og Venner*

61. Sculpture, 2006. ***Rituel Økse*** (Ritual axe)

Stoneware, iron; modelled, muffle-fired. H 45 x W 11. Mark: none. Mus.no. 197/2006
ACQUISITION: *Ceramicisten Aage Birck*, 2006, Roskilde Kunstforening. Donation from *C. L. Davids Legat for Slægt og Venner*

62. Lidded jug, 1987

Stoneware, celadon-glazed, bamboo; thrown, slip, fired at 1285°. H 50.3 x Diam 11.2. Mark: 'Birck 87' inscribed on base. Mus.no. D 1673
ACQUISITION: *Heidi Guthmann Birck – Aage Birck. Unika i keramik*, 1988, Kunsthallen Nikolaj. On deposit from *Statens Kunstfond*, 1989

BLOCH, MERETHE 1946 –

Ceramicist

1963-67 Kunsthåndværkerskolen
1970- Own studio workshop, Glamsbjerg, Funen
www.merethebloch.dk

Merethe Bloch (MB) has worked both with ceramics for everyday use and with unique creations, including sculptures and commissioned ceramic works. Among the latter are several fine examples of water installations, ceramic reliefs and columns, e.g. for Assistens churchyard, Odense, in 1990. In terms of form MB's bowls are classical and simple, thrown in stoneware and porcelain. At the museum's summer exhibition in 1986, '*Fynske Kunsthåndværkere*', the museum purchased a porcelain bowl decorated with a rhombus pattern **(63)**. In the same year MB made a series of 40 porcelain bowls with turquoise glaze which were sold as 'Souvenir of the Month' in the museum **(64)**. MB was represented in the exhibition '*Dansk Keramik 1850-1997*' at Sophienholm in 1997.

63. Bowl, 1986

Porcelain, feldspar-glazed, partially unglazed; thrown, masking, painted, reduction-fired at 1300°. H 16 x Diam 20.5. Mark: 'M Bloch 1986' painted on base. Mus.no. 87/1986. ACQUISITION: *Fynske kunsthåndværkere*, 1986, Kunstindustrimuseet. Donation from *Kunstindustrimuseets Venner*

64. Bowl, 1986

Porcelain, feldspar-glazed; thrown, masking, painted, reduction-fired at 1300°. H 7.6 x Diam 13. Mark: 'M. Bloch 86' painted on base. Mus.no. 320/1989 ACQUISITION: *Månedens souvenir*, Kunstindustrimuseet's shop

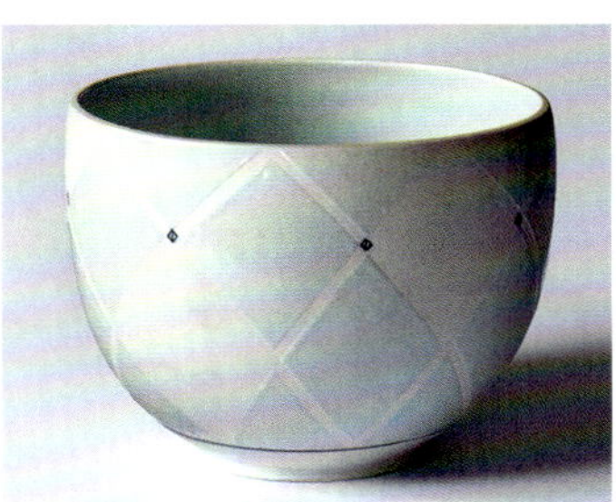

63 87/1986 **64.** 320/1989

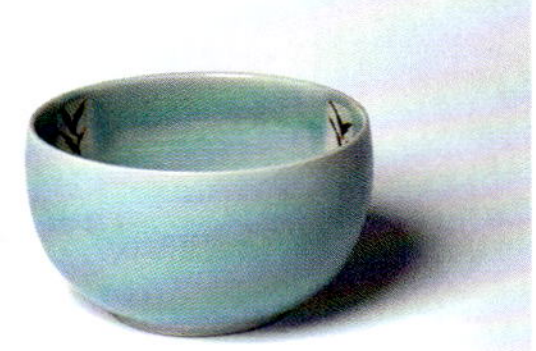

BLOCH, OLE 1942 –

Ceramicist, engineer

1977-81 Aarhus Kunstakademi
1980- Own studio workshop, Jutland

Ole Bloch made his debut at '*Kunstnernes Påskeudstilling 1982*' and took part in several exhibitions in the 1980s. He later took a qualification as an electronic engineer and worked for the firm of Danfoss. The museum's lidded pot was acquired at the '*Påskeudstilling*', Aarhus, in 1984 and is a work in raku typical of its time **(65)**.

65. Lidded pot, 1984

Stoneware, alkali-glazed; thrown, relief-carved ridges, raku, fired at 1000°. H 18.5 x Diam 11.5. Mark: Stamped mark on rim. Mus.no. 125a-b/1984 ACQUISITION: *Kunstnernes Påskeudstilling*, 1984, Århus Kunstbygning. Donation from *Finansieringsinstituttet for Industri og Håndværks Jubilæumslegat*

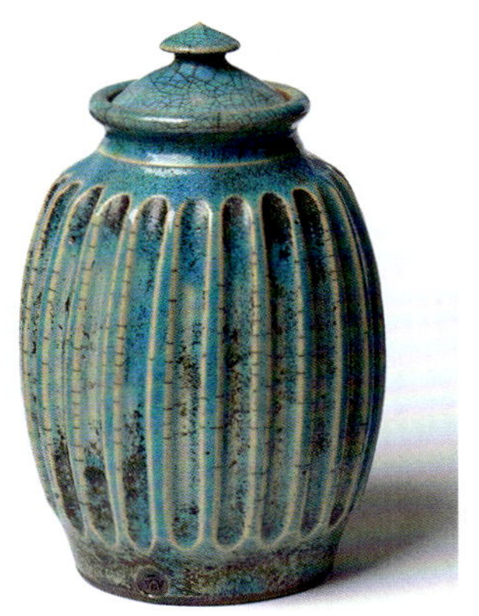

65. 125a-b/1984

BRANDES, PETER 1944 –

Artist, sculptor, photographer, ceramicist
Autodidact
1972- Own studio workshop, Paris

Peter Brandes (PB) is a prominent Danish artist who has worked within many disciplines and with many materials. He became fascinated with clay at an early point and has remained faithful to that engagement through much of his life. He began to stand out as an actual ceramic artist from the end of the 1980s and has since then made an extensive series of works, including many large-scale commissions in the form of freestanding sculptures, ceramic walls and reliefs, church decorations and smaller works such as pots and dishes.

A particular chapter in PB's *oeuvre* consists of the monumental stoneware vases, the earliest from 1992, which were made in Tommerup Keramiske Værksted in collaboration between the artist and the workshop's ceramic staff and craftsmen. Until now 12 giant vases have been made, their height varying from 4.65 to 5.25 m. Several of them are located in Denmark (Roskilde, the Royal garden at Marselisborg, and Nyborg) and others are in the USA, Germany and Israel.

PB works with successive series of works, exploring motifs in drawings, graphics, book illustrations, photography, glass and ceramics, with a special sensitivity to the diverse materials and processes. Recurrently found motifs are from classical antiquity and the pictorial worlds of Judaism and Christianity.

Central themes of PB's ceramic works are represented in the museum's collection. The earliest object is the pot from 1991 made of earthenware, with many layers of coloured slip and incised lines that create the characteristic movement of structures in the surface, supporting the progress of the decoration and the range of its colours **(66)**.

66. 303/1992

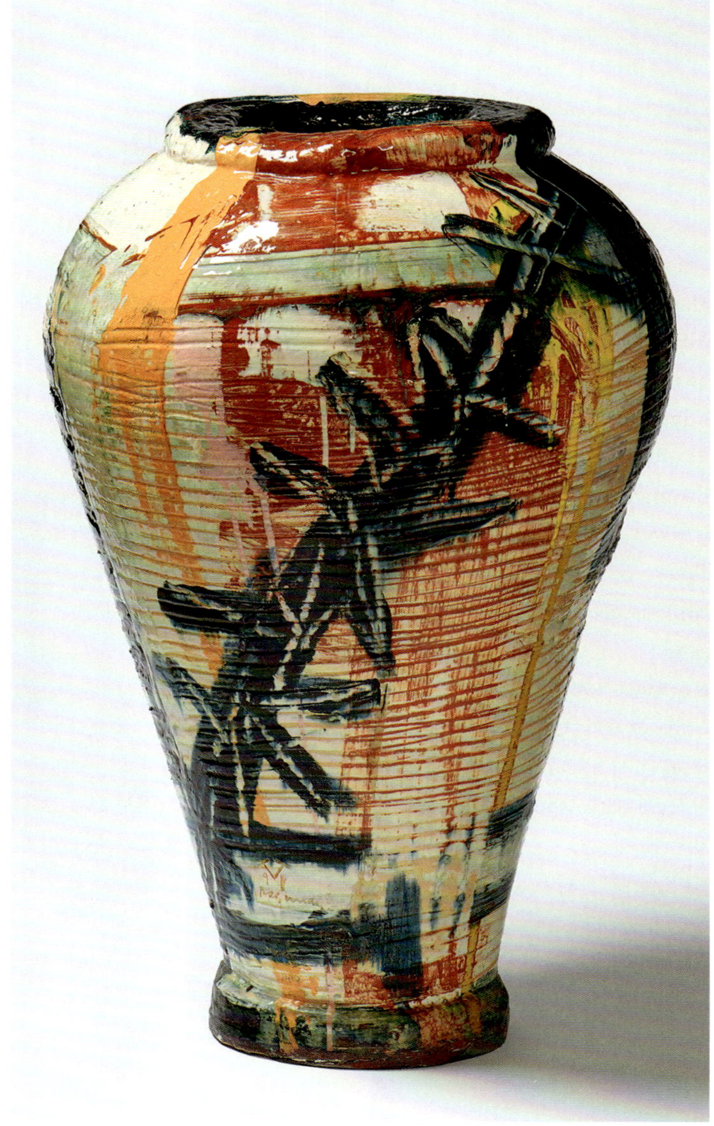

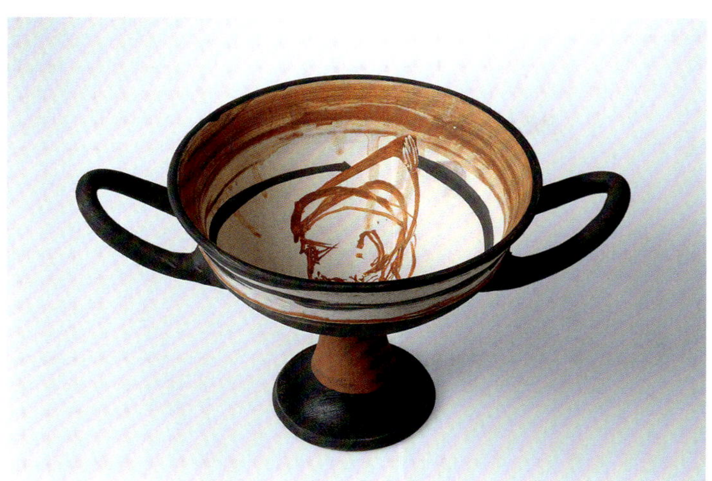

68. 189/2001

From around the same time there is the fine and intense sculpture *Hyrden* (the shepherd), with a reddish colouring that seems to flow like blood from the wounded animal on the figure's shoulder, down over his body onto the ground **(67)**. This biblical but also general human motif is one to which PB returned in sculptures from 2014.

Inspiration from classical antiquity is found in two of the museum's works. One, from 2001, is in the form of a *kylix* (drinking bowl); like its Greek predecessors it is made of red clay and covered with a whitish slip that lends itself to be drawn and painted on. The motif inside the centre of the bowl is a man's head clad in a Phrygian hat, as Odysseus is often depicted **(68)**. The museum's other and most recent work is from 2008 and consists of five oval plates with the shared title *Den 11. sang*, (The 11th song) referring to the Odyssey, a work that has been a recurring focus for PB and which he has been engaged in illustrating over the course of many years. In the '11th Song' Odysseus makes sacrifices to the dead in the Underworld (Hades) to obtain advice as to how he can return home. The dead are described in the song as gruesome figures, and this has perhaps suggested the tortured expressions in the five clay depictions donated to the museum by its most generous donor throughout many years, *Ny Carlsbergfondet* **(69-73)**.

66. Vase, 1991

Earthenware, layers of slip, glazed; modelled using a plaster mould, scratched indentations, slip colours on pre-fired earthenware fired at 1040°, then fired with lead glaze at 1025°, made at Tommerup Keramiske Værksted. H 90. Mark: none. Mus.no. 303/1992. ACQUISITION: Galerie Moderne, Silkeborg. Donation from the estate of L. E. Sandberg, consultant doctor

67. 363/1993

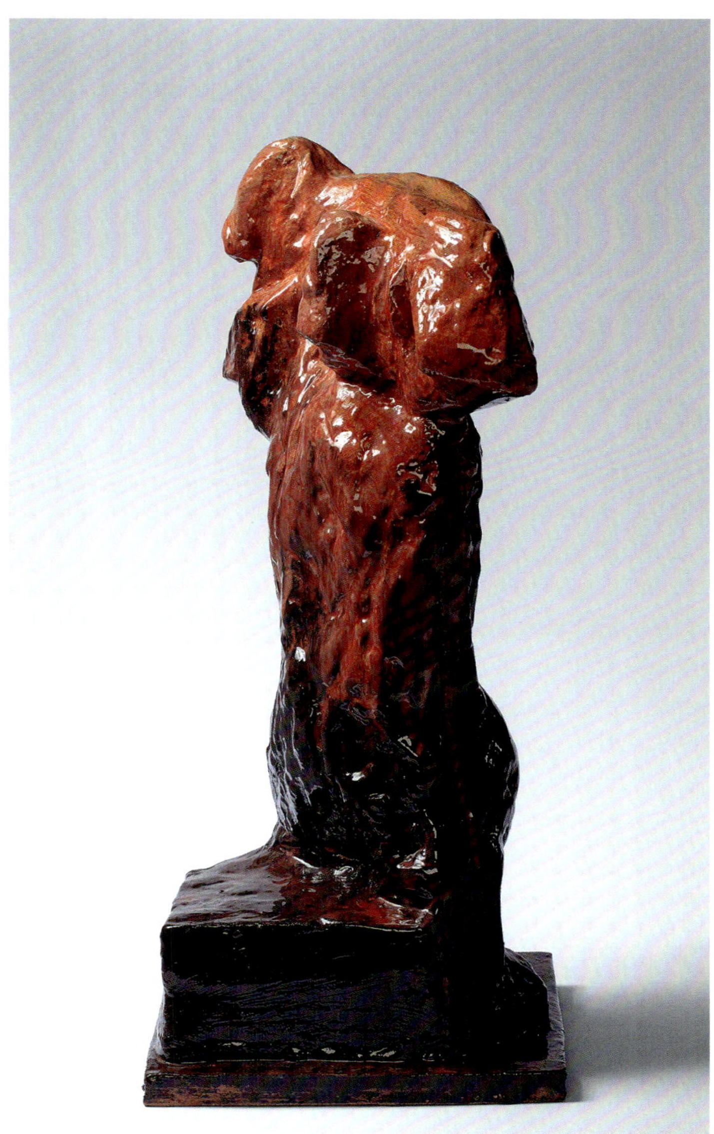

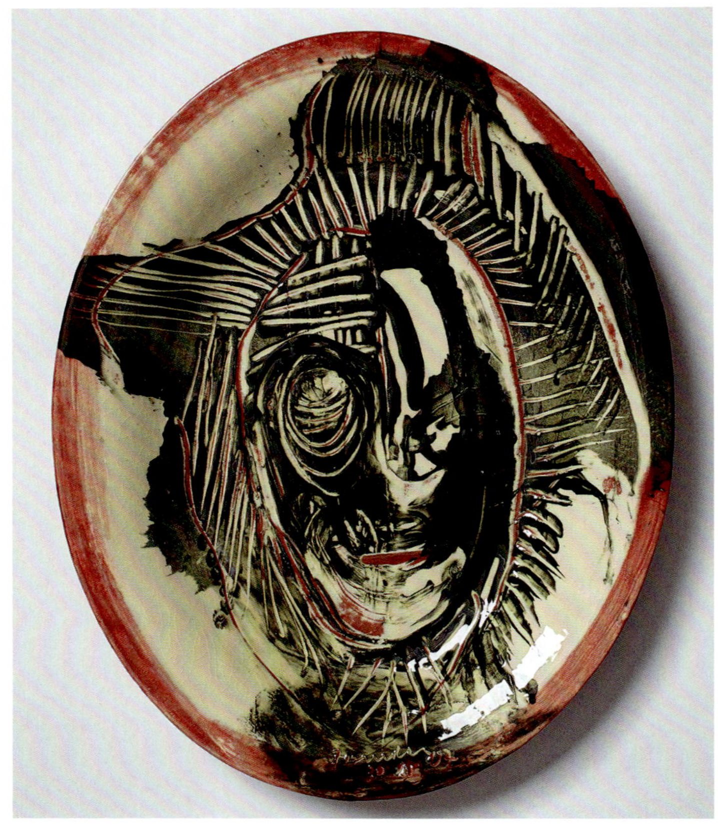

69. 127/2009

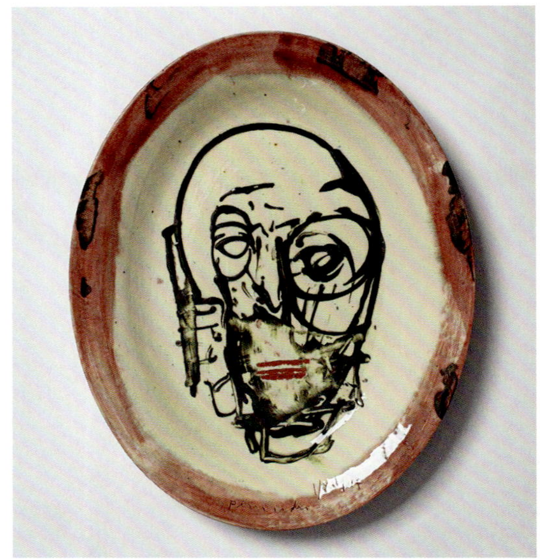

70. 128/2009

71. 129/2009

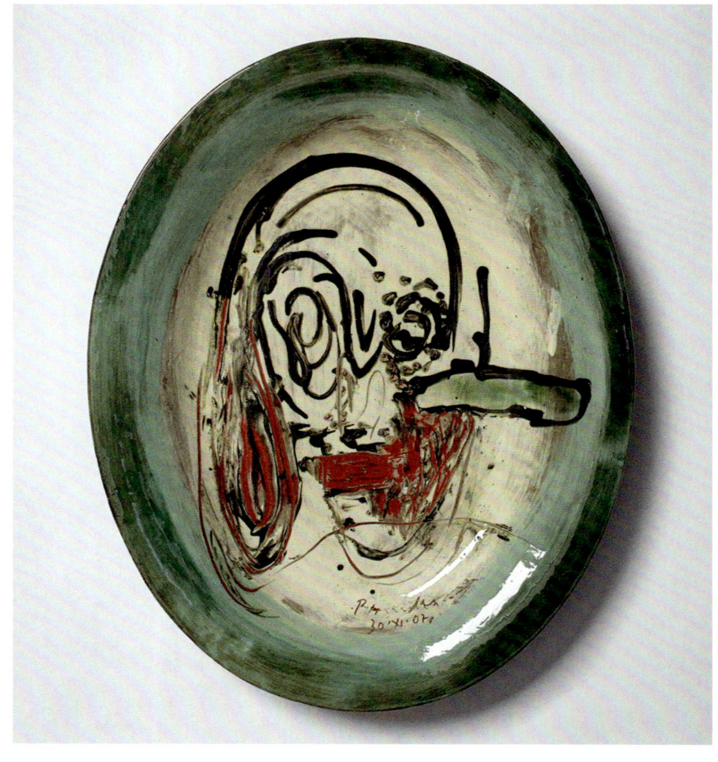

67. Sculpture, 1990-1991. *Hyrden* (The shepherd)
Earthenware, lead-glazed; roughly shaped in plaster mould, modelled, slip, fired at 1025°. Made at Tommerup Keramiske Værksted. H 53 x W 24. Mark: 'P Brandes' painted on base. Mus.no. 363/1993
ACQUISITION: Galerie Moderne, Silkeborg. See: Dybdahl, L., 1997

68. Bowl, 2001. *Kylix*
Red clay, unglazed; thrown by ceramicist Sverre Holmen in the presence of PB and in accordance with his directions, slip colours, sgrafitto, brush-painted decoration, fired at 1020°. H 16 x Diam 19. Mark: 'P Brandes 2001' inscribed on the foot along with Sverre Holmen's mark. Mus.no. 189/2001
ACQUISITION: *Peter Brandes Phaidon – Det Antikke Grækenland,* Søllerød Kunstforening, Gl. Holtegaard, 2001.
Donation from *Kunstindustrimuseets Venner*

69. Oval plate, 2007. (Part of) *Odysseen – Den 11.sang*
(The Odyssey – the 11th song)
Earthenware, glazed; glaze painted. H 43 x W 34. Mark: 'Brandes XI 07' painted and inscribed on base. Mus.no. 127/2009
ACQUISITION: Donation from *Ny Carlsbergfondet*

70. Oval plate, 2007. (Part of) *Odysseen – Den 11.sang*
The Odyssey – the 11th song)
Earthenware, glazed; glaze painted. H 43 x W 34. Mark: 'P Brandes I/XII/07' painted and inscribed on upper surface. Mus.no. 128/2009
ACQUISITION: Donation from *Ny Carlsbergfondet*

71. Oval plate, 2007. (Part of) *Odysseen – Den 11.sang*
(The Odyssey – the 11th song)
Earthenware, glazed; glaze painted. H 43 x W 34. Mark: 'P Brandes 30.XI.07' painted and inscribed on upper surface. Mus.no. 129/2009
ACQUISITION: Donation from *Ny Carlsbergfondet*

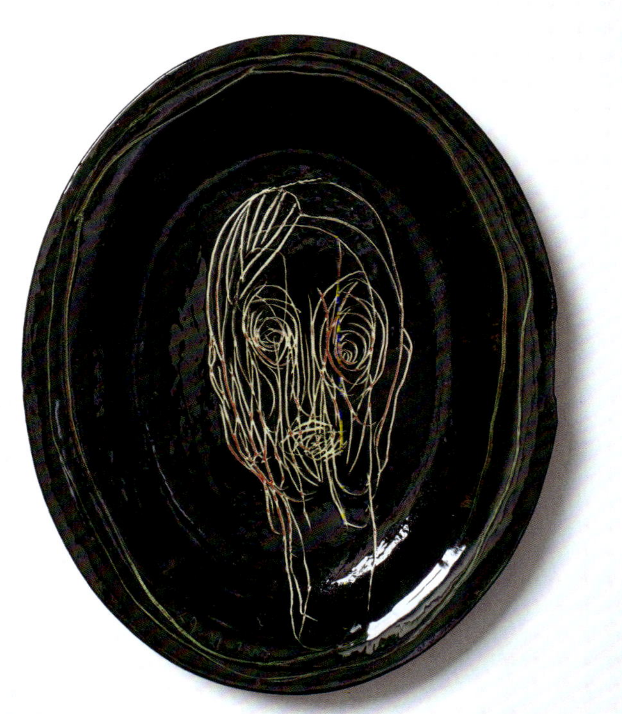

72. 130/2009

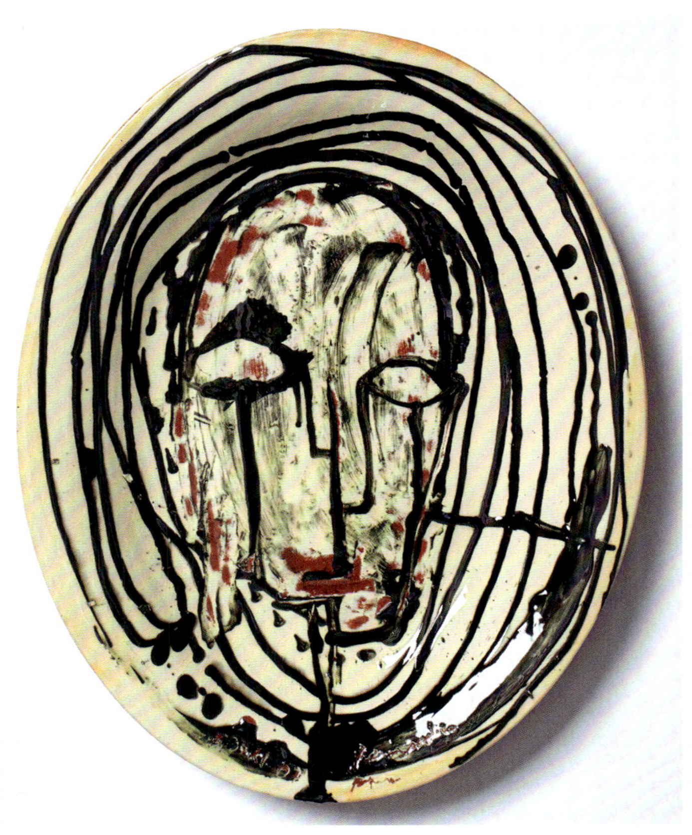

73. 131/2009

72. Oval plate, 2007. (Part of) *Odysseen – Den 11. sang*
(The Odyssey – the 11th song)
Earthenware, glazed; glaze painted. H 43 x W 34. Mark: 'P Brandes I/XII/07' painted and inscribed on upper surface. Mus.no. 130/2009
ACQUISITION: Donation from *Ny Carlsbergfondet*

73. Oval plate, 2007. (Part of) *Odysseen – Den 11. sang*
(The Odyssey – the 11th song)
Earthenware, glazed; glaze painted. H 43 x W 34. Mark: 'P Brandes 26-XI-07' painted and inscribed on upper surface. Mus.no. 131/2009
ACQUISITION: Donation from *Ny Carlsbergfondet*

BROKSØ, TINE see CLAYDIES p. 97

BRUHN, INGER 1948 –

Ceramicist

1981-85 Aarhus Kunstakademi

1997- Participated in *Lertøj* group, Aarhus

2005- Studio workshop in Horsens

www.ingerbruhn.dk

Inger Bruhn (IB) started her career as a ceramicist relatively late, but has worked intensively since leaving Aarhus Kunstakademi, where she was taught by Kim Holm. She mostly uses raku-firing for her works, which are sometimes freely modelled, thrown or in other cases slab-built; triangular forms can refer to sails and sailing which is an important source of inspiration for IB.

Other impressions come from travelling, which has brought her into contact with Native American culture, and from studies of older ceramics in museum collections.

The work in the museum's collection is slab-built and its colours exemplify the green, brown and whitish shades that are to be found in many of IB's works. The sculpture has the form of a little stool, topped by a representation of a cushion **(74)**.

74. Sculpture, 1991. ***Trekantet skammel med pude***
(Triangular stool with cushion)
Stoneware, frit- and ochre-glazed; slab technique, brush-painted, sgrafitto, raku, fired at 980°. H 15 x W 23. Mark: 'IB' stamped on base. Mus.no. 159/1990
ACQUISITION: *A'TI,* Gavlhuset, Århus. Donation from *Forenede Legater*

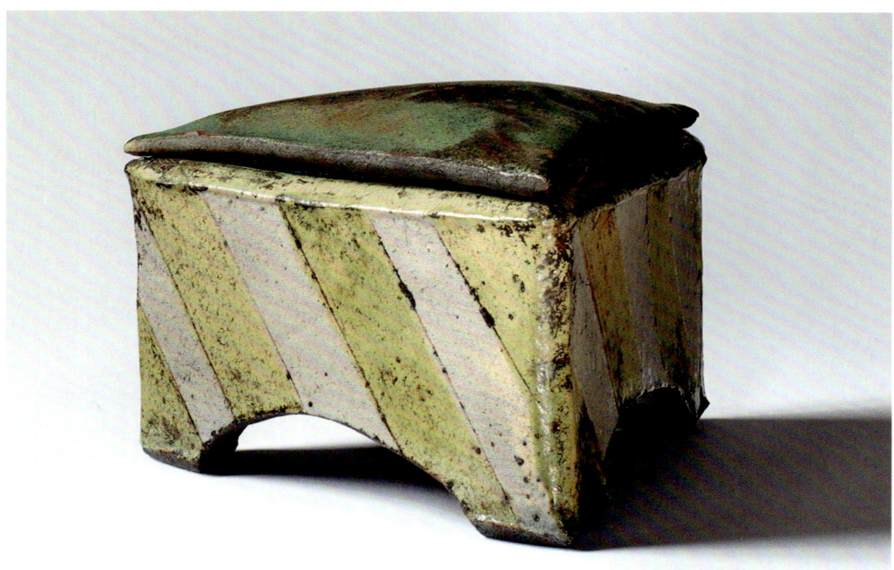

74. 159/1990

BRUUN, CHRISTIAN 1963 –

Ceramicist

1990 Completed studies at Skolen for Brugskunst

1991- Own studio workshop, Copenhagen
External consultant, instructor and external examiner at Kunstakademiets Designskole, Bornholm
www.christianbruun.com

One can detect inspiration taken from Japanese ceramic culture, with which CB became fascinated after visits to the museum and on journeys to Japan. In recent years CB has developed an interesting production of large stoneware pots made in cooperation with a factory in Vietnam.

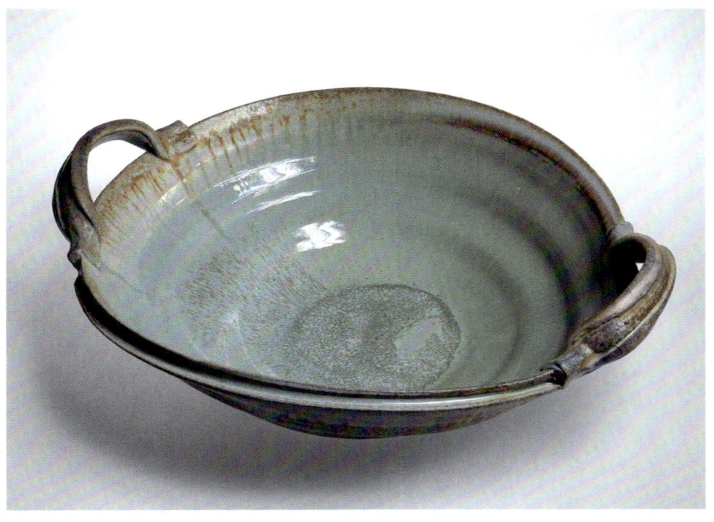

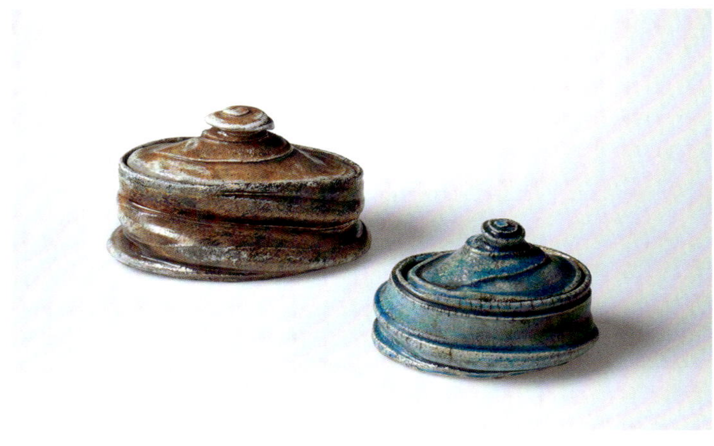

75. 31/2002 **76.** 416a-b/2008

In 2002 the museum acquired a massive dish with two sturdy handles and a thrown but organically and freely modelled corpus – a dish, but with sculptural qualities **(75)**. It was wood-fired, over six days, at the International Ceramic Research Center at Guldagergaard. It is glazed on the inside with a Korean celadon glaze and on the outside with a thinly applied clear glaze. Christian Bruun (CB) developed the basic form of the dish further in making the *Venus* table service, in thin hand-thrown white porcelain; he still produces it, and it belongs to the ranks of the finest porcelain for household use currently being produced in Danish private studios. In the museum's collection there are also two thrown lidded stoneware pots which radiate the same pleasure in clay and robust treatment of shape; here this has been achieved by 'tossing' the thrown form onto the worktop so that the shape becomes an oval that cannot be completely controlled **(76)**.

75. Dish, 2002
Porcelain, Korean celadon glaze with ochre; thrown, modelled, fired at 1350°. H 18 x Diam 52. Mark: 'CB' painted on base. Mus.no. 31/2002
ACQUISITION: *Nuancer af hvid*, 2002, Galleri Nørby, Copenhagen. Donation from *Kunstindustrimuseets Venner*

76. Two lidded pots, 1994
Stoneware, alkali-glazed; thrown, worked into an oval shape, raku-fired at c. 1100°. a: H (with lid) 9 x L 13.3 x W 12; b: H (with lid) 7.3 x L 11 x W 10. Mark: a: 'CB 94' painted on base; b: 'CB' (combined) painted. Mus.no. 416a-b/2008.
ACQUISITION: Donation from estate of Ambassador Niels Christian Tillisch, Copenhagen, 2008. See: Gelfer-Jørgensen, M., 2013, p. 315.

BRYNJOLF, JØRGEN 1931 – 1993

Painter, sculptor, graphic artist, ceramicist

1955-58	Mogens Andersens tegneskole, Copenhagen
1960-62	Stanley W. Hayter's Graphic Art School, Paris
1975-	Own studio workshop, Odsherred, NW Sealand

After moving to Odsherred in 1975 Jørgen Brynjolf (JB) found his painting developing towards a free naturalism under the influence of the grand-scale landscapes surrounding him. In addition to painting and sculpture JB used enamel technique e.g. in connection with commissioned work, but very little is known about his ceramic works. Nevertheless, the museum owns a signed dish from 1984 with the title *Himmel og hav* (Sky and sea), donated by the artist **(77)**. This work, with its freely painted natural composition, with broad spontaneous brushstrokes, clearly has close connections to JB's other artistic works.

77. Dish, 1984. *Himmel og hav* (Sky and sea)

Stoneware, glazed; painted glaze. H 5.5 x Diam 37. Mark: 'Brynjolf 1984 Denmark' painted on base. Mus.no. 109/1990

ACQUISITION: Donated by the artist

77. 109/1990

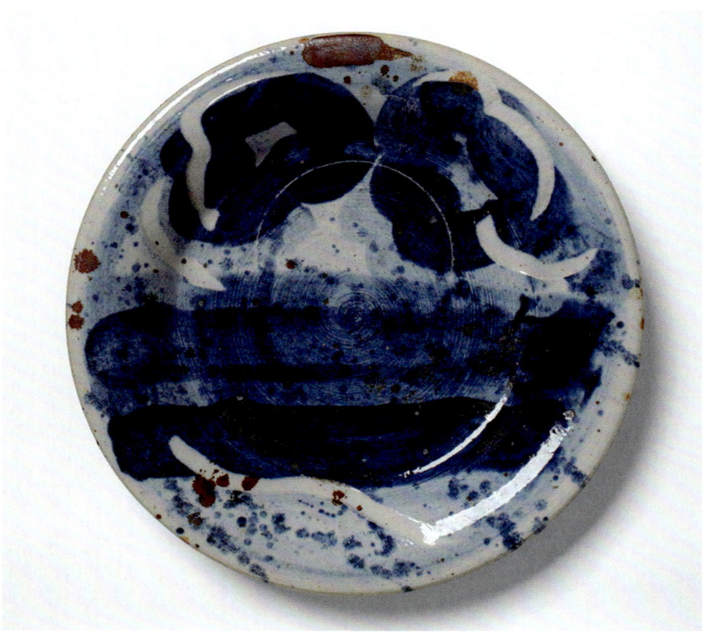

BÆCH, GUDRUN MEEDOM 1915 – 2011

Ceramicist

1945	Completed studies at Kunsthåndværkerskolen
1945-46	Saxbo ceramic works
1946-53	Bing & Grøndahl's stoneware workshop
1953-	Own studio workshop, Viborg
1984	Det Jyske Kunstakademi, instructor

Gudrun Meedom Bæch (GMB) was highlighted as the classical Danish ceramicist *par excellence* by the two distinguished foreign connoisseurs of Danish ceramics in the period 1950-1990, Dorris U. Kuyken-Schneider, Museum Boijmans Van Beuningen, Rotterdam, and William Hull, Museum of Art, Pennsylvania State University, who organised the first international presentation of Danish ceramics in the USA in 1982. The reasons given for this accolade were GMB's fine mastery of interplay between form and decoration and in the balance of use of different techniques: painting with slip, inlays, overglaze decoration, and finally the understated beauty of all of GMB's works. '*These beautiful and unassuming pieces have come to be [seen as among] the most Danish of the Danish Modern period of the postwar era outside of Denmark*'. (*Brændpunkter* 1990, p. 100)

Danish writers emphasise GMB's commendable work to revive and develop earthenware made of red clay from Jutland. GMB took up the use of this technique in connection with the setting up of her studio in Viborg in 1953. Before that she had shown herself to be a fine stoneware artist in the context of her time at Saxbo and later as artist-in-residence in Bing & Grøndahl's stoneware workshop.

As a result of donations from the artist this development can be followed in the museum's collection in the form of ten works; seven of them were made in her own studio, and three are from the years with Bing & Grøndahl **(78-79,84)**. The last-mentioned unique works are carefully marked with the artist's signature and the factory's mark. From the collection one can gain a lively impression of GMB's work with form, glaze and stylized ornamentation, progressing from the paler and more colourful glazes of the early works to the later works in red clay and subdued-toned glazes with added wood ash from e.g. poplar and apple trees. Several of the works have low recessed and unglazed base which shows the red clay.

GMB was represented at major exhibitions both in Denmark and internationally, and her works were acquired by knowledgeable collectors. She also carried out several large commissions in the form of ceramic sculptures and reliefs, and prepared designs for pictorial woven works, often for churches. (See: '*Gudrun Meedom Bæch – en keramikers livsværk*', Skovgaard Museet, 2006. ISBN 87-87191-11-3.)

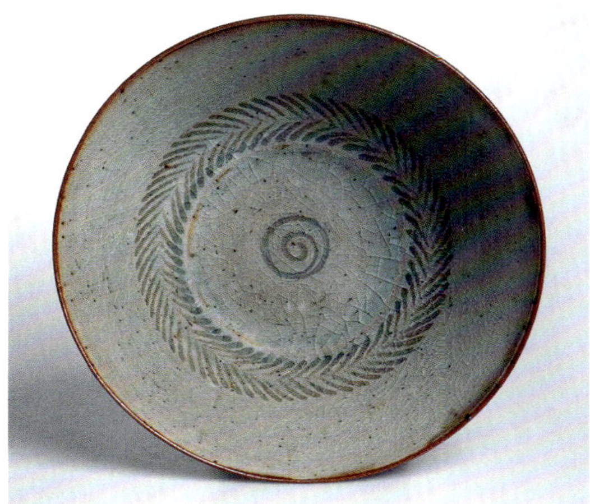

79. 13/1953

78. 50/1950

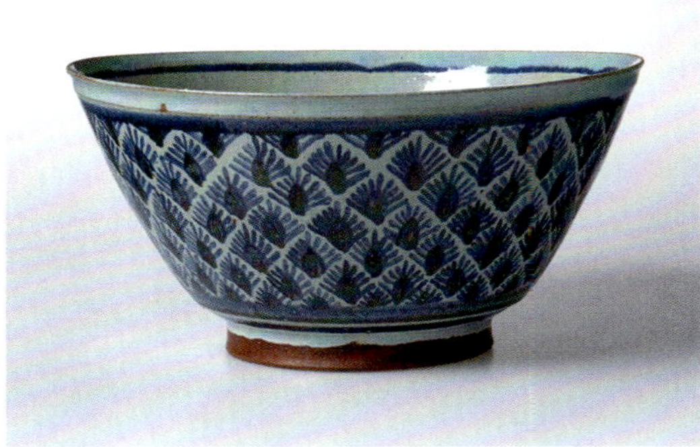

80. 1/1957

82. 234/1990

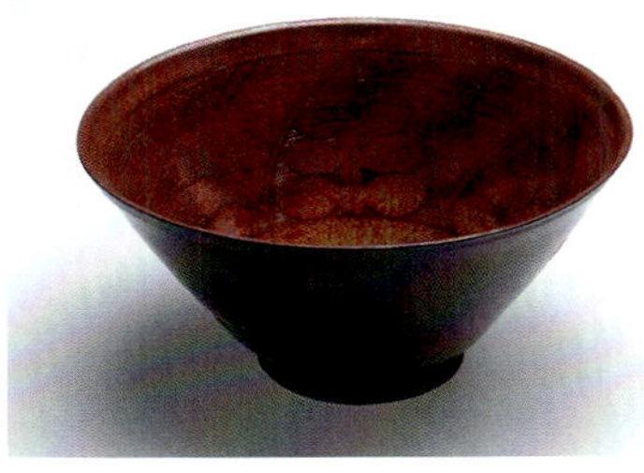

83. 235/1990

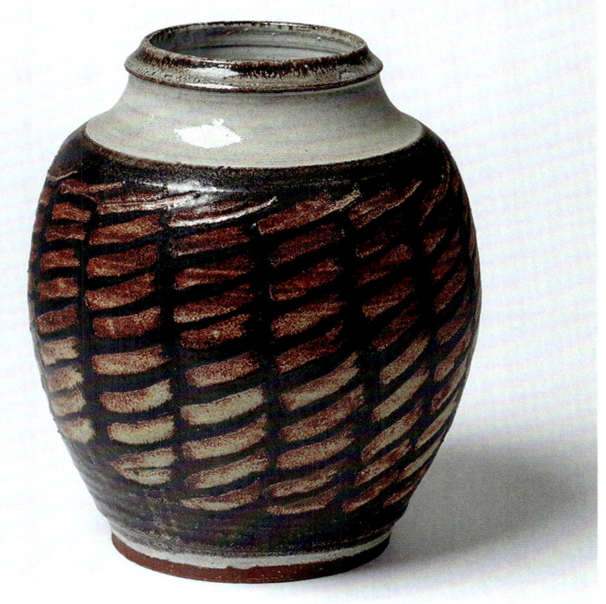

81. 233/1990

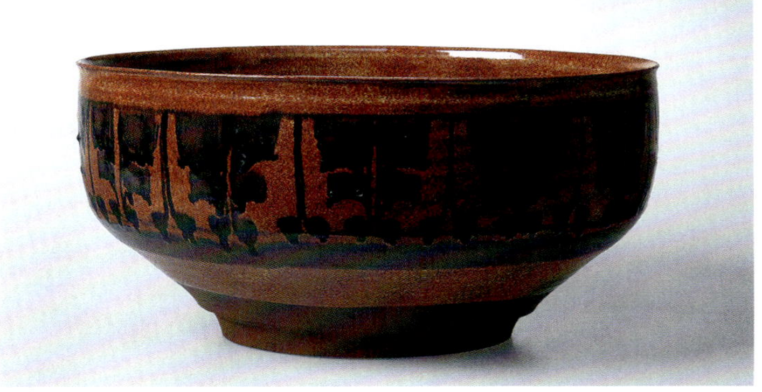

78. Bowl, 1950

Stoneware, clear glaze; thrown, slip, decoration. H 8 x Diam. 12.5.

Mark: 'G Mee' inscribed on base, with stamped 'B & G'. Mus.no. 50/1950

ACQUISITION: *Landsforeningens forårsudstilling*, 1950, Kunstindustrimuseet. Donation from *Kunstindustrimuseets 50-års Jubilæumslegat*. See: Lassen, E., 1978

79. Bowl, 1953

Stoneware; thrown, slip. H 8 x Diam 17.5. Mark: 'G Mee' inscribed on base, with stamped 'B & G'. Mus.no. 13/1953

ACQUISITION: Bing & Grøndahl, 1953.

Donation from *Benny Dessaus Mindelegat*. See: *Brændpunkter*, 1990

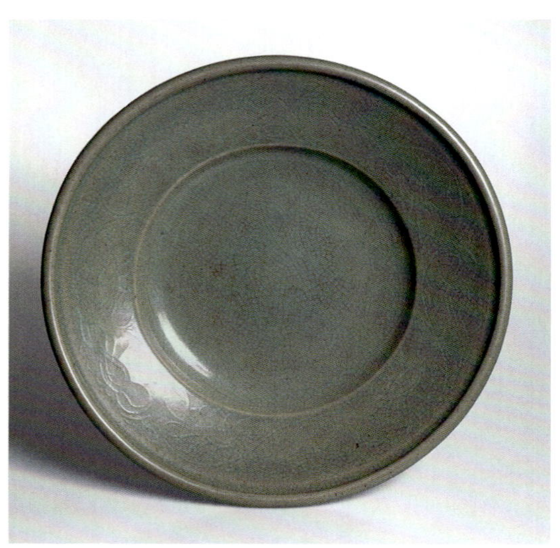

84. 362/1993

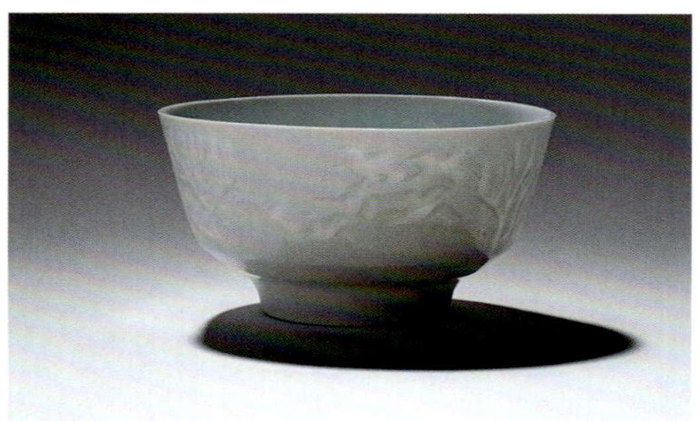

85. 460/2007

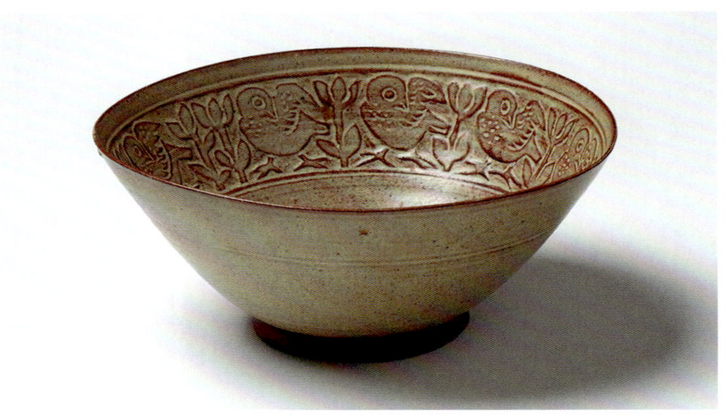

86. 463/2007

80. Bowl, 1956

Earthenware, glaze; thrown, slip, brush-painted decoration.

H 11.2 x Diam 23.2. Mark: 'G Mee Danmark' inscribed on base.

Mus.no. 1/1957

ACQUISITION: Den Permanente, 1956, Copenhagen. See: Dybdahl, L., 1997

87. 464/2007

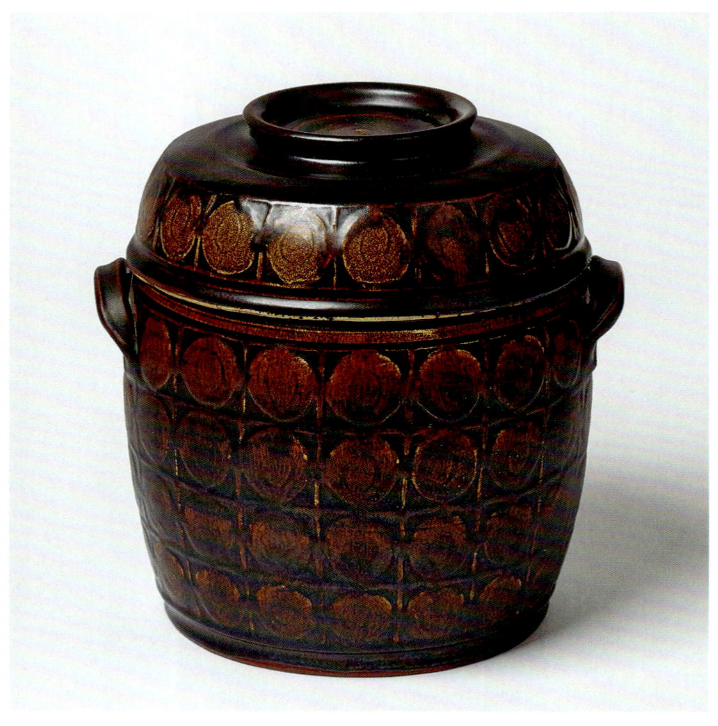

81. Bowl, 1981

Stoneware, glaze; thrown, brush-painted decoration. H 15.5 x Diam 31. Mark: 'G Mee 1981' inscribed on base. Mus.no. 233/1990.

ACQUISITION: Gudrun Meedom Bæch. Donation from *Kunstindustrimuseets Venner*

82. Bowl, 1981

Earthenware; thrown, wax resist. H 11 x Diam 21. Mark: 'G Mee 1981' inscribed on base. Mus.no. 234/1990.

ACQUISITION: Gudrun Meedom Bæch. Donation from *Kunstindustrimuseets Venner*

83. Pot, 1981

Stoneware, glazed; thrown, decorated. H 21 x Diam 20. Mark: 'G Mee' inscribed on base. Mus.no. 235/1990.

ACQUISITION: Donation from Gudrun Meedom Bæch for Kunstindustri-museet's 100-year Jubilee. See: Dybdahl, L., 1997

84. Dish, 1946-1953

Stoneware, celadon-glazed; thrown. H 9.4 x Diam 39. Mark: 'G Mee' inscribed on base with stamped 'B&G'. Mus.no. 362/1993

ACQUISITION: Art Deco, Copenhagen

85. Bowl, 1950s

Porcelain, clear glaze; carved decoration. H 7.2 x Diam 13.6. Mark: indecipherable mark on base. Mus.no. 460/2007

ACQUISITION: Donation from Gudrun Meedom Bæch

86. Bowl, c.1970

Earthenware, apple-ash-glazed; carved decoration, hard fired. H 8.5 x W 20. Mark: indecipherable, obscured by repair. Mus.no. 463/2007

ACQUISITION: Donation from Gudrun Meedom Bæch

87. Lidded pot, c.1965

Earthenware, glazed with wood ash and iron; slip, relief. H 23 x Diam 18. Mark: 'G Mee' inscribed on base. Mus.no. 454/2007

ACQUISITION: Donation from Gudrun Meedom Bæch

BÆKHØJ, POUL 1942 –

Sculptor, ceramicist

Cheminova, Lemvig, laboratory technician

1970	Autodidact ceramicist
1970-	Own studio workshop, Århus

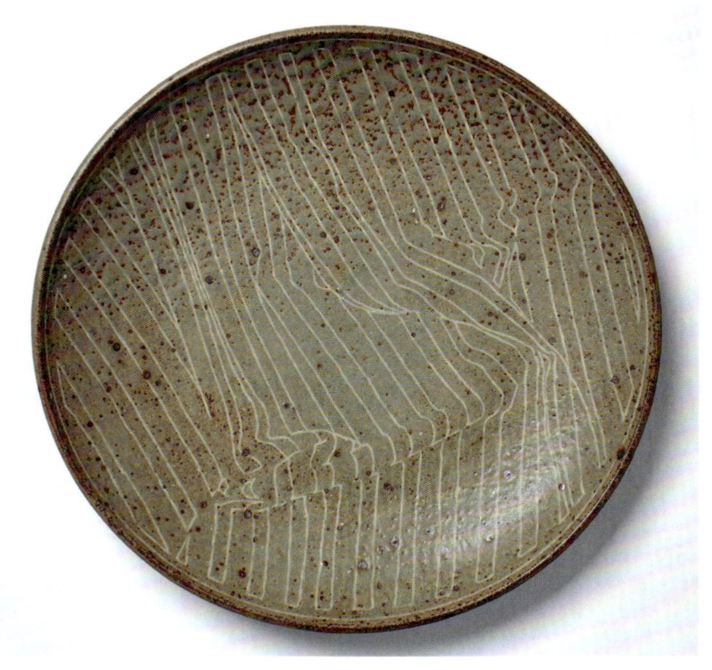

88. 103/1983

After Poul Bækhøj set up his own workshop in combination with a gallery in Århus in 1970 he dedicated himself to ceramic pictorial art for a decade; after that he transferred his focus to working with stone sculpture. The museum's work, dated 1983, is a dish with a large plain shape and an elegant inlaid whitish line-decoration, with a glaze which has a deeply textured and subdued colour effect **(88)**. This form of play with lines can also be seen in the artist's later sculptures in granite.

88. Dish, 1983

Stoneware, matte, colourless glaze; thrown, inlaid clay, fired at 1300°. H 6.8 x Diam 48.5. Mark: 'Bækhøj' stamped on base. Mus.no. 103/1983

ACQUISITION: Poul Bækhøj. Donation from *Ny Carlsberg Museumslegat*

BÖRJESON, BIRGITTE 1939 –

Ceramicist

1956-60 Kunsthåndværkerskolen

1960-62 Harry and May Davis, Crowan Pottery, Cornwall, England

1963- Studio workshop shared with Hans Börjeson, Fulby, Sealand

2016 Retrospective exhibition at CLAY

www.fulby.com

BÖRJESON, HANS 1932 –

Ceramicist

1952-56 Slöjdforeningens Skola, Göteborg, Sweden

1958-62 Harry and May Davis, Crowan Pottery, Cornwall, England

1963- Studio workshop shared with Birgitte Börjeson, Fulby, Sealand

2016 Retrospective exhibition at CLAY

www.fulby.com

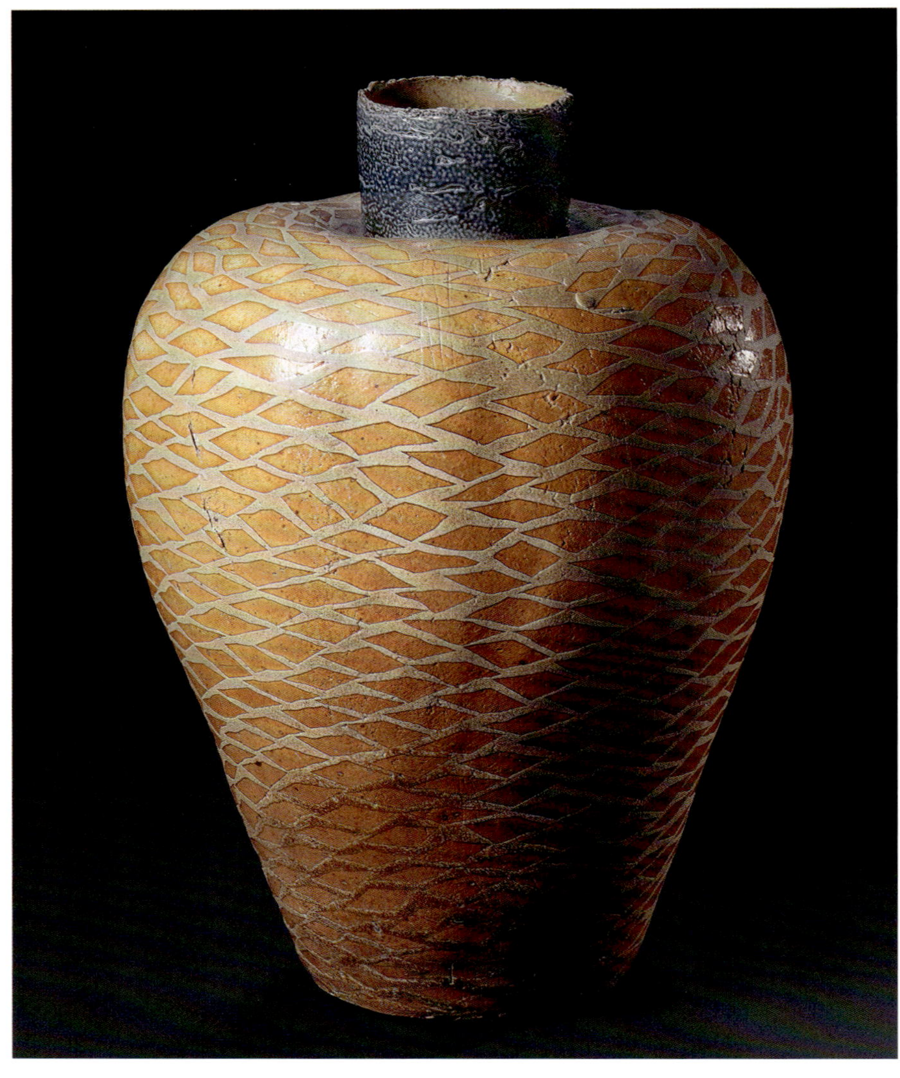

90. 153/1994

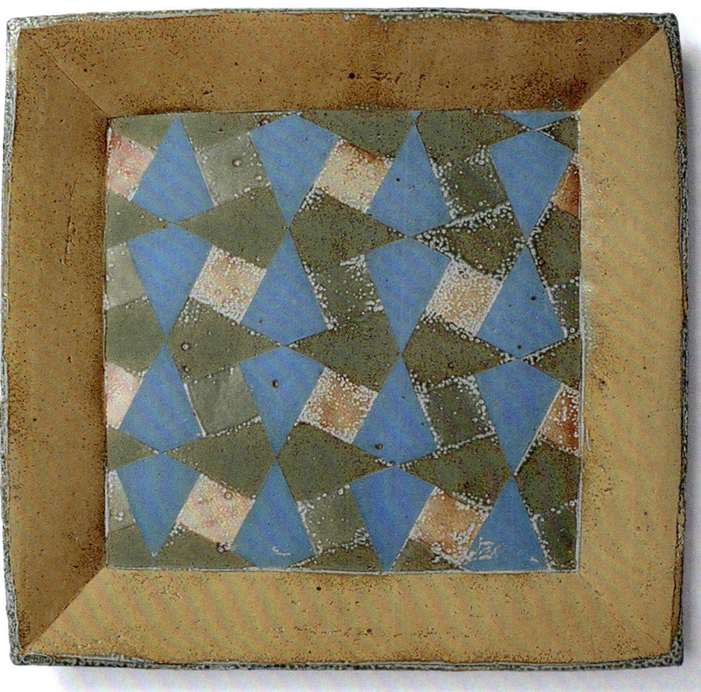

93. 41a-b/2000

Birgitte and Hans Börjeson (BHB) together form an institution in Danish ceramics because of the quality and quantity of their products, because of their partnership with joint signing of their works, and because of the openness, humanity and perseverance they have shown throughout 50 years at their shared workshop *FULBY* near Sorø. In brief, they have made studio-ceramic history in Denmark, and apart from a few years in Africa working for Danida in the early 1970s, the departure-point for all they have achieved has been their studio in Fulby.

Just two years after setting up the studio, in 1965, BHB became members of Den Permanente, and during a period of over 20 years thereafter the majority of their works were sold there. Their table service with black tenmoku glaze was a bestseller, and many young pupils spent time in their workshop in the course of the years. Gradually, after Den Permanente and other sales points found they had to close, BHB increasingly focused on markets for ceramics further afield in Europe, and over time that became a lifestyle and international pivot for their activities. Contacts with customers, fellow ceramicists, collectors and museums were forged thanks to the couple's characterful products and open-minded disposition. A point worth noting is that it was BHB who took the initiative in 1983 to set up the now annual craft market at Frue Plads in the centre of Copenhagen.

Ceramic pieces from FULBY are to be found all around the world in museums and collections. BHB have participated in innumerable exhibitions and carried out about 20 ceramic commissions, some of them with very tall assembled columns, glazed and weight-bearing, or else large benches for residential areas, which involve difficult and demanding work. A completely different and untraditional project was undertaken in 1999 for Vejen Kunstmuseum: a 'Pathfinder-path', in which ceramic bricks shaped like cobblestones show visitors the way from the station to Vejen Kunstmuseum. In 2005 the Kunstindustrimuseum acquired several examples of these ceramic paving stones with inscriptions **(92)**.

BHB's results were achieved by means of a persistently experimental attitude to the work, both with regard to research related to materials and techniques and in matters of artistic development, which was a process that constantly moved forward. Early in the 1970s work began on developing a porcelain paste which could make it possible to fire transparent porcelain. Throughout the 1980s many objects were produced in porcelain, but at the beginning of the 1980s a new era started for FULBY with experiments using salt glaze; that was to become the workshop's major speciality and to build up an international reputation for BHB. In the museum's collection there are five works from FULBY from the years 1986-2005. The earliest is a salt-glazed flask from 1986, from which it can be seen that salt glaze has by that time been incorporated in earnest into the workshop's products **(89)**, and from 1994 there is a large vase with a fine shape that is encircled and supported by a net-like decoration made by applying a layer of slip coloured using various oxides. The colouring of the vase, its proportions and the vivacious modelling make it a masterpiece. **(90)**.

91. 174/2005

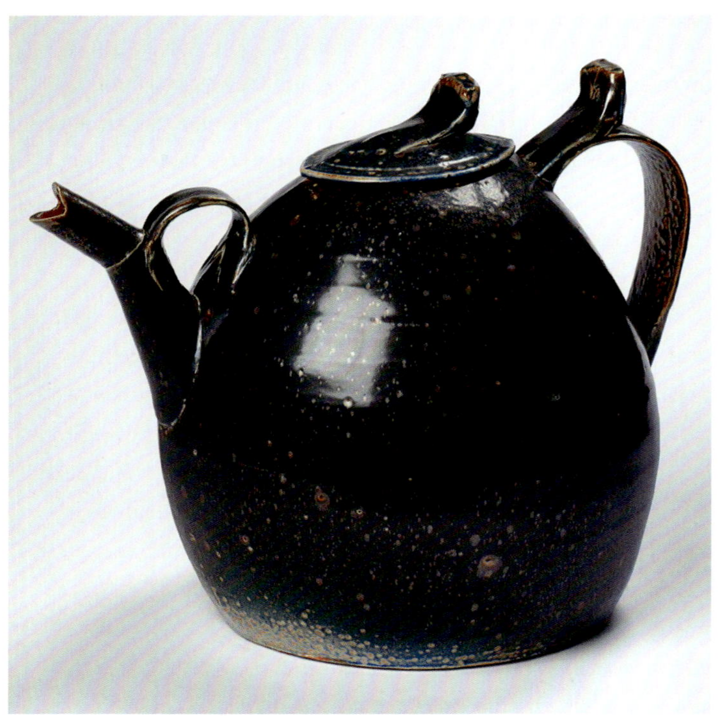

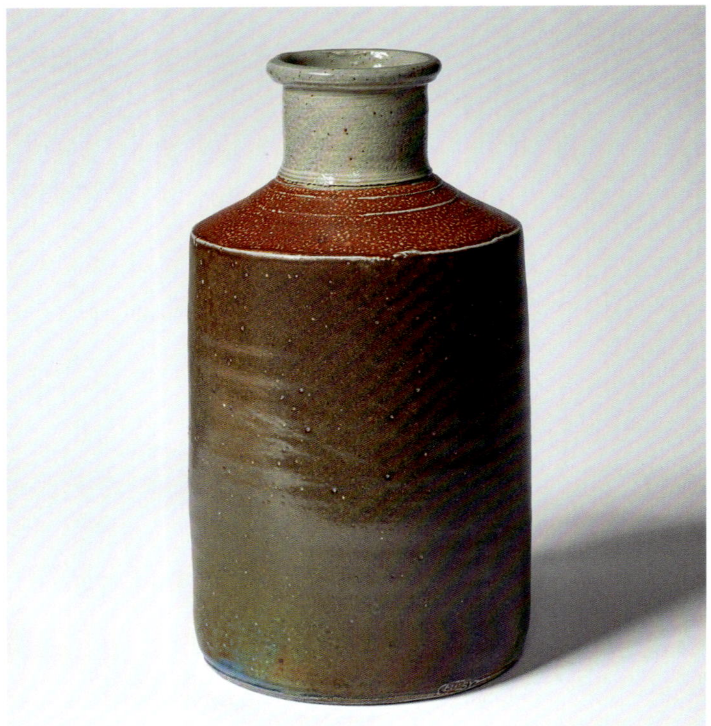

89. 101/1986

Among the most characteristic pieces in the workshop's production are the jugs that are thrown by Hans Börjeson and that through the years have taken on fantastical forms, anthropomorphic and decorated with rich variations of salt glazes and textures. The museum's example is a splendid large teapot with a salt glaze that shimmers in blue, green and black **(91)**. Another salt-glazed work that illustrates the workshop's impressive precision and control of the seemingly uncontrollable process is the large dish with the Moorish-inspired decoration that was acquired at the retrospective exhibition '*Fuld Form Fulby*' in 2005 in the museum **(93)**. A large selection of BHB's many types of work from the years 1963-2005 was shown there, including examples of the very large thrown pots and dishes with figurative narrative depictions of often ferocious encounters between animals and people; these works are thrown by Hans Börjeson, while Birgitte Börjeson was responsible for the painted decoration. In 2013 FULBY celebrated its 50th jubilee with a retrospective publication, '*fifty/fifty/fulby*'. In 2016 FULBY received the honour of having a comprehensive retrospective exhibition devoted to it at Denmark's Museum of Ceramic Art, CLAY, in Middelfart, Funen.

89. Flask, 1986

Stoneware, salt-glazed; thrown, slip, fired at 1300°. H 32 x Diam 16. Mark: 'Fulby' stamped on base. Mus.no. 101/1986

ACQUISITION: *Kunstforeningen Gl. Strand*, 1986.

Donation from *Kunstindustrimuseets Venner*. See: *Brændpunkter*, 1990

90. Vase, 1993

Stoneware, salt-glazed; thrown, paper resist, salt-fired at 1300°. H 65.5 x Diam 39. Mark: none. Mus.no. 153/1994. ACQUISITION: Galleri Nørby, 2001, Copenhagen. Donation from *Politiken Fonden*. See: Dybdahl, L., 1997

91. Teapot, 1999

Stoneware, salt-glazed; thrown, fired at 1300°. H 32. Mark: none. Mus.no. 41a-b/2000. ACQUISITION: Galleri Nørby, 2001, Copenhagen. Donation from *Kunstindustrimuseets Venner*

92. Four paving stones with texts, 2005. *Rokoko, Anarki, Teori, Populær*

Stoneware, salt-glazed; cast, fired at 1300°. H 5.5 x W 9.5 x D 9.5. Mark: none. Mus.no. 206a-d/2005.

ACQUISITION: *Fuld Form Fulby*, 2005, Kunstindustrimuseet

93. Dish, 2000

Stoneware, salt-glazed; oxide slip, paper resist, fired at 1300°. L 64 x W 64. Mark: none. Mus.no. 174/2005. ACQUISITION: *Fuld Form Fulby*, 2005, Kunstindustrimuseet

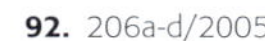
92. 206a-d/2005

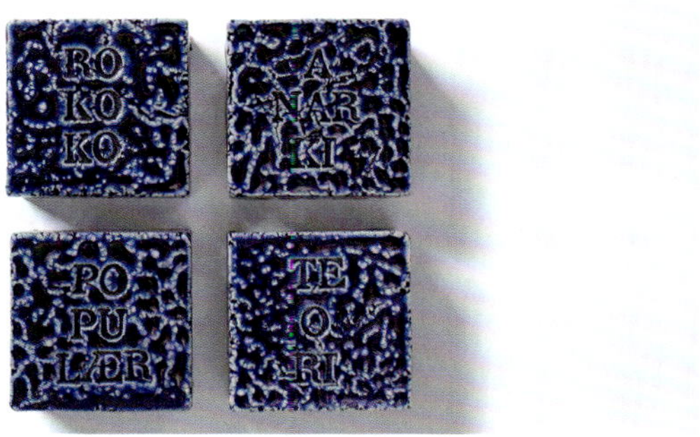

VON BÜLOW, ANE KATRINE 1952 –

Ceramic designer

1974-80 Skolen for Brugskunst

1983-2007 Danmarks Designskole, ceramics and glass, instructor

1994- Own studio workshop, Hellerup

www.anekatrinevonbulow.dk

Work with 'Graphic Porcelain' is the expression used by Ane-Katrine von Bülow (AKvB) for her ceramic endeavours, which she has developed over a number of years as a practising ceramicist as well as through her many years of teaching at Danmarks Designskole with ceramic decoration as the field of her courses. Her teaching is collected in the compendium '*Serigrafi på keramik og glas*' published in 1999 by AKvB and Ørnulf Opheim. Before she was employed at Danmarks Designskole she travelled to Japan to study Sumi-e (brush painting).

AKvB works with bowls as her basic choice of form, often in monumental sizes. They are double cast in porcelain, and shape and pattern are worked on via computer so that a rare degree of integration can be achieved. This complicated technique, involving interplay between skilled craftsmanship and advanced computer technology, has resulted in unique works of convincing aesthetic vigour which have won international reputation. They are exhibited around the world and have earned the artist well-deserved accolades such as the Westerwald Prize in 2004.

The four works in the museum's collection show the range of graphic expression, including examples both of geometric, rhythmic pattern composition in the *Net bowls* **(94-95)**, and of organic decoration, as on the two very fine bowls on which entwined leaves and branches unite the interior and exterior surfaces in a single form of expression **(96-97)**. The works show an exceptional mastery of black-and-white graphic idiom.

94. Bowl, 2008. *Netskål* (Net bowl)

Porcelain, matte transparent glaze; cast, computer-processed serigraphy, transferred from silk screen prints, fired at 1280°. H 8 x Diam 16.5. Mark: 'AKB' painted in a square on the base. Mus.no. 11/2009

ACQUISITION: Ann Linnemann Studie Galleri, Copenhagen

95. Bowl, 2008. *Netskål* (Net bowl)

Porcelain, matte transparent glaze; cast, computer-processed serigraphy, transferred from silk screen prints, fired at 1280°. H 20.5 x Diam 41.3. Mark: 'AKB' painted in a square on the base. Mus.no. 12/2009

ACQUISITION: Ann Linnemann Studie Galleri, Copenhagen

96. Bowl, 2009

Porcelain, soda-glazed; cast, computer-processed serigraphy, transferred from silk screen prints, reduction-fired at 1280°. H 23.5 x Diam 48.

Mus.no. 37/2010

ACQUISITION: *2D til 3D – fotografier af Ole Akhøj og porcelæn af Ane-Katrine von Bülow*, Ann Linnemann Studie Galleri, Copenhagen

97. Bowl, 2009

Porcelain, soda-glazed; cast, computer-processed serigraphy, transferred from silk screen prints, reduction-fired at 1280°. H 23.5 x Diam 48.5.

Mus.no. 38/2010

ACQUISITION: *2D til 3D – fotografier af Ole Akhøj og porcelæn af Ane-Katrine von Bülow*, Ann Linnemann Studie Galleri, Copenhagen

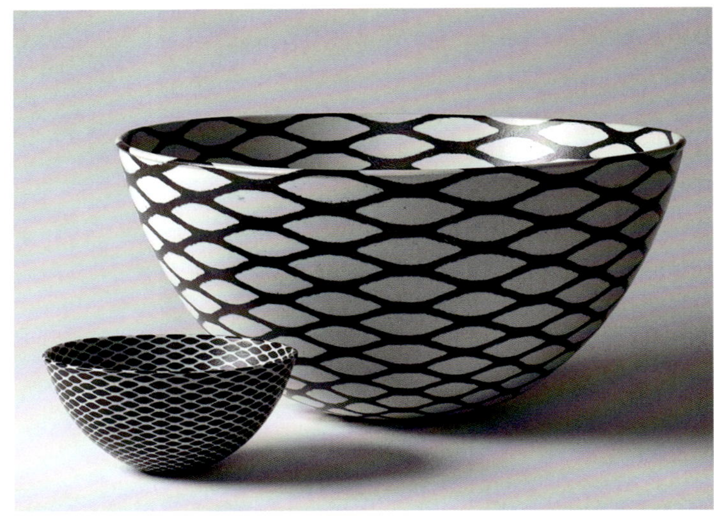

94. 11/2009 **95.** 12/2009

96. 37/2010 **97.** 38/2010

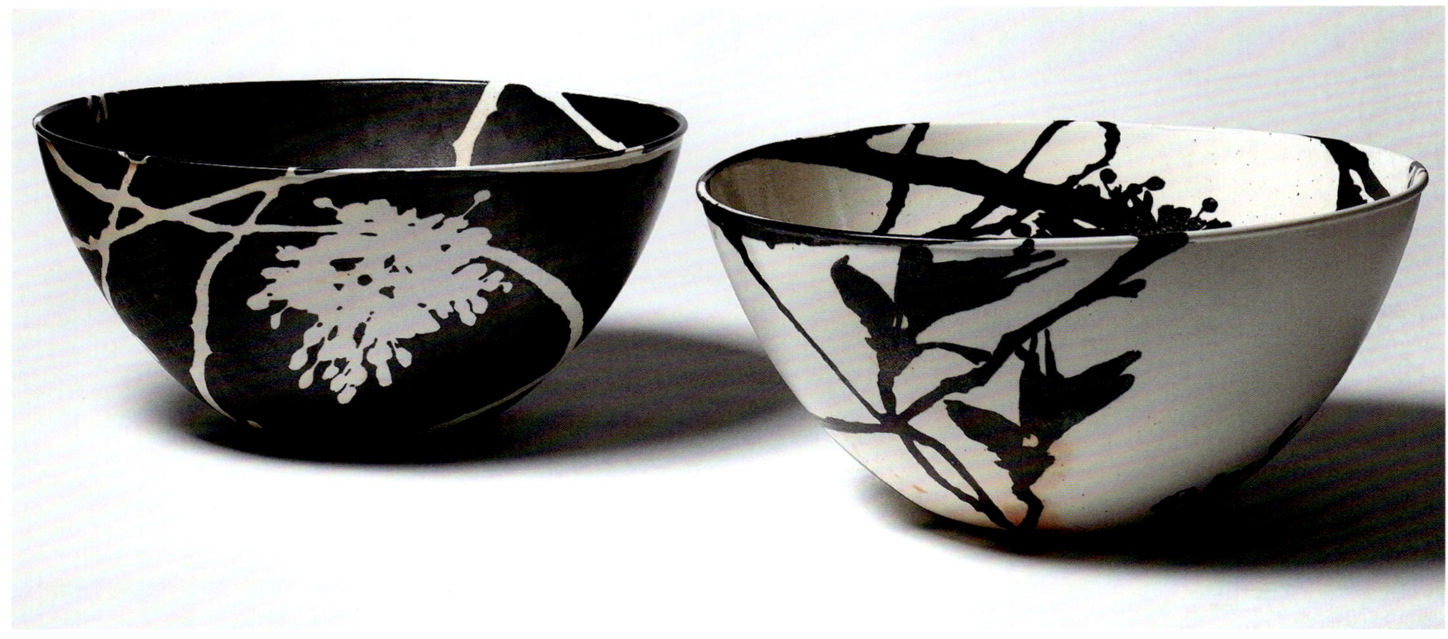

BØRSTING, STEN 1946 –

Ceramicist

Autodidact

1986- Own studio workshop, Ribe
www.stenboersting.dk

In the summer of 1989 the museum had the opportunity to hold a large exhibition of Jutland craft works, with all the classical areas of craftsmanship represented: textiles, glass, metal and of course ceramics. In all 40 artist craftsmen took part, 17 of them ceramicists. The museum acquired a number of works in this context, including two by Sten Børsting (SB) **(98-99)**.

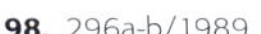

98. 296a-b/1989

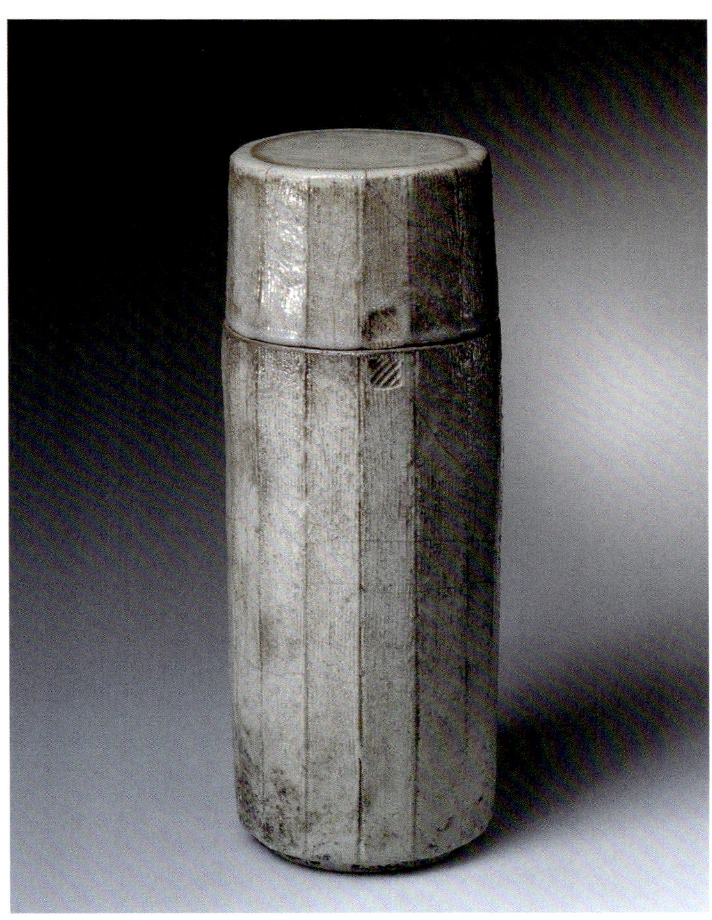

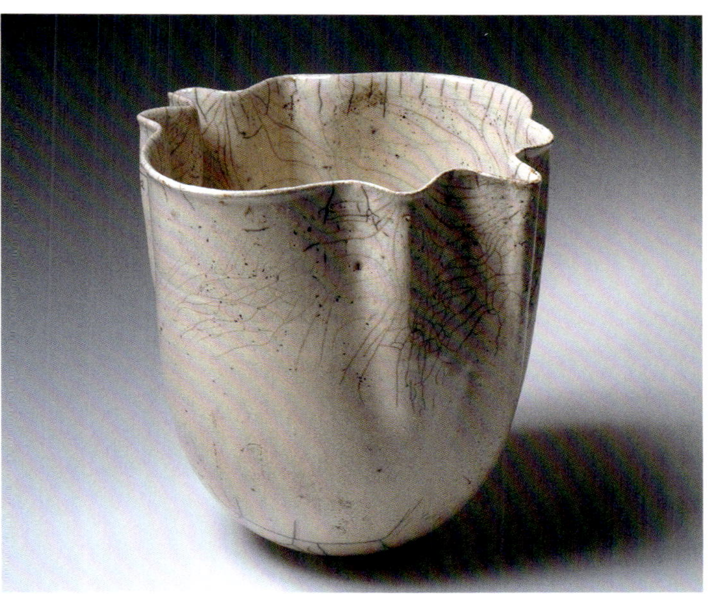

99. 342/1989

SB qualified as a teacher but in 1986 he took the plunge to start working with ceramics full time, setting up his own studio workshop. While being firmly anchored in the Danish ceramic tradition he has also sought knowledge and inspiration from travels and visits to many places around the world, and has developed a personal form of expression in his works, based on ceramic culture from both Denmark and further afield. The museum's two works are made in glazed raku-fired earthenware, which is still SB's preferred medium. Through the years his repertoire of shapes has developed in more experimental and more free directions.

98. Lidded pot, 1989

Earthenware, raku- and frit-glazed; thrown, cut, facetted, raku, fired at 1050°.
H 27.3 x Diam 9.2. Mark: 'SB' stamped on base. Mus.no. 296a-b/1989
ACQUISITION: *Jysk sommer*, 1989, Kunstindustrimuseet. Donation from *Ny Carlsberg Museumslegat*

99. Vase, 1988

Earthenware, raku- and frit-glazed; thrown, folded, raku, fired at 1050°.
H 17 x W 17. Mark: 'SB' stamped on base. Mus.no. 342/1989
ACQUISITION: *Jysk sommer*, 1989, Kunstindustrimuseet

BAARSTRØM, GERD 1946 –

Ceramicist

1979-82 Aarhus Kunstakademi

1982- Own studio workshop and gallery, Resenbro, Silkeborg www.gerd-baarstroem.dk

Soon after completing her studies at Århus Kunstakademi Gerd Baarstrøm(GB) opened the studio workshop in central Jutland where she has worked ever since, building up a fine career involving participation in exhibition activities and ceramic commissions, alongside working on the unique creations that can be seen in and bought from the gallery. GB first took part in *'Kunstnernes Sommerudstilling'* (the Artists' Summer Exhibition), the annual adjudicated exhibition that is held in Tistrup, in central Jutland, in 1983. In 1989 GB was selected by the Kunstindustrimuseum as one of the 17 ceramicists to be represented in the museum's exhibition *'Jysk Sommer'* (Jutland Summer) In that context the museum acquired the interesting sculpture *På vej mod bjergets top*, made in the same year that the exhibition was held **(100)**. The work's 16 glazed column-shaped containers with slanting lids are raku-fired and vary in size; arranged together they make up a curling spiral sequence which is highlighted by their geometric decoration. Inspiration for the work came from the spiral ramp of the Round Tower in Copenhagen.

100. Sculpture, 1989. (16 lidded pots) *På vej mod tårnets top* (On the way to the top of the tower)
English stoneware clay, ochre-glazed; modelled, slab technique, brush-painted, raku, fired at 1000°. H from 34.6 to 11.8. Mark: Sequential number and directional arrows on base. Mus.no. 124/1990. ACQUISITION: *Jysk sommer*, 1989, Kunstindustrimuseet. Donation from *Kunstindustrimuseets Venner*

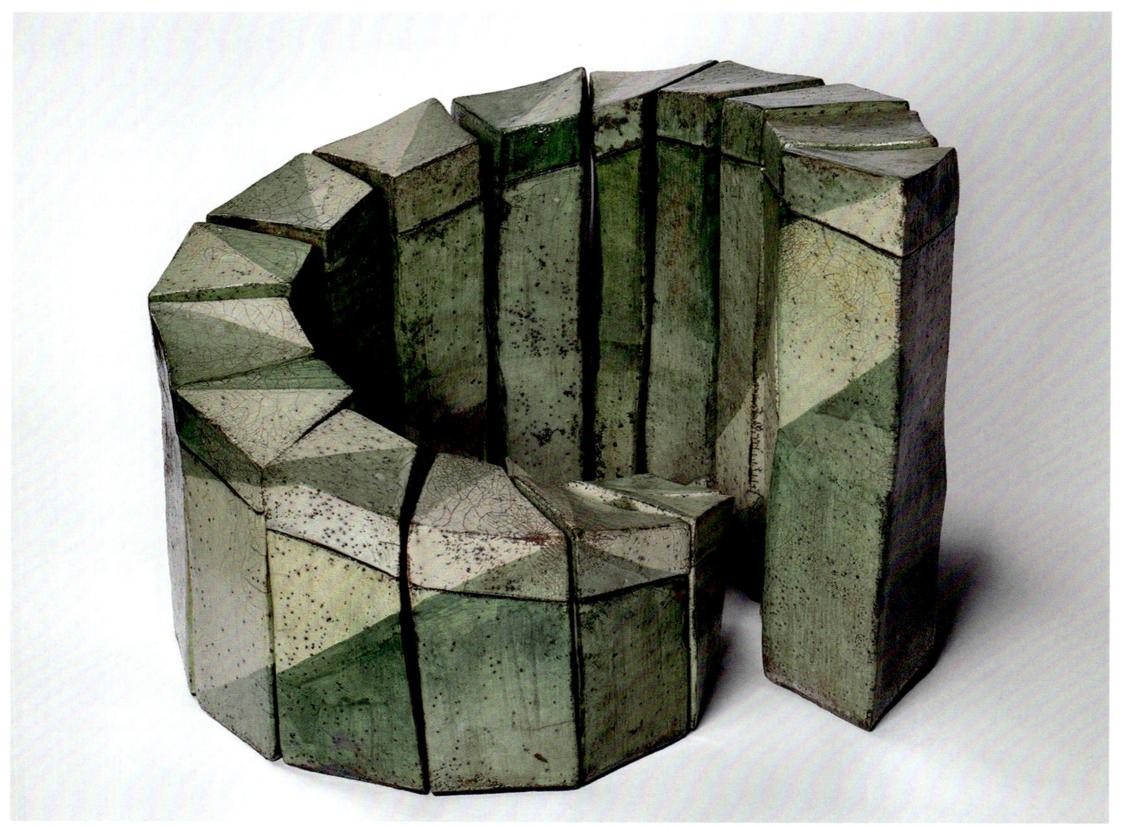

100. 124/1990

CHRISTENSEN, KIRSTEN 1943 –

Artist

1964-69	Kunsthåndværkerskolen, Ceramic department
1969-75	The Royal Danish Academy of Fine Arts, School of Walls and Space
1979-83	School of Walls and Space, tutor
1984-	Own studio workshop, Copenhagen
1991	Statens Kunstfonds honorary lifelong stipend
	www.kirstenchristensen.dk

With a background as a ceramicist, and having completed studies from Kunsthåndværkerskolen and subsequently the Royal Academy, Kirsten Christensen (KC) has created, with clay as her chosen medium, a pictorial *oeuvre*, with poetic, political and narrative qualities that are unique in Danish art.

Since the 1970s KC has developed and refined the special ceramic technique in which she inscribes/scores and brush-paints motifs on thin clay plaques, covered with slip, which are fired like stoneware. In her clay pictures KC has created a series of universally human narratives about childhood, family, love, sex, illness and death out of her own memories and experiences. Many of the pictures are composed of several assembled pieces, as is necessary because of the size of the kiln and the character of the material, but that possible limitation is converted to pictorial strength by the artist's technique of scoring and cutting out the individual elements.

KC exhibited her clay pictures in the Kunstindustrimuseum as early as 1975, but the earliest work in the museum's collection is *Blå Grav* (Blue grave), from 1983, which was shown in a large presentation of the artist's work at Nordjyllands Kunstmuseum in that year **(101)**. The work is part of a series of 5 large 'grave-pictures' and belongs among the many moving and unsentimental depictions of illness, old age, death and burial that the artist was absorbed with from the end of the 1970s, including her breakthrough work, *Min mor og mig* (My mother and me) from 1978.

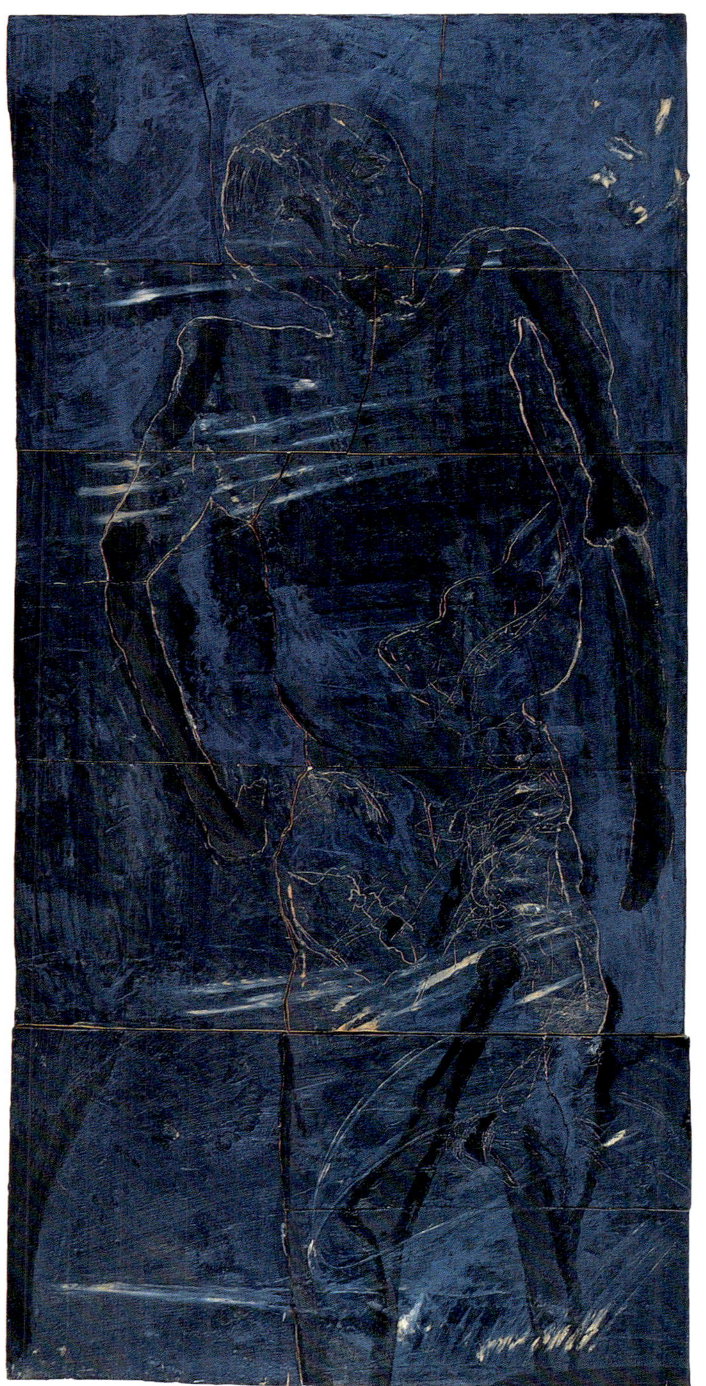

101. 125/1986

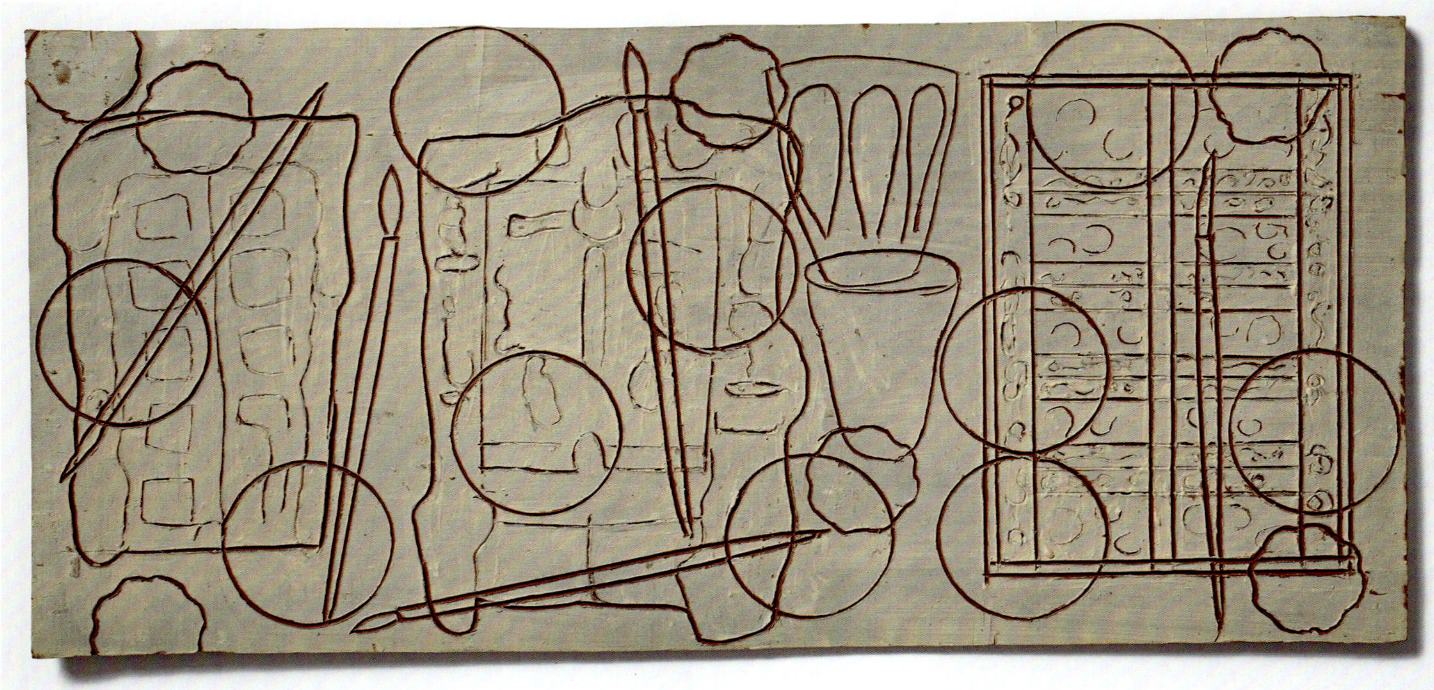

102. 115/2000

Interest in craftsmanship has been a constant factor for KC, and through the years this has shown itself in constructive cooperation over many exhibitions with KC as organiser, architect and consultant, helping both individual craftsmen and groups. As a teacher at both Kunsthåndværkerskolen and the Royal Academy's School of Walls and Space she has a great deal of experience and expertise to offer in the field of ceramics.

In 2001 KC put her commitment to full use in an exhibition of her own new clay pictures held in the premises of the Danish Crafts and Design Association, with the title '*KUNST – KUNSTHÅNDVÆRK*'. The purpose was set out as follows: '*In these years there is much discussion about the degree to which some craftsmen are artists, and since I am an artist and hold exhibitions among craftspeople, I decided to work with this issue.*' The very poetic and perceptively-focused exhibition contained nearly 50 new works in a novel and attractive installation/aesthetic arrangement with the clay pictures directly on the floor on large pink and olive-coloured boards. Several significant elements were hung up in mid-air, such as Ursula Munch-Petersen's first cup for the Royal Porcelain Factory (more beautiful than the one later produced), tools for modelling, large photographs and flower petals with texts. At that exhibition the museum acquired two pictures, one of them a portrait of the celebrated abstract painter Piet Mondrian, surrounded by palette and brushes **(103)**, and the other with brushes, glass and cup and three stylised cupboards (perhaps a reference to concern about material things) as well as circle patterns **(102)**.

Other works in the exhibition contained references to ceramic artists such as Christian Poulsen and Birthe Weggerby, and other modernists such as Picasso, Monet, and Brancusi, and over all there were floating cups, jugs, pots, glasses, brushes, palettes, tools and patterns. It was an exhibition that became a declaration of love to craftwork and to art. In recent years KC has recurrently worked with oil crayon sketches and in 2015, for the first time, in the exhibition '*Poesi og Skattegæld*' (Poetry

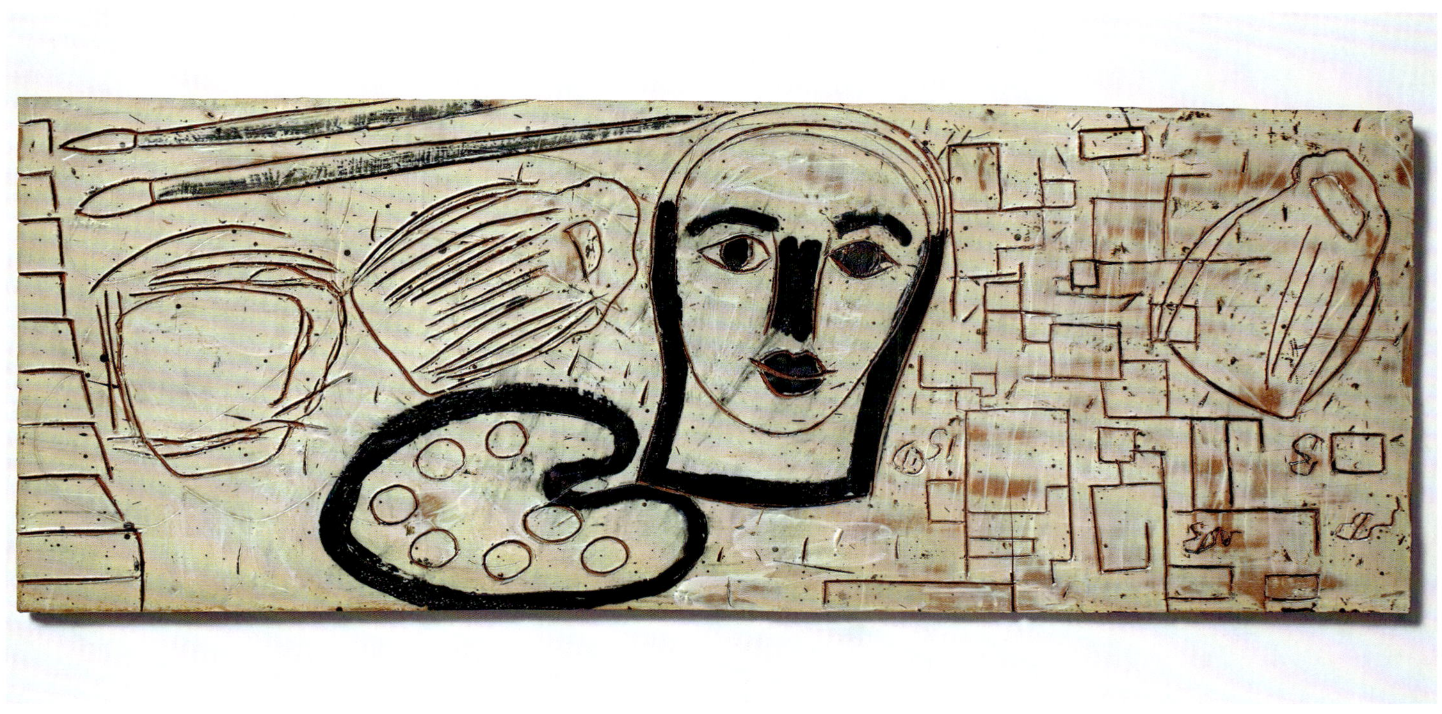

103. 116/2000

and tax-debt) she showed several composite works with both drawings and ceramic expressions; the latter display brownish red surface-slashes against the white slip and depict a gruesome story about the Danish tax authorities.

KC has been responsible for a number of commissioned works in ceramics and other materials around Denmark, and is a member of the artists' association which was called *Kammeraterne* from 1978 and *Den Frie Udstilling* from 1986.

101. Clay picture, 1983. *Blå Grav* (Blue grave)

Stoneware, fibre glass; composite picture, thin stoneware plates glued onto fibre glass, slip, scored, brush-painted, fired at 1260-1300°. H 173.5 x W 83. Mark: none. Mus.no. 125/1986

ACQUISITION: Donation from Kirsten Christensen. Exhibited in *Døden til sidst for os*, Nordjyllands Kunstmuseum, 1983. See: *Kirsten Christensen – Keramiske Billeder*, Nordjyllands Kunstmuseum, 1995

102. Clay picture, 2000

Stoneware; cast, slip, scored, brush-painted, fired at 1260-1300°.

L 45 x W 25.5. Mark: 'Kirsten Christensen 1 2000' on back. Mus.no. 115/2000

ACQUISITION: Exhibition by Kirsten Christensen, *Kunst-Kunsthåndværk,* 2001, *Danske Kunsthåndværkere, Officinet*. Donation from *Kunstindustrimuseets Venner*

103. Clay picture, 2000

Stoneware; cast, slip, scored, brush-painted, fired at 1260-1300°.

L 56 x W 21. Mark: 'Kirsten Christensen 24' on back. Mus.no. 116/2000.

ACQUISITION: Exhibition by Kirsten Christensen, *Kunst-Kunsthåndværk*, 2001, *Danske Kunsthåndværkere, Officinet*. Donation from *Kunstindustrimuseets Venner*

CHRISTIANSEN, JESPER 1955 –

Artist

1979-80 Kunsthåndværkerskolen

1981-88 The Royal Danish Academy of Fine Arts

2003-08 The Royal Danish Academy of Fine Arts, Professor

In 1998 gallery-owner Michael Andersen, Copenhagen, initiated a development project with three artists, Jesper Christiansen, Per Arnoldi and Günther Förg, with the firm of Kähler as working partner. Taking their departure-point in the glazed earthenware of traditional pottery, the three artists designed forms of pot that were thrown at Kähler's and decorated by the artists. The results of the project were displayed at the gallery around the turn of the year 1998/99, and at that time the museum acquired 2 works by Jesper Christiansen (JC), thrown by Bjarne Puggaard.

In the museum's department of prints and drawings there are 45 sketches (lead, Indian ink, water colours, gouache) by JC for pots with colour samples and notes, including directions for the museum's two pots, which have the same basic shape. Through these sketches one can follow how JC seeks to achieve an interplay/counterplay between rounded three-dimensionality and surface painting, between the spatial and the flat – a constant thread in JC's *oeuvre*. The motifs on the two pots are very different; on one, with dark blue-grey shiny glaze **(104)** there is a staircase that leads in or out of the undulating shapes and creates a connection, while the other **(105)** is decorated with large geometric 'windows' in clear, bright colours in an optical manoeuvre. JC has not himself decorated ceramic pots since then, but in several of his paintings of interiors one can see some bold-coloured patterned pots – owned by the artist, and found by him in diverse markets.

104. Pot, 1998. *Trappe* (Staircase)
Earthenware, glazed; thrown, slip, brush-painted. H 43.5.
Mark: 'Jesper Christiansen 1998' painted on base. Mus.no. 11/1999
ACQUISITION: *Malerkrukker - Keramik fra Kähler*, 1998/99, Galerie Mikael Andersen, Copenhagen. Donation from *Ny Carlsbergfondet*

105. Pot, 1998. *Rendez-vous #2*
Earthenware, glazed; thrown, slip, brush-painted. H 44.5.
Mark: 'Jesper Christiansen 1998' painted on base. Mus.no. 12/1999
ACQUISITION: *Malerkrukker - Keramik fra Kähler*, 1998/99, Galerie Mikael Andersen, Copenhagen. Donation from *Ny Carlsbergfondet*

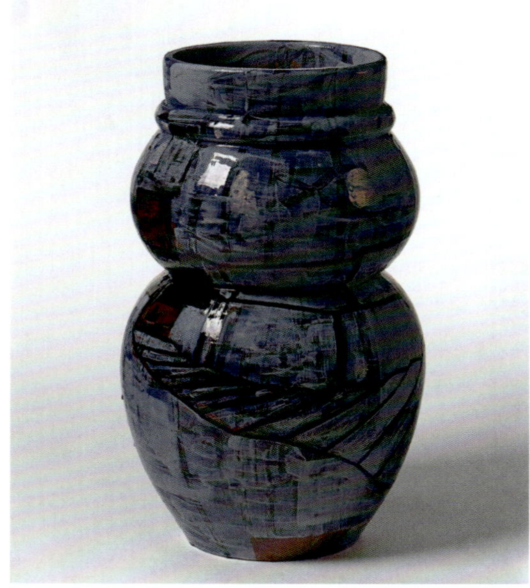

104. 11/1999

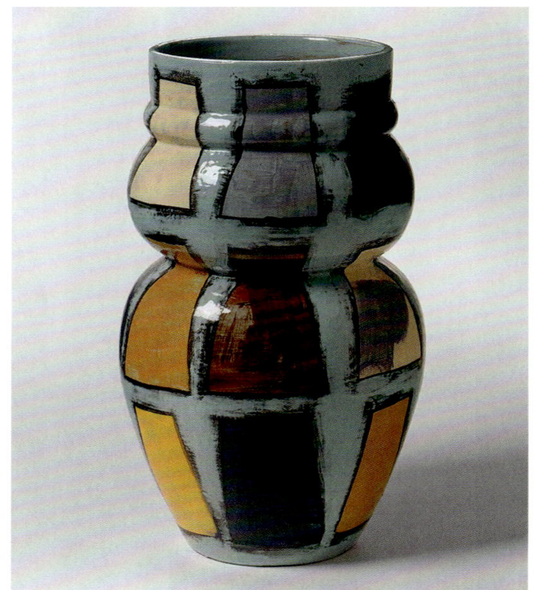

105. 12/1999

CLAYDIES:

BROKSØ, TINE 1971 –

Ceramicist

1995-2000	Danmarks Designskole, Ceramics and Glass
1998	University of Art and Design, Helsinki
2000-	Claydies, artists' group and workshop shared with Karen Kjældgård-Larsen, Copenhagen www.claydies.dk

KJÆLDGÅRD-LARSEN, KAREN 1974 –

Ceramicist

1995-2000	Danmarks Designskole, Ceramics and Glass
1999	Glasgow School of Art, exchange visit
2000-	Claydies, artists' group and workshop shared with Tine Broksø, Copenhagen www.claydies.dk

In 2000 Tine Broksø and Karen Kjældgård-Larsen set up the artist-duo *Claydies*, and in the years since then they have attracted attention with their conceptual artworks and design, carried along by their desire and ability to renew the potential and practice of ceramics. At the '*Biennale for Kunsthåndværk og Design*' at Trapholt Museum in 2007 their project for a blue coffee service, *Blueclay*, modelled with a blindfold over the eyes, was one of the most discussed features, with its break with virtually all the main 'given' norms in Danish functional ceramics; the concept of the coffee service was presented in a ceramic manifesto named '*Dogme07*'. The coffee service was worked on further and launched in 2009 by Normann Copenhagen with the name *True Feelings*, and as in the case of other projects by Claydies the ideas have proved strong enough to transfer from the dogma-like, handmade original version to mass production – and indeed without becoming hackneyed.

As early as in 2003 Claydies could claim a far-reaching breakthrough when they paraded on the catwalk with a collection of 25 very varied ceramic hairstyles and hats, from cycle helmets to cocktail hats – and

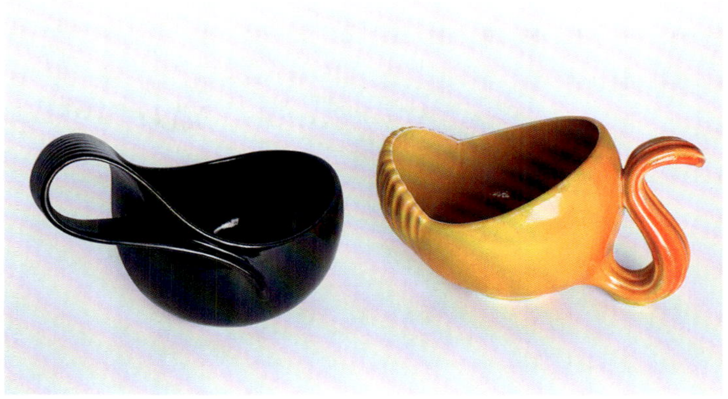

107. 198/2012 **106.** 197/2012

as a brilliant invention, if one turns the hairdos over, one has some extremely delightful bowls for household use. The idea was born out of a kind of irritation with the fashion world's ability to take over the front pages, compared with the less sexy appeal of ceramics, and it succeeded in occupying a number of front pages with the charming concept and the well-made objects. In the museum's collection there are two hair-style-bowls, one for Sally and one for Billy **(106-107).**

From 2011 the museum has acquired examples from one of Claydies's more recent projects, *Wallpieces*, in which the traditional 'wall-plate' is given a new interpretation **(108-110)**. There is no doubt that Claydies's distinctive way of working at the crossroads between ceramic innovation, communication design and dialogue with consumer culture has created new interest among young people in ceramics and has opened eyes to other aspects of the potential of ceramics as a contemporary means of expression.

In 2012 Claydies received *Annie & Otto Johs. Detlefs'* prize for ceramics, the purpose of which is to support ceramicists who pursue new approaches in ceramics through experimental means.

106. Hair-style bowl, 2010. *Sally*

Stoneware, glazed; modelled, fired at 1280°. H 17.5 x W 31. Mark: stamped 'claydies'. Mus.no. 197/2012

ACQUISITION: Donation from *Designmuseets Venner*

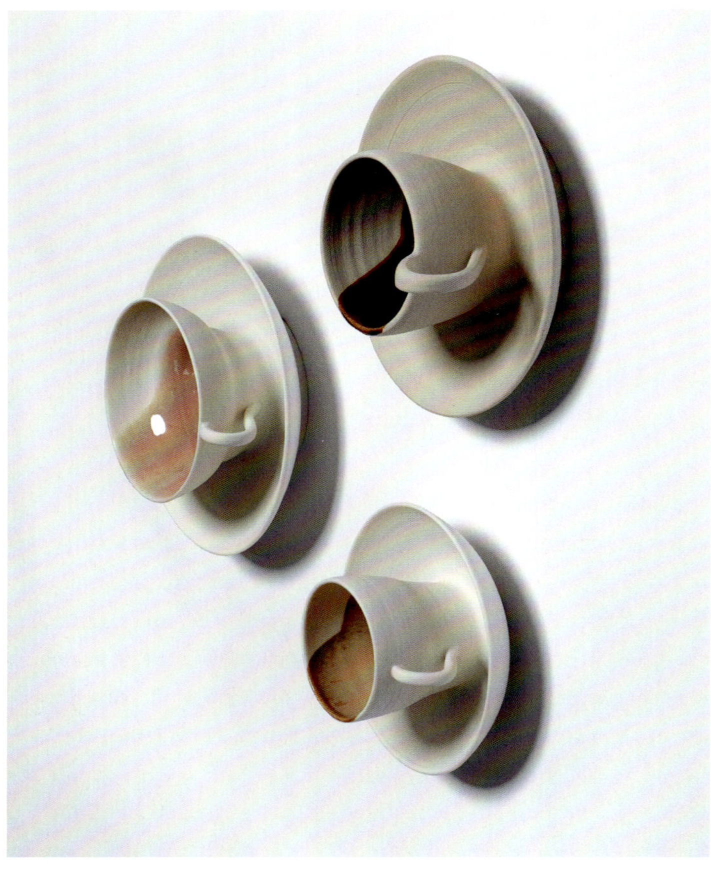

108-110. 199-201/2012

107. Hair-style bowl, 2010. *Billy*
Stoneware, glazed, iron and cobalt; modelled, fired at 1280°. H 21.5 x W 28. Mark: stamped 'claydies'. Mus.no. 198/2012
ACQUISITION: Donation from *Designmuseets Venner*

108-110. Wallpieces, 2011. *Chokolade, Kaffe, Mokka* (Chocolate, coffee, mocha)
Porcelain, glaze pre-coloured with iron; thrown, shaped, fired at 1280°. 199: H 6 x Diam 15, 200: H 8.5 x Diam 15, 201: H 7 x Diam 12. Mark: stamped 'claydies'. Mus.nos. 199-201/2012
ACQUISITION: Donation from *Designmuseets Venner*

DAVIDSEN, MOGENS 1962 –

Ceramicist

1984-88 Kunsthåndværkerskolen, Kolding, Jutland
Own studio workshop, Højer, S Jutland
www.davidsen-keramik.dk

In 1993 a group of young ceramicists combined to arrange an exhibition under the title '*Keramikkens underskov*' (The undergrowth of ceramics); it was a protest action against the many exhibitions with established ceramicists that provided no access for the new generation. The exhibition was shown in the Round Tower in Copenhagen and subsequently in Ridehuset in Aarhus, and it contained works by 33 younger ceramicists, many of them newly finished with their studies. The museum acquired from the exhibition the modelled and abstract brush-painted pot by Mogens Davidsen (MD) **(111)**. In recent years MD has worked in particular with ceramic sculptures and has also expanded his area of work with painting.

111. Pot, 1993
Stoneware, metallic salts; modelled, slip, brush-painted, raku, fired at 1000°. H 45 x W 30. Mark: 'MB 20' inscribed on base. Mus.no. 370/1993
ACQUISITION: *Keramikkens underskov*, 1993, Rundetårn, Copenhagen

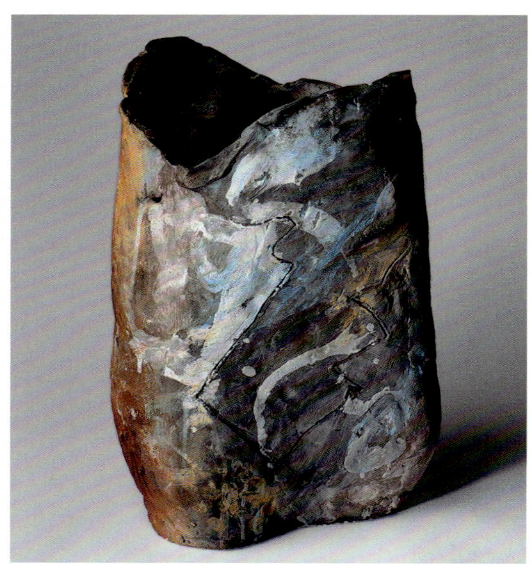

111. 370/1993

DAVOLIO, SANDRA 1951 –

Ceramicist

1985 Ccompleted studies, Danmarks Designskole
1985- Own studio workshop, Copenhagen
www.sandradavolio.dk

Sandra Davolio (SD) was born in Italy and has lived in Denmark since 1974. After completing her studies at Danmarks Designskole she set up her own studio workshop in Copenhagen, and from there she has developed a personal profile within Danish and international ceramics, exhibiting frequently in Denmark and around Europe. As a teacher SD has worked at Holbæk Kunsthøjskole and at Lundtofte Gamle Skole's Ceramic Workshop.

SD works in stoneware and porcelain, mostly on the basis of pots and vases. Her approach is experimental with regard to materials and methods of firing; she has used electric and gas kilns, wood-firing and raku. Over the years SD has achieved a particular aesthetic expression in terms of form and material, with her visually elegant and delicate works, in which she creates a quivering light-and shadow effect by integrating thin 'discs' into the basic shape. The discs may be organic, resembling foliage or feathers, on ivory-white poetic pots and porcelain objects with a refined transparency, or they may create dense horizontal layers upon layers, as seen in other series of stoneware with matte glaze, often in mellow colours.

The work from 2004 which the museum acquired in the same year **(112)** belongs in the latter category. SD's works are distinguished by displaying a refined cross-fertilization between Danish and Italian culture and between the ceramic and design traditions of those countries.

112. Vase, 2004

Stoneware, zinc-barium-glazed; thrown, modelled. H 52. Mark: 'SD' painted on base. Mus.no. 200/2005

ACQUISITION: Galleri Nørby, Copenhagen

112. 200/2005

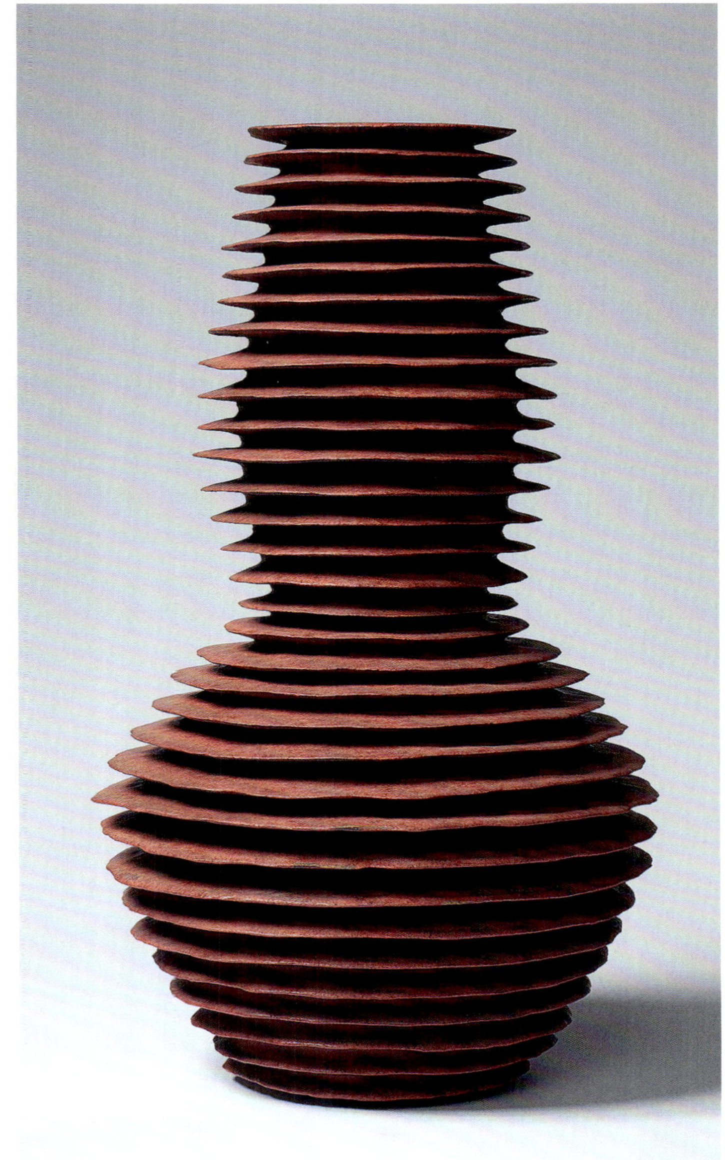

EHRENREICH, LIS 1953 –

Ceramicist

1976-81 Det Jyske Kunstakademi

1981- Own studio workshop, Aarhus

Lis Ehrenreich (LE) studied at the Jyske Kunstakademi, where Gutte Eriksen was a teacher for a number of years and passed on to her students a basic attitude to working with ceramics that insisted on the use of natural materials and simple methods of work. These are demanding conditions; without artistic sensitivity – and skilled craftsmanship – ceramics of high quality would be unlikely to result from such a departure-point. After completing her studies LE rapidly set up her own workshop, and from it she has developed her strong and distinctive shapes in earthenware, reaching, not least through many experiments, a high degree of skill in the use of ash glazes from e.g. wheat and rye straw or elm and beech, each with their own colour and texture.

Dishes, which may be square, 6- or 8-sided, round or rectangular, are the perfect form to work with for LE, allowing her to combine slip, ash glazes and painstaking firings to reach a dramatic and characterful texture and richness of colour. In the museum's collection there are two fine 6-sided dishes with different patterns and colouring **(113-114)**. In recent years LE has worked with the form of the *albarello*, inspired by ceramics from Spanish-Moorish culture.

LE is involved with the international professional ceramic network with both individual and group exhibitions, and is represented in leading ceramic museums in the Nordic region and Europe. LE is a member of the group *8 keramikere*, with colleagues from the Jyske Kunstakademi.

113. Dish, 1984

Earthenware, semi-transparent ash- and borax- glazed; thrown, cut, pipeclay- and cobalt- slip, paper resist, sgrafitto, reduction-fired in electric kiln at 1180°. H 5.3 x Diam 39.5. Mark: none. Mus.no. 142/1984

ACQUISITION: *Danske Kunsthåndværkeres Landssammenslutning - Århus-gruppen*, 1984, Kunstindustrimuseet. Donation from *Finansieringsinstituttet for Industri og Håndværks Jubilæumslegat*

114. Dish, 1983

Earthenware, celadon-glazed; thrown, cut, slip, paper resist, sgrafitto, reduction-fired at 1180°. H 4.2 x Diam 40.5. Mark: 'LE' stamped on base. Mus.no. 111/2009

ACQUISITION: Donation from *Ny Carlsbergfondet*

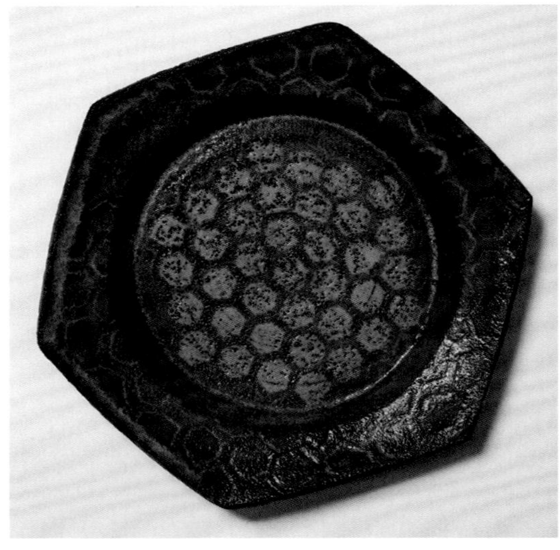

113. 142/1984

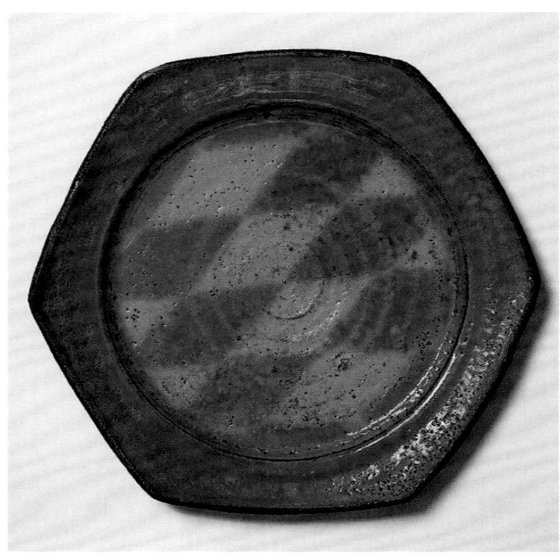

114. 111/2009

ENGQVIST, LISA 1914-1989

Ceramicist

1935	Completed studies at Kunsthåndværkerskolen
1935-38	Worked for Saxbo
1952-54	Worked for Saxbo
1948-89	Own studio workshop, Lyngby, near Copenhagen
1965-70	Worked as artist for Bing & Grøndahl
1980s	Det Jyske Kunstakademi, teacher

Lisa Engqvist (LE) occupied a special position in Danish earthenware in the second half of the 20th century. LE is also widely admired and recognized by her fellow-professionals, and this was expressed, e.g. in the establishment of the exhibition group *Keramiske Veje* in 1985, when a group of young ceramicists specialising in work with stoneware collected around LE as a central figure. At the first exhibition, in 1987, LE displayed, at the insistence of the group, a selection of some of her older and more recent works and wrote in the catalogue about her ceramics:

> *'Transformation – that is what fascinates me in ceramics. The transformation, through firing, of clay into a firm body, and of the glazing substance, in interplay with the corpus, into colours, clarity, light, sheen and textural character.'*

It was precisely the ability to make ceramic objects live and light up, her will to constantly experiment and create new expressions and approaches to earthenware's traditional materials and techniques, that made LE a great ceramicist. Her strong artistic grasp was founded in respect for the ceramic craftsmanship which she knew through and through and mastered supremely. She took inspiration from Islamic ceramics, seeking across ages and cultures to find the old anonymous potters' art. LE's lively interest in young people coming into the profession made her a respected teacher of ceramics courses at the Jyske Kunstakademi (the Jutland Art Academy) in the 1980s. She also became engaged in work with her colleagues, e.g. in the group *Strandstræde Keramikerne* (members of *Keramiske Veje*), with whom LE exhibited collages and sculptures in paper and cardboard in 1984.

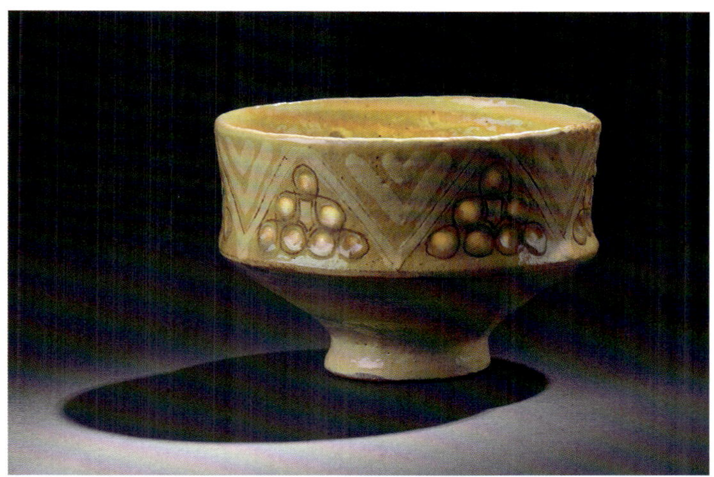

115. 3/1959

116. 14/1967

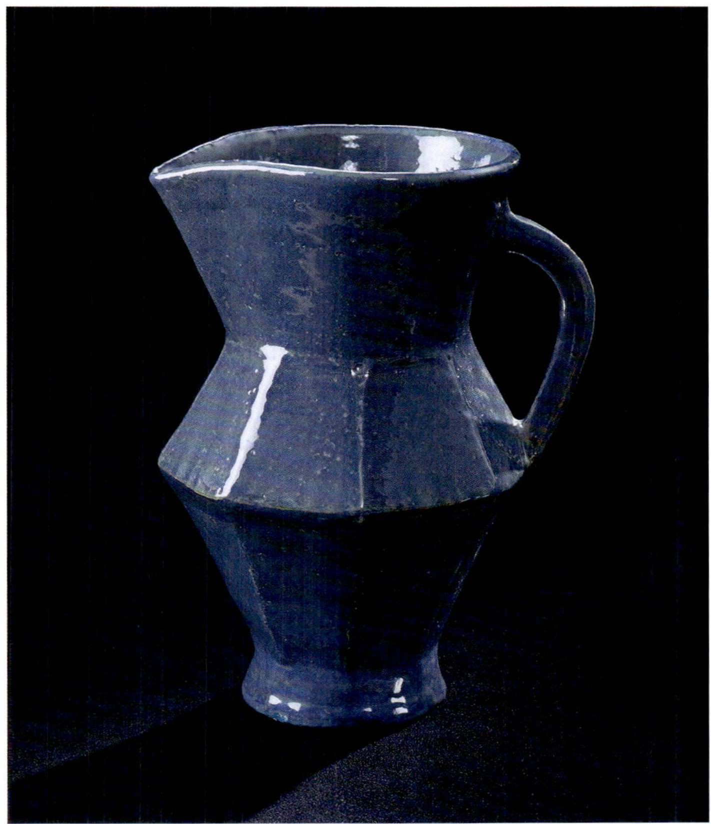

Work with paper led to LE for instance making stencil decorations on a series of small dishes in the 1980s, several of them now in the museum's collection **(118,120-121,129-131).** The same technique was used by LE on white porcelain during her time at Bing & Grøndahl, from 1965 to 70; in those years she designed a series of vases and lidded pots decorated with coloured stencilled patterns, which the factory put into production.

As a result of donations from LE's family after her death this gifted ceramicist is well represented in the museum's collection, with in all 18 works from the mid 1950s up to 1987, and through the rich combinations and variety of forms, colours and decoration in these works LE stands out as a ceramic artist and exceptional interpreter of earthenware in her own time. In the collection there are dishes, bowls, jugs and vases which are all distinctively radiant and strong in colour, with blue, reddish, white tones, and not least with wonderful yellow glazes and slip, showing her particular mastery and originality in the use of coloured slip. Even though LE worked with the familiar types of ordinary household ceramics, the objects she made, through her handling and plastic modelling, became re-created in surprising shapes and particular textures, as can be seen for instance in the iconic radiant blue jug with its facetted sculptural corpus, from which the handle and spout sprout organically; on several lidded jugs the spout takes the form of a bird's head **(116)**.

One of LE's most impressive works is the stele **(128)** from 1970, with two asymmetrically positioned large snail shells on the side as a strong shaping element that, along with the brownish slip and matte glaze, creates the experience of a 'piece of nature' from a far-off (fossil) age. The inspiration for this and similar works possibly came from a period in 1966 when LE visited the old and much respected Farnham Pottery in Wrecclesham, Surrey, England. It was perhaps in that connection that LE met Lucie Rie and brought back a fine yellow-glazed bowl that is now in the museum's collection.

In 1948 LE established her own studio workshop, but before that she worked for a while for the Saxbo company, and later, from 1965 to 70, she worked for Bing & Grøndahl, where she also had exhibitions in 1969 and 1972. LE exhibited for the first time in '*Kunstnernes Efterårsudstilling*' in 1948 and exhibited regularly throughout her whole professional life. She was the recipient of many awards, including the Academy Council's Thorvald Bindesbøll Medal in 1984.

117. 23a-b/1975

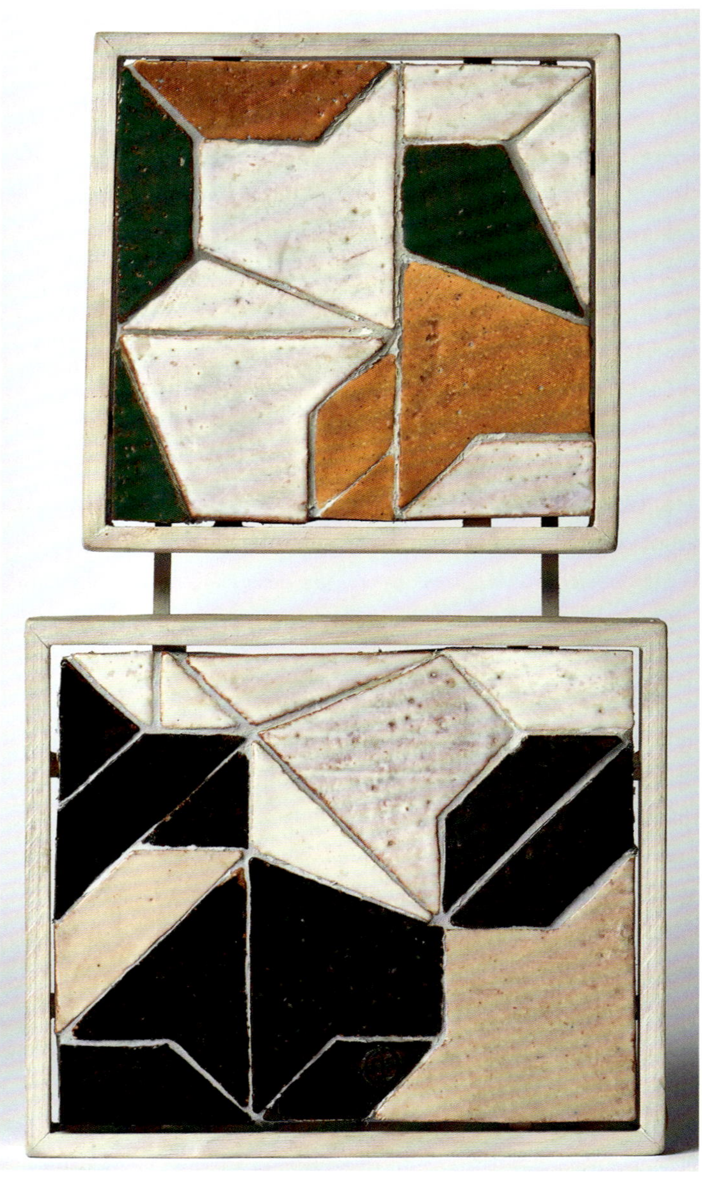

115. Bowl, 1955

Earthenware, lead-glazed; slip, sgrafitto, painted decoration, scattered 'rice-grain holes': H 8.8 x Diam 12.5. Mark: 'LE', reversed, stamped on base. Mus.no. 3/1959.
ACQUISITION: Den Frie Udstillingsbygning, 1959. Donation from *Dansk Kunsthåndværks 50-års Jubilæumslegat*. See: *Brændpunkter*, 1990

116. Jug, 1959

Earthenware, clear glaze; thrown, shaped, slip. H 24.5. Mark: 'LE', reversed, stamped on base. Mus.no. 14/1967. ACQUISITION: Lisa Engqvist. Donation from *Dansk Kunsthåndværks 50-års Jubilæumslegat*. See: Dybdahl, L., 1997

117. Two tile pictures, 1974-75

Earthenware, clear glaze; modelled, slip, tile mosaics, mounted in wood frames. a: H 22.5 x W 19.5; b: H 19 x W 19. Mark: 'LE' in a clay seal attached to the front. Mus.no. 23a-b/1975.
ACQUISITION: *Sommerudstilling*, 1975, Helsingborg Stadsmuseum. Donation from *Kunstindustrimuseets 50-års Jubilæumslegat*

118. Dish, 1980

Earthenware, clear glaze; thrown, modelled, slip, stencil decoration. H 3.6 x W 24.1. Mark: 'LE' stamped on upper surface. Mus.no. 4/1981
ACQUISITION: Lisa Engqvist. Donation from *Benny Dessaus Mindelegat*. See: *Brændpunkter*, 1990

119. Dish, 1950s

Earthenware, lead-glazed; thrown, slip, decorated. H 6 x Diam 35. Mark: 'LE' stamped on base. Mus.no. 220/1987.
ACQUISITION: *Keramiske Veje*, 1987, Den Frie Udstillingsbygning. Donation from *Nationalbankens Jubilæumsfond*

120. Dish, 1987

Earthenware, clear glaze; modelled, slip, stencil decoration. H 2.5 x W 23. Mark: indecipherable. Mus.no. 221/1987
ACQUISITION: *Keramiske Veje*, 1987, Den Frie Udstillingsbygning

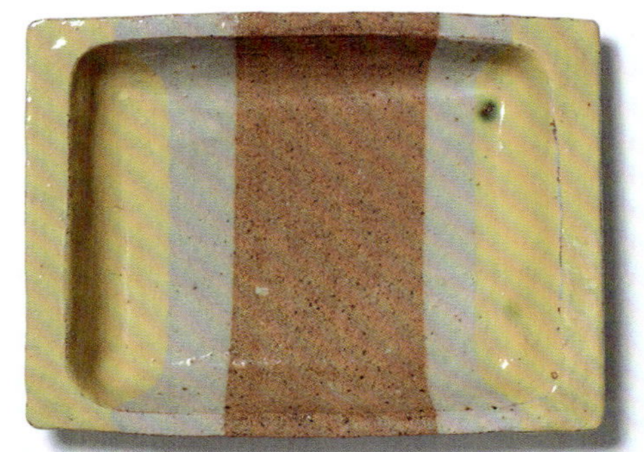

120 221/1987

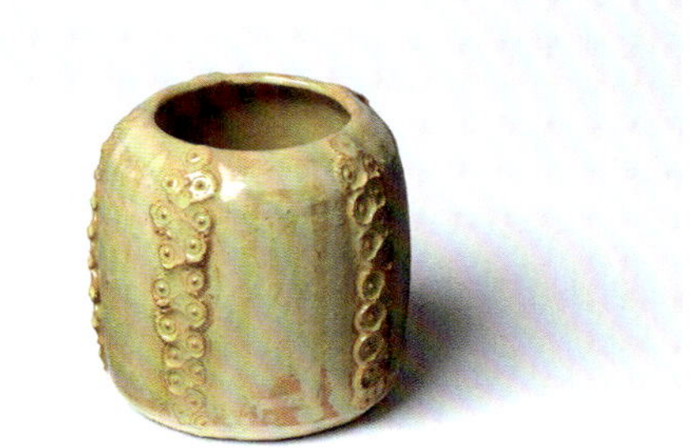

122 103/1990

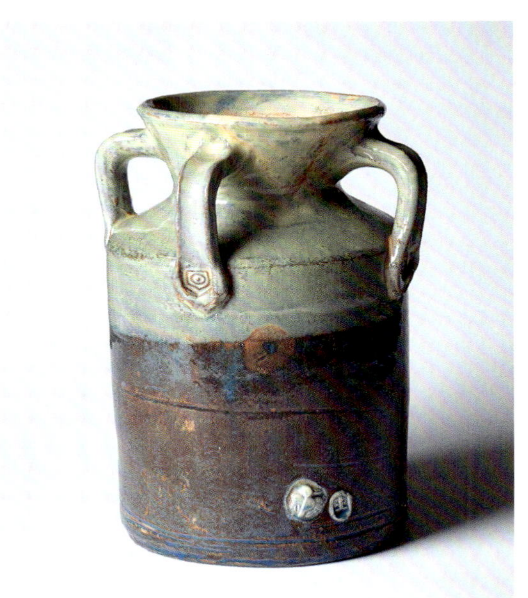

123 104/1990

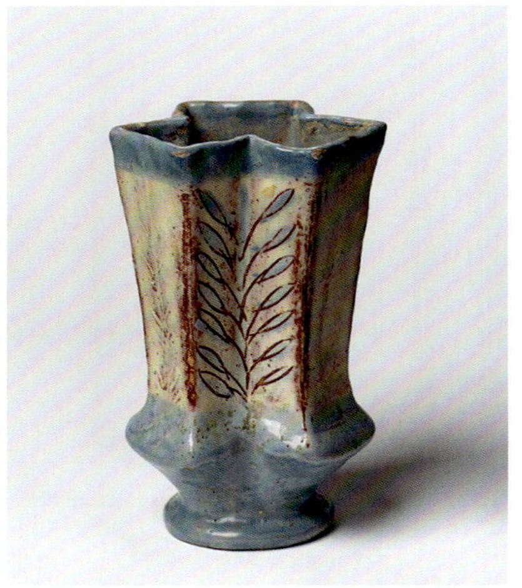

125 193/2001

121. Bowl, 1955

Earthenware, clear glaze; thrown, slip, stamped decoration, painted with zig-zag pattern. H 9 x Diam 29. Mark: 'LE', reversed, stamped on base. Mus.no. 102/1990. ACQUISITION: Donation from Hans Henrik Engqvist, Lyngby. See: *Brændpunkter*, 1990

121. 102/1990

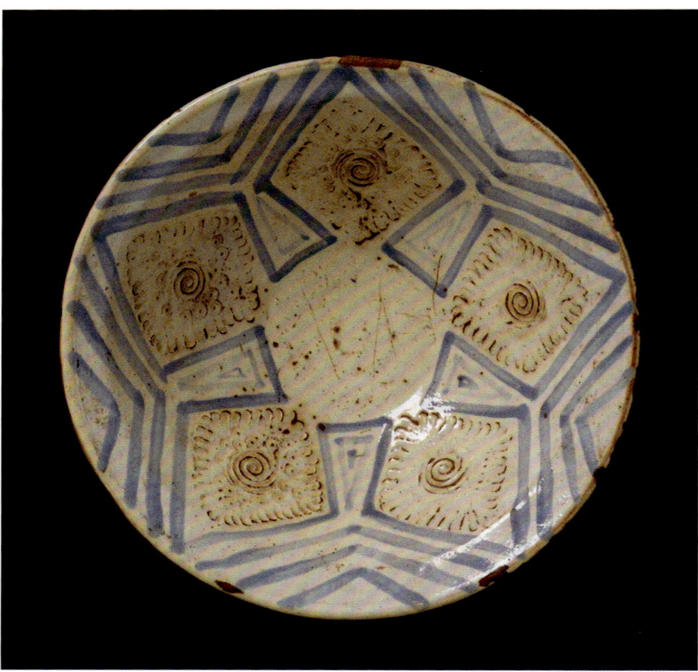

122. Vase, 1956

Earthenware, clear glaze; thrown, slip, stamped decoration in relief. H 8.5 x Diam 7.5. Mark: 'LE 56' stamped on base. Mus.no. 103/1990
ACQUISITION: Donation from Hans Henrik Engqvist, Lyngby

123. Pot, 1956-60

Earthenware, glazed; stamped decoration, dipped. H 23 x Diam 18. Mark: 'LE', reversed, stamped on base. Mus.no. 104/1990.
ACQUISITION: Donation from Hans Henrik Engqvist, Lyngby.
See: Dybdahl, L., 1997

124. Lidded pot, date unknown.

Earthenware, clear glaze; thrown, slip, stamped decoration in relief. H 9 x Diam 7.5. Mark: 'LE', reversed, stamped at the base. Mus.no. 143a-b/1999
ACQUISITION: Donation from C. B. Andersen, Bank Director, Copenhagen

125. Vase, 1955

Earthenware, clear glaze; thrown, modelled, sgrafitto. H 15.5 x Diam 10. Mark: 'LE 55' stamped on base. Mus.no. 193/2001
ACQUISITION: Donation from Hans Henrik Engqvist, Lyngby

126. Coffee pot, date unknown.

Earthenware, clear glaze; thrown, modelled, slip. H 15 x W 15 x Diam 7.5. Mark: 'LE' stamped on base. Mus.no. 194a-b/2001
ACQUISITION: Donation from Hans Henrik Engqvist, Lyngby

127. Dish, date unknown.

Earthenware, chamotte clay, matte glaze; thrown, modelled, dark slip. H 6 x Diam 34.5. Mark: 'LE', reversed, stamped on base. Mus.no. 195/2001
ACQUISITION: Donation from Hans Henrik Engqvist, Lyngby

128. Stele, 1970

Earthenware, chamotte clay, matte glaze; modelled, dark slip, decorated with snail shapes. H 66. Mark: none. Mus.no. D 1547
ACQUISITION: On deposit from *Statens Kunstfond*, 1982

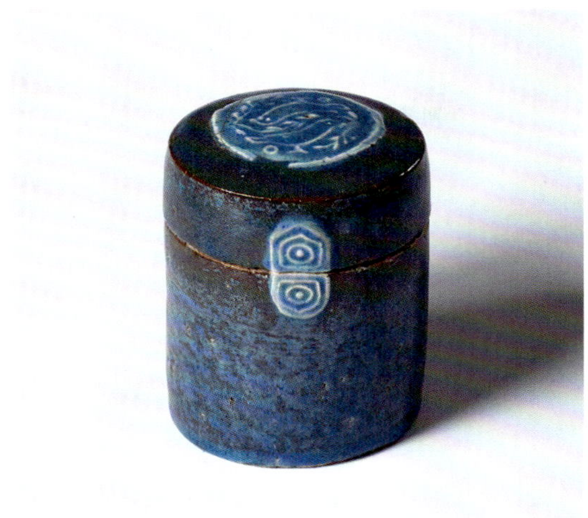

124 143a-b/1999

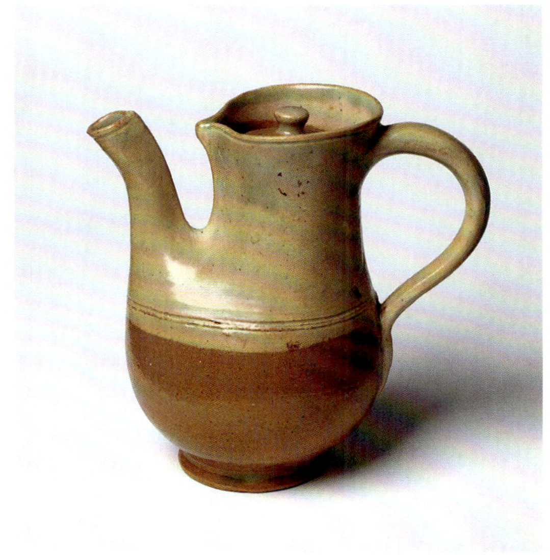

126 194a-b/2001

119. 220/1987

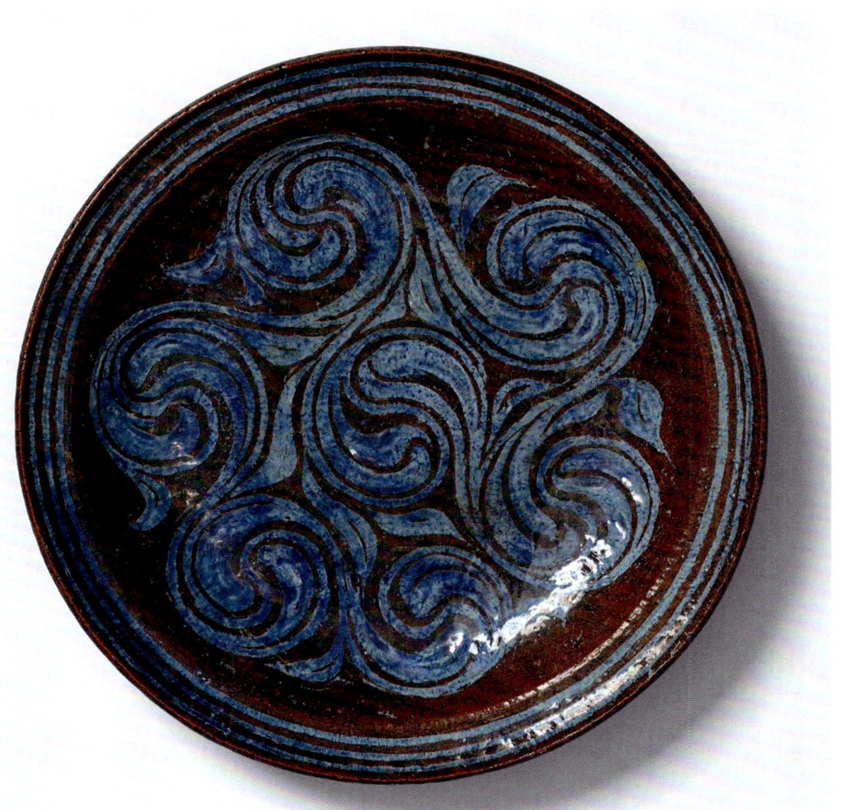

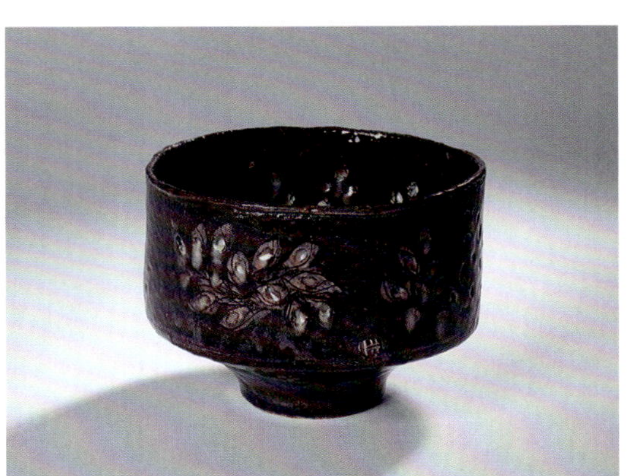

132 D 1667

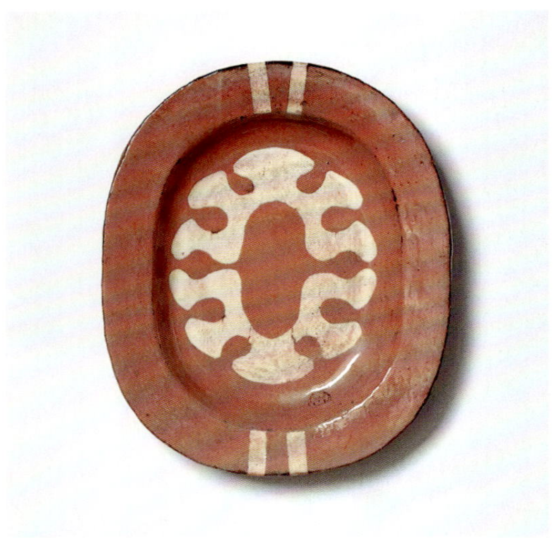

118. 4/1981

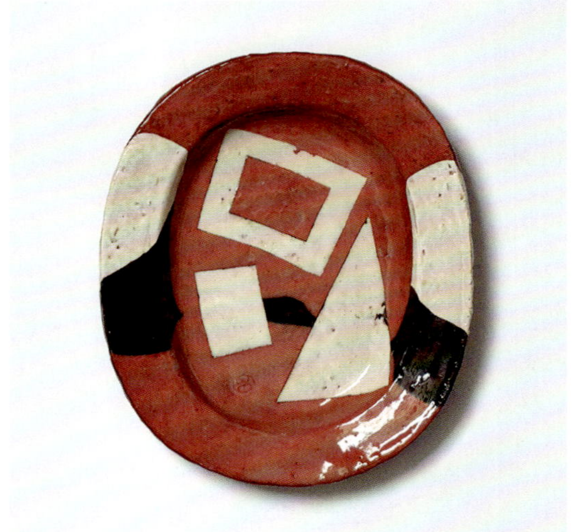

130 D 1549

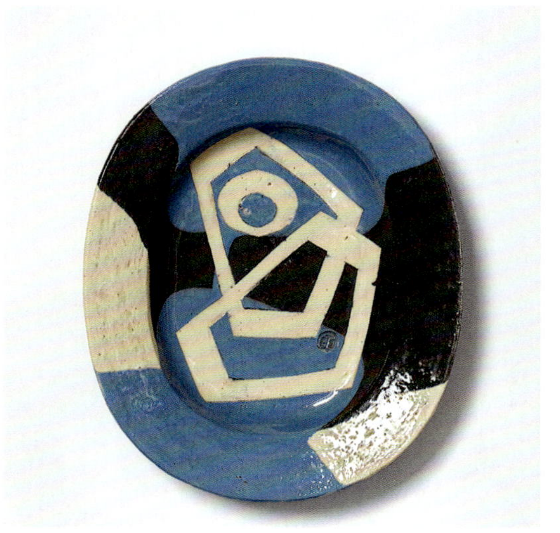

129 D 1548

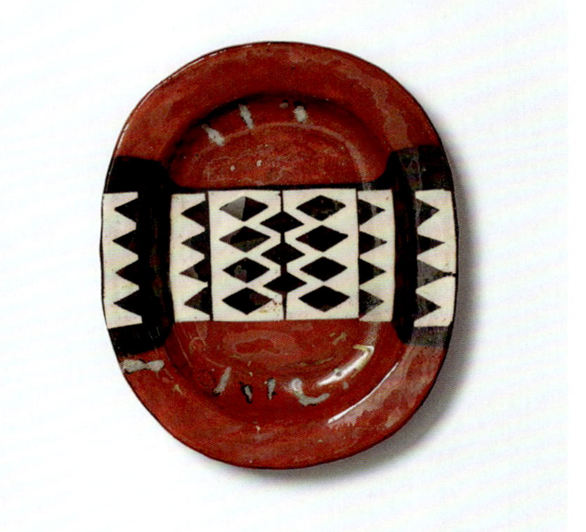

131 D 1666

129. Dish, 1980

Earthenware, glaze; modelled, slip, stencilled decoration. H 4 x W 21.5 x L 25.6. Mark: 'LE' stamped on upper surface. Mus.no. D 1548

ACQUISITION: On deposit from *Statens Kunstfond*, 1982

130. Dish, 1980

Earthenware, glaze; modelled, slip, stencilled decoration. H 3.5 x W 24.5. Mark: 'LE' stamped on upper surface. Mus.no. D 1549

ACQUISITION: On deposit from *Statens Kunstfond*, 1982

131. Dish, 1987

Earthenware, glaze; modelled, slip, stencil-decorated. H 3.7 x W 23.5. Mark: 'LE' stamped on upper surface. Mus.no. D 1666

ACQUISITION: *Keramiske Veje*, 1987, Den Frie Udstillingsbygning. On deposit from *Statens Kunstfond*, 1989

132. Bowl, 1950s

Earthenware, clear glaze; thrown, slip, openwork leaf decoration. H 12.5 x Diam 17. Mark: 'LE' stamped on base. Mus.no. D 1667

ACQUISITION: On deposit from *Statens Kunstfond*, 1989

127 195/2001

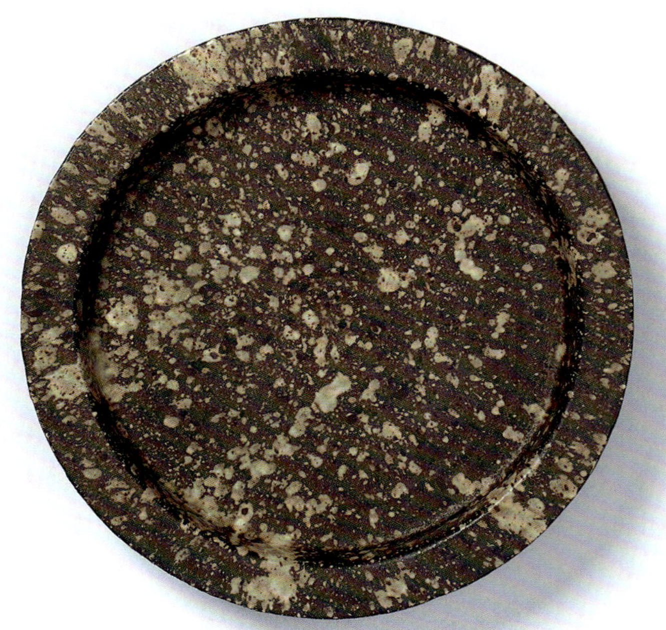

128 D 1547

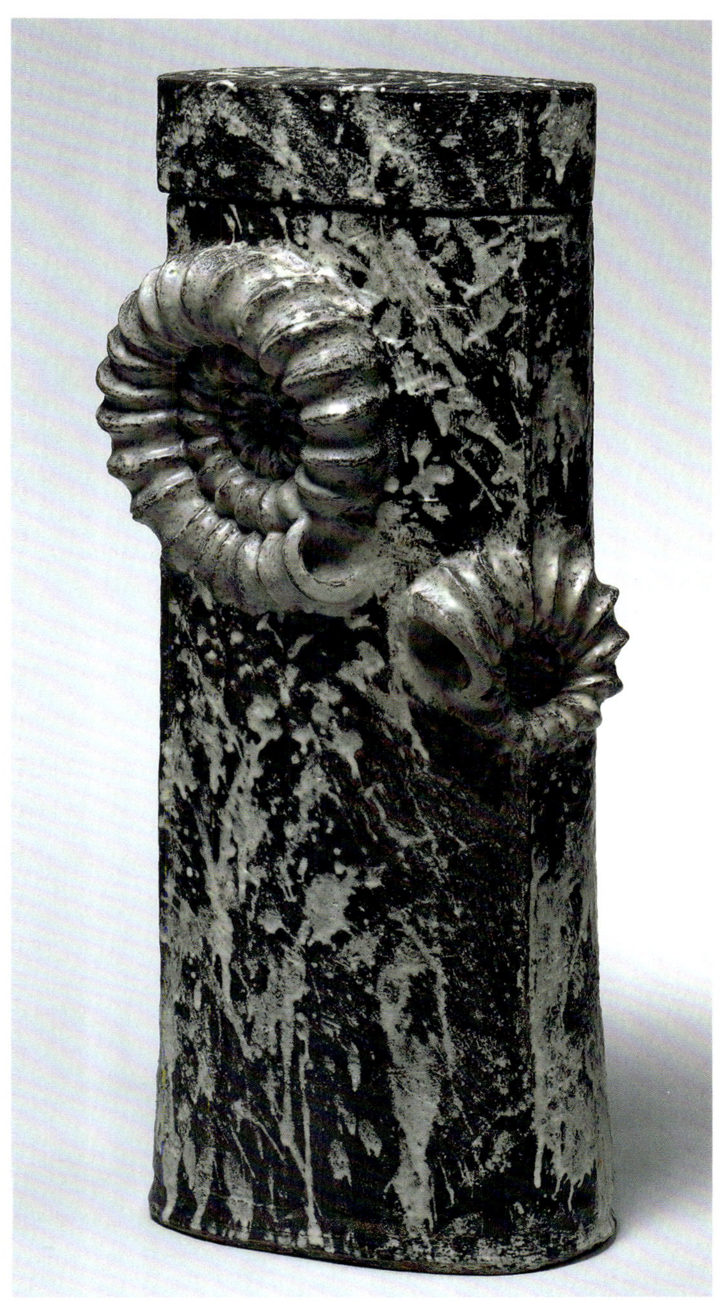

ERIKSEN, GUTTE 1918 – 2008

Ceramicist

1936-39	Kunsthåndværkerskolen
1942	Own studio workshop, Kastrup
1953-2008	Hundested, N Sealand
1948	Study-visits to Bernard Leach, St. Ives, Cornwall; Pierre Lion, Saint-Amand; Vassil Ivanoff, La Borne
1968-71, 1973-74, 1976-78	Det Jyske Kunstakademi, Head of Ceramics course
1987	Retrospective exhibition in Kunstforeningen Gl. Strand, Copenhagen
1991	Awarded Statens Kunstfond's honorary lifelong stipend

Gutte Eriksen (GE) is centrally placed in the history of Danish ceramics from the second half of the 20th century, with the status of a major and internationally recognised ceramic artist. Through GE's many years of teaching the Ceramics course at the Jyske Kunstakademi she came to influence a generation of ceramicists, stimulating interest in the strong textures and robust simple forms of ceramic materials. While she herself never abandoned earthenware as the fundamental material, over the course of years she developed a hard-fired earthenware which almost had the character of stoneware. This, in combination with the use of a glaze composed of borax, quartz, clay and ash, which GE worked with from the mid 1950s, is characteristic of much of her production. As can be seen from her works, the colours can vary almost endlessly depending on the firing. There can be no doubt that GE was also open to what the whims of the kiln could produce in the way of surprising effects, and to incorporating them in her results.

GE herself said that inspiration came to her from a young age from visits to the National Museum's Prehistoric and Classical Antiquity collections, and this was supplemented by interest in ceramic cultures in Korea, China and particularly Japan. For GE impressions from these sources became decisive for the attitudes and ideals that formed the basis for her ceramic work. GE's main focus of interest, in whatever epoch or culture, was the anonymous old craft of pottery, and through her own approach to the ceramic evidence of the past she succeeded in creating a contemporary and convincing *oeuvre*. GE made a strong international reputation for herself, and her works are represented all over the world in leading ceramic museums.

In 1942 GE set up her own studio workshop, but she had already exhibited in '*Kunstnernes Efterårsudstilling*' in 1938, which testifies to

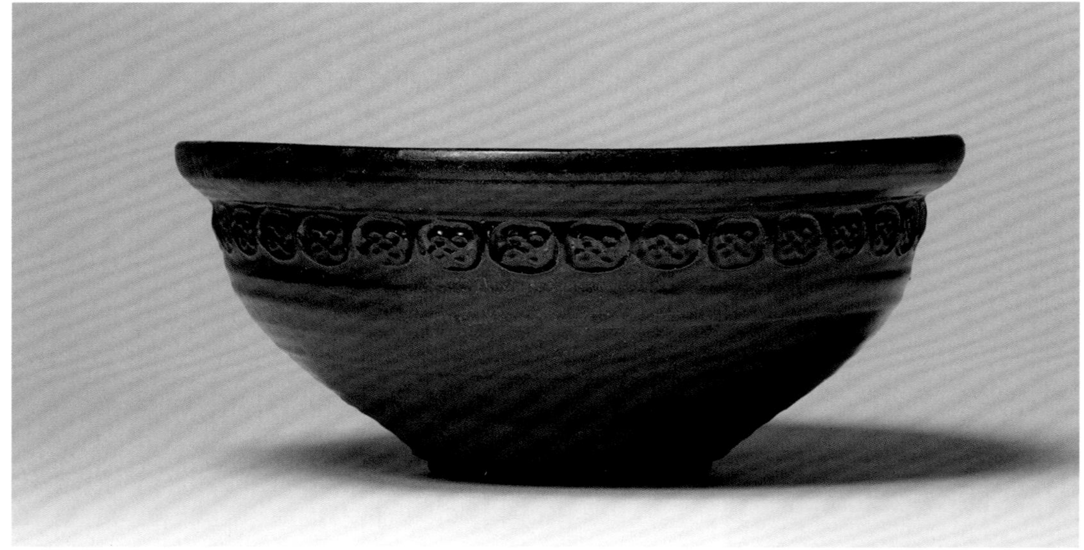

136 7/1956

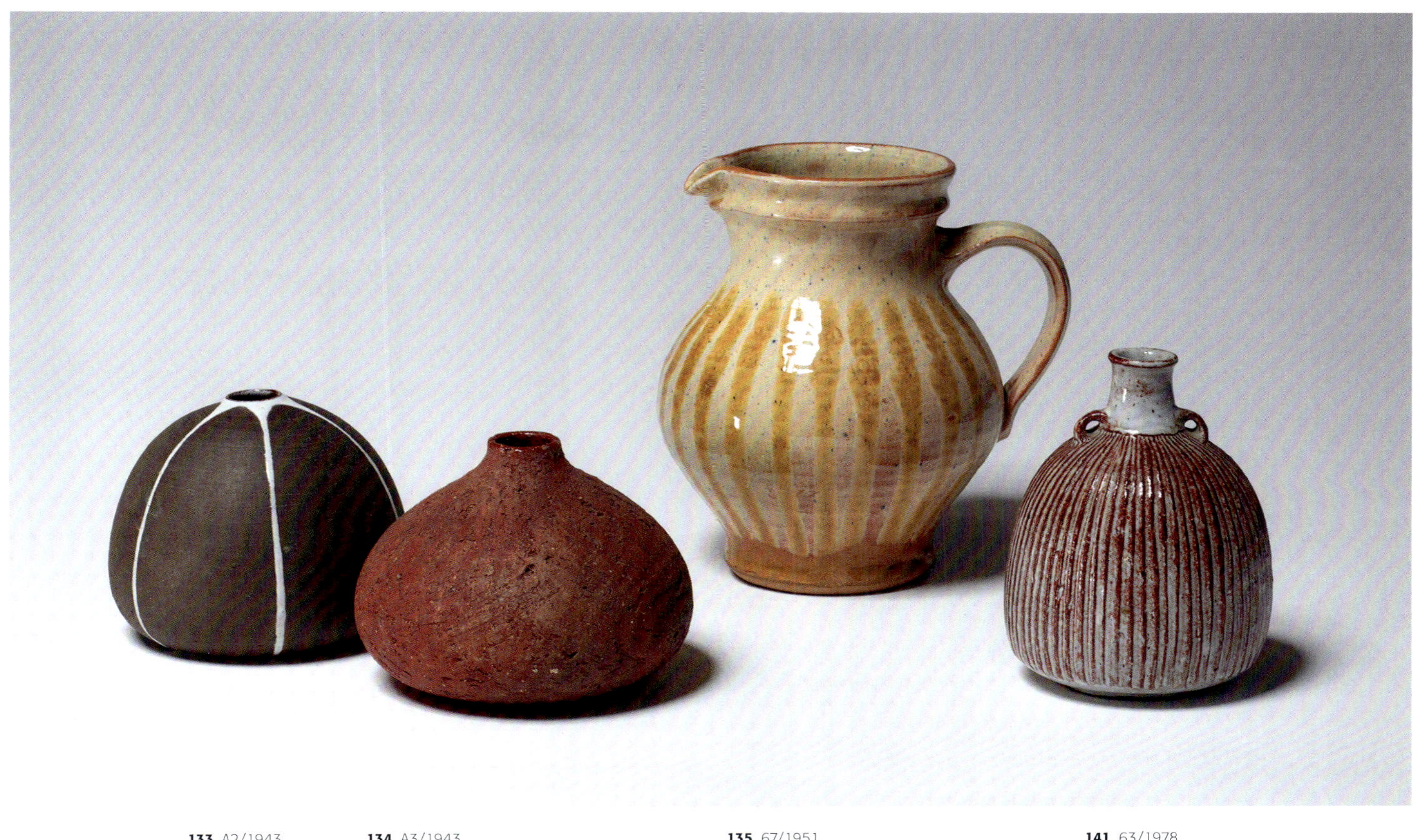

133 A2/1943 **134** A3/1943 **135** 67/1951 **141** 63/1978

the strength of impact of her ceramics. The Danish earthenware tradition was the focus of her work e.g. while she was with Felix Møhl, in Allerød, N. Sealand, from 1951-53.

GE's encounter with Japan's ceramic culture came to have landmark significance for her. She came into contact with that culture in 1948, when she spent several months in England with the influential ceramicist Bernard Leach (1887-1979), who had been in Japan for many years before setting up his workshop in St. Ives, Cornwall, in 1920. In 1940 he published *'A Potter's Book'*, about Japanese raku, among other techniques, and the book became a bible for the new wave of studio ceramicists, in Denmark as well. In 1948 GE travelled on to the important French pottery centres at Saint-Amand-en-Puisaye and La Borne, where work with stoneware was the main focus; this contributed to GE's later decision to use a coarser clay than that favoured by Bernard Leach. These visits to England and France were supplemented by two important study visits that GE made to Japan in 1971 and 1973.

GE is represented in the museum's collection by 21 works, distributed fairly evenly over the years 1941-95. The four earliest works are from 1941; three made at the workshop in Hareskoven and the fourth at Felix Møhl's. The museum acquired *Søpindsvinet* (Sea urchin) **(133)** and the onion-shaped vase **(134)** at the exhibition '*Dansk Kunsthåndværk*' in the museum in 1943 and the striped jug from '*Dansk Kunsthåndværk*' in 1953 **(135)**. These early works are made of red clay; in several cases they have been inspired by nature and have lead-glazed decoration with clear links to Danish pottery traditions. The same is true of a fine glazed bowl, covered with slip, from 1955 **(136)**, decorated with a stamped quatrefoil pattern. The bowl is the earliest work in the museum that came from GE's workshop in Hareskoven, and represents the phase of GE's work before her journeys abroad. From the time after, in the 1960s, there are four works with shapes that are found repeatedly in the works of the following many years. The vase with the five finely modelled loop-handles at the rim **(138)**, for example, became a classic, of which the collection includes several examples from the 1980s and 1990s **(144,150,152)**.

The bowls are another recurrent category, and the museum has two quatrefoil examples, both with horizontal ridging and four vertical indentations, between which the sides bulge out **(139,153)**. This shape is part of GE's work with many-sided containers, which includes another form of solution in an octagonal pot from 1984, acquired at *Kammeraterne's* exhibition that year (98/1984), and a similar octagonal bowl from 1970 decorated with herringbone pattern under the glaze, acquired at the retrospective exhibition in *Kunstforeningen* **(143)**.

146 98/1994

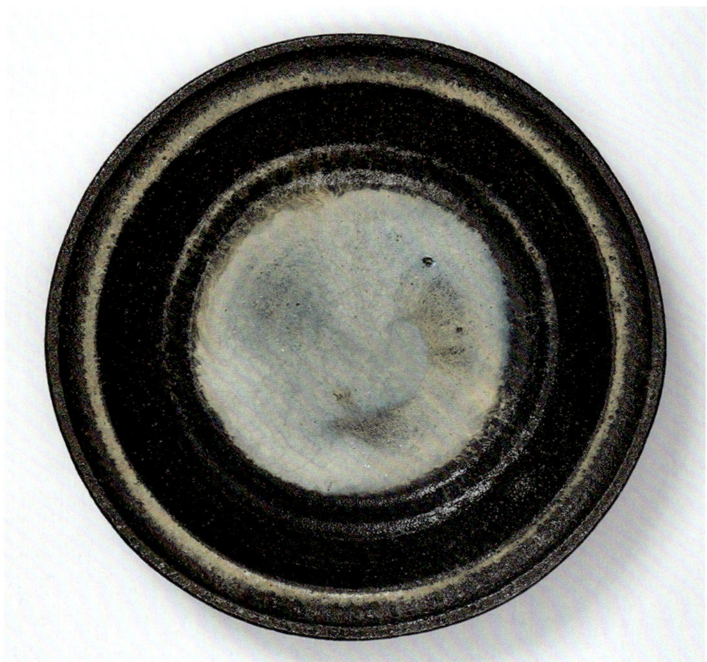

In addition to the types of work mentioned here, the collection has examples of teapots, a demanding household object which GE was interested in throughout much of her career **(147-149,151)**.

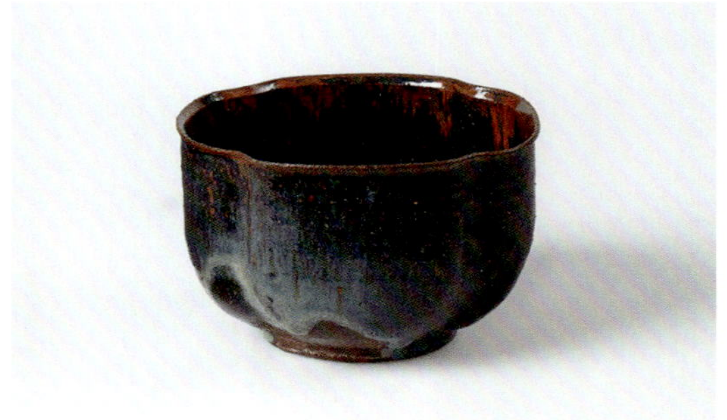

139 48/1967

The museum's 21 works by GE provide a varied and impressive picture of GE's ceramic universe, in which she achieved results of lasting beauty within a distinct selection of types of object, as a result of her skill with firing techniques and a wide range of glazes. It is well-known that GE often fired her works many times over in order to reach the desired effect with the borax glaze she chose to work with, as the only form of decoration, from the mid 1950s, while throughout a lifelong process she worked to refine and strengthen her form of expression. It is precisely the universal human and cultural expressions and experiences that GE sought and gave substance to in her works that have won affection and admiration for them.

133. Vase, 1941. *Søpindsvin* (Sea urchin)
Earthenware, tin-glazed; thrown. H 8.6 x Diam 10. Mark: 'Gutte oku' (the workshop in Hareskoven shared with Aase Feilberg and Christian Frederiksen 1941-42) inscribed on base. Mus.no. A2/1943. ACQUISITION: *Dansk kunsthåndværk*, 1943, Kunstindustrimuseet. See: *Brændpunkter*, 1990

134. Vase, 1941
Red clay, glazed; modelled, onion-shaped. H 8.4 x Diam 11.2.
Mark: 'Gutte oku' (the workshop in Hareskoven shared with Aase Feilberg and Christian Frederiksen 1941-42) inscribed on base. Mus.no. A3/1943
ACQUISITION: *Dansk kunsthåndværk*, 1943, Kunstindustrimuseet

135. Jug, 1951
Earthenware, lead-glazed; slip. H 16. Mark: 'Gutte' inscribed on base. Mus.no. 67/1951
ACQUISITION: Gutte Eriksen. Donation from *Benny Dessaus Mindelegat*. See: *Dansk Kunsthåndværk*, 1967-68

136. Bowl, 1955
Earthenware, glazed; thrown, slip, stamped decoration, hard-fired. H 15.8 x Diam 37.5. Mark: 'G' inscribed on side. Mus.no. 7/1956
ACQUISITION: *Forårsudstillingen*, 1956, Charlottenborg

137. Bowl, 1963
Earthenware, borax-glazed with iron oxide; thrown, shaped, hexagonal, hard-fired. H 12.5 x Diam 23.3. Mark: 'Gutte Danmark' inscribed on base. Mus.no. 11/1964
ACQUISITION: *Gutte Eriksen, Håndarbejdets Fremme*

138. Vase, 1967
Earthenware, glazed; thrown, modelled, 5 loop-handles at the rim, hard-fired. H 42.5 x Diam 15. Mark: none. Mus.no. 47/1967
ACQUISITION: *Efterårsudstillingen*, 1967, Charlottenborg. Donation from *Dansk Kunsthåndværks 50-års Jubilæumslegat*. See: *Dansk Kunsthåndværk*, 1967-68

139. Bowl, 1967. *Lotusskål* (Lotus bowl)
Earthenware, borax-glazed; thrown, shaped, hard-fired. H 8 x W 11.5. Mark: none. Mus.no. 48/1967
ACQUISITION: *Efterårsudstillingen*, 1967, Charlottenborg. Donation from *Kunstindustrimuseets 50-års Jubilæumslegat*. See: *Brændpunkter*, 1990

140. Bowl, 1969
Earthenware, glazed; thrown, decorated using cow-horn, hard-fired. H 11.8 x Diam 31.5. Mark: none. Mus.no. 133/1969
ACQUISITION: Donation from *Den Permanente* for Kunstindustrimuseum's 75th jubilee

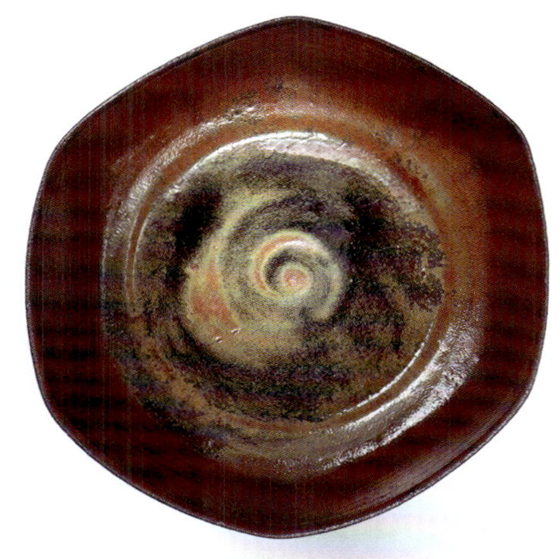

137 11/1964

144 144/1987

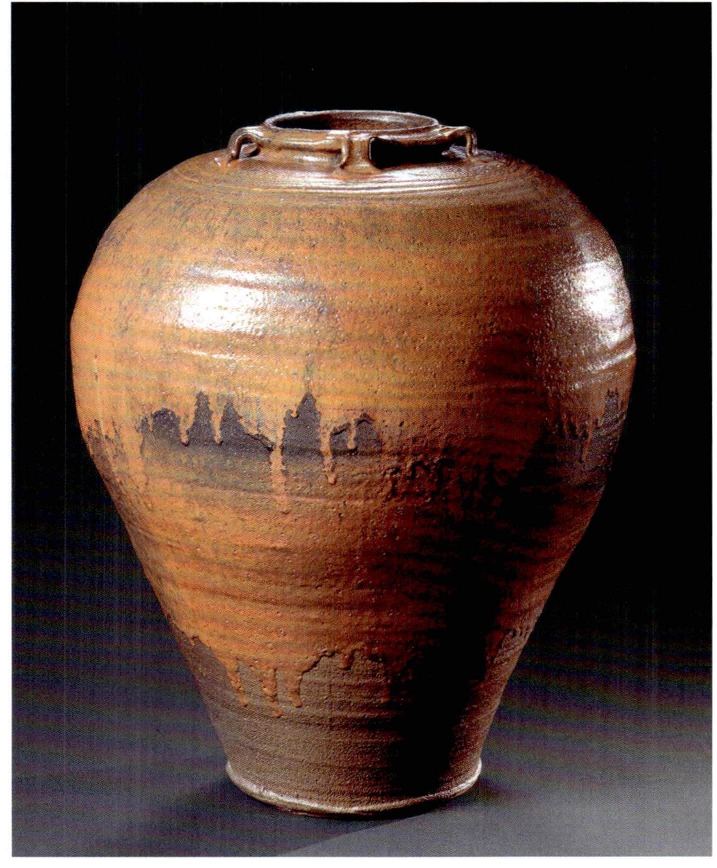

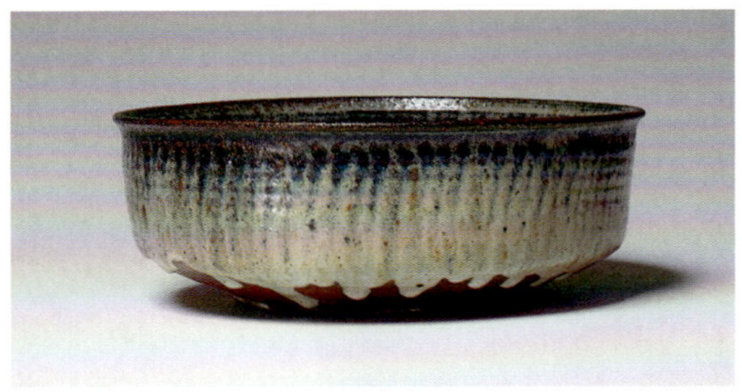

140 133/1969

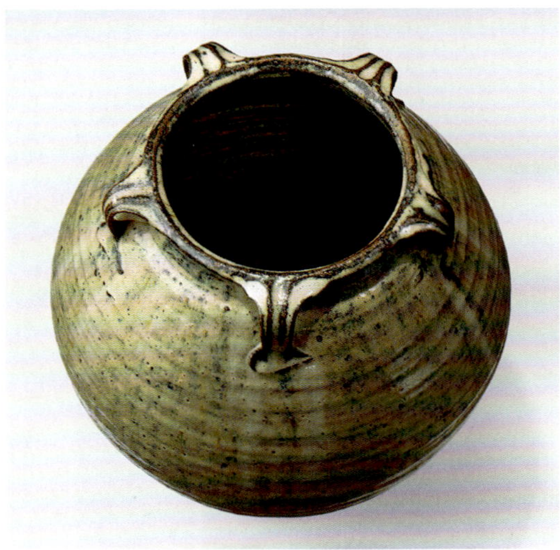

138 47/1967

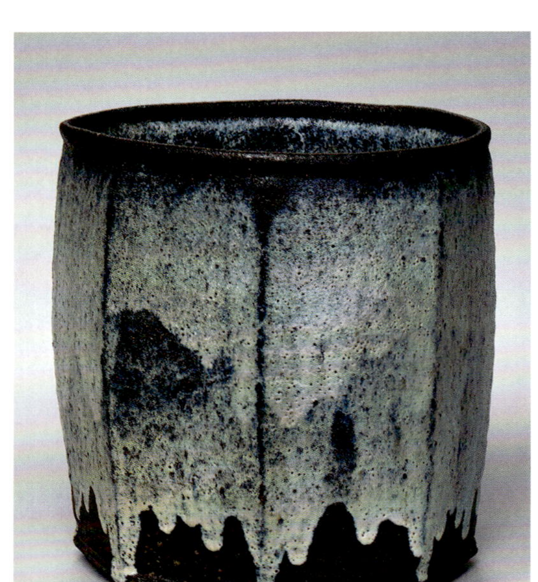

142 98/1984

150 133/1999

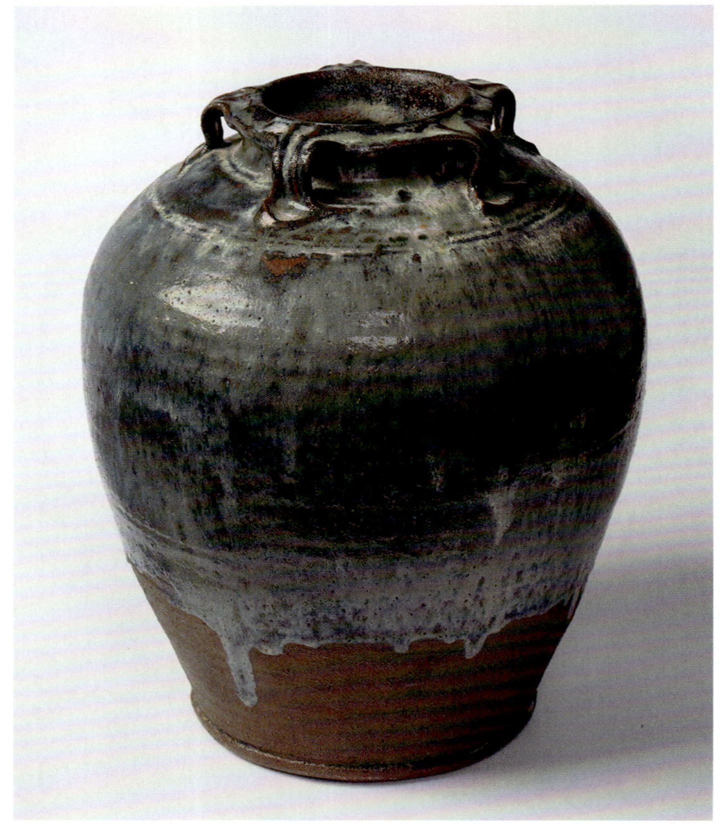

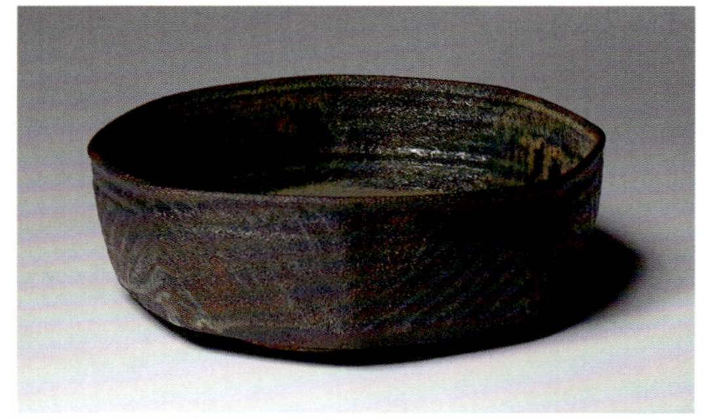

143 97/1985

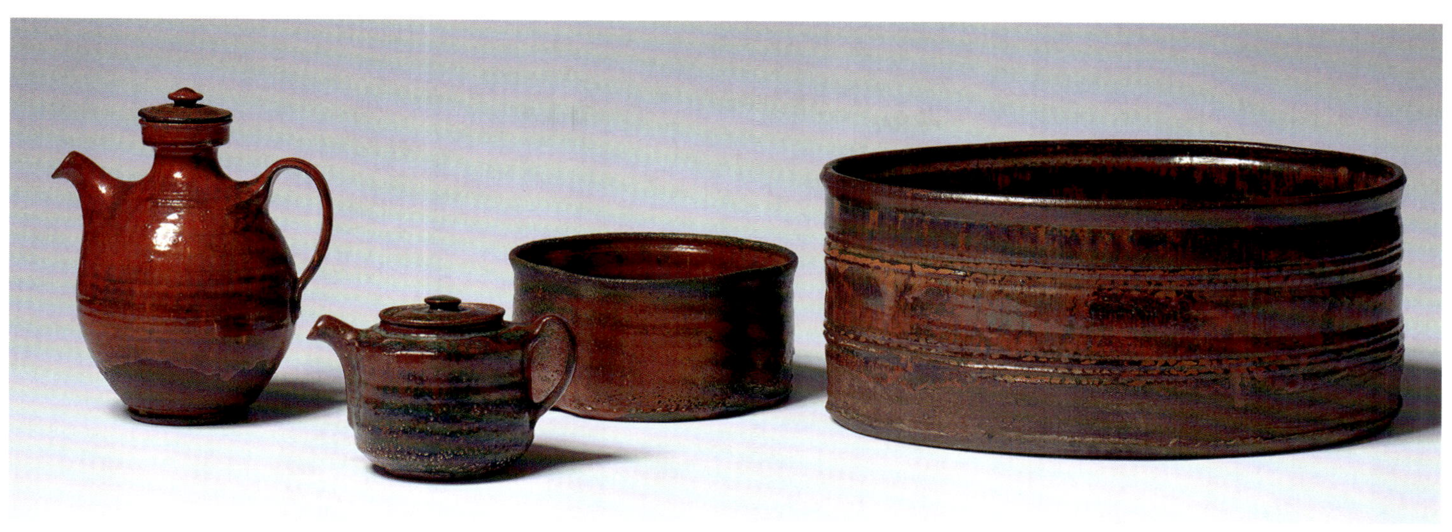

151 134a-b/1999 **147** 103a-b/1994 **153** D 1584 **145** 158/1990

152 202/2003

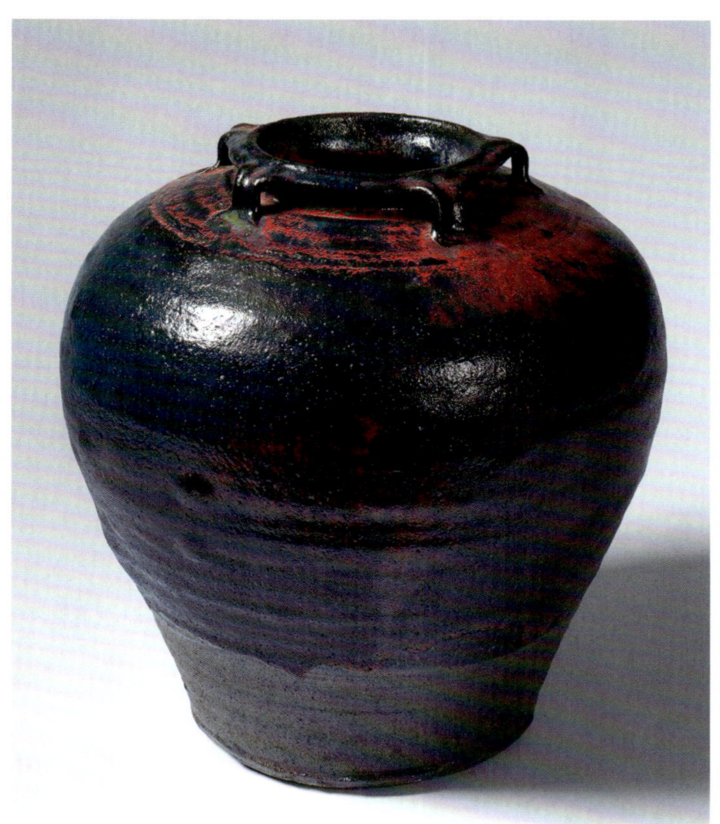

141. Vase, 1941

Earthenware, tin-glazed; thrown, fluted, hard-fired. H 11.4 x W 8.7.

Mark: 'Gutte' inscribed on base. Mus.no. 63/1978

ACQUISITION: Anker Nørregaard. Donation from *Helge Jacobsens Legat*. See: *Brændpunkter*, 1990. *Dansk Design 1910-1945 – Art Deco og funktionalisme*, 1998. Dybdahl, L., 1997

142. Pot, 1984

Earthenware, borax-glazed; thrown, shaped, octagonal, hard-fired.

H 31.5 x Diam 30. Mark: none. Mus.no. 98/1984

ACQUISITION: *Kammeraterne*, 1984. Donation from *Finansieringsinstituttet for Industri og Håndværks Jubilæumslegat*. See: *Brændpunkter*, 1990

143. Bowl, 1970

Earthenware, borax-glazed; thrown, shaped, octagonal, patterned, hard-fired.

H 11 x Diam 32. Mark: none. Mus.no. 97/1985

ACQUISITION: *Gutte Eriksen-50 års keramiske arbejder,* 1987, *Kunstforeningen*. Donation from William Hull, USA

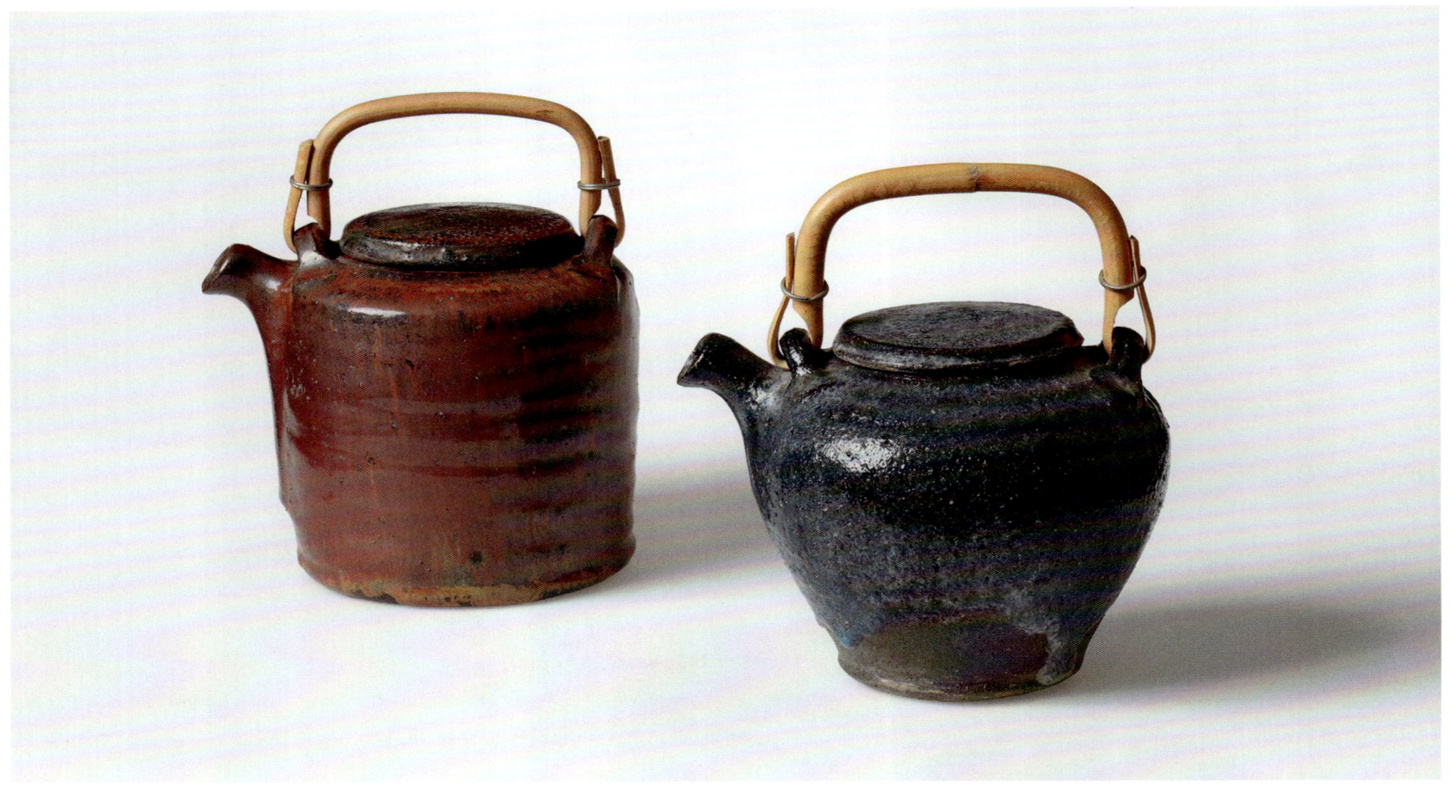

148 104a-b/1994 **149** 105a-b/1994

144. Vase, 1987

Earthenware, borax-glazed; thrown, modelled, 5 loop-handles at the rim, hard-fired. H 69 x Diam 56. Mark: none. Mus.no. 144/1987
ACQUISITION: *Gutte Eriksen-50 års keramiske arbejder,* 1987, *Kunstforeningen*. Donation from *Nationalbankens Jubilæumsfond*. See: Dybdahl, L., 1997

145. Basin, 1990

Earthenware, borax-glazed; thrown, shaped, hard-fired. H 37 x Diam 28.3. Mark: 'G' stamped on base. Mus.no. 158/1990
ACQUISITION: Gutte Eriksen. Donation from *Kunstindustrimuseets Venner*

146. Dish, 1993

Earthenware, borax-glazed with ash; thrown, modelled, hard-fired. H 9.8 x Diam 58. Mark: 'G' stamped on base. Mus.no. 98/1994
ACQUISITION: Galleri Borreby, Skælskør. Donation from *Poul og Hildur Kongo Pedersens Mindelegat*

147. Teapot, 1976-77

Earthenware, borax-glazed; thrown, modelled, hard-fired. H 10.8 x Diam 7.5. Mark: none. Mus.no. 103a-b/1994. ACQUISITION: Klassik, Copenhagen. Donation from *Kunstindustrimuseets Venner*

148. Teapot, 1984-85
Earthenware, bamboo, borax-glazed; thrown, modelled, hard-fired.
H 11.5 x Diam 7.3. Mark: 'G' stamped on base. Mus.no. 104a-b/1994.
ACQUISITION: Klassik, Copenhagen. Donation from *Kunstindustrimuseets Venner*

149. Teapot, 1984-85
Earthenware, bamboo, borax-glazed; thrown, modelled, hard-fired.
H 12. Mark: none. Mus.no. 105a-b/1994. ACQUISITION: Klassik, Copenhagen.
Donation from *Kunstindustrimuseets Venner*

150. Vase, 1989
Earthenware, borax-glazed; thrown, modelled, 5 loop-handles at the rim, hard-fired. H 40 x Diam 35. Mark: 'Gutte' inscribed on base. Mus.no. 133/1999
ACQUISITION: Donation from C. B. Andersen, Bank Director, Copenhagen

151. Jug with lid, 1963
Earthenware, glazed; thrown, modelled, hard-fired. H 22 x W 20 x Diam 14.
Mark: 'Gutte Danmark' inscribed on base. Mus.no. 134a-b/1999
ACQUISITION: Donation from C. B. Andersen, Bank Director, Copenhagen

152. Vase, 1995
Earthenware, borax-glazed; thrown, modelled, 5 loop-handles at the rim, hard-fired. H 41.5 x Diam 36.5. Mark: 'G' stamped on base. Mus.no. 202/2003
ACQUISITION: Gutte Eriksen

153. Bowl, 1980-81. *Lotusskål* (Lotus bowl)
Earthenware, borax-glazed; thrown, modelled, hard-fired. H 10 x W 19.5.
Mark: 'G' stamped on base. Mus.no. D 1584
ACQUISITION: Den Frie Udstillingsbygning.
On deposit from *Statens Kunstfond*, 1985.
See: *Statens Kunstfonds beretning*, 1981

ESPERSEN, MORTEN LØBNER 1965 –

Ceramicist

1987-89	Skolen for Brugskunst, Copenhagen
1989-90	École Supérieure des Arts Appliqués, Duperré, Paris
1990-92	Danmarks Designskole, Copenhagen
1999-05	Designskolen Kolding, lecturer
2005-11	Högskolan for Design och Konsthandverk (HDK), Gothenburg, Sweden, Visiting Professor
1992-95	Studio workshop, Kulturfabrikken
1995-2011	'Fusion', Kigkurren
2011-	The Clay Hotel, Copenhagen
	www.espersen.nu

Morten Løbner Espersen (MLE) belongs to the generation of prominent ceramicists who were born in the 1960s, educated in the 1980s, began to make names for themselves in the 1990s, and who have since, in the course of a few years, established a position for themselves both nationally and internationally. MLE works with galleries in the USA, Germany and Belgium, and has made a substantial contribution to teaching at the design schools in Denmark and Sweden.

In 1993, the year after leaving Danmarks Designskole, MLE participated in the exhibition '*Keramikkens Underskov*'(The undergrowth of ceramics), an initiative that aimed to set out what the young 'new' ceramicists were making in their own studios around the country and to display the variety of ceramic forms of expression characteristic of the time. In the same year MLE received the Arts and Crafts Award of 1879, silver medal (highest award) and the subsequent exhibition of works by prize-winners revealed a young ceramicist who was already on track for a promising ceramic career.

From his earliest works MLE has shown himself to be not only someone skilled at shaping clay and using a range of techniques, but also a scientist and an explorer. He determinedly explores the possibilities of ceramic material and of chemical and technological processes; his work is to a great extent experimental, incorporating surprising effects and results from what are often repeated firings of individual works. Within his chosen boundaries MLE constantly dares to go to the outermost extremes and has found a fine balance between new minimalistic forms and sumptuous bold colouring, structures and textures in glazing.

The museum owns six of MLE's works from the period 1993-2001, and they demonstrate the development from the early white-grey, matte and crusty glazes **(154-155)** to the shiny objects with deeper colouring **(157-158)**. The two more recent works, from 1998 **(156)** and 2001 **(157)** respectively, are examples of the strong colours and thickly flowing glazes, often applied layer on layer, which point in the direction of MLE's commissioned work for Hillerød Viden- og Kulturpark, from 2003, for which he made nine monumental vessels positioned on a shelf 2.5 m above floor level.

There was a period of many years during which MLE concentrated on glazes, with the container as the 'canvas' for his splendid glazed painting, but then he decided to engage with modelled work, and in recent years, on the basis of complex and carefully registered experiments,

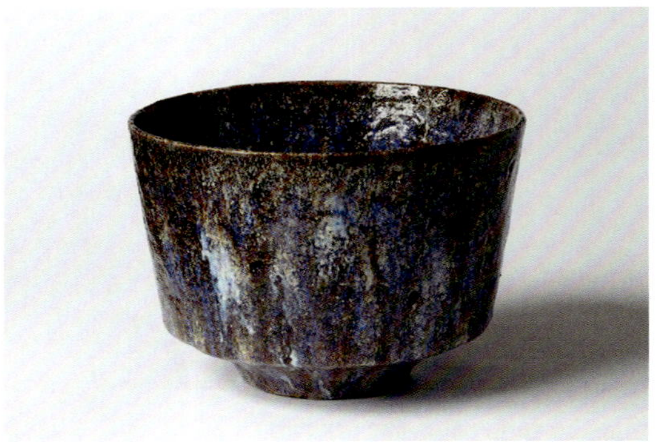

157 414/2008

he has made several remarkable series of works. Among them is the strong and innovative *Horror Vacui*, from 2011-12, with expressive organically modelled works that reinterpret the relationship between the classic pot/vase and its decoration, in that the decoration in this case takes an independent three-dimensional and dramatic form and in a sense embraces/smothers the pot. Another series from the same time has the title *Vacui*, and consists of rows of cylinder-shaped pots with sumptuous and novel glazed effects. A third series from that period, entitled *Errata*, consisting of a sequence of polychrome

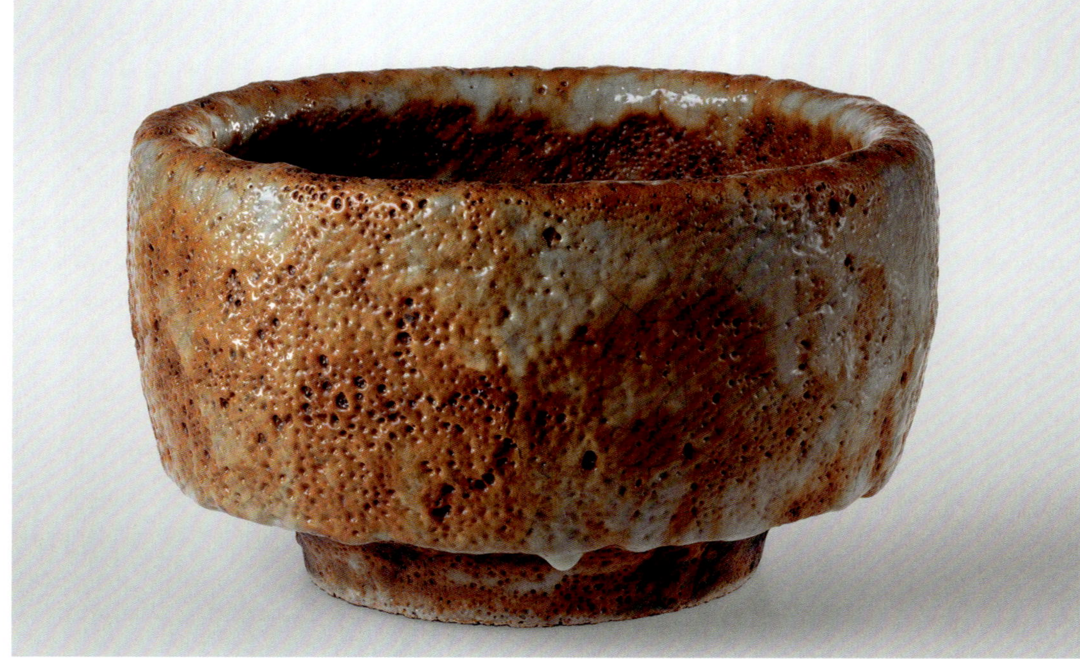

156 127/1998

ceramic pictures with numerous layers of glaze, was included, along with those already mentioned, in the comprehensive solo exhibition held for MLE at Trapholt in 2012, together with a selection of the artist's graphic works (See: *Horror Vacui*, Trapholt, 2012). MLE was a member of the exhibition-group *New Danish Ceramics* from 2004 to 2008. He has exhibited in many parts of the world, is represented in influential museums in the Nordic region, Europe, the USA and Japan, and has been awarded numerous prizes and distinctions.

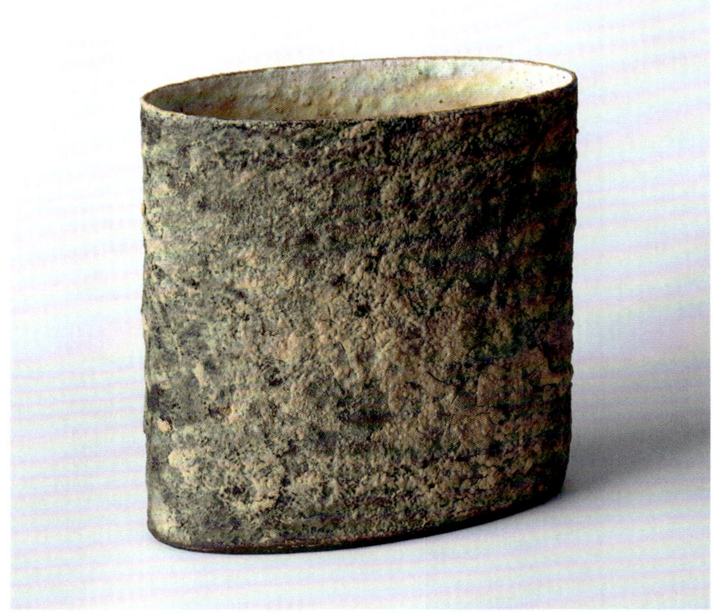

154 201/1994

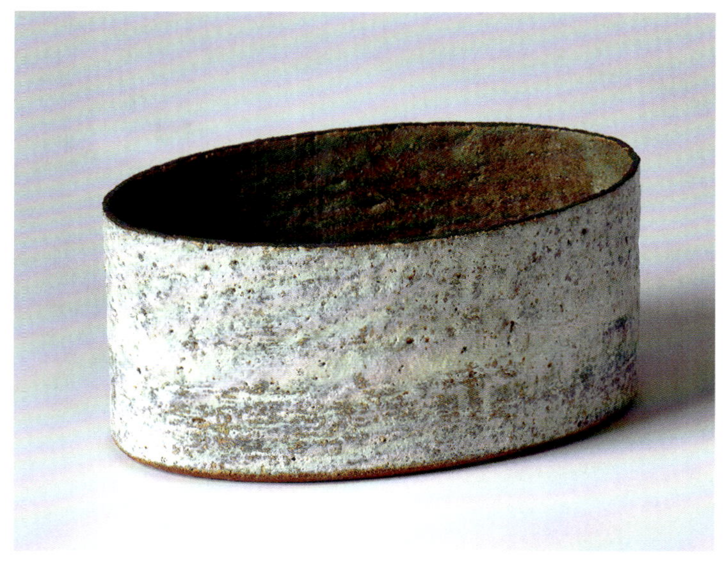

155 202/1994

154. Pot, 1993

Stoneware, several layers of glaze; modelled, hard-fired at 1268°. H 21.5 x Diam 20.5. Mark: Stamped monogram on base. Mus.no. 201/1994
ACQUISITION: *Kunsthåndværkerprisen,* 1993, Kunstindustrimuseet

155. Pot, 1993

Stoneware, several layers of glaze; modelled, fired at 1268°. H 10.5 x W 23.5. Mark: Stamped monogram on base. Mus.no. 202/1994
ACQUISITION: Galleri Stylvig, Iceland

156. Vessel, 1999

Stoneware, shino glaze; modelled, fired at 1268°. H 20.5 x Diam 34.5. Mark: 'M 400' stamped on base. Mus.no. 127/1998
ACQUISITION: Solo exhibition in Galleri Nørby, 1998, Copenhagen. Donation from *Kunstindustrimuseets Venner*. See: Gelfer-Jørgensen, 2013, p. 317.

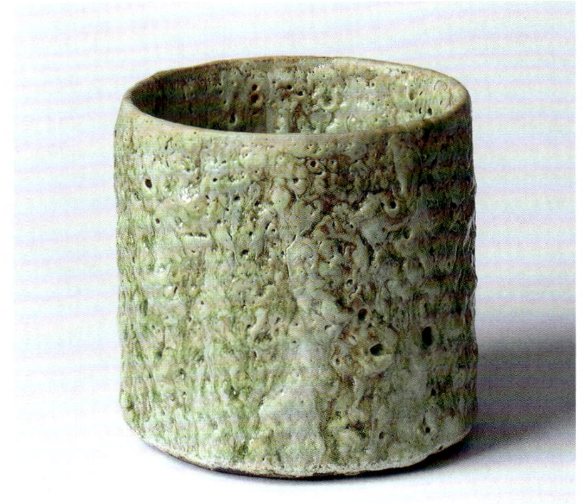

158 415/2008

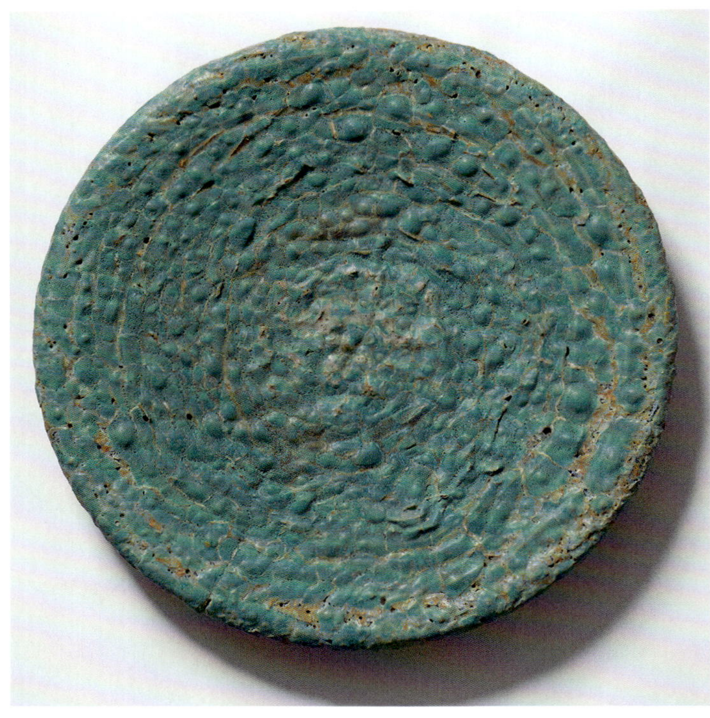

159 117/2009

FISCHER-HANSEN, ELSE 1905 – 1996

Painter, ceramicist

1921-25,	
1928-29	Rannows School of Painting, porcelain painting
1929	Life-drawing course, Nice
1928-38	Kunstnernes Efterårsudstilling
1950-54	Grønningen
1980-	Koloristerne
1960	Own studio workshop, Vanløse, Copenhagen

The museum owns three works by Else Fischer-Hansen (EFH), all of them from around 1960; they are very different in colour and expression, but were all made in the artist's own studio with the same technique, i.e. brush-painted tile pictures in different sizes and with different numbers of tiles sunk in cement and framed for wall-hanging. One of the works was acquired in connection with an exhibition in the museum - '*Keramiske Fliser af Else Fischer-Hansen*' in 1960 **(160)** – and another fine work from the same exhibition, from 1960 **(161)**,

157. Bowl, 1998

Stoneware, thick-flowing layer of glaze; thrown. H 12. Mark: 'M 532' stamped on base. Mus.no. 414/2008

ACQUISITION: Willed donation from the estate of Ambassador Niels Christian Tillisch, Copenhagen

158. Pot, 2002

Stoneware, thick-flowing layer of glaze; modelled. H 13. Mark: 'M 986' stamped on base. Mus.no. 415/2008

ACQUISITION: Willed donation from the estate of Ambassador Niels Christian Tillisch, Copenhagen

159. Dish, 2001

Stoneware, thick-flowing layer of glaze; thrown at Tommerup Teglværk, glaze fired twice. Diam 73. Mark: none. Mus.no. 117/2009

ACQUISITION: Donation from *Ny Carlsbergfondet*

162 18/1977

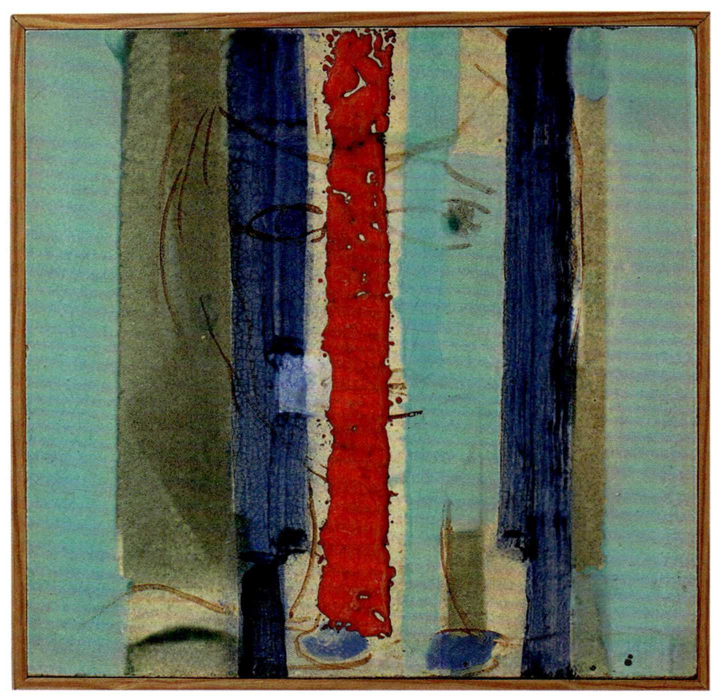

was acquired later. The third work **(162)** was donated to the museum in 1977. Under the vertical stripes in its glaze it has a faintly sketched female portrait, possibly a self-portrait; at any rate the picture allegedly belonged to the artist's husband, the painter and children's book author Egon Mathiesen (1907-1976), with whom EFH had several exhibitions. EFH worked in various materials, including ceramic tiles, coloured mosaics – e.g. for the commissioned work for the entrance to Herlev hospital – and pictorial weaving. From the 1930s EFH developed great colouristic talent for abstract, nature-inspired, poetic painting, and it is that form of expression that EFH transfers, with refined sensitivity, to the ceramic tile-pictures.

160. Tile-picture, 1960. *Komposition*

Earthenware, glazed; 6 tiles laid in cement, metal suspension. H 45 x W 33.5. Mark: none. Mus.no. 61/1960. ACQUISITION: Else Fischer-Hansen. Donation from *Statens 50-års Jubilæumslegat*. Probably exhibited in *Keramiske fliser af Else Fischer-Hansen,* Kunstindustrimuseet 1960

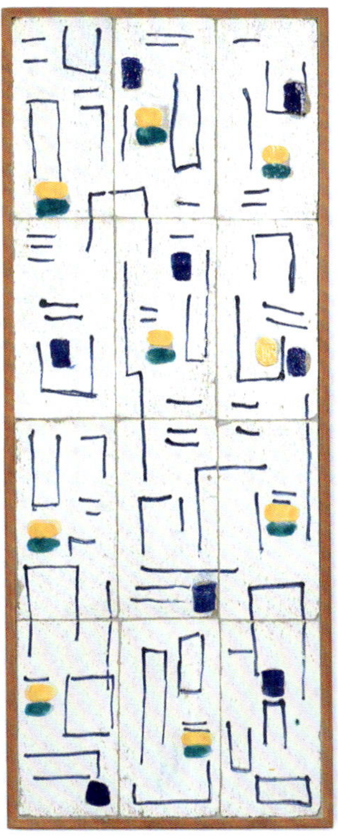

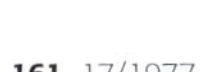

161 17/1977

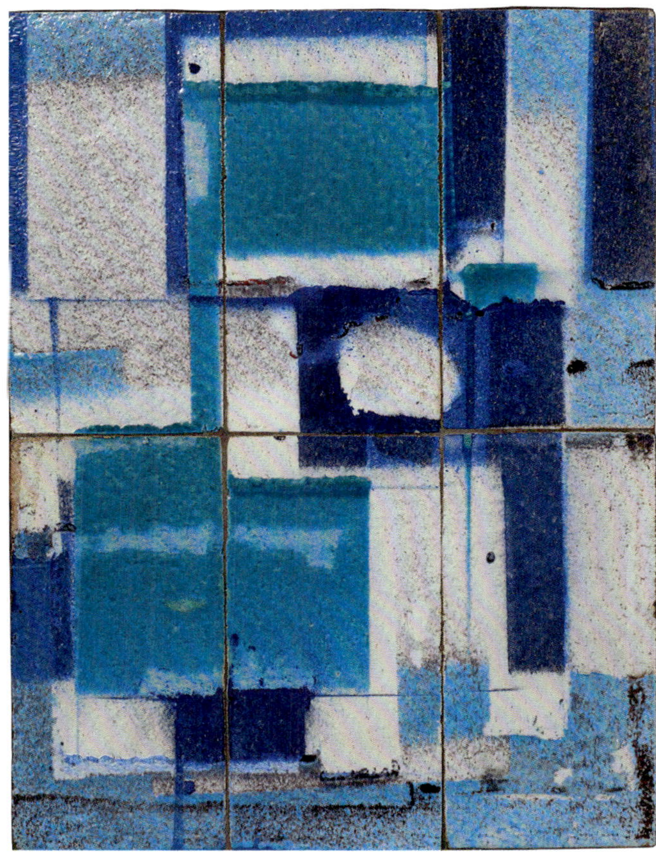

160 61/1960

161. Tile-picture, 1960

Earthenware, glazed; 3 x 4 tiles laid in cement, frame in wood. H 93.5 x W 36. Mark: 'Else Fischer-Hansen' painted on back. Mus.no. 17/1977 ACQUISITION: Else Fischer-Hansen. Donation from *Kunstindustrimuseets 50-års Jubilæumslegat*. Exhibited in *Keramiske fliser af Else Fischer-Hansen*, Kunstindustrimuseet 1960

162. Tile-picture, 1962

Earthenware, glazed; tile laid in cement, female portrait (self-portrait) sketched under the glaze, metal frame. H 29 x W 29. Mark: 'Else Fischer-Hansen 1962, belongs to Egon Mathiesen' painted on back. Mus.no. 18/1977 ACQUISITION: Else Fischer-Hansen. Donation from *Kunstindustrimuseets 50-års Jubilæumslegat*

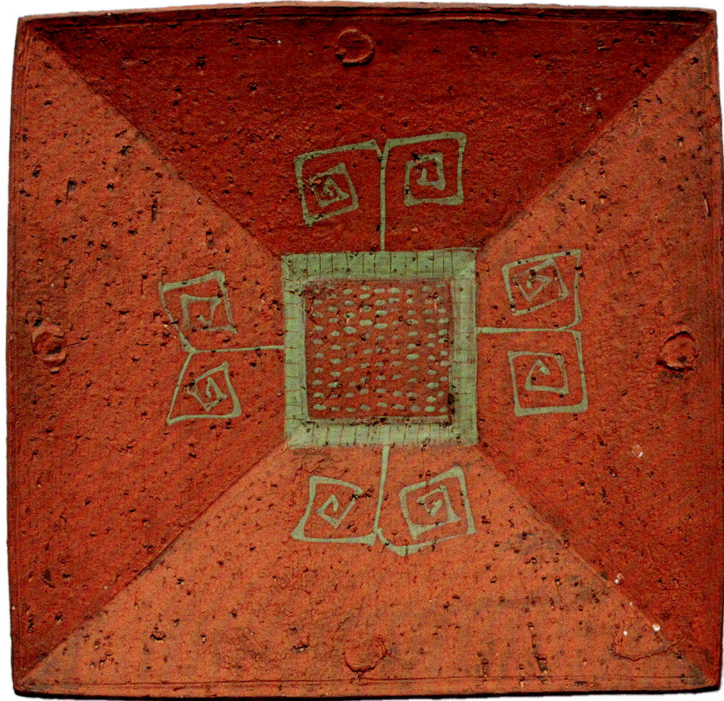

166 307/2004

FLØCHE, ANNE 1952 –

Ceramicist

1973-78	Det Jyske Kunstakademi
1975	Silapakorn University, Bangkok
1978-	Own studio workshop, Århus
1984-	in Knebel, Djursland, shared with Hans Vangsø
1988-91	Det Jyske Kunstakademi, teacher
1993-2008	Aarhus Kunstakademi, teacher
	www.annefloche.dk

Anne Fløche (AF) was aware from an early age that she wanted to pursue an artistic path, and when she met Erik Nyholm at Brandbjerg Højskole and appreciated his approach to working with ceramics she decided to choose clay as her material. AF was offered a place at Det Jyske Kunstakademi and became a pupil of Gutte Eriksen, but in her works in more recent years AF has abandoned forms for household use in favour of a poetic, experimental, free expression.

AF considers herself first and foremost as a ceramicist and has the expanse of knowledge about the materials and ceramic processes that is associated with skilled craftsmanship. This makes it possible for her to transform into material reality the concepts and inspirations from travels, nature and poetry that are the hub, the thought-substance, of her ceramic art. AF paints and creates poetry in clay; her universe of shapes, textures and ornamentation contains characters, letters, concepts, words, texts, quotations and poetry which AF integrates into her works, thereby creating metaphysical space to enhance shared culture and the experience of beauty. While she was still studying AF went off

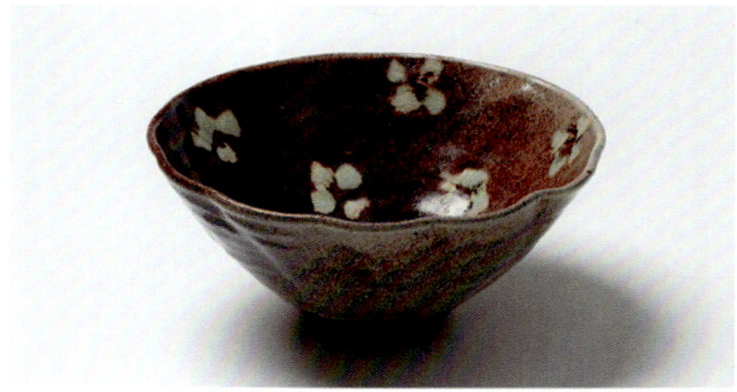

164 300/1989

travelling and spent a year at Silapakorn University in Bangkok. Later journeys and study visits took her among other places to the Danish Institute in Damascus, and have clearly made a mark in her works, which show relations with the great ceramic traditions of the Mediterranean countries, Turkey and Persia. In 2008 AF had a solo exhibition in Danmarks Keramikmuseum, CLAY, with a series of gigantic vessel-shapes, on which the surface decorations she had used in recent years were successfully applied to the rounded forms of the vessels.
AF is represented with four works in the museum's collection, three of them from around 1990, and the fourth from 2004. While the three earlier ones are thrown, glazed and decorated with nature-inspired motifs **(163-165)**, the large unglazed square dish has been shaped and stands matte in the classical red coarse *terra sigillata* like an architectural fragment from a sun-baked building in the Orient, with a delicate stylised brush-painted ornament in the centre of the dish **(166)**.

AF was a member of the exhibition-group *8 keramikere* (1987-96), she has taken part in a large number of exhibitions in Denmark and abroad, and she is associated with galleries in Stockholm, Paris, London and Philadelphia.

163. Dish, date unknown
Earthenware, feldspar- and iron-glazed; thrown, hard-fired at 1200°. H 6 x Diam 31.3. Mark: 'A' stamped on base. Mus.no. 299/1989. ACQUISITION: *Jysk sommer*, 1989, Kunstindustrimuseet. Donation from *Ny Carlsberg Museumslegat*

164. Bowl, 1989
Earthenware, glazed; thrown, brush-painted, wax, fired at 1200°. H 9 x Diam 19.5. Mark: 'A' stamped on base Mus.no. 300/1989 ACQUISITION: *Jysk sommer*, 1989, Kunstindustrimuseet. Donation from *Ny Carlsberg Museumslegat*. See: *Brændpunkter*, 1990

165. Pot, 1991
Earthenware, feldspar- and iron- glazed; thrown, brush-painted, raku, reduction-hard-fired at 1200°. H 22. Mark: 'A' stamped on base. Mus.no. 10/1992 ACQUISITION: Anne Fløche. See: Dybdahl, L., 1997

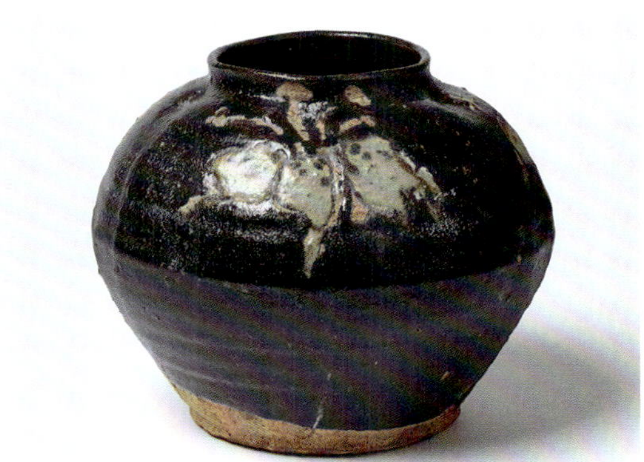

165 10/1992

166. Dish, 2004
Pibe-clay, perlite, iron oxide, *terra sigillata*; slab-work, shaped, brush-painted, hard-fired at 1100°. H 8 x Diam 44.5. Mark: none. Mus.no. 307/2004 ACQUISITION: *Anne Fløche-nyeste keramiske arbejder*, 2004, Galleri Nørby. Donation from *Kunstindustrimuseets Venner*

163 299/1989

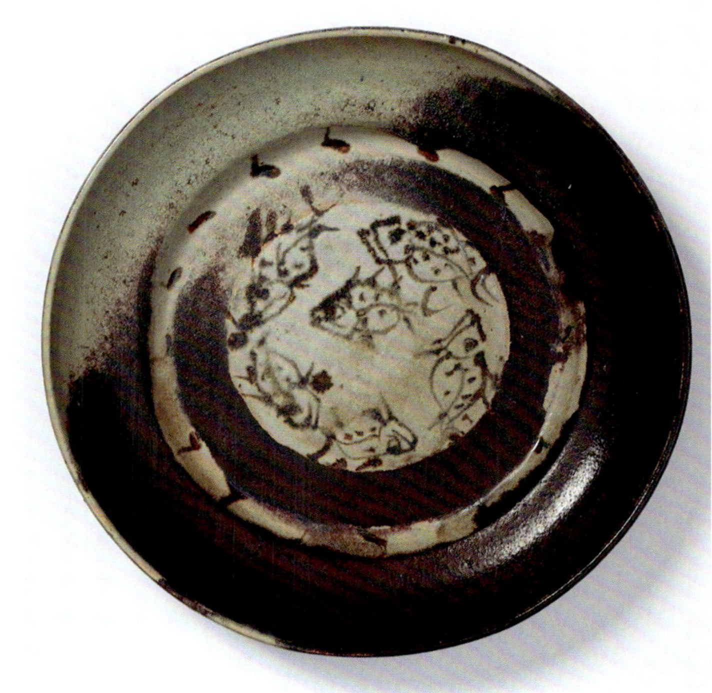

GAIHEDE, JYTTE 1943 –

Ceramicist

Own studio workshop, Løkken, NW Jutland
www.keramikogbilleder.dk

In the summer of 1989 the museum held the exhibition '*Jysk Sommer*' (Jutland Summer) with 17 invited ceramicists, mainly from the north, west and south Jutland areas. In all forty workshops were represented, and in addition to ceramics the fields of textiles, glass, metalwork and book-craft were included. From the little catalogue of the exhibition it appears that it was the large number of workshops spread around in Jutland that spurred the museum to mount the exhibition. Prior to this there were about ten workshops represented in the museum's collections.

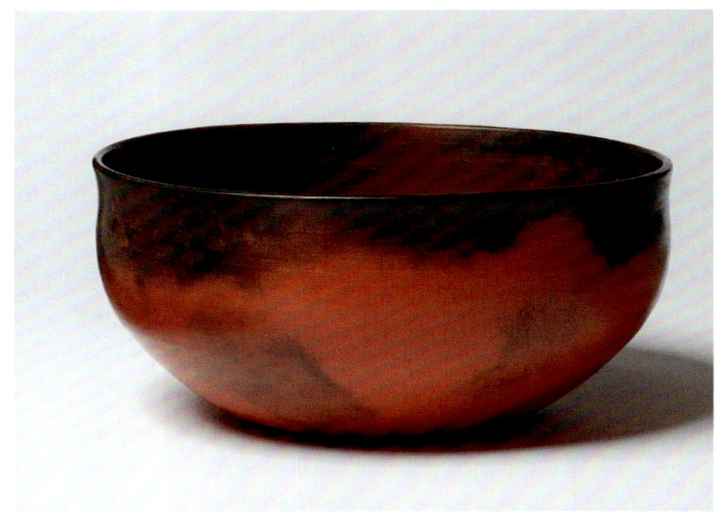

167 298/1989

A number of pieces from the exhibition were acquired by the museum, including two bowls by Jytte Gaihede (JG). Both are made with the same technique; they are thrown earthenware, fired with the charcoal-burning technique known from prehistoric times – a slow firing on an earth-covered fire. After firing the surface is polished so that it becomes shiny and smooth. The works are meticulously made and harmonious in effect, displaying a refined sense of restrained decoration **(167-168)**. JG has had a workshop and shop for many years in Ingstrup near Løkken, and has taken part in exhibitions in Denmark and abroad.

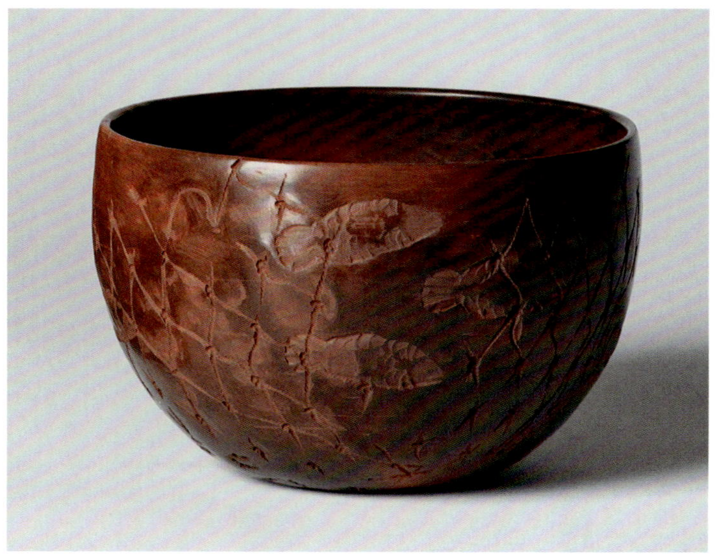

167. Bowl, 1988

Earthenware, un-glazed; thrown, polished, charcoal-fired at 1000°.
H 12.3 x Diam 26. Mark: Plant motif stamped on base. Mus.no. 298/1989
ACQUISITION: *Jysk sommer*, 1989, Kunstindustrimuseet. Donation from *Kunstindustrimuseets 50-års Jubilæumslegat*

168. Bowl, 1988

Earthenware, un-glazed; thrown, decorated, polished, fired at 1000°, charcoal-fired at 850-950°. H 10.5 x Diam 15.5. Mark: 'Gaihede 88' inscribed on base. Mus.no. 345/1989
ACQUISITION: *Jysk sommer*, 1989, Kunstindustrimuseet.
See: *Fire elementer – to temperamenter,* 1996

168 345/1989

GEERTSEN, MICHAEL 1966 –

Ceramicist, industrial designer

1984-88 Trained as a potter
1988-91 Skolen for Brugskunst, ceramics and glass
1991-1993 Danmarks Designskole, industrial design
1993- Own studio workshop, Copenhagen
1995- Worked for Ikea, Kähler Keramik, Muuto, Paustian, By- og Boligministeriet, Skandinavian Tobacco, Royal Scandinavia, and as a freelance designer
1999-2000 Udstillingssted for Ny Keramik (Exhibition venue for New Ceramics), Copenhagen, co-owner
1999, 2002-03 Designskolen Kolding, external examiner
1999-2000, 2006 Danmarks Designskole, guest teacher, external examiner
www.michaelgeertsen.com

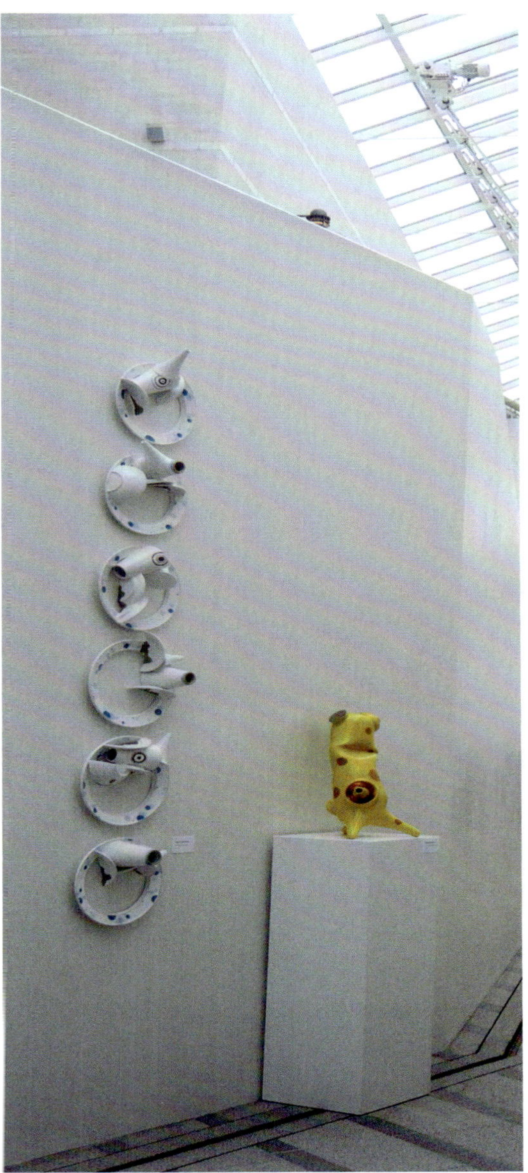
172 108a-f/2011

Michael Geertsen (MG) belongs to the group of ambitious and successful ceramicists who were educated in the 1980s and became known in the early 90s. Through the years MG has combined being a celebrated ceramic *avant garde* artist, represented in the most prestigious and influential international museums, with a freelance career as designer of functional household objects for (mainly Danish) manufacturers. This combination has a century-long tradition in Denmark, where the two great porcelain factories, and many smaller ceramic companies as well, brought in successive people with artistic skills, employing them to contribute to the design of products. One could well wish that many more of MG's stylishly interesting and refined prototypes from the 1990s for functional objects relating to tableware and dining had been put into production.

MG is both technically and theoretically well-informed, and his works are often linked to existing artistic and craft traditions as a springboard for further reflection and new interpretations. Evidence that MG has the necessary knowledge, professional skill and artistic nerve to carry off this method was presented e.g. in the exhibition *Geertsen VERSUS* at Næstved Museum in 2014, when MG, in dialogue with that museum's unique collection of Kähler Keramik from 1839 to 1974 showed his own earlier and very new works in an inspiring, playful and convincing juxtaposition. (See: *Michael Geertsen VERSUS*, Næstved Museum, 2014).

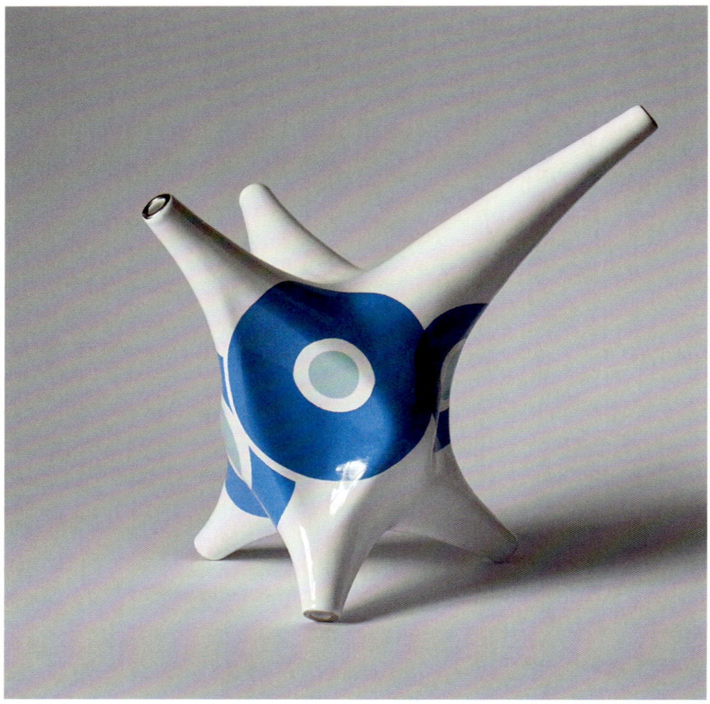

171 217/2007

impressive mural commission which MG carried out in Hanoi, Vietnam in 2009. From 2007 there is a work in the museum's collection which is an organic biomorphic sculpture and a type of work which is still a central concern to MG **(171)**. The work of most recent date is from 2010 **(172)**, and consists of 6 white-glazed plate-shaped open rings decorated with blue and red circular fields which refer back to the Russian propaganda porcelain decorated by Kasimir Malevich in the early 20th century; the same decoration is to be seen on the sculpture *Objekt #21* from 2007. The work *Untitled- the plates* was included in the adjudicated European Ceramic Context 2010 at Bornholms Kunstmuseum. In 2012 MG received Annie & Otto Johs. Detlefs' Ceramic Prize for his ground-breaking ceramic work.

169. Object, 2001. ***Blåt vægobjekt*** (Blue wall-object)
Earthenware, tin-glazed, prepared stains; thrown, cut, modelled, fired at 1020-1030°. H 15.5 x W 31 x D 45. Mark: none. Mus.no. 110/2002
ACQUISITION: Galleri Nørby, Copenhagen

MG came into focus in earnest from the mid 1990s, when he showed the first of his fragmented deconstructivist objects, with their piled up elements, which call to mind early 20th century modernism. In these works MG throws entirely ordinary domestic pieces such as cups, jugs and plates and then cuts them up and piles them together into new stacked sculptures in which the original shapes can still be traced, but are given new life through the completely-covering monochrome glazes, often in matte sprayed-on colours. The sculptures acquire a spatial presence as wall-mounted objects when they are transferred from table or podium to take possession of wall space. In the museum's collection there are two of these wall objects from around the year 2000 **(169-170)**. A particularly complicated and splendid work with shiny grey glaze was shown on a table-like podium in the exhibition '*New Danish Ceramics*' in the museum in 2004 held by the newly-formed exhibition-group of that name, of which MG is a member; the work was later acquired by MAD, Museum of Arts & Design, New York. A very large number of wall-objects were incorporated into an

169 110/2002 **170** 111/2002

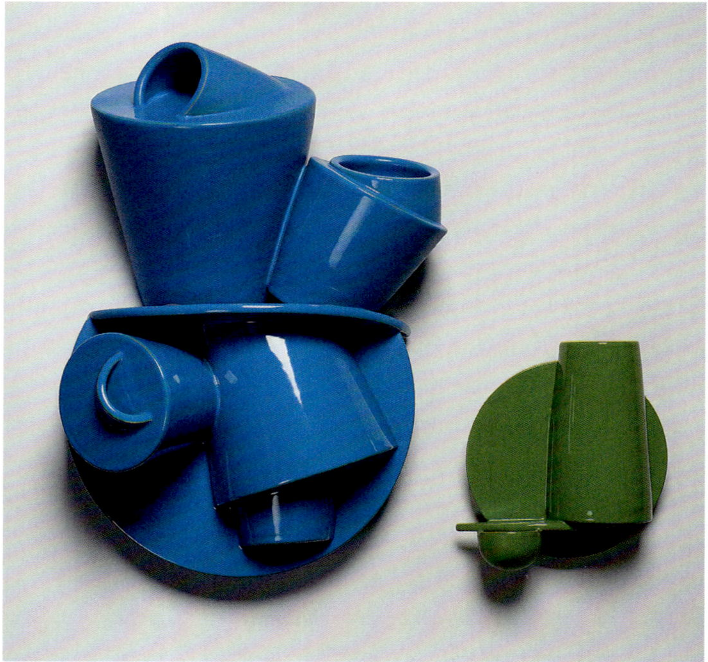

170. Object, 2002. *Grønt vægobjekt* (Green wall-object)
Earthenware, tin-glazed, prepared stains; thrown, cut, modelled, fired at 1020-1030°. H 8 x W 20 x Diam 17. Mark: none. Mus.no. 111/2002
ACQUISITION: Galleri Nørby, Copenhagen. See: *From the Kilns of Denmark, 2002*

171. Object, 2007. *Objekt #21*
Earthenware, glazed, decals, platinum lustre; thrown, modelled, assembled, decorated. H 24 x W 36 x D 40. Mark: none. Mus.no. 217/2007
ACQUISITION: *Black Holes and Revelations*, 2007, Drud & Køppe Gallery, Copenhagen

172. Six wall-objects, 2010. *The Plates*
Earthenware, glazed, platinum; thrown, transfer, majolica. Diam 35.
Mark: none. Mus.no. 108a-f/2011. ACQUISITION: Michael Geertsen.
See: *European Ceramic Context*, Bornholm, 2010, p. 152

GJERDEVIK, NILS ERIK 1962 – 2016

Artist

1982-83	H.C. Høiers Malerskole
1984	Kunstakademiet, Prague
1993-96	Det Jyske Kunstakademi, Head of Graphic Department
	Own studio workshop, Copenhagen
	www.gjerdevik.com

Niels Erik Gjerdevik (NEG) worked with ceramics from an early age. Since the 1980s he has made a large number of glazed stoneware sculptures that he exhibits together with his paintings, drawings and graphic works. While many pictorial artists only explore using clay for a short period, NEG has constantly used it in his *oeuvre*.
The museum 's sculpture by NEG was made in 1988 and has the title *Danmarkskort* (Map of Denmark) **(173)**. The map motif can be seen at the end of two 'tongues of land' with lizard-like creatures on them, one of them ending in an outline of Jutland and the other with Funen and Sealand. While the sculpture is glazed, the outlines of Denmark are matte pink and without decoration. One can detect a mildly sarcastic undertone in the work. From the same year there are several sculptures that show various sections of the northern hemisphere in neo-expressive works which were displayed in Galleri C, Aarhus, in 1989. As an extension of the works mentioned above, in 1988 NEG also completed two large ceramic commissions, one in Elektronik Centralen in Hørsholm, and the other in the Panum Institute in Copenhagen.

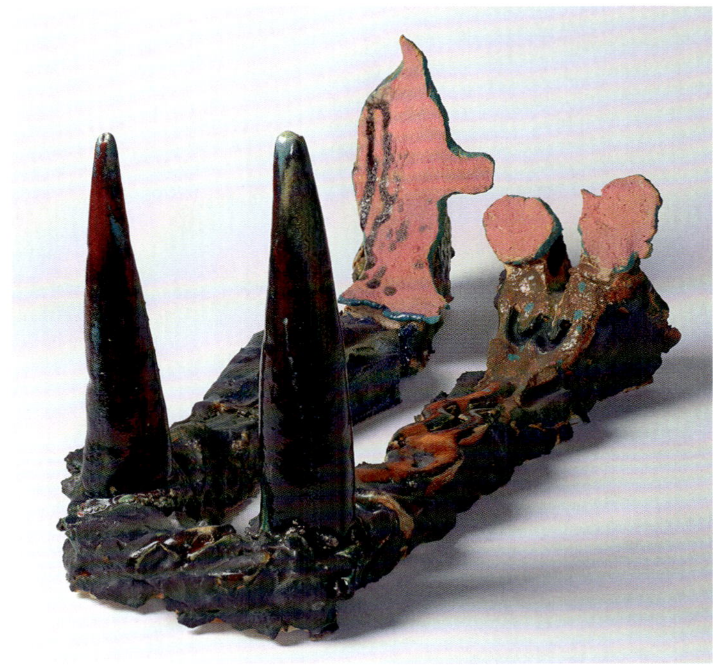

173 227/1989

The 7.5 m-long ceramic relief in Hørsholm in particular testifies to a relation with the Cobra-movement (Asger Jorn, *Det store relief*, Århus Statsskole, 1959) and the Eks-skole. NEG moved to Berlin in 1989, and lived and worked there for a number of years.

173. Sculpture, 1988. *Danmarkskort* (Map of Denmark)
Earthenware, glazed; modelled. Made in Bent Skytte Rasmussen's workshop, Mors. H 30 x L 57 x D 23.5.
Mark: 'Gjerdevik 1988' painted on base. Mus.no. 227/1989
ACQUISITION: Galleri Stadshill, Copenhagen. Donation from *Kunstindustrimuseets 50-års Jubilæumslegat*

GLOB, LOTTE 1944 –

Ceramicist

1959-63	pottery apprenticeship with Gutte Eriksen; Knud Jensen, Sorring, E Jutland
1963-64	Philip Pierce, Ireland
1964-65	David Illingworth, Scotland
1965-67	Own studio workshop, Djursland, E Jutland
1968-	Own studio workshop, Durness, Scotland
	www.lotteglob.co.uk

174 217/1974

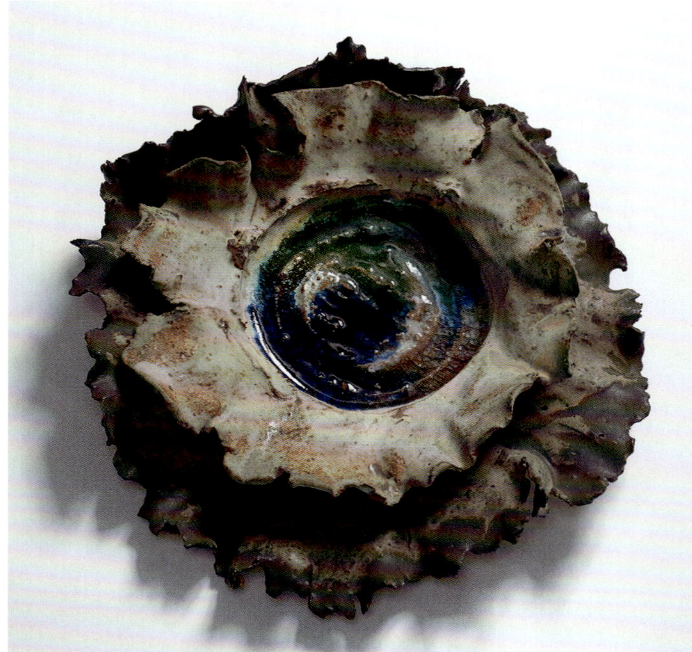

Perhaps inspired by her time as apprentice with Gutte Eriksen and by the latter's connection to the English master-potter Bernard Leach, Lotte Glob (LG) travelled to England, went on a study visit to Ireland and then went on to Scotland, which became her home and workplace from 1968 onwards. LG's life and career has encompassed many journeys, but since the 1990s she has made her life in NW Scotland's magnificent and deserted landscape, creating a workshop-and-nature area which is open to visitors walking through, where her ceramic sculptures are integrated into the landscape.

In the years prior to 1990 LG exhibited regularly in Denmark, and the two works owned by the museum are the result of exhibitions held by the museum in 1974 **(174)** and in Galleri Gammelstrand in 1977 **(175)**. The nature-inspired and expressively modelled works are made in Scottish clay, which when unglazed has a brownish-grey earth colour. LG has at times used strongly coloured glazes as a feature in the centre of her sculptures.

174. Sculpture, 1974. *Måneblomst* (Moonflower)
Earthenware, stoneware, powdered glass, dolomite- and oxide-glazed; modelled, reduction-fired in oil kiln. Diam 42. Mark: none. Mus.no. 217/1974
ACQUISITION: *Lotte Glob – stoneware*, 1974, Kunstindustrimuseet. Donation from *Kunstindustrimuseets 50-års Jubilæumslegat*

175. Sculpture, 1976/77. *Stenblomst* (Stone flower)
Stoneware, glazed; modelled. H 42. Mark: none. Mus.no. 78/1977
ACQUISITION: Galleri Gammelstrand, Copenhagen, 1977. Donation from *Overretssagfører Odin Kaysers Legat*

175 78/1977

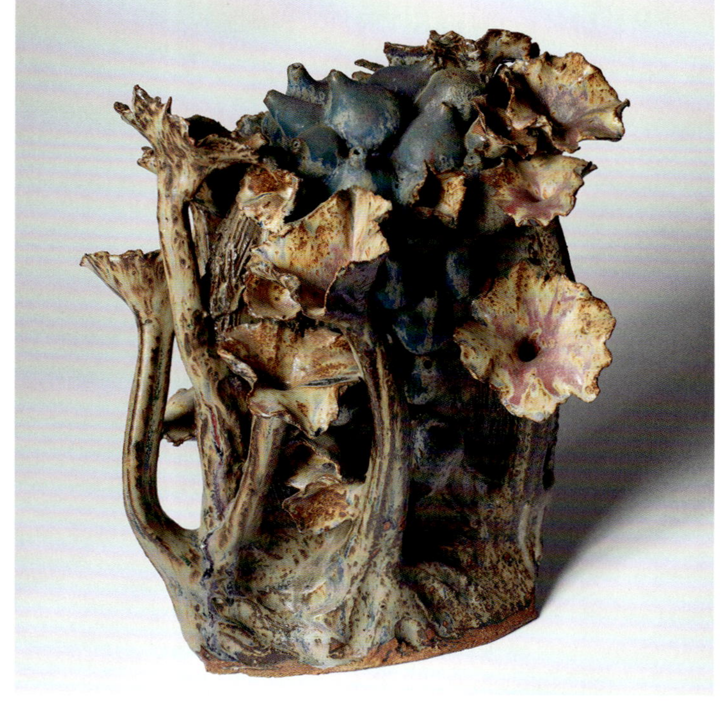

GOLDENBERG, LENNY 1937 –

Ceramicist

1959-62 Vancouver School of Art, Montreal

1963- Own studio workshop on Bornholm
www.goldenbergceramics.dk

Lenny Goldenberg (LG) was born in Montreal, but has had a workshop on Bornholm since 1963. In his early work he was influenced by Bernard Leach, whom he met, and in particular by Leach's Japan-influenced aesthetics; later, via pop art, his work developed towards topical contemporary issues. Both functional objects and unique works have been produced from his studio over the years. A particular category of late consists of ceramic books, made in stoneware with many types of text and illustrations, printed digitally in iron oxide and transferred to the ceramic book page.

The work in the museum's collection takes as subject the artist's own *métier*, ceramic art. The object shows a passage in a ceramic reference book, dealing with samples of glazes where letters are pressed into the wet clay and after pre-firing are filled with ceramic colours **(176)**.

176. Object, 1990. *Keramisk håndbog* (Ceramic reference book)
Stoneware; pressed into a mould, modelled, relief print, brush-painted, fired at 1280°. H 13.5 x W 45 x D 31. Mark: 'LENNY GOLDENBERG' stamped on side.
Mus.no. 221/2006
ACQUISITION: Lenny Goldenberg

176 221/2006

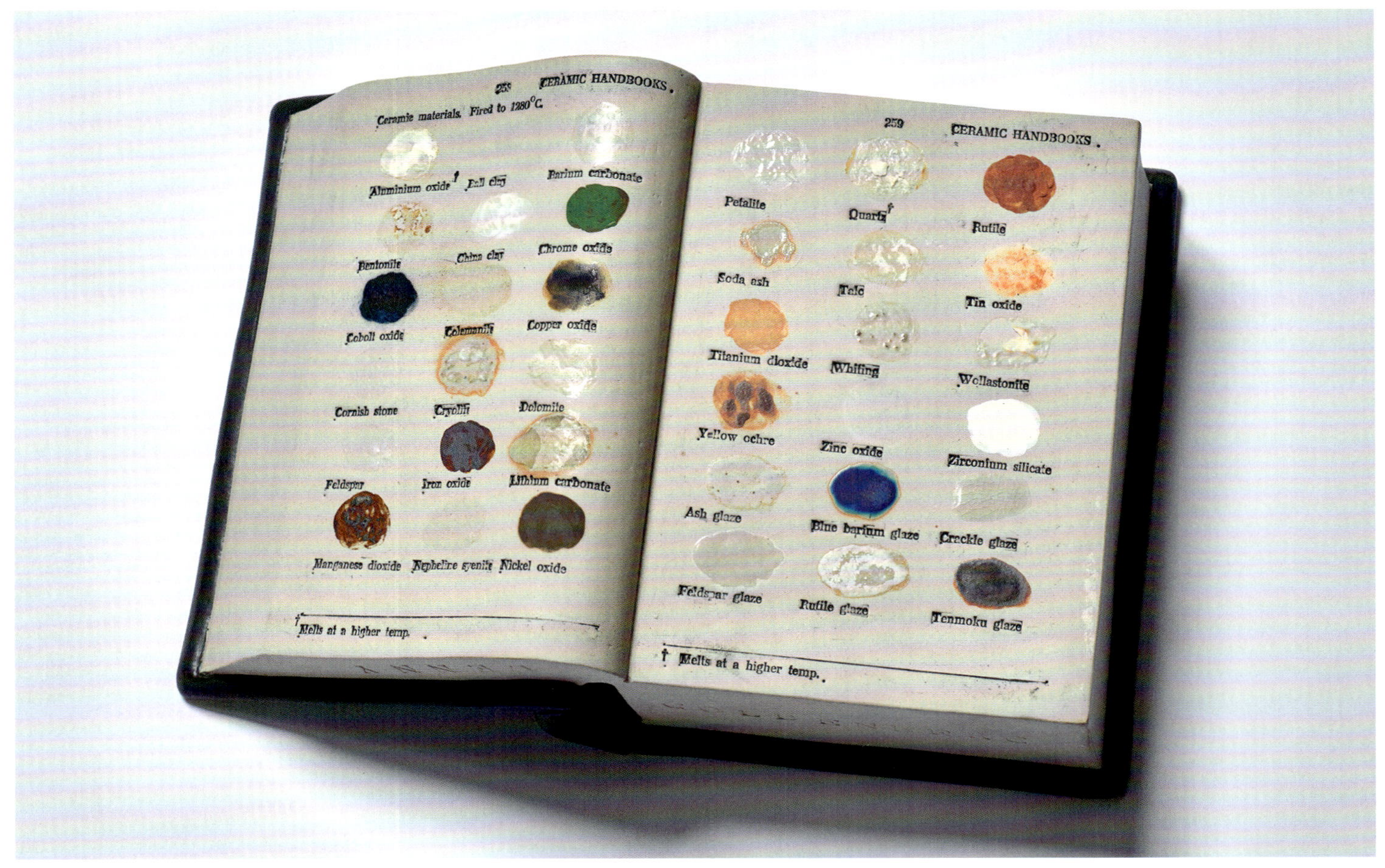

HANSEN, BENTE 1943 –

Ceramicist

1960-64	Kunsthåndværkerskolen
1964-70	Bing & Grøndahl, employed as artist
1968-	Own studio workshop, Copenhagen
1978-82	The Royal Porcelain Factory, employed as artist
1992-96	Danmarks Designskole, Head of Ceramics and Glass
2001	Alfred University, College of Ceramics, USA, Visiting Associated Professor
	www.bentehansen.dk

Bente Hansen (BH) is among her generation's most important ceramicists and masters sculptural form as few others do; her works centre around ceramic containers and include a long and impressive series of pots and other works in which BH analyses and revolves around the duality of inner and outer spatial relations. She has pursued this theme with its philosophical and meditative undercurrents through constant experimentation with expressions, materials, techniques and shapes, including her exquisite double pots. An exhibition at the museum in 2001, together with her husband, Ole Palsby, had the title '*VOID*', and the works exhibited explored the approach to creating shape in an artistic and searching form of work.

BH studied at Kunsthåndværkerskolen under the guidance of Richard Kjærgaard, and was thereby set on track to pursue the idealistically orientated work with functional ceramics that has been a recurrent theme in BH's work through the years. On completing her studies in 1964 BH was immediately employed as an artist working for Bing & Grøndahl, and with the factory's free and generous conditions for artists she was able both to work with industrial production and to develop her own free products. BH's talent was valued, and she and the factory gained appreciation and recognition at exhibitions. Her employment there lasted until 1970, but by 1968 BH had already established her own studio workshop and so had provided for herself the space and freedom to experiment and develop at her own pace.

BH's interest in functional household objects led to several projects, including, in 1975, '*PROJEKT 75*', in which a group of ten ceramicists collaborated in a programme aiming both to produce functional objects well-suited to industrial production and to create contacts with firms. As a consequence of this BH was employed as an artist at the Royal Porcelain Factory. BH worked there until 1982 and made vases, pots, etc. and unique pieces with a view to possible production. BH participated in two further projects concerning functional products; one was *Lærkestellet* (the Lark Service) in 1994 (see p. 346) and the other

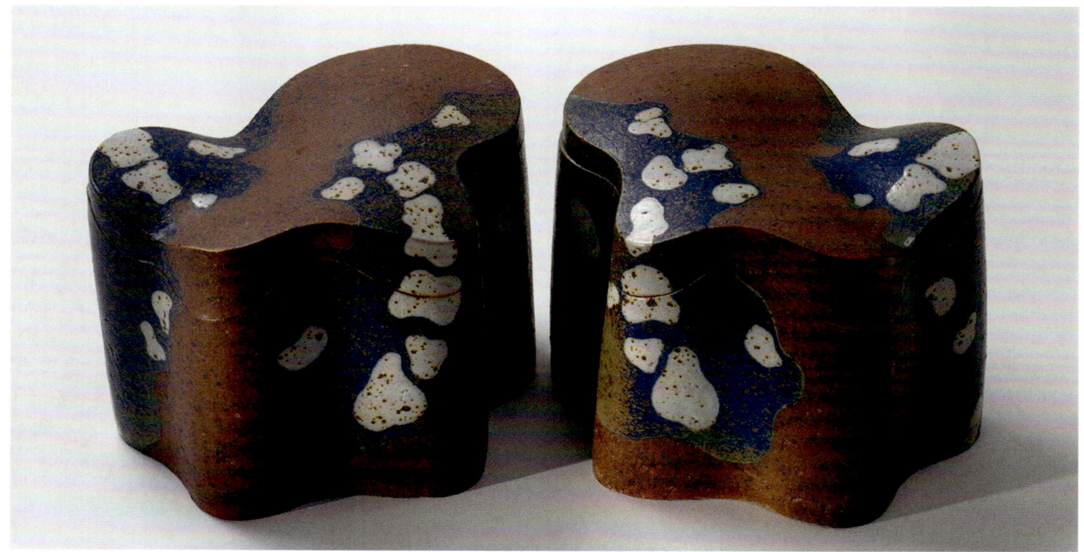

185 D 1550a-d

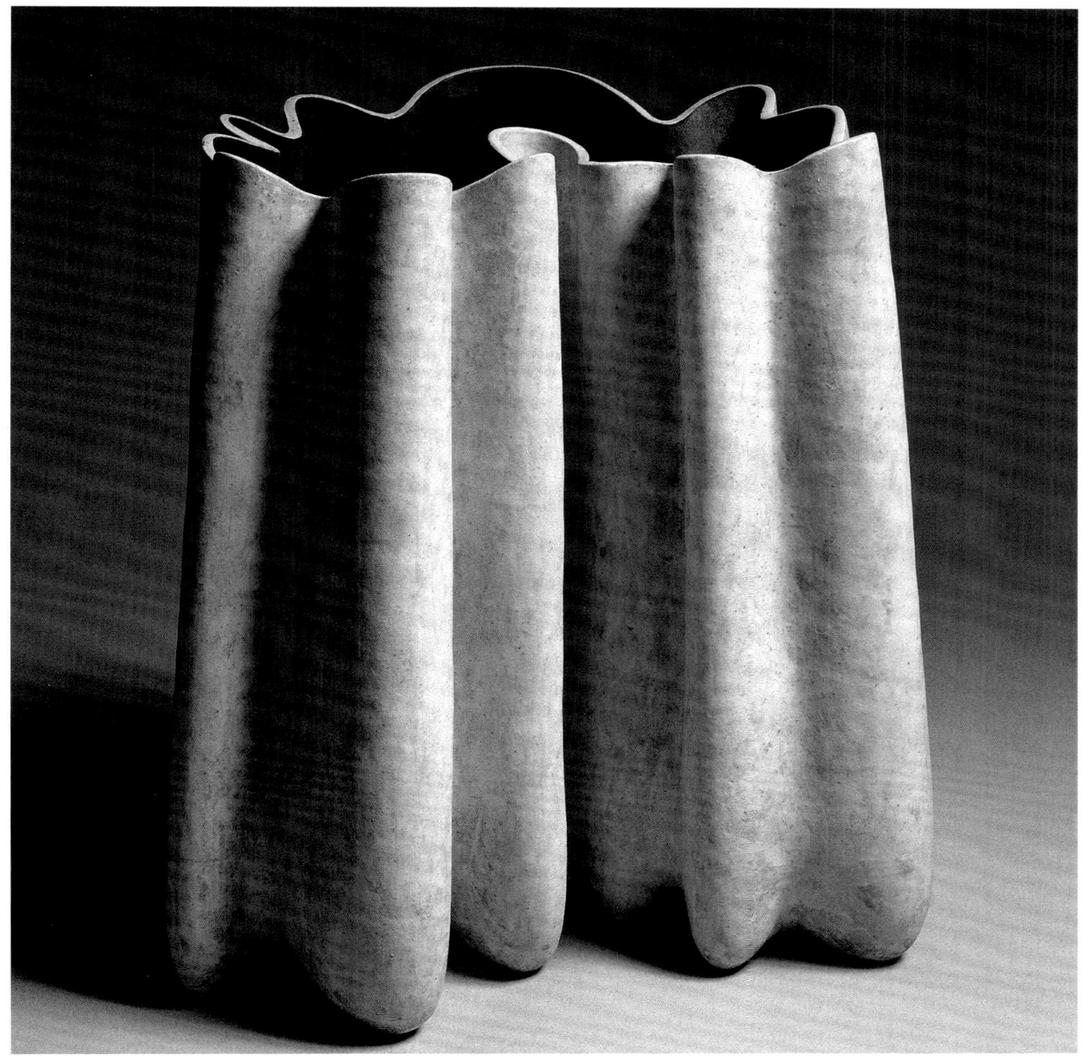

184 305/2004

Fremtidens stel (Tableware for the future) on the occasion of the Royal Porcelain Factory's 225th Jubilee, in the year 2000. For that project BH developed a 'table service for ready-made meals', and its well-designed components were later put into production by the firm of Stelton.

Among the functional objects that BH over time has returned to, is the sculptural teapot – an object that offers many challenges if it is to be beautiful, functional and a daily pleasure to use and look at. In the solo exhibition *The-Tid* (Tea-time) in Galleri Nørby in 1998 BH displayed a selection of six different teapots with cups, jug and sugar-bowl/tea-light holder. The teapots were given suggestive and amusing names, e.g. *The Hen*, *The Egg*, *The Duck* and *The Parrot*, and there was a relationship between the shape of several of the teapots and that of BH's modelled and decorated unique works, e.g. the pot **(178)** and the teapots *Oval vugge* (oval cradle) **(179,187)**.

The museum's collection of Danish studio ceramics contains 12 works by BH, all of them made in her own studio by her most frequently-used technique – stoneware, covered with slip and salt-glazed. The earliest of the works are two sculptural lidded pots from 1976 in an organic idiom with nature-inspired decoration **(185)**. From 1983 there is another lidded pot **(177)**, which is significantly different from the earlier ones. It is strict in shape, with straight sides, a slightly convex lid and a decoration of vertical stripes that unifies lid and corpus. The fine colourplay in the stripes is produced by layers of slip, and this points in the direction of the mastery achieved in subsequent years in geometric slip decoration on clear severely-shaped pots and bowls **(178,186)**. It was with those works in particular that BH won international recognition.

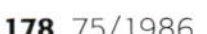

178 75/1986

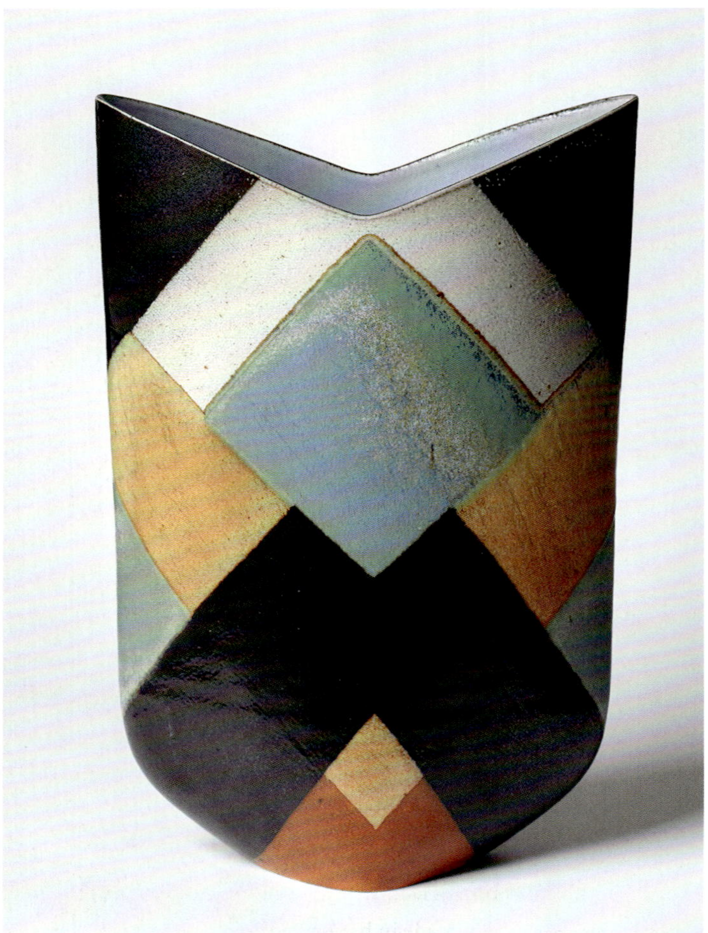

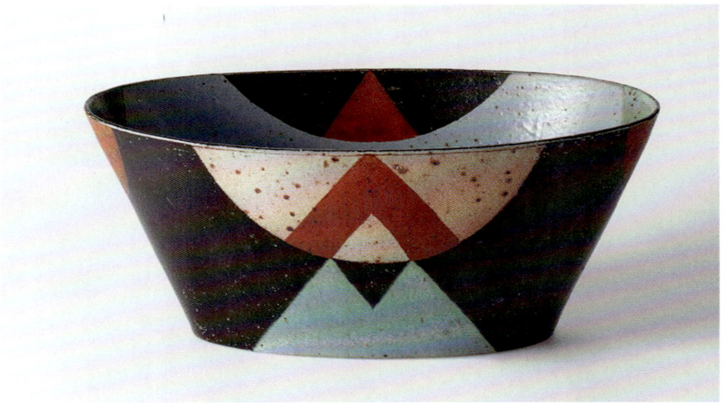

186 D1641

At the beginning of the 1990s, while BH was head of Ceramics and Glass at Danmarks Designskole, she began to develop a whole new type of work with strongly sculptural shapes, in which the sides of the pot bulge and fold in a wavy course around a dark-glazed interior hollow space. The pots are salt-glazed with fine surface structures and colour nuances. The museum has a fine work of this type from 1994 **(180)**, and another monumental and exquisitely modelled work, the curvaceous *Mæanderkrukken* from 2003, which has a matte white slip, fired at a low temperature in a salt kiln **(184)**. This tall slightly inward-sloping pot tightly encloses its black interior, with the contours emphasised by the white edge. Also from 2003 there are two large smooth monolithic pots, one black and one white, with matte surfaces. They are entitled *Hældende form* (Sloping form) and belong to a type of work that BH developed for the exhibition '*VOID*' in 2001. The shapes are copious and give a strong impression of gravity; the energy in the works emanates from the black interior, which like the mystical 'black holes' in space attract and trap all that comes near **(183)**.

BH has had a long career path with many important roles, responsible positions and distinctions; she has taught and taken high positions in the international professional context. She has participated in exhibitions around the world and her work is represented in leading museums. In Denmark BH exhibits on a continuous basis with the group *Keramiske Veje*, which she helped to set up in 1984, and since 1999 she has been a member of the artists' group *CORNER*.

177. Lidded pot, 1983

Stoneware, salt-glazed; thrown, shaped, slip, fired at 1300°. H 21.5 x W 19.
Mark: 'BH 83' painted on base. Mus.no. 172a-b/1984.
ACQUISITION: *Efterårsudstillingen*, 1984, Charlottenborg. Donation from *Finansieringsinstituttet for Industri og Håndværks Jubilæumslegat*. See: *Brændpunkter*, 1990

178. Pot, 1985

Stoneware, salt-glazed; thrown, cut, slip, fired at 1300°. H 37 x W 12.
Mark: 'BH 85' painted on base. Mus.no. 75/1986
ACQUISITION: *Keramiske Veje*, 1985, Den Frie. Donation from *Kunstindustrimuseets Venner*

179. Teapot, 1990

Stoneware, salt-glazed; slip, cast, fired at 1300°. H 19.5 x W 29.
Mark: 'BH 90' painted on base. Mus.no. 247a-b/1990
ACQUISITION: *Design – håndværk eller industri*, 1990, Den Frie.
See: *The-tid*, 1998

180 7/1994

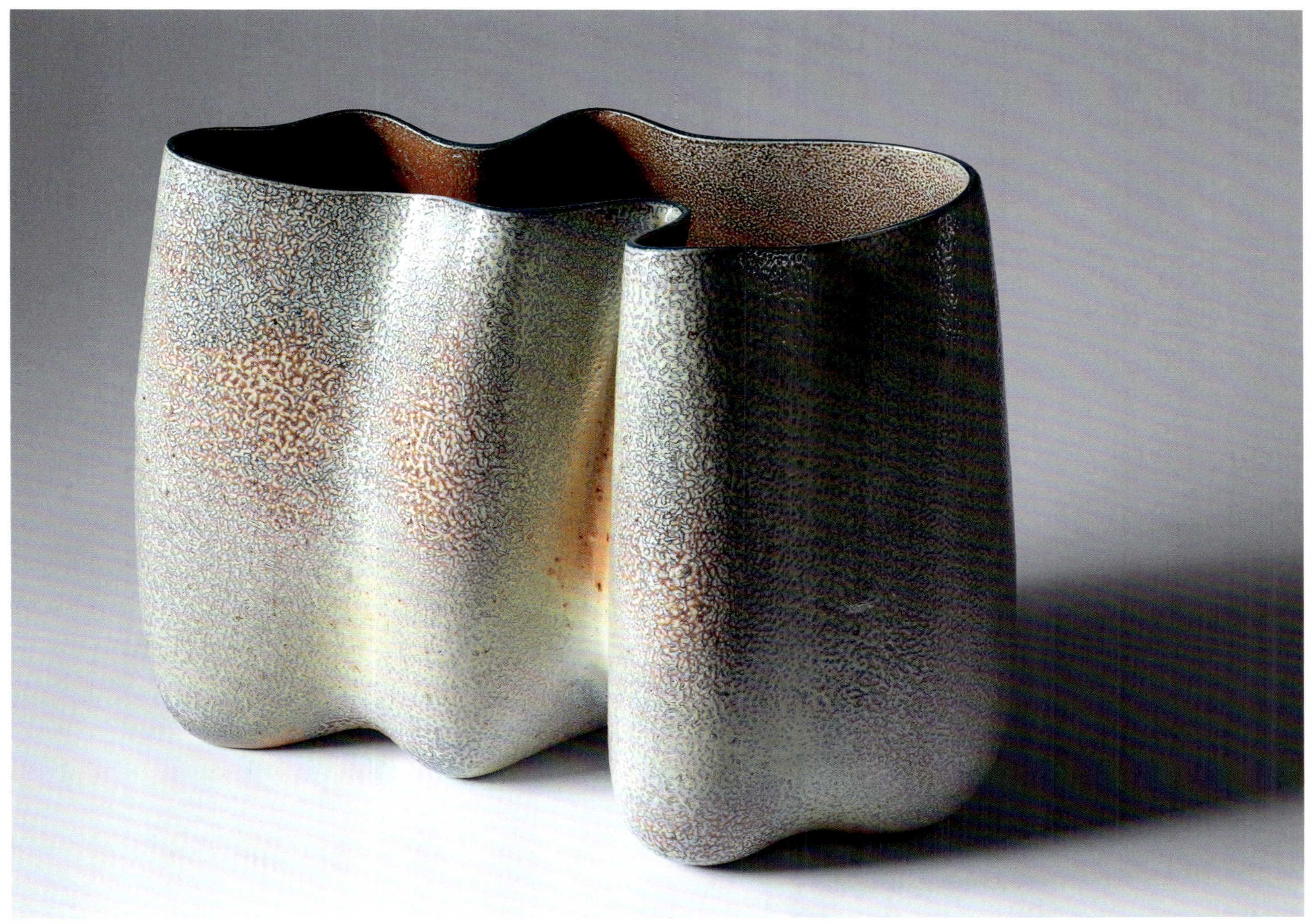

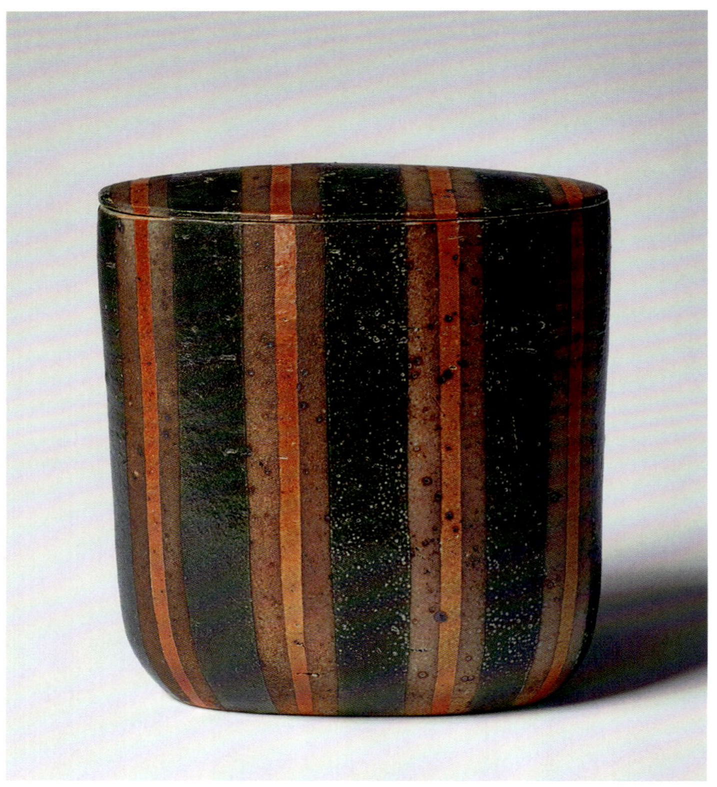

180. Pot, 1994. *Mæanderkrukke* (Meander pot)
Stoneware, salt-glazed; modelled, slip, fired at 1300°. H 37.5 x W 44.
Mark: 'BH 94' painted on base. Mus.no. 7/1994.
ACQUISITION: *Ler*, 1994, Kunstmuseum Trapholt

181. Pot, 1996
Stoneware, salt-glazed; modelled, slip, fired at 1300°. H 68.5 x W 53.
Mark: 'BH 96' painted on base. Mus.no. 130/1998
ACQUISITION: Galleri Nørby, Copenhagen. Donation from *Politikens Fond*

182. Teapot, 1998. *Ægget* (The egg)
Stoneware, salt-glazed; cast, slip, fired at 1300°. H 15 x W 28.
Mark: 'BH 98' painted on base. Mus.no. 13a-b/1999
ACQUISITION: *The-tid*, 1998, Galleri Nørby, Copenhagen

183. Two sculptures, 2003. *Hældende form* (Sloping form)
Stoneware; modelled, slip, fired in a salt kiln at 1280°. H 53 x W 50 x D 32.
Mark: 'BH 99' painted on base. Mus.no. 204a-b/2003
ACQUISITION: Bente Hansen. Donation from *Kulturstyrelsen og Kunstindustrimuseets Venner*

177 172a-b/1984

187 D 1733 **179** 247a-b/1990

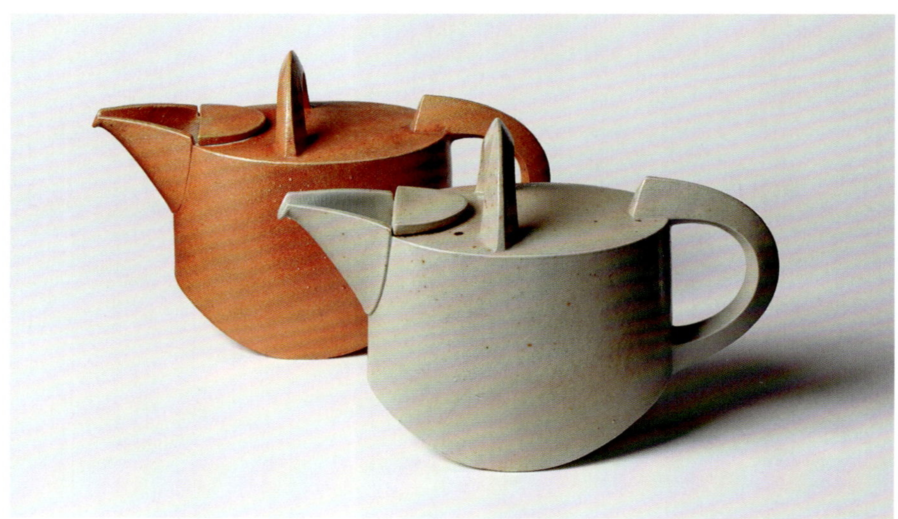

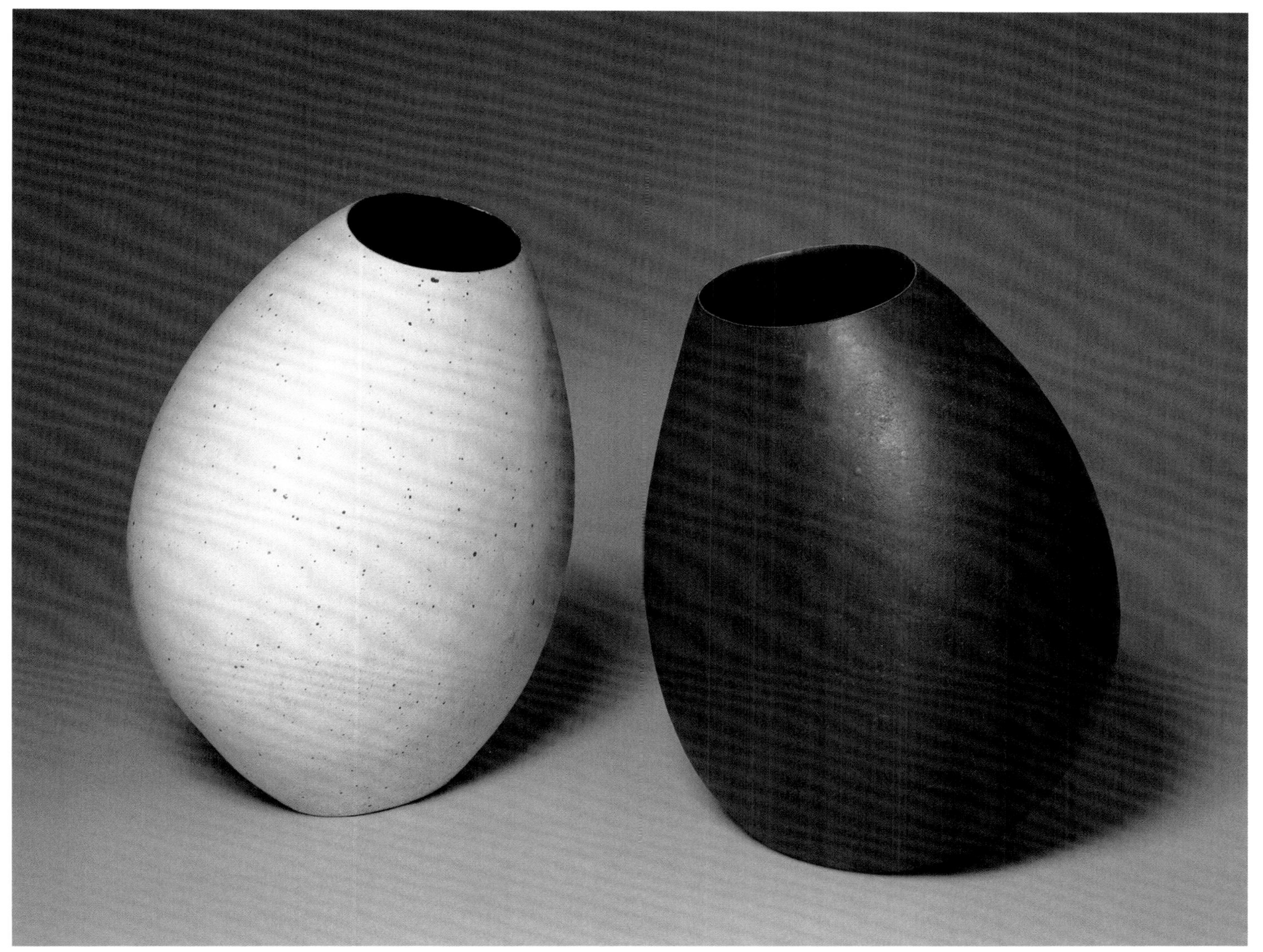

183 204a-b/2003

184. Pot, 2003. *Mæanderkrukke* (Meander pot)

Stoneware; modelled, slip, fired in a salt kiln at 1280°. H 64 x W 46. Mark: none. Mus.no. 305/2004

ACQUISITION: Galleri Nørby, 2003, Copenhagen. Donation from *Augustinus Fonden og L. F. Foghts Fond*

185. Two lidded pots, 1976

Stoneware, salt-glazed; thrown, shaped, matte slip, fired at 1300°. H 20.9 x W 24.5. Mark: 'Bente 1976' inscribed on base. Mus.no. D 1550a-d

ACQUISITION: On deposit from *Statens Kunstfond*, 1982

186. Bowl, 1985

Stoneware, salt-glazed; thrown, modelled, slip, fired at 1300°. H 16 x W 37.5. Mark: 'BH 85' painted on base. Mus.no. D 1641

ACQUISITION: On deposit from *Statens Kunstfond*, 1987

187. Teapot, 1990

Porcelain, salt-glazed; cast, slip, fired at 1300°. H 19.5 x W 29. Mark: none. Mus.no. D 1733

ACQUISITION: On deposit from *Statens Kunstfond*, 1995. See: *The-tid*, 1998

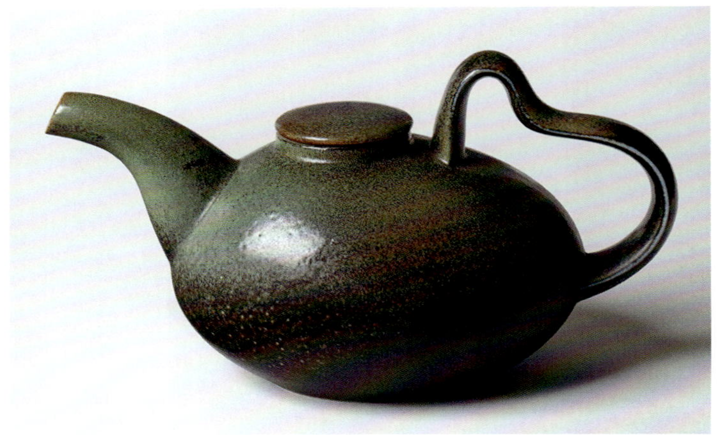

182 13a-b/1999

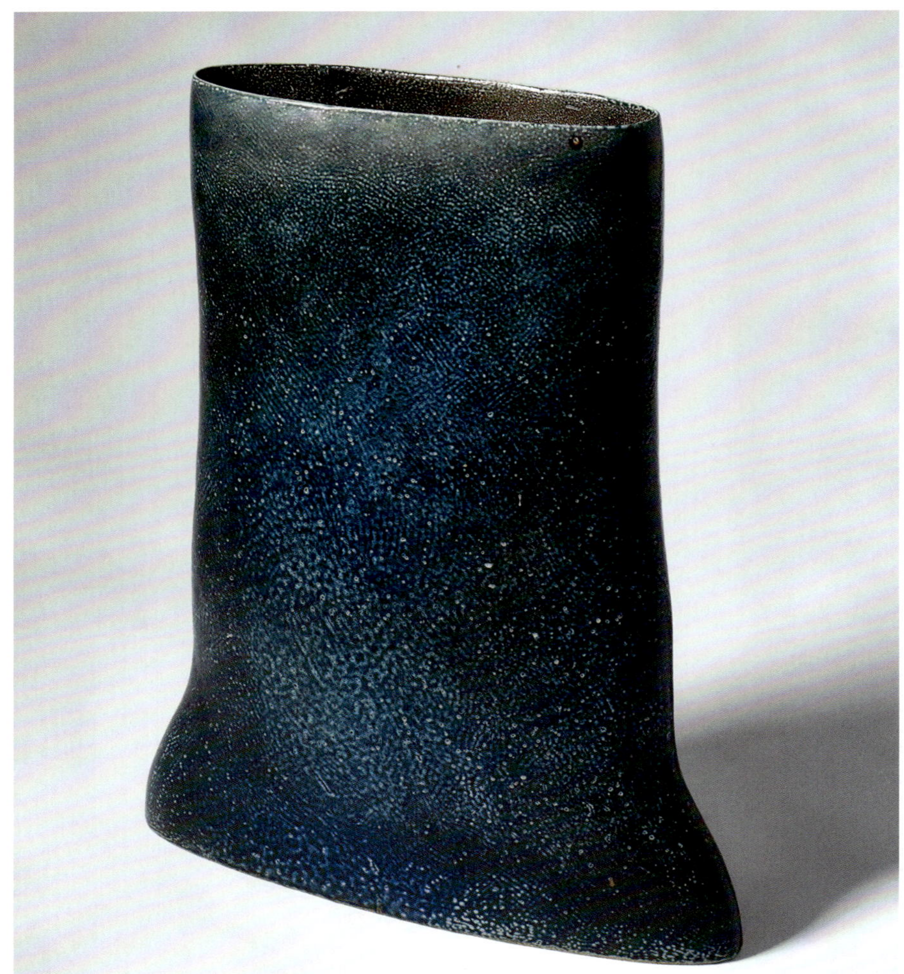

181 130/1998

HANSEN, FLEMMING TVEDE 1966 –

Ceramicist

1990-95 Danmarks Designskole, Ceramics
1994 Glasgow School of Art, Scotland, Ceramics
1995-05 Own studio workshop, Copenhagen
1997-98 Shigaraki Ceramic Cultural Park, Japan
1999-2000 Multimedia Institute (MMI), School of Architecture of the Royal Danish Academy of Fine Arts, Copenhagen
2005-06 Danmarks Designskole, teacher
2006-10 Danmarks Designskole, Design, Ph.D.
2011-15- The Royal Danish Academy of Fine Arts, Schools of Architecture, Design and Conservation, Post-Doctoral Research Fellow; 2015- Associate Professor, Product Design
www. flemmingtvede.dk

Flemming Tvede Hansen (FTH) studied at Danmarks Designskole, specialising in Glass and Ceramics, supplemented with studies in multimedia design – a combination that formed the departure-point for his research into the interplay between digital technology and ceramic material, in an interactive experimental process about development of form. Ceramic material and the ceramicist's knowledge and skill in processing are an important activating element in the design process.

Before his research studies at Danmarks Designskole, which concluded with his Ph.D. thesis on 3D digital design ('Materialedreven 3d digital formgivning') in 2010 and his subsequent employment at the Design School, first as teacher and from 2015 as Associate Professor, FTH had his own workshop. He became known as an experimental

188 121/2009

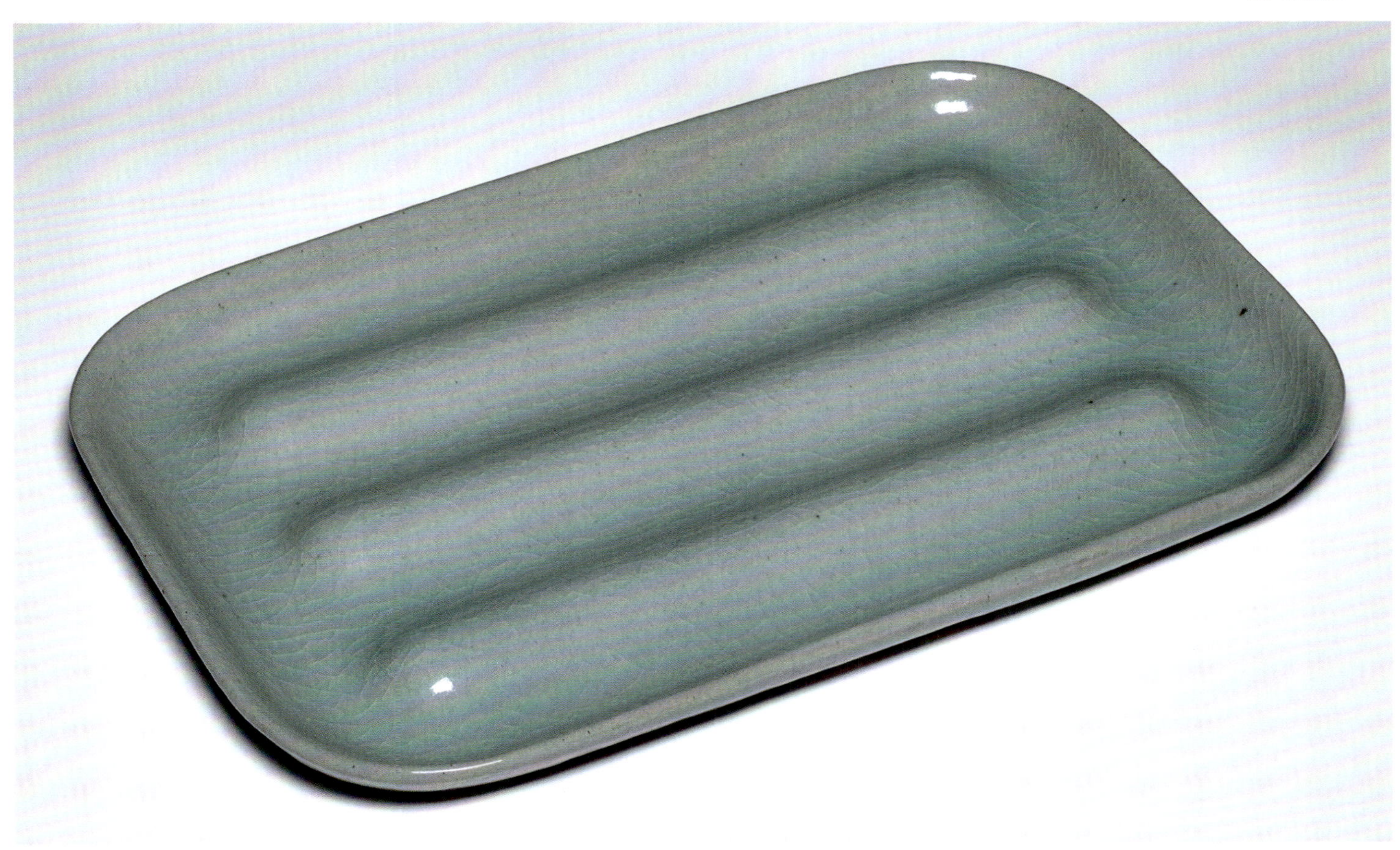

and talented ceramicist and won the Danish Biennale prize in 1997, with a subsequent exhibition in the museum in 1999, and went on to win the Triennale prize in 2000 at Trapholt Museum.

FTH belongs to the group of ceramicists who exhibited in 'Udstillingssted for Ny Keramik' (Exhibition Centre for New Ceramics), in Copenhagen, where for example in 1997 in conjunction with Gitte Jungersen he held the interesting exhibition '*Deform 1*', which illustrated the de-structuring of a series of spherical shapes in clay under the effect of heat while being fired in a ceramic kiln. The aim was to investigate sculptural expression on the basis of the chemical process during firing. A further exhibition, '*Deform 2*' was held in 1998 in Kyoto, Japan. In the same year FTH exhibited in Galleri Nørby, Copenhagen, a series of powerfully effective dishes in stoneware that were shaped on the same module, with rounded relief-lines on the base, but in varying sizes, and all with completely covering slightly crackled celadon glaze, in pale pastel colours. The museum has a very large dish acquired from that exhibition **(188)**.

In 2003 the exhibition group *NEW DANISH CERAMICS* was created; its nine members joined forces to promote the recent work of Danish ceramicists through international exhibitions. They themselves emphasise that it is characteristic of this group, born in the 1960s, to have a research-based approach to their work, involving systematic and in-depth experiments with materials, methods and forms of expression. FTH belongs to this group, which held its first exhibition in the museum, and it is exactly that approach to ceramics that has shaped his career both as a ceramicist and as a researcher.
See: Flemming Tvede Hansen, *Materialedreven 3d digital formgivning*. Danmarks Designskole, 2010

188. Dish, 1998

Stoneware, celadon, crackle-glazed; modelled, shaped over a mould, reduction-fired at 1280°. H 4 x W 45.5 x L 67. Mark: stamped 'FTH'.
Mus.no. 121/2009
ACQUISITION: Galleri Nørby, 1998, Copenhagen.
Donation from *Ny Carlsbergfondet*

HANSEN, JØRGEN 1945 –

Ceramicist

1965-72	Attached to workshops in France, England and Canada
1972-	Own studio workshop, Tirstrup; 1989- Hyllested, E Jutland
1989-	Guest teacher at Kunsthåndværkerskolen in Kolding, Glass and Ceramics, and Keramikskolen, Bornholm, Kunstakademiet in Reykjavik and elsewhere
1992-93	Aarhus Kunstakademi, instructor
	www.jorgenhansen.com

Jørgen Hansen (JH) has worked with clay ever since his childhood, and threw his first pots in a potter's workshop when he was 13 years old. After he left Gymnasium he travelled far and wide with clay as his passport and worked in ceramic workshops, with reputed ceramicists and artists in Brittany and later in the well-known ceramic centre at La Borne, where the tradition of firing stoneware goes back to the Middle Ages. In the years that followed he travelled to England and thanks to his skilled craftsmanship worked for a time with Bernard Leach, where he met Soshi Hamada and encountered Japanese ceramic culture, which came to take root, alongside the Danish earthenware tradition, in his subsequent work. From there JH went on to Ireland, Spain and Canada, where for a time he had a workshop in Nova Scotia.

On return to Denmark in 1972 JH started his own studio workshop near Ebeltoft, and through the years he developed an extensive range of workshop products, including animal sculptures, but first and foremost he has carried out many public commissions, not least the monumental location-specific fired sculptures – 21 of them in all – which JH and assistants have made and fired in Denmark and elsewhere in the world since 1994.

At the '*Biennale for kunsthåndværk og design 07*' the museum acquired the work *Pisces*, which is part of a series of 3 large sculptural fish, made in 2007 taking inspiration from the coelacanth (also known as the 'The blue fossil') **(189)**. JH's nearly-black fish is like an ur-type that is stranded in a strange world where it is doomed to perish.

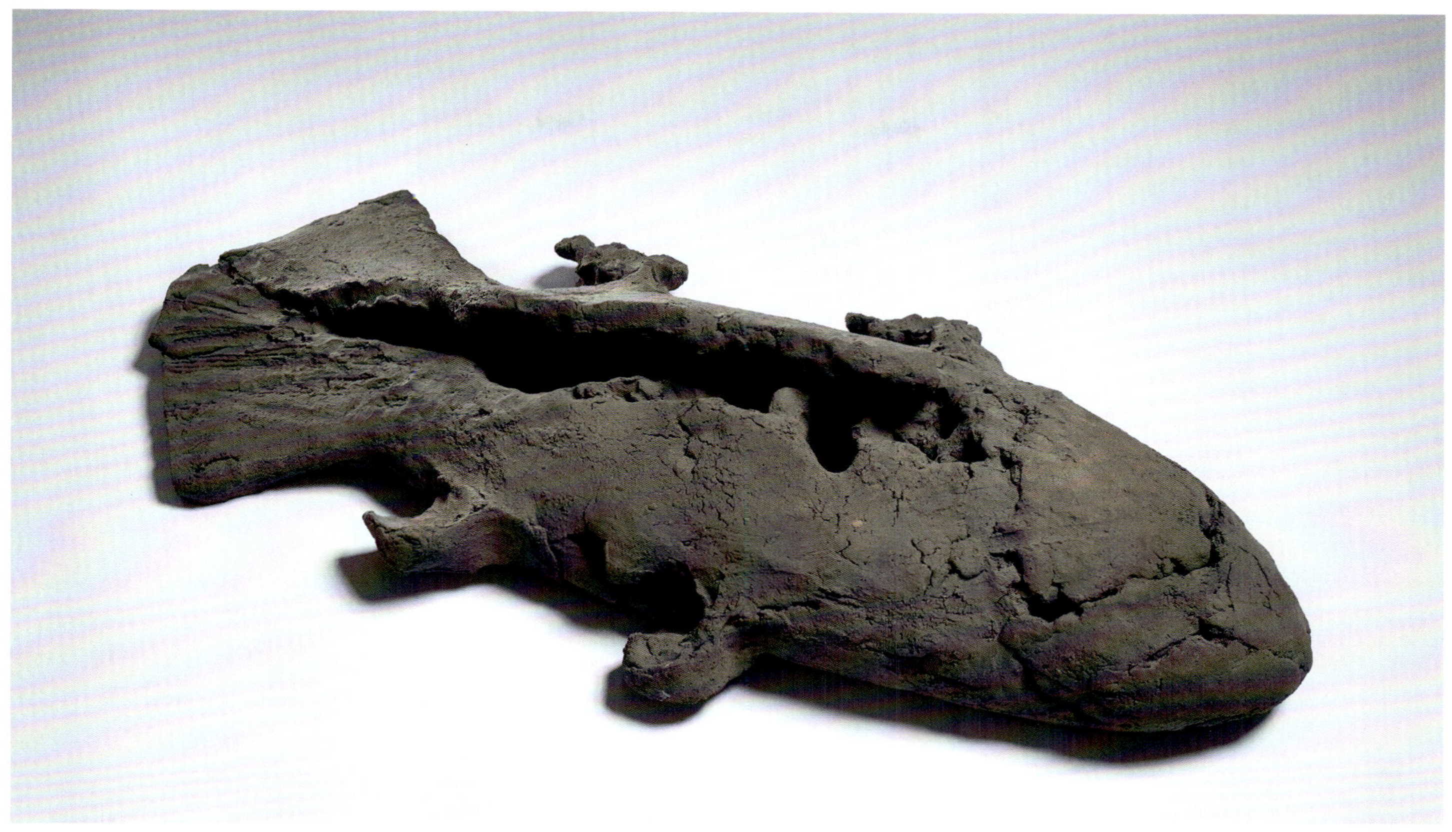

189 387/2007

JH has been awarded many bursaries and distinctions, including the first prize in 'European Ceramics 99', Westerwald Keramikmuseum, Germany, and in 2008 the Jury's Special Prize at the 7th Mashiko Competition, Japan.

189. Sculpture, 2007. *Pisces*

Earthenware; modelled, fired twice, the second time as a black-firing at 1040°. L 110 x W 45. Mark: none. Mus.no. 387/2007. ACQUISITION: *Biennalen*, 2007, Trapholt. See: *Biennalen for kunsthåndværk og design 07*, 2007

HARRISON, ANNE MARIE 1928 – 2005

Ceramicist

1940	Knabstrup Teglværk, Sealand
1949	Bernard Leach, St Ives, Cornwall
1945-51	Knabstrup Teglværk
1950	Completed studies at Kunsthåndværkerskolen
1952	National Diploma of Industrial Design, Stoke-on-Trent, England
1963-	Own studio workshop, Holbæk

Anne Marie Harrison (AMH) studied at Kunsthåndværkerskolen in Copenhagen. In 1949 she spent time at Bernard Leach's studio in England, and there became interested in Japanese and Chinese ceramics; she continued studying in England in Stoke-on-Trent, historically well-known for its ceramics. AMH kept in contact with the Leach family and for a time David Leach's younger son, Jeremy, worked at her studio in Holbæk.

Before the time she spent in England AMH was attached to Knabstrup Brickworks; she established her own studio workshop in Holbæk in 1963. AMH was known for her skill and had a fine production of robust functional articles in stoneware **(190)**, but she also worked with porcelain. In 1974 the museum acquired two works by AMH at an exhibition she held with Tove Reiff and the ceramicist Erik Reiff, with whom she had a shared interest in Oriental ornamentation, as is apparent from the fine calligraphy of the brush-painted decoration on the museum's porcelain bowl **(191)**. Because of an injury AMH had to give up ceramics and worked with patchwork instead.

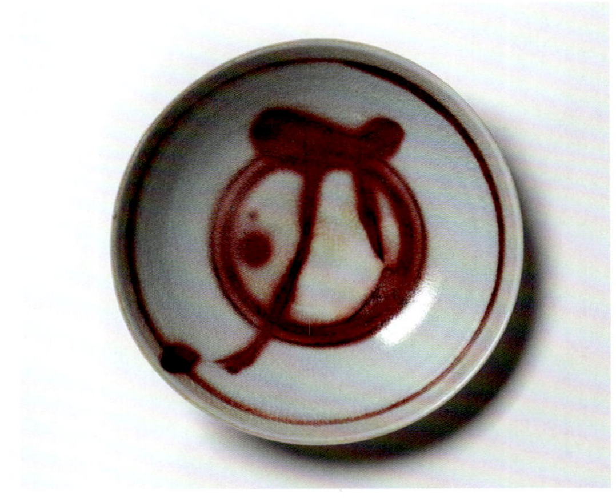

191 216/1974

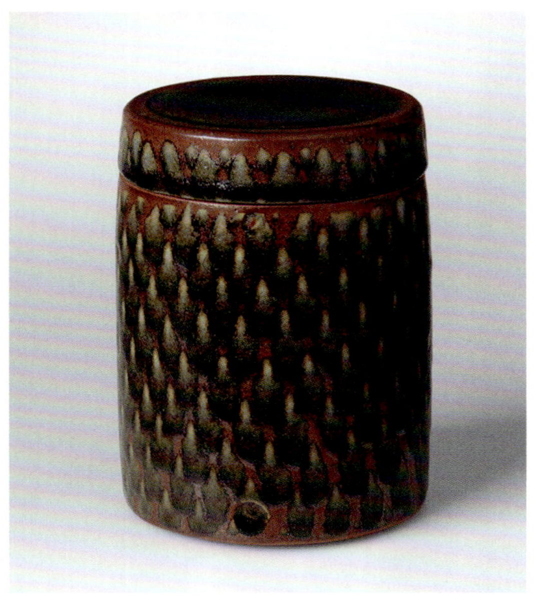

190 215/1974

190. Lidded pot, 1974

Stoneware, glazed; thrown, decorated. H 12.6 x Diam 9.5. Mark: Monogram stamped on foot. Mus.no. 215/1974

ACQUISITION: *Anne Marie Harrison, Erik Reiff og Tove Reiff*, 1974, Butterupgaard, Holbæk. Donation from *Kunstindustrimuseets 50-års Jubilæumslegat*

191. Bowl, 1974

Porcelain, crackle-glazed; thrown, brush-painted decoration. H 4.4 x Diam 15.6. Mark: Monogram stamped on base. Mus.no. 216/1974

ACQUISITION: *Anne Marie Harrison, Erik Reiff og Tove Reiff*, 1974, Butterupgaard, Holbæk. Donation from *Kunstindustrimuseets 50-års Jubilæumslegat*

HEIDE, DORTE SCHIERUP 1942 – 2005

Ceramicist

1961-65 Kunsthåndværkerskolen

1968-69 The Royal Porcelain Factory

1975- Own studio workshop, Aarhus

Dorte Schierup Heide (DSH) belonged to the generation of talented ceramicists who qualified from Kunsthåndværkerskolen at the beginning of the 1960s; after a brief period at the Royal Porcelain Factory she moved with her family to Aarhus and set up a workshop there in 1975. By the time of her death in 2005 DSH had won considerable recognition, both in Denmark and internationally, for her ceramic work. SH was selected to participate in several official Danish Design exhibitions in the 1970s and 80s, and her classical and restrained pots and vase-shapes in blue/white tones struck a fine harmony with the style-idiom of Danish Design.

Over the years DSH perfected her ceramic and graphic expressions in many works which superficially have a certain common character, but on closer examination they reveal wide variations in their decoration – which often covers the whole surface, with changing rhythms and intensity in the complex line-patterns that were traced out in order to achieve a strongly simplified effect. The decoration is carried out in coloured slip, usually cobalt-based, ranging from pale blue to blue-black, with hatching or inlaid lines on the surface, often in a combination of those techniques, and is subsequently glazed with transparent ash glazes. DSH found inspiration for this decoration in nature, and in order to obtain optimal conditions for the decoration she preferred the simple form of the pot, which she always threw in pale stoneware-clay.

The museum has four of DSH's works, and they show the variety in her decorative treatment of forms of pot **(192-195)**; she had pots displayed in many exhibitions and they have been acquired by influential museums in Denmark and elsewhere. DSH was also awarded a number of bursaries and distinctions.

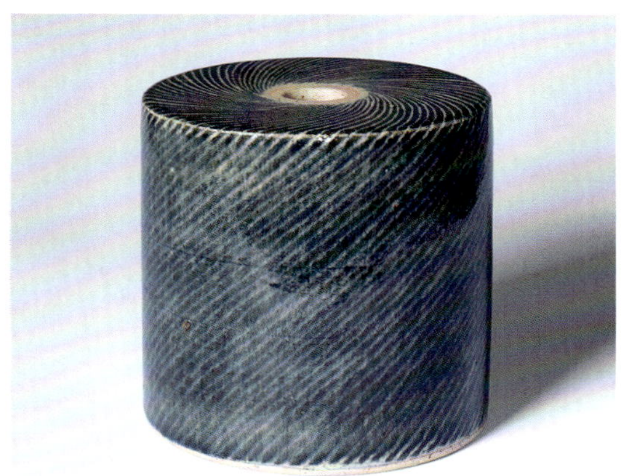

192 90/1985

192. Vase, 1985

Stoneware, slip, clear-ash-glazed; thrown, line ornamentation. H 18 x W 17.8.

Mark: 'Dorte S. Heide' inscribed on base. Mus.no. 90/1985

ACQUISITION: *Hanne Vedel – Dorte S. Heide*, 1985, Galleri for kunsthåndværk, Toftegårds Kunsthandel, Copenhagen.

See: *Brændpunkter,* 1990. Dybdahl, L., 1997

193 93/2002

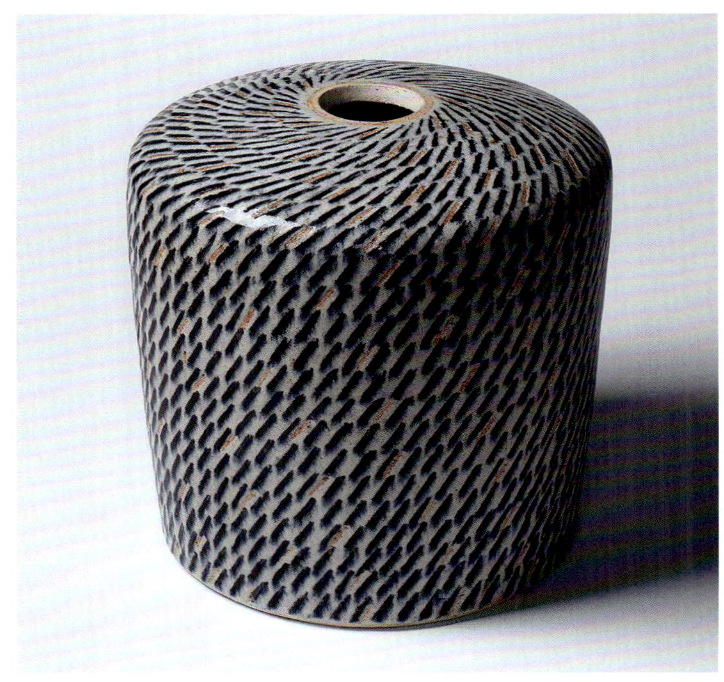

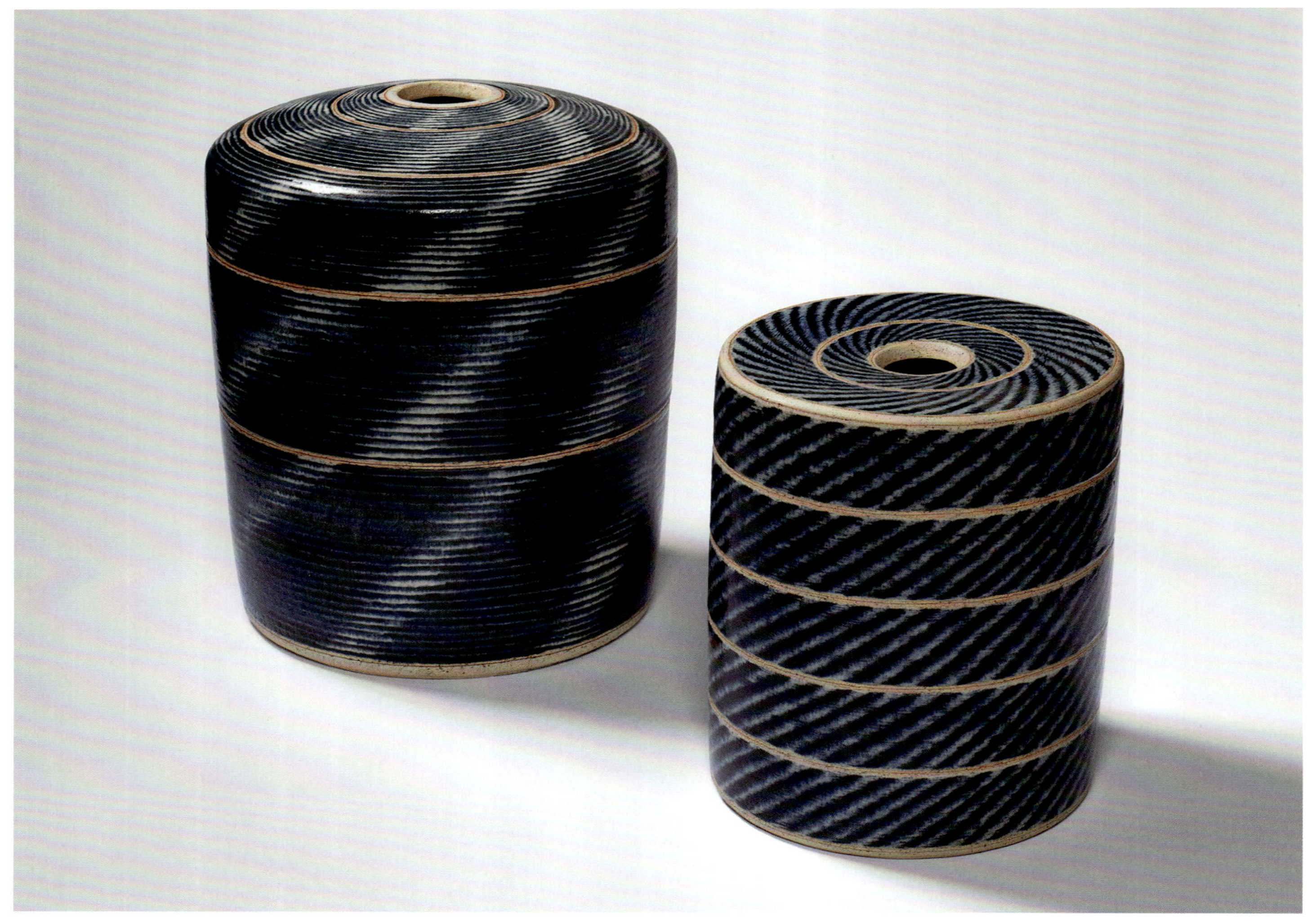

195 D 1644 **194** 332/2007

193. Pot, 2002

Stoneware, slip, iron-oxide, clear ash-glazed; thrown, inlaid line ornamentation. H 28 x Diam 30. Mark: Signature inscribed on base. Mus.no. 93/2002
ACQUISITION: Galleri Nørby, Copenhagen. Donation from *Kunstindustri-museets Venner*

194. Pot, 1990

Stoneware, slip, clear ash-glazed; thrown, line ornamentation. H 65 x Diam 50. Mark: 'Dorte Heide' inscribed on base with butterfly mark. Mus.no. 332/2007
ACQUISITION: Hans-Henrik Schierup. Donation from *Højesteretssagfører C. L. Davids Legat for Slægt og Venner*

195. Pot, 1986

Stoneware, slip, glazed; thrown, hatched ornamentation. H 40 x Diam 33. Mark: 'Dorte S. Heide' inscribed on base. Mus.no. D 1644
ACQUISITION: On deposit from *Statens Kunstfond*, 1987

HERLUFSDATTER, MARIANNE 1931 –

Painter, ceramicist

1949-50	The Royal Danish Academy of Fine Arts, School of Painting
1951	The Royal Swedish Academy of Arts, Stockholm
1952-70	Studio workshop shared with Lars Thirslund, Birkerød, Sealand
1970	Moved to Sweden

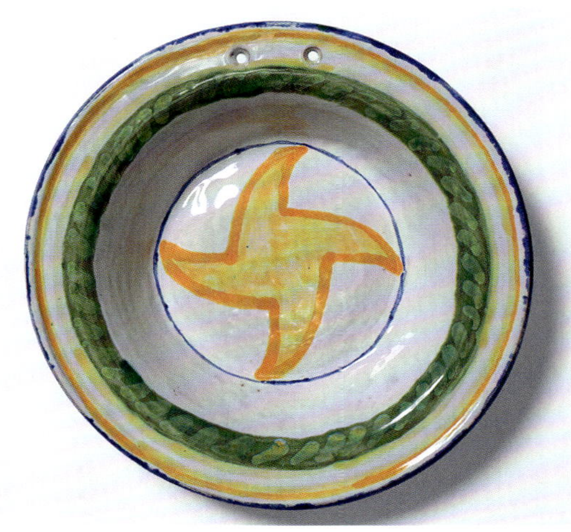

196 68/1956

Marianne Herlufsdatter (MH) studied as a painter at the Art Academies in Copenhagen and Stockholm, but after her marriage to ceramicist Lars Thirslund in 1951 she dedicated herself to ceramics. MH has worked mostly with glazed and stamped-decorated earthenware in the form of bowls, vases, dishes and pots. MH's work features in particular what are referred to as 'wall plates' with two holes in the rim intended to be used for suspension; the surface is thus decorated for display, often with a motif in relief like the stylised bird on the museum's example. This typical dish is glazed on both sides with white tin glaze and the surface and rim are decorated with coloured oxides **(196)**.

196. Wall plate, 1956

Earthenware, glazed; thrown, two holes in the rim for suspension. H 8 x Diam 23. Mark: 'Marianne Herlufsdatter 10 + 56, Danmark, fugl i relief' underneath. Mus.no. 68/1956 ACQUISITION: *Trefoldigheden*, 1956, Copenhagen. Donation from *Statens 50-års Jubilæumslegat*

HERMANSEN, INGE MARIE BULLER 1945 –

Ceramicist

1961-65	Holbæk Lervarefabrik; Lillerød Lervarefabrik; Felix Møhl
1965	Own studio workshop
c.1985-	Dyngby, Odder, E Jutland
1994-2000	Courses at Århus Kunstakademi
2015	Retrospective exhibition in Odder Kunstsamling
	www.bullerhermansen.dk

Buller Hermansen (IMBH) belongs among the ceramicists who established a studio on the basis of a potter's training with solid know-how about working with clay, firing and production of glaze and slip. Her first workshop, from 1965, was in Ammendrup near Helsinge in N Sealand, and in the years that followed IMBH developed a hard-fired earthenware, glazed and/or covered with slip, in the classical potter's shapes with roots in ceramic folk art and with her own individual development of the inherited shapes and styles of decoration. IMBH began at an early stage to work with patterns and decoration, taking inspiration e.g. from her study years with Felix Møhl, but became

198 344/1989 **199** 304/1989

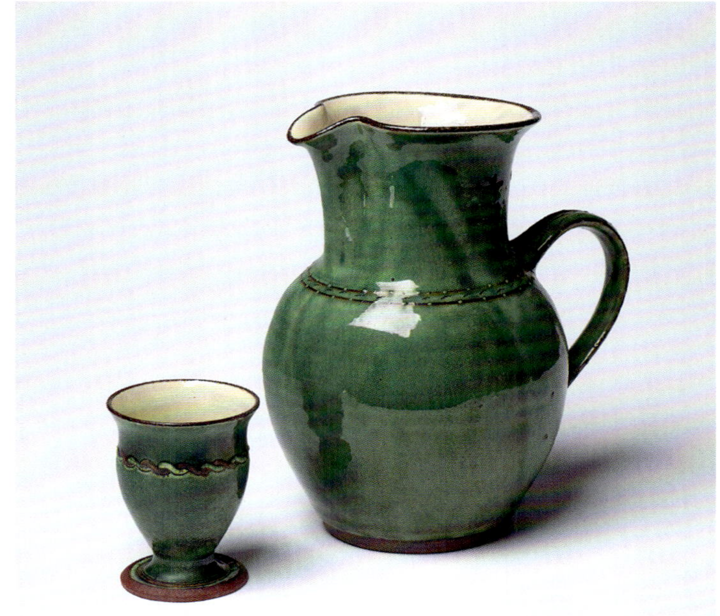

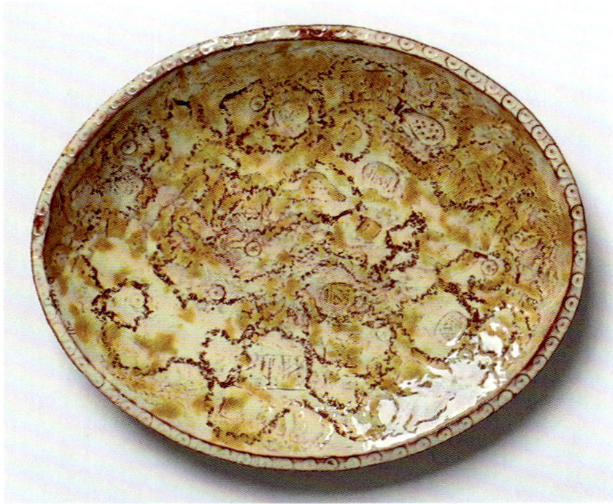

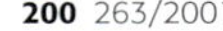

200 263/2001

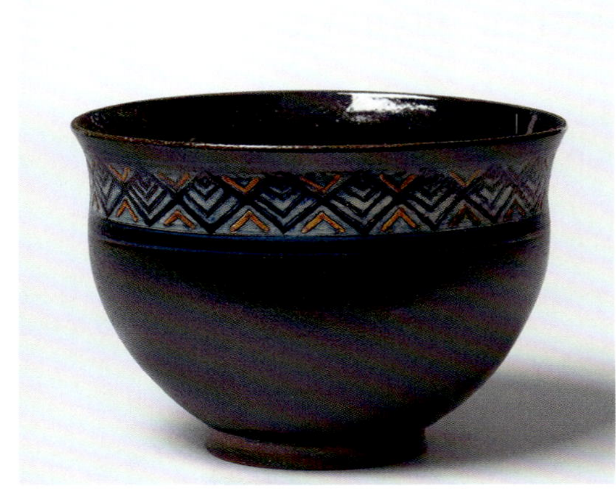

197 297/1989

increasingly independent in the painted tiles and tile pictures that have been a recurring feature in her work.

In the early 1970s IMBH moved to Bornholm, and contact with the rich ceramic environment there in the following decade was very significant for her work. Over the years IMBH has refined the thin-walled earthenware she uses for household objects with variations of decoration that are sometimes nature-inspired, or geometric or classical, and she has created a personal form of expression in her work.

From the mid 1980s IMBH has run her studio workshop in Dyngby, and since 2006 she has also experimented and worked there with wood-fired stoneware and porcelain. This development is in part the result of demands arising from several outdoor commissioned works, including the relief, nearly 6 m tall, from 2009, named *Livstræet* (Tree of life), in Skovbakkeskolen, Odder.

The museum owns four works by IMBH, three of them from 1988-89, which are good representative examples of IMBH's 'classical' functional ceramics **(197-199)**, while the oval dish from 2001 is an expression of a more abstract and freer form of work, with impressed and poetic traces and shapes in the pale yellow glaze that allow the red clay to shine through with a refined textural effect **(200)**.

197. Bowl, 1988

Earthenware, frit-glazed; thrown, covered with slip, painted using horn, incised decoration, reduction-fired at 1085-1100°. H 22 x Diam 24. Mark: 'Buller' inscribed on base. Mus.no. 297/1989

ACQUISITION: *Jysk sommer*, 1989, Kunstindustrimuseet. Donation from Ny Carlsberg Museumslegat. See: Dybdahl, L., 1997

198. Beaker, 1989

Earthenware, frit-glazed; thrown, slip, painted using horn, decorated with curved lines, reduction-fired at 1085-1100°. H 9.2 x Diam 7. Mark: 'Buller' inscribed on base. Mus.no. 344/1989

ACQUISITION: *Jysk sommer*, 1989, Kunstindustrimuseet

199. Jug, 1989. *Grøn kande* (Green jug)

Earthenware, frit-glazed; thrown, slip, painted using horn, fired at 1085-1100°. H 22. Mark: 'Buller' inscribed on base. Mus.no. 304/1989

ACQUISITION: *Jysk sommer*, 1989, Kunstindustrimuseet. Donation *from Statens 50-års Jubilæumslegat.* See: *Brændpunkter*, 1990

200. Dish, 2001

Earthenware, frit-glazed; modelled, fired at 1085-1100°. H 4 x W 33 x D 39. Mark: 'Buller 01' inscribed on base. Mus.no. 263/2001

ACQUISITION: Buller Hermansen. Donation from *Kunstindustrimuseets Venner*

HESSELHOLDT & MEJLVANG:

201 67/2006

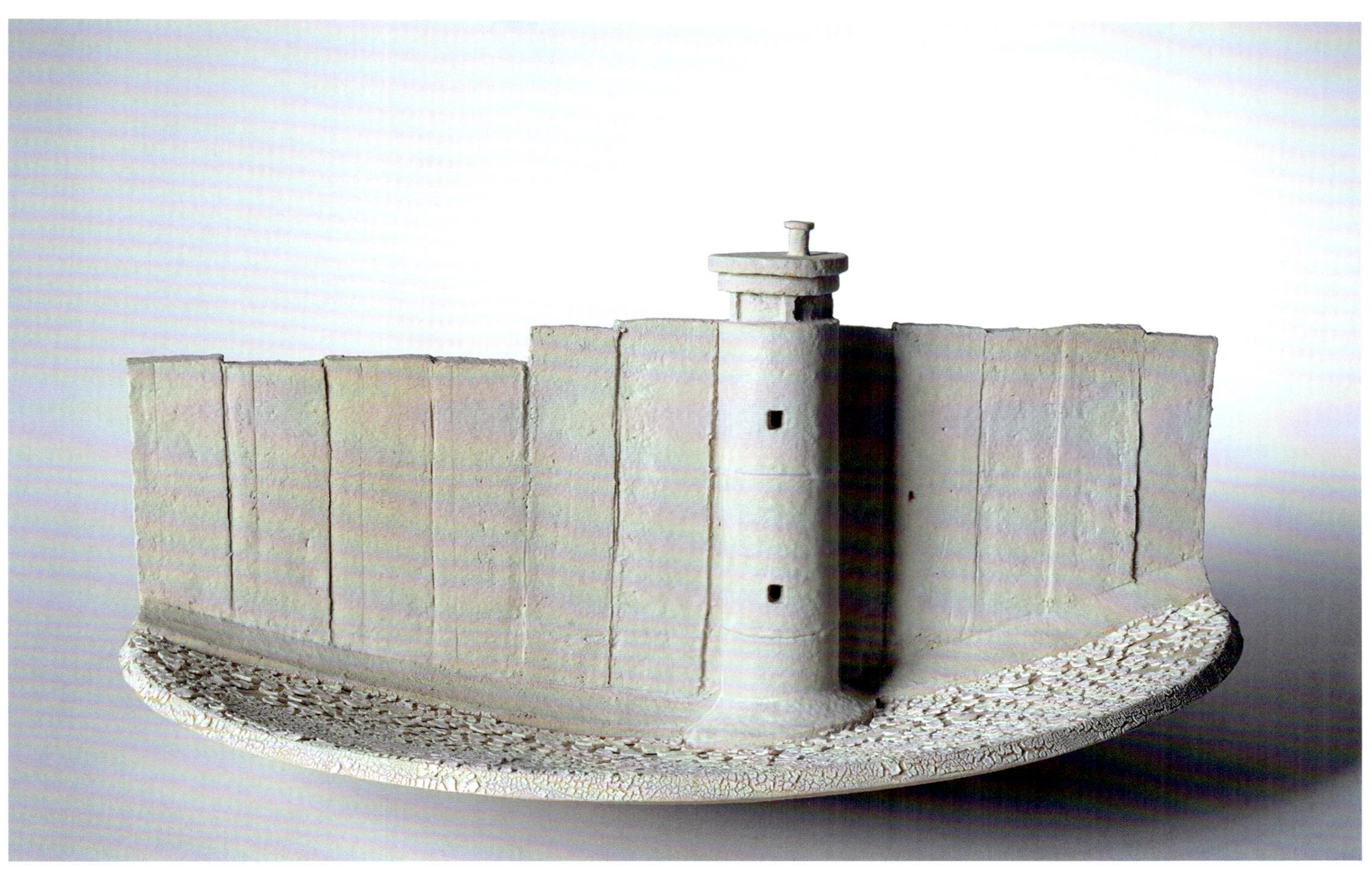

HESSELHOLDT, SOFIE 1974 –

Sculptor

1995-1998	Art History, Copenhagen University, BA
1999-2000	Det Fynske Kunstakademi
1999-	Artists' group Hesselholdt & Mejlvang
2000-06	The Royal Danish Academy of Fine Arts
	www.hesselholdt-mejlvang.dk

MEJLVANG, VIBEKE 1976 –

sculptor

1999-2000	Det Fynske Kunstakademi
1999-	Artists' group Hesselholdt & Mejlvang
2005	Kunst- og Designhøjskolen, Bergen, Norway
2000-06	The Royal Danish Academy of Fine Arts, MFA
	www.hesselholdt-mejlvang.dk

Sofie Hesselholdt and Vibeke Mejlvang began their artistic cooperation in 1999 and since 2000 they have used ceramic material both in smaller-scale sculptural works and in large ceramic assignments, e.g. *Det flyvende tæppe* (The flying carpet), in Ventemøllegården, Sorø. They have extensive exhibition activities with acknowledged politically motivated installations.

Inspiration for the work owned by the museum came from the time when the Wall in the West Bank was built; the piece shows a section of the wall with a control tower in a stretch of empty, desert-like landscape. The artists are referring more broadly to walls and fences around the world, and are thus sadly topical in current times. The work can also be interpreted on a more abstract level, with the choice of the traditional dish form, associated with domestic functional use, drawing attention to the walls that are to be found even in the safe bastion of the home. This rigorously-made work, with its political and ceramic power, is part of the museum's continuous collection of contemporary ceramic works made by artists. *The Wall* was made in the Art Academy's ceramic workshop **(201)**.

201. Sculpture, 2005. ***The Wall***

Stoneware, crawling glaze; cast in a plaster mould, added modelled elements.
H 30 x Diam 55. Mark: none. Mus.no. 67/2006
ACQUISITION: Galerie Mikael Andersen, Copenhagen. Donation from *Kunstindustrimuseets Venner*

HINDSGAVL, LOUISE 1973 –

Ceramicist

1994-99 Designskolen Kolding, Institute for Ceramic Conceptual Art
2000- Own studio workshop, Copenhagen
www.louisehindsgavl.dk

White glossy porcelain has fascinated Europeans ever since the first porcelain objects arrived in western Europe via the Silk Road in the 15th century, and later the hunt began for the formula for making the 'white gold'. It was not until the beginning of the 18th century, at the court of August the Strong in Saxony, that the secret behind the production of white porcelain was finally uncovered, leaving the road open to the decorative ceramic art of the rococo period, with its cherished small figures of shepherds and shepherdesses in idyllic and piquant scenes, and other more caricature-like and louche figure representations of the elegant and risqué lifestyle of the higher classes. These table decorations and conversation pieces made by the early porcelain factories such as Meissen, Sèvres and the Danish Royal Porcelain Factory, were the incarnation of an ideal of beauty and of a certain social order, and around the turn of the millennium they were taken up again for 'tender' treatment by several international artists who use porcelain figures as a material and as a form of reference in their hard-hitting critique of presentday values in a hypocritical, media-created and power-corrupted world.

Louise Hindsgavl (LH) has created a reputation for herself in a short time, in Danish and international ceramics; already in her final project as a student in 1999 she showed that she had found her medium in the white porcelain figures that were the basis for her individual narrative form, which takes features of folk-tales, animal fables and the media of popular culture to set up excoriating surreal scenes. Linguistic and literary communication takes place through the artist's titles for her works, which provide precise summaries of the figure-compositions' content and action. LH boldly uses white porcelain to take up the cudgels against 'niceness', against suppression of opinions and against taboos that allow injustices to continue; she creates grotesque tales that distance her work by innumerable miles from the DNA of the porcelain figures from the 18th and 19th centuries. LH demonstrated her full potential in a major exhibition in 2014 with the title '*Power. Porcelæn. Poesi. /Power. Porcelain. Poetry.*', which was shown at Rønnebæksholm and at Skovgaard Museum (see: exhibition catalogue, ISBN 978-87-995000-5-5). A large number of earlier and recent works were displayed in eight separate tableaux in a scenography that released and added nuances to the sculptures' throng of grotesque and burlesque creatures, often hybrids between people, animals, male and female, assembled in part from casts of ready-mades. The artist puts her finger on the horrendous things that surround us in society and in the human psyche, and makes us confront them by letting the figures go to extremes with their often monstrous (mis)deeds. Genial black humour and moving poetry and yearning are also to be found in this ferocious theatre. In the museum's collections there are three works by LH, made in 2005, 2007 and 2009 respectively, all with two or three figures in different situations, from the amusing *Overraskelsen* (Surprise) **(202)**, which turns out to be a hen, to the astonishment of the three figures concerned on the little podium, to the morbid *Step Two* **(203)** with two figures, one of which has a fox head and is instructing the other, with a rhinoceros head, in how to carve up one's own legs. The third work, entitled *The New State of the Graces* **(204)** is a paraphrase of the classical motif with 'The Three Graces' and can be interpreted as a protest against oppressive ideals of female beauty.

LH is known and respected in national and international contexts and has sustained an impressive exhibition participation through the years; her works are represented in museums in Denmark and beyond. She has received a number of prestigious bursaries and prizes, including, in 2006, *Annie & Otto Johs. Detlefs' Ceramic Prize.*

203 401/2008

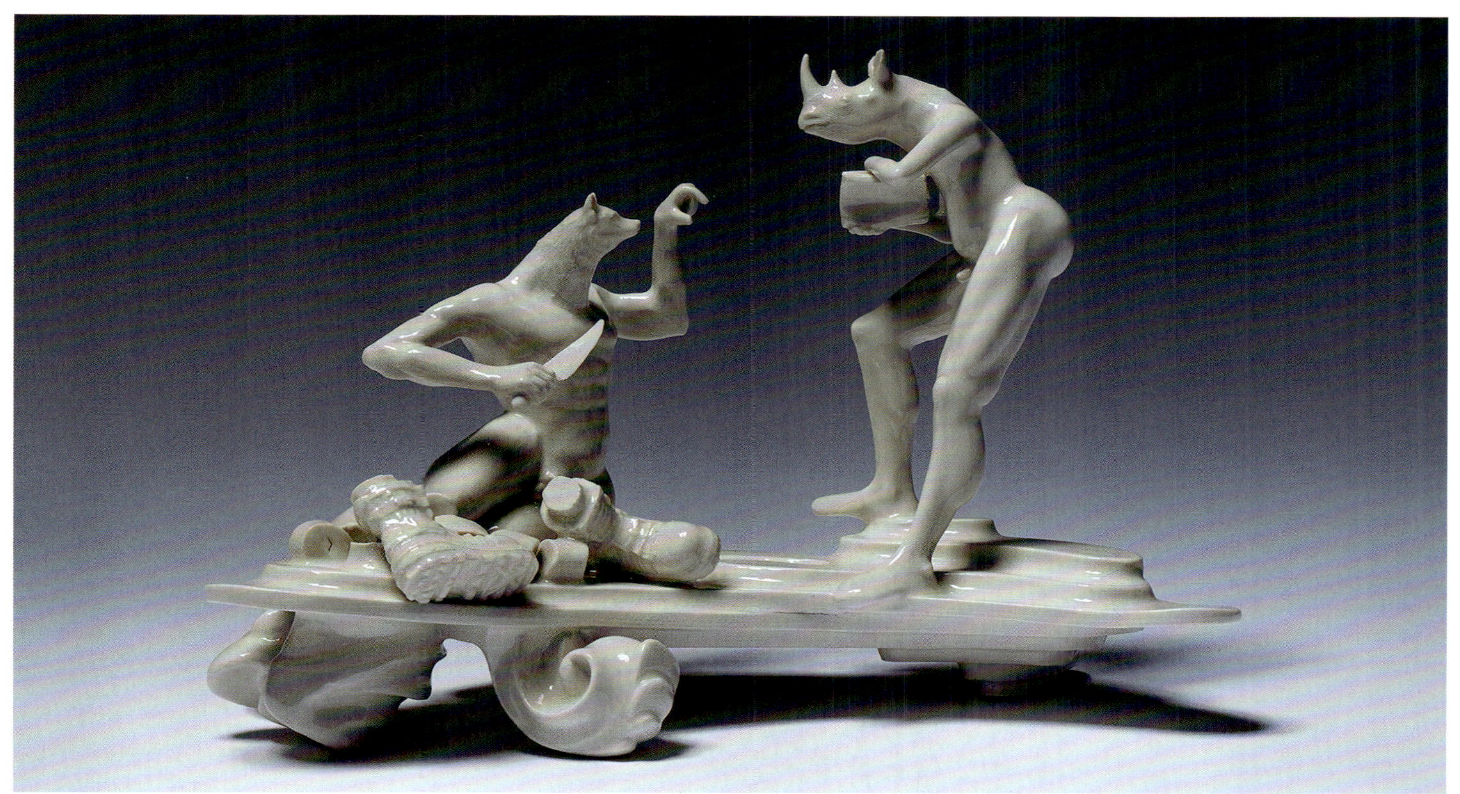

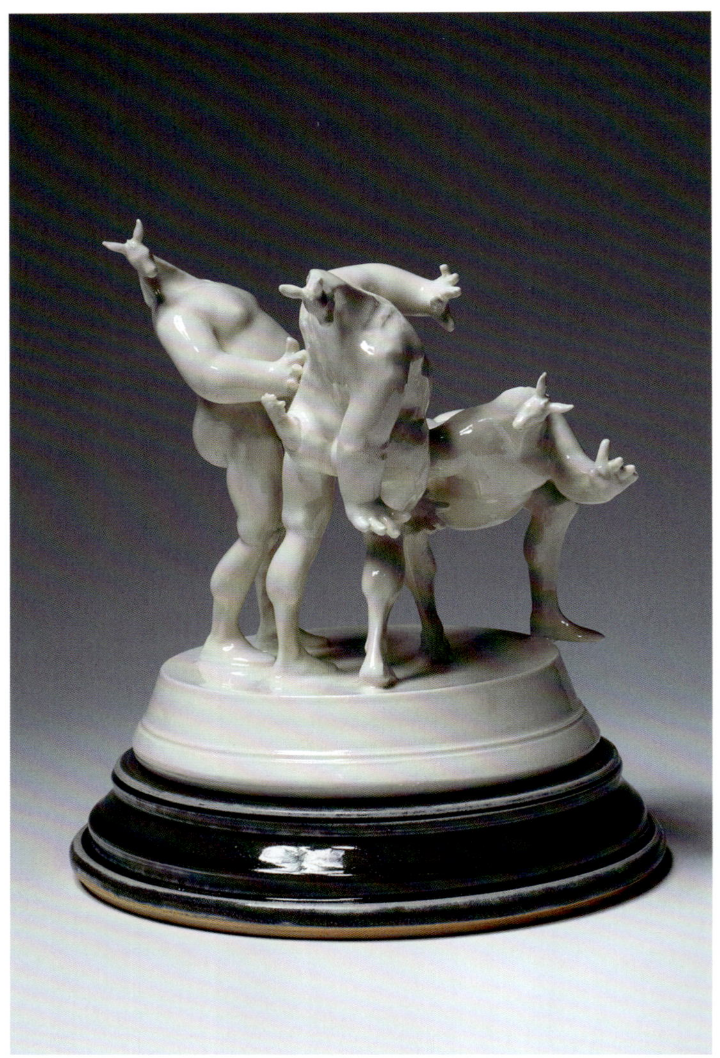

202 214/2005

202. Figure-group, 2005. *Overraskelsen* (The surprise)
Porcelain, stoneware, feldspar-glazed; thrown, modelled, cast, fired at 1280°.
H 31 x Diam 26. Mark: 'LH 07'. Mus.no. 214/2005
ACQUISITION: Galleri Nørby, 2005, Copenhagen. Donation from *Kunstindustrimuseets Venner*. See: *Louise Hindsgavl Ceramics*, 2005

203. Figure-group, 2007. *Step Two*
Porcelain, stoneware, feldspar-glazed; modelled, cast, fired at 1280°.
H 22 x W 34 x D 16. Mark: 'LH 07'. Mus.no. 401/2008
ACQUISITION: *The Edge of Innocence*, Drud og Køppe Gallery, 2008, Copenhagen. Donation from *Kunstindustrimuseets Venner*

204. Figure-group, 2009. *The New State of the Graces*
Porcelain, stoneware, feldspar-glazed; thrown, modelled, cast, fired at 1280°.
H 19.5. Mus.no. 113/2010. ACQUISITION: Donation from *Sølvsmed Kay Bojesen og hustru Erna Bojesens Mindelegat*

204 113/2010

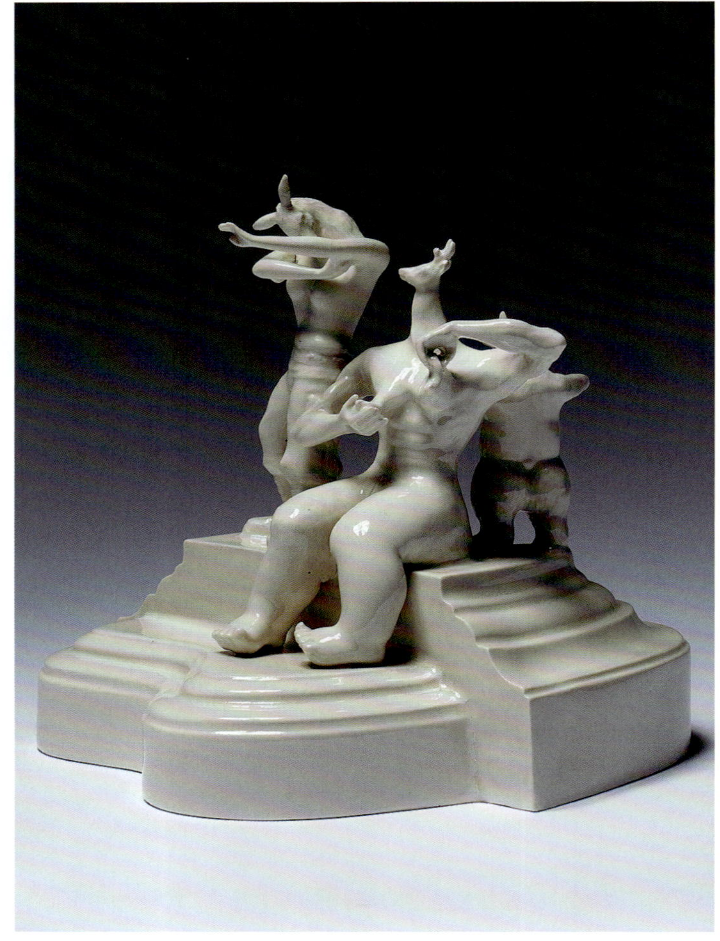

HJORTH, MARIE 1941 –

Ceramicist

1960-64	Kunsthåndværkerskolen
1973-76	Own studio workshop, Tejn, Bornholm
1982-92	ran Hjorths Fabrik (Ceramic Works), Rønne, Bornholm, with Ulla Hjorth
1992-	Studio Ceramicist and day-to-day head of the Ceramic Museum, Hjorths Fabrik

Marie Hjorth (MH) is closely bound to the history of Bornholm ceramics, in that she belongs to the fourth generation of the Hjorth family and is the day-to-day head of Hjorths Fabrik, which was taken over by the local authority in 1992 and is run as a working museum of ceramics. Apart from a few years in the mid 1970s when MH had her own studio workshop, her ceramic production has come from the factory's workshop. MH has also carried out commissions for large tile paintings and has taken part in exhibition activities both in Denmark and elsewhere.

Through the years MH has developed very confident shapes and distinctive use of materials in several series of functional ceramics for sale from the factory, but at the same time she has pursued an experimental line in fine unique pieces in stoneware and low-fired porcelain, in which the interplay between form, decoration and glaze is very personal and convincingly ceramic in expression, with a wide range of types of decoration.

The two works by MH in the museum represent the two areas of her work; the square lidded pot with the distinctive chess-patterned fields on the unglazed body is a unique piece **(206)**, while the little glazed lidded bowl with leaf decoration is cast and is one of a series of 100 that was produced for sale specially for the museum **(205)**.

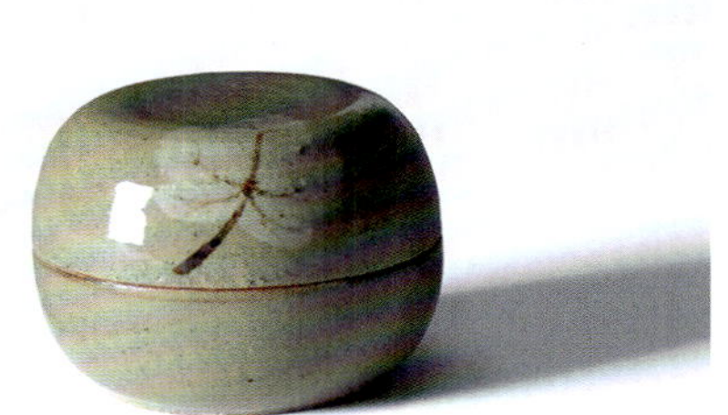

205 316a-b/2010

205. Small lidded bowl, 1984

Stoneware, glazed; cast, covered with slip, decorated. H 7 x Diam 9.5.

Mark: 'MH' painted on base. Mus.no. 316a-b/1989

ACQUISITION: *Månedens Souvenir*, no. 1, Kunstindustrimuseum's shop

206. Lidded pot, square, 1980-81

Stoneware, glazed; reduction-fired at 1280°. H 12.5 x W 7.

Mark: 'Marie L Hjorth' painted on base. Mus.no. D 1590

ACQUISITION: L. Hjorth. On deposit from *Statens Kunstfond*, 1985

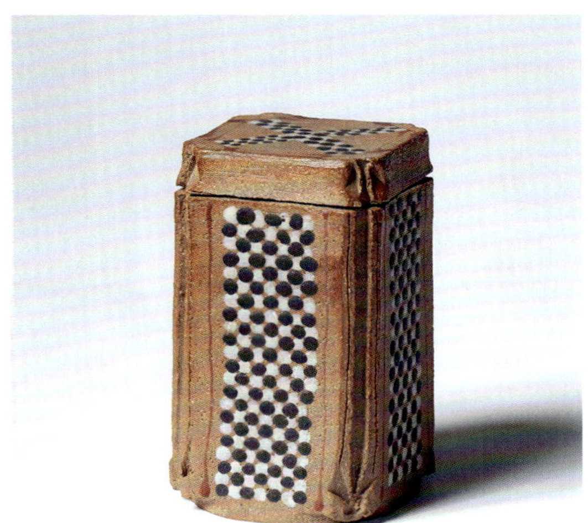

206 D 1590

HJORTH, ULLA 1945 –

Ceramicist

1965-69	Kunsthåndværkerskolen
1969-	Employed in Hjorths Fabrik (Ceramic Works), Rønne, Bornholm
1982-92	Ran Hjorths Fabrik with Marie Hjorth
1969-	Studio ceramicist in the Ceramic Museum, Hjorths Fabrik

Ulla Hjorth (UH) and Marie Hjorth together ran Hjorths Fabrik in Rønne during a ten-year period from 1982 to 92; they were the fourth generation of ceramicists in the well-known Bornholm family. After leaving the Kunsthåndværkerskolen UH was employed at Hjorths Fabrik, where she developed prototypes for production of the familiar range of brown-glazed household objects, and she also made many smaller series of cups, plates, bowls, etc. For other works UH used white tin glazes and decoration with patterns in cobalt oxide in fine shades of blue. UH has also experimented with soft-fired porcelain.

207 215/1992

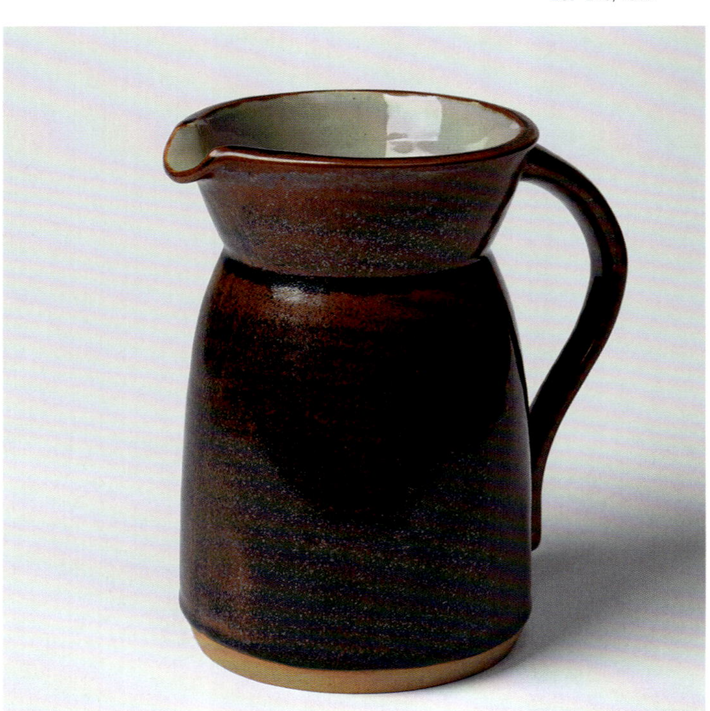

UH took part in *'Projekt 75'*, in which a group of 10 ceramicists agreed to develop new functional objects and create contacts with a view to having them produced; the other participants included Bente Hansen and Malene Müllertz. For the project UH developed the model of a well-proportioned and balanced cast jug, with tenmoku glaze on the outside and transparent greyish glaze inside **(207)**. The results of the project were exhibited in the museum in 1976 and 1977, and UH's jug was presented to the museum by Lars Serena, the knowledgeable historiographer of Bornholm ceramics.

Along with many of the other skilled studio ceramicists who have Bornholm as the departure-point for their work, UH has participated in exhibitions both in Denmark and internationally. She sells her works from the shop in the Factory.

207. Jug, 1976

Stoneware, Tenmoku-glazed, transparent glaze; cast in a plaster mould, reduction-fired at 1280°. Mark: Composite 'UH' and 'L HIORTH' painted on base. Mus.no. 215/1992.

ACQUISITION: *Projekt 1975*, 1976, Kunstindustrimuseum. Donation from Lars Serena. See: Serena, L., 2004. Hjorth, L., 2006

HOLE, NINA 1941 – 2016

Ceramicist

1961-63	Kunsthåndværkerskolen
1963-66	Glyptotekets Malerskole (Painting School)
1969-72	Ceramic workshop, New York, USA
1972-75	Chatauqua Arts Institute, New York
1975-77	Fredonia State College, New York
1984-	Own studio workshop, Skælskør, W Sealand
1990	Co-founder of the group Clay Today
1994	Co-founder of Danmarks Keramikmuseum Grimmerhus, Middelfart
1998	Co-founder of the International Ceramic Center – Guldagergaard, Skælskør
	www.ninahole.com

Nina Hole (NH) had a special position in Danish ceramics from around 1980, when she returned to Denmark after 10 years in the USA and became a bridge-builder between, on the one hand, the international expressive sculptural ceramics which had grown up particularly in the USA in the mid-1950s, with charismatic artists such as John Mason, Ken Price and Peter Voulkos, and on the other the Danish tradition for ceramics of a more function- and design- orientated character. In the USA NH acquired expertise with the time-honoured and still current Japanese raku technique, which she later mainly used.

On her return to Denmark NH became a catalyst for the formation of the *Clay Today* movement in Denmark, which held international workshops and seminars that created a fruitful and inspiring environment, bringing together talented people of many nationalities, including American, Japanese and Australian studio ceramicists. This led, in 1998, again with NH as one of the driving forces, to the establishment of the International Ceramic Research Center at Guldagergaard, which developed through the years into an important centre for the *Clay Today* group and has become an international forum for both young and established ceramicists from the whole world. At Guldagergaard experiments are carried out with for instance the wood-firing of ceramics in the large kilns there, built by the participants themselves, and expert advice on firing is available to visiting ceramicists who want to fire their work using this technique. NH was also active in the founding of Denmark's Museum of Ceramic Art (now CLAY) in 1994, which created a new platform for publicising international ceramic art.

NH covered an exceedingly large range in her work. From the mid 1990s onwards she worked both on smaller scale studio pieces and also on the outdoor monumental fired sculptures, several metres tall, that have made her known and respected in the whole ceramic universe. These place-specific installations have had an important role in collecting groups of assistants in connection with the construction of the architecturally-inspired, often house-like, structures. After the first

208 172/1997

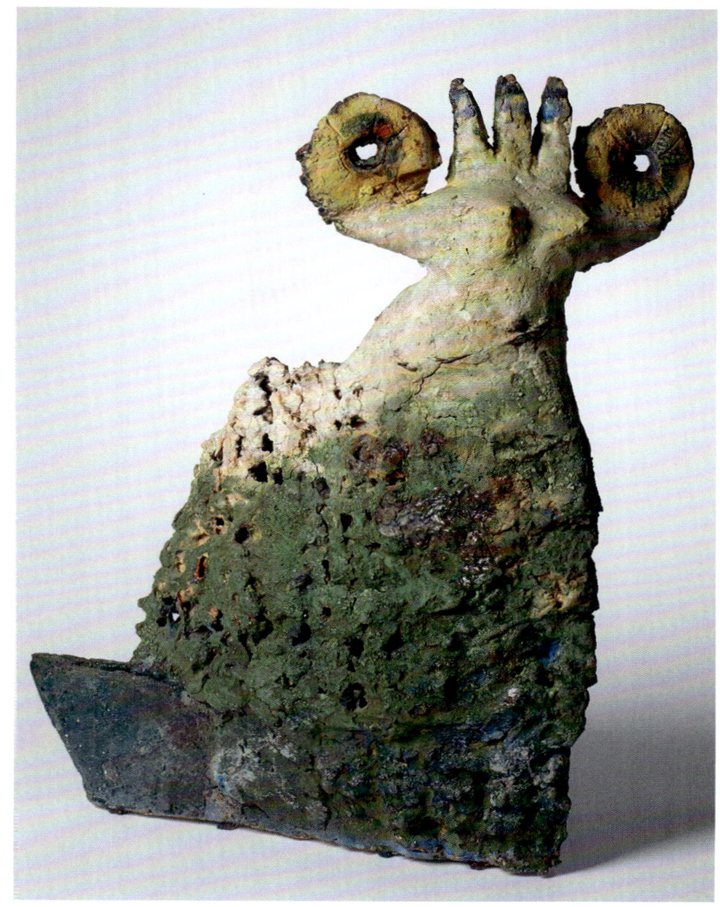

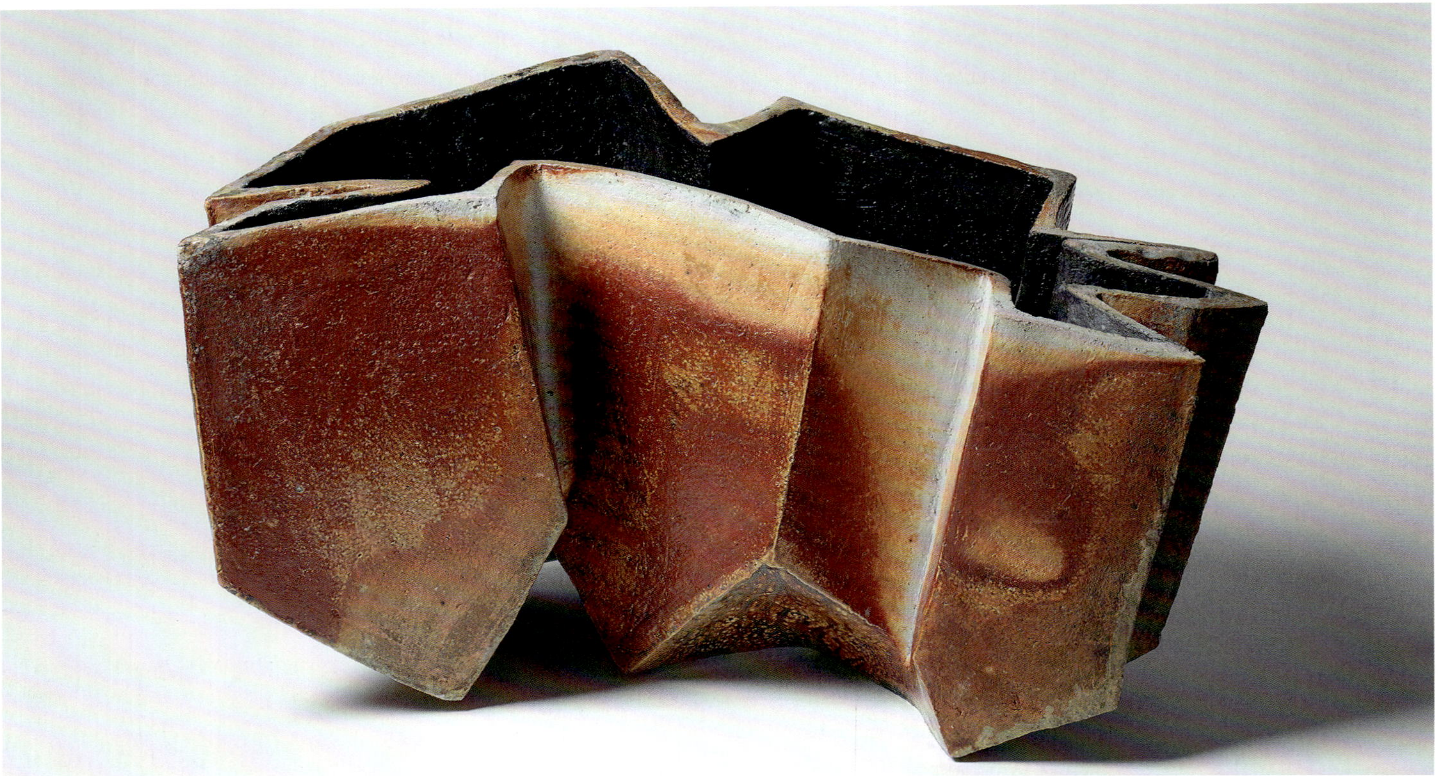

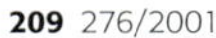

209 276/2001

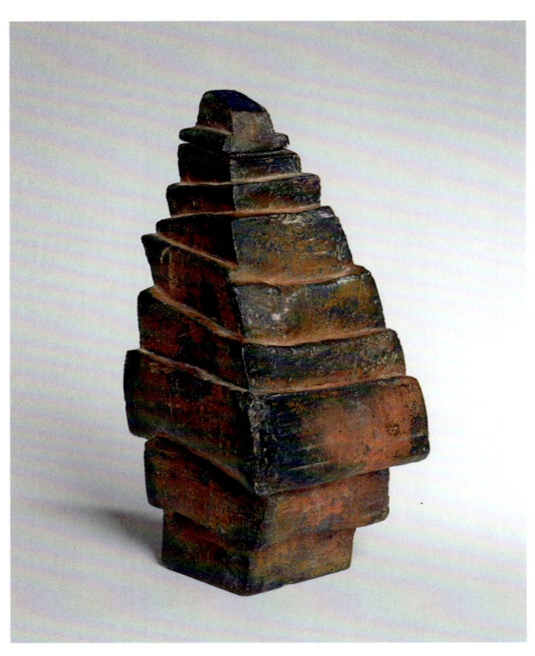

210 118a-b/2009

firings in the early 1990s NH carried out about 25 around the whole world – an impressive and dedicated effort, sustained by NH's intense engagement with the nature of clay and its expressive qualities, and with the primordial magic force of the processes and the red structures. In the museum's collection there are four works by NH, and they illustrate well some of the significant shapes, inspirations and techniques in her work. The two earliest were made in 1988, one of them an urn **(210)** and the other a boat-shaped sculpture **(211)**. They represent motif groups that NH worked with for a number of years and which are fundamental to her artistic endeavours. Urns, houses and boats are universal human symbols, framing conditions of human existence. In many works NH took history as a source of inspiration, in some cases classical antiquity, like the Etruscan Necropolises which provide the basis for the urn sculptures, but also North European prehistory, as in the sculpture *Bodeacea* (Boudica), the name of a Celtic heroine **(208)**.

With the sculpture *Deep River* **(209)** NH summarises, in a dramatic, sharply truncated form, an association with nature, but equally a deep emotional undercurrent, while she also reaches back to the Danish ceramic tradition, in which the container is a primordial form. For NH there was never a gulf between 'free' and 'stringent' form.

NH carried out a number of large-scale commissions and is represented in art and ceramic- museums in Denmark and abroad. Throughout her whole career she held lectures and contributed to innumerable workshops, seminars and panel discussions.

208. Sculpture, 1997. *Bodeacea* (Boudica – Celtic queen who led the uprising against the Romans in the year 61 AD)
Stoneware, earthenware, paper clay, terracotta mesh, magnesium carbonate- and lead- glazed; modelled, raku-fired at 1030°. H 55 x W 4. Mark: 'Nina Hole' painted on base. Mus.no. 172/1997. ACQUISITION: Galleri Nørby, Copenhagen

209. Vessel, 2000. *Deep River*
Stoneware, ash-glazed, manganese-glazed; slab technique, wood-fired at 1360° at Guldagergaard, then in an electric kiln at 1020o.
H 39 x W 66 x D 27. Mark: none. Mus.no. 276/2001. ACQUISITION: Galleri Nørby, Copenhagen. Donation from *Kunstindustrimuseets Venner*

210. Urn, 1988
Stoneware, earthenware; modelled, raku-fired at 1030°. H 33. Mark: none. Mus.no. 118a-b/2009 ACQUISITION: *Nina Hole Retrospektiv*, Grimmerhus 2008. Donation from *Ny Carlsbergfondet*. See: *Nina Hole Retrospektiv*, Danmarks Keramikmuseum 2008, pp. 14-15

211. Boat-shaped sculpture, 1988. *Energy*
Stoneware, earthenware, several layers of glaze; modelled, raku-fired.
H 45 x L 53. Mark: none. Mus.no. 119/2009. ACQUISITION: *Nina Hole Retrospektiv,* Grimmerhus 2008. Donation from *Ny Carlsbergfondet*

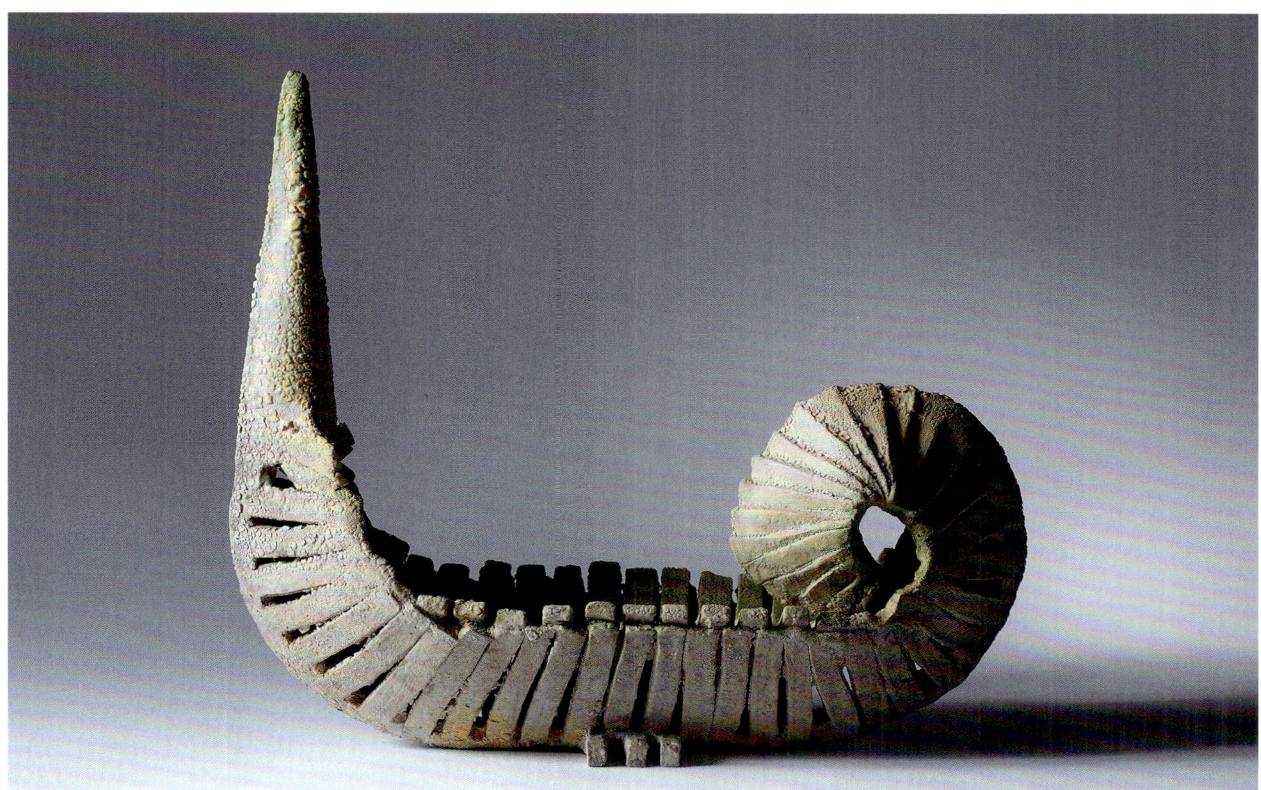

211 119/2009

HOLM, KIM 1952 –

Ceramicist

1968-72	Aarhus Kunstakademi
1972-2015	Aarhus Kunstakademi, teacher
1977-	Own studio workshop, Århus
2012-	Brabrand, studio shared with Ann Sloth, weaver
1989-90	Det Jyske Kunstakademi, guest teacher
	www.kimholm.net

Kim Holm (KH) chose the basic form for his work, the cylinder, at an early point in his career; from this departure-point he developed a ceramic *oeuvre* that is sustained by in-depth exploration of the textural expression of a range of glazes and styles of decoration. This insistence on a basic form evokes metaphorical connotations with the painter's frame with the stretched canvas or the composer's 'theme with variations'. The cylinder or container is a primordial type, not least in Danish ceramics, where its significance-laden history still makes it a vital and challenging form that is worked on both factually and symbolically in current ceramic art.

215 124/2009

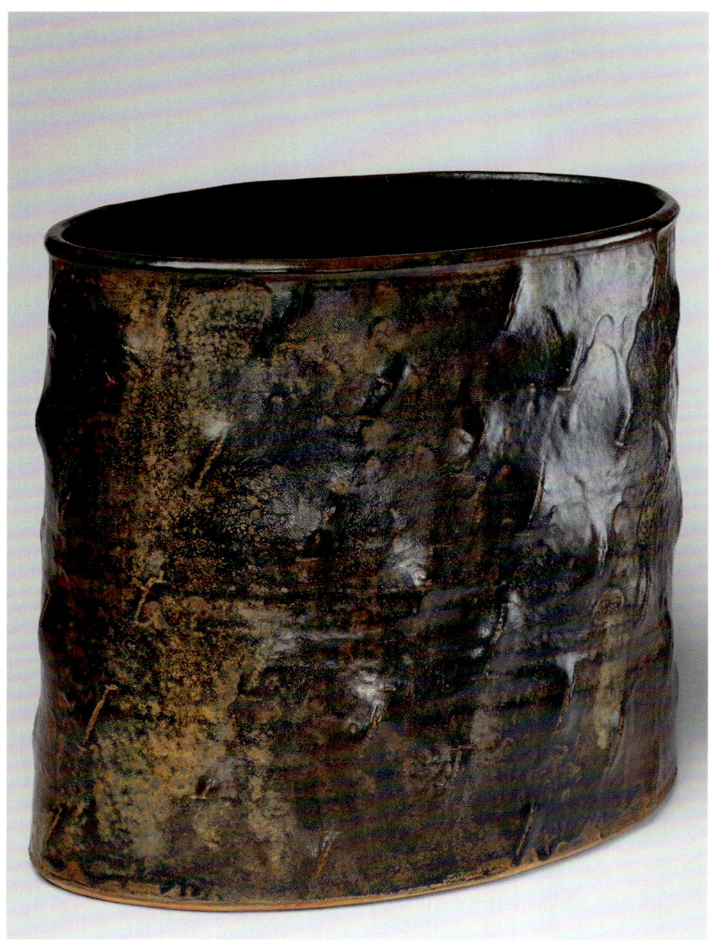

KH throws his cylinders and pots, shapes and processes both the inside and outside into a single entity, glazes them and fires them, often using raku-technique, which he experiments with. Through the years the glazes have come to play an ever-larger role, often applied layer on layer and fired several times, and KH has achieved an impressive range of textures, sheen and colour in interplay between glaze and decoration. The works radiate a dimensionally stable calm and concentration that is founded on great professional skill, certainty in the choices during the process and strong discipline.

Of the five works by KH in the museum's collection, four are from the 1980s and one is from 1999. None of these works represents the very boldly-glazed cylinders of recent years, but they are early examples of functional shapes, for instance the bowl from 1989 **(213)** and the dish from the same year **(216)**. Both works are decorated, the first with sgrafitto on a pale slip and the dish with slip decoration made using horn in a delicate orientally-inspired pattern. Thanks to a donation from *Ny Carlsbergfondet* the museum owns a fine example of KH's larger pieces, a tall, oval, brown-glazed vessel with regularly-placed cuts that have been pressed from inside so that they widen towards the exterior surface **(215)**.

Alongside teaching for many years at Aarhus Kunstakademi, KH has participated in many group exhibitions, some as a member of *8 keramikere* (1987-96); he has also had solo exhibitions in Japan, Europe and the Nordic countries. KH has an established international position as the recipient of diverse prizes and distinctions, and his work is to be found in several leading public museums and collections.

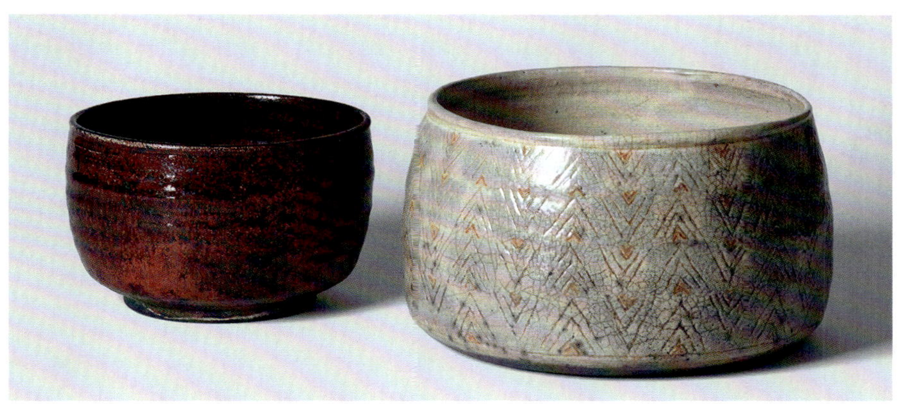

212 39/1985 **213** 301/1989

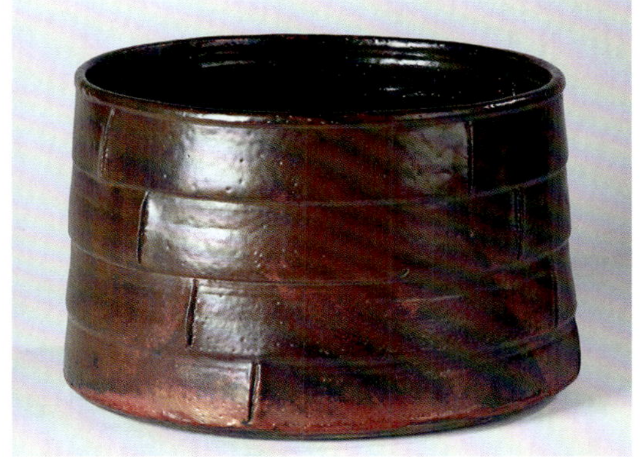

214 420/2008

212. Bowl, 1984

Stoneware, oxblood-glazed; thrown, raku-fired at 1100°. H 11.3 x Diam 18.2. Mark: 'KH' with a bird in a circle stamped on base. Mus.no. 39/1985 ACQUISITION: *Danske Kunsthåndværkeres Landssammenslutning* – Århus-gruppen, 1985, Århus Kunstmuseum. Donation from *Kunstindustrimuseets 50-års Jubilæumslegat*. See: *Brændpunkter*, 1990

213. Bowl, 1988

Stoneware, raku- and clay-glazed; thrown, slip, sgrafitto, raku-fired at 1100°. H 14 x Diam 21.5. Mark: 'KH' with a bird in a circle stamped on base. Mus.no. 301/1989.
ACQUISITION: *Jysk sommer*, 1989, Kunstindustrimuseet. Donation from *Ny Carlsberg Museumslegat*

214. Pot, 1980s

Stoneware, glazed; thrown, modelled, raku-fired at 1100°. Mark: 'KH' with a bird in a circle stamped on base. H 15.2. Mus.no. 420/2008
ACQUISITION: Donation from the estate of Ambassador Niels Christian Tillisch, Copenhagen, 2008

215. Oval vessel, 1999

Stoneware with chamotte; thrown, shaped, cut and pressed decoration, reduction-fired with raku technique at 1100°. H 35 x W 37. Mark: 'K' inscribed on base. Mus.no. 124/2009. ACQUISITION: Galleri Nørby, Copenhagen, 1999. Donation from *Ny Carlsbergfondet*

216. Dish, 1988

Stoneware, clear raku-glazed; thrown, slip decorated with horn, raku-fired at 1100°. H 6.5 x Diam 37. Mark: 'KH' with a bird in a circle stamped on base. Mus.no. D 1692. ACQUISITION: *Jysk Sommer,* Kunstindustrimuseet, 1989. On deposit from *Statens Kunstfond*, 1989

216 D 1692

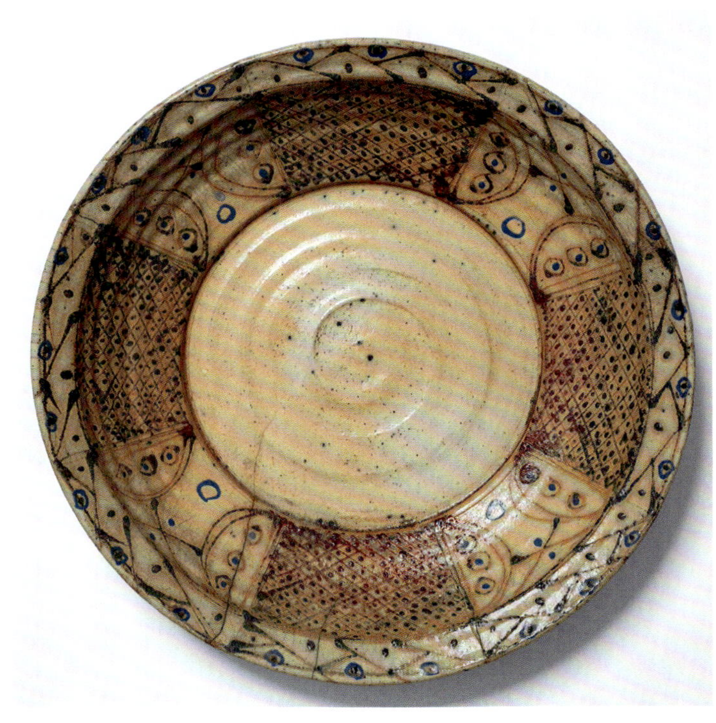

HOUGAARD, KARIN 1960 –

Ceramicist

1980-85 Det Jyske Kunstakademi
1983-1984 Athens School of Fine Arts, Athens
1985-2005 Own studio workshop, Aarhus
2005- Own studio workshop, Copenhagen

Karin Hougaard (KH) studied at the Jyske Kunstakademi with Lisa Engqvist as teacher. While she was a student she was awarded a Greek state bursary to study at the School of Fine Arts in Athens and in the Cyclades, and since then she has worked on the basis of the Greek ceramic traditions. Under inspiration from Minoan mural paintings and ceramics KH has through the years developed an up-to-date and universally valid idiom with strict geometric shapes and sometimes inlaid coloured fields and dots on oblong monumental whitish vessels.

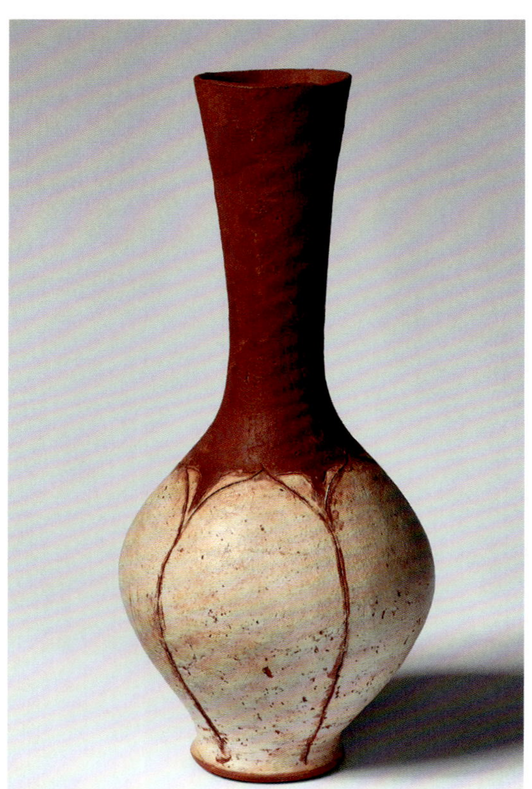

217 235/1989

In 1989 the museum acquired one of KH's works from the early period when she worked with classical shapes of pots and vases **(217)**.

217. Vase, 1989

Earthenware; modelled, inlaid clay, slip, fired at 1020°. H 36.8. Mark: 'Karin Hougaard' inscribed on base. Mus.no. 235/1989. ACQUISITION: Galleri Birkdam, Copenhagen. Donation from *Kunstindustrimuseets 50-års Jubilæumslegat*

HØM, JULIE 1944 –

Ceramicist

1962-65 Kunsthåndværkerskolen
1968- Own studio workshop, Holkadalen, Bornholm; 1968-75 shared with husband Bo Kristiansen

There are two main tracks in the ceramics works made by Julie Høm (JH) – one consists of the delicately decorated unique pieces in the form of vases, bowls and dishes, and the other takes the form of the many commissioned works she has completed from 1970 until the present day. These ceramic commissions can be found in churches and public institutions around Denmark and include e.g. ceramic reliefs, floor-standing vases and sculptures as well as a number of adornments for organs. JH has taken part in many exhibitions in the Nordic region, in the rest of Europe and in the USA, and is represented in highly reputable ceramic museums in many countries. As the fourth generation in the Bornholm ceramicist Hjorth family (daughter of Lisbet Munch-Petersen and the artist Poul Høm), JH rented the house in Holkadalen where her maternal aunt Gertrud Vasegaard and her husband, the painter Sigurd Vasegaard, had had their workshop, but in 1972 she moved to the other property in Holkadalen, where she still has her studio workshop. JH is represented in the museum by four works from between the mid 1970s and 1997, all precisely and handsomely shaped and finished. The decoration consists of abstract, inlaid fields of slip and glazing, and bears witness to strong inspiration from elements of nature, transformed into lively and varied expression. Rocks, sea, vegetation, colour and light are revealed in JH's works, which are

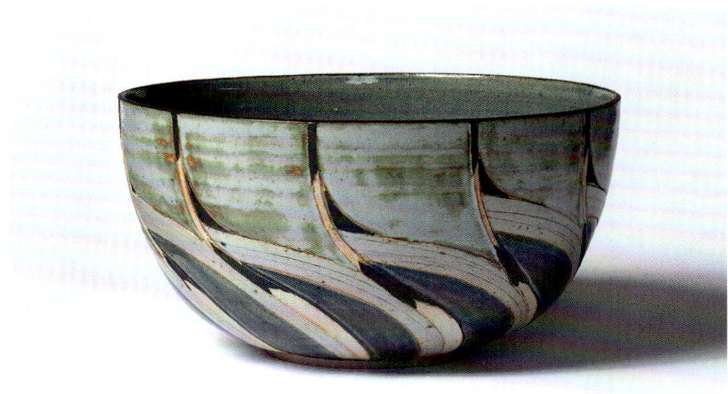

220 2/1990

an appreciable addition to the rich artistic heritage of Bornholm. The most recent of these works was acquired in 1997 in connection with an exhibition in the museum **(221)**.

218. Bowl, 1975-76

Stoneware, feldspar-glazed; thrown, scored with a knife in inlaid slip- and glazed- fields, fired at 1310°. H 10 x Diam 15. Mark: 'JH' inscribed on base. Mus.no. 43/1978. ACQUISITION: Julie Høm. Donation from *Kunstindustri-museets 50-års Jubilæumslegat*

219. Bowl, 1982

Stoneware, feldspar-glazed; thrown, scored with a knife, iron oxide in hollows, fired at 1310°. H 9.3 x Diam 11. Mark: 'JH' inscribed on base. Mus.no. 50/1983. ACQUISITION: *Glas og keramik*, 1983, Illums Bolighus, Copenhagen. Donation from *Kunstindustrimuseets 50-års Jubilæumslegat*

220. Bowl, 1990

Stoneware, feldspar-glazed; thrown, slip, scored with a knife in inlaid slip- and glazed- fields, fired at 1310°. H 14.8 x Diam 27.5. Mark: 'JH 90' inscribed on base. Mus.no. 2/1990. ACQUISITION: Danske Banks Kunstforening, 1990. Donation from *Kunstindustrimuseets Venner*. See: Dybdahl, L., 1997

221. Bowl, 1997

Stoneware, feldspar-glazed; thrown, scored with a knife in inlaid slip- and glazed- fields, fired at 1310°. H 26 x Diam 31. Mark: 'JH 97' inscribed on base. Mus.no. 178/1997 ACQUISITION: *Julie Høm – keramik*, 1997, Stensalen, Kunstindustrimuseet

218 43/1978

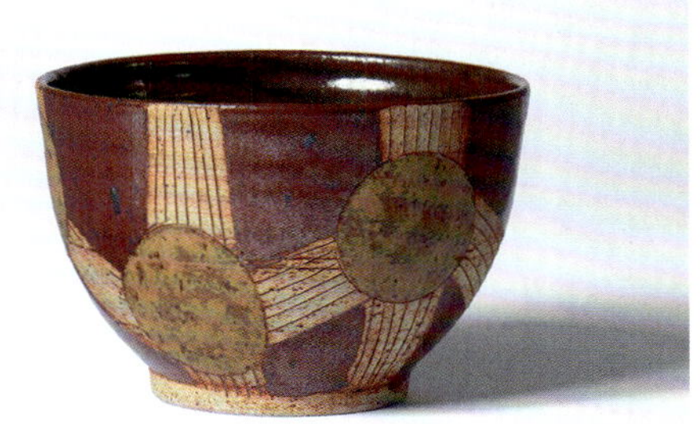

219 50/1983

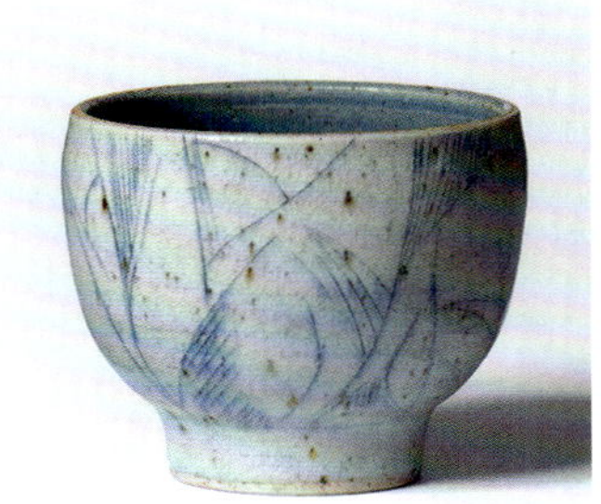

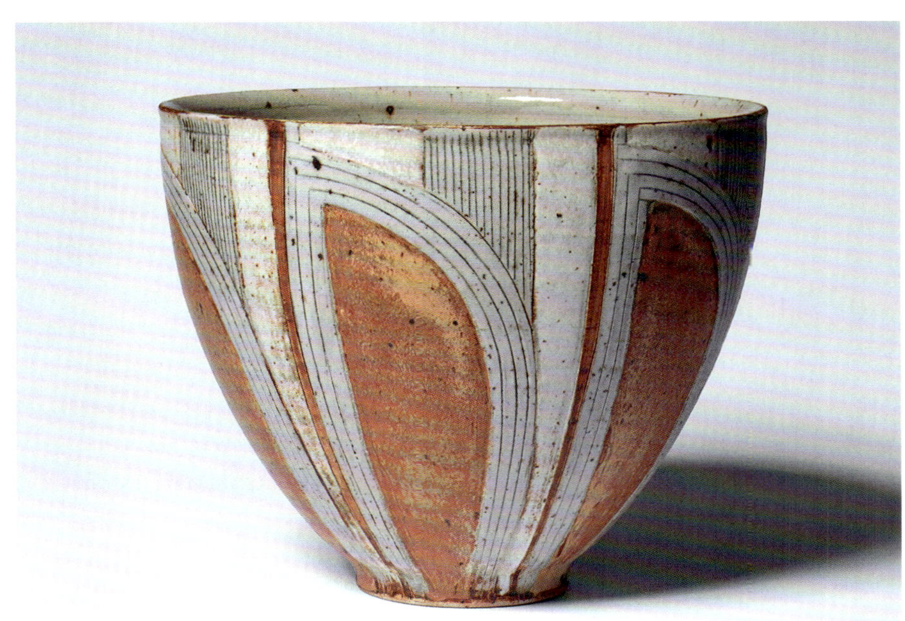

221 178/1997

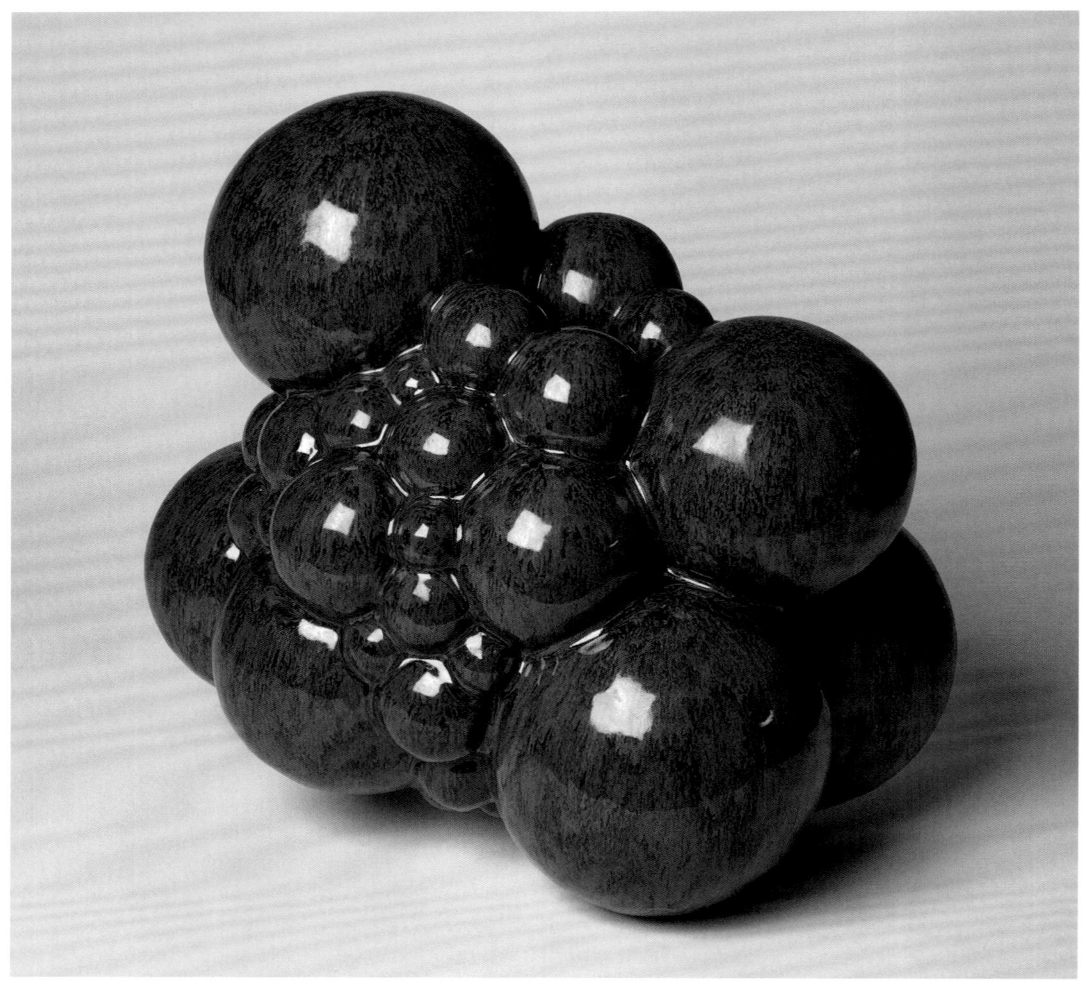

222 415/2003

IPSEN, STEEN 1966 –

Ceramicist

1984-87 Skolen for Brugskunst
1987-90 Kunsthåndværkerskolen in Kolding
1990- Own studio workshop, Studio Steen Ipsen, Copenhagen
1996-04 Danmarks Designskole, head of Ceramics and Glass department
2005-07 Designskolen Kolding, teacher
2012-14 Copenhagen Ceramics, exhibition centre, co-founder and -owner
www.steen-ipsen.dk

There is a consistency and fine quality in all that has come from the workshop of Steen Ipsen (SI) since he first exhibited in '*Kunstnernes Efterårsudstilling*' in 1992. Alongside stringency and well-maintained tempo in his career SI has made a considerable contribution as a teacher in the design schools in Kolding and Copenhagen, in the latter as head of the courses in Glass and Ceramics during an eight-year period. In other areas as well, as an external examiner and jury member, he has represented and supported the Danish ceramic milieu.SI's ceramic works can in general be seen as an artistic development exercise, a research effort, through which he has methodically and intensively explored his own defined themes. In this way he has worked

224 329/2007

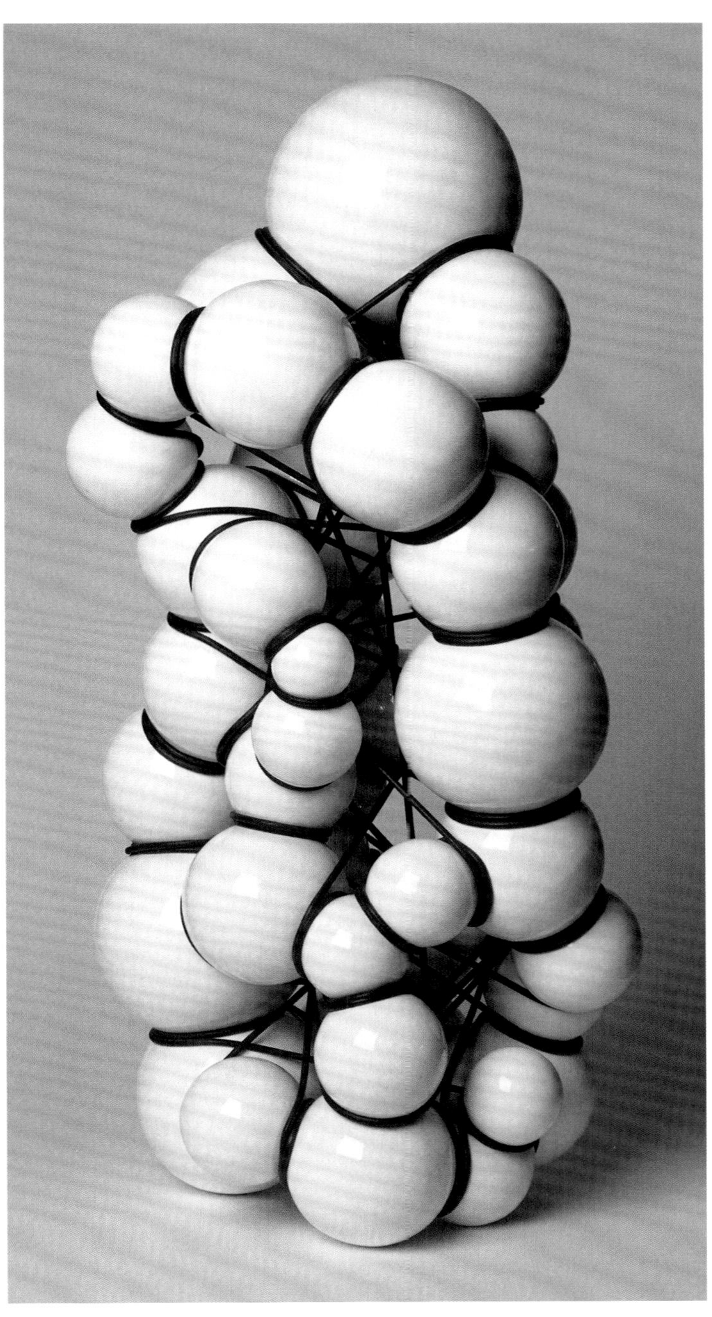

through vocabularies of form that range from the organic to the geometric, from spikes to bubbles and spheres, from the monochrome to the polychrome and from the unique modelled piece to modular repetition. Thanks to his skill as a ceramicist and his creative drive, SI has succeeded in carrying through these very complex and demanding series of works. This might sound like a dry and formal approach to working with malleable clay and magnificently coloured glazes, but the actual core of the process is a quite different matter, as SI himself has said:

> *'I work with a decorative ceramic expression that involves both form and decoration. The decoration is integrated into the form, and the form in itself is spatially decorative. The different layers of decorative agents combine in a complex interplay, where they succeed one another in being prominent, in disappearing and in making up a whole again. The decorative, including the shape as decoration, is the fulcrum of my work.' (Fremadrettet tilbageblik. In: Steen Ipsen, Ceramic Works 1990-2005, p. 14. ISBN 87-990222-8-1).*

The container as a ceramic archetype, particularly in Danish ceramics, has been explored by SI in several series of works from the 1990s; the cast basic forms are transformed into a cubist-inspired optical interplay between the faceted corpus, the line decorations and the coloured markings. It was this type of work that was used in a project for the Police Headquarters (Politigården) in Copenhagen in 1998; five-metre tall giant pots, with convincing spatial significance, form the central dynamic hub in a large public area. The museum owns one of SI's works from this period which also exemplifies the complexity of his artful geometric pots and their optical effect **(223)**.

Since then, however, SI has moved in a quite different direction, away from the functional Danish ceramic tradition and towards freely modelled works, in which he succeeds in giving solidity and meaningful shape to tendencies in the present rapidly-moving world. Form and decoration are integrated, producing sculptures in which we are reflected in radiant glossy surfaces and attracted by the living, growing and bubbling organisms that are played through in an infinite number of variations of changing colour and expression. In the exhibition '*New Danish Ceramics*' in the museum in 2004 SI displayed new modelled organic sculptures built up out of large and small bubbles and covered with shiny and partly pastel-coloured glazes. The museum acquired one of those works **(222)**.

Bubbles or rather spheres or balls are also the theme of the museum's latest work by SI, from the series *Tied-Up*, from 2007 **(224)**. These series with monochrome sculptures of balls bound together with complicated coils of leather, or PVC laces in contrasting colours, lead to masses of associations and interpretations (scientific, erotic, science-fiction related) and have resulted in a breakthrough for SI in the international art market, where he is represented by influential galleries.

222. Sculpture, 2003. *Sculptural Bubbles II*
Stoneware, running glaze; modelled, fired at 1225°. H 32 x W 70 x D 60. Mark: none. Mus.no. 415/2003. ACQUISITION: *New Danish Ceramics,* 2004, Kunstindustrimuseet. See: *Steen Ipsen – Ceramic Works 1990-2005,* 2005

223. Basin, 1993. *Vessel #1*
Stoneware, glazed; cast, printed 3D decoration. H 39.5 x Diam 45. Mark: 'IPSEN 93' painted in a square on base. Mus.no. 328/2007 ACQUISITION: Drud & Køppe Gallery, Copenhagen. Donation from *Højesteretssagfører C. L. Davids Legat for Slægt og Venner*. See: Køppe og Mazanti, 2005

224. Sculpture, 2007. *Tied-up 9*
Stoneware, earthenware-glazed, leather laces; modelled, assembled balls, fired several times at 1060°. H 66 x W 32. Mark: none. Mus.no. 329/2007 ACQUISITION: Drud & Køppe Gallery, Copenhagen

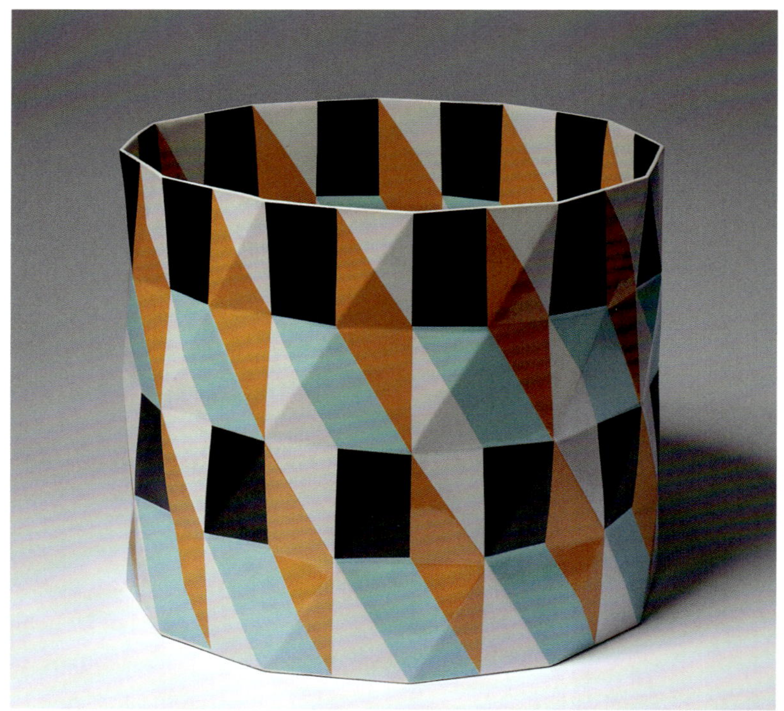

223 328/2007

JENSEN, BERIT HEGGENHOUGEN 1956 –

Researching artist

1978-83,	
1989-90	The Royal Danish Academy of Fine Arts, painter
1999,	
2000-2004	École des hautes études en sciences sociales, Paris, doctorate student
2004	Institut for Kunst- og Kulturvidenskab, Copenhagen University, external lecturer and researching artist www.berit-heggenhougen-jensen.com

In the early 1980s, several former art students of the Experimental Art School, *Eks-skolen*, began to show an interest in experimenting with ceramic sculpture, and this resulted in some remarkable exhibitions, some of them revolving around Horsens Kunstmuseum. In 1985 five 'wild' young artists were given the chance to work with ceramics in the studio of ceramicist Aage Würtz in Haldrup near Horsens, and there the kilns and professional help were made available to Peter Bonde, Claus Carstensen, Erik A. Frandsen, Christian Lemmerz and Berit Jensen (later Heggenhougen Jensen). The result was an impressive collection of 130 very experimental works that were displayed in the exhibition '*Ler-Etuder II*' in Horsens Kunstmuseum in May-June 1985.

Berit Heggenhougen Jensen (BHJ) participated with 36 expressive works, seven with the title *Neutron-ler* (Neutron-clay); one of them, no. 7 in the exhibition catalogue, later came to the museum as a donation from John Hunov, the dynamic collector who had had the original idea for these exhibitions of ceramic sculpture **(225)**. The first '*Ler-Etuder I*' was shown at *Eks-Skolens Forlag* (Publishing House) and the second, as mentioned, followed shortly afterwards in Horsens Kunstmuseum with the same group of artists.

BHJ has not since then produced ceramic works as such, but has expanded into an interesting conceptual art field, and from around the year 2000 she has pursued research studies in Paris. BHJ has carried out commissions for public projects and official portraits, and has written a number of texts and publications.

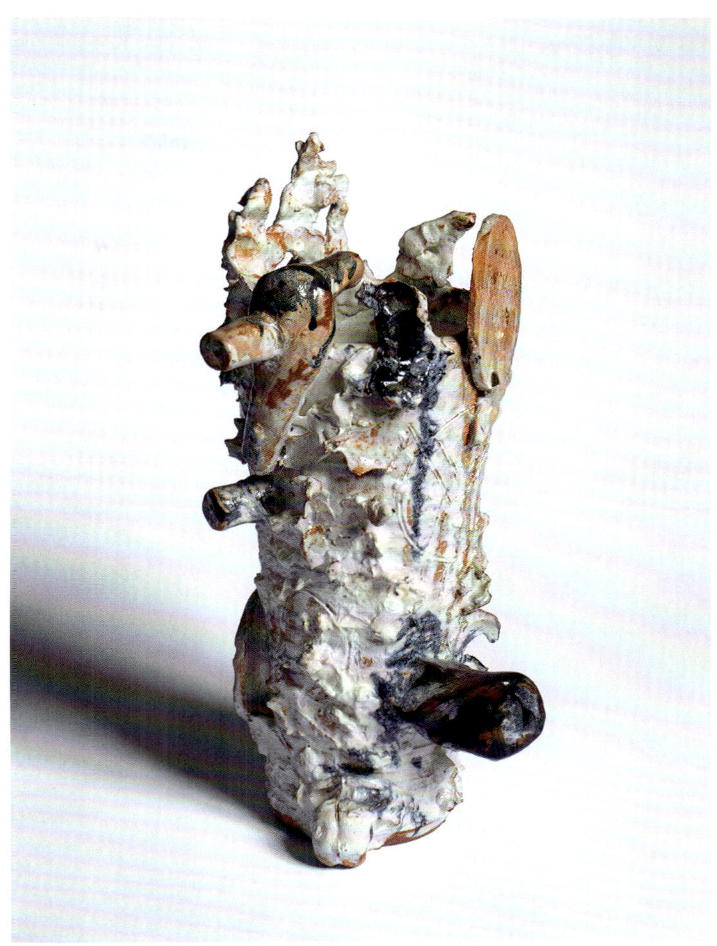

225 81/1987

225. Sculpture, 1985. *Neutron-ler* (Neutron-clay)
Earthenware, glazed; thrown, modelled, collage, relief, assembling elements.
H 37.5 x Diam 14. Mark: 'B.J. -85' painted on base. Mus.no. 81/1987
ACQUISITION: Donation from John Hunov, Frederiksberg. See: *Ler-Etuder II*, 1985. L. Dybdahl, 1997

JENSEN, ELSE KAMP 1937 – 2007

Ceramicist, designer

1970-74 Kunsthåndværkerskolen in Kolding
1967-70 Own studio workshop, Ribe
1974-77 Own studion, Vamdrup
1977-86/87 Worked for Bing & Grøndahl
1987-1990s Worked for Royal Copenhagen

At the exhibition '*Stentøj og Tekstil*' held at the museum in 1976 a work by the interesting ceramicist Else Kamp Jensen (EKJ) was acquired by the museum **(226)**; her works were unusual and noteworthy stoneware creations with impressions of coarse patterns, from thick knitting and sacking, worked into the surface of elegantly shaped oval sculpted vases, balanced by extending the sides out into stabilising wings. EKJ had her own studio workshop in Ribe and then in Vamdrup until 1977, when she began to work for Bing & Grøndahl. There she made for instance thin-walled, funnel-shaped bowls of porcelain, some of which had surfaces of unglazed *bisquit* with gold edges, while others were decorated with under-glaze painting and glazed. EKJ was represented at the major exhibition of '*Danish Ceramic Design*' mounted in the USA in 1982, and her works were mentioned in terms of high praise as the most sophisticated examples of contemporary ceramics in the world. After the fusion in 1987 of the two Danish porcelain factories EKJ became employed in Royal Copenhagen, and worked there until the beginning of the 1990s.

226. Vase, 1976

Stoneware, feldspar-glazed; slab technique, modelled, impressed decoration, fired at 1320°. H 39.5 x W 33. Mark: 'EK 76' inscribed on base.
Mus.no. 42/1976.
ACQUISITION: *Stoneware og Tekstil*, 1976, Kunstindustrimuseet. Donation from *Kunstindustrimuseets 50-års Jubilæumslegat*. See: *Brændpunkter*, 1990

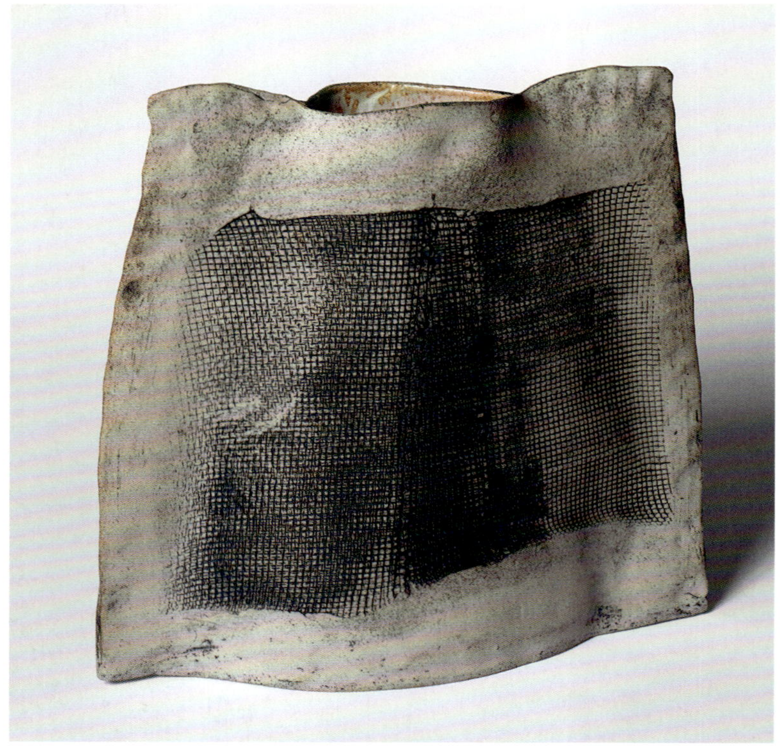

226 42/1976

JENSEN, OLE 1958 –

Ceramicist / designer

1979	Car mechanic
1985	Kunsthåndværkerskolen in Kolding, ceramic designer
1985-90	The Royal Danish Academy of Fine Arts
1985- 2000	Worked for Bing & Grøndahl, from 1987 for Royal Copenhagen
1992-99	Danmarks Designskole, head of Institute for Product Design
1995	Studio workshop with Henrik Lund Larsen and others
1999-	Studio workshop with Bente Skjøttgaard, Frederiksberg
2007	Curator, with Lars Dybdahl, of '*Biennalen for Kunsthåndværk og Design 2007*'
2009	Awarded Statens Kunstfond's honorary lifelong stipend
2013	Alfred University, New York State, Guest Professor
	www.olejensendesign.com

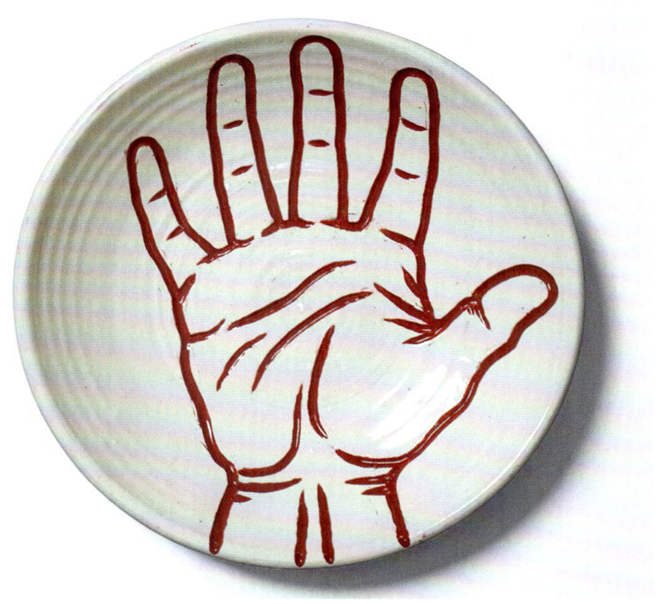

228 321/2003

Ole Jensen (OJ) is among the most original and internationally recognized designers of his generation. He has reinvented our everyday functional objects for table-and kitchen-use and created a unique and subtle design-universe with awareness of the user's needs, bringing daily pleasure, for the eye and the hands, in using objects he has designed. OJ is also one of the few who has succeeded in breaking through the media's reluctance to take up subjects related to craft and design, because of the unique character of his works and his original and nuanced style of communication, emphasising the necessity of free artistic development for achieving high quality design. Education at the Academy of Fine Arts was the essential foundation for OJ's independent and thoroughly considered attitudes to creative activity.

227 155a-b/1987

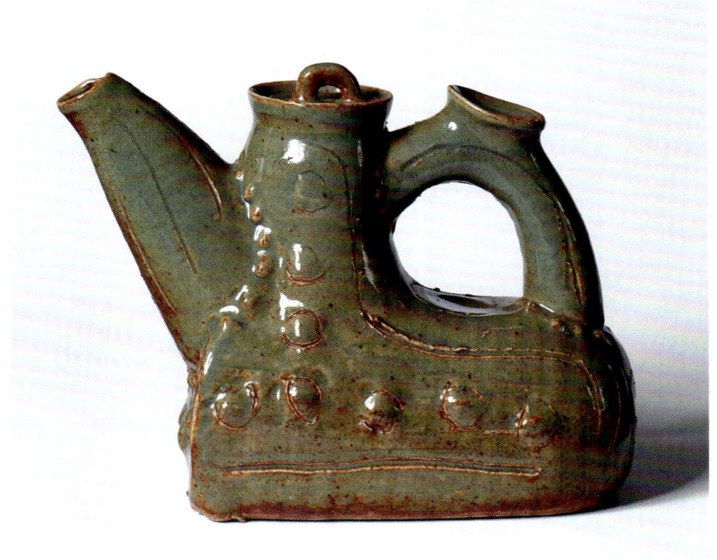

Ceramics became the departure-point for OJ, in that it was clay that inspired him in his youth, and it was training as a ceramicist at Kunsthåndværkerskolen in Kolding that later led him to the Academy in Copenhagen and at the same time to employment with Bing & Grøndahl (1987 Royal Copenhagen). The association with the old major factories gave OJ access to technical and production expertise, giving him valuable knowledge and opening up the way for him to jump from unique works to industrial production on the strength of his talent. In 1993 OJ's breakthrough arrived, with what became a design classic: the three-legged teapot with lid shaped like a measuring spoon,

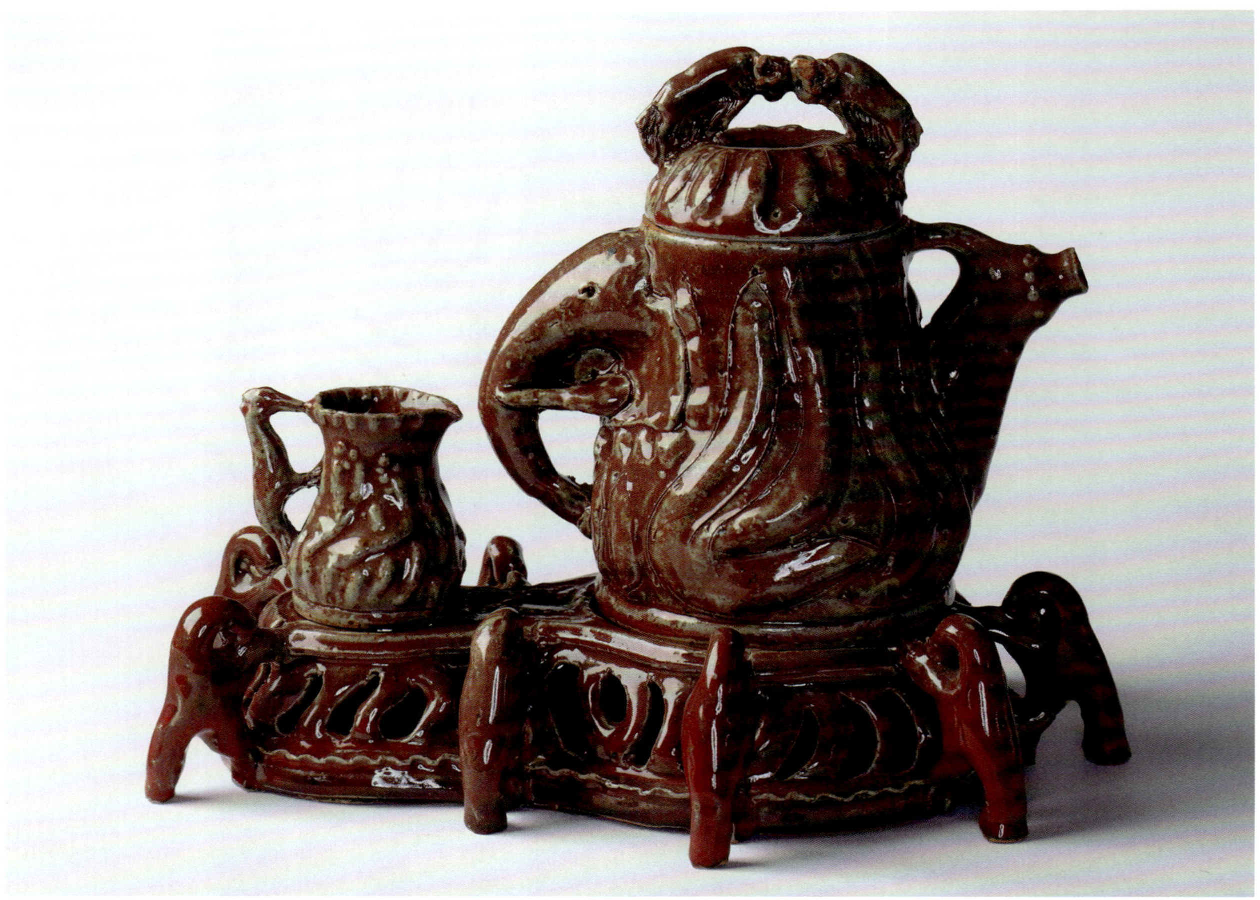

229 48a-d/2010

commissioned by the furnishing firm Paustian and produced in limited series by Royal Copenhagen.

In the museum's collection there are two works by OJ from the time before the three-legged teapot, one of them a coffee service from 1985 that is splendidly modelled with two rams on the lid of the coffee pot and a handle in the form of an elephant's trunk **(229)**, and the other a teapot from 1986 **(227)**; both were shown in his first exhibition at B&G, where they were bought respectively by *Statens Kunstfond* and the museum. It is interesting to see these early experiments in which the vitality of the modelling and treatment has a personal radiance and grasp that can be recognized again in the decisive and organic design of the 1993 teapot.

This humanistic attitude and approach to design has been a constant influence in OJ's distinguished design career, which has included e.g. the kitchenware series O L E for Royal Copenhagen from the mid 1990s, the internationally known rubber washing-up bowls and dustpan-and-inbuilt brush for Normann Copenhagen, and lamps for Louis Poulsen. Even though the museum's collections contain many examples of OJ's designs, their materials fall outside the scope of this catalogue; it has to be mentioned, however, that clay has gone on being the departure-point in the development of his objects, even though they are produced in other materials. That OJ had not abandoned clay became clear in connection with an exhibition in Galleri Nørby in 2003, with the title '*Brugskunst*', which partly arose out of the exhibition '*Lertøj*' in *Udstillingssted for Ny Keramik* in 2000. In both exhibitions OJ presented an impressively varied range of large and small thrown round dishes and bowls in traditional red clay with white slip and clear glaze. In Galleri Nørby these were supplemented with sturdily designed jugs and mugs. The whole lot was produced in his own workshop, and the abundant register of decorations speaks tellingly of OJ's capacity in the area of graphics also, in this *tour de force* in earthenware's eternal attractiveness, charm and potential for new development. In the exhibition '*Brugskunst*' the museum acquired the bowl with the 'potter's open hand' as a powerful symbol of the producer of the work **(228)**.

OJ has been awarded many notable prizes and distinctions for his designs and artistic activities, including the Thorvald Bindesbøll Medal in 2004, Statens Kunstfond's honorary lifelong stipend in 2009, and *Danmarks Nationalbanks Jubilæumsfonds hæderslegat* in 2012.

227. Teapot, 1986

Stoneware, celadon-glazed; thrown, modelled, relief, sgrafitto, fired at c. 1380°. H 18.5 x L 23. Mark: 'OLE 86 B&G' stamped on base. Mus.no. 155a-b/1987 ACQUISITION: *Birthe Spanggaard og Ole Jensen*, 1987, Bing & Grøndahl. Donation from *Kunstindustrimuseets Venner*. See: *Brændpunkter*, 1990

228. Bowl, 2003

Earthenware, transparent glaze; thrown, slip, sgrafitto, fired at c. 1050°. H 5.5 x Diam 33.5. Mark: 'OJ 03 malet Ole Jensen' inscribed on base. Mus.no. 321/2003. ACQUISITION: Ole Jensen, *Brugskunst*, 2003, Galleri Nørby, Copenhagen. Donation from *Kunstindustrimuseets Venner*. See: Erik Steffensen, *Ole Jensen.* Danske Designere, Aschehoug Dansk Forlag A/S, Louisiana for Moderne Kunst, 2002

229. Coffee service, 1985

Stoneware, oxblood-glazed; modelled, glazed. H 21 x L 29. Mark: 'OLE 85 mærke' painted on base. Mus.no. 48a-d/2010. ACQUISITION: *Birthe Spanggaard og Ole Jensen*, 1987, Bing & Grøndahl. Donation from *Statens Kunstfond* 2010

JOCHIMSEN, JOBIM A.M. see SOUVENIX p. 291

JORN, ASGER 1914 – 1973

Artist

1936-37 Académie Contemporaine, Paris
1938-40 Royal Danish Academy of Fine Arts
1953-73 Ceramic production, Silkeborg, Sorring, Albissola

Alongside his work as a pictorial artist, Asger Jorn (AJ) was an active ceramicist whose work in that field culminated in 1958/59 with the sculpturally demanding work entitled *Det store Relief* (The Great Relief), for the long entrance hall to the Statsgymnasium in Aarhus. The relief, c. 3 m in height and 27 m in length, was commissioned from the artist by *Statens Kunstfond*, and AJ chose to have it made in the Italian ceramic town of Albissola, to which he had moved, with his family, in 1954, and where he had organised, in the same year, an international meeting between artists and writers with artistic ceramic experiments as the central focus of the meeting. This is mentioned

230 42/1955

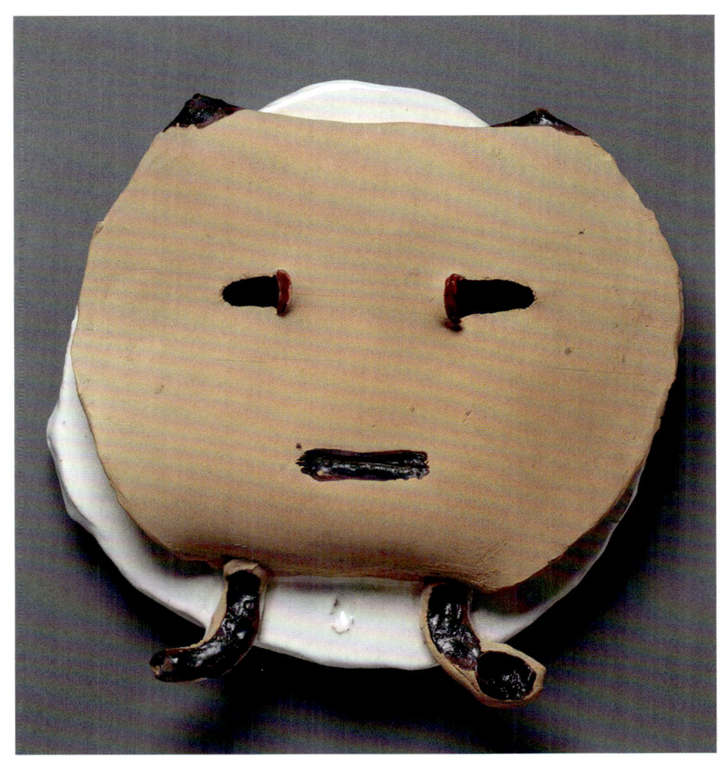

here because AJ's ceramic works from the meeting were displayed in the museum in 1955.

But AJ's interest in ceramics began much earlier. In 1929 he moved with his mother and siblings to Silkeborg, in Jutland, which he came to consider his hometown, and to which he presented extensive collections of his own works, together with noteworthy works from the international experimental art of the second half of the 20th century – collections that form the kernel of Museum Jorn (Silkeborg Art Museum). AJ had a keen interest in crafts and had worked with ceramics back in the early 1930s. After contracting tuberculosis in 1951/52 he spent a period in Silkeborg Tuberculosis Sanatorium and later visited local pottery workshops, inspired in particular by his artist friend Erik Nyholm, who lived nearby and was himself engaged in ceramic experiments. In 1952 AJ made a series of oval egg-shaped dishes with bird motifs in relief in the workshop of his former teacher at Silkeborg Seminarium, O. Randlev Petersen. One of these was acquired by the museum in 2001 **(233)**, while another is in Museum Jorn.

231 48/1966

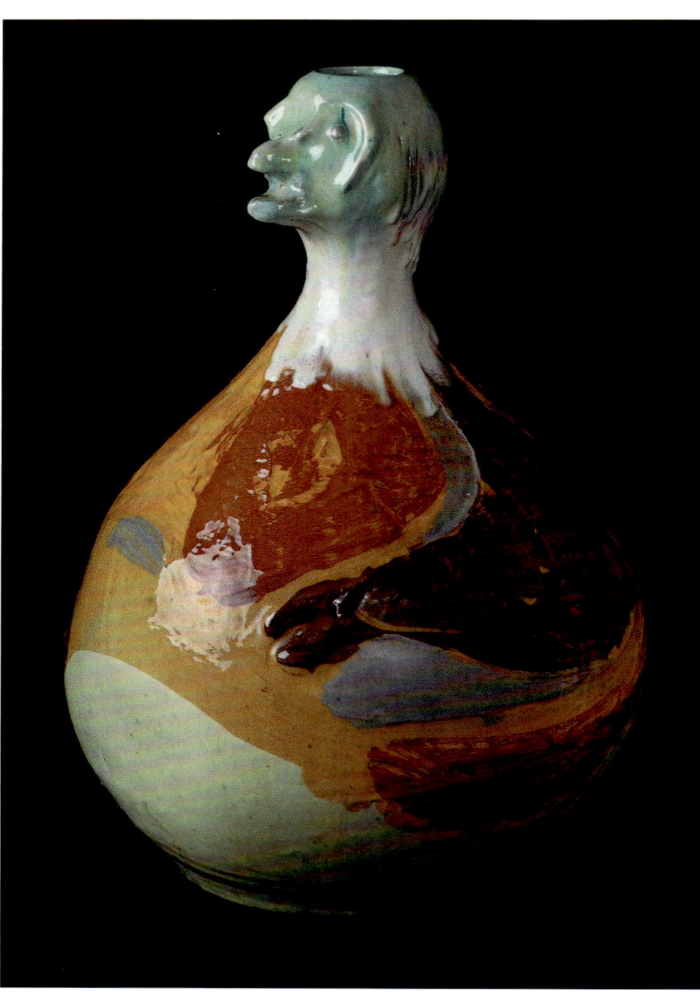

AJ found more space and resources in the studio of Knud Jensen, a potter in Sorring near Silkeborg, and thanks to a grant from Silkeborg Museum in 1953 he threw himself into ceramic work with intense energy and produced some sixty dishes, pots and bowls, thrown by Knud Jensen and then completed by AJ in expressive shapes that he painted and glazed, often with glazes he mixed himself. Many of these works went to Silkeborg Museum as had been agreed, and on a photo from 1953, where that museum's board is seen in the process of selecting works, among the newly-fired objects one can make out *Krukkemanden* (The pot man), which was presented to Kunstindustrimuseet in 1966 **(231)**. (See: *Asger Jorn Keramik*, 1991, p. 13). The sculpture is a good example of AJ's ceramics from Sorring, with the traditional potter's pot as departure-point for AJ's re-modelling and decorating of the upper area, in this case ending up with a bird-like man's head. There is another work from AJ's Sorring-era in the museum's collection – a bowl **(232)**, which was finished by AJ and decorated with colourful and painterly layers of slip, sgrafitto and running glazes.

In 1955 AJ brought to the museum a proposal for an exhibition of his new ceramic experiments, made in Albissola, which had been well-received when shown at the Xth Triennale in Milan in 1954 and subsequently in Cannes. The proposal was accepted; in an internal memo Erik Lassen, later director of the museum, recommended mounting the exhibition with the words: 'I know Jorn and his works in Albissola well. He is muddleheaded, but the muddle is on the boil. He is a living protest against the all-too-perfectable, tasteful and streamlined, which is characteristic of some aspects of Danish craftwork.' (Translation of

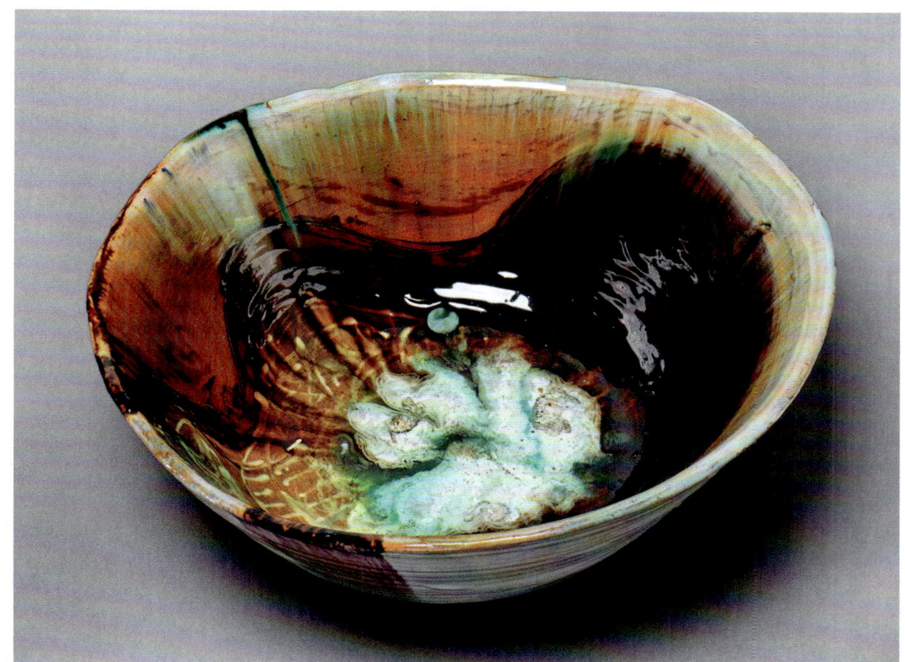

232 121/1983

quotation from the museum's archives, see *Brændpunkter*, pp. 82-83). Two months later the exhibition opened in the museum with a poster and a little catalogue with texts by Robert Dahlmann Olsen and AJ (in the museum's archives, and published in '*Asger Jorn i Italien*', 2007, pp. 213-16). The catalogue contains a list of the 20 works in the exhibition listed in five categories; two of the works are described as 'free form'. One of them, with the title *Maske. Fri form* (Mask, free form) was acquired by the museum, and it was unfortunately the only piece sold from the exhibition **(230)**. The mask, which is intended to be suspended, is an interesting work in which several techniques and surfaces are used to create the shiny and expectant duplicitous expression which is associated with the function of the mask.

If one reads the reviews of Jorn's exhibition written at the time, one can understand how ground-breaking and provocative it was, but even though those in the museum responsible for the exhibition were criticised by some who usually supported them, several of the trendsetting critics welcomed the provocation. 'This is the most unorthodox and fantasy-filled thing that has been shown in [the museum] in a long time. Magical and fantastic, for Jorn defies all good basic doctrine and experiments for all he's worth' wrote Pierre Lübecker in *Politiken* on 7 November 1955. As already mentioned, AJ's experimental ceramic work in the mid 1950s led, in 1957, to the creation of *Det store Relief* in Aarhus, an exceptional artistic and ceramic achievement.

230. Sculpture, 1954. *Maske, fri form* (Mask, free form)
Earthenware, partially glazed; modelled. Made in Albissola. H 30. Mark: 'JORN 1954 M.G.' inscribed on back. Mus.no. 42/1955
ACQUISITION: *Keramiske arbejder af Asger Jorn*, 1955, Kunstindustrimuseet. Donation from *Kunstindustrimuseets 50-års Jubilæumslegat*.
See: *Brændpunkter,* 1990. *Asger Jorn Keramik,* 1991. *Asger Jorn i Italien,* 2003

231. Pot, 1952/53. *Krukkemanden* (The pot man)
Earthenware, glazed; modelled, low relief, glaze-painted. Made in Knud Jensen's workshop, Sorring. H 41.5. Mark: 'Asger Jorn' inscribed on base. Mus.no. 48/1966. ACQUISITION: Donation from *Ny Carlsbergfondet*.
See: *Brændpunkter*, 1990. *Asger Jorn Keramik,* 1991. Dybdahl, L., 1997

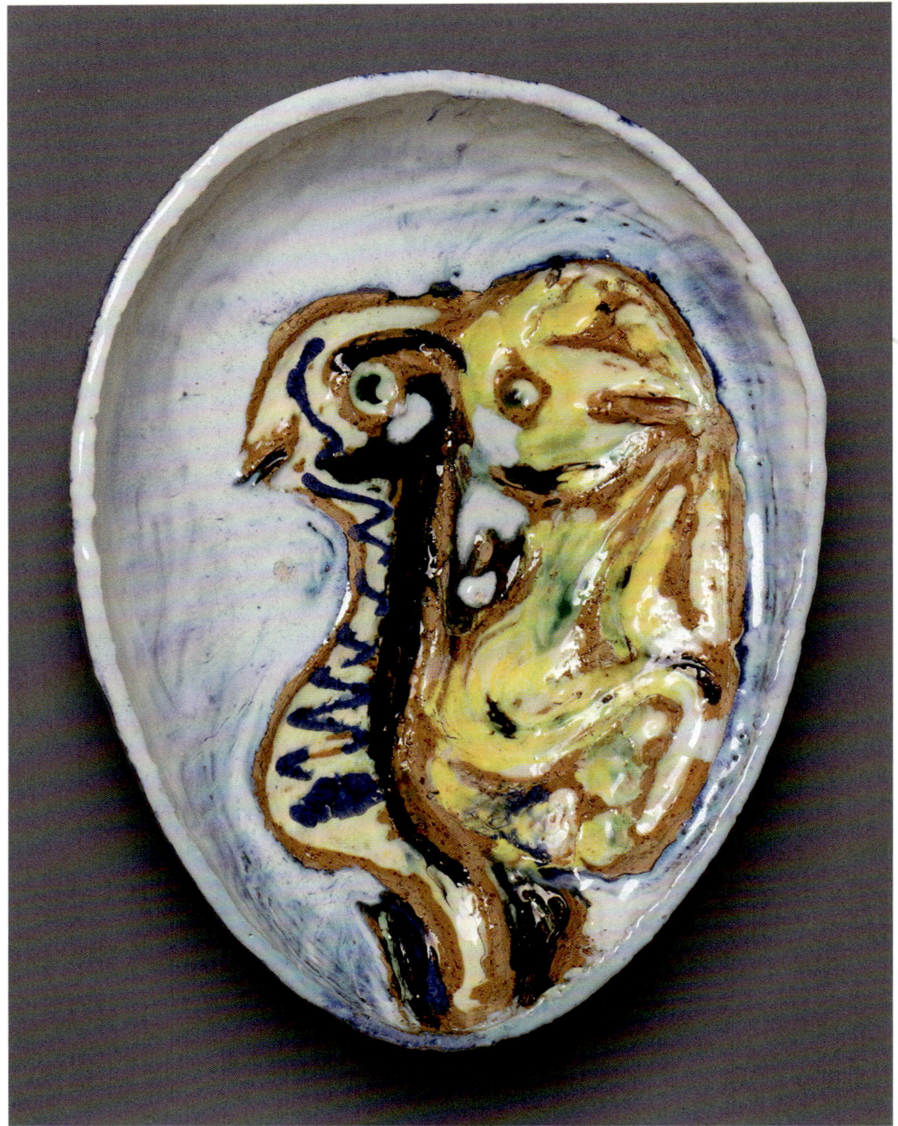

233 190/2001

232. Bowl, 1953

Earthenware, glazed; thrown, shaped, slip. Made in Knud Jensen's workshop, Sorring. H 12.5 x Diam 33. Mark: 'Jorn 19' inscribed on base. Mus.no. 121/1983.

ACQUISITION: Edith Dam. Donation from *Kunstindustrimuseets Venner*

233. Oval dish with bird motif, 1952-53

Earthenware, glazed; thrown, shaped, relief, slip. H 6.5 x L 34.5 x W 27.5. Mark: 'jorn' with an indecipherable date painted on base. Mus.no. 190/2001

ACQUISITION: Jens S. Bork, Copenhagen. Donation from *Højesteretssagfører C. L. Davids Legat for Slægt og Venner*. See: *Asger Jorn Keramik*, 1991. *Asger Jorn i Italien*, 2003

JUNGERSEN, GITTE 1967 –

Ceramicist

1988-93	Danmarks Designskole, School of Ceramic Conceptual Art; 1992 College of Art and Design, Bergen
1993-95	Workshop at Kulturfabrikken, Copenhagen
1995-2002	Studio workshop shared with Bente Skjøttgaard, Michael Geertsen, Turi Heisselberg and Lone Skov Madsen
1997	Shigaraki Ceramic Cultural Park, Japan, artist-in-residence
2003	Own studio workshop, Copenhagen
	www.gittejungersen.dk

Gitte Jungersen (GJ) studied at Danmarks Designskole and belongs to the experimental group of ceramicists who have searched for strong and expressive combinations of glazes, clay and firing, aiming at finding new and evocative structures. From the beginning GJ chose to go to the outer boundaries (and beyond) of the familiar, in opposition to the aesthetic and harmonious norms adopted by earlier generations of Danish ceramicists, and she has broken through both nationally and internationally with works that provoke and at the same time contain strongly classical ceramic qualities.

Research into glazes has been a particular preoccupation for GJ; she has invented new combinations with strong textural character, as well as a pop-style range of synthetic colours in shades of acid green, poisonous yellow and fuchsia. The fierce firing temperatures to which GJ subjects her works cause bubbles, spitting and melting of the glazes and this is fixed into surrealistic formations through sudden cooling. Experiments with clay were also an early focus, and at the 'Udstillingssted for Ny Keramik' (Exhibition Centre for New Ceramics) in 1997 GJ, together with Flemming Tvede Hansen, mounted the exhibition '*Deform*' with a collection of strange and collapsed shapes that documented the many stages of disintegration and meltdown in the process of firing a round pot-shape into fluid lumps of lava-like character. A '*Deform 2*' exhibition took place in Kyoto in 1998, that time with pipe-shaped objects. Through the years GJ has worked with a range of basic forms which have provided different departure-points for the interplay between clay and glaze. From the mid 1990s there is a series of containers of two main types, one with tall, narrow and flat pieces, and the other with open cube forms. In the museum's collection GJ is represented by an early example of the cubes from 1995; its fine glazing plays with black, yellow and grey nuances while flowing in a controlled course over the sides of the cube **(234)**. GJ has returned at intervals over the years to working with the cube form in continual new glazing experiments.

From the beginning of the 2000s GJ created several series of sculptural works with titles such as *Place for a Secret* (KIM 2008) and *Place to Be Lost* (Copenhagen Ceramics 2014), in which ready-mades such as little porcelain figures or plastic toys were included in narrative scenarios associated with psychological or existential issues. The latest works from GJ are the results of new experimental glazing trials on a monumental scale and in a minimalist idiom. GJ has received many prizes and bursaries, and exhibits frequently in Denmark and abroad.

234. Vessel, 1995. *Gul kube* (Yellow cube)
Stoneware, glazed; cast, double glazed, fired at 1280°. H 21.5 x W 21.5.
Mark: none. Mus.no. 15/1999. ACQUISITION: Galleri Nørby, Copenhagen

234 15/1999

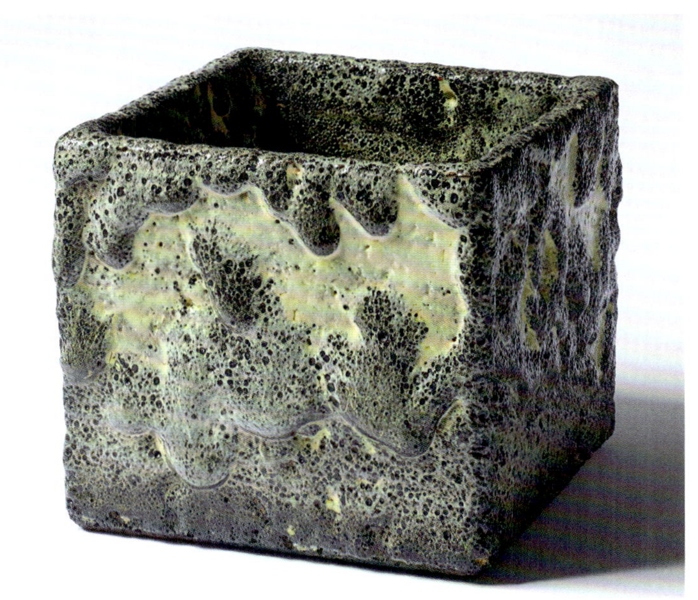

KALDAHL, MARTIN BODILSEN 1954 –

Ceramicist

1974-77	Aarhus Kunstakademi; 1977-81 workshop experience in France, England, Denmark
1981-88	Own studio workshop, Odder
1991-97	Own studio workshop, Aarhus
1997-2008	Own studio workshop, Copenhagen
2008-	Own studio workshop, Roskilde
1988-90	Royal College of Art, London, MA
1993-97	Det Jyske Kunstakademi, teacher
1997-2004	Danmarks Designskole, Product Design, Ceramics and Glass, teacher
2004-05	Danmarks Designskole, Ceramics and Glass, head of course
2005-08	Danmarks Designskole, Guest designer (The Digital Clay Project)
2009-10	Danmarks Designskole, teacher
2010-	Danmarks Designskole, SuperFormLab/Ceramic Design, co-founder and instructor
2012-14	Copenhagen Ceramics, exhibition venue, co-founder and -owner
	www.martinkaldahl.com

Over the last 40 years Martin Bodilsen Kaldahl (MBK) has been active within Danish ceramics, and at the same time he has played a role, through his international network and perspective, in forging links with the present-day ceramics environment in Britain, with the influential ceramicists there. MBK has a Master's degree from the Royal College of Art in London in 1990, and since then many young Danish ceramicists have followed in his footsteps.

Through MBK's curating of the major exhibition '*British Ceramics 2000*' at Grimmerhus Museum of Ceramic Art, the links between Danish and British ceramics were strengthened, and this was followed by a later exhibition with the title '*END*' in 2007 with English, Norwegian and Danish ceramicists taking part, arranged by MBK, Karen Bennicke and Peder Rasmussen in the museum.

235 205/2003

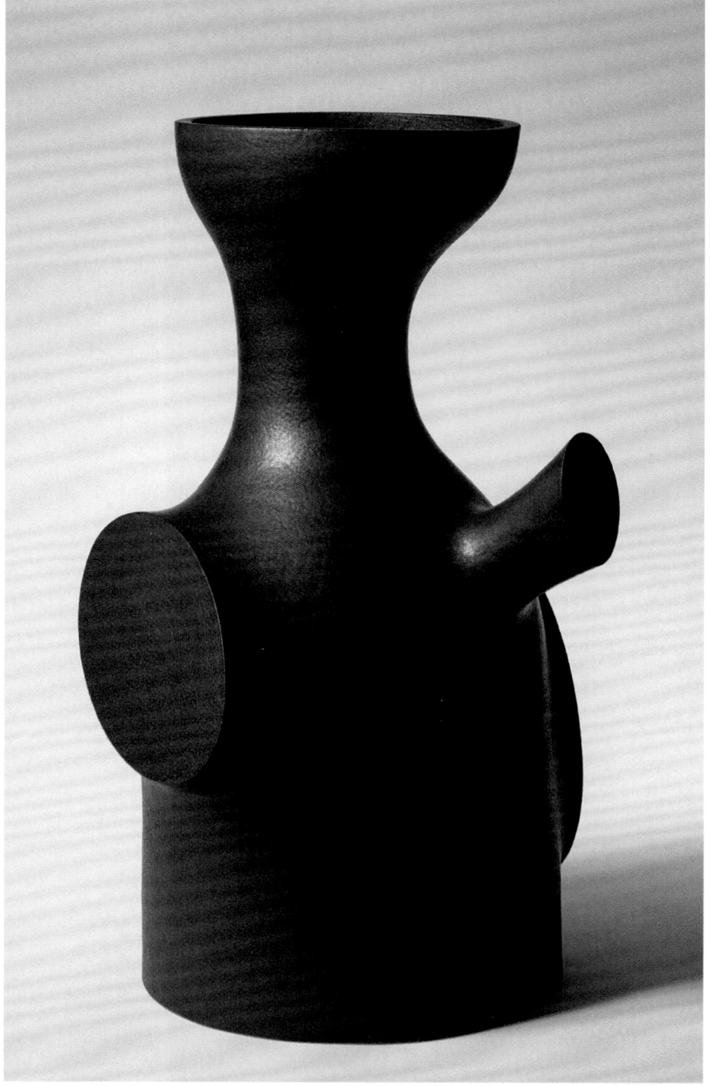

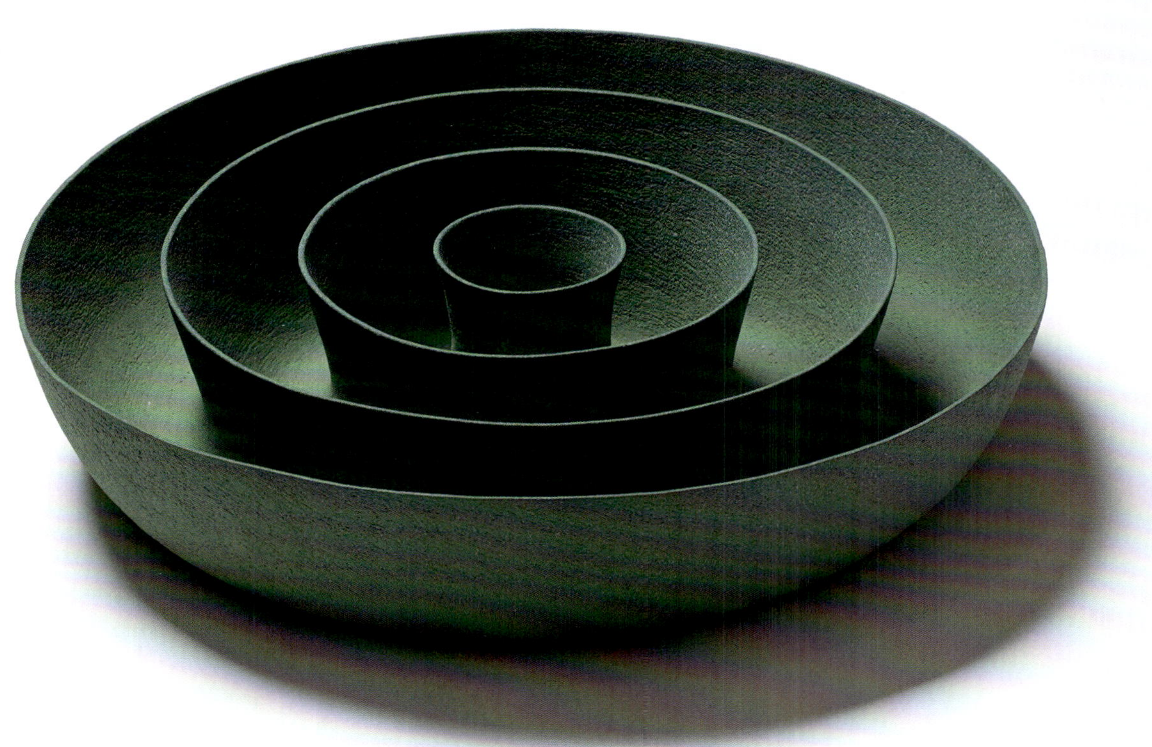

236 10/2009

After his basic education as a ceramicist, and then workshop experience abroad, MBK set up his own studio workshop in 1981, and from there produced functional pieces which were sold at fairs in Norway and Switzerland in a cooperative arrangement with colleagues. During this time MBK became more interested in working with the form of objects rather than their function, and this led to his further studies at the Royal College of Art in London and a different focus in his work as a ceramicist. Later still, however, he developed new forms for functional objects, some of them in connection with Royal Copenhagen's 225th jubilee in 2000, when MBK was invited to present an idea for a 'Service of the Future'. MBK has carried out independent research into the use of digital media (2D and 3D) as tools in development of form and pattern for ceramic objects. This is an area which MBK has cultivated, as a researcher and teacher at Danmarks Designskole, since 2005, most recently as co-founder of SuperFormLab/Keramisk Design. He has used his experience of digital development for art purposes for instance in producing works with compositions of natural impressions and branches and digitally-modelled shapes in 'branch objects', which he exhibited *i.a.* in the museum in 2007.

The archetypical ceramic pot has been a central theme in MBK's exploratory practical work since 1990, as his departure-point for new ways of conceptualising or looking at the form of the pot and its significance as a bearer of tradition. The experiment has been the sustained element in his working processes and has contributed to expanding his comprehension of shape and decoration, understood as a combination of patterns, structures and the total perception of the work as an entity in an architectural space. MBK's works range from large organic sculptures at the beginning of the 1990s, through geometric containers with striped decoration, to the 'branch objects' with their symbiosis between digital and organic idioms. The most recent developments are complicated modelled abstract sculptures, labelled

'Spatial Drawings', which incorporate experience from his other types of work, e.g. the *knotpots* (2003-2006) and the *branch objects*.

There are two works by MBK in the museum's collection. The earlier one has the title *Four Green Circles* and is from the year 2000; it belongs to a number of works from those years that have the circle as theme **(236)**; the same theme is explored in connection with a specific form of decoration: round and oval surfaces that grow out of the sides of the cylindrical pot and carry associations with the scars on treetrunks where branches have been taken off. This motif also characterises the museum's other work, from 2003 **(235)**, with the title *Saltoid - Other Planes* – a reference to a sculptural ceramic vessel in the museum, from 1956, by the artist Axel Salto (1889-1961). Inspiration from this work can clearly be seen in MBK's re-interpretation, which expresses his appreciation of the ceramic tradition.

MBK maintains an extensive exhibition activity in Denmark and abroad; he has been awarded many bursaries and prizes and is represented by works in influential museums and private collections. He has associations with galleries in London, Paris and Brussels.

235. Sculpture, 2003. *Saltoid – Other Planes 14*
Stoneware, matte stoneware-glazed; modelled, sinter slip, fired at 1260-70°. H 87 x Diam 53. Mark: 'MBK -03'. Mus.no. 205/2003
ACQUISITION: *Marit Tingleff – Martin Bodilsen Kaldahl: Ceramics 2003*, Galleri Nørby, 2003, Copenhagen. See: Jorunn Veiteberg, *Eit forsvar for ornamentet / In Defence of Ornament*. Catalogue, Galleri Nørby, 2003

236. Sculptural pot, dish form, 2000. *Four Green Circles*
Stoneware; modelled, sinter slip, fired at 1280°. H 11 x Diam 49.5.
Mark: 'MBK 2000' inscribed on base. Mus.no. 10/2009
ACQUISITION: Martin Bodilsen Kaldahl

KJÆLDGAARD-LARSEN, KAREN
see **CLAYDIES** p. 97

KJÆRGAARD, RICHARD 1919 – 1999

Ceramicist

1944	Completed studies at Kunsthåndværkerskolen
1945	Own studio workshop, Kastrup
1956-99	Kunstnerbyen, Hjortekær, Copenhagen
1955-	Kunsthåndværkerskolen (later Skolen for Brugskunst), Ceramics teacher
1969-85	Kunsthåndværkerskolen, Head of department
1958-62	Bing & Grøndahl, designer
1963-	The Royal Danish Academy of Fine Arts, School of Walls and Space, consultant, teacher

Richard Kjærgaard (RK) is an important figure in Danish ceramics in the second half of the 20th century. He worked both as an independent ceramicist and course leader for Ceramics and later Glass at Skolen for Brugskunst for a period of 20 years. As a charismatic teacher and source of inspiration RK has had decisive influence on many of the ceramicists who took his courses in his time as a teacher, and who in turn have contributed to creating the high level of Danish studio ceramics and its reputation abroad in recent times.

RK's teaching was based on an exploratory and intellectual working method, which students found challenging and provocative. Critical and demanding are two words that have been used by several of his students, but at the same time RK instilled a basic approach and an enthusiasm for ceramics as an idea and as a process which had long-term and wide-ranging effects on students. The essence of his teaching was its focus on practical applications, which to RK were anchored in a strong professional, idealistic and social foundation. This engagement led to many public commissions and official duties. RK contributed to promoting crafts in public in a vigorous and direct way for many years.

After finishing his studies at Kunsthåndværkerskolen in 1944 RK was given access to the studio in Kastrup, south of Copenhagen, which Gutte Eriksen had established in 1942. He rapidly began producing functional wares, both in ordinary earthenware with slip and glazes and in hard-fired earthenware with the emphasis on tautness of form.

In 1956 RK moved to Kunstnerbyen (the artists' village) in Hjortekær, to the north of Copenhagen. There he established his own studio workshop and began to work with stoneware, which became his preferred material and which also featured strongly in his teaching. Already in his student years RK began to make his mark in the exhibition context, where his sense of design and mastery of techniques were lauded time after time in reviews. As early as in 1948 he exhibited in Den Permanente together with six other ceramicists in the same age-group, and on that occasion Christian Poulsen and RK were singled out with a remark that 'some of these two artists' works deserve a place in the Kunstindustrimuseum' (*Berlingske Tidende*, 7.12.1948). The message was understood, and the museum acquired two glazed and well-shaped stoneware objects by RK from the exhibition **(237-238)**.

RK's interest in ceramic functional craftwork led to him being employed as a designer by Bing & Grøndahl for a 4-year period, during which he designed a service of porcelain ovenware 'Pyrodan', which was in production for a limited number of years.

Throughout his life RK was someone who took initiatives related to functional craft activities. An example was the *Kunsthåndværkersammenslutningen 16+2* (graphic designers), which was a group of 16 established craft practitioners (mainly teachers at Skolen for Brugskunst)

238 7/1949

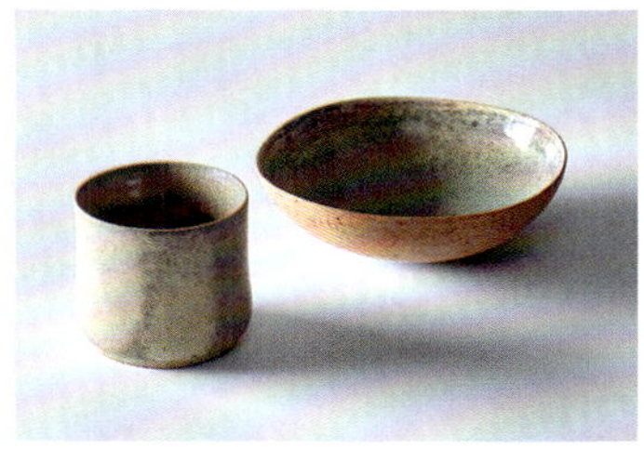

237 6/1949

who set out to explain to the surrounding world the difference between buying a random object in a department store and a unique piece from a craftsman, and how it is worthwhile saving up for the real thing which is both good to use and at the same time has qualities in terms of 'decorative function in the local environment'. The aim was to communicate this in such a way that it reached out beyond the narrow circles of the elite, and it was hoped that new and different groups would join this campaign across the whole country: 'we want to stamp out Copenhagen snobbery in our profession' (interview in *Kristeligt Dagblad* 11.6.1981). The group's first exhibition in 1981 in the museum was a great success and the same can be said of another, '*16+3*', exhibition in 1984 in the museum garden, Grønnegården, when an outdoor café was installed with Camilla Plum's food and the craft products were displayed in use in a fusion of design, execution and purpose. RK contributed to this with brown-glazed coffee-pots and matching cups which are now in the museum's collection **(240)**.

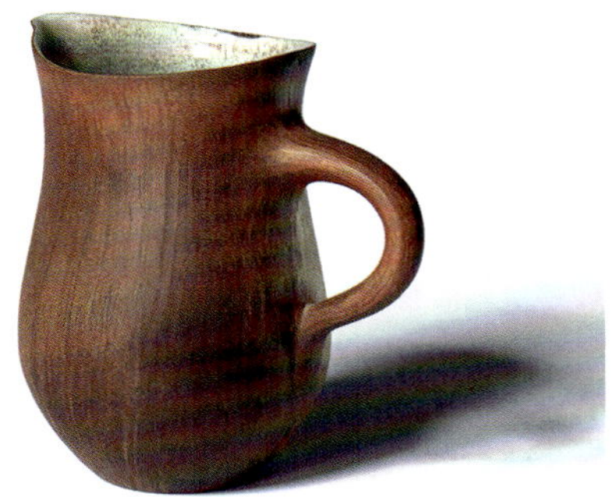

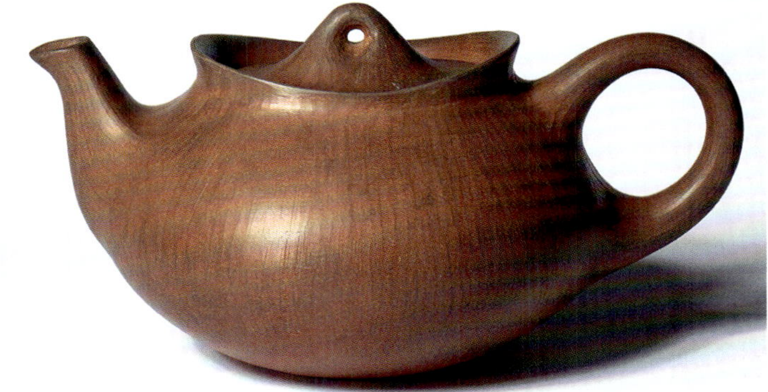

244 205a-c/2005

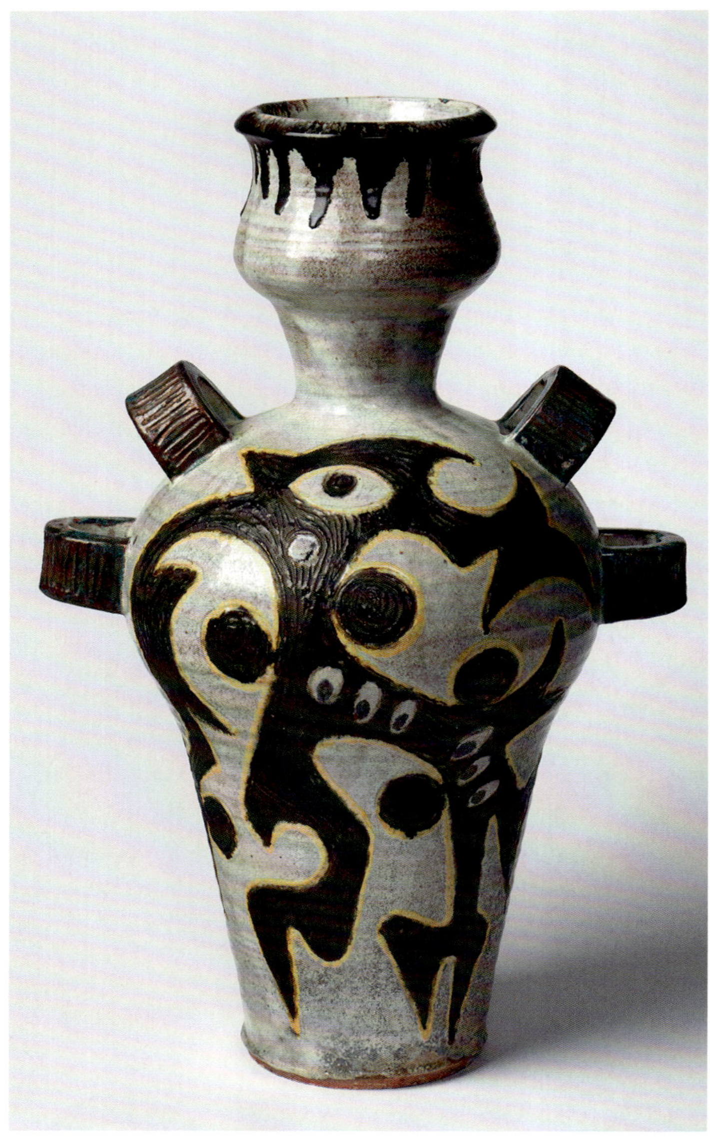

243 204/2005

Despite his teaching duties RK managed through the years to pursue an interesting career as an independent ceramicist with comprehensive exhibition activities in Denmark, the Nordic region, USA and France. In the many international promotional campaigns in the 1950s he contributed ceramic ware for household use as an exponent of Danish Design and functionalism; his iconic teapots and jugs in an organic idiom in brown, glazed and hard-fired earthenware were admired and featured in publications and they are to be found in the museum in a version from *c.*1945 **(244)**. In all his work RK focused on ceramic decoration, through experiments and research that gained extra momentum after he retired from teaching in 1985 (cf. the thorough analysis in Gerd Bloxham Zettersten's '*Richard Kjærgaard – A Modernist in Danish Ceramics*', Scandinavian Journal of Design History, 4, 1994, pp. 81-107).

But from the mid 1950s onwards there were also larger-scale works, made of earthenware with colourful abstract or partially figurative decoration, which were indicative of RK's interest in the spontaneous expressions of the Cobra movement. Thanks to the generosity of the artist's widow, Gurli Kjærgaard, it has been possible for the museum to acquire several major unique pieces of RK's *oeuvre*, including the large vase in earthenware decorated with a black fantasy animal on white glaze, from *c.*1955 **(243)**. Another important and well-known work, from 1962, is the cylindrical stoneware pot, freely modelled with applied slip and glazes in a modernist abstract relief decoration **(245)**. RK received the gold diploma for this work at the '*Exposition Internationale de la Céramique Contemporaine Prague*', 1962. In an interview from 1981 (*Kristeligt Dagblad*, 11.6.1981) RK distances himself from modernism (and perhaps this pot), because he came to feel that his 'things became aggressive'. He sought clarity of thought, not in conflict with anything extreme, but as the outcome of the effort to come to a decisive conclusion. As already mentioned, from the mid 1980s RK resumed his experiments with the development of decoration, its motifs and techniques and the interplay between form and ornament. In the museum's collection there are several works with new styles of ornamentation from those years, showing the use of different techniques, including stencils, stamps, transfers, glazing, etc. **(241-242,246-248)**.

In honour of the master-teacher, in 1995 Galleri Nørby, together with a group of 11 of RK's former pupils and teacher-colleagues, arranged the exhibition '*Lærer og elev*' (Teacher and pupil), which also displayed recent and earlier works by RK. There his early functional works could be seen side by side with samples of the later decorated works. The classical items for everyday use are to be found today all round the world in influential museums, but for RK time did not stand still. Until the end ceramics continued to tempt his curiosity and lead him to new experiments and research.

237. Bowl, 1949

Stoneware, glazed; thrown. H 3.5 x W 11.8. Mark: 'RK' painted on base. Mus.no. 6/1949. ACQUISITION: Den Permanente, 1949, Copenhagen. Donation from *Statens 50-års Jubilæumslegat*

238. Beaker, 1949

Stoneware, glazed; thrown. H 5.7 x Diam 6. Mark: 'RK' painted on base. Mus.no. 7/1949. ACQUISITION: Den Permanente, 1949, Copenhagen. Donation from *Statens 50-års Jubilæumslegat*

239. Bowl, 1976

Stoneware, zircon- and rutile- glazed; thrown. H 14.5 x Diam 19. Mark: 'RK [monogram] Danmark 76' painted on base. Mus.no. 66/1977 ACQUISITION: *Danske kunsthåndværkere*, 1977, Kunstindustrimuseum. Donation from *Overretssagfører Odin Kaysers Legat*. See: *Brændpunkter*, 1990.

240. Coffee pot and 2 cups with saucers, 1984

Stoneware, glazed; thrown, shaped, reduction-fired. a: H 16.7 x W 14; b: H 6.3 x W 9.4; c: H 1.5 x W 13.6. Mark: 'RK [monogram]1984 Danmark' painted on base. Mus.no. 159a-f/1984. ACQUISITION: Richard Kjærgaard. Donation from *Benny Dessaus Mindelegat*

241. Dish, 1986

Stoneware, glazed; thrown, shaped, slip. H 5 x W 44.5. Mark: 'RK [monogram] Danmark 1986' painted on base. Mus.no.108/1986. ACQUISITION: Galleri K, Copenhagen. Donation from *Kunstindustrimuseets Venner*

242. Dish, 1988

Stoneware, zircon- and rutile- glazed, thrown, shaped. H 5 x W 43.5 x D 37.5. Mark: 'RK [monogram] Danmark 1988' painted on base. Mus.no. 203/2005 ACQUISITION: Donation from Gurli Kjærgaard, Copenhagen

243. Sculptural vase, *c.*1955

Earthenware, tin-glazed; thrown, modelled, decorated with an 'amoeba-like pattern', reduction-fired. H 50 x Diam 24. Mark: 'RK Danmark Kastrup' painted on base. Mus.no. 204/2005. ACQUISITION: Donation from Gurli Kjærgaard, Copenhagen. See: *Brændpunkter*, 1990, p. 73

244. Teapot and jug, 1945

Earthenware, interior glazed, unglazed; thrown, shaped, polished. a-b: H 13 x W 26; c: H 14 x W 16. Mark: 'RK Danmark' painted on base. Mus. no. 205a-c/2005. ACQUISITION: Donation from Gurli Kjærgaard, Copenhagen. See: *Brændpunkter*, 1990, p. 65

245 69/2006

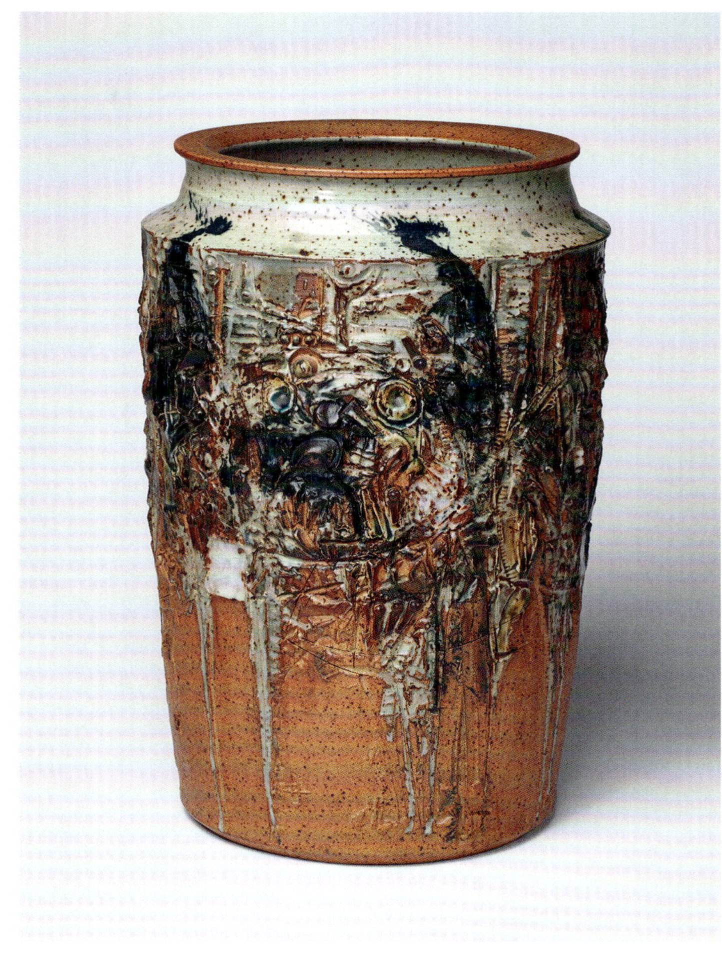

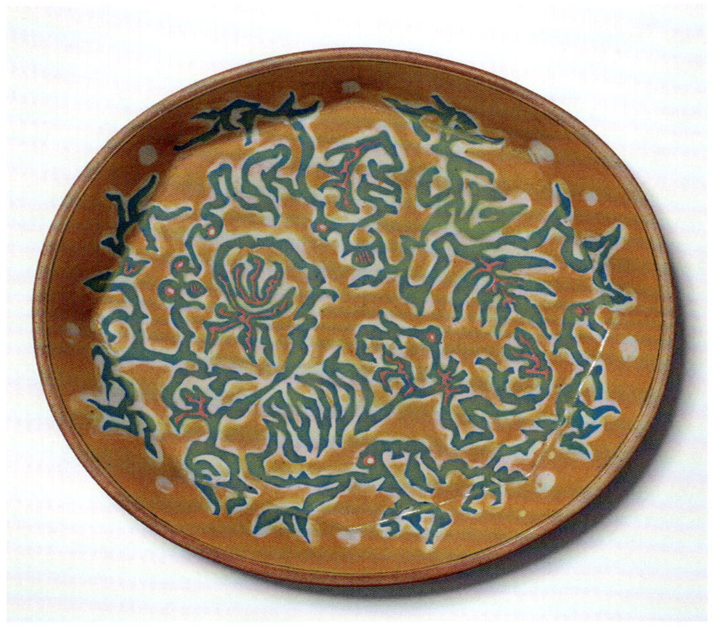

242 203/2005

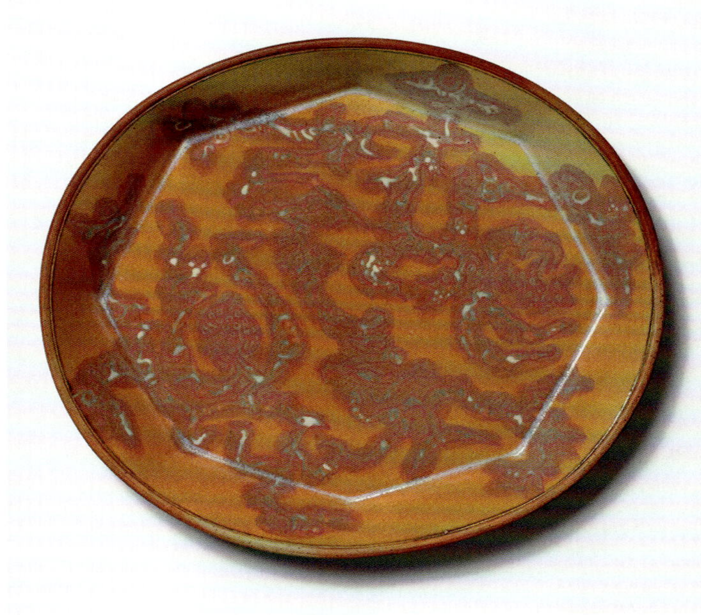

241 108/1986

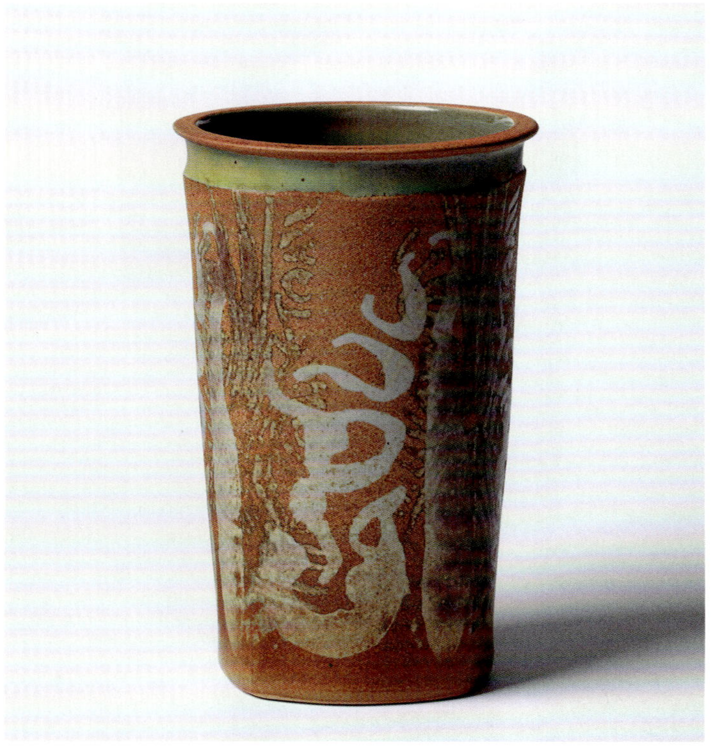

246 106/2010

245. Pot, 1962

Stoneware, glazed; thrown, modelled, scored, hard-fired. Gold diploma at the *Exposition Internationale de la Céramique Contemporaine Prague*, 1962. H 40 x Diam 30. Mark: 'RK Danmark' painted on base. Mus.no. 69/2006.
ACQUISITION: Gurli Kjærgaard. Donation from *Helge Jakobsens Mindelegat*

246. Vase, 1999

Stoneware, glazed; thrown, slip, brush-painted. H 19.3 x Diam 12.3.
Mark: 'RK[monogram] Danmark 1999' painted on base. Mus.no. 106/2010
ACQUISITION: Donation from Gurli Kjærgaard, Copenhagen

247. Bowl, 6-sided, 1998

Stoneware, transparent glaze; thrown, shaped, arabesque-like ornament in 6 fields. H 14.3 x Diam 21.3. Mark: 'RK [monogram] Danmark 1998' painted on base. Mus.no. 107/2010.
ACQUISITION: Donation from Gurli Kjærgaard, Copenhagen

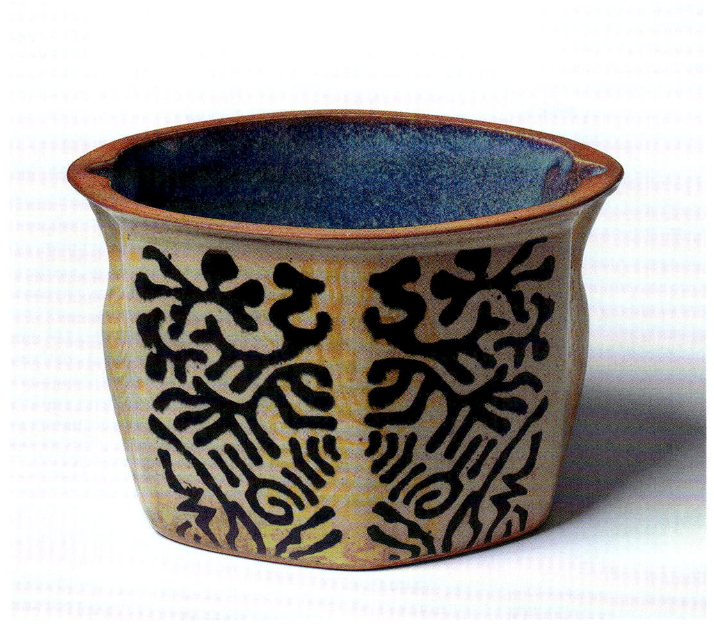

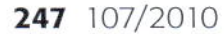

247 107/2010

248. Dish, 1986

Stoneware, glazed; thrown, shaped, slip, decorated. Mus.no. 108/2010

Mark: 'RK Danmark' painted on base.

ACQUISITION: Donation from Gurli Kjærgaard, Copenhagen

239 66/1977

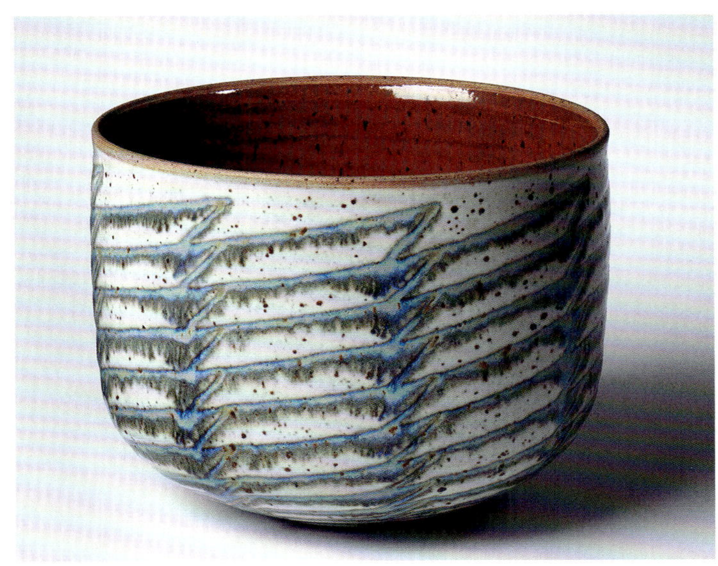

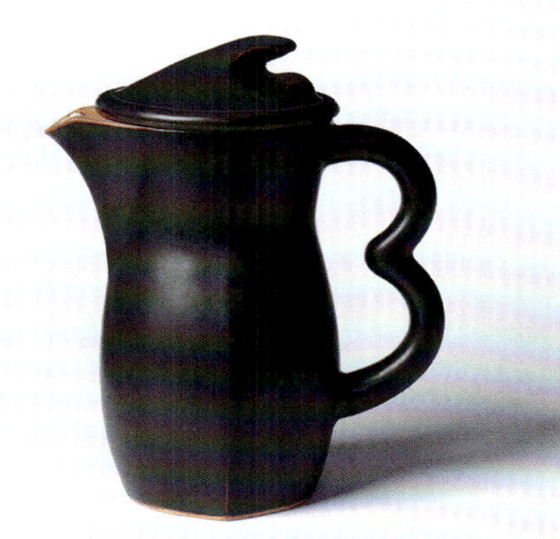

249 1089a-b/2010

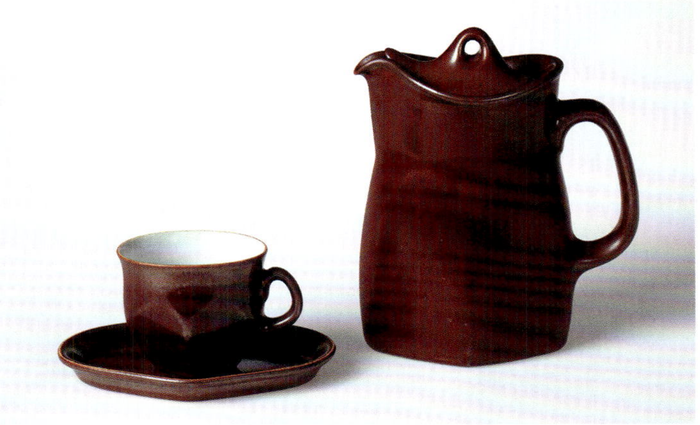

240 159a-f/1984

249. Jug with lid, 1996

Stoneware, glazed; thrown, shaped, pointed-oval cross-section, glazed inside.

H 19.5. Mark: 'RK Danmark 1996' painted on base. Mus.no. 109a-b/2010

ACQUISITION: Donation from Gurli Kjærgaard, Copenhagen

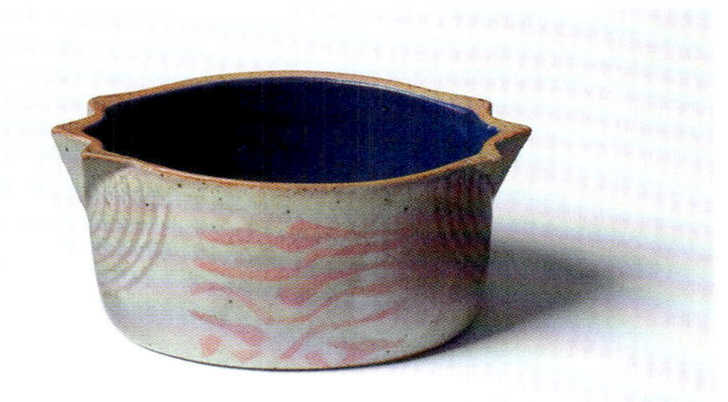

248 108/2010

KJÆRSGAARD, ANNE 1933 – 1990

Ceramicist

1951-55	Kunsthåndværkerskolen; workshop experience in 8 studios in Denmark and Norway
1955	Own studio workshop, Ringsted
1956-58	Bernard Leach, St. Ives, Cornwall, workshop experience
1958-90	Own studio workshop, France: La Borne, Laspeyres, La Borne
1976-77	Boulder University, Colorado, USA, guest teacher

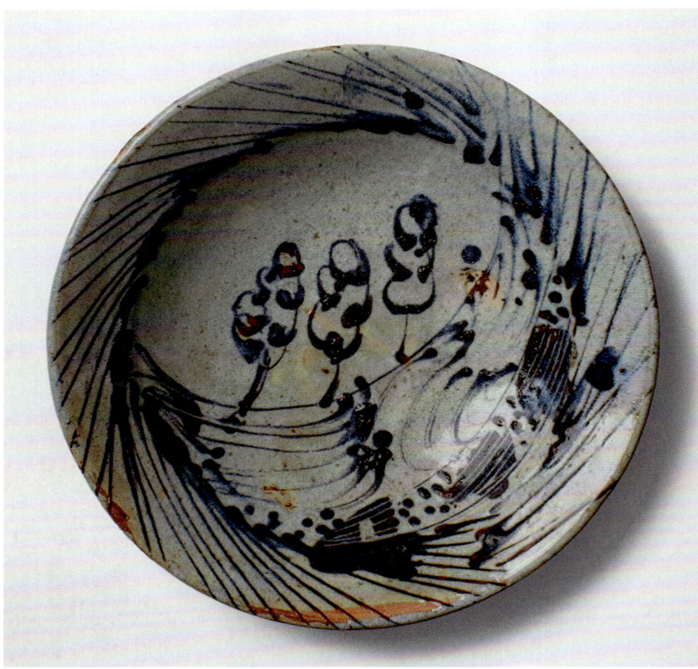

250 1/1983

Anne Kjærsgaard (AK) studied in Denmark, but moved to France in 1958, and there she developed a respected ceramic *oeuvre*, based in and around La Borne, with its rich ceramic tradition, its natural supply of fine stoneware clay and ready access to fuel from nearby forests for wood-firing, which became AK's preferred technique. AK set up workshop(s) with wood-fired kilns and began production of functional domestic objects in glazed stoneware, building, in terms of design, on French traditions. But AK also had other significant experience to

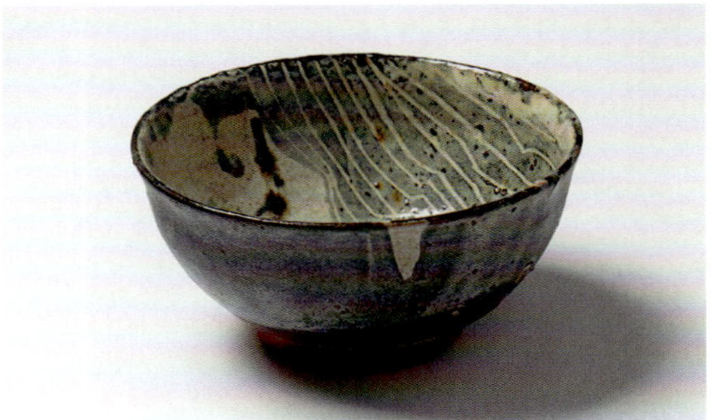

251 2/1983

bring to bear on her new work, from the two years she had spent with the influential English potter Bernard Leach and from the Japanese-inspired stoneware which was the hallmark of Leach's workshop. AK remained in contact with Leach, who supported her, and in the area of glazing in particular she built on the knowledge she had acquired in his workshop. In Denmark AK exhibited her work in Galleri Birkdam, Copenhagen, in 1965, 1977 and again in 1982, when the museum acquired two works **(250-251)**; later a third was added, in the form

252 40/2010

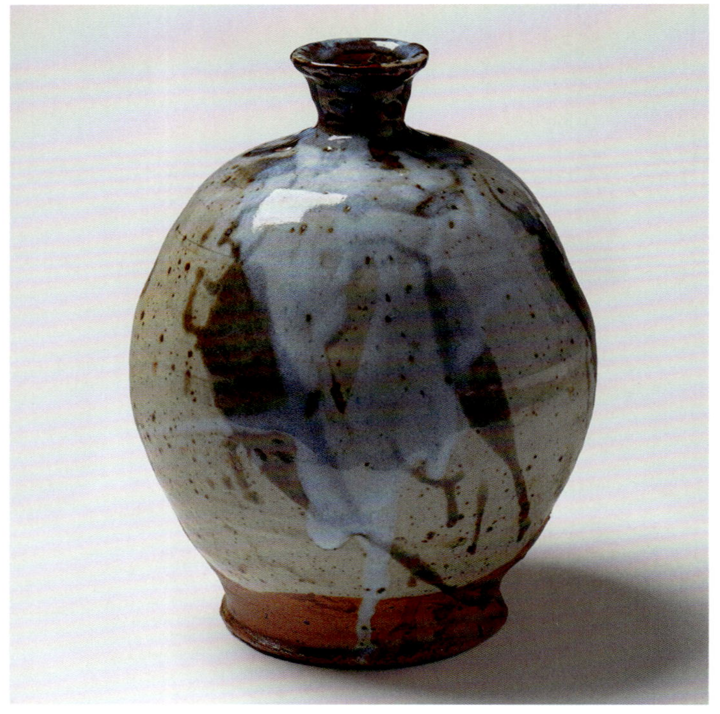

of a private donation of a sturdy pot from 1989 which demonstrates the artist's mastery of glazing, shown not least in the works from the 1980s **(252)**. These three works radiate a personal animus, in which the artistic expression stands firm throughout the kiln's melting of clay, slip, glaze and decoration. AK took as her departure-point the styles of the French potters, but over the course of her life she developed a free painterly nature-inspired decoration of traditional objects for domestic use: dishes, pots, jugs, bowls and plates, and she stuck to those designs. Through the 1980s AK nurtured exhibition activities on a large scale in France, the Netherlands, Sweden and Denmark. AK kept up her links with Danish ceramics through friendships with fellow ceramicists, especially from the group around Gutte Eriksen and Det Jyske Kunstakademi, whose appreciation of her work remains alive. In Denmark in general AK was not well-known, but this was rectified with a comprehensive retrospective exhibition at Grimmerhus in 2009 (see: exhibition catalogue '*Anne Kjærsgaard*', Museum of Ceramic Art, Grimmerhus, 2009). The lifework of this fine ceramicist was unfolded, showing how she succeeded, despite hard conditions, in creating works whose appeal to the spirit and the senses, through their ceramic originality and beauty, has given her a notable position in both French and Danish ceramics.

250. Dish, 1982

Stoneware, clear-glazed; thrown, slip, horn-decorated, wood-fired. H 7 x Diam 29.8. Mark: 'A' painted on base. Mus.no. 1/1983. ACQUISITION: Galleri Birkdam, 1982, Copenhagen. Donation from *Statens 50-års Jubilæumslegat*

251. Bowl, 1982

Stoneware, clear-glazed; thrown, slip, decorated, wood-fired. H 9.5 x Diam 19.3. Mark: 'Anne' painted on base. Mus.no. 2/1983
ACQUISITION: Galleri Birkdam, 1982, Copenhagen. Donation from *Statens 50-års Jubilæumslegat*. See: *Brændpunkter i dansk keramik 1890-1990.*

252. Pot, 1989

Stoneware, glazed; thrown, slip, wood-fired. H 25.3. Mark: indecipherable signature painted on base. Mus.no. 40/2010. ACQUISITION: Galerie Epona, 1991, Paris. Donation from André and Nadine Laviolette

KNUDSEN, PER BØRGLUM 1947 – 2004

Potter

1964-68	Kähler Keramik, Næstved, trained as a potter
1968-70	Kunsthåndværkerskolen
1970s	Employment with the Royal Porcelain Factory
1980s	Pottemagerskolen, Sønderborg, instructor
	Own studio workshop at intervals

Per Børglum Knudsen (PBK) trained as a potter in the firm of Kähler Keramik and was exceptionally skilled at throwing. He became Nordic champion in throwing pots in 1981.For a time PBK was attached to the Royal Porcelain factory and worked independently with coloured porcelain clay. In 1984 the museum acquired two very precisely- and skilfully- made works from that year.

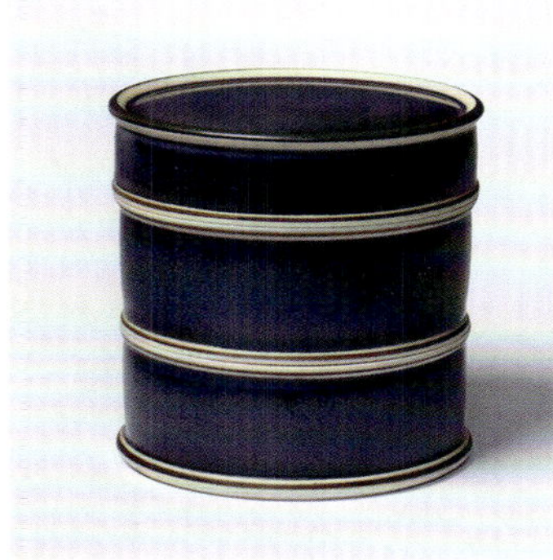

253 116a-c/1984

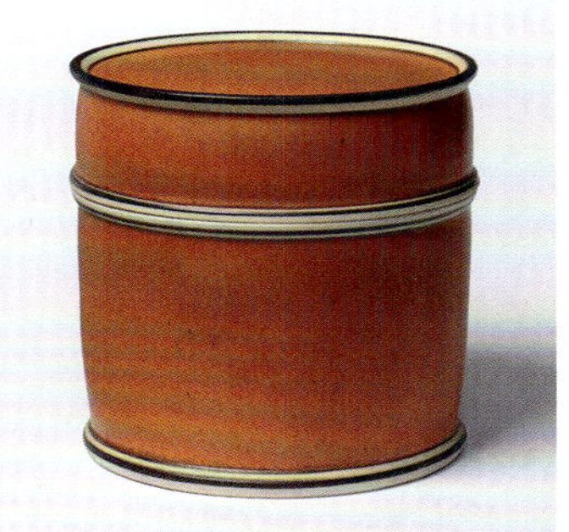

254 150a-b/1984

253. Lidded pot, 1984

Porcelain clay, glazed; cast. H 15.7 x Diam 15.4. Mark: 'Per Børglum Knudsen 84' painted on base. Mus.no. 116a-c/1984
ACQUISITION: *Forårsudstillingen*, 1984, Charlottenborg. Donation from *Finansieringsinstituttet for Industri og Håndværks Jubilæumslegat*

254. Lidded pot, 1984

Porcelain clay, glazed; cast. H 18.8 x Diam 18.5. Mark: 'Per Børglum Knudsen 84' painted on base. Mus.no. 150a-b/1984
ACQUISITION: Per Børglum Knudsen. This work was awarded a bronze medal and exhibited in the display *'Kunsthåndværkerprisen af 1879'*, Kunstindustrimuseum 1984. Donation from *Benny Dessaus Mindelegat*

KRISTENSEN, KNUD 1948 –

Sculptor, ceramicist

1982-83 Aarhus Kunstakademi
1983-89 Det Jyske Kunstakademi, sculpture, ceramics
1989-91 Own studio workshop, Aarhus
91-92 Own studio workshop, Odder
92-2002 Own studio workshop, Høng
2002-11 Own studio workshop, Velling Kirkeby
2012- Own studio workshop, Velling

Ceramic works by Knud Kristensen (KK) can clearly be distinguished from other contemporary Danish ceramics, despite the fact that his favourite shapes are bowls, dishes and pots. He specialises in delicately shaped and finished lidded pots, which bear references to the ancient cultures of Egypt and Greece, but also to African objects and sculptures. The surface treatment and decoration in particular provide the associations with distant times and cultures.

KK throws his works and covers them with several layers of slip, and then inscribes patterns, often in vertical bands running from the top to the bottom and crossed by horizontal borders where the lid and lower part meet. With the layers of slip KK achieves very fine colours – yellow, aubergine, dark blue, etc. The pots are unglazed and matte in appearance, but when the surfaces are polished a soft sheen is produced. The museum's lidded pot is a good example of KK's refined works **(255)**. Since the 1990s in particular KK has participated in many exhibitions in the Nordic region, and in 2004 he produced a commissioned work for the library in Høng municipality. After a break of some years KK has recently resumed ceramic activities.

255. Lidded pot, 1990

Stoneware; thrown, modelled, slip, inlaid decoration, hatching, polished, fired at 1100°. H 24 x Diam 35. Mark: 'Knud Kristensen' inscribed on base. Mus. no. 39/1991. ACQUISITION: Jubilee donation from *Justitsråd J. F. Møllmanns Legatfond*. See: Dybdahl, L., 1997

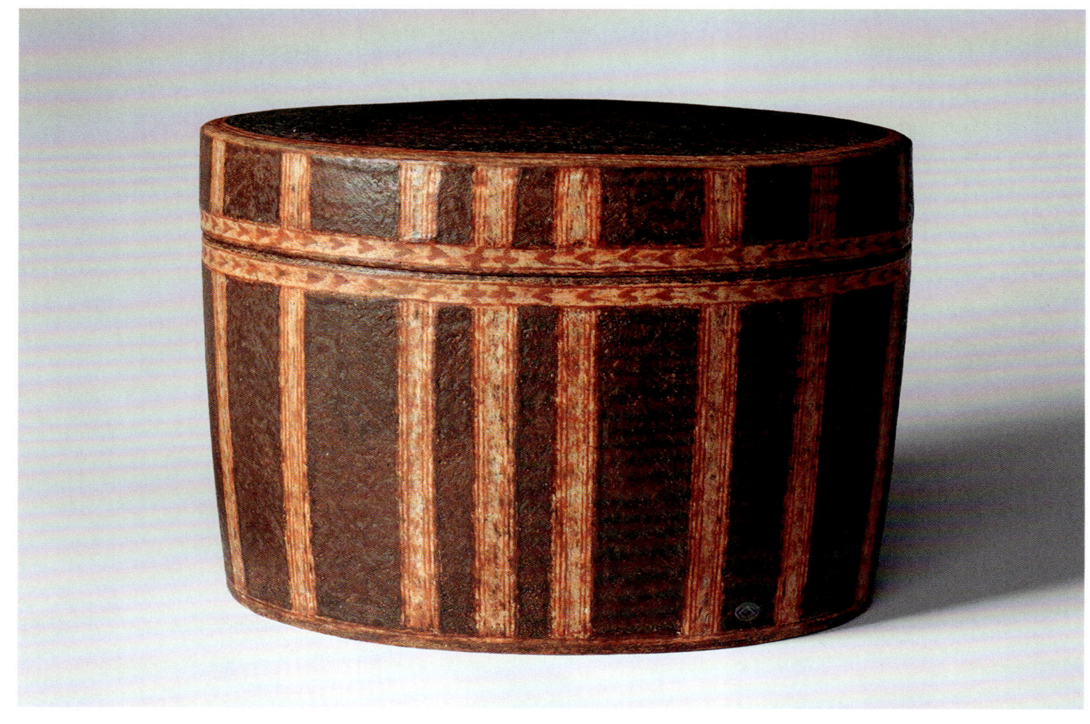

255 39/1991

KRISTENSEN, NINA MØLLER 1946 –

Ceramicist

1965-69 Kunsthåndværkerskolen

1969-72 The Royal Danish Academy of Fine Arts, School of Walls and Space

1972-74 School of Art Education

1979- Own studio workshop, Copenhagen

www.ninamk-keramik.dk

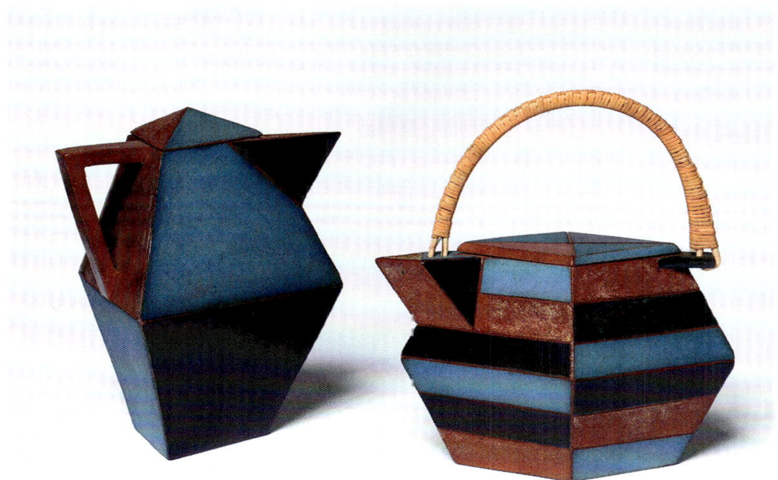

257 123a-b/1999

256 122a-b/1999

From an early stage in her career Nina Møller Kristensen (NMK) established a clear framework of norms for her ceramic work and set herself goals of achieving luminously simplified design with correlations both between shape and colour and between shape and decoration. Her works – often functional objects such as jugs, pots, bowls and cups – display discipline but combine this with movement because of her choice of surprisingly asymmetrical 3- or 5-sided basic shapes, with a geometry which is carried over into many facets, making up a characterful system in combination with coloured glazes and layers of slip. NMK chose earthenware, Danish red clay, as her material because of its softness and warmth. Even though her works are fired at a rather high temperature for earthenware, she finds it possible to cultivate particular colours in the glazes and layers of slip that she produces herself in the workshop, with the certainty that they are lead-free.

In 1999 the museum acquired two works by NMK **(256-257)** that are characteristic of this precise and skilled ceramicist, who studied both at the Kunsthåndværkerskolen and at the Royal Danish Academy of Fine Arts, and was also trained in the Skole for Kunstpædagogik, set up by Helge Bertram. NMK has moreover worked e.g. with fluoride glazes, which Bertram experimented with in the mid 1960s, and she has been inspired by his investigative methods.

256. Teapot, 1999

Earthenware, borax-, frit- and fluoride-glazed, partly unglazed; slab technique, slip, brush-painted, fired at 1055°. H 17.5 x W 17 x Diam 9.5.

Mark: 'NKM 1 99' inscribed on base. Mus.no. 122a-b/1999

ACQUISITION: *Lertøj – brugsting*, 1999, Galleri Nørby, Copenhagen

257. Jug with lid, 1999

Earthenware, borax-, frit- and fluoride- glazed, partly unglazed; slab technique, slip, filled, brush-painted, fired at 1055°. H 17 x W 17 x Diam 13.

Mark: 'NMK 1.99' inscribed on base. Mus.no. 123a-b/1999

ACQUISITION: *Lertøj – brugsting*, 1999, Galleri Nørby, Copenhagen

KRISTIANSEN, BO 1944 – 1991

Ceramicist

1962-65 Kunsthåndværkerskolen
1968-79 Studio workshop shared with ceramicist Julie Høm, Bornholm
1974-80 Attached to the Royal Porcelain Factory
1979-91 Own studio workshop, Copenhagen

Despite the fact that he died before reaching the age of 50, Bo Kristiansen (BK) created a ceramic *oeuvre* that won a place in the history of Danish ceramics in the second half of the 20th century, through its originality and confident execution, achieved through the methodical cultivation and refinement of one basic idea: a form of ceramic decoration consisting of letters of the alphabet. The font he chose was inspired by Latin antiqua fonts, which he worked with and cut or

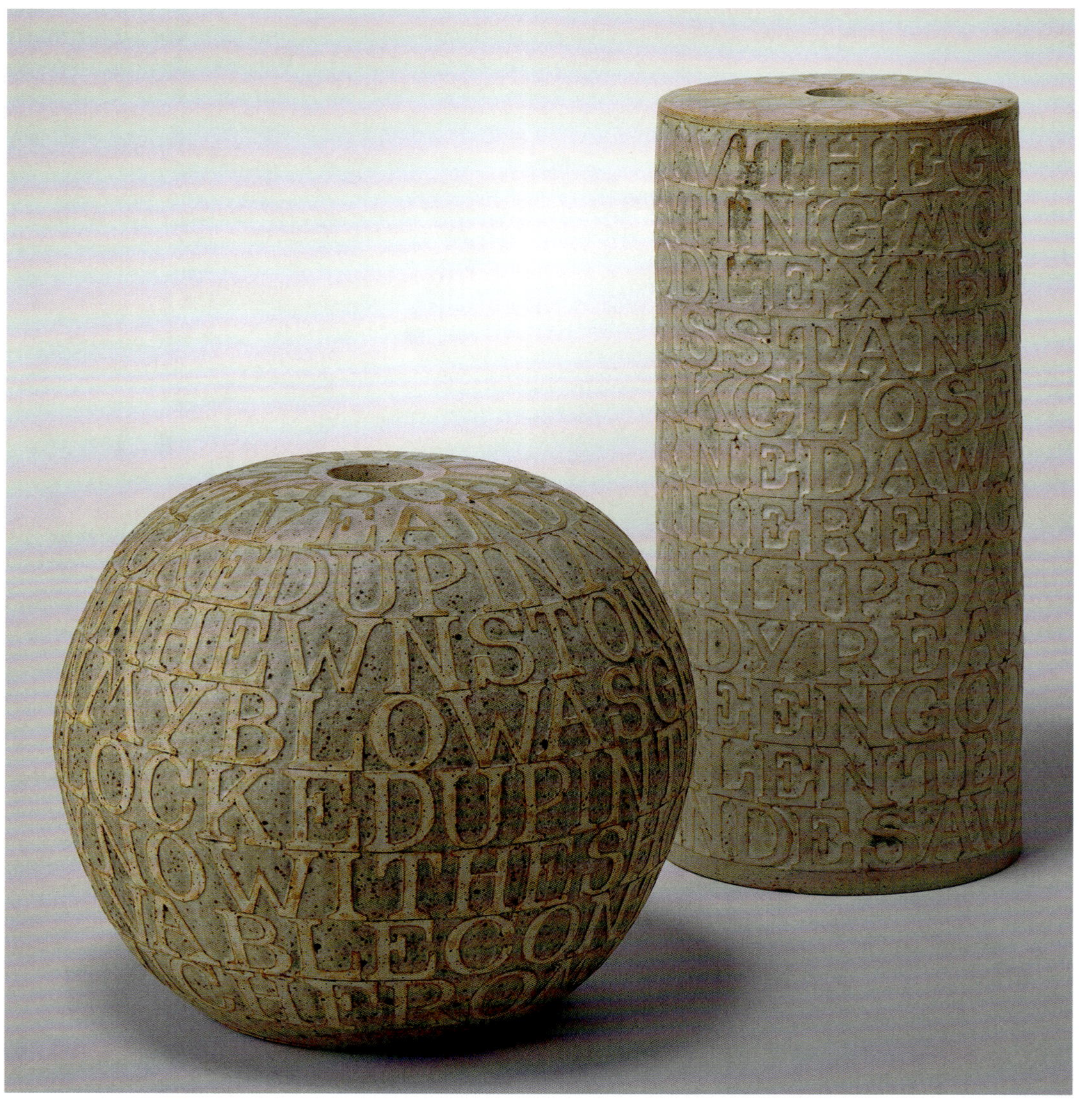

258 34/1973 **261** 115/2009

scratched by hand into the wet clay of the thrown object. The shapes BK decorated were mostly traditional bowls, lidded pots, spherical pots and cylinders, made and thrown by BK with great precision in stoneware clay which he mixed himself and to which he added a special greyish Bornholm clay. The decoration consists of regular rows of letters, in two sizes, running round the shape, with the large letters covered by two smaller ones, and then slip in various colours is painted on the fields between. The painted surface is polished before firing, which is done twice. Some of the works are subsequently decorated with gold leaf using cold gilding. For a number of years BK was employed by the Royal Porcelain Factory, which was planning to put in production 'semi-unique' stoneware, of which there are several known examples by BK. But he also worked with faience, transferring alphabet decoration onto it by silk screen printing.

See: Lautrup-Larsen, L., 2007.

In the museum's collection there are four works by BK, representing various types of shapes and decoration. The earliest is from 1971 **(258)**, and is a perfect sphere covered with white slip, with a little opening and letters cut in relief. On this work the letters form a continuous text from the poem 'The Stone' by Gustaf Munch-Petersen; through his marriage to Julie Høm BK found himself in the inner circle of ceramicists on Bornholm with the Hjorth family in its centre. On other works BK used lines from Walt Whitman or Dylan Thomas, always in

259 9a-b/1982

260 134a-b/1988

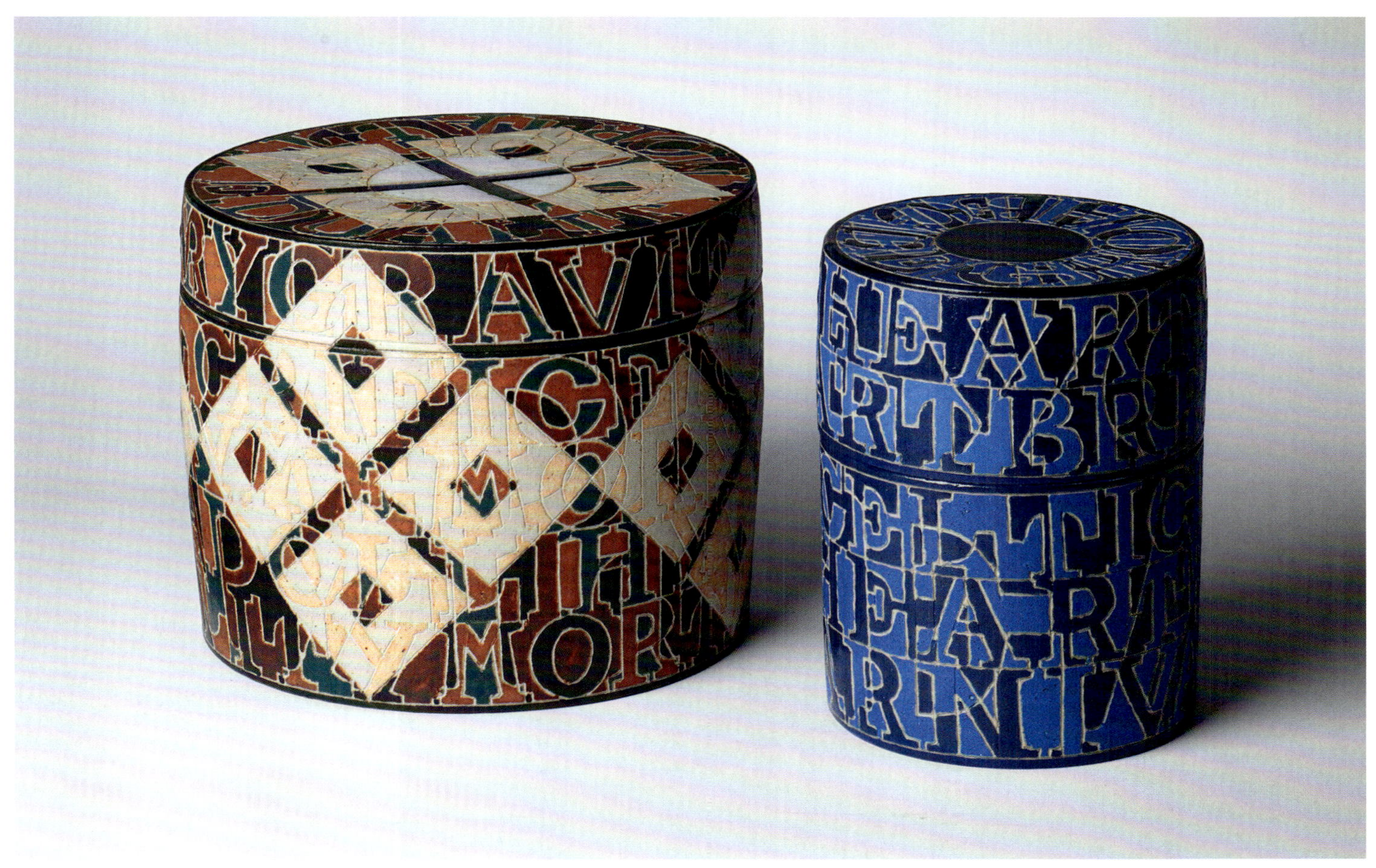

English to avoid the special Danish letters Æ, Ø and Å, but it was only on the earliest works that there was a continuous legible text.

From 1975 there is a very vital and delicately shaped bowl **(261)** with inscribed letters and an abstract decoration running across parts of the letters. The bowl is glazed and covered with slip inside and out in a warm, subdued colour range with blue and red shades. From 1981 **(259)** and 1988 **(260)** respectively there are two cylindrical lidded pots, both with inscribed letter-decoration. The pot from 1981 has an atypical combination of letters and geometric fields.

In 1979, after many years on Bornholm, BK moved to Copenhagen, where he continued to be attached to the Royal Porcelain Factory. He exhibited in Denmark and abroad; his work was well-received from an early stage, and is represented in leading museums and collections.

258. Spherical pot, 1971.

Stoneware, glazed; thrown, slip, letter-decoration in relief (part of Gustaf Munch-Petersen's poem 'The Stone'), fired at c. 1320°. H 32.
Mark: 'K' inscribed on base. Mus.no. 34/1973
ACQUISITION: *Bo Kristiansen – stentøj,* 1973, Kunstindustrimuseet.
Donation from *Kunstindustrimuseets 50-års Jubilæumslegat*

259. Cylinder-shaped lidded pot, 1981

Stoneware, glazed; thrown, slip made of pipe clay coloured with oxides and pre-stained, inscribed letter-decoration, fired at c. 1320°. H 16.5 x Diam 19.5.
Mark: none. Mus.no. 9a-b/1982
ACQUISITION: Galleriet, Kolding. Donation from *Benny Dessaus Mindelegat*

260. Cylinder-shaped lidded pot, 1988

Stoneware, glazed; thrown, slip of pipe-clay, coloured with oxides and pre-stained, inscribed letter-decoration. H 16.3 x Diam 12.3. Mark: none.
Mus.no. 134a-b/1988
ACQUISITION: Galleri Weinberger, 1988, Copenhagen. Donation from *Kunstindustrimuseets Venner og Den Weinbergske Familiefond.*
See: *Brændpunkter*, 1990

261. Cylinder-shaped pot, 1975

Stoneware, glazed; thrown, slip of pipe-clay, coloured with oxides and pre-stained, inscribed letter-decoration. H 20.5 x Diam 25. Mark: 'K' inscribed on base. Mus.no. 115/2009
ACQUISITION: Donation from *Ny Carlsbergfondet*

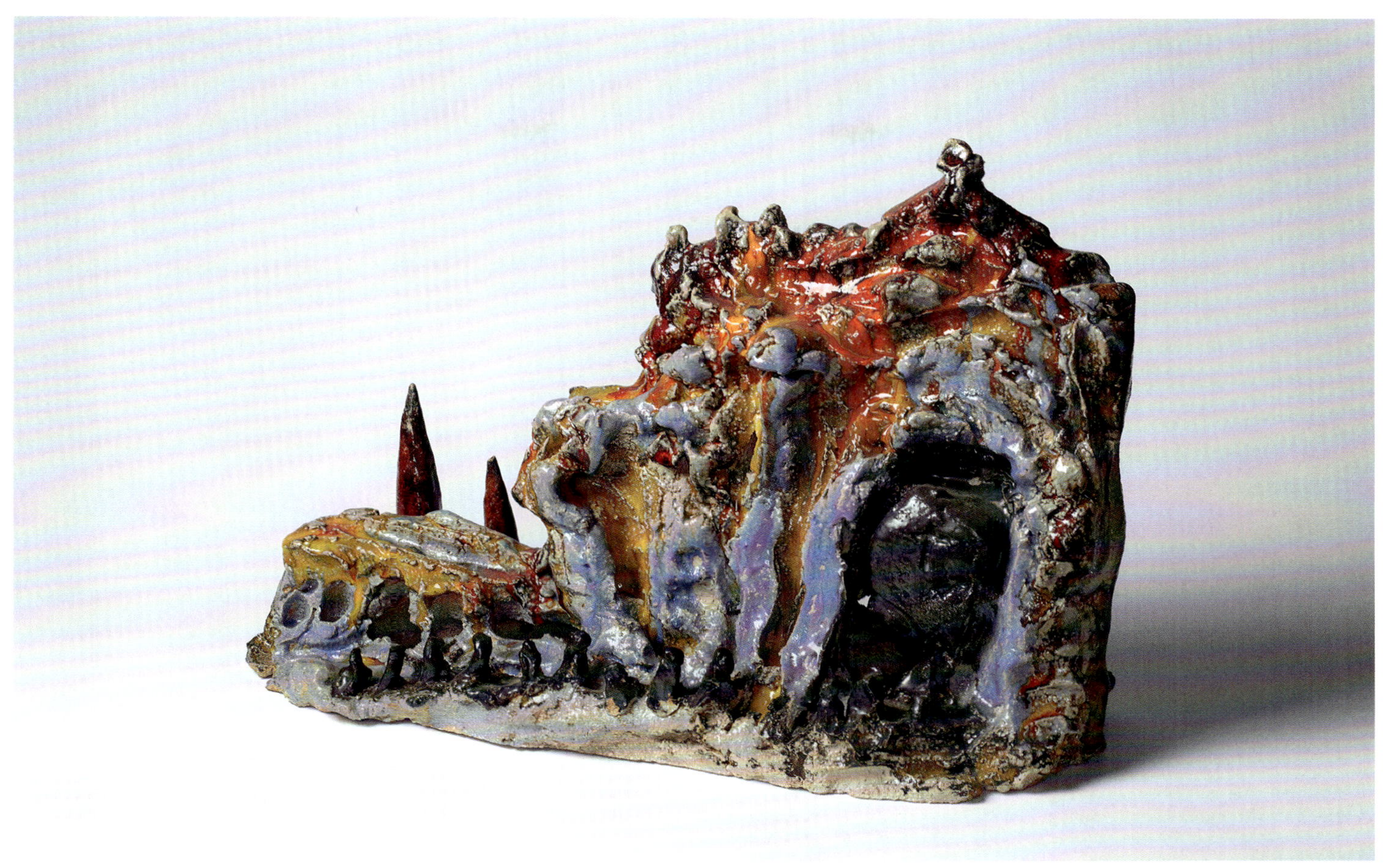

262 149/1990

KRÜGER, ANDERS 1960 –

Sculptor

1985-91	Royal Danish Academy of Fine Arts, School of Sculpture
1996-97	University of California, San Diego, guest lecturer
1997-2000	Umeå University, Sweden, Professor
2004-05	Kunstakademiet, Stockholm, Architecture
2008-10	Grafikens Hus, Mariefred, Sweden, Artistic Director

Anders Krüger (AK) was born in Sweden, educated at the Art Academy in Copenhagen as a student of Bjørn Nørgaard, and then studied architecture at the Art Academy in Stockholm. He has developed his experimental methods around the world, and has created sculptures; he has worked with film and in museums, has curated exhibitions and has taught courses in various institutions. AK lives in Sweden. The museum has one work by AK, made in 1990 and acquired in the same year **(262)**.

This strongly expressive sculpture is reminiscent of some of Lene Adler Petersen's works from the mid 1980s. (See: Sculptural Considerations, Vandalorum, Centre for Art and Design, Värnamo, Sweden, 2012.)

262. Sculpture, 1990

Earthenware, glazed; modelled. H 39 x W 60 x D 20. Mark: 'A.K. 98' painted on base. Mus.no. 149/1990. ACQUISITION: Galleri Stadshil, Copenhagen. Donation from *Forenede Legater*

KÄHLER, HERMAN JØRGEN 1904 – 1996

Ceramicist

1918-20	Kähler Keramik, Næstved, trained as a potter
1925-28	(c.) Norway, in charge of a small workshop
1928	Kähler Keramik, Næstved, journeyman
1940-60	Kähler Keramik, technical/administrative superintendent
1960-69	Kähler Keramik, director
1974 (70)	Own studio workshop, Viemose, SE Sealand

As part of the fourth generation of the legendary Kähler pottery dynasty and the eldest son of the powerful Herman H.C. Kähler (1876 – 1940), Herman Jørgen Kähler (HJK), like his 2-year-younger brother Nils, was predestined to go into the firm after training as a potter in the same place, but his métier turned out to be instead as a technical and business manager.

Before HJK took up his place in the family business in earnest he went to sea for some years and also spent some time as workshop manager for the Norwegian artists and ceramicists Lalla Hvalstad and Lili Scheel, who worked with decorated earthenware.

With HJK as the last director in the family and with the sale of Kähler Keramik to Næstved municipality in 1974 there came the end of an important epoch. There was a large production of Kähler Keramik from the middle of the 19th century to the closure of the firm in 1974; it became a focus of international attention in the decades around 1900, and it was used daily in many Danish homes. Kähler Keramik forms an important chapter in Danish ceramic culture and history See: Rasmussen, P., 2002.

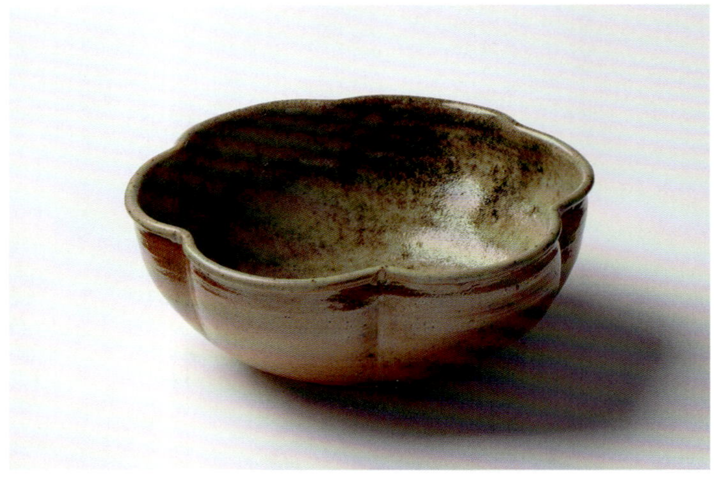

263 61/1983

264 229a-e/1994

266 136a-b/1996

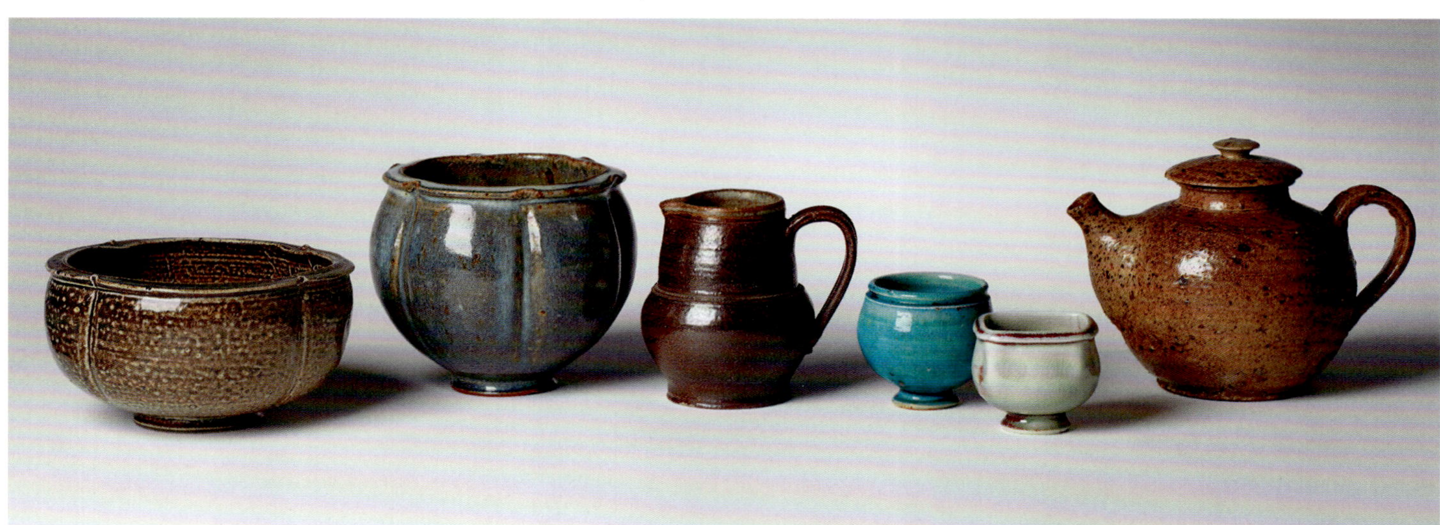

The ceramic production of the factory falls outside the remit of the present catalogue, which deals only with unique works from individual studio workshops, but the museum has a little collection of works by HJK that he made after the break away from Kähler Keramik at the beginning of the 1970s, when HJK set up his own workshop. Despite the many years when HJK had been engaged mainly in business and technical matters concerning production, but also advising artists on the execution of decoration, etc., he found the will and initiative to go back to the wheel and begin again working for himself, choosing glazed stoneware as his material. Right up to his death HJK exhibited his own works e.g. in Den Permanente and Illums Bolighus.

The museum's works by HJK date from the 1980s and 90s and are representative examples of the objects for functional use that he made in his own workshop **(263-266)**.

263. Bowl, 1983

Stoneware, iron grains, saltglazed; thrown, slip. H 7.3 x Diam 18.4.
Mark: 'HJK' inscribed on base. Mus.no. 61/1983
ACQUISITION: *Dagens ret*, 1983, Kunstindustrimuseet. Donation from *Benny Dessaus Mindelegat*. See: Thomsen, S., 1983

264. Jug and four bowls, 1980s

Stoneware, saltglazed; thrown. a: H 8.5 x W 15; b: H 11.5 x W 14; c: H 10.5 x W 10.5; d: H 4.5 x W 7; e: H 6.5 x W 7. Mark: 'HJK' inscribed on base. Mus.no. 229a-e/1994.
ACQUISITION: Donation from ceramicis Peter Winkel, Møen

265. Bowl, 1900s (No photo)

Stoneware, saltglazed; thrown. H 9 x W 15. Mark: 'HJK IX' inscribed on base. Mus.no. 230/1994.
ACQUISITION: Hermann Jørgen Kähler

266. Teapot, 1980s

Stoneware, saltglazed; thrown. H 12 x W 18. Mark: 'HJK' inscribed on base. Mus.no. 136a-b/1996
ACQUISITION: Donation from ceramicist Sys Thomsen

LINDBLAD, GRETHE 1926 –

Ceramicist

1955	Qualified from Kunsthåndværkerskolen
1956-57	Workshop shared with Signe Boesen, Lyngby, Sealand
1960-67	Own studio workshop, Hjortekær
1967-71	Own studio, Bornholm

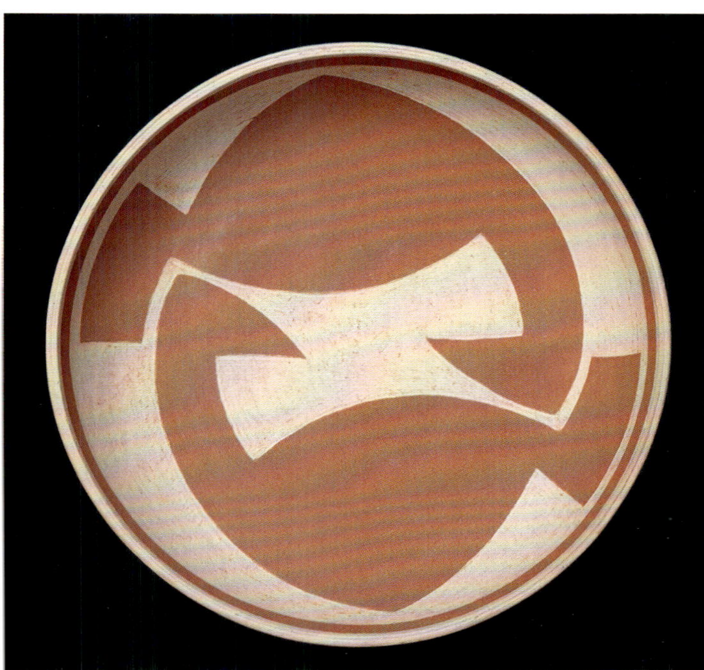

267 33/2002

Grethe Lindblad (GL) studied at Kunsthåndværkerskolen until 1955; after sharing a workshop for a short time with a school friend, Signe Boesen, she set up a new studio on her own in Hjortekær in 1960 – a studio that Bjørn Wiinblad took over in 1967 when GL moved to Bornholm. By that time GL was a known and respected ceramicist with experience of international exhibitions, and her works had been sold to museums in Denmark and elsewhere. She had been awarded official prizes and bursaries.

GL won recognition not least for her nature-inspired works, with delicate decoration often in under-glaze painting, which had a particularly luminous effect thanks to a glazing technique that she used, involving spreading coloured and transparent glazes over a white slip. During firing the glaze and the body melt together into one substance.

GL used some of the same technique in a series of large dishes and bowls from c. 1960, decorated with stylised bird-motifs that stand out starkly against the surrounding white slip, giving a fine graphic effect. See: Bloxham, G., 1990, p. 28. Serena, L., 2004

267. Bowl, 1960

Earthenware; thrown, slip, hard-fired, sgrafitto. H 10.6 x Diam 37.8.
Mark: 'Grethe Lindblad Danmark 60' inscribed on base. Mus.no. 33/2002
ACQUISITION: Grethe Lindblad, Bornholm

LINNEMANN, ANN 1957 –

Ceramic designer

1979-83	Kähler Keramik, Næstved, trained as a potter
1983-89	Danmarks Designskole
1993-94	Arizona State University, USA, graduate research scholar
1993	Archie Bray Foundation, Montana, USA, artist-in-residence
1994-95	Banff Arts Centre, Alberta, Canada, artist-in-residence
1996-	Own studio workshop, Copenhagen
1999-07	Guldagergaard, International Ceramic Research Center, Skelskør; 2005-07 Director
2008-	Ann Linneman Studie Galleri, Copenhagen www.annlinnemann.blogspot.com

268 171/1997

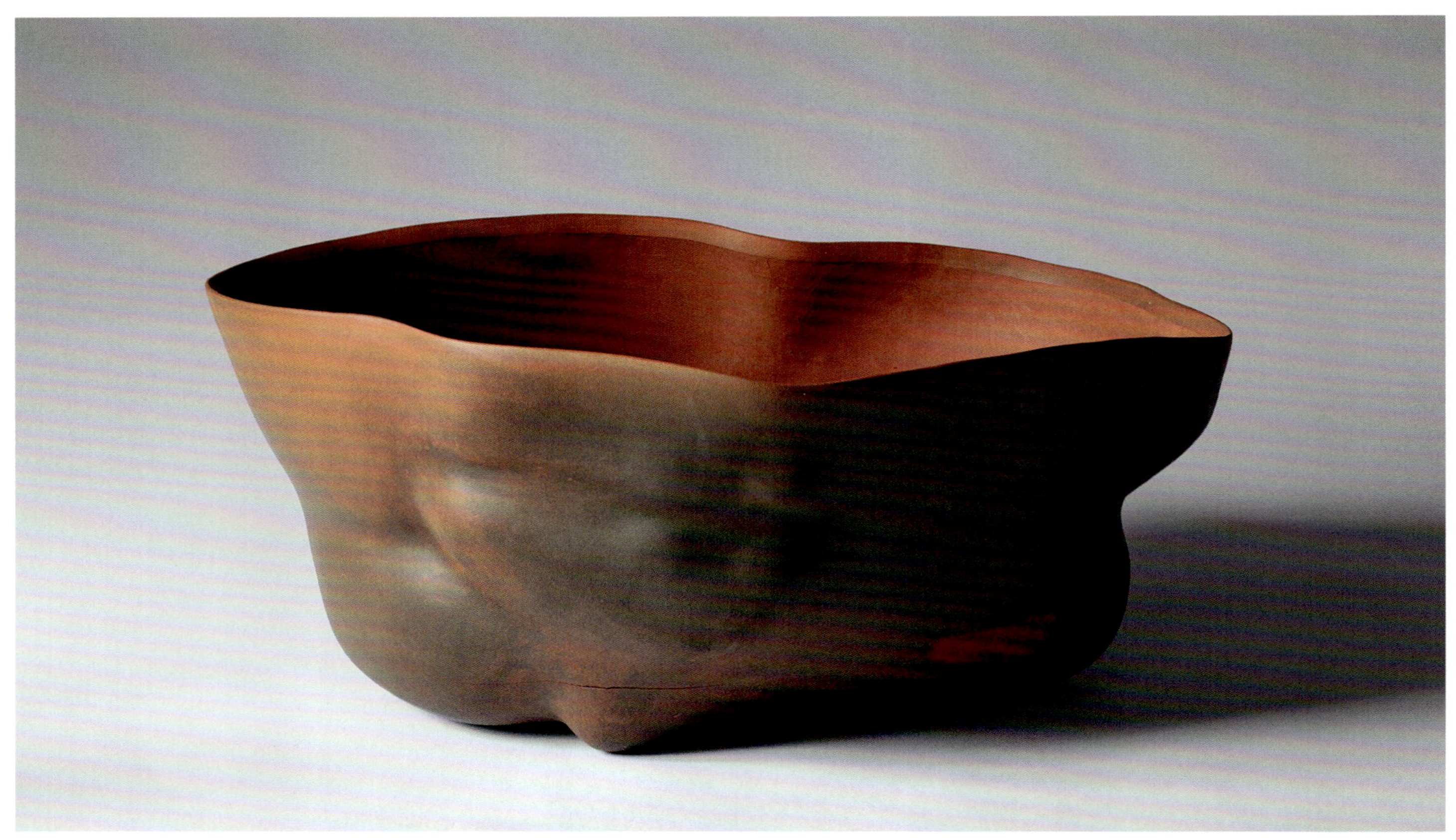

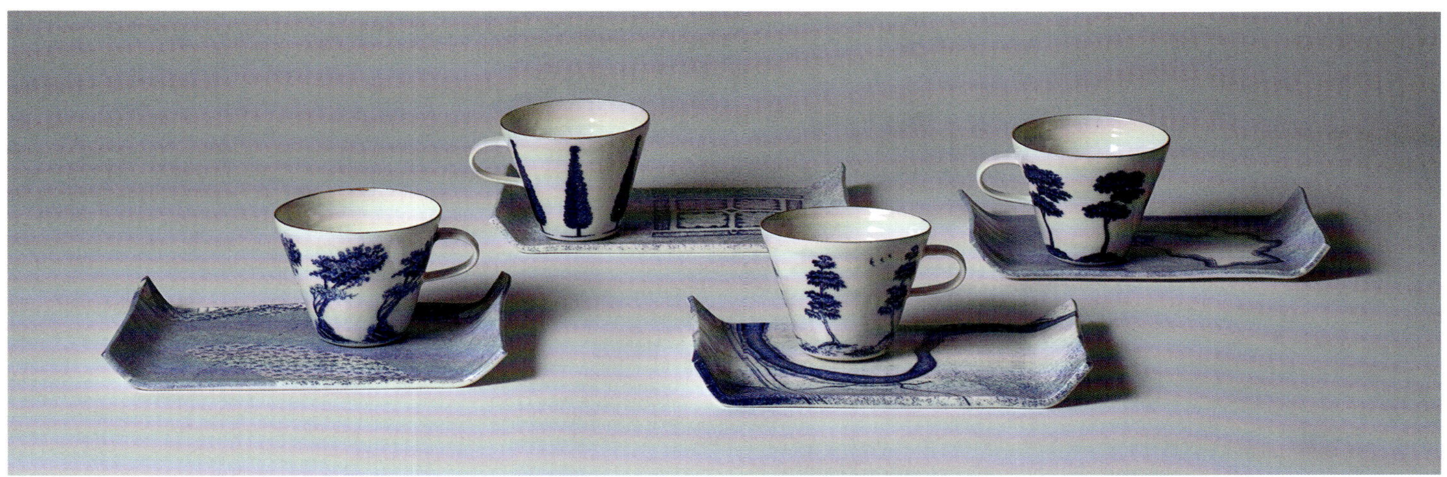

269 100a-h/2011

Ann Linnemann (AL) has a broad education, first as a potter in the firm of Kähler Keramik, then as a student at Danmarks Designskole, supplemented by several years of studying in the USA and Canada. AL was therefore well-equipped to develop a personal career with several strands in it, not only as a ceramicist, but also taking up appointment as director of the institution of Guldagergaard, and since 2008 running a professional gallery.

As a result of her extensive international network, built up through many years of participating around the world in exhibitions, workshops, seminars, commissions, and symposia, and guest lecturing and board memberships, AL has since 2008 put in place an exhibition programme, in her studio-gallery in the centre of Copenhagen, of great interest and high quality, involving both Danish and foreign ceramicists; now, alongside Galleri Pagter in Kolding, AL's Studie Galleri is the only specialised ceramic gallery in Denmark. In spite of these efforts, AL has succeeded in pursuing her work as a studio ceramicist, and has continuously produced series of small functional objects in porcelain, earthenware and stoneware, as well as large sculptural works which are mostly abstract, but often with the human torso as the departure-point. A case in point is the large earthenware vessel from 1995 which the museum acquired in 1997; it evokes organic and anthropomorphic qualities despite its form as a vessel **(268)**.

In recent years AL has experimented with decoration of these body-like shapes in a type of work which she calls 'Body Landscape', where the basic shape is painted with landscapes, trees and motifs from the many journeys, impressions and moods she has experienced. AL is a particularly gifted ceramicist who masters her craft and can throw porcelain so that it is really transparent, thin and delicate. This exceptionally skilled craftwork also characterises the household objects that can be seen in the museum's series of cups with plates from 2011, decorated with silk screen printed garden plans and trees from different periods, made in collaboration with the English ceramicist Paul Scott **(269)**.

268. Vessel, 1995. *Menneskeform* (Human shape)
Earthenware, unglazed; thrown, modelled, polished, hard-fired at 1100°.
H 22 x Diam 53. Mark: none. Mus.no. 171/1997
ACQUISITION: *Earthenware*, 1995, Galleri Nørby, Copenhagen

269. Four cups with plates, 2011. *Landscape Blue and Garden Plates (Formal Garden, Pond Garden, River Garden, Dune Garden)*
Porcelain, gold, silver; thrown, cut, silk screen print decoration. Cups: H 7.5-8 x Diam 9, plates: L 21 x W 13.5. Mark: 'Ann Linnemann og Paul Scott'. Mus.no. 100a-h/2011
ACQUISITION: Ann Linnemann Studie Galleri, Copenhagen

LÜBBERT, BETTER 1955 –

Ceramicist

1988-90 Danmarks Designskole, Ceramics and Glass
1991-94 Danmarks Designskole, Ceramic Conceptual Art
1998- Own studio workshop, Hundested, N Sealand
www.better-lubbert.com

Better Lübbert (BL) began studying at Danmarks Designskole after several years of travelling in the Middle East, South America and North Africa, and a year spent in the Caribbean. BL has successfully integrated elements of the rich ceramic cultures she encountered on her travels with Danish traditions of design and craftwork, creating an individual and original ceramic body of work.

At the Design School BL first took Glass and Ceramics courses and then developed her interest in unique art pieces. Combining glass and ceramics, at the end of the 1990s she created a number of conceptual works with a ceramic corpus and sand-cast superimposed shapes. In 1999 the museum acquired a technically complex work of this kind with the title *Sienna Adventure*, made of stoneware and glass with the reddish-brown colour that is called 'Sienna' and has its origins in a soil pigment with iron oxides extracted in areas of southern Tuscany **(270)**.

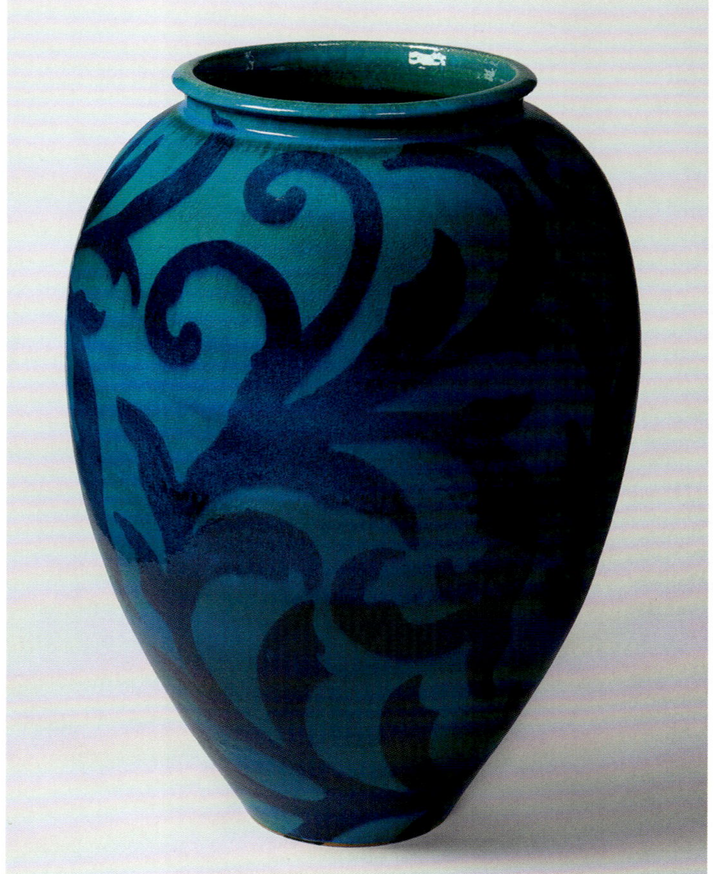

271 301/2005

270 125a-b/1999

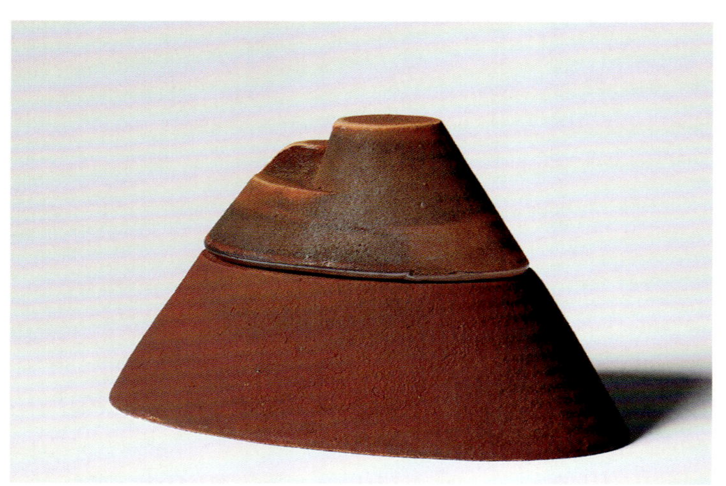

From the time around 2000 BL has worked mostly with large pots which she throws herself in stoneware clay with a technique learnt on Crete. The subsequent glazing takes place in several firings, with different glazes of Middle Eastern origin. BL has experimented throughout her career with glazes of different compositions; she has studied in Istanbul and Iznik with the aim of achieving the desired intensity and palette of colours. The pots are mostly monochrome, but BL also often uses decoration inspired by classical and oriental patterns, which she integrates in some cases with elements from present-day pictorial images and motifs. In 2005 the museum purchased, from an exhibition at Sophienholm, a pot with a smooth surface and a luminous glossy turquoise base-colour; it is decorated with a darker organic plant pattern which embraces and emphasises the form of the pot **(271)**. BL has been an active participant in exhibitions nationally and internationally ever since she completed her studies, and works commissioned from her are to be found in many places in Denmark; she has also received grants and commendations.

270. Lidded pot, 1999. *Sienna Adventure*
Stoneware, sand-cast glass, ash-glazed, sinter slip with iron oxide; modelled corpus, slip, fired at 1260°, upper part (lid) of sand-cast glass. H 16 x L 26. Mark: 'BL 99 I' painted on base. Mus.no. 125a-b/1999
ACQUISITION: Galleri Susanne Højriis, Copenhagen

271. Vase, 2005
Stoneware, alkali-, lead- and crackle- glazed; thrown, painted slip, decorated, fired at 1260°, then glazed with several kinds of glaze and fired at 1040°. H 69 x Diam 31. Mark: 'BL 05' painted on base. Mus.no. 301/2005
ACQUISITION: *My Room*, 2005, Sophienholm. Donation from *Kunstindustrimuseets Venner*

LYNGGAARD, FINN 1930 – 2012

Ceramicist, glass artist

1951	Journeyman painter
1951-56	Royal Danish Academy of Fine Arts, School of Painting, School of Ceramics
1956-60	Own studio workshop, Guldbergsgade, Copenhagen
1960-80	Own studio workshop, Kokkedal
1966	Portland State College, USA, Guest Professor
1974-90	Skolen for Brugskunst, Ceramics and Glass, teacher
1985	Glasmuseet Ebeltoft, co-founder and director
1980-2012	Glass workshop with Tchai Munch, Ebeltoft
2010	*Status 80*, retrospective exhibition, ceramics and glass, Glasmuseet Ebeltoft

Finn Lynggaard (FL) is a distinctive figure in Danish craftwork. He was in the best sense of the word an entrepreneur; because of his lively curiosity and openness towards social and international trends, his impressive technical and craft skills and an engaging ability to communicate, he was able to influence both the field of ceramics and the

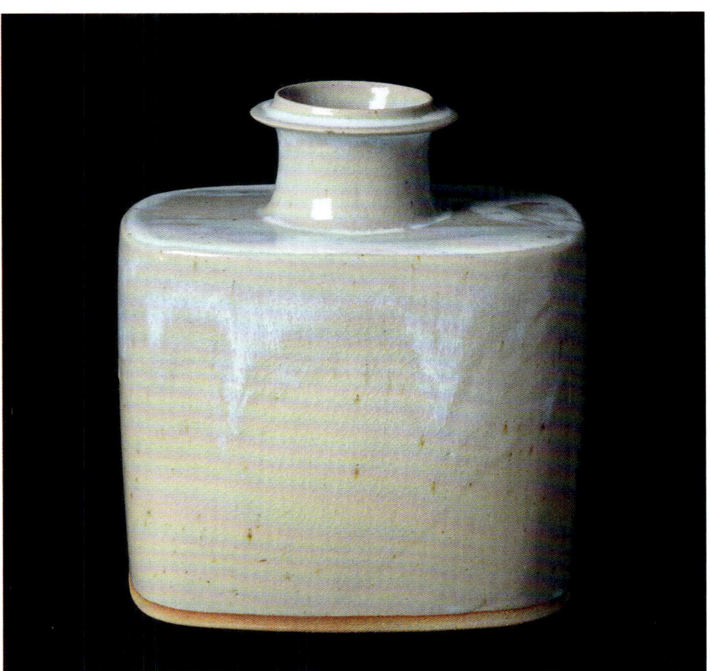

272 236/1990

development of studio-made glass in Denmark in his lifetime. His career fell into two main time-blocks, from c.1956-80, when ceramics were his focus, and from 1980 onwards, when studio glass was his favoured medium, laying claim to both his artistic and his organisational energy and culminating in the founding and opening of the Glass Museum in Ebeltoft in 1986. But clay did not let go of its hold on FL, and in 1996 he was honoured by the mounting, at the Ceramic Museum at Grimmerhus (now CLAY), of the exhibition '*Finn Lynggaard – keramiker – 40-års jubilæumsudstilling*', which included new ceramic works from the mid 1990s. In an associated publication with the same title (ISBN 87 899 75-38-3) FL's memoirs can be found, with a good introduction to his personality, his active life and work and professional tenets, forming an interesting picture of conditions for craftworkers in the second half of the 20th century.

At the Academy, where he sought entry as a painter in 1951, he was captivated by ceramics and in his last years there went to Peter Hald's classes in the Ceramics School. As soon as he completed his studies in 1956 he set up his own workshop, and in record time created a production of functional ceramics and unique pieces which were exhibited in Dansk Kunsthåndværks exhibitions and Charlottenborg's spring

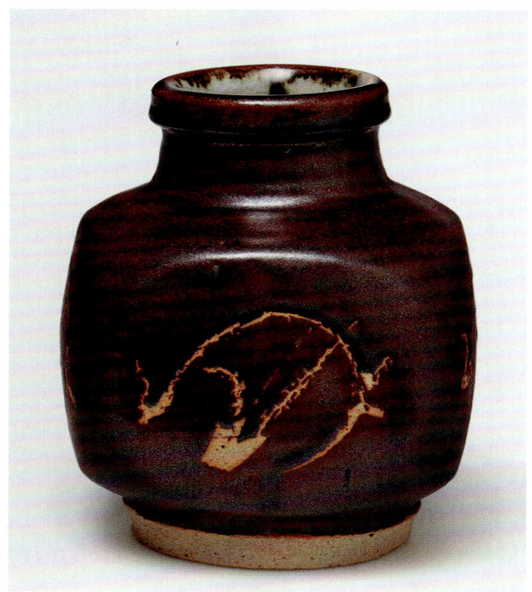

273 237/1990

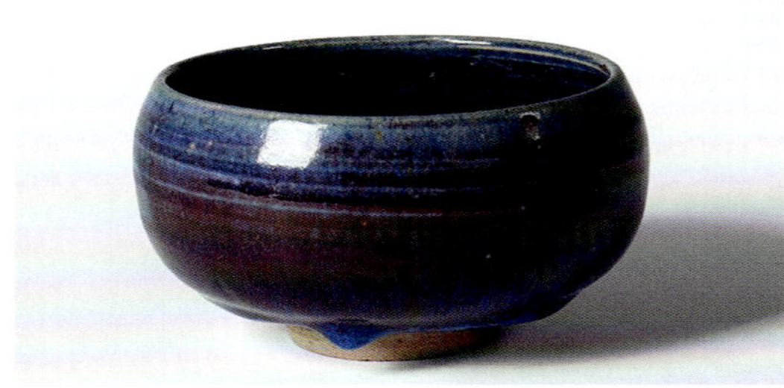

274 238/1990

and autumn exhibitions and were sold via Den Permanente and elsewhere. The golden era for Danish arts and crafts in the 1950s, carrying through to the 1970s, in combination with FL's great capacity for hard work, created the basis for the workshop's economy.

Alongside his ceramic activities FL developed a life-work with an impressive range of activities in Denmark and beyond, and through many journeys, exhibitions and participation in international symposia etc. he built up a broad international network that was beneficial to Danish craftwork and made him a leading figure and pioneer, especially in the field of studio glass. His activities included many official positions on boards and councils, he taught Ceramics and founded the course in Glass at Skolen for Brugskunst from 1974 – 1990, and he was also the author of an impressive number of textbooks – a total of six about ceramics, among them the classic *Keramisk Håndbog*, 1968, (in Danish, Swedish and Spanish editions) and *RAKU*, 1970, (Danish and English editions) as well as seven publications about glass. His textbooks were widely distributed and stimulated many people to try their hand at craftwork. In 1973 FL also translated into Danish and edited for Nyt Nordisk Forlag the book by the Spanish ceramicist José Llorens Artigas, *Artigas' Glasurbog*, which most ceramicists use, professionals and amateurs alike. Travelling gave FL inspiration which can be discerned in his works. He went on study visits, during his time at the Academy, to Turkey and Greece, and in the mid 60s this resulted in several unique pieces in stoneware with towers and onion cupolas, and there is also a connection with FL's largest commissioned work, a fountain-arrangement with numerous cupola-crowned gold-decorated pillars in stoneware for the newly built Hotel Scandinavia, in 1993. Journeys to the USA, for the first time in 1966, followed by many others, resulted in FL's interest in Pop-art, and he is the ceramic artist in Denmark who most clearly represents that art movement, with a number of humourous and provocative works from the beginning of the 1970s.

Several long visits, the first of them in 1970, were made by FL to Japan, and Japanese ceramic culture came to have great significance for him. '*The greatest inspiration for me has always been Japan – and I recognise that that can be traced in many of my things*', Fl wrote in his memoirs (p. 21). This can also be seen in his return to ceramics in the 1990s, when most of the new works for the jubilee exhibition were Japanese-inspired bowls and pots. But already in 1970 FL had published his book about Raku, its origins, history and technique, which he had earlier become familiar with through Bernard Leach's *A Potter's Book* and its interpretation of Japanese ceramics.

FL is represented in the museum with four works, three of which were donations from the artist in connection with the museum's 100-years' jubilee. They are all from the 1970s and belong among the Japanese-inspired works **(272-274)**; this is particularly true of the traditionally-shaped tea bowl **(274)**, made in raku technique. The teapot **(275)** is one of the many good functional pieces that FL made at the workshop in Kokkedal. Despite his textbooks' detailed information about materials and production processes, tools and design of workshops, FL described his own work processes as being based on an experimental approach e.g. to glazes; he highlighted the pleasure in making one's own glazes, with all the risks, rather than using the 'safe' readymade bought ones. FL was attracted by the fast processes that are characteristic of studio glass and raku technique, and his work had an infectious influence, both constructive and critical, that was of significance for art craftwork as a whole; FL had a broad reach and he brought international trends into the Danish context.

272. Large bottle-shaped vase, 1970s

Stoneware, celadon- and crackle- glazed; thrown, modelled.
H 30 x L 25 x W 19. Mark: 'Finn L.' painted on base with stamp 'DENMARK'.
Mus.no. 236/1990 ACQUISITION: Donation from Finn Lynggaard on the occasion of Kunstindustrimuseet's 100-years' Jubilee

273. Pot, 1978

Stoneware, tenmoku-glazed; thrown, modelled, wax resist, decorated, fired at 1300°. H 19.3. Mark: 'Finn L.' painted on base with stamp 'DENMARK'.
Mus.no. 237/1990.
ACQUISITION: Donation from Finn Lynggaard on the occasion of Kunstindustrimuseet's 100-years' Jubilee

274. Tea-bowl, c. 1969

Earthenware, glazed; thrown, raku technique. H 7.3 x Diam 12. Mark: 'Finn L.' painted on base with stamp 'DENMARK'. Mus.no. 238/1990
ACQUISITION: Donation from Finn Lynggaard on the occasion of Kunstindustrimuseet's 100-years' Jubilee

275. Teapot, 1960s

Stoneware, glazed, bamboo; thrown, relief, decorated. H 22 x Diam 16.
Mark: Stamped 'Finn L. Denmark' on base. Mus.no. 131a-b/1999.
ACQUISITION: Donation from Bank Director C. B. Andersen, Copenhagen

275 131a-b/1999

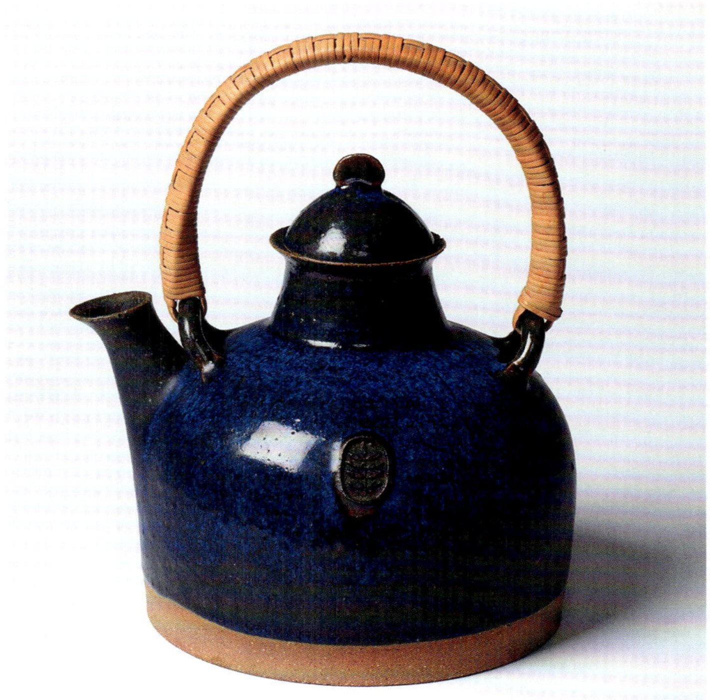

MADSEN, LONE SKOV 1964 –

Ceramicist

1984-88 Skolen for Brugskunst
1988-89 Instituto Statale d'Arte per la Ceramica, Faenza, Italy
1989 Cooperative workshop, Copenhagen
2010- Workshop shared with Turi Heisselberg Pedersen
1995-96 Atelierzentrum Schloos Ringenberg, Hamminkel and Düsseldorf, Germany
1996-2000 Udstillingssted for Ny Keramik, Copenhagen, co-founder and -owner
www.loneskovmadsen.dk

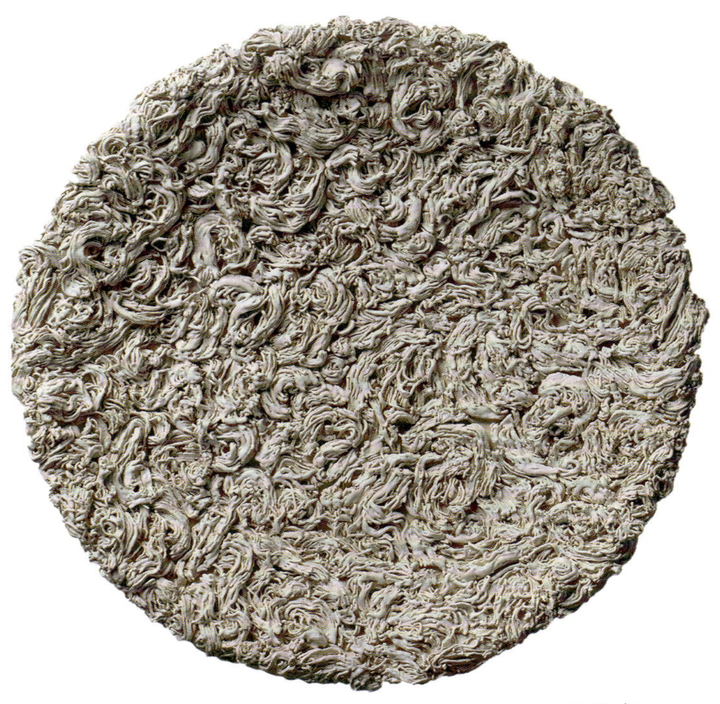

276 160/2001

At the 3rd Danish Ceramic Triennial, held at Trapholt in 2000, Lone Skov Madsen (LSM) exhibited a series of 15 circular wall-hung dishes, c. 50 cm in diameter, decorated with a rich variety of textures covering the whole surface, glazed with whitish, bluish and black shades in an interplay of shiny and matte glazes. This was a major achievement by LSM, who was able in this way to usher the dish form, so rich in tradition in Danish ceramics, directly into present-day ceramic art forms, while at the same time sending thoughts back to the great predecessors in the history of unique dishes, such as Thorvald Bindesbøll in the 19th century and Erik Nyholm in the 20th. In these and other works LSM renews ceramic decoration by integrating surfaces and textures with the essential form, so that the ornamentation itself becomes the form. The dishes from 2000 are represented in the museum's collection by a work in white whose densely-covering decoration of small bundles of clay threads seems to undulate in constant motion **(276)**. The magic of these works arises in part from the difficulty of deciding whether the motifs are microscopic details or immense natural phenomena seen from a distant perspective. They invite inspection and reflection.

Like other prominent ceramicists from the 1960s generation, LSM has been active in groups and projects with a focus on presenting new trends in ceramics to a wider public. One of the important initiatives was the establishment in 1996 of the exhibition centre 'Udstillingssted for Ny Keramik' in Kompagnistræde, Copenhagen. Through the four years that it existed it became a centre for young ceramicists and for those interested in ceramics, who had a unique opportunity there to keep abreast of new developments in an important period for Danish ceramics. LSM was co-founder and -owner and had two important solo exhibitions there, displaying new departures in her work. The first of those exhibitions was in 1997, with the unusual title *20.623 sorte punktnedslag på hvide beholdere* (20,623 black dot-impacts on white containers); here LSM displayed a series of works with organic abstract forms decorated with black glaze dots that have a strong effect on the perception of the form. The museum acquired for the collection a group of three objects from this exhibition which highlight the serial approach which LSM often works with **(277)**, as also shown in the exhibition *28 + -* in 2000, with e.g. a series of white folded objects covered with white glazed dots.

The main driving forces behind 'Udstillingssted for Ny Keramik' joined up in a new exhibition group, *New Danish Ceramics*, which presented, in 2003, their first and impressive exhibition in the museum.

LSM contributed a new series of 11 white-glazed dishes with the results of her continuing exploration of structures and materials with the circular form of the dish as a staple symbol.

In 2009 LSM and Turi Heisselberg Pedersen collaborated on an interesting exhibition project in the museum, in dialogue with the museum's collections. This became an impressive *tour de force* for the exhibiting artists, involving development of many new sculptural works that were displayed in close proximity to the selected museum pieces, both furniture and objects, which in the process became enriched with new significance. *Statens Kunstfond* awarded a prize to this inspiring and interesting exhibition. (See: *Time Out*, Exhibition Catalogue 2009)

SLM has a good international network and a large range of exhibition activities in Denmark, Europe and the USA. She has received many prizes and grants. In 2009 she was awarded *Annie og Otto Johs. Detlefs'* prize for ceramics.

276. Dish, 2000
Stoneware, zinc- and barium- glazed; thrown on a mould, strands of clay through metal netting. H 10 x Diam 54. Mark: none. Mus.no. 160/2001
ACQUISITION: Galleri Nørby. Donation from *Kunstindustrimuseets Venner*.
See: *Keramiske arbejder*, 2000

277. 3 vases, 1997. ***20.623 sorte punktnedslag på hvide beholdere***
(20,623 black dot-impacts on white containers)
Stoneware, zinc- and barium- glazed; modelled, slip, dots applied level with surface, fired at 1260°. H 20; H 27.5; H 36. Mark: none.
Mus.nos. 234-236/2006. ACQUISITION: Lone Skov Madsen. Donation from *Kunstindustrimuseets Venner*. See: *Ceramic Works/Keramiske arbejder*, 2001. *Udstillingssted for Ny Keramik,* 2002. *Lava*, 2005

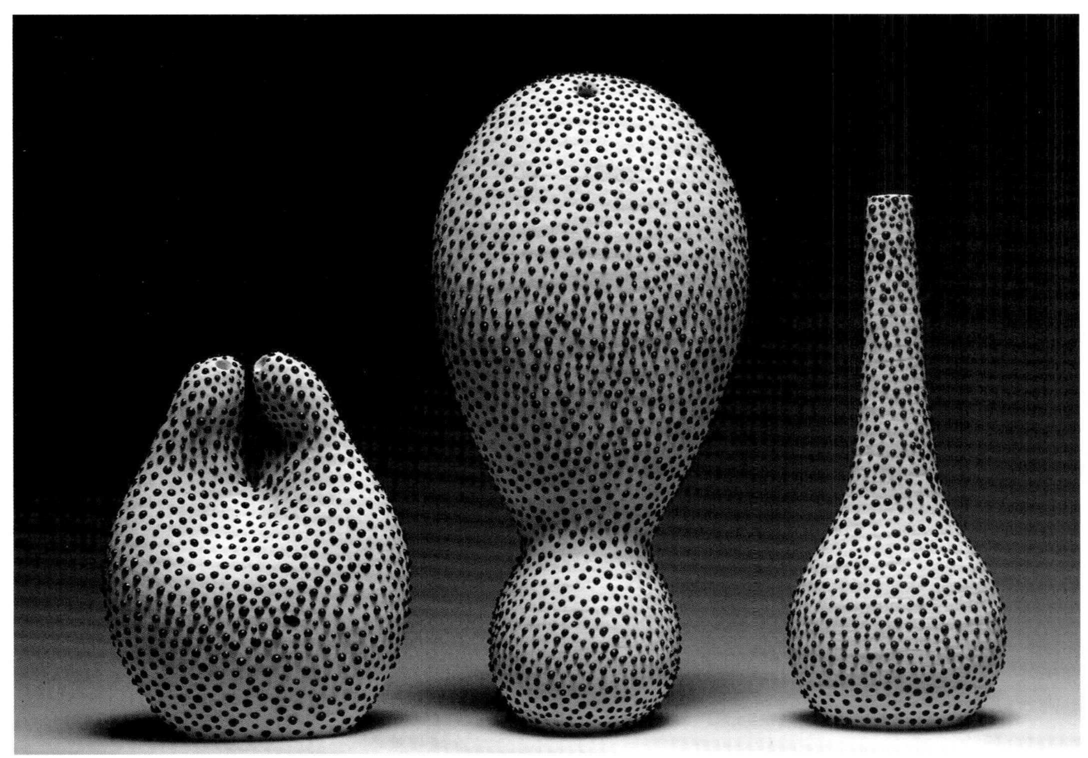

277 234-236/2006

MADSEN, STEN LYKKE 1937 –

Ceramicist

1954-58	Kunsthåndværkerskolen
1958-59	Kähler Keramik, Næstved, S Sealand
1959-62	Own studio workshop, shared with Henrik Jensen, Cph.
1962-87	Attached to Bing & Grøndahl
1987-2003	Attached to Royal Copenhagen
2009-	International Ceramic Research Center Guldagergaard, artist-in-residence

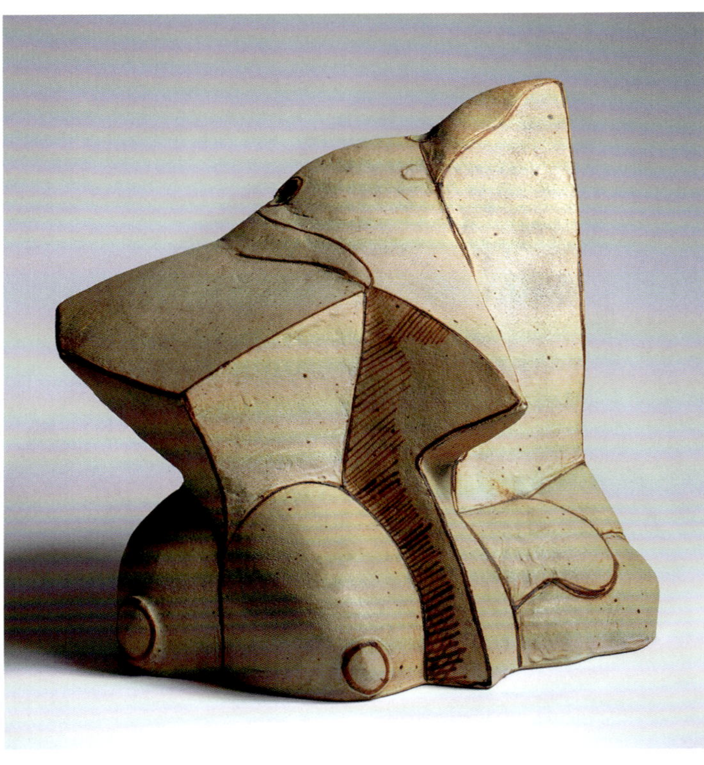

278 10/1971

Throughout his long career Sten Lykke Madsen (SLM) has created a multitude of figures and sculptures with his starting point in a personal pictorial world that consists largely of animals, female figures and fantasy beings. Through SLM's perspective we gain access to a world of fantasy in which fables and folktales develop freely and are given body and soul in often burlesque and sensual juxtapositions of animals and people. The figures are not harmless; they bare their teeth and engage in unruly pursuits which may arouse a certain disquiet in the observer.

SLM contemplates his surroundings and the doings of other people, and sees individuals hampered by loneliness and constraints; this finds expression in several of the figures in the museum's collection, e.g. in *Kassedamen* (The check-out girl) **(282)**, whose static fixed position at work is pin-pointed in the shaping of the check-out assistant as a chair, and in the touching depiction of *Grønt pukkelrygget fabeldyr* (Green hunchbacked fantasy animal) **(287)**. The latter is the museum's most recent work by SLM, made at Guldagergaard after he left Royal Copenhagen in 2003.

SLM is a particularly skilled ceramicist who demonstrates mastery of craftwork, form and materials at a high level. Clay is for him the central focus, and together with his extensive stock of everyday sketches and drawings of people and situations it forms the departure-point for his works. He studied at Kunsthåndværkerskolen, and then gained experience at Kähler's in Næstved. From 1959-62 he had his own studio workshop in Copenhagen, until in 1962 he joined Bing & Grøndahl's artistic workshop. There he worked on ceramic sculpture when the factory had to find a successor to Jean Gauguin, after the latter's death in 1961. In the factory's many exhibitions in the 1960s and 70s SLM was a natural contributor with his abstract stoneware sculptures that heralded modernism and new styles of expression within the figurative genre.

There is no doubt that SLM has certain favourite animals that recur in his figures: fish, birds, frogs, rhinoceros and sheep are treated fondly, appearing in innumerable amusing and bizarre situations, and they always look at us with the same round, slightly bemused and sad eyes. A familial relationship with the Cobra-movement and Asger Jorn is often mentioned, while SLM himself sees Henry Heerup as a related artist. The museum's collection includes nine works by SLM, evenly distributed over the years 1971 to 2007. The earliest is a distinctive sculpture, an abstract modernist female bust from 1971, made of unglazed stoneware, on which the artist has used contours and hatching to emphasize the shapes of the sculpture **(278)**. From the 1980s there are two vase-shapes, both decorated with slip and painted glaze motifs of women. The more monumental of the two is a slightly angular cylinder-shaped pot with a rectangular mouth, completely covered by a painterly representation with seven female figures, two goats, two chairs and a table **(279)**. The other work, *Dame med slanger* (Lady with snakes) is a vase shape with an interesting decoration: a finely-drawn female face in profile surrounded by undulating snakes and other animals painted in pale glazed colours can be seen on the lower half of the vase; above the decoration the reddish-brown colour of the clay corbels outwards **(280)**.

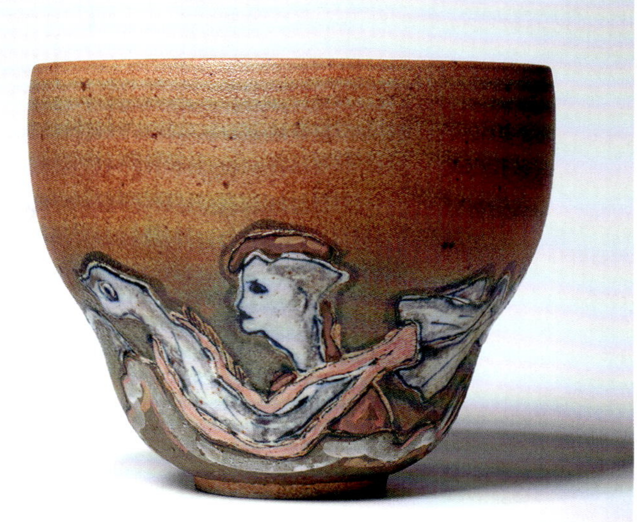

280 174/1988

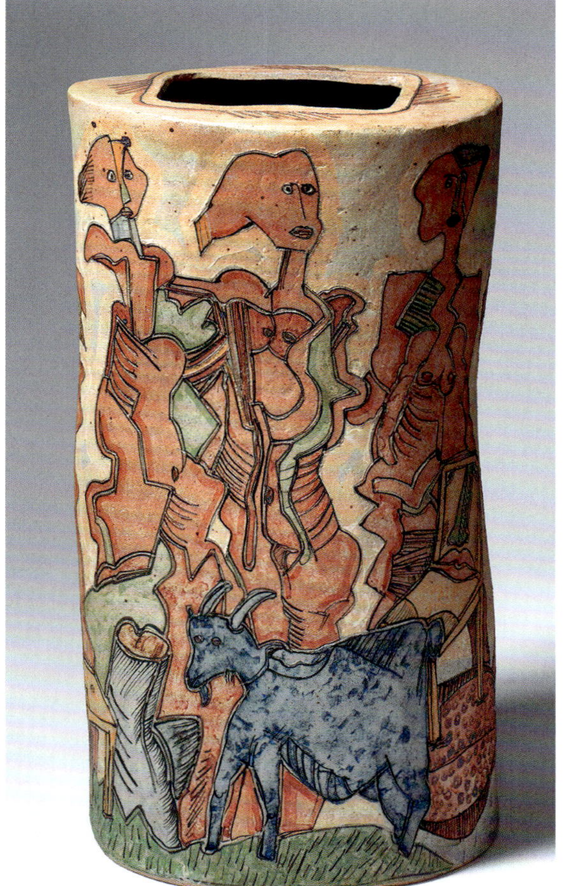

279 68/1984

After the fusion of the two major porcelain factories in 1987 SLM became part of the staff of Royal Copenhagen, where he was allocated a studio workshop in the factory's buildings in Smallegade in Frederiksberg, and from there he produced a strange flat asymmetrical object, decorated inside with a large dark bird-like fantasy animal of an outline that is almost repeated in the shape of the dish **(283)**.

The museum purchased the work at an exhibition in Royal Copenhagen, since SLM continued to exhibit under the auspices of the firm until 2003; after that he had the use of a workshop at Guldagergaard. At the same time SLM carried on constant and intense exhibition activities in Denmark and further afield, where his highly appreciated works have been acquired by major museums and collections, and he is still active in exhibition life and a member of the exhibition group *Keramiske Veje*. Together with the group's other ceramicists he contributed works to the *Lærkestellet* project (see p. 346).

In 2003 SLM held a solo exhibition in the museum. The title of the exhibition was 'Salt' and it contained many examples of ingeniously sculptural salt-cellars, two of which the museum acquired: one is made of porcelain and is a yellow-glazed salt-container with a curly fantasy sheep which clings to its lid **(285)**, while the other is a

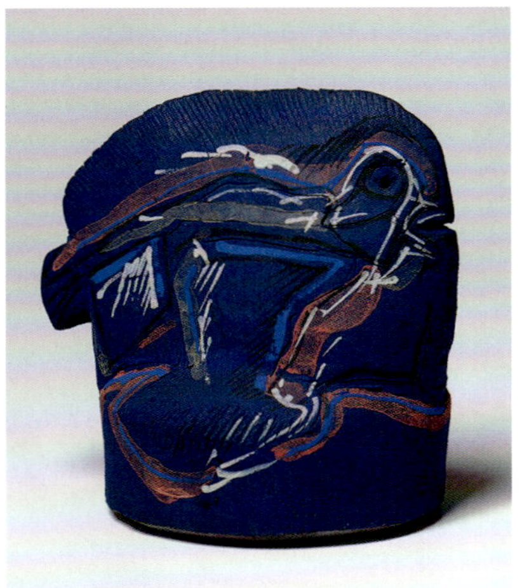

281 175/1988

pure-styled cubist sculpture, with many elements with edges that are marked with dark line-decoration **(286)**. The latter relates in an interesting way to the earliest works by SLM, in which his figure compositions heralded a new modernist development at Bing & Grøndahl. SLM has executed many gable-decoration projects, in Copenhagen for instance at Vesterbrogade 147 (1978), Sølvgade 14 (1993) and at the High School for the Deaf, Castberggård, near Hedensted, Jutland (2002), as well as a ceramic fountain *Sct. Jørgen og Dragen* (St George and the Dragon) at Store Torv in Holstebro (1986).

278. Sculpture, 1971. *Kvindebuste* (Female bust)
Stoneware with carborundum; slab technique, modelled, decorated, fired up to 1380°. H 43.5 x Diam 40.5. Mark: 'STEN B&G' inscribed on side. Mus.no. 10/1971. ACQUISITION: Donation from *Statens 50-års Jubilæumslegat.* See: Lassen, Erik, 1978

279. Pot, 1981
Stoneware with carborundum; modelled, slip, underglaze colour, inscribed and painted figure decoration, fired up to 1380°. H 80 x W 42. Mark: '49.81' painted in black on base. Mus.no. 68/1984
ACQUISITION: Donation from *Finansieringsinstituttet for Industri og Håndværk*

280. Vase, 1988. *Dame med slanger* (Lady with snakes)
Stoneware with carborundum; modelled, slip, underglaze colour, inscribed, decorated, fired up to 1380°. H 27 x Diam 31. Mus.no. 174/1988
ACQUISITION: Exhibition at Royal Copenhagen. Donation from *Kunstindustrimuseets Venner.* See: *Brændpunkter*, 1990

281. Sculpture, 1988. *Fisk* (Fish)
Stoneware with carborundum; modelled, slip, underglaze colour, decorated, fired up to 1380°. H 17.5. Mark: 'STEN 1998 B&G' inscribed on base. Mus.no. 175/1988. ACQUISITION: Exhibition at Royal Copenhagen. Donation from *Kunstindustrimuseets Venner*

282. Figure, 1993. *Kassedame* (The check-out girl)
Porcelain, glazed; modelled, underglaze painting, glazed. H 41 x Diam 21. Mark: 'STEN 1993' inscribed on base. Mus.no. 70/1994.
ACQUISITION: Exhibition at Royal Copenhagen. Donation from Royal Copenhagen

282 70/1994

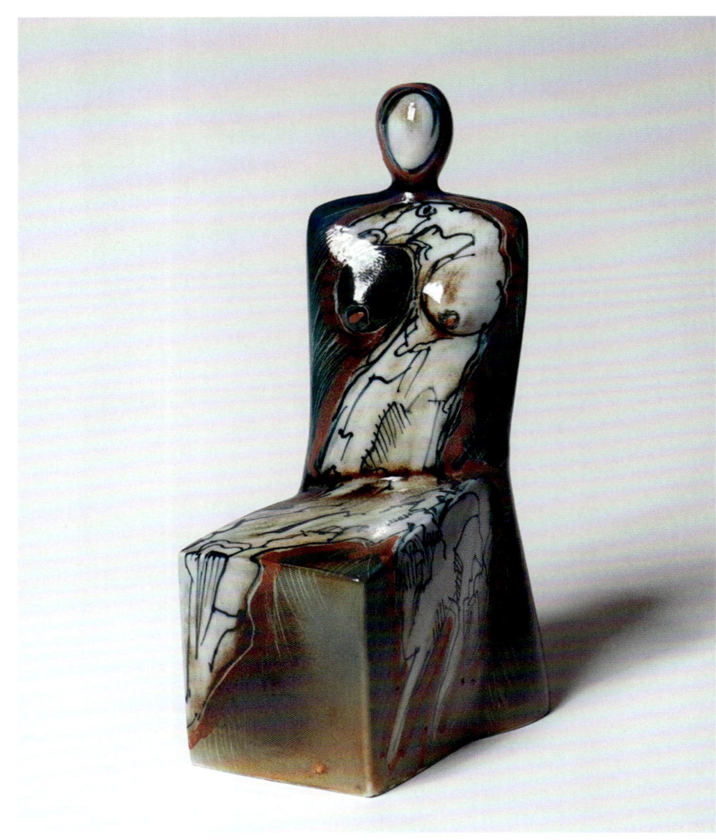

283. Dish-shape, 1994

Stoneware with carborundum; slab technique, modelled, organic and multi-sided shape, slip, decorated inside with fantasy animal, fired up to 1380°. H 11 x Diam 59. Mark: 'STEN', and 3 waves, inscribed on base. Mus.no. 71/1994. ACQUISITION: Exhibition at Royal Copenhagen, 1994

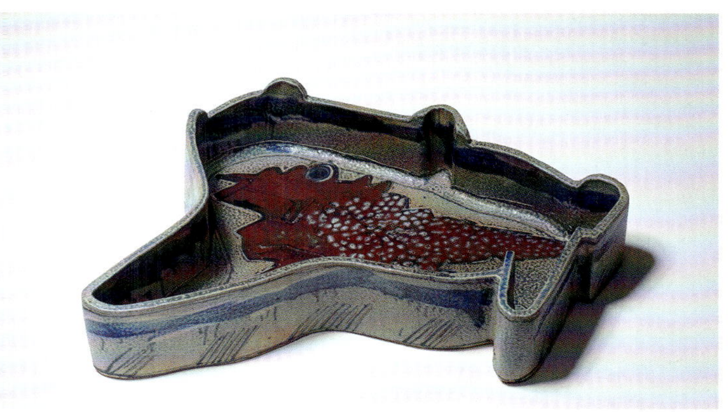

283 71/1994

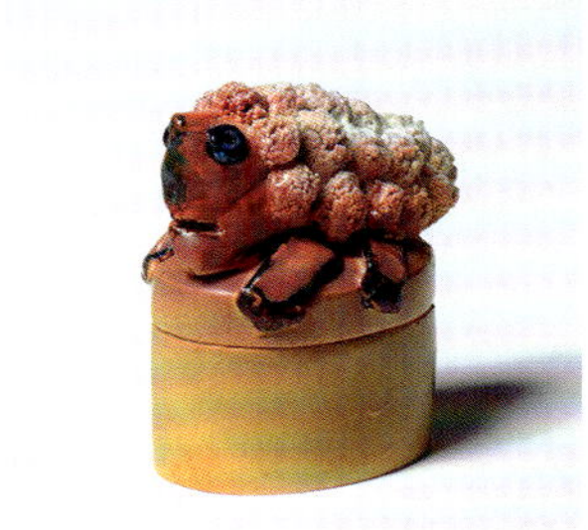

285 2a-b/2003

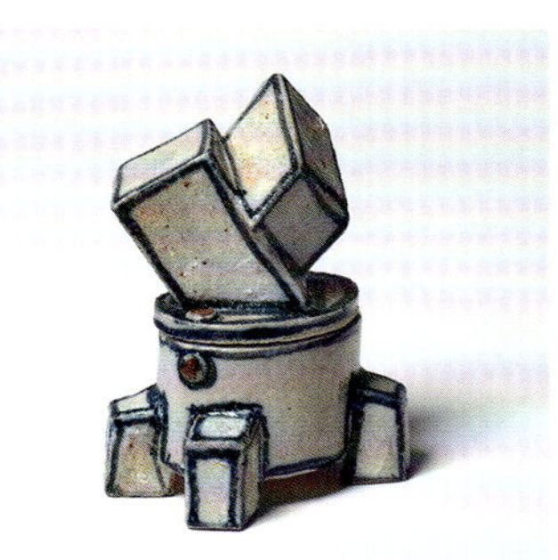

286 3a-b/2003

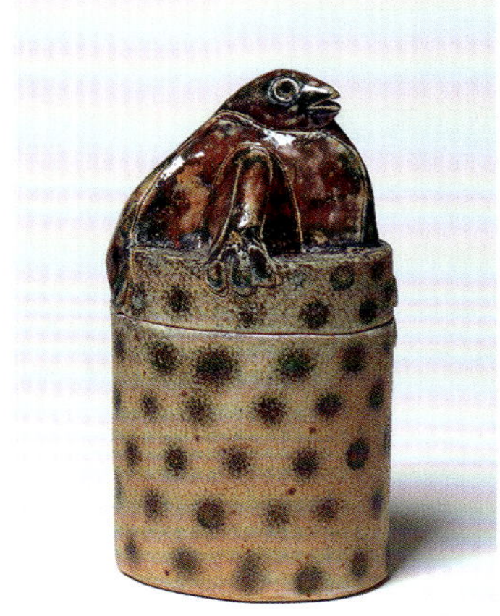

284 165a-b/1995

286. Salt-cellar with lid, 2001. *Kubistisk æske* (Cubist box)

Stoneware, glazed; modelled, underglaze colour, decorated, fired up to 1380°. H 15 x W 11.5 x D 7.2. Mark: 'STEN' and 3 waves, with '2001', inscribed on base. Mus.no. 3a-b/2003. ACQUISITION: *Salt,* 2002, Kunstindustrimuseet

287. Figure, 2007. *Grønt pukkelrygget fabeldyr* (Green hunchbacked fantasy animal)

Stoneware, glazed; modelled, slip, decorated, fired up to 1380°. H 24.5 x W 12.5 x L 28.5. Mark: 'STEN 2007' inscribed on base. Mus.no. 303/2007 ACQUISITION: Steen Lykke Madsen, 2007. Donation from *Sølvsmed Kay Bojesen og hustru Erna Bojesens Mindelegat*

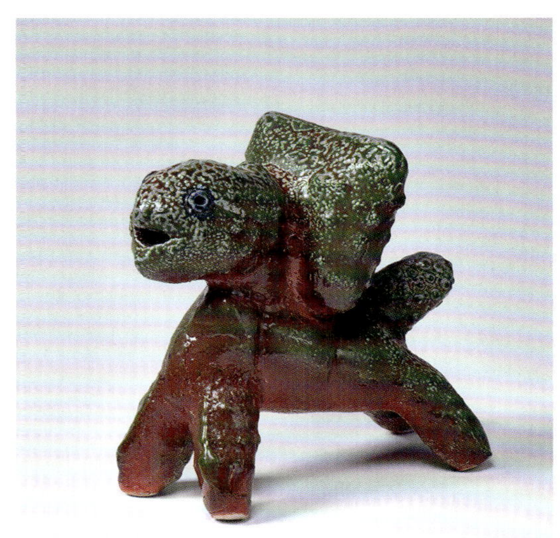

287 303/2007

284. Lidded pot with fish, 1995

Stoneware with carborundum; modelled, slip, underglaze colour, decorated, fired up to 1380°. H 25.5 x Diam 13.7. Mark: 'STEN 1995', and 3 waves. Mus.no. 165a-b/1995

ACQUISITION: Galleri Nørby, Copenhagen. Donation from ISS Facility Services

285. Salt-cellar with lid, 2002. *Fabelfår* (Fantasy sheep)

Porcelain, glaze; modelled, decorated, underglaze painted, glazed, wood-fired. H 9.5 x W 7.5 x D 5.5. Mark: 'STEN', and 3 waves with '2002', inscribed on base. Mus.no. 2a-b/2003. ACQUISITION: *Salt,* 2002, Kunstindustrimuseet

MANZ, BODIL 1943 –

Ceramicist

1961-65	Kunsthåndværkerskolen
1965	Gustavsberg Porslinsfabrik, Stockholm
1967-	Workshop shared with Richard Manz, Den Gamle Skole, Starreklinte, W Sealand
1966	Escuela de Desinio y Artisanias, Mexico City
1966	Berkeley University, San Francisco
1982-85	Bing & Grøndahl, freelance
	www.bodilmanz.dk

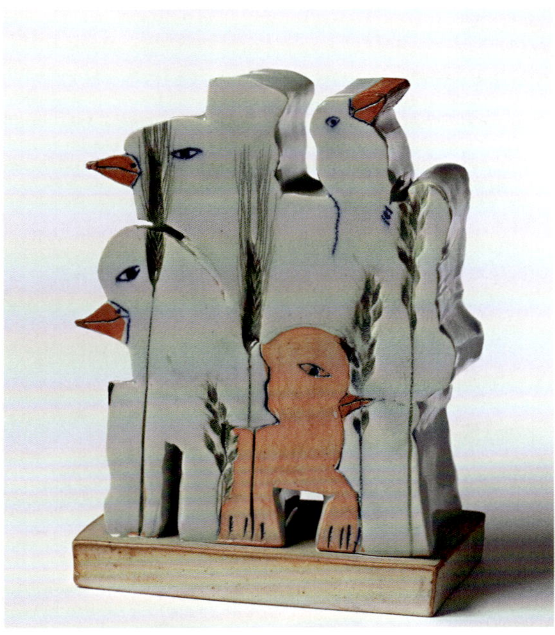

288 71/1977

During the last decades of the 20th century the international scene around ceramic exhibitions and connections with well-known galleries came to have increasing importance for Danish ceramicists, and several of them succeeded in making impressive reputations for themselves. Bodil Manz (BM) belongs to the absolute elite, and her signature pieces, the transparent, paper-thin porcelain cylinders, cast in plaster moulds, have been made by her in constantly varying and developing forms. With a graphic mastery she decorates them using coloured transfers, a technique she became acquainted with through her work at Bing & Grøndahl. Her cylinder has become an international icon, represented in leading museums and in private collections worldwide. Alongside the cylinders BM has developed an experimental range of activities, working with new sculptural forms in cast porcelain, including sand-cast works, paper-making with integrated ceramic clay colours and sand, graphic works, etc.

Bodil and Richard Manz were married in 1966, and after a journey to Mexico and Berkeley University, USA, where they met the charismatic and expressive ceramic artist Peter Voulkos, in 1967 they set up a shared studio workshop in the Old School in Starreklinte, W Sealand; BM has carried on the workshop after Richard Manz's death in 1999. In this professional and technically well-functioning workshop the couple launched an impressive and richly varied production of household objects in their own design of cast porcelain, which was sold through Den Permanente. Over the course of the years, together and independently, they carried through a number of commissions in the context of public buildings, involving a sand-cast porcelain technique which also became an important technique for their individual artistic work.
The museum's collection of BM's work contains in all 24 objects, from the years 1977-2008, which means that virtually all phases of her work over 38 years are illustrated. The earliest, from 1977, consists of two pieces cut out of massive porcelain, small, strong and personal objects that were acquired at the museum's exhibition entitled '*Bodil og Richard Manz - variation i porcelæn*' (1977), in which the workshop's comprehensive production of both functional objects and unique pieces was shown to full advantage **(288-289)**.

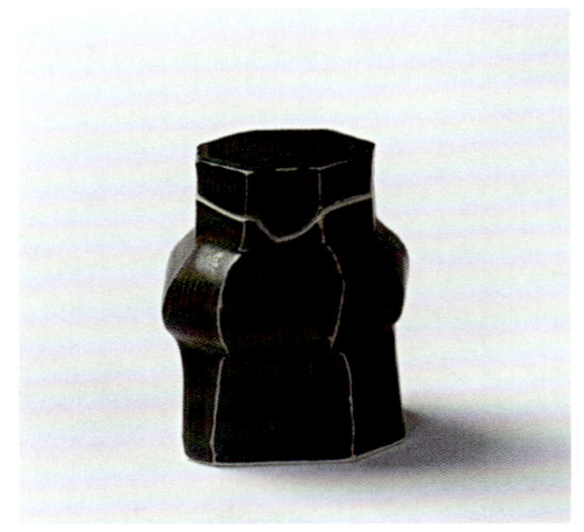

289 72a-b/1977

At the beginning of the 1980s BM was inspired by the Arabic geometric motif world, in connection with the preliminary work for an assignment for the national museum in Bahrain, designed by the Danish architect firm of K+HR. As part of an associated background for this ornamental context BM developed the *firkantsfade* (square dish) in stoneware, of which the museum owns an example from 1981 **(299)**.

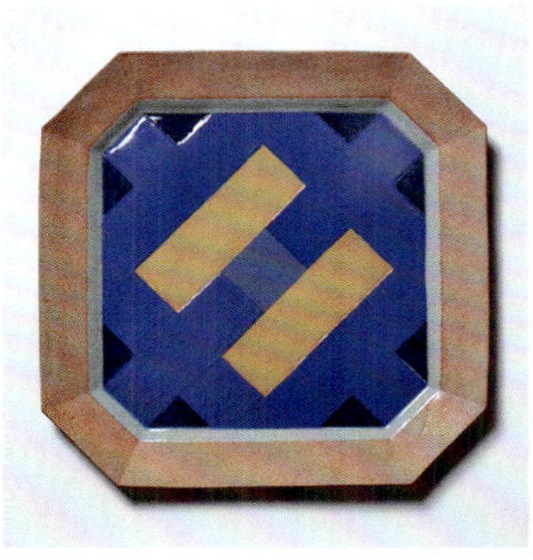

299 318/1990

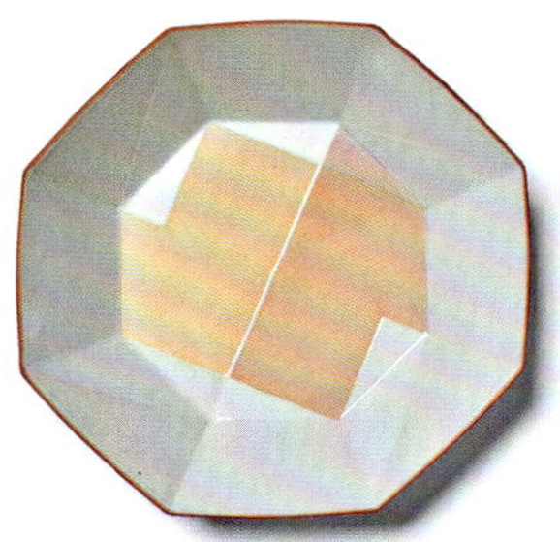

291 157/1985

There are direct lines that can be drawn from fascination with the abstract, geometric pattern in interplay with architecture to BM's later works. The fine line-decoration also characterises the *Facet* service, which BM made for Bing & Grøndahl, and of which the museum acquired a prototype in 1984, an octagonal bowl **(291)**; an angled form

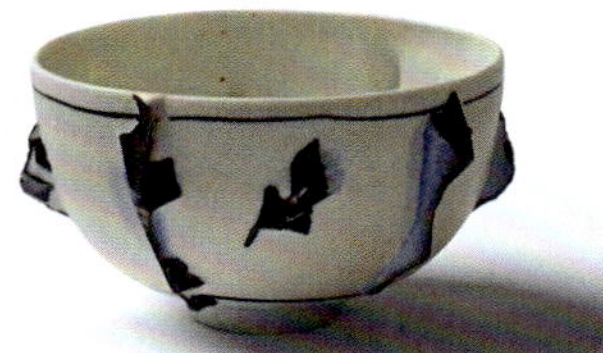

293 150/1989

is to be found again in the hexagonal vase in cast porcelain, decorated in black and gold, from 1987 **(292)**. Together with the cylinder these angled shapes are a recurrent aspect of BM's works, as can be seen e.g. from the series of *sekskantede kandeformer* (hexagonal jug shapes) **(297-298)** and from 1986 the *16-kantede ovale fad* (16-sided oval dish) with brush-painted decoration **(311)**.

From the end of the 1980s the study of flintstone became a source of inspiration for both water-colours and several large and small *flinteskåle* (flint bowls), made with sand-cast technique, in which the flint is pressed into the shape of the bowl and then the imprint is decorated by BM, following sketched material. In the museum's collection there is a massive, monumental example of such a bowl, from 1989 **(305)**.

As already mentioned the cylinders play a distinctive part in BM's *oeuvre*, and they are represented in the museum's collection. Particu-

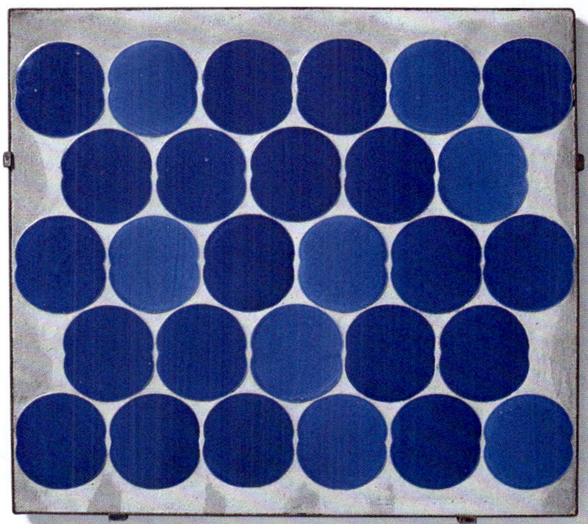

290 38/1978

lar mention can be made here of the large cylindrical vessel **(301)** with the title *Vinterskygge* (Winter shadow), which was exhibited in '*Keramiske Veje 2000*' in Den Frie Udstillingsbygning, made in sandcast porcelain and fired many times with several layers of colour, glazes and slip, in a wild expressionist idiom. The work is one of 13 that BM created in the year after Richard Manz's death. Through this grief-fuelled work BM came to master in earnest the sandcast technique, for both porcelain and plaster, that has become her favourite technique in the interesting experimental direction of development that she has explored alongside the moulded cylinders.

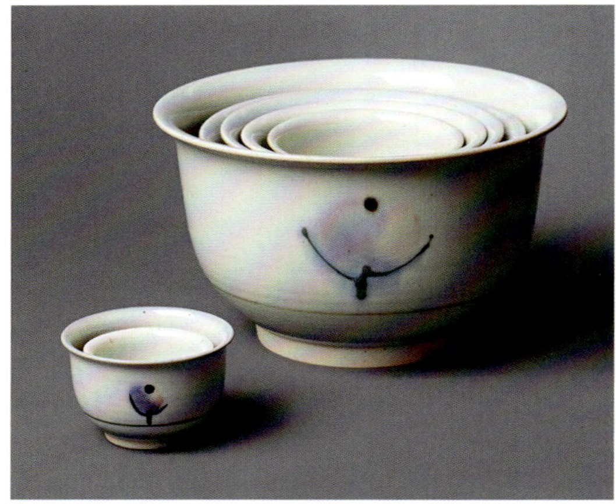

296 246a-g/1990

In 2008 the museum held a comprehensive retrospective exhibition of BM's work, and in that context it acquired several works, three of them with support from *Ny Carlsbergfondet*. The monumental sandcast porcelain vessel with the title *Sand* from 2001 **(309)** shows the mastery BM rapidly gained in both the size of the work and the exploitation of the potential of the technique for exploring and using many different materials. Other experiments from recent years are the slab-built *Samplings*, which play with the 'classical' cylinder in bringing together in one work different elements in compositions with constructivist influences, as can be seen in the museum's two works in this category **(307-308)**. The last work acquired from the exhibition was *Erindringer* (Memories), consisting of five pictures/tablets made of plaster with inlaid fragments of canvas and paper, strips of diverse notes by the family, bills, etc., which are fixed within the abstract compositions of the tablets **(310)**.

BM is co-founder and member of the exhibition group *Keramikkens Veje* and engages in extensive international exhibition activities. She was awarded Statens Kunstfonds honorary lifelong stipend in 1998. See: Bruun, N.,and Laursen, B.B. (eds), 2008.

288. Sculpture, 1977. ***Fugle i kornmark*** (Birds in a cornfield)
Porcelain, transparent glaze; cut from solid porcelain, reduction-fired at 1300°. H 21.5 x W 15.5. Mark: none. Mus.no. 71/1977
ACQUISITION: *Bodil og Richard Manz – variation i porcelæn,* 1977, Kunstindustrimuseet. Donation from *Overretssagfører Odin Kaysers Legat*

289. Lidded pot, 1975. ***Buddha***
Porcelain, hare's-fur-glazed; cut from a lump and hollowed out, reduction-fired at 1300°. H 9 x W 6. Mark: 'BODIL MANZ' painted on base, with 'BM 75'in a square mark. Mus.no. 72a-b/1977
ACQUISITION: *Bodil og Richard Manz – variation i porcelæn,* 1977, Kunstindustrimuseet. Donation from *Overretssagfører Odin Kaysers Legat*

297 248a-c/1990

298 249a-b/1990

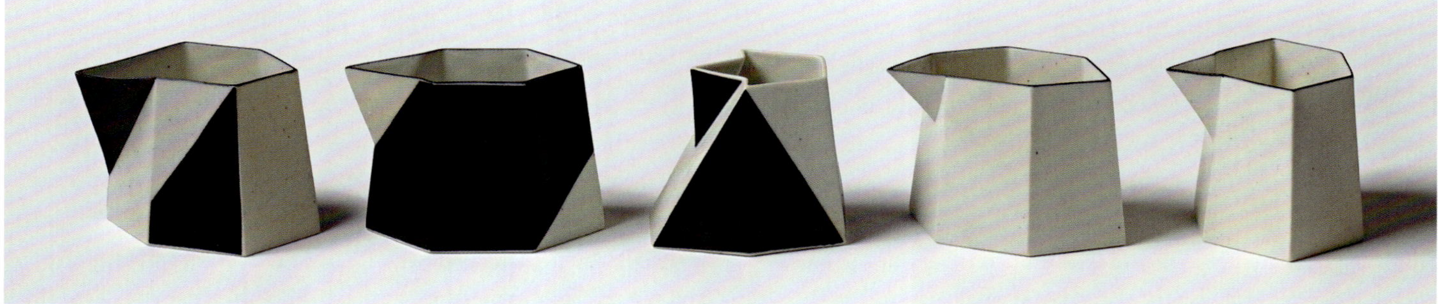

290. Tile picture, 1972. *Blåt flisebillede* (Blue tile picture)
Porcelain, glazed; brush-painted, set with cement into an iron frame, reduction-fired at 1300°. H 65 x W 65. Mark: 'BODIL MANZ' painted on back and 'BM 1972' in square mark. Mus.no. 38/1978
ACQUISITION: Bodil and Richard Manz. Donation from *Overretssagfører Odin Kaysers Legat*

291. Bowl, 1984. *8-kantet skål* (Octagonal bowl) No photo
Porcelain, service-glazed; cast, slip, fired at 1400°. H 7.5 x Diam 31. Mark: 'Bodil Manz' painted on base with 'BM' in a square mark.
Mus.no. 157/1985
ACQUISITION: Launch of *Facet*, Bing & Grøndahl. Donation from *Finansieringsinstituttet for Industri og Håndværk*. See: *Brændpunkter*, 1990

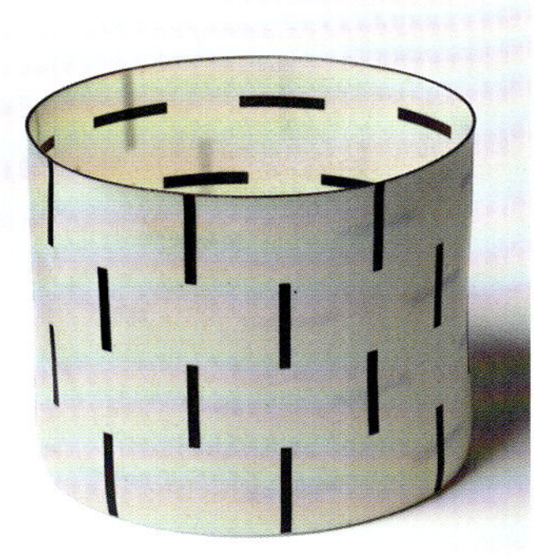

304 60/204

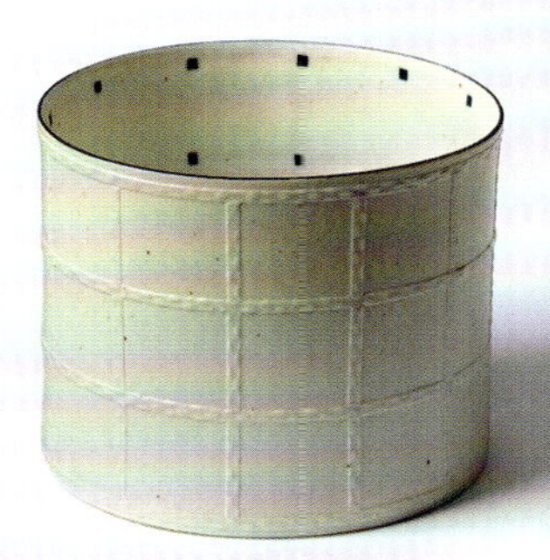

294 127/1990

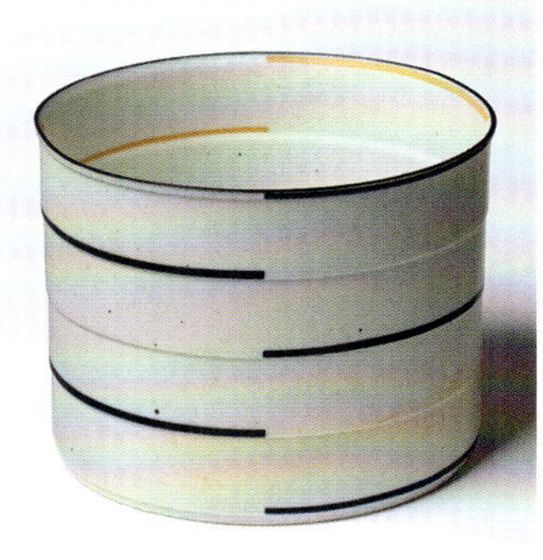

295 128/1990

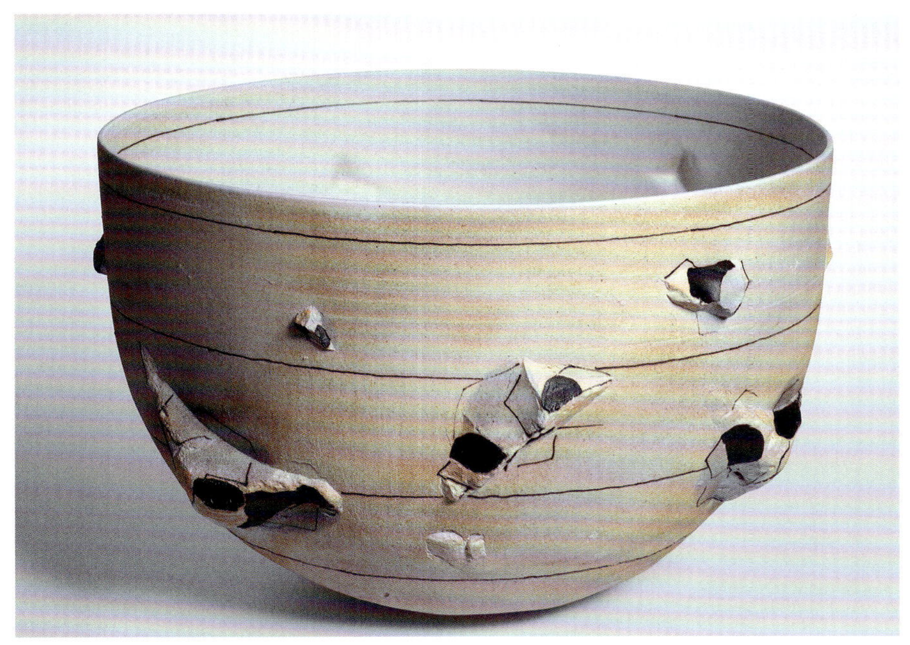

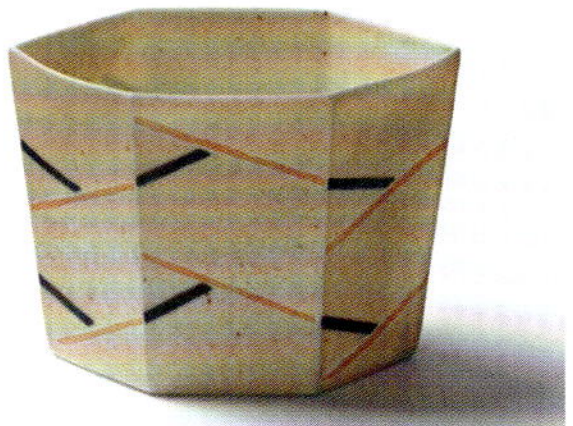

292 42/1987

305 348/2004

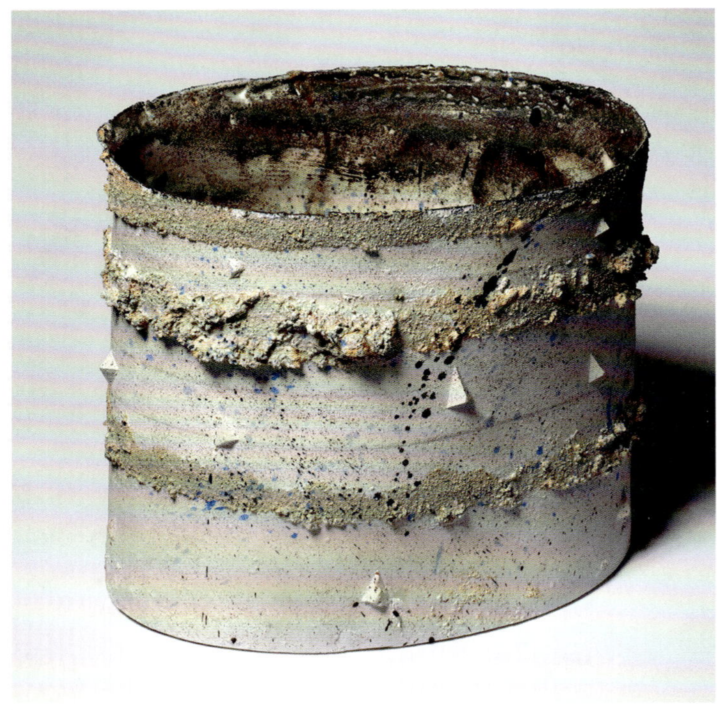

309 440/2008

295. Cylinder, 1990. *Cylinder med gult og sort*
(Cylinder with yellow and black)
Porcelain, matte glaze; serigraphy, reduction-fired at 1300°. H 15.5 x W 19.6. Mark: 'BODIL MANZ' painted on base and 'BM' in a square mark. Mus.no. 128/1990. ACQUISITION: Donation from *Sølvsmed Kay Bojesen og hustru Erna Bojesens Mindelegat*. See: Dybdahl, L., 1997

296. Set of bowls, 1989/1990. *Syv æbleskåle* (Seven apple bowls)
Porcelain, celadon-glazed; thrown using jiggering process, removed by hand, porcelain slip with cobalt-chloride, decorated. Largest measurements: H 16.5 x Diam 26.2. Mark: 'MANZ' painted on base. Mus.no. 246a-g/1990
ACQUISITION: Kunstindustrimuseet. Donation from *Sølvsmed Kay Bojesen og hustru Erna Bojesens Mindelegat*

292. Vase, 1987. *6-kantet med sort og gult*
(Hexagonal vase with black and yellow)
Porcelain, matte glaze; cast, brush-painted, reduction-fired at 1300°. H 9.5 x W 12.5. Mark: 'BODIL MANZ' painted on base and 'BM' in a square mark. Mus.no. 42/1987. ACQUISITION: Galleri Q, 1987. See: *Keramik – min elskede jeg hader dig*, 1987

293. Bowl, 1989. *Flinteskål* (Flint bowl)
Porcelain, cobalt-chloride glazed; sand-cast, reduction-fired at 1300°. H 8 x Diam 11. Mark: 'BODIL MANZ' painted on base and 'BM' in a square mark. Mus.no. 150/1989. ACQUISITION: Donation from *Kunstindustrimuseets Venner*

294. Cylinder, 1990. *Cylinder med relief og sort*
(Cylinder with relief and black)
Porcelain, matte glaze; cast, relief, serigraphy, reduction-fired at 1300°. H 12 x Diam 14,3. Mark: 'BODIL MANZ' painted on base and 'BM' in a square mark. Mus.no. 127/1990. ACQUISITION: Bodil Manz. Donation from *Sølvsmed Kay Bojesen og hustru Erna Bojesens Mindelegat*

301 9/2000

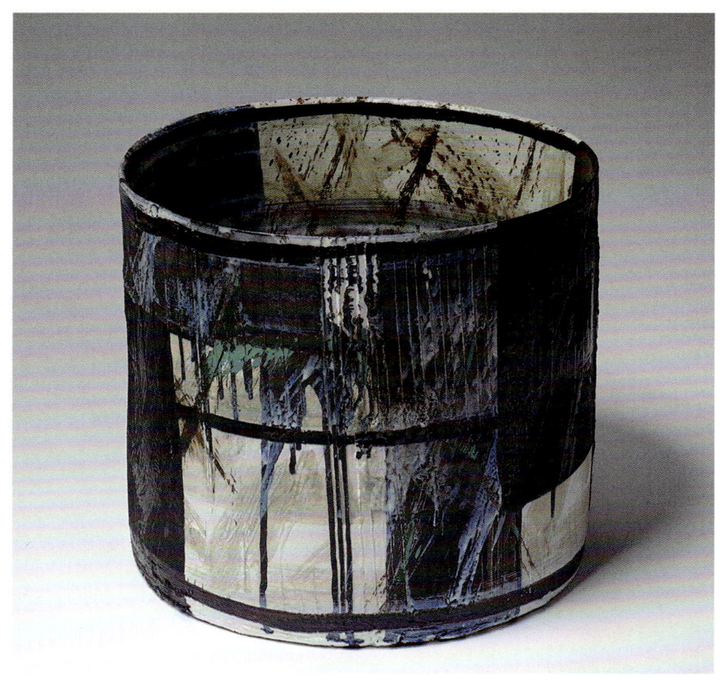

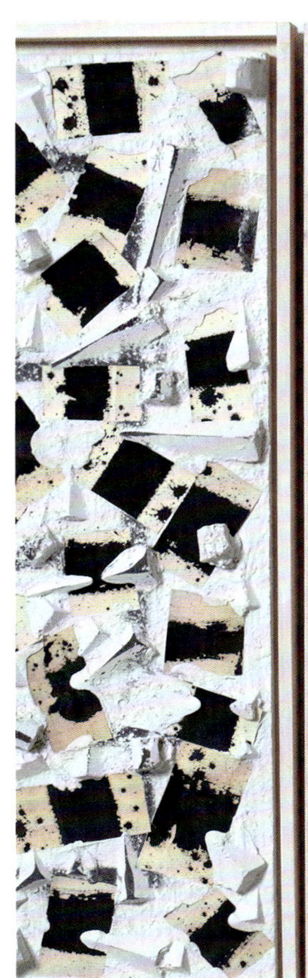
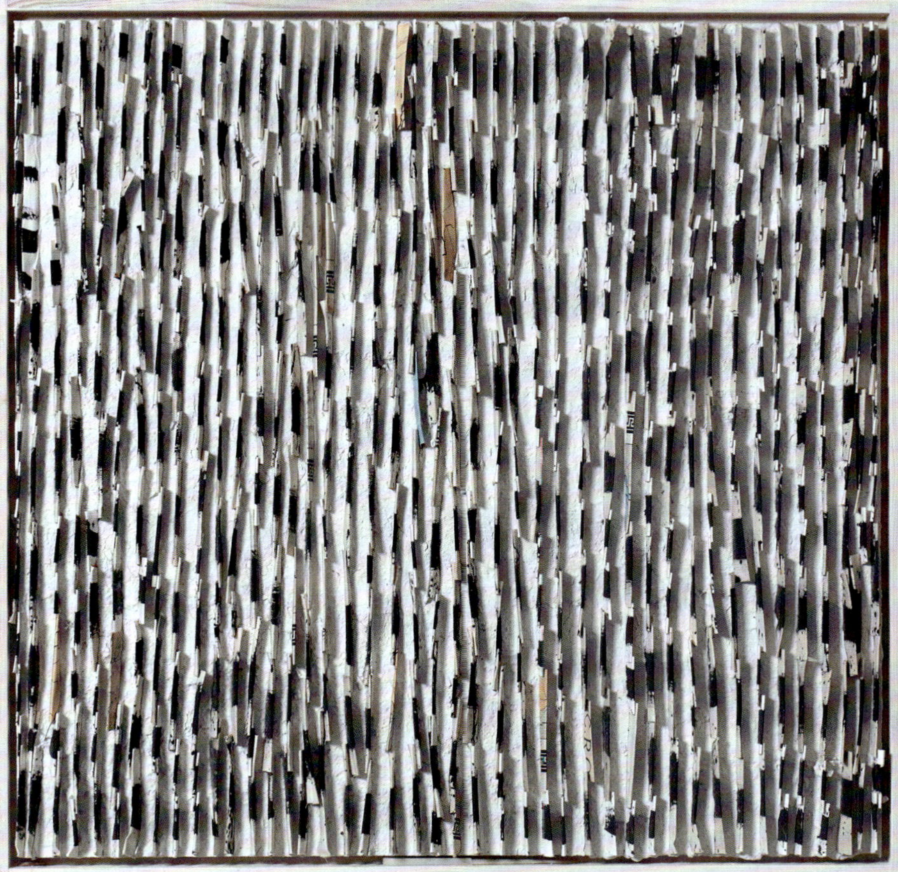
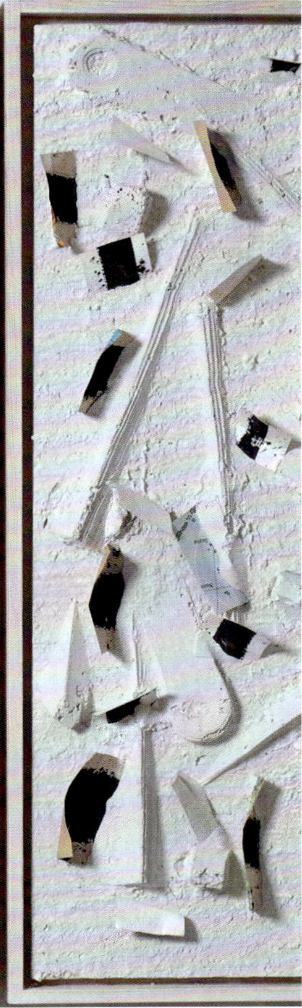

310 143c/2009

297. Three jugs, 1990. *6-kantede kandeformer* (Hexagonal jug shapes)
Porcelain, matte glaze; cast, serigraphy, fired at 1300°. a: H 9.5 x Diam 11.5; b: H 9.5 x Diam 12.5; c: H 9.5 x Diam 7.5. Mark: 'BODIL MANZ' and 'BM' in a square mark. Mus.no. 248a-c/1990
ACQUISITION: *Design – håndværk eller industri*, Den Frie, 1990

298. Two jugs, 1990. *6-kantede kandeformer* (Hexagonal jug shapes)
Porcelain, matte glaze; cast, reduction-fired at 1300°. a: H 9.5 x Diam 11.5; b: H 9.5 x Diam 10.5. Mark: 'BODIL MANZ' painted on base and 'BM 90' in a square mark. Mus.no. 249a-b/1990
ACQUISITION: *Design – håndværk eller industri*, 1990, Den Frie. Donation from *Kunstindustrimuseets Venner*

299. Dish, 1981. *Firkantsfad med blåt, brunt og sort* (Square dish with blue, brown and black)
Stoneware, transparent glaze; slab technique, shaped over a mould, sgrafitto, reduction-fired at 1300°. H 34 x W 45.5. Mark: 'BODIL MANZ' painted on base and 'BM' in a square mark. Mus.no. 318/1990
ACQUISITION: Donation from Bodil Manz

300. Bowl, 1994. *Stjernevase* (Star vase)
Porcelain, matte glaze; cast, serigraphy, reduction-fired at 1300°. H 9.3 x Diam 8.4. Mark: 'BODIL MANZ' painted on base and 'BM' in a square mark. Mus.no. 64/1994
ACQUISITION: Donation from *Helge Jacobsens Legat*

301. Cylindrical vessel, 1999. *Vinterskygge* (Winter shadow)
Porcelain, barium-glazed; sandcast, fired many times at temperatures from 760 to 1260°. H 30 x Diam 34. Mark: 'BODIL MANZ' painted on base and 'BM' in a square mark. Mus.no. 9/2000. ACQUISITION: *Keramiske Veje*, 2000, Den Frie Udstillingsbygning. Donation from *Kunstindustrimuseets Venner*

302. 2 bowls, 2000. *Oval form og oval form med snit*
(Oval shape and oval with cut)
Porcelain, glazed; cast, reduction-fired at 1300°, glaze fired at 775°. a: H 7.5 x W 24.5 x D 6.5; b: H 7.5 x W 16.5 x D 12.5. Mark: 'BODIL MANZ' painted on base and 'BM' in a square mark. Mus.no. 187a-b/2000. ACQUISITION: Galleri Nørby, Copenhagen. Donation from *Kunstindustrimuseets Venner*

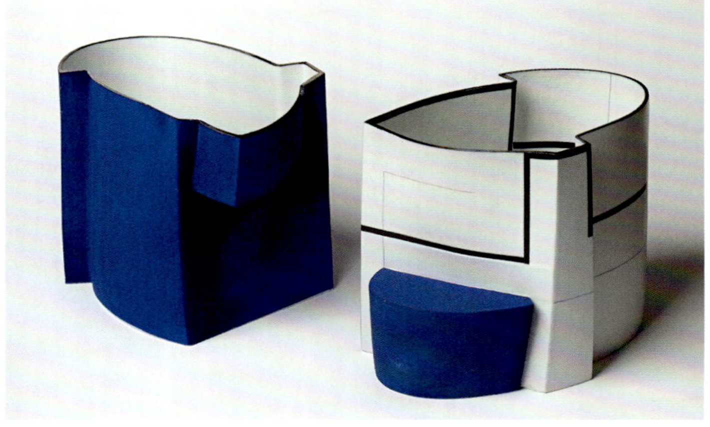

308 439/2008 **307** 438/2008

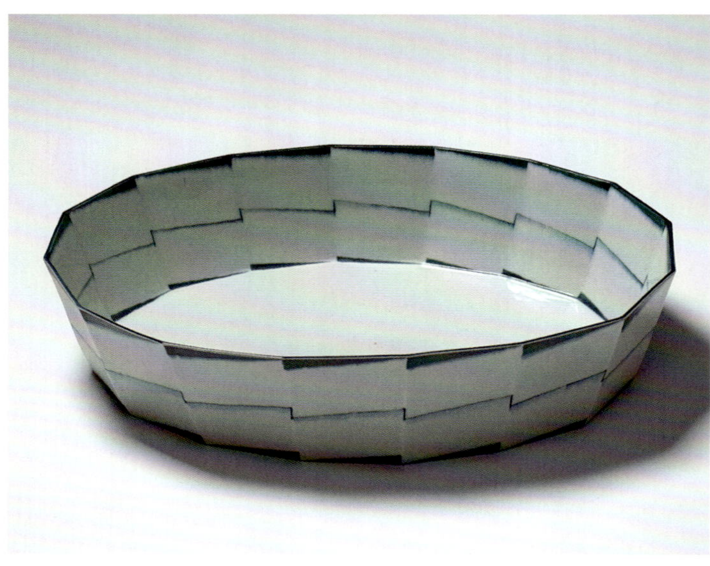

311 D 1649

303. Object, 2001. *Random Grid*
Porcelain, matte glaze, wood; cast, serigraphy, reduction-fired at 1300°. Cylinder: H 8 x Diam 9. Wooden construction: H 25.5 x W 14.5. Mark: 'BODIL MANZ' painted on base of cylinder and 'BM' in a square mark. Wooden construction made by Cecilie Manz. Mus.no. 215a-b/2001
ACQUISITION: Bodil Manz and Cecilie Manz. Donation from *Kunstindustrimuseets Venner*

304. Cylinder, 2004. *Cross*
Porcelain, matte glaze; cast, serigraphy, reduction-fired at 1300°. H 16 x Diam 18.5. Mark: 'BODIL MANZ' painted on base and 'BM' in a square mark. Mus.no. 60/2004. ACQUISITION: Donation from *Kunstindustrimuseets Venner* and *Knud V. Engelhardts Mindelegat*

305. Vessel, 1989. *Flinteskål* (Flint bowl)
Porcelain, barium-glazed; sand-cast, brush-painted, reduction-fired at 1300°. H 35 x Diam 54. Mark: 'BODIL MANZ' painted on base and 'BM' in a square mark. Mus.no. 348/2004. ACQUISITION: Bodil Manz. Donation from *Ny Carlsbergfondet* and *Oak Foundation*

306. Pot, 1991
Porcelain, glazed; cast, relief. H 15.3 x Diam 18.7. Mark: 'BODIL MANZ' painted on base. Mus.no. 85/2006. ACQUISITION: Jørgen L. Dalgaard. Donation from *Højesteretssagfører C. L. Davids Legat for Slægt og Venner*

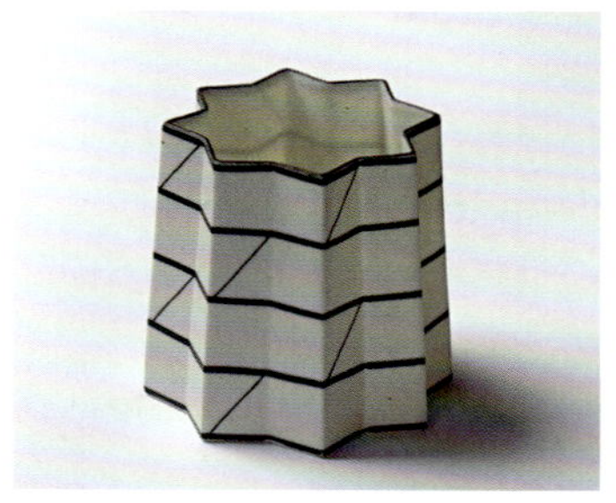

300 64/1994

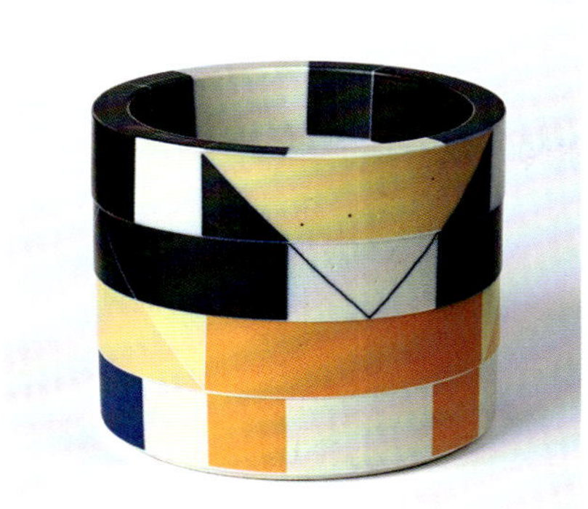

306 85/2006

307. Vessel, 2007. *Sampling #9E*

Porcelain, glazed, transfers; cast, four assembled shapes with applied high-fired transfers, fired at 1300°. Mark: 'BODIL MANZ' painted on base and 'BM' in a square mark. H 20. Mus.no. 438/2008

ACQUISITION: *Bodil Manz*, 2008, Kunstindustrimuseet. Donation from *Ny Carlsbergfondet*. See: *Laursen, Bodil B.*, 2008

308. Vessel, 2007. *Sampling #9F*

Porcelain, glazed, transfers; cast, four assembled shapes with applied high-fired transfers, fired at 1300°. H 20. Mark: 'BODIL MANZ' painted on base and 'BM' in a square mark. Mus. no. 439/2008

ACQUISITION: *Bodil Manz*, 2008, Kunstindustrimuseet. Donation from *Ny Carlsbergfondet*

309. Vessel, 2001. *Sand*

Porcelain, matte glazed; thrown, sand-cast, inlaid sand-structures, melted pieces of glaze, brush-painted. H 41 x L 46.5. Mark: 'BODIL MANZ' painted on side and 'BM' in a square mark. Mus.no. 440/2008

ACQUISITION: *Bodil Manz*, 2008, Kunstindustrimuseet. Donation from *Ny Carlsbergfondet*

310. 5 tablets, 2008. *Erindringer* (Memories)

Plaster, paper, canvas; painted, mounted in wooden frames. H 90 x W 90 (each tablet). Mus.nos. 139-143/2009.

ACQUISITION: *Bodil Manz*, 2008, Kunstindustrimuseet. Donation from *Højesteretssagfører C. L. Davids Legat for Slægt og Venner*

311. Dish, 1986. *16-sided oval dish*

Porcelain, transparent glaze; cast, brush-painted, reduction-fired at 1300°. H 12.5 x W 42 x L 54. Mark: 'BODIL MANZ' painted on base and 'BM 1986/41' in a square mark. Mus.no. D 1649

ACQUISITION: On deposit from *Statens Kunstfond*, 1987

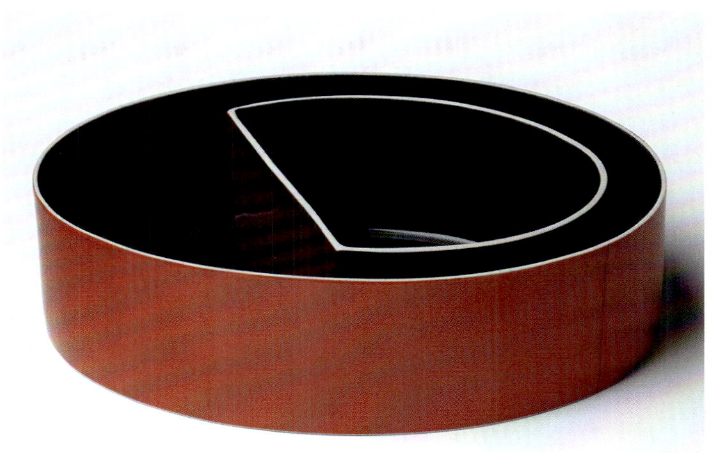

302 187a-b/2000

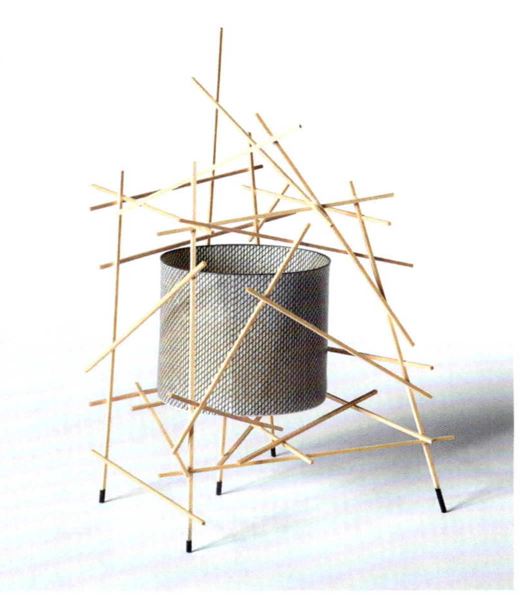

303 215a-b/2001

MANZ, RICHARD 1933 – 1999

Ceramicist

1950	Trained as a potter in Germany
1955-65	Gustavsberg, Sweden
1956	Konstfackskolan, Stockholm
1966	Escuela de Desiñio y Artisanias, Mexico City
1966	Berkeley University, San Francisco
1967-	Studio workshop shared with Bodil Manz, Den gamle Skole, Starreklinte, W Sealand
1970s	Holbæk Kunsthøjskole, Det Jyske Kunstakademi, teacher
1980	Metropolitana Azcapotzalco, Mexico City, guest teacher

On completion of his education as a potter in Germany the young Richard Manz (RM) began his journey northwards in 1955 and was employed by the major Swedish ceramics factory Gustavsberg, near Stockholm. Because of his technical skill in throwing he became an assistant to the most important designers in the factory's artistic workshop, whose role was to bring new designs forward into industrial production. There he became familiar with stoneware and porcelain and the experimental technique with sand-cast porcelain which he later developed in the workshop he shared with Bodil Manz in Starreklinte, W Sealand, from 1967. That workshop became the setting for the couple's substantial and significant contribution to Danish ceramics, with porcelain as the main material, used in their work both for functional household objects and in their creations in the context of their individual artistic careers.

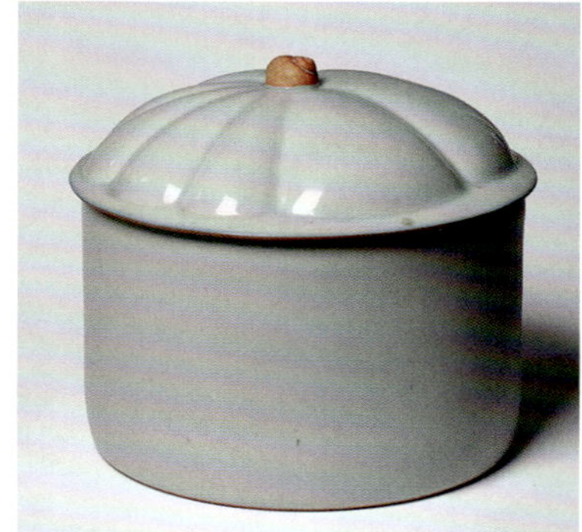

312 73a-b/1977

Functional ceramic objects were the departure-point for the workshop in Starreklinte, and over the years, not least thanks to RM's consciously goal-directed work, it developed into a fully professional workshop with capacity to turn out a standardized high-quality production of various small series of household ceramics of their own design. Apart from development of the design aspect, there had to be basic research into production of the materials to be used, and rational as well as craft skills invested in the organisation of the process from the casting of plaster moulds to the throwing of the objects. A distinguishing characteristic of the Manzs' workshop through all the years has been that the materials used were their own products prepared on the spot; Bodil Manz has kept up this policy.

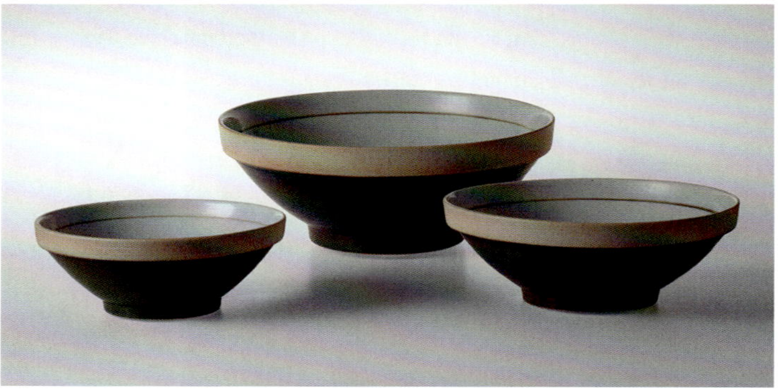

313 74a-c/1977

Amazingly fast after the setting up of the workshop, so many well-worked-out functional objects had been created that exhibition activity could be embarked on with the début exhibition *'Ler og tråd'* (Clay and thread) in 1969, in collaboration with weaver Bodil Bødtker-Næss, at 'Den Permanente', from where Richard and Bodil Manz, in common with the leading art craftsmen of the time, sold their work and were important contributors to the exhibition activities that took place under its auspices.

The development of the workshop was strongly influenced by a study visit to Japan in 1975, including time spent working in the 'porcelain town' of Arita, with the aim of gaining knowledge about the production of functional objects in porcelain. The results of that visit could be seen in a large exhibition held in the museum in 1977, entitled '*Variation i porcelæn*'. It was evident then that RM had succeeded in reaching a quality of mould-thrown porcelain, a transparency and colour, of exceptional beauty. From this copious exhibition, which included both functional objects and unique works in porcelain and stoneware, the museum acquired several works, among them RM's stringently shaped tureen with a snail-shell on the lid **(312)**, and what was to become a classic in the workshop's production, *Risskålene* (The rice bowls – a nod to Japan), consisting of a set of bowls in six sizes, glazed on the outside with a greenish-black hare-fur glaze **(313)**. This set of bowls was also later included in the *Lærkestellet* (see p. 346). Another set of bowls was added to the museum's collection in 1987, this one of stoneware with a deep blue cobalt glaze **(314)**. In 1999 the public had another opportunity to see a comprehensive range of RM's functional pieces in the exhibition '*Form-Transformation*' held by the museum; it included examples of RM's five prize-winning proposals for a service which unfortunately never came into production.

RM worked on creating sculptural unique pieces throughout his active career, from his time in Mexico and the USA in the mid 1960s and up to the time of his death in 1999; these works were often made for the many exhibitions he took part in, in Denmark and abroad. The works are based on simple geometric forms such as the sphere, the cone, the pyramid or the cylinder, and display an exceptional level of rigour and consistency. In the museum's collection there are several significant works that represent this aspect of RM's sculptural pieces **(315,317,320,323)**.

RM developed sand-casting of porcelain through the years, in particular in connection with 13 commissioned works in which the workshop was involved in the period 1978-1990, and which placed challenging demands on its artistic and technical capacity.

But the technique of sand-casting was also to find use in a number of sculptures of convincing artistic strength, in which expression, materials and technique are united in a higher entity. Major pieces from the mid 1990s, from this final important phase of RM's life, are to be found in the museum's collection; in particular the sculptures *Culture Morte* **(322)** and *Erindringer* (Memories) **(321)** will stand as central works in the history of Danish ceramics in the latter half of the 20th century. See: Manz, C., (ed.), 2015.

312. Lidded pot, tureen, 1977
Porcelain, celadon-glazed; thrown, fired at 1300°. H 22.5 x Diam 25.
Mark: 'Richard Manz' painted on base. Mus.no. 73a-b/1977
ACQUISITION: *Bodil og Richard Manz – variation i porcelæn*, 1977, Kunstindustrimuseet. Donation from *Overretssagfører Odin Kaysers Legat*

313. Set of bowls (three out of six bowls), 1977. ***Risskåle*** (Rice bowls)
Porcelain, hare's fur glaze, transparent glaze; jigged, decorated, wiped rims. Largest dimensions: H 12.4 x Diam 33. Mark: 'Manz' (indistinct) painted on base. Mus.no. 74a-c/1977
ACQUISITION: *Bodil og Richard Manz – variation i porcelæn*, 1977, Kunstindustrimuseet

314. Set of bowls (three bowls), 1987
Stoneware, cobalt-glazed; thrown. Largest dimension: H 13.5 x Diam 26.5.
Mark: 'Manz' painted on base. Mus.no. 43a-c/1987
ACQUISITION: *Keramik – min elskede, jeg hader dig*, 1987, Galleri Q. Donation from *Nationalbankens Jubilæumsfond*

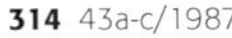
314 43a-c/1987

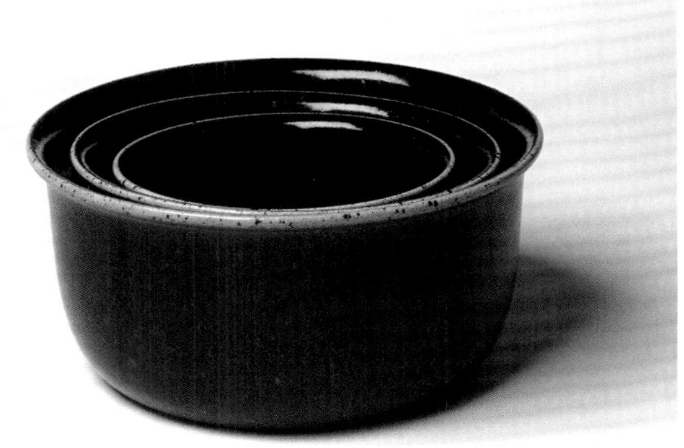

315. Vessel, dual form, 1980

Stoneware, transparent alkali glaze; handbuilt, slab technique. H 33 x W 35. Mark: 'Richard Manz' painted on base with 'R' in a square mark. Mus.no. 154/1987

ACQUISITION: *Keramik – min elskede, jeg hader dig*, 1987, Galleri Q. Donation from *Nationalbankens Jubilæumsfond.* See: *Brændpunkter*, 1990

316. Bowl, 1989

Stoneware, celadon- glazed; thrown, soft-fired at 1300°. H 9 x Diam 28.5. Mark: 'R' in a square mark painted on base with '-89'. Mus.no. 147/1989

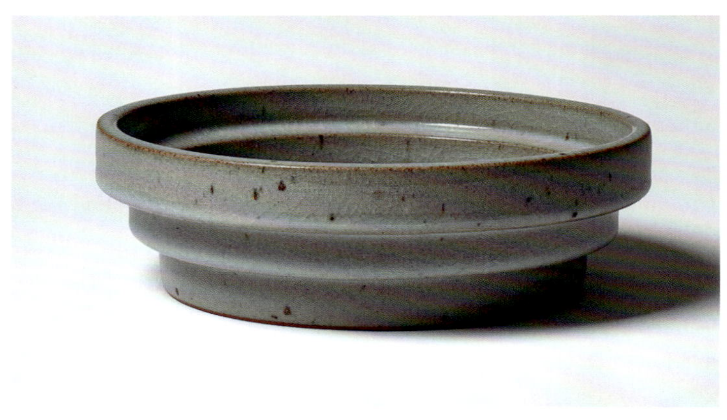

316 147/1989

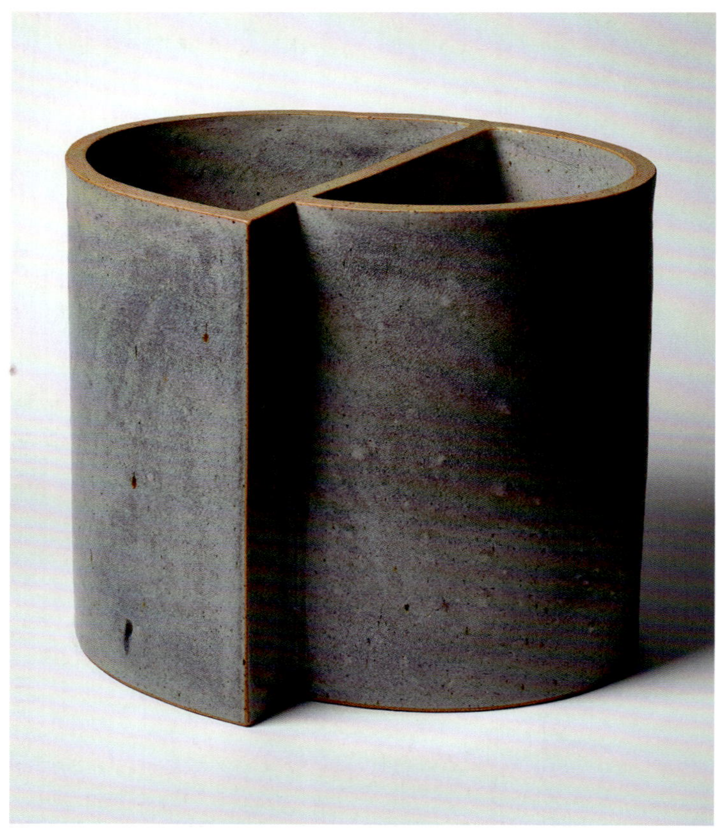

315 154/1987

317. Pot, 1989

Stoneware, oxblood-glazed; thrown. H 36 x Diam 21. Mark: 'Richard Manz' in a square mark painted on base. Mus.no. 148/1989.

ACQUISITION: Donation from *Kunstindustrimuseets Venner.*

See: Dybdahl, L., 1997

318. Two beakers and jug, 1990. From the 'zig-zag' series

Porcelain, glazed, transparent glaze; cast in a mould. Beakers H 8.5 x Diam 7.5 (a-b), jug H 22.2 x Diam 10.7 (c). Mark: (a-b): 'R Manz' painted on base.; (c): 'Richard Manz'. Mus.no. 129a-c/1990

ACQUISITION: Donation from *Sølvsmed Kay Bojesen og hustru Erna Bojesens Mindelegat*

319 11/1992

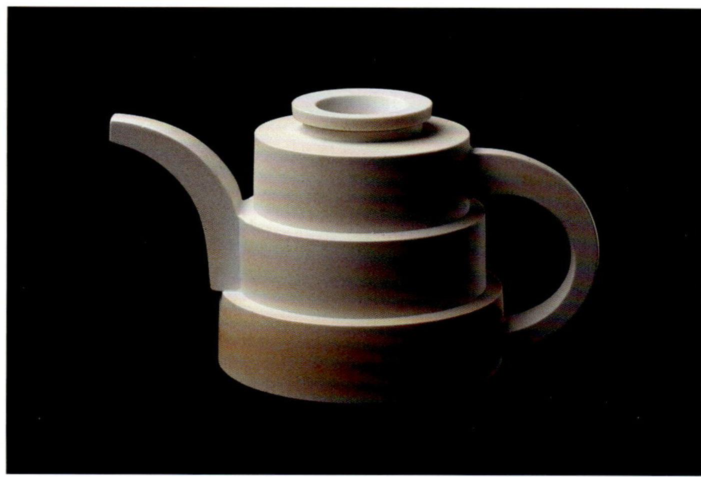

ACQUISITION: Donation from *Kunstindustrimuseets Venner*

319. Teapot, 1991

Porcelain, unglazed; cast, fired at 1300°. H 15 x Diam 16. Mark: 'Richard Manz' painted on base with 'R' in a square mark. Mus.no. 11/1992

ACQUISITION: Donation from *Fonden af 26. maj 1978*.

See: Dybdahl, L., 1997

320. Sculpture, 1995. *Stilleben* (Still life)

Porcelain, unglazed; slab technique, sand-cast. H 10 x L 62 x W 50. Mark: 'R' inscribed in a square on base. Mus.no. 161/1995

ACQUISITION: *Porcelæn 95 – Bodil & Richard Manz*, 1995, Galleri Nørby, Copenhagen

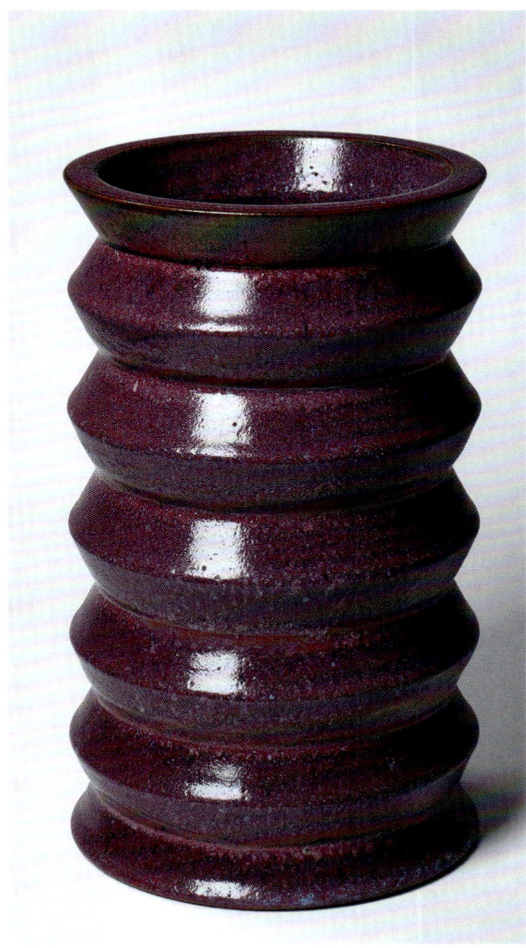

317 148/1989

321. Sculpture, (seven parts), 1997. *Erindringer* (Remembrances)

Porcelain, partially glazed with matt white slipping; sand-cast, fired at 1300°. H 18 x L 200 x W 47. Mus.no. 102a-h/1999

ACQUISITION: Donation from *THE VELUX FOUNDATIONS*

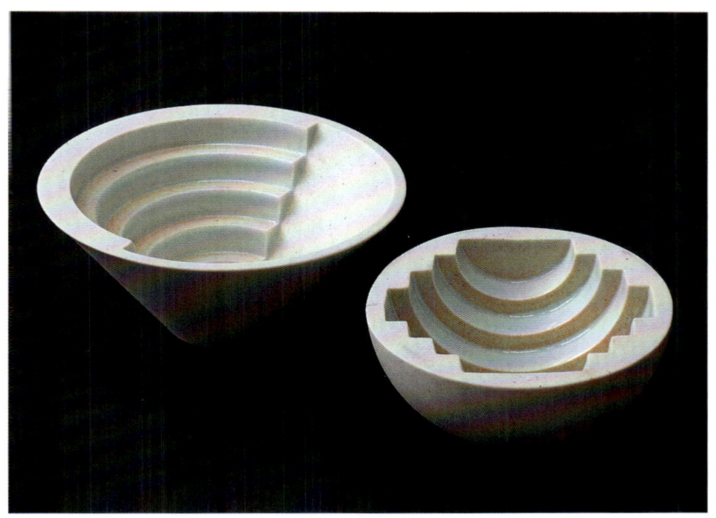

324 og 325 D 1751 og D1752

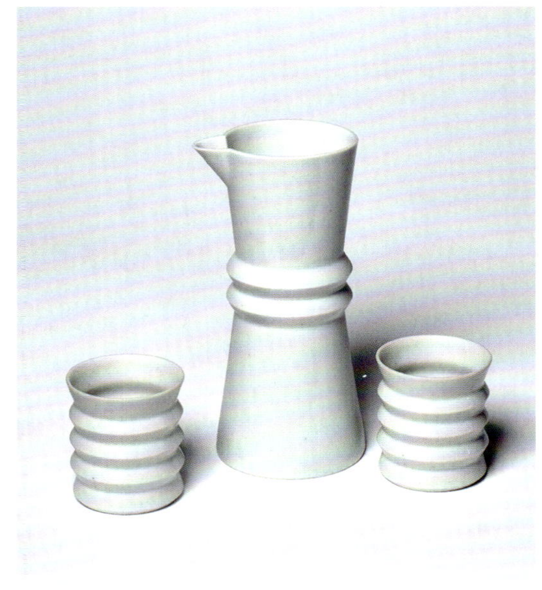

318 129a-c/1990

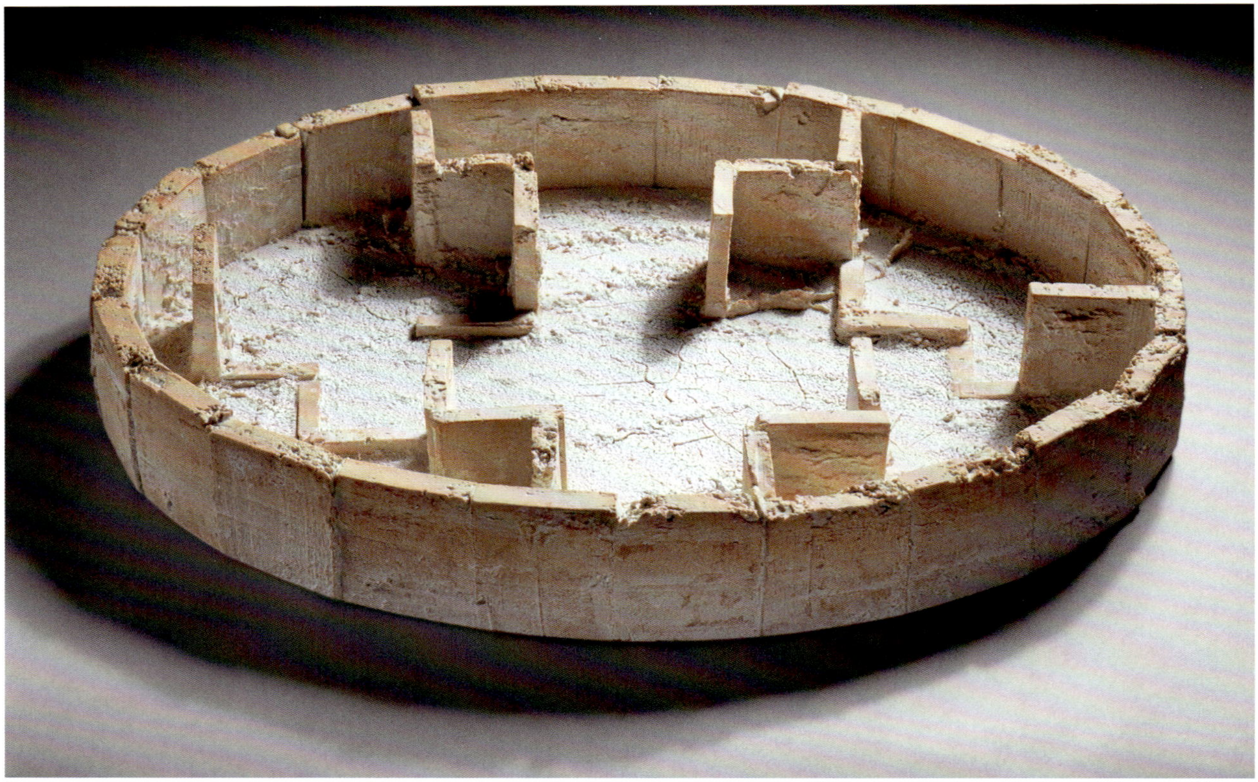

320 161/1995

322. Sculpture, 1995. *Culture Morte*

Porcelain, unglazed; modelled, sand-cast, fired at 1300°. H 31.5 x Diam 30.

Mark: 'R. Manz' painted on base. Mus.no. 103/1999

ACQUISITION: Donation from Bodil Manz.

See: *Form – transformation 1966-1999*, 1999

323. Basin, 1991. *Tromsø*

Stoneware, partially glazed; thrown, fired at 1300°. H 22.5 x Diam 53.

Mark: 'Richard Manz' painted on base in a square mark. Mus.no. D1750

ACQUISITION: Charlottenborgs Efterårsudstilling 1991.

On deposit from *Statens Kunstfond*, 2000

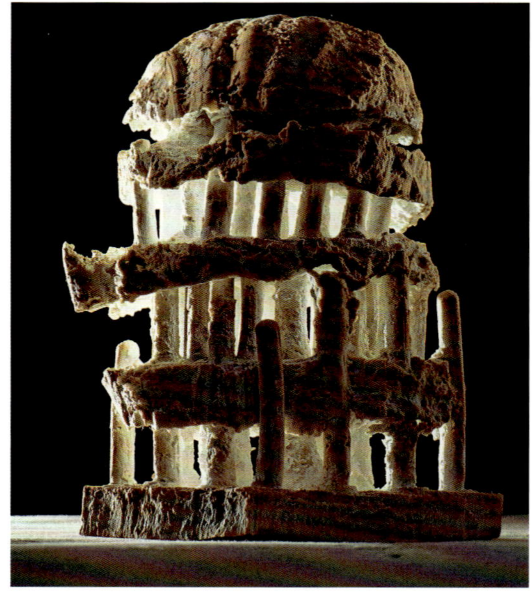

322 103/1999

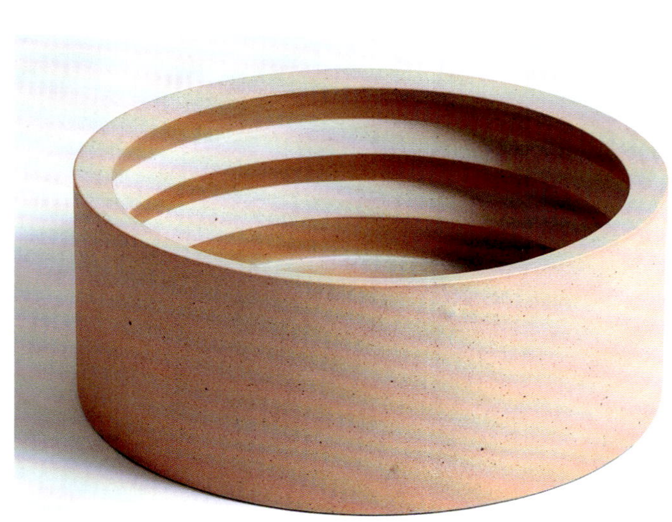

323 D1750

324. Small bowl, 1992

Porcelain, partially glazed, transparent glaze; thrown in mould (jiggering process), modelled, fired at 1300°. H 8 x Diam 18. Mark: 'R Manz' and 'RM' painted in a square mark on base. Mus.no. D 1751

ACQUISITION: On deposit from *Statens Kunstfond*, 2000

325. Small bowl, 1992

Porcelain, partially glazed, transparent glaze; thrown in mould (jiggering process), modelled, fired at 1300°. H 7 x Diam 15. Mark: 'R Manz' painted in a square mark on base. Mus.no. D 1752

ACQUISITION: On deposit from *Statens Kunstfond*, 2000

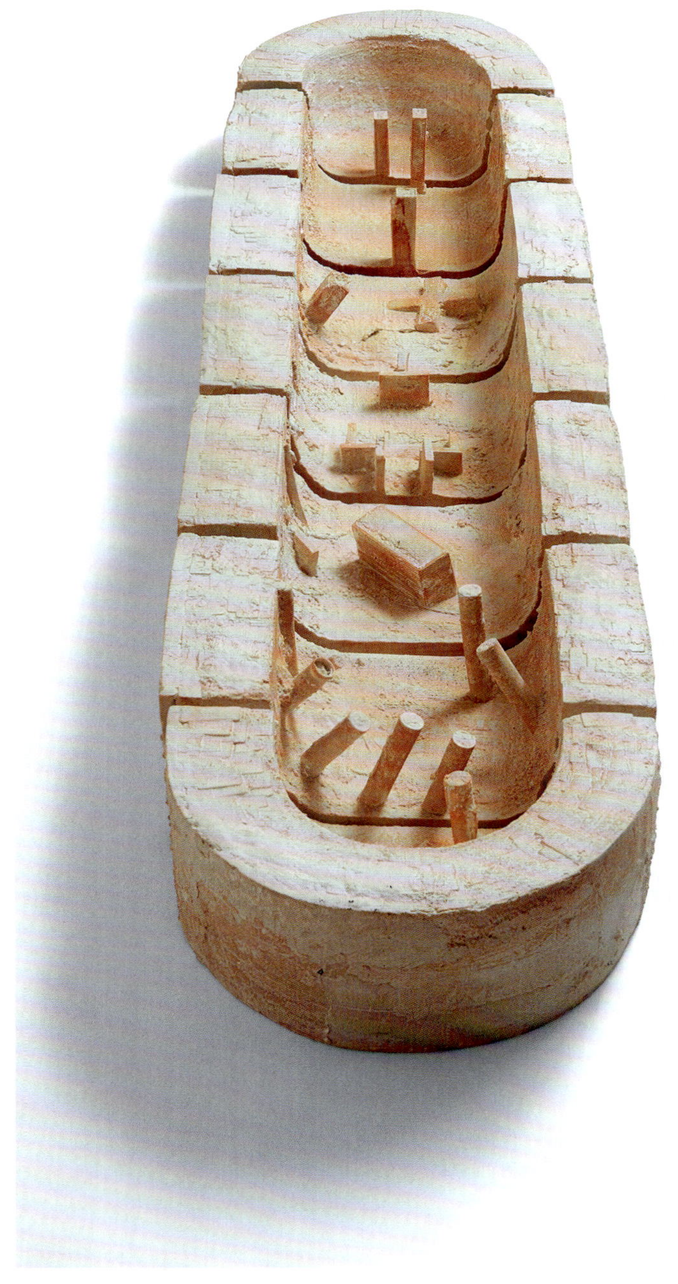

321 102a-h/1999

MAY, MARIANNE 1943 –

Ceramicist

1959-63 Trained as potter with Bjørn Wiinblad

1964-85 Shared workshop with Jac Hansen, Copenhagen, later in Ebeltoft, Jutland

1987- Own studio workshop, Ebeltoft

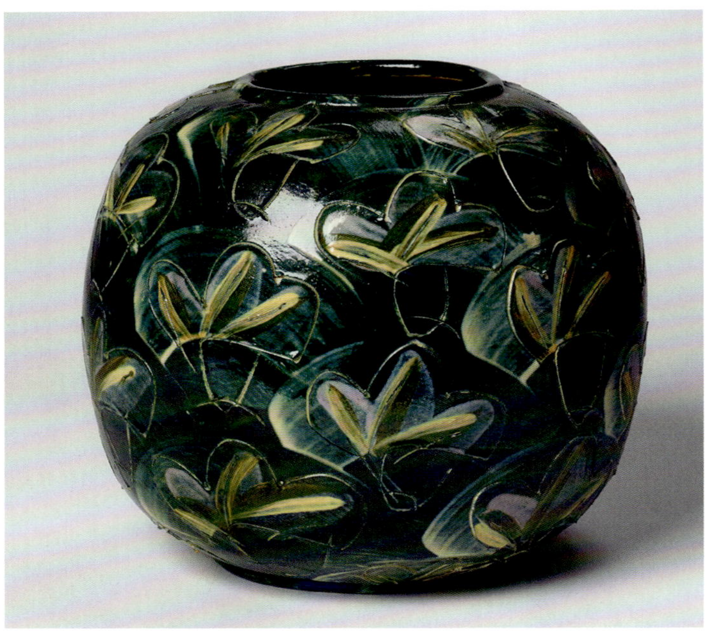

326 343/1989

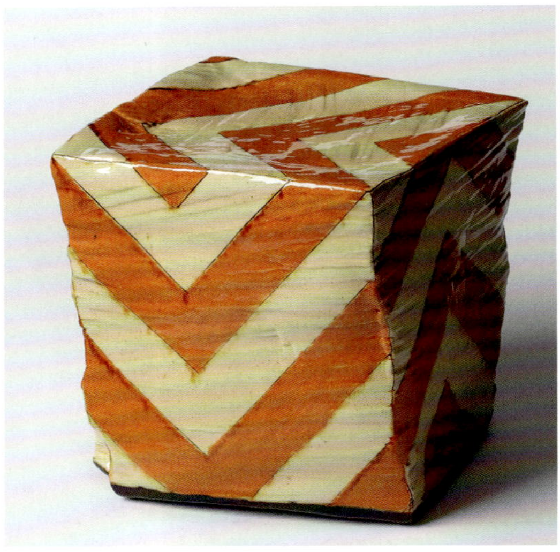

327 D 1670

326. Spherical vase, 1989. *Gaia*

Faience, lead frit; thrown, brush-painted, fired at 1040°. H 24 x Diam 12.
Mark: 'May' inscribed on base. Mus.no. 343/1989
ACQUISITION: *Jysk sommer*, 1989, Kunstindustrimuseet

327. Sculpture, date unknown. *Sten* **(Stone)**

Earthenware, glazed; modelled, slab technique. Mark: none.
H 18 x W 17.5 x L 16.5. Mus.no. D 1670
ACQUISITION: On deposit from *Statens Kunstfond*, 1989

Marianne May (MM) learned pottery in Bjørn Wiinblad's workshop and has worked with decorative ceramics and pastel drawings. MM has travelled widely and sought inspiration in nature, mythology, Islamic art and pre-historic cultures. She has also worked with church decoration.

MM was invited by the museum to participate in its exhibition entitled '*Jysk Sommer*' (Jutland Summer) in 1989; 17 ceramic workshops from Jutland were represented. From the exhibition the museum acquired MM's spherical vase *Gaia*, made in faience with a brush-painted flower motif (343/1989). In 1989 *Statens Kunstfond* deposited with the museum a characteristic work by MM, a square sculpture with zigzag decoration **(327)**.

MEJLVANG, VIBEKE see HESSELHOLDT, SOFIE p. 143

MEYER, LILLER 1943 –

Ceramicist

1967-68 Aarhus Kunstakademi
1969-72 Det Jyske Kunstakademi, Ceramics and Sculpture
1973 Central School of Art and Design, London
1970-2000 (c.) Own studio workshop, Samsø
2004 Moved to Flensburg, Germany
www.liller-meyer-helm.dk

Liller Meyer (LM) studied in Aarhus and had her own ceramic workshop and gallery on Samsø until she moved to Flensburg, in Germany, in 2004. She has in particular made use of the raku technique.

Soon after completing her studies LM began to participate in exhibitions, including the '*Danske Kunsthåndværkere*' exhibition held in the museum in 1984; at that time the museum acquired from her a raku-fired bowl which was later exhibited in '*Brændpunkter*' in 1990 **(328)**. In the following years LM exhibited in the Nordic region, elsewhere in Europe and in Japan. She is represented in several museums and public institutions.

328. Bowl, 1984

Earthenware, lustre-glazed; thrown, raku-fired. H 8 x Diam 15.5. Mark: 'Liller Meyer' inscribed on the base rim. Mus.no. 144/1984 ACQUISITION: *Danske Kunsthåndværkeres Landssammenslutning – Aarhus-gruppen,* 1984, Kunstindustrimuseet. Donation from *Finansieringsinstituttet for Industri og Håndværks Jubilæumslegat*. See: *Brændpunkter*, 1990

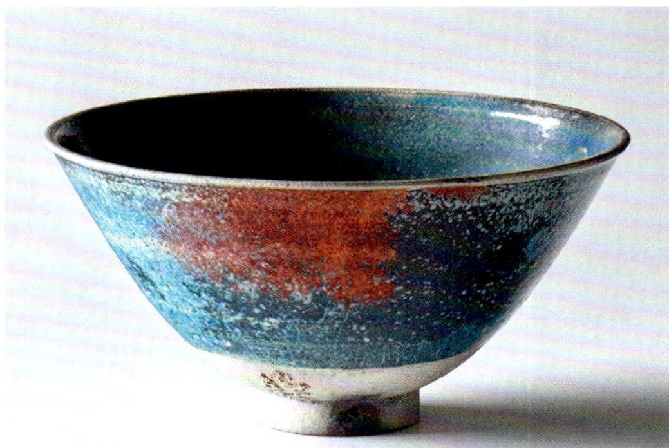

328 144/1984

MORTENSEN, IDA HOLM 1950 –

Painter, ceramicist, graphic artist

1972-77 Det Fynske Kunstakademi, School of Painting; various ceramic workshops
1978- Own studio workshop, Kerteminde, Funen
www.idaholmmortensen.dk

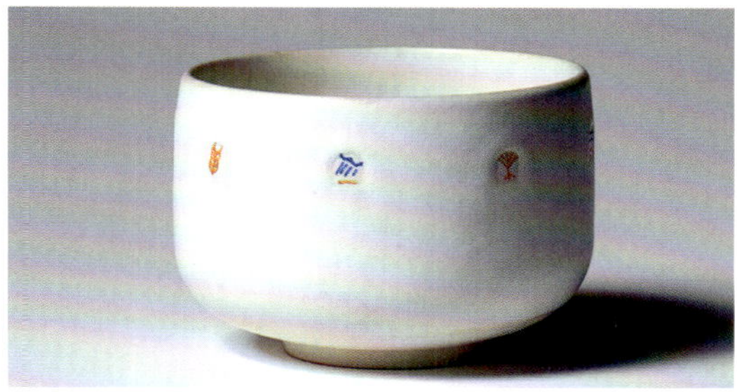

329 86/1986

Ida Holm Mortensen (IHM) studied at the Fynske Kunstakademi in the School of Painting, and supplemented this with training in ceramic workshops. Since setting up her own studio workshop in 1978 IHM has achieved an extensive production of diverse types of work, ranging from painting, drawing and unique ceramic bowls and sculptures to a large number of commissioned works in the form of reliefs. Her many commissions for public institutions are mostly figurative, and are to be found both indoors and out, while several of them include large decorated 'sitting globes' made of stoneware. IHM's commissioned art works can be seen in many locations in Denmark, and she has been a diligent participant in exhibitions over the whole Nordic region as a member of the exhibition group *Fynske Kunsthåndværkere*.

Fynske Kunsthåndværkere exhibited in the museum in 1986, and on that occasion the museum acquired the matte white bowl in stoneware with fine little brush-painted decorations in blue and ochre **(329)**.

329. Bowl, 1986. *Årets Gang* (The course of the year)

Stoneware, zinc- and barium- glazed; thrown, decorated, indented areas brush-painted with oxides, fired at 1240°. H 9 x Diam 13. Mark: 'IHM -86' painted on base. Mus.no. 86/1986. ACQUISITION: *Fynske kunsthåndværkere*, 1986, Kunstindustrimuseet. Donation from *Kunstindustrimuseets Venner*

MUNCH-PETERSEN, LISBET 1909 – 1997

Ceramicist

1928-30 Kunstindustrimuseet's course in Ceramics
1931-33 Hans and Grete Syberg's pottery, Valby, Copenhagen
1933-36 Workshop shared with Gertrud Vasegaard, Gudhjem, Bornholm
1937-97 Own studio workshop, Gudhjem
1961-66 Attached to Bing & Grøndahl
1983 Awarded an honorary lifelong stipend by Statens Kunstfond

Lisbet Munch-Petersen (LMP) is the third generation in the ceramicist family from the L. Hjorth factory in Rønne on Bornholm, and she became a pivotal influence on Bornholm ceramics throughout the many years that she lived and worked in Gudhjem. LMP was active in the development of the ceramic milieu on Bornholm, especially through her involvement with the setting up of the open craft workshop '*Bornholms Frie Værksteder for Kunst og Håndværk*'. LMP also has to be seen as having a significant artistic role in the general development and continuity of Danish studio ceramics in the 20th century.

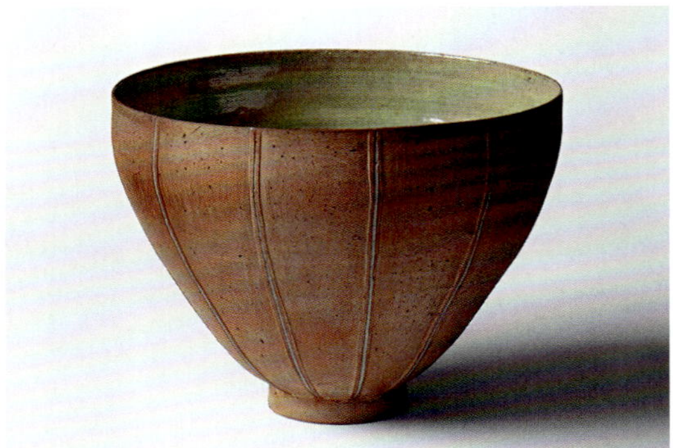

330 A1/1943

In 1989 LMP celebrated her 80th birthday and on that occasion a retrospective exhibition was held in Bornholms Kunstmuseum and she was presented with the publication of a *festschrift* with contributions from colleagues, including the ceramicist Christian Poulsen, a friend from her youth, who produced a fine formulation of the aura of LMP's works (see: *Gudinden fra Holkadalen – Lisbet Munch-Petersen*, Bornholms Kunstmuseum, 1989, p. 45):

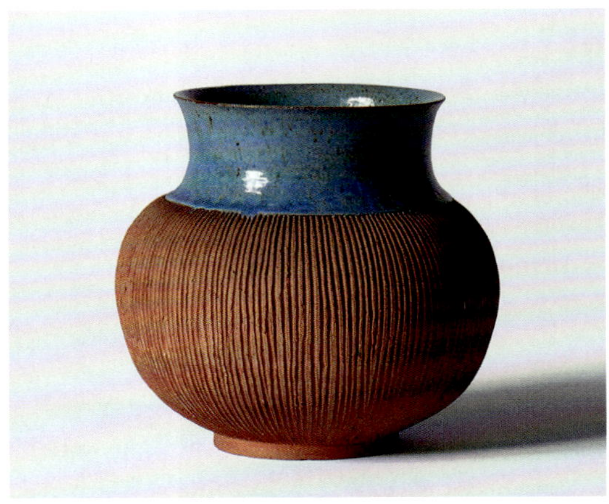

331 B24/1944

The farmer, the fisherman, and the hunter interpret the signs of nature; the artist and craft worker feel the mystic power of nature, its soul, and unconsciously give it expression in matter and shape, as Lisbet has managed to do in her timeless ceramic art.

That Bornholm's rich and splendid nature, with light, sea, rocks and vegetation, were the material that LMP so unaffectedly and handsomely translated into her life's many ceramic works and commissioned projects can be seen and sensed, but she also found inspiration outside Bornholm, as is evidenced by traces of prehistoric ceramics and African decoration in some of her works (See: Bloxham, G., 1990, p. 16) **(341)**. She moved in richly artistic circles on Bornholm and in Copenhagen and forged lasting friendships at the

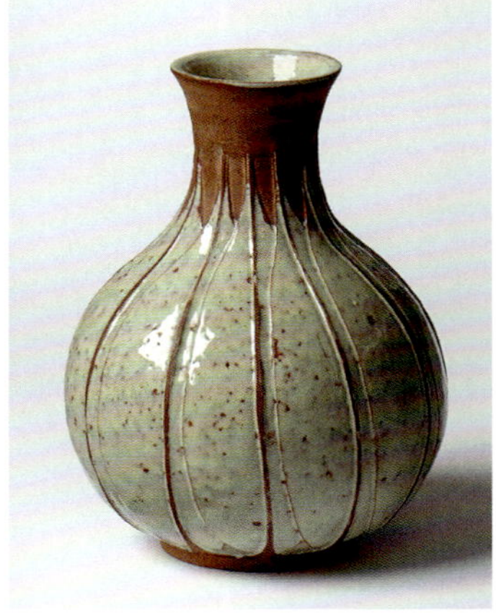

332 B26/1944

Kunsthåndværkerskolen, e.g. with Richard Mortensen, Ejler Bille and Sonja Ferlov. She herself was first married to the author and artist Gustaf Munch-Petersen, who was killed in 1938 in the Spanish Civil War, and then to the artist Poul Høm.

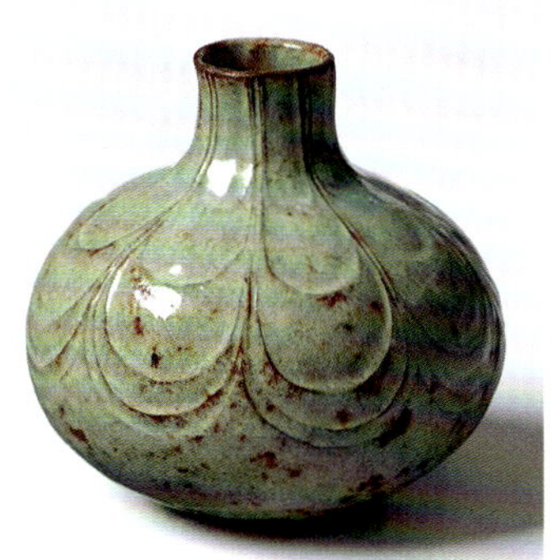

333 B28/1944

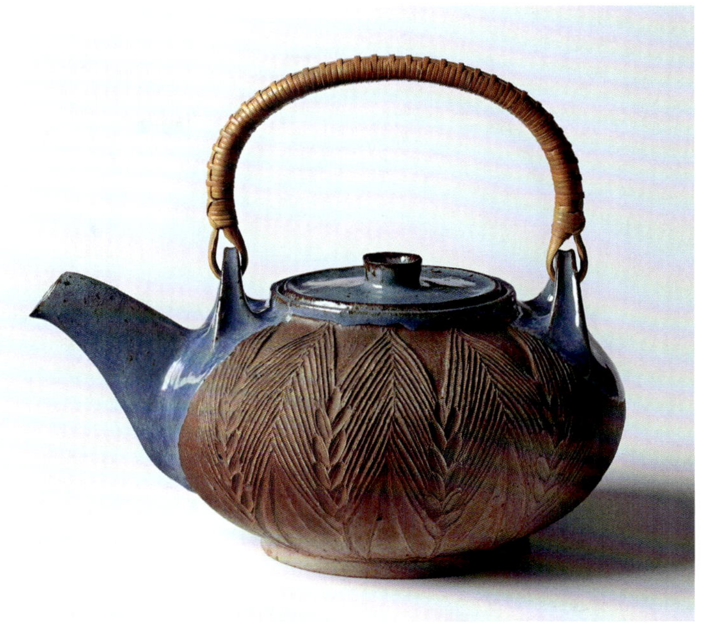

335 87/1950

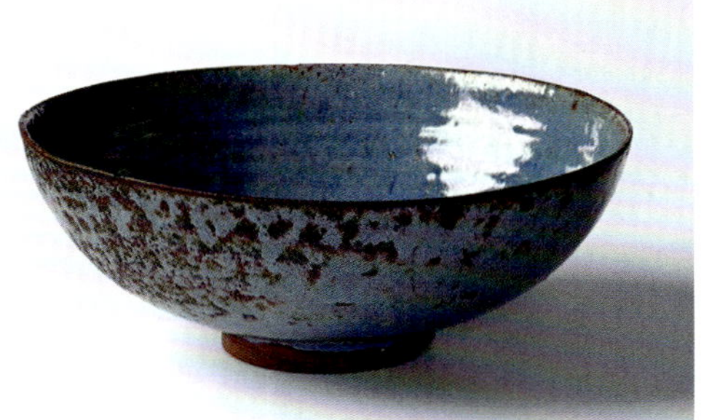

334 B29/1944

After some years in Copenhagen, where LMP took classes in ceramics and also worked in Hans and Grete Syberg's pottery, LMP went home to Bornholm, where she and her sister Gertrud Hjorth (Vasegaard), with the help of their father, Hans Hjorth, set up a workshop which they shared until 1936, when they both started families. From then until her death LMP worked from her own workshop in Gudhjem, producing hard-fired earthenware which did not require as high a firing temperature as stoneware. The decoration she used was often nature inspired, but sometimes also geometric; she embossed, modelled and incised it into the clay before glazing with pale blue, brownish black and yellow glazes that were based on glaze recipes from the time she spent at the firm of Saxbo in the winter of 1939/40 and subsequent experiments in Christian Poulsen's laboratory at the Polyteknisk Læreanstalt. (See: Bloxham, G., 1990, pp. 15-16, 34). From around 1960 LMP devoted more of her time to a series of commissioned works. Chief among these was the unique series of four large ceramic reliefs with the seasons as the theme, for the Danish sports hall in Flensburg,

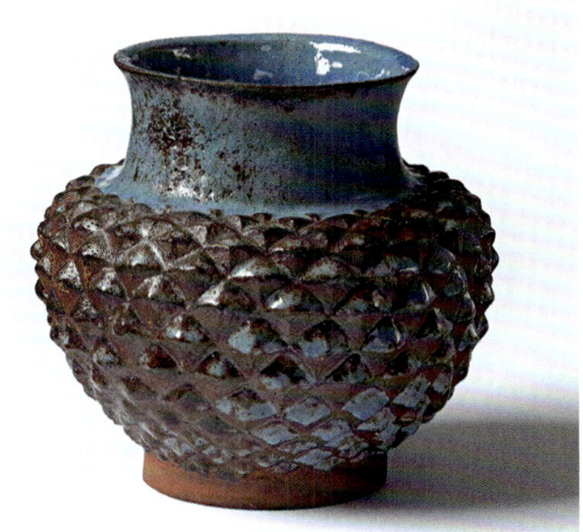

336 88/1950

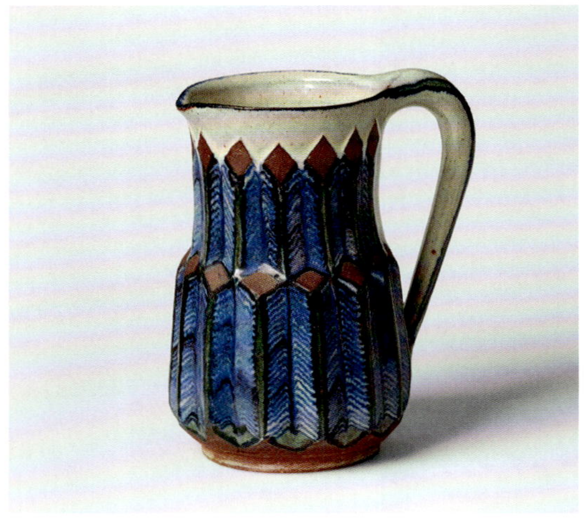

337 128/1958

dating from 1966-70, commissioned by *Statens Kunstfond*. She also carried out several large commissions for churches in collaboration with Poul Høm, and other works, including a ceramic relief for Nexø Town hall in 1984, with her daughter, Julie Høm.

The museum has a good representative collection of 14 vases and bowls by LMP from 1934 to 1982, with particular weight on the 1940s and 50s. Most of the works show a fine mastery of the contrast between glazed sections and unglazed sections (usually the neck and base) that reveal the reddish brown colour of the body; all the works are glazed inside.

In 1943 the museum acquired its first work by LMP, an elegantly-shaped conical bowl **(330)**, at the exhibition *'Dansk Kunsthåndværk'*, and then followed a group of four works donated by *Ny Carlsbergfondet* and bought from the firm of Fischer & Krarup, booksellers and art dealers in Bredgade, Copenhagen. The pot **(331)** is remarkable, with its grooved spherical corpus, which is unglazed, while the neck and the inside are covered in fine lavender blue glaze. Two glazed vases **(322-333)** have relief decoration based respectively on foliage and on onion scales. Nature-inspired decoration is also to be seen on the teapot from 1950 **(335)**, with large areas of indented stylised ears of barley, placed close together on the unglazed sides, and clear blue glaze on the spout, lid and inside. Both this work and the fir-cone vase **(336)** were acquired at the artist's exhibition in 1950 at Bruun Rasmussen, Copenhagen. The collection also contains two works with geometric glaze-painted patterns; a pot with a triangular motif **(343)**, and a bowl with a lively painted rhombus pattern **(340)**, which is the last work by LMP in the collection.

As the history of these acquisitions shows, the artist maintained connections with the Copenhagen exhibition scene and was involved in Danish, Nordic and international exhibition contexts. Works by LMP are represented in influential museums, and she was the recipient of many distinctions in the form of bursaries and honour awards, including the Thorvald Bindesbøll medal in 1986.
See: Bloxham, G., 1990; Serena, L., 2004.

330. Bowl, c.1940

Earthenware, glazed; thrown, decorated with 12 radial double lines with inlaid glaze matching that on the inside. H 17.4 x Diam 23. Mark: 'LMP' inscribed on base. Mus.no. A1/1943.

ACQUISITION: *Dansk Kunsthåndværk*, 1943, Kunstindustrimuseet

331. Pot, 1943

Earthenware, glazed; grooved, partially glazed. H 18 x Diam 18.5. Mark: 'LMP' inscribed on base. Mus.no. B24/1944

ACQUISITION: Fischer og Krarup, Copenhagen, 1944. Donation from *Ny Carlsbergfondet*

332. Vase, 1943

Earthenware, glazed; thrown, decorated with a leaf motif in relief. H 21 x Diam 16.5. Mark: 'LMP' inscribed on base. Mus.no. B26/1944. ACQUISITION: Fischer og Krarup, Copenhagen, 1944. Donation from *Ny Carlsbergfondet*

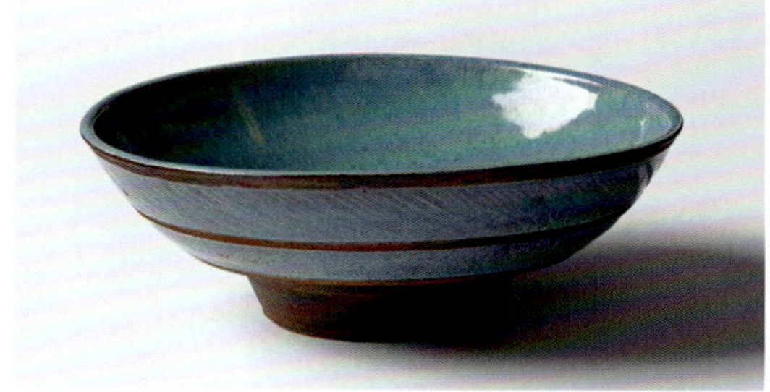

338 692/1962

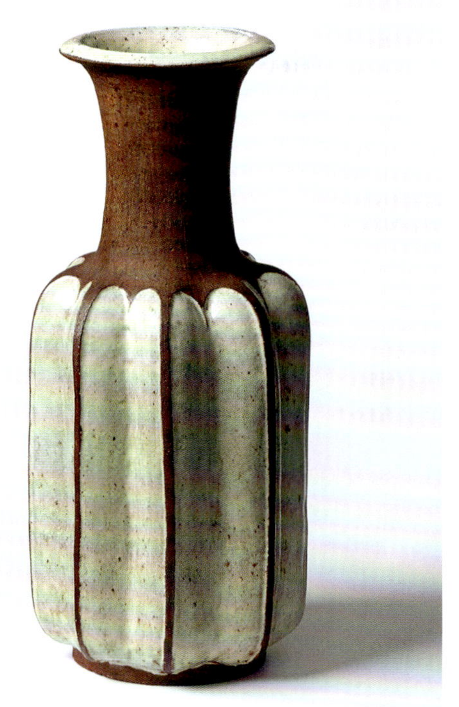

339 36/1966

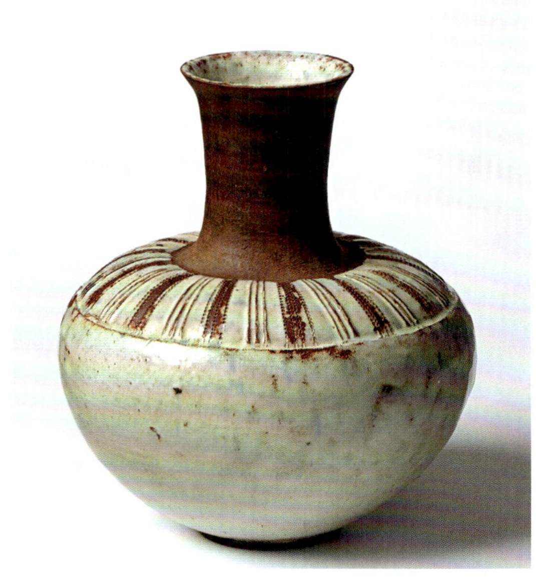

342 392/2004

333. Pot, 1944

Earthenware, glazed; thrown, decorated with onion scales in relief. H 10.9 x Diam 11.2. Mark: 'LMP' inscribed on base. Mus.no. B28/1944

ACQUISITION: Fischer og Krarup, Copenhagen, 1944. Donation from *Ny Carlsbergfondet*

334. Bowl, 1944

Earthenware, glazed; thrown, shaped. H 7.7 x Diam 20.8. Mark: 'LMP' inscribed on base. Mus.no. B29/1944

ACQUISITION: Fischer og Krarup, Copenhagen, 1944. Donation from *Ny Carlsbergfondet*

335. Teapot, 1950

Earthenware, glazed; thrown, modelled, decoration in the form of ears of barley in relief on unglazed body, partially glazed. H 12 x Diam 22. Mark: 'LMP' inscribed on base. Mus.no. 87/1950

ACQUISITION: Artist's exhibition at Bruun Rasmussen, Copenhagen, 1950. Donation from *Benny Dessaus Mindelegat*. See: Dybdahl, L., 1997

336. Vase, 1950

Earthenware, glazed; thrown, modelled fir-cone in relief. H 15 x Diam 15. Mark: 'LMP' in a square inscribed on base. Mus.no. 88/1950

ACQUISITION: Artist's exhibition at Bruun Rasmussen, Copenhagen, 1950. Donation from *Benny Dessaus Mindelegat*. See: *Brændpunkter*, 1990. Dybdahl, L., 1997

337. Jug, 1958

Earthenware, glazed; thrown, modelled, fluted corpus, polychrome glazed. H 15 x W 10. Mark: 'LMP' inscribed on base. Mus.no. 128/1958

ACQUISITION: Den Permanente, Copenhagen. Donation from *Benny Dessaus Mindelegat*. See: *Brændpunkter*, 1990

338. Bowl, 1962

Earthenware, glazed; thrown, inscribed decoration of striations, unglazed encircling band. H 7.8 x Diam 22.2. Mark: 'LMP' inscribed on base. Mus.no. 692/1962 .

ACQUISITION: *Nordisk keramik I*, 1962, Lunds Konsthal, Sweden. Donation from *Benny Dessaus Mindelegat*

339. Vase, 1954

Earthenware, glazed; shaped like a seed pod, cast corpus, thrown neck, partially glazed. H 36 x Diam 15. Mark: 'LMP' inscribed on base. Mus.no. 36/1966

ACQUISITION: Donation from Karen Prehn. See: Dybdahl, L., 1997

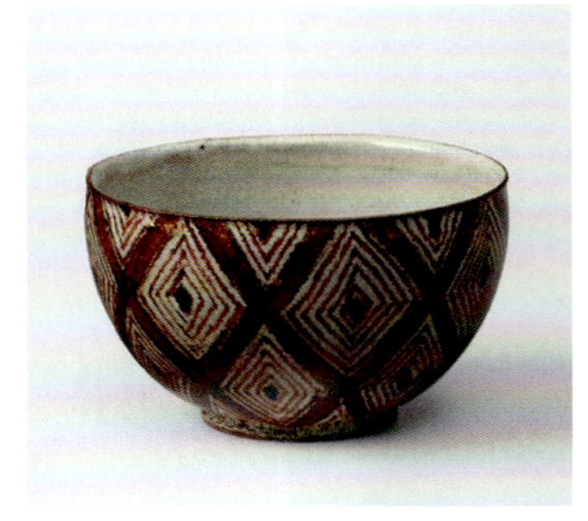

340 49/1983

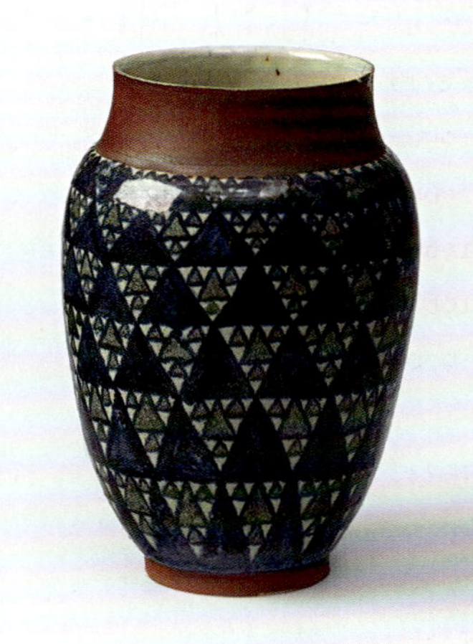

343 393/2004

340. Bowl, 1982

Earthenware, glazed; thrown, outside decorated with painted rhombus motif. H 8.5 x Diam 13.8. Mark: none. Mus.no. 49/1983

ACQUISITION: *Glas og keramik*, 1983, Illums Bolighus. Donation from *Kunstindustrimuseets 50-års Jubilæumslegat*

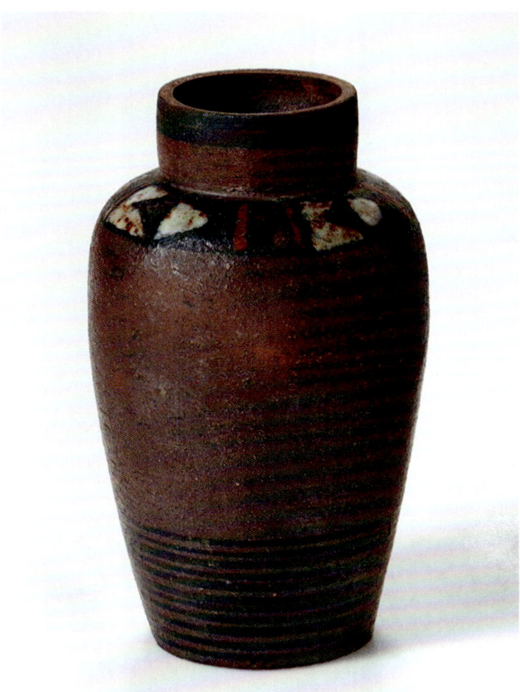

341 150/1990

341. Vase, 1934

Earthenware, glazed; thrown, slip, brush-painted decoration and glazed fields. H 19 x Diam 11.5. Mark: 'G.H.L.' (monogram for Gertrud and Lisbet Hjort) stamped on base. Mus.no. 150/1990

ACQUISITION: Donation from Lisbet Munch-Petersen.

(See: Bloxham, G., 1990, p. 16. *Brændpunkter*, 1990, pp. 58-60)

342. Vase, date unknown

Earthenware, partially glazed; thrown, decorated. H 23.1 x Diam 19.7. Mark: 'LMP' inscribed on base. Mus.no. 392/2004

ACQUISITION: Donation from Carl M. Dahl

343. Vase, date unknown

Earthenware, glazed; thrown, decoration of glaze with triangular motif. H 20.8 x Diam 14. Mark: 'LMP' inscribed on base. Mus.no. 393/2004

ACQUISITION: Donation from Carl M. Dahl

MUNCH-PETERSEN, URSULA 1937 –

Ceramicist

1956-60	Kunsthåndværkerskolen
1960-61	L. Hjorths Fabrik, Rønne, Bornholm
1961-68	Bing & Grøndahl, artists' workshop
1968	Visiting student, Escuela de Diseño y Artesanias, Mexico
1970-72	Royal Danish Academy of Fine Arts, School of Walls and Space
1973-88	Skolen for Brugskunst, instructor
1978-	Own studio workshop, Copenhagen
1989-	Own studio workshop, Møn
1987-2002	Attached to Royal Scandinavia
1998	Awarded Statens Kunstfond's honorary lifelong stipend

Since the 1960s Ursula Munch-Petersen (UMP) has had an important career within Danish ceramics, combining cooperation with industry and many years of teaching at Skolen for Brugskunst with a rich production as a practising studio ceramicist. Wherever UMP has invested her talents she has stood up for art craftsmanship and for artistic development as a precondition for creating good new household objects for ordinary use, to give pleasure to people through excellent functional qualities and appeal to the eye. UMP belongs to the fourth generation in the ceramicist family that created and still runs the ceramic firm named L. Hjorth in Rønne on Bornholm. She studied at Kunsthåndværkerskolen and worked intermittently in the family's factory. While working there in 1960-61 she undertook her first major commission, a project for the ferry M/S Bornholm; she made a ceramic relief at L. Hjorth, using a motif from the river Læså, a piece of Bornholm nature with water, rocks and glimpses of fish. Examples of trial sections were shown at the exhibition held by the National Association of Danish Crafts at Charlottenborg in 1961 and were highly praised. In the museum's collection there is one of these trial pieces, with a swimming snake **(357)**. Another work by UMP, made in 1986, renders eternally flowing water material in a green-glazed modelled wreath, a free sculpture with strong pictorial power **(348)**. Preparatory studies for this work are in Vejen Kunstmuseum and in Erik Veistrup's collection at CLAY.

Through the museum's collection one can follow several of the many activities that UMP has engaged in over the course of the years. The works show the development of forms and expressions and document the manual experimental methods that have created functional objects with a strong aura of the values of art craftwork. Many of UMP's products have been made in connection with exhibition projects, not all of which can be mentioned here, but by way of introduction the landmark exhibition in Den Permanente, in 1972, entitled *'At være Keramiker'* (Being a ceramicist) should be included here. It was a cooperative endeavour by nine ceramicists: UMP, Hans and Birgitte Börjeson, Hans Munck Andersen, Marie Hjorth, Bodil and Richard Manz, Gerd Hiort Petersen and Anne-Marie Trolle (married name Oxmund). The purpose was *inter alia* to discuss the justification for being a ceramicist in the context of contemporary social and economic conditions – raising important, still topical issues which this critical and innovative exhibition set before the surrounding world (see Nielsen, T., 2004, pp. 70-77).

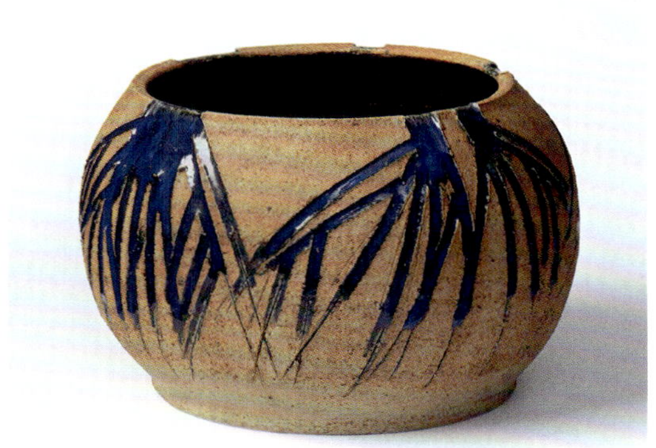

359 211/1999

The following is a brief summary of the projects from which the museum's collection of UMP's works arose; characteristically they were often developed in cooperation with others.

The first collective proposal for a table service, whose prototypes are to be found in the museum's collection, was a dining- and serving-set for 'Huset' in Magstræde, Copenhagen, where an informal restaurant was being planned. UMP was asked to provide a proposal and she worked out models in Bornholm stoneware clay at the Hjorth factory **(350, 355)**. The simple and robust pieces in the service were suited to limited factory production. Despite interest from many quarters, and diligent work by UMP, it never proved possible to put it into production. As always the idea lost out because of the cost in comparison to mass-produced cheap imported goods, but it provided experience, and that gave the starting signal for the laborious journey towards the URSULA service, which came into production at Royal Copenhagen in 1993.

A major event was born out of cooperation with Skolen for Brugskunst (formerly Kunsthåndværkerskolen), whose director, Richard Kjærgaard, took the initiative for an exhibition project involving 16 teachers and other craftworkers and furniture designers associated with the school. The project was entitled '16+' – the plus sign indicating that guests could be invited to participate. The exhibition was held in 1981 in the museum, and UMP created for it a new generation, in terms of design, of functional objects based on a technique of shaping the object over a mould, so that with simple aids objects could be produced in a small series. The material was stoneware, glazed inside and unglazed outside, and the objects were for instance a herring pot with lid, decorated with little brush-painted crests of waves **(344)** and a butter-dish with lid, decorated with plant motifs **(345-346)** The exhibition was a success and was followed in 1984 by a further '*16+*' arrangement, this time in the museum's garden, 'Grønnegården', where during the summer visitors could have lunch in greenhouses with food made by Camilla Plum and Nanna Simonsen. The food was served on items from table services made by UMP, consisting of 10 very diverse little bowls, each produced in an edition of 50, along with centrepieces, flower vases and large salad bowls **(351-354, 361)**. UMP herself expressed pleasure in the project, which for her was part of having the feeling of contributing to produce healthy and good food; a

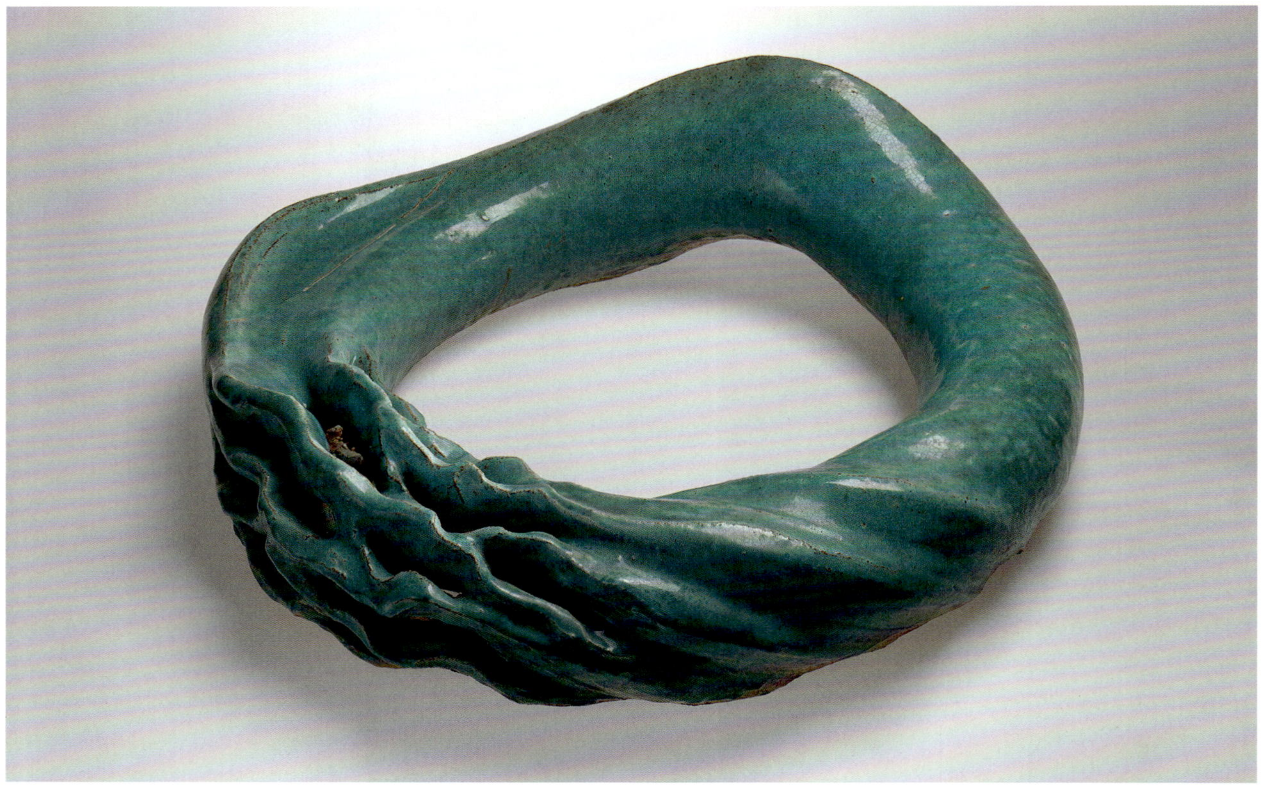

348 145/1987

kind of symbol of a 'better' and more aesthetic existence. (See: exhibition catalogue '*De Danske*', Kulturhuset, Stockholm, 1984/85).

Another major undertaking, carried out in cooperation with selected pupils from Skolen for Brugskunst during the 1980s, was the development of unique and serially-produced flower-pots for the Botanical Garden in Copenhagen; the project continued in 1997 with flower-pots for Vejen at the time of the retrospective exhibition at Vejen Kunstmuseum. The work with the pots for the Botanical Garden is one of many examples of UMP's dedicated efforts throughout her 15 years as a teacher at Skolen for Brugskunst; her work there only came to an end when the development of the URSULA service took off with great strides towards its presentation in Royal Copenhagen in 1991, where it was described in the catalogue as a service for everyday use, 'A trial production in faience'.

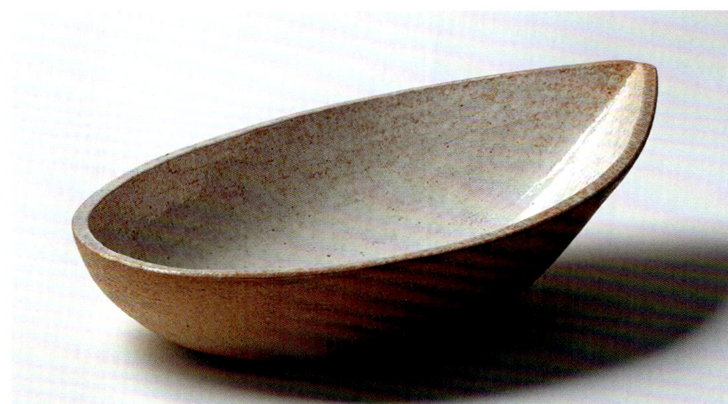

347 128/1984

The museum's design collection naturally includes the URSULA service, but the present catalogue includes only the unique works that are related to the development of the forms of the service. From 1983 there is the very robustly-shaped three-segment beak-pitcher, which the artist donated to the museum in 1987 **(356)**. Two bowls also point the way forward to the eventual design of the components of the URSULA-service – from 1984 an example of the 'squint' bowl-type and a preparatory work for the service's oval bowls, in this case glazed inside with a pale blue glaze that has similarities with that of the finally produced service **(347)**. Finally, in 1997 the museum acquired a work that is a poetic and strong image of one of the basic shapes

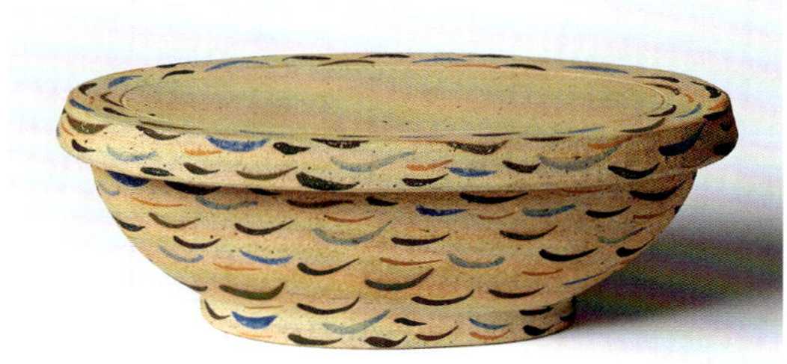

344 31a-b/1981

of the service, the sculpture *Søen* (The lake), in which on the superficially calm dark blue surface of water one can just discern a slight disturbance, and taken together with the raw concrete of the base this results in the idyll acquiring nuances **(358)**.

Items from the URSULA-service are included in the Lærkestellet (the Lark service), which resulted from a remarkable initiative led by Louise Lerche-Lerchenborg; her idea, based on a Japanese model, was to create a service with many individual parts that would be made by different ceramicists for whom work with functional objects had a particular appeal. Nine ceramicists, including UMP, rallied to this cause (see *Lærkestellet*, p. 346).

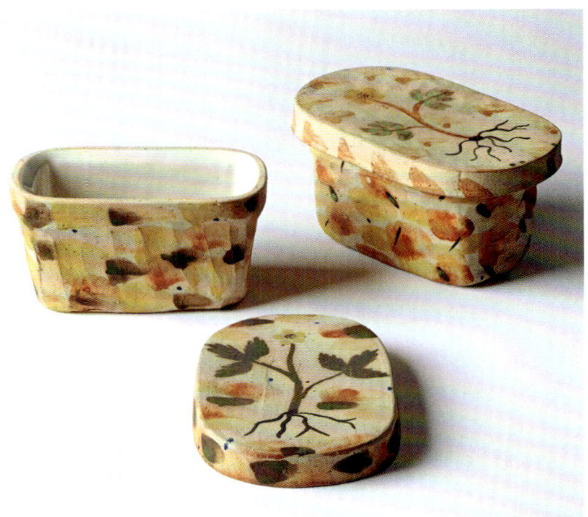

346 79a-b/1983

345 32a-b/1981

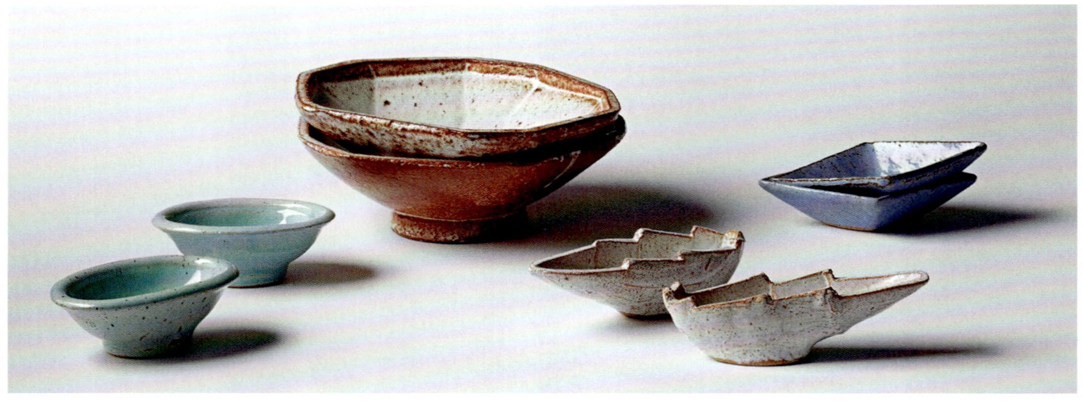

354 151a-b/1987 **351** 148a-b/1987 **352** 149a-b/1987 **353** 150a-b/1987

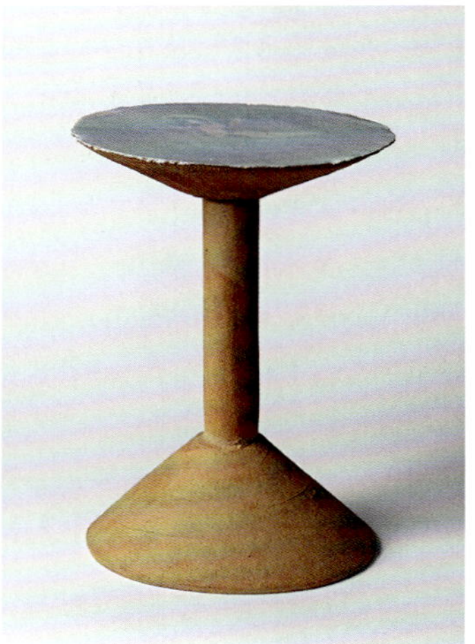

349 146/1987

The last work by UMP in the museum's collection is *Mit dukkestel* (My doll's tea-set) comprising 46 pieces, from 2003. UMP made a total of 10 doll's sets inspired by childhood memories and playing with grandchildren **(362)**.

There is a keynote of strong idealism and social motivation in UMP's form of work and attitudes, and this finds expression in the ceramic works and many articles, contributions, textbooks, periodicals, and catalogues, in which UMP, with courage and idealism, has stood up for a humane society, for the cause of craftsmanship and for the importance of good-quality everyday functional household objects. 2004 saw the publication of the book '*Ursula Munch-Petersen*' by Teresa Nielsen, in which UMP's work and significance are documented with insight. See: Nielsen, T., 2004.

344. Lidded pot, 1981. ***Sildekrukke*** (Herring pot)
Stoneware, glazed, partially unglazed; brush-painted decoration, fired at 1240°. H 11.7 x W 28.6. Mark: 'UM-P' inscribed on base. Mus.no. 31a-b/1981 ACQUISITION: *16+,* 1981, Kunstindustrimuseet. Donation from *Benny Dessaus Mindelegat*. See: *Brændpunkter*, 1990

345. Butterdish, 1981
Stoneware; shaped over a mould, brush-painted decoration, fired at 1240°. H 9 x W 15. Mark: 'UM-P' inscribed on base. Mus.no. 32a-b/1981. ACQUISITION: *16+*, 1981, Kunstindustrimuseet. Donation from *Benny Dessaus Mindelegat*

346. Butterdish, 1982
Stoneware; shaped over a mould, brush-painted decoration, fired at 1240°. H 9.2 x W 14.5. Mark: 'UM-P' inscribed on base. Mus.no. 79a-b/1983 ACQUISITION: Ursula Munch-Petersen. Donation from *Kunstindustrimuseets 50-års Jubilæumslegat*

347. Dish, 1984
Stoneware, glazed; thrown, shaped, fired at 1240°. H 12.8 x W 48. Mark: none. Mus.no. 128/1984. ACQUISITION: Illums Bolighus. Donation from *Finansieringsinstituttet for Industri og Håndværks Jubilæumslegat*

350 147/1987; 157a-f/1987 **355** 158a-b/1987

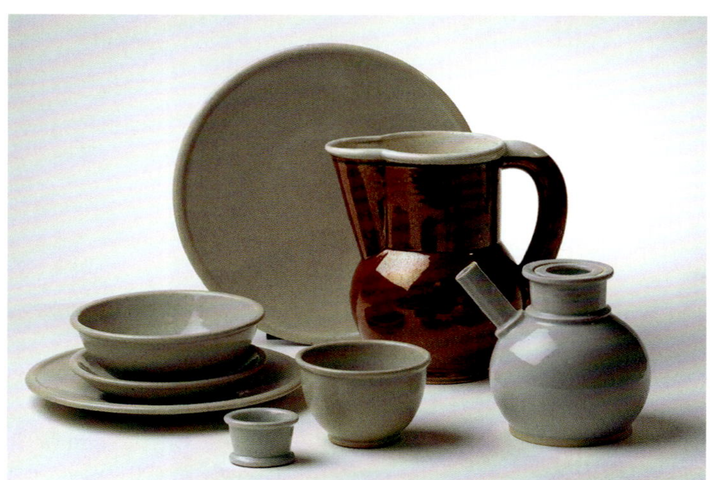

348. Sculpture, 1986. *Krans af Stentøj* (Stoneware wreath)
Stoneware, glazed; modelled, fired at 1240°. H 15 x Diam 53.
Mus.no. 145/1987. ACQUISITION: Ursula Munch-Petersen. Donation from Kunstindustrimuseets Venner. See: *Brændpunkter*, 1990

349. Centrepiece, 1984
Stoneware, glazed, partially unglazed; thrown, modelled, fired at 1240°.
H 31.5 x Diam 23. Mark: none. Mus.no. 146/1987. ACQUISITION: Ursula Munch-Petersen. Donation from *Kunstindustrimuseets Venner*

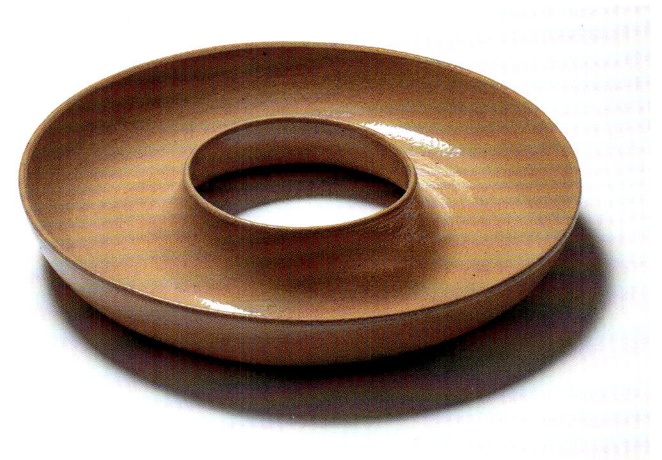

363 126/2009

356 159/1987

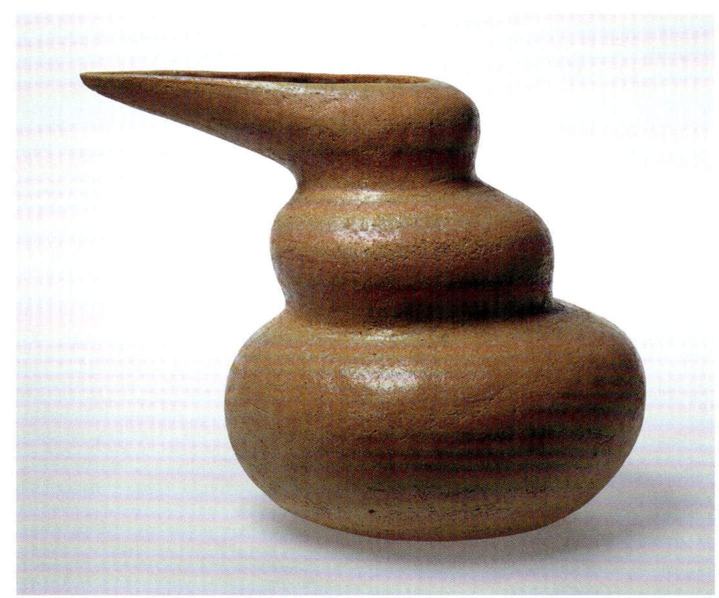

350. Jug and pieces of table service, 1975
Stoneware, iron-glazed; cast, fired at 1240°. Prototype, made as a supplement to the service for Husets Restaurant, Rådhusstræde, Copenhagen (cf. Mus.no. 157a-f/1987, 158/a-b/1987). H 19.4 x W 19.4 x Diam 11.4. Mark: none. Mus.no. 147/1987.
ACQUISITION: Ursula Munch-Petersen. Donation from *Kunstindustrimuseets Venner*

351. Bowls, 1984. *Spiseskåle* (Portion bowls)
Stoneware; shaped on a plaster core, hard-fired at 1240°. H 6.9 x Diam 20.6.
Mark: none. Mus.no. 148a-b/1987.
ACQUISITION: Ursula Munch-Petersen, *16+*, 1984, Kunstindustrimuseet.
Donation from *Kunstindustrimuseets Venner*

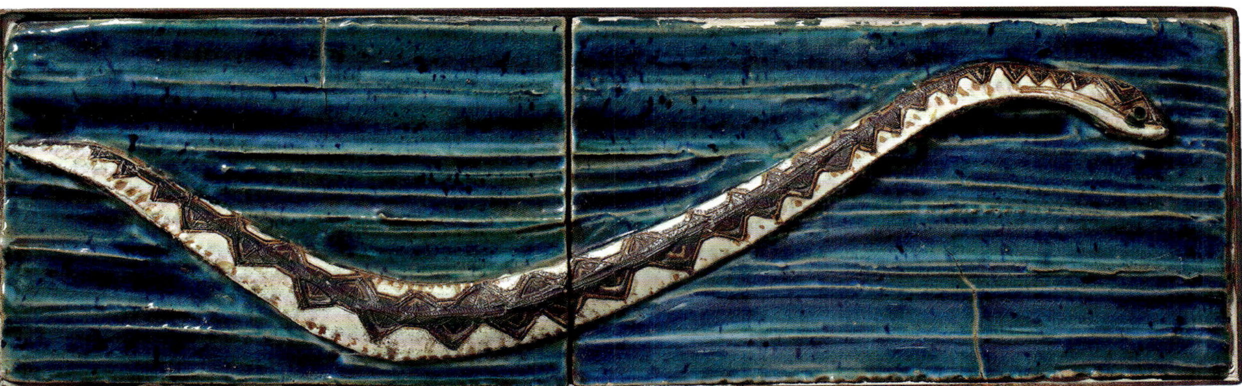

357 180/1987

352. Pitcher, 1983. ***Næbkande*** (Beak pitcher)
Stoneware, thin glaze; modelled. H 23 x Diam 27.8. Mark: 'UM.P 83' inscribed on base. Mus.no. 159/1987.
ACQUISITION: Donation from Ursula Munch-Petersen

353. Bowls, 1984. ***Rejeskåle*** (Shrimp bowls)
Stoneware; shaped on a plaster core, hard-fired at 1240°. H 4.4 x W 14.3 x Diam 4.7. Mark: none. Mus.no. 149a-b/1987. ACQUISITION: Ursula Munch-Petersen. Donation from Kunstindustrimuseets Venner

354. Bowls, 1984
Earthenware; hard-fired at 1240°. H 3 x W 13.5 x Diam 9.2. Mark: none. Mus.no. 150a-b/1987. ACQUISITION: Ursula Munch-Petersen. Donation from *Kunstindustrimuseets Venner*

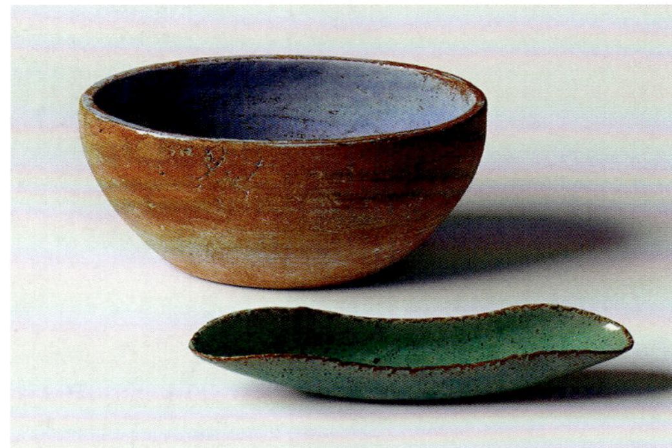

360 175/2000

361 176/2000

355. Bowls, 1984
Stoneware, glazed; modelled, fired at 1240°. H 4.3 x W 10.8 x Diam 7.8. Mark: 'UMP' in a circle on base. Mus.no. 151a-b/1987
ACQUISITION: Ursula Munch-Petersen. Donation from *Kunstindustrimuseets Venner*

356. Teapot, 1973
Stoneware, glazed; thrown. Prototype for Husets Restaurant, Copenhagen. a: H 13 x W 14.3; b: H 2.9 x Diam 5. Mark: 'UM-P-73' inscribed on base. Mus.no. 158a-b/1987
ACQUISITION: Donation from Ursula Munch-Petersen

357. Relief, 1961. ***Slange*** (Snake)
Stoneware, glazed; modelled, mounted in a metal frame. Trial firing for decoration for the ferry 'Bornholm', made at L. Hjorth, Bornholm.
H 59 x W 19 x Diam 4. Mark: none. Mus.no. 180/1987
ACQUISITION: Donation from Ursula Munch-Petersen.
See: *Schou-Christensen, J.*, 1977

358. Sculpture, 1997. ***Søen*** (The lake)
Stoneware, cement, glazed; modelled, fired at 1240°.
H 17.5 x W 44 x Diam 71. Mark: none. Mus.no. 210/1997
ACQUISITION: Clausens Kunsthandel, 1997

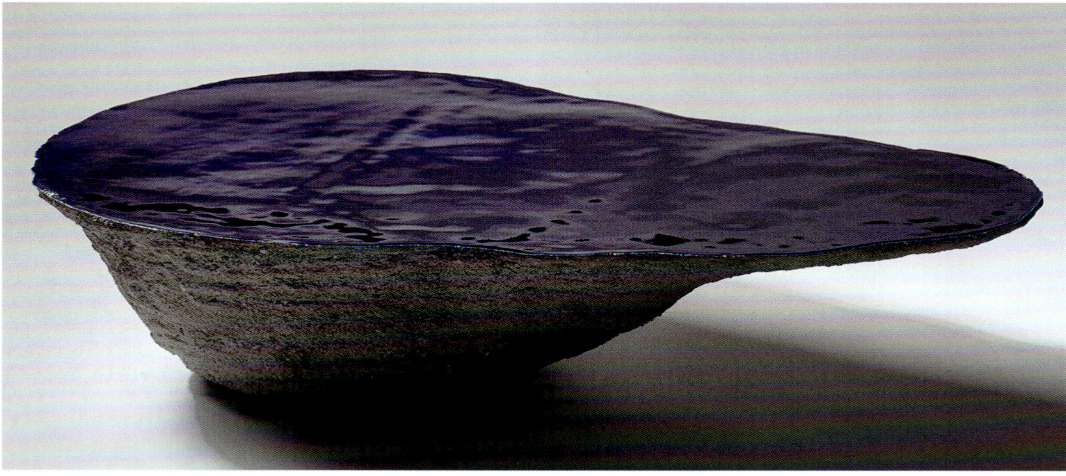

358 210/1997

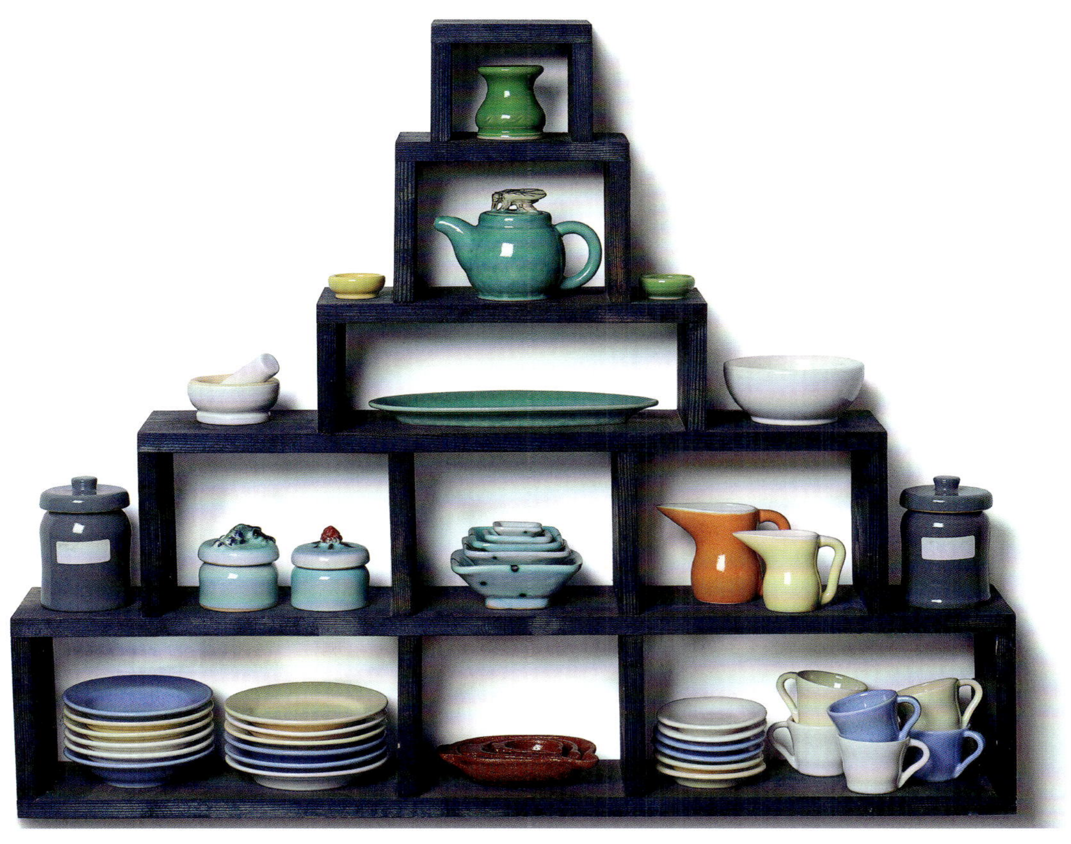

362 206a-z og 207a-ø/2003

359. Pot, date unknown

Stoneware, glazed; thrown, plant decoration. H 19.5 x Diam 20 (at mouth). Mark: 'UMP B&G' inscribed on base. Mus.no. 211/1999

ACQUISITION: Donation from Bank Director C.B. Andersen, Copenhagen

360. Bowl, date unknown

Stoneware, glazed; shaped over a mould. Preparatory work for the 'Ursula'service, Royal Copenhagen. H 12 x W 20 x Diam 14. Mark: none. Mus.no. 175/2000. ACQUISITION: Donation from Royal Copenhagen

361. Asparagus dish, 1984

Stoneware, glazed; modelled. H 4.5 x W 5.5 x L 21.5. Mark: none. Mus.no. 176/2000. ACQUISITION: Donation from Ursula Munch-Petersen. Part of service for exhibition '*16+*' in Grønnegården, 1984, Kunstindustrimuseet

362. Doll's table-service, 2003. *Mit dukkestel* (My doll's table-service)

Stoneware, porcelain clay, glazed; thrown, modelled, shaped over a mould, fired with access of oxygen, at 1240°. With accompanying wooden shelf. H 57.5 x W 12 x L 69.8. Mark: 'UM-P' inscribed on base (206a-b: no mark). Mus.nos. 206a-z og 207a-ø/2003

ACQUISITION: Clausens Kunsthandel, Copenhagen. Donation from *Kunstindustrimuseets Venner*. See: Bendtsen, T., 2003

363. Dish, 1995

Stoneware, glazed; thrown, modelled as a ring mould, glazed. H 8 x Diam 47. Mark: 'UM-P 95' inscribed on base. Mus.no. 126/2009

ACQUISITION: Donation from *Ny Carlsbergfondet*

MÜLLERTZ, MALENE 1949 –

Ceramicist, designer

1965-70	Kunsthåndværkerskolen
1970-73	Bing & Grøndahl, artists' workshop
1973-75	The Royal Danish Academy of Fine Arts, School of Architecture, Department of Industrial Design
1975-	Own studio workshop, Copenhagen
1977, 1982	The Royal Porcelain Factory, employed as artist
2007	Awarded Statens Kunstfond's honorary lifelong stipend
	www.malenemüllertz.dk

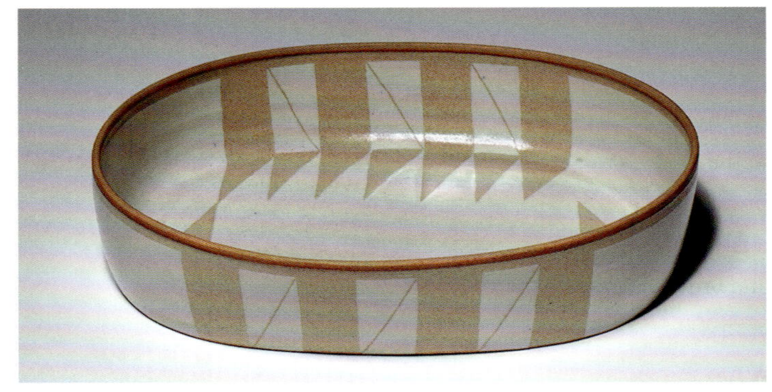

367 76/1986

Malene Müllertz (MM) belongs among the nationally and internationally recognized elite of Danish ceramicists. Her talents were noticed at the time of her earliest works and she went on to develop through original creativity and uncompromising efforts for more than forty years. MM's work is distinguished by certainty in the proportions and choice of techniques and materials in relation to textures, by a special and personal colour universe and a clear design focus that produces balance and harmony. Many of her works are technically complicated and demanding to make, requiring a high degree of working confidence and patience, and perhaps because of that they have a particular equilibrium. At the same time the works are subtle and immediately endearing; some rattle and make noises, becoming personal and making their presence known. Behind the works there lies an artistic context of sketching and drawing on journeys, with impressions of places, landscapes, crafts and architecture, and instructive preparatory drawings which MM has laid out in catalogues in connection with two solo exhibitions in the museum in 1997 and 2007.

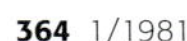

364 1/1981

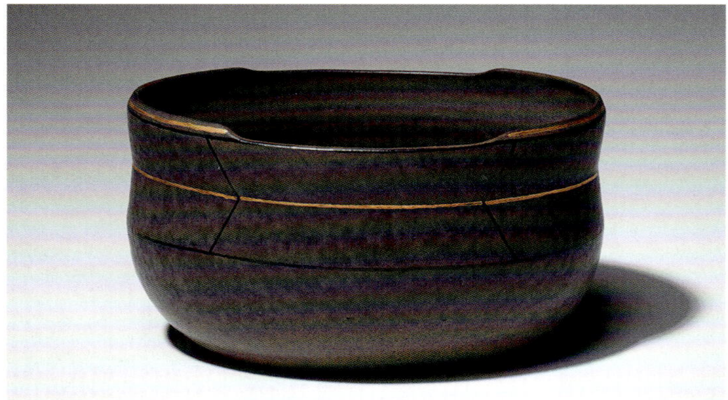

MM began her ceramic studies in 1965, and ten years later she set up her own studio workshop. By then she had completed her studies at Kunsthåndværkerskolen, supplemented by two years in the Academy's Design department, and had been employed for a 3-year period as an artist in the Royal Porcelain Factory. MM was thus an experienced ceramicist in 1975, when she started her own workshop, and she had already, while she was at the factory, exhibited her work and won appreciation of it. Like other ceramicists who studied at Kunsthåndværkerskolen under Richard Kjærgaard's leadership, MM was interested in working with the design of functional objects. In 1975 she took part in *'PROJEKT 75'*, in which a group of 10 young Danish ceramicists cooperated on a programme to design functional pieces suitable for industrial production and to form contacts with potential production firms. The results were shown in the museum in 1976, and as an extension of the project in 1977 MM and Bente Hansen were employed in the Royal Porcelain Factory, where MM made a number of works in stoneware, including a series of lidded pots which were not put into production because of problems in the factory (see: Lautrup-Larsen, L., 2007, pp. 305-07).

In 1983 MM was invited by the museum to hold a solo exhibition – an unusual proposal in relation to such a young artist. From the exhibition the museum acquired a large vessel modelled in pale stoneware, scraped to leave a thin body and decorated with stripes and ridges in different colours of glaze **(365)**. Another work from the exhibition is in the collection – an oval porcelain box with a gold 'cloud' decoration inspired by lacquer ware from the East **(366)**. The museum had previously bought a work by MM from 1980, a bowl with a matte black glaze and brush-painted decoration with stripes in black and gold **(364)**. From MM's workshop in the last 40 years there has come a flow of works which can be described in thematic terms but cannot be categorized chronologically, since MM often returns to ceramic forms and geometrical patterns she has used in different periods. MM masters the whole range from little delicate containers to monumental vessels and bowls like the mighty outward-sloping striped bowl from 1990 **(368)**, from the exhibition '*Design - Håndværk eller Industri*' in Den Frie's building in 1990. Among the smaller works are the boxes or small containers which one can think of as signature works for MM, made continuously throughout the years. In the museum's collection there are examples from 1982 to 1995. Most are made in porcelain and cast using MM's original model, either oval or with angled sides, often many-sided, with flat or pyramid-shaped lids and with very diverse decoration, in some cases brush-painted with over-glaze technique. The museum has a fine little collection of 'stepped pyramid' boxes, built up using clay sticks, acquired at the exhibition '*Design – Håndværk eller Industri*', including two small ones **(370-371)** and a larger version, a lidded pot **(369)**. At the exhibition '*Nye keramiske æsker*' (New ceramic boxes), in the museum in 1997, an oval stoneware box with a complicated optical decoration, made by dipping into grey slip and then scraping off half of the surfaces, was acquired for the collection; the original model is made of sticks placed at a slanting angle **(372)**.

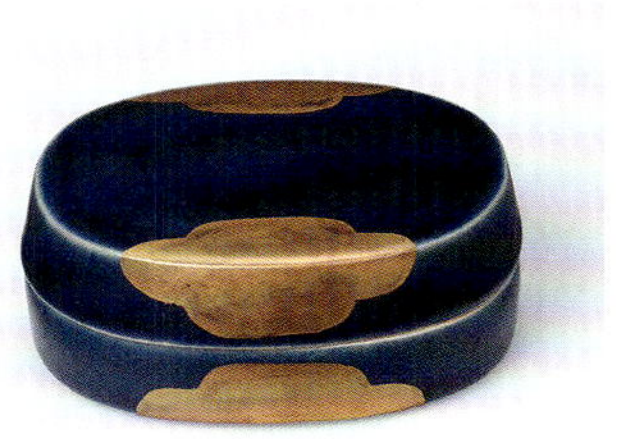

366 52a-b/1983

365 51/1983

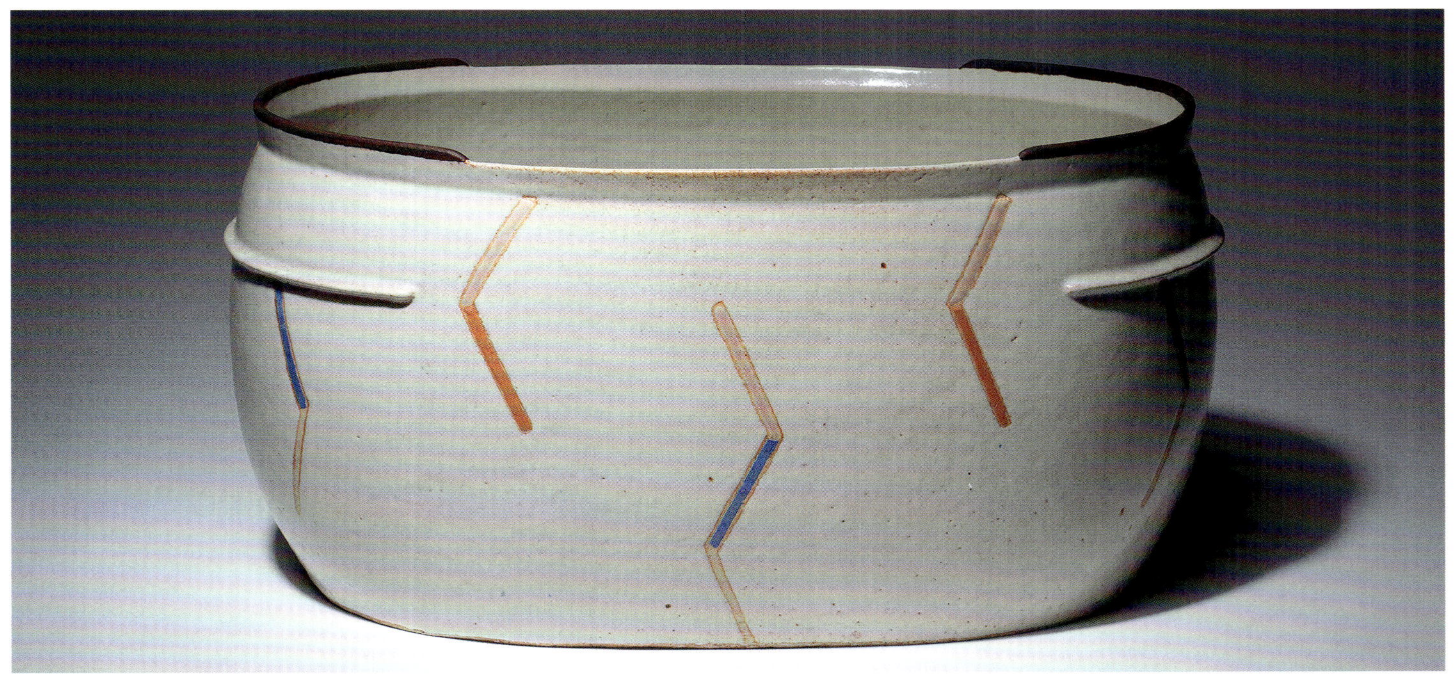

Geometric ornamentation is displayed on two of MM's dishes in the collection, both with upright sides. The earlier one is from 1985 and is oval in shape, decorated with white porcelain slip with masked-off rectangular fields meeting a zig-zag pattern around the edges of the base; the dish was exhibited in 1985 in '*Keramiske Veje*' **(367)**. The other dish, square with grey and brown stripes, was acquired in 2000 in Galleri Nørby and has stripes made with alternate blocks of pale and dark slabs and glazed with a clear matte glaze **(374)**. In the 1990s MM took up a new main motif, which is inspired by basketwork from its rich worldwide culture heritage and from Moorish architecture. These works take their departure-point in adding perforations to the classic cylinder, forming structures that are reminiscent of basketwork and netting, and which provide effects of light and shadow. The museum has two works of this type which show the range of diversity in MM's achievements. The earlier one is *Spiralnet* from 1999, exhibited in '*Keramiske Veje* in 2000, and is constructed with a single pale strip of clay divided into layers by little black balls of clay **(373)**, while the other, *Rødtjørn* (Red thorn) from 2001 is constructed

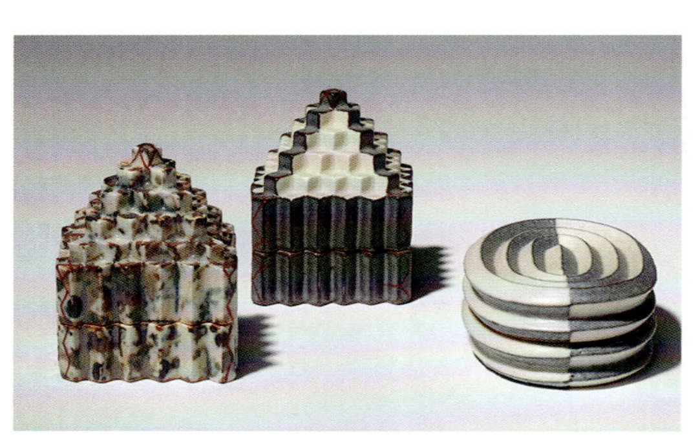

370 251a-b/1990 **371** 252a-b/1990 **372** 173a-b/1997

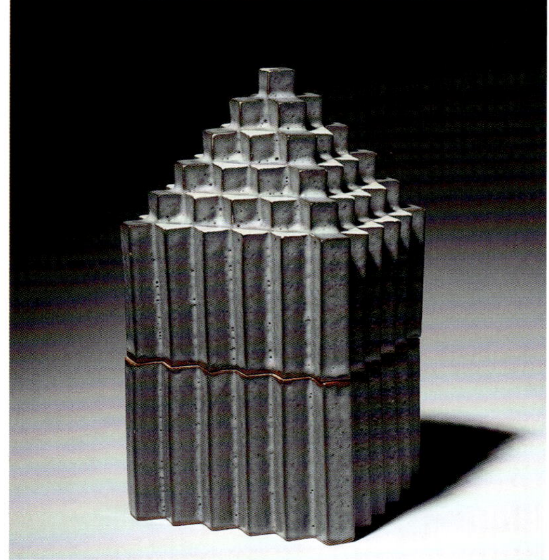

369 250a-b/1990

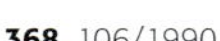

368 106/1990

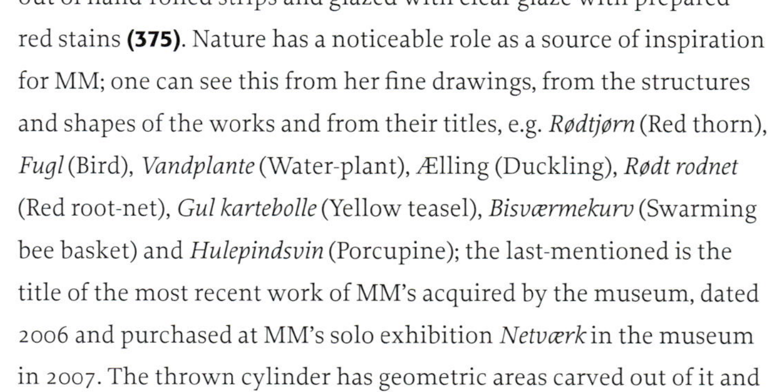

out of hand-rolled strips and glazed with clear glaze with prepared red stains **(375)**. Nature has a noticeable role as a source of inspiration for MM; one can see this from her fine drawings, from the structures and shapes of the works and from their titles, e.g. *Rødtjørn* (Red thorn), *Fugl* (Bird), *Vandplante* (Water-plant), *Ælling* (Duckling), *Rødt rodnet* (Red root-net), *Gul kartebolle* (Yellow teasel), *Bisværmekurv* (Swarming bee basket) and *Hulepindsvin* (Porcupine); the last-mentioned is the title of the most recent work of MM's acquired by the museum, dated 2006 and purchased at MM's solo exhibition *Netværk* in the museum in 2007. The thrown cylinder has geometric areas carved out of it and 150 hand-rolled spikes attached to it, obscuring the basic form of the cylinder **(376)**.MM is a co-founder and member of the exhibition-group *Keramiske Veje*. MM has also participated in a wealth of exhibitions in Denmark and further afield, and is represented in influential museums and collections all over the world.

364. Bowl, 1980. *Sort oval skål* (Oval bowl, black)
Stoneware, zirkon-, chrome- and iron-glazed; thrown, modelled, brush-painted decoration, pre-fired at 980°, fired at 1280°, post-fired at 820°.
H 10.8 x W 19.7. Mark: 'M. 80' inscribed on base. Mus.no. 1/1981.
ACQUISITION: Malene Müllertz. Donation from *Benny Dessaus Mindelegat*.
See: *Brændpunkter,* 1990

365. Vessel, 1982. *Lyst kar* (Pale vessel)
Stoneware, cobalt-, talcum- and tin- glazed; modelled, fired at 1280°.
H 27 x W 54. Mark: none. Mus.no. 51/1983.
ACQUISITION: *Krukker, kander og kar – Stentøj af Malene Müllertz,* 1983, Kunstindustrimuseet. Donation from *Ny Carlsberg Museumslegat*

373 36/2000

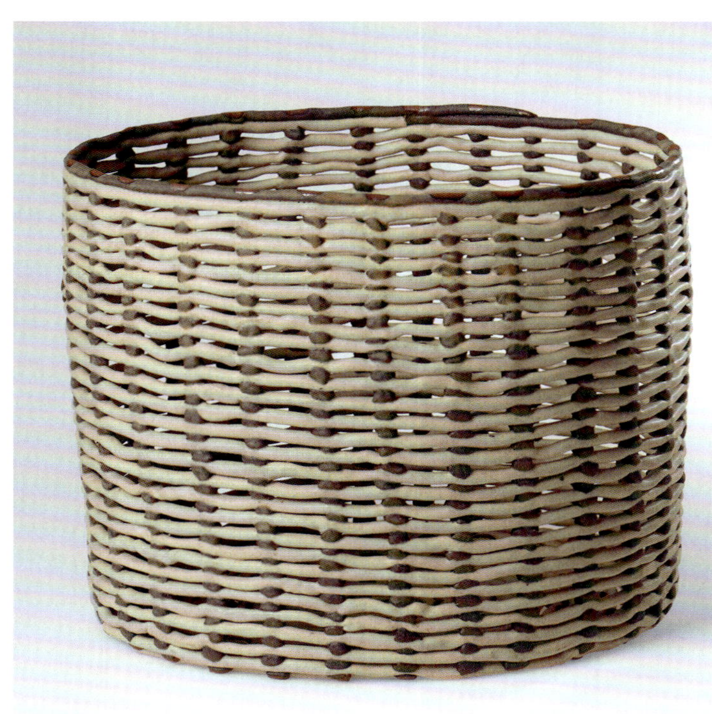

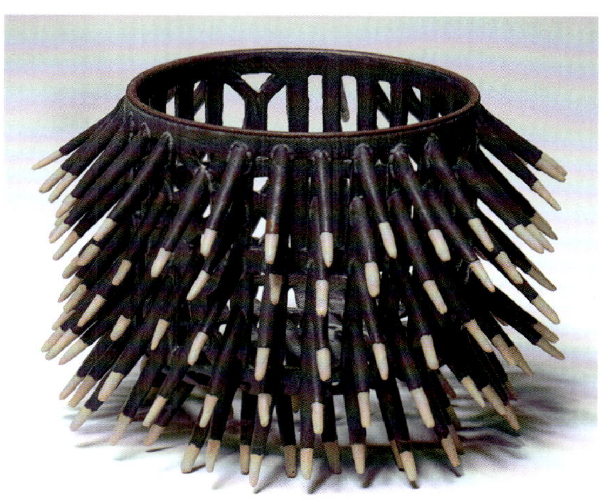

376 211/2007

366. Box, 1982. *Lav oval æske med guld 'sky' dekoration*
(Low oval box with gold 'cloud' decoration)
Porcelain, cobalt-, chrome- and iron- glazed; cast, fired at 1280°, post-fired with buffing-gold at 820°. H 4 x W 10. Mark: 'M' inscribed on base. Mus.no. 52a-b/1983. ACQUISITION: *Krukker, kander og kar – Stentøj af Malene Müllertz,* 1983, Kunstindustrimuseet. Donation from *Ny Carlsberg Museumslegat*

367. Dish, 1985. *Ovalt fad med hvid porcelænsbegitning*
(Oval dish with white porcelain slip)
Stoneware, syenite-, chalk-, kaolin- and quartz- glazed; thrown, modelled, porcelain- and iron- slip, fired at 1280°. H 7.5 x W 35. Mark: 'Malene 1985' inscribed on base. Mus.no. 76/1986
ACQUISITION: Den Frie, 1986. Donation from *Kunstindustrimuseets Venner*

368. Bowl, 1990. *Stor stribet skål* (Large striped bowl)
Stoneware, clear- and half-matte syenite-, chalk-, kaolin- and quartz- glazed; modelled, slip. H 34.5 x Diam 54. Mark: 'M. 1990' inscribed on base. Mus.no. 106/1990. ACQUISITION: Donation from *Ellen og Knud Dalhoff Larsens Fond ved Kunstindustrimuseets 100*-års *' jubilæum*

369. Lidded pot, 1990. *Stor trappepyramide* (Large stepped pyramid)
Stoneware, clear and matte glaze; cast, iron-oxide slip, fired at 1280°. H 30.
Mark: 'M. 1990' inscribed on base. Mus.no. 250a-b/1990
ACQUISITION: *Design – håndværk eller industri,* 1990, Den Frie, Copenhagen

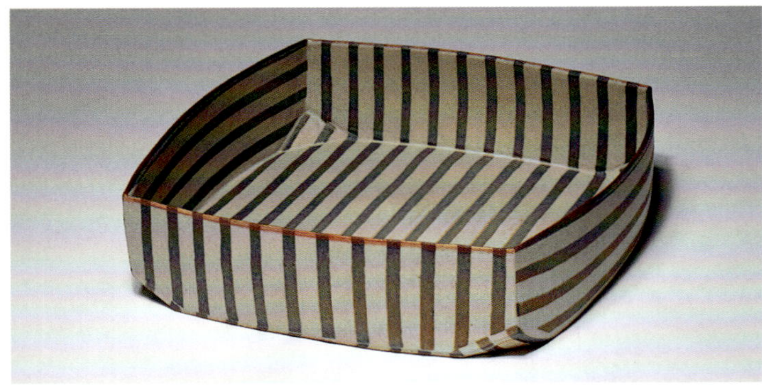

374 45/2000

370. Box, 1990. *Trappepyramide* (Stepped pyramid)
Porcelain, clear glaze; cast, iron slip, brush-painted, fired at 1280°, post-fired at 720°. H (with lid) 9.2 x L 6.5 x W 6.5. Mark: 'M. 1990' inscribed on base. Mus.no. 251a-b/1990. ACQUISITION: *Design – håndværk eller industri,* 1990, Den Frie, Copenhagen. See: *Keramiske Veje*, 1989

371. Box, 1989. *Trappepyramide* (Stepped pyramid)
Porcelain, clear half-matte syenite-, chalk-, kaolin- and quartz- glazed; cast, sprinkled, brush-painted, pre-fired at 1000°, fired at 1280°, post-fired at 720°. H (with lid) 9.2 x L 6.5 x W 6.5). Mark: 'M. 89' inscribed on base.
Mus.no. 252a-b/1990
ACQUISITION: *Design – håndværk eller industri,* 1990, Den Frie, Copenhagen

372. Box, 1995. *Zig-zag*
Stoneware, clear matte glaze; cast, slip, scraped, pre-fired at 890°, fired at 1280°. H 4 x L 11. Mark: 'M. '95' inscribed on base. Mus.no. 173a-b/1997
ACQUISITION: *Nye keramiske æsker*, 1997, Kunstindustrimuseet

373. Basin, 1999. *Spiral-net*
Stoneware, clear matte syenite-chalk- glazed; wax resist, fired at 1270°. H 23.5 x W 29. Mark: 'M. 1999' painted on base. Mus.no. 36/2000
ACQUISITION: *Keramiske Veje*, 2000, Den Frie, Copenhagen. Donation from *Kunstindustrimuseets Venner*

374. Dish, 1999. *Stribet fad i agatteknik* (Striped dish in agate technique)
Stoneware, clear matte syenite- chalk-glazed; slab technique, fired at 1270°. H 9 x Diam 38. Mark: 'M. 99' inscribed on base. Mus.no. 45/2000
ACQUISITION: Galleri Nørby, Copenhagen. Donation from *Kunstindustrimuseets Venner*

375. Container, net, 2001. *Rødtjørn – cylinder basket* (Red thorn)
Stoneware, coloured chalk-syenite clear glaze, prepared stains; hand-rolled clay strands, fired with access of oxygen at 1260°. H 45.5 x Diam 44. Mark: 'M. 2001' inscribed on base. Mus.no. 30/2002
ACQUISITION: Malene Müllertz. Donation from *Højesteretssagfører C.L. Davids Legat for Slægt og Venner*. See: Nørregård-Nielsen, H. E., 2002

376. Pot, 2006. *Hulepindsvin* (Porcupine)
Stoneware; thrown, slip, cut, brushed, 150 hand-rolled spikes attached, fired upside-down at 1280°. H 19 x Diam 20. Mark: 'M. 2006' inscribed on base. Mus.no. 211/2007.
ACQUISITION: *Nye keramiske arbejder*, 2007, Kunstindustrimuseet

375 30/2002

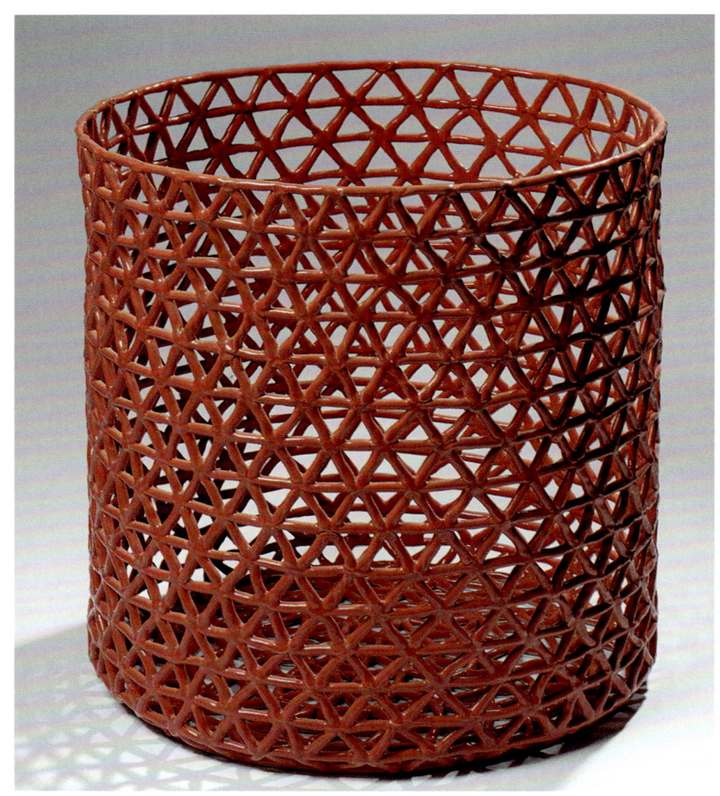

MØHL, FELIX 1906 – 1985

Ceramicist

1927-30	Kunstindustrimuseets Ceramics classes
1932-34	Lillerød Lervarefabrik (Ceramics factory, N Sealand)
1934-	Own studio workshop, Allerød, N Sealand

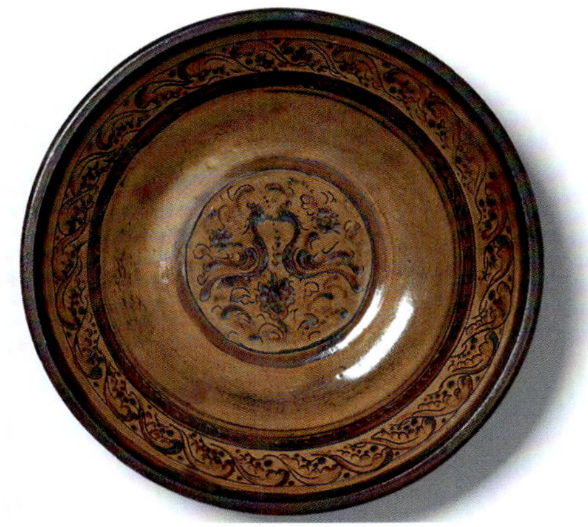

377 17/1990

Felix Møhl (FM) has a special place in Danish ceramics from the beginning of the 1930s and the decades that followed, because of her refined pursuit of the rich traditions of popular folk ceramics. FM's education as a potter took place in a little school of ceramics run by an architect, Aage Rafn, in a wing of the premises – newly opened in 1926 – of the Kunstindustrimuseum. FM worked for some years at Lillerød Lervarefabrik, until she opened her own studio workshop in 1934 in Allerød. In the workshop in Allerød FM produced functional objects with delicate and charming horn-painted decoration, often with flower or bird motifs. Gutte Eriksen worked with FM in 1951-53 and is said to have taught her how to use reduction-firing, resulting in objects with a characteristic brownish/greyish tinge, as can be seen in the case of the museum's bowl, dated to c.1980 **(377)**. FM took part in exhibitions for many years, especially in the context of the craft association *'Haandarbejdets Fremme'*. See: Bloxham, G., 1990, Nielsen, T.,2009.

377. Bowl, c.1980

Earthenware, glazed; thrown, horn-painted decoration, reduction-fired. H 4.5 x Diam 20.8. Mark: 'Felix MiV'. Mus.no. 17/1990. See: *Brændpunkter*, 1990

MØLLER, DORTHE 1932 – 2010

Ceramicist

1950-55	Kunsthåndværkerskolen
1984-86	Det Jyske Kunstakademi, Ceramics teacher, also in the 1960s
1964-2010	Own studio workshop, Elsinore, N Sealand

Dorthe Møller (DM) had her own studio workshop during more than 40 years, and was a deeply dedicated ceramicist who found lifelong inspiration in the ceramic cultures of Korea and Japan; she took a Bachelor's degree in Korean language from Copenhagen University. In a fine little article DM has set out her view of what it means to be a ceramicist, of ceramics as a language, and defended the point of view that a spiritual transmutation can be achieved in work with ceramics as in other artistic disciplines (see: *Keramikkens Væsen*, 1999). DM chose to work with stoneware and with ash glazes, which she made herself, and to express herself through the shapes of functional ceramics. In the museum's collection there is only one work by DM, a partially glazed hexafoil lidded bowl **(378)**. The base and lid of the bowl can be used independently, but together make up a fruit form, and radiate the calm and harmony that is characteristic of all DM's *oeuvre*.. DM exhibited regularly. She received a number of prizes and is represented in the Victoria and Albert Museum. See: Gelfer-Jørgensen, M., 2013.

378. Lidded pot, 1983

Stoneware, ash-glazed; thrown, shaped, fired at 1200°. H 12 x Diam 12. Mark: 'D' on base. Mus.no. 102a-b/1987. ACQUISITION: *Dagens Ret*, 1983, Kunstindustrimuseet. See: Thomsen, Sys, 1983

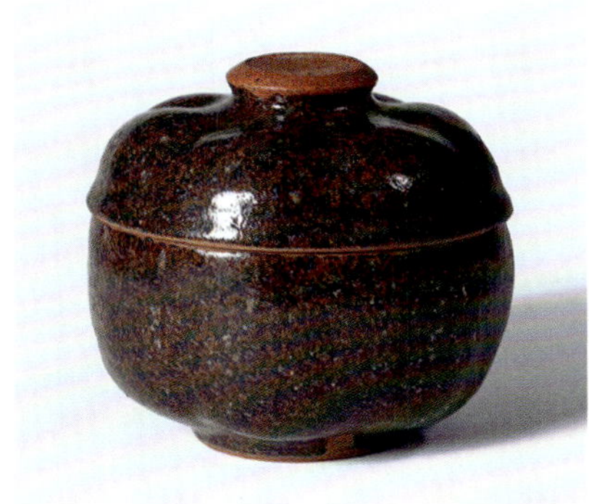

378 102a-b/1987

NYHOLM, ERIK 1911-1990

Ceramicist, painter,
Autodidact

1931	Askov Højskole, Jutland
1938-39	Landbohøjskolen (College of Agriculture), Chemistry student
1951	Début as a painter
1950-	Ceramic workshop, Funder, Silkeborg
1966-73	Brandbjerg Højskole
1973-78	Kunsthøjskolen, Holstebro, Ceramics teacher
1968, 1974	Rochester Institute of Technology, School for American Crafts, Rochester, N.Y., guest teacher

385 131/1991

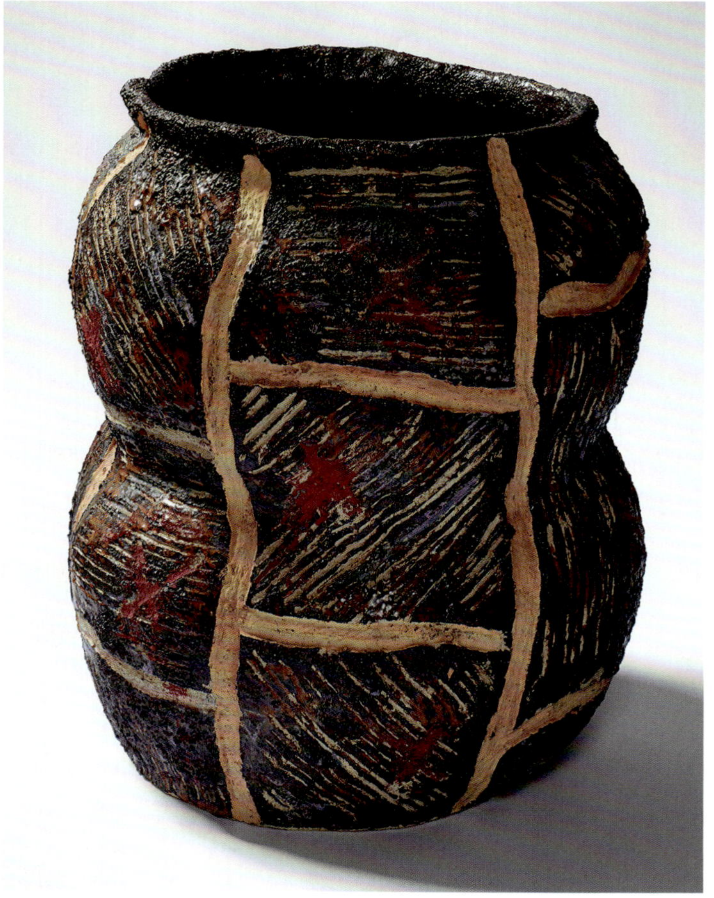

Erik Nyholm (EN) settled down in 1942 near Silkeborg as a pond-keeper and trout-breeder. Silkeborg has been known since ancient times as a pottery region; there are many pottery workshops in the area, and both EN and Asger Jorn made use of them when they began working with ceramics in around 1950.

EN had his first kiln built in 1950 with help from the potter Knud Jensen from the nearby village of Sorring. Both EN and Jorn can be seen as pioneers of the revival of Danish artists' interest in ceramics that took place from the middle of the 20th century and has continued until now. This development forms an extension of the art ceramics from the last decades of the 19th century, and was borne forward by children of Golden Age artists, Thorvald Bindesbøll, the Skovgaard siblings, Joakim, Niels and Suzette (Holten), Elise Konstantin *et al.* The artistic force field that grew around Silkeborg through cooperation between EN, Asger Jorn and the Cobra-artists Appel, Corneille and Constant, attracted EN to advance further on the artistic track which began with painting and then from the 1950s focused more and more on ceramics.

In 1976 EN became involved, at the request of Troels Andersen, the director of Silkeborg Art Museum, in the planning and execution of a ceramic stoneware relief, 100 m² in size, for the museum; it was to be made according to a design sketched by Jean Dubuffet. EN was responsible for the complicated process of transferring the artist's sketches to the ceramic substance, developing the glazes, etc., and then the actual technical process of firing 600 large tiles.

The firing process took place in cooperation with a newly established workshop, 'Ild & Ler', with the ceramicists Bent Skytte-Rasmussen and Esben Lyngsaa Madsen. The latter was a pupil of EN's from Holstebro Kunsthøjskolen, who became a lifelong friend and co-worker via 'NEES Fællesværksted' (1980-84) and then in 'Tommerup Teglværk' from 1987. The large-scale works which EN made, including the massive dish for Hørsholm Kulturhus in 1988 and many other commissioned projects, were thus produced in Tommerup, and the same is true of many of the works by EN that are to be found in the museum's

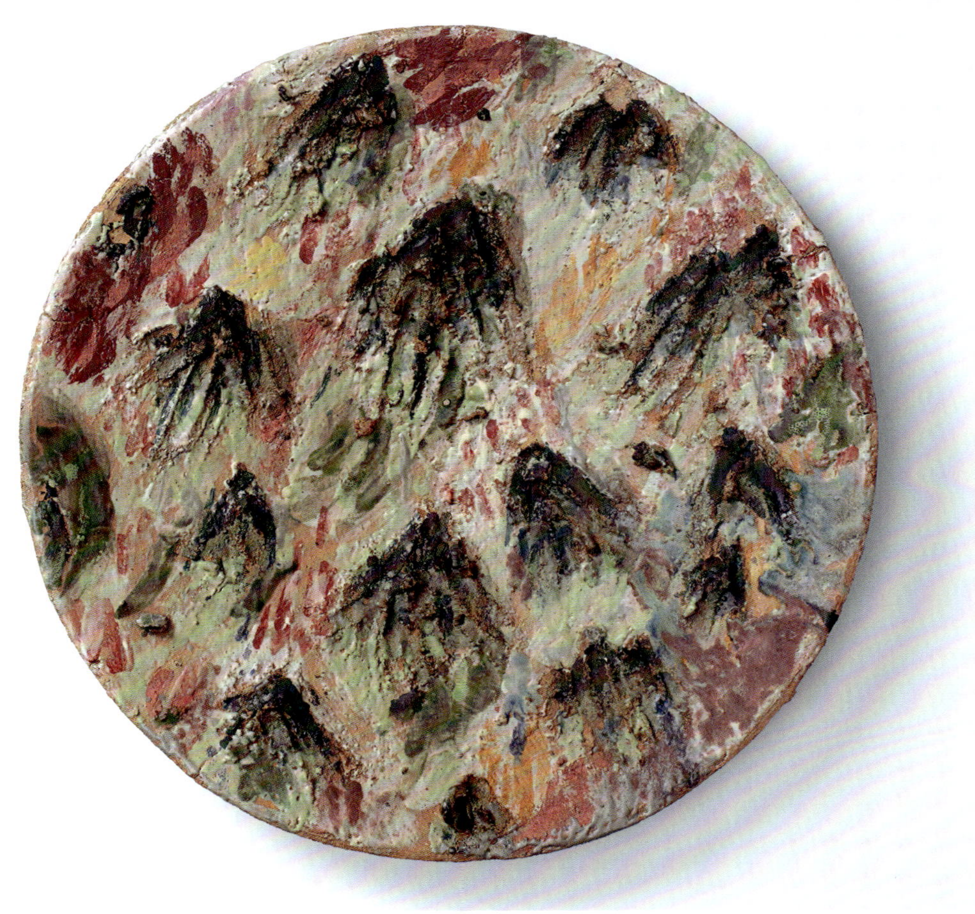

379 163/1984

collection. The monumental relief *Epohké*, following Dubuffet's sketch, was completed in 1977 and became an eye-opener for others, including Bjørn Nørgaard and Lene Adler Petersen, who, in the 1980s, after seeking advice from EN, made a number of large ceramic decorations with Esben Lyngsaa Madsen as the technical anchorman.

As a ceramicist EN was strongly experimental, using processes that had never been tried before, and materials that he found locally or brought back from travels, integrating them into expressive pictures with titles that often referred to impressions of nature and places he had visited. In a number of texts EN has provided valuable insights into his relationship with ceramics:

It was the many possibilities of clay that turned me into a professional amateur in the world of ceramics – a world full of surprises. The conversation with nature that lies behind the creation of pictures can go in many directions. In ceramics the material has so strong a presence that sometimes it pushes away the pictures that one dreamt of making.

The museum has a well-rounded collection of works by EN, seven of them in all, and four of these are large dishes – a form that has made EN a worthy successor to Thorvald Bindesbøll. EN was awarded the Thorvald Bindesbøll Medal in 1985.The museum's dishes are all from the 1980s; EN explained how they came into existence in a conversation with Lars Ravn, held shortly before his death, in the context of

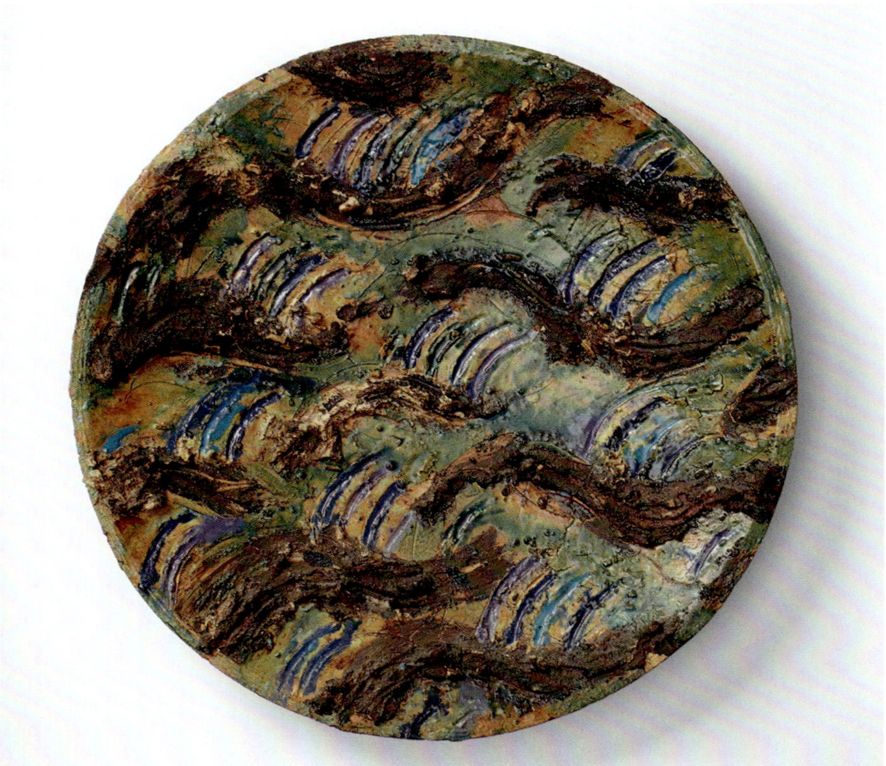

382 119/1988

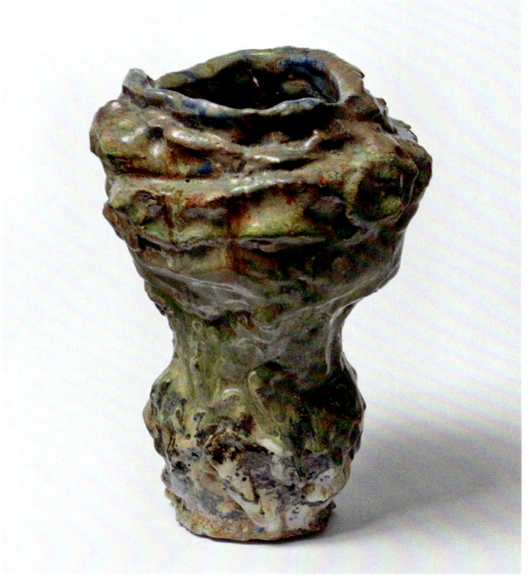

381 82/1987

380 93/1985

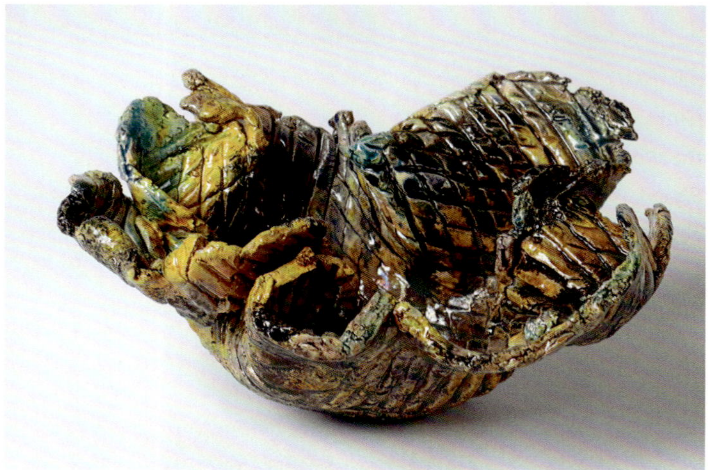

the exhibition *Fra skitse til færdigt arbejde – En keramisk proces* (From sketch to finished work – a ceramic process) mounted in Brøndsalen in Frederiksberg and in Silkeborg Art Museum in 1990 (see exhibition catalogue, p. 79). From the conversation it was apparent that EN in his final years worked on the motifs for the dishes with sketches on paper and ceramic sketches, a process used in the work on the large commissions where mistakes could not be made. From the exhibition mentioned above comes the work *Green Sleeves* **(384)**, for which there is a ceramic sketch, but the finished dish is more concentrated, with fewer and larger applied green-glazed surfaces raised above the brown earth. There is another work from 1990 in the collection, the large organic-shaped pot *Afrika*, with reminiscences from a journey earlier in that year **(385)**. About that work Gunhild Rudjord, who together with Esben Lyngsaa Madsen runs the Tommerup Keramiske Værksted and who assisted EN with his last works, relates that it was

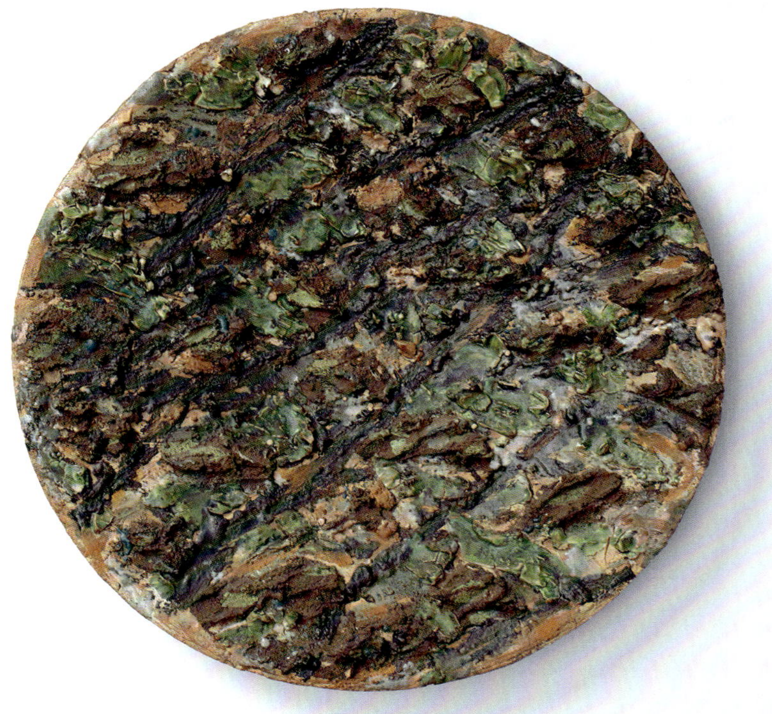

383 128/1988

intended to be lop-sided in the right way, or as EN said, 'as lop-sided as life itself' ('*8 kunstnere omkring Nyholm*', published for the exhibition *Omkring Nyholm*, Silkeborg Kunstmuseum 2002, p. 26). From 1983 there is the dish *Færøerne* II (The Faroe Islands II) **(383)**, and from 1987 *Skyen og Regnbuen* (The cloud and the rainbow) **(382)**, which are both penetrating ceramic studies of organic structures; the latter is related to and shares its title with the massive dish for Hørsholm Kulturhus, Trommen.

EN had two exhibitions in the museum, in 1972 and again in 1977, when the large, beautiful and very diverse blue-glazed stones that today can be seen in Museum Jorn in Silkeborg were displayed in the museum's garden, Grønnegården. Those stones and their way of breaking up the horizontal line preoccupied EN and form a recurrent motif in the work of this significant ceramic pioneer and artist.

384 17/1991

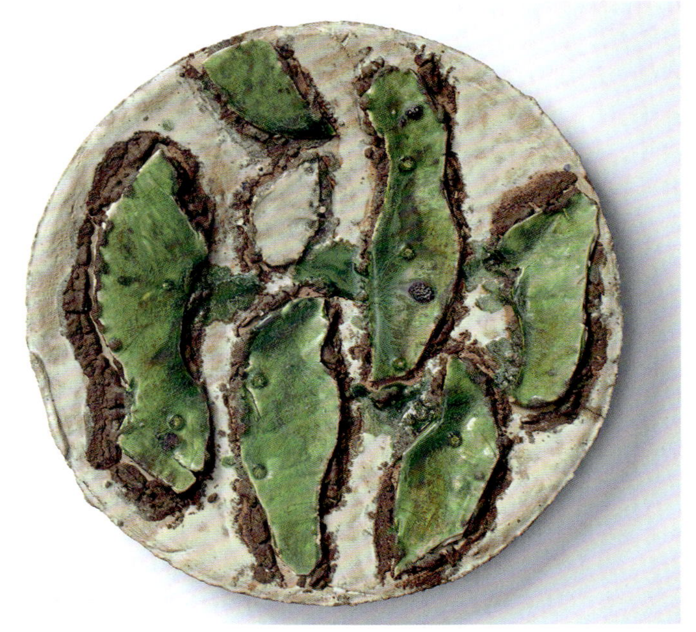

379. Dish, 1982. *Ariba*
Stoneware, glazed; thrown, modelled, decorated. H 9.5 X Diam 72. Mark: 'E:N: -82 ARIBA' inscribed (with felt tip pen) on base. Mus.no. 163/1984
ACQUISITION: Erik Nyholm. Donation from *Finansieringsinstituttet for Industri og Håndværks Jubilæumslegat*. See: *Brændpunkter*, 1990

380. Sculpture, 1985. *Blomst* (Flower)
Earthenware, glazed; modelled, sgrafitto, raku-fired. H 11 x W 19.5. Mark: none. Mus.no. 93/1985
ACQUISITION: *Erik Nyholm – Raku*, 1985, Galleri Marius, Copenhagen. Donation from *Statens 50-års Jubilæumslegat*

381. Vase, 1985-86
Earthenware, lead-glazed; modelled, fired twice. H 25.5 x Diam 11. Mark: none. Mus.no. 82/1987. ACQUISITION: Donation from Erik Nyholm

382. Dish, 1987. *Skyen og regnbuen* (The cloud and the rainbow)
Stoneware, glazed; thrown, modelled, decorated. Diam 70. Mark: 'EN 87' inscribed. Mus.no. 119/1988. ACQUISITION: *Erik Nyholm,* 1988, Galleri Marius, Copenhagen. Donation from *Gutenberghus Gruppen, Copenhagen*

383. Dish, 1983. *Færøerne II* (The Faroe Islands II)
Stoneware, glazed; thrown, modelled, decorated. Diam 70. Mark: 'EN 83' on base. Mus.no. 128/1988. ACQUISITION: Erik Nyholm. Donation from *Kgl. Brand*

384. Dish, 1990. *Green Sleeves*
Stoneware, glazed; thrown, modelled, decorated with glazed clay fields. H 7 x Diam 53. Mark: 'EN 90' on base. Mus.no. 17/1991.
ACQUISITION: *Fra skitse til færdigt arbejde – en keramisk proces*, 1990, Brøndsalen, Det kongelige Haveselskab, Frederiksberg. Donation from *Forenede Jubilæums- og Mindelegater*

385. Pot, 1990. *Afrika*
Stoneware, glazed; modelled, inscribed, decorated. H 53 x Diam 32.5. Mark: none. Mus.no. 131/1991.
ACQUISITION: *Fra skitse til færdigt arbejde – en keramisk proces*, 1990, Brøndsalen, Det kongelige Haveselskab, Frederiksberg

NØRGAARD, BJØRN 1947 –

Sculptor

1964-	Attached to Den Eksperimenterende Kunstskole (Eks-Skolen)
1972-78(9)	Eks-Skolens Trykkeri ApS, co-founder and co-owner
1985-94	The Royal Danish Academy of Fine Arts, Sculpture, Professor
	www.bjoernnoergaard.dk

Bjørn Nørgaard (BN) is notably the Danish sculptor who has since the end of the 1970s carried out the most comprehensive and diverse commissioned projects in ceramic materials. From the 1980s the list includes Gladsaxe Public Library (1981), *Menneskemuren* (1982), *Komedien eller Den Guddommelige*, Horsens Town Hall, together with Lene Adler Petersen (1986), Panum Instituttet, Copenhagen (1986) and ceramic fountain-sculptures, including a 12 m- long ceramic snake and full-length sculptures, Hjørring (1989). Several large and small collected or individual works in BN's extensive *oeuvre* can be mentioned, but the 1980s specifically are relevant to the context of the only work by BN in the museum's collection: the model for a fountain dated 1981-82 **(386)**.

The commissioned work for Gladsaxe Public Library was initiated at the end of the 1970s, and BN decided to use ceramic material. He consulted Erik Nyholm and through him contacted the NEES Fællesværkstedet, a cooperative workshop in Holstebro set up in 1980 by a group including Esben Lyngsaa Madsen, who in 1984 moved to Tommerup Teglværk. In cooperation with Fællesværkstedet and later Tommerup Teglværk, BN was able to arrange the firing of the many sculptural components of the project, including the model for the fountain, later acquired by the museum.

Historical reference to the baroque period is clear in the shape of the model for the fountain, with its segmented construction: at the bottom an octagonal base, and above that the distended forms of four putti-like naked figures, supporting a basin divided into four sections by scaly lizards. The basin supports an upper construction with four

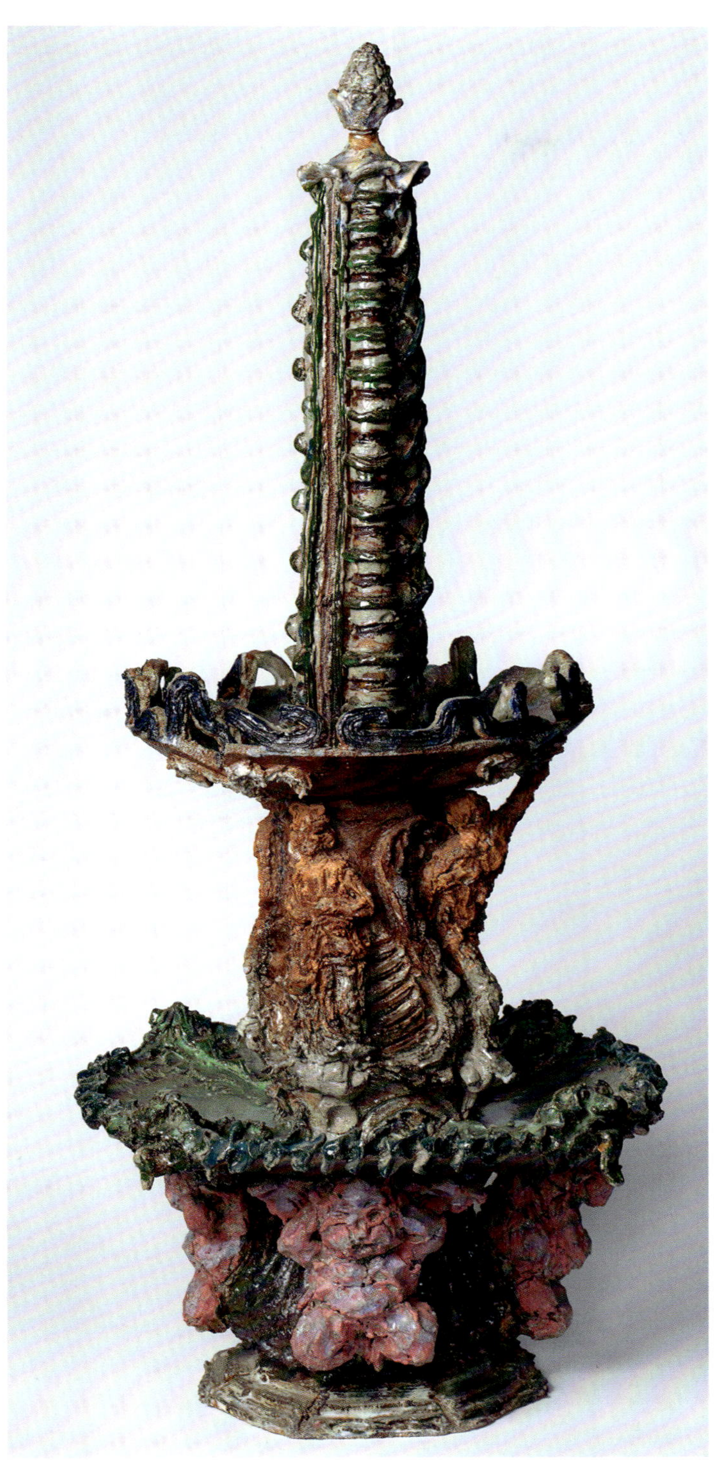

imitation-antique figures, two male and two female, supporting a smaller basin. The fountain is crowned by a spire of stylized, segmented plant-stems, topped by a pine cone. The model is expressively, fluidly, formed, and yet very detailed; there is no information about the plan for its location.

Some years later, in 1986, a monumental work by BN called *Tårnet* (The tower) was inaugurated at Høje Tåstrup Station Square. The construction of the technically very complicated tower incorporated a wealth of materials and of art-historical and general cultural references. If one compares *Tårnet* and BN's fountain model, however, one could be tempted to put forward the hypothesis that the model could have a place in that context, as an early element in the longer-range planning. See: Krogh, L., 1989. Seisbøll, L., 1991

386. Model for fountain, 1981-82

Stoneware, glazed; modelled, decorated. H 107 x Diam 50. Mark: none. Mus.no. 4/1983.

ACQUISITION: Veksølund Skulptur 1982. Donation from *Kgl. Brand*

386 4/1983

PACKNESS, JESPER 1948 –

Ceramicist

1963-66	Palshus Stoneware, training as a potter
1967-68	With potter Henrik Ejgil Jensen, Copenhagen
1969-	Own studio workshop, Copenhagen
1982-	Shop and workshop, Copenhagen
	www.packness.dk

387 125/1992

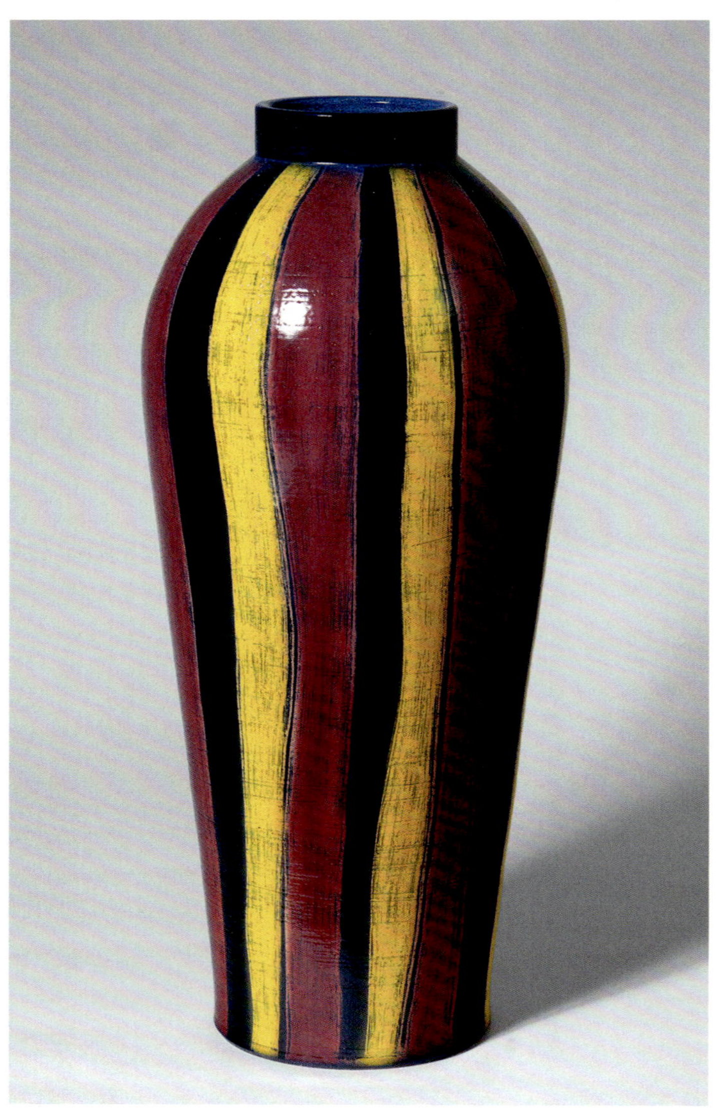

Jesper Packness (JP) trained as a potter and at the end of his apprenticeship with Henrik Ejgil Jensen i Linnésgade in Copenhagen he bought the large workshop there and went on to run it, selling products through Den Permanente, Trikan Art and participation in commercial fairs in Herning. In 2006 JP set up a workshop and shop in Store Kongensgade 95 in the centre of Copenhagen.

JP was one of the first Danish post-modern ceramicists; taking inspiration from Memphis Milano, he has developed his own brilliantly-coloured and decorated form of expression, with vivid shades, chessboard patterns and gold and silver additions to many of the works he produces in his workshop; the premises offer passers-by in the street the opportunity to observe what is going on there and be inspired.

JP makes both functional products and sculptural pieces in many variations, often with fine humorous details. He has concentrated his activities on his own workshop and shop, creating a niche in Danish ceramics from where he can best continue the solo-workshop tradition. The museum has a fine characteristic work by JP from 1992, a striped pot made in majolica technique with clear, colourful earthenware glazes **(387)**.

387. Pot, 1992

Faience, white and clear glaze; thrown, airbrushed, sgrafitto, majolica technique, fired at 1050°. H 81 x Diam 16.5. Mark: 'J. Packness Denmark' inscribed on base. Mus.no. 125/1992

ACQUISITION: Jesper Packness. Donation from *Justitsråd J.F. Møllmanns Legatfond*

PEDERSEN, ANNE LISE BRUUN 1931 – 2004

Ceramicist

1954	School teacher
1969-73	Skolen for Brugskunst
1973-	Own studio workshop, Copenhagen
1982-87	Kunsthåndværkerskolen in Kolding, teacher

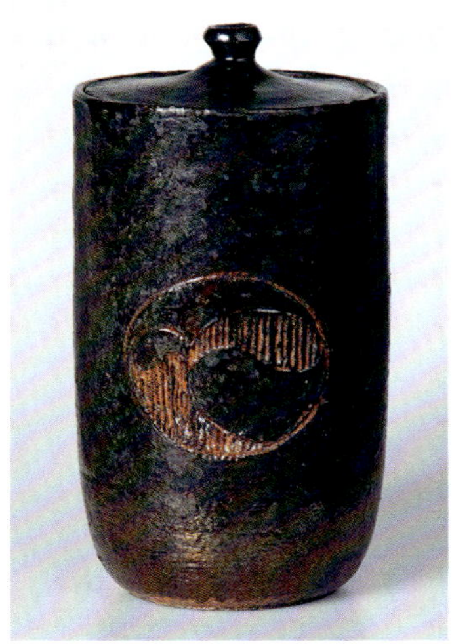

388 47a-b/1981

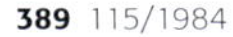

389 115/1984

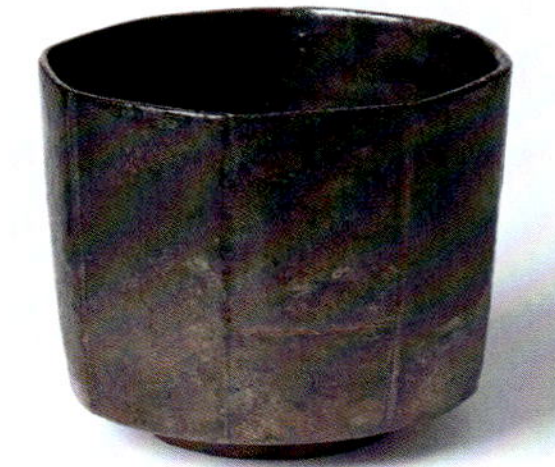

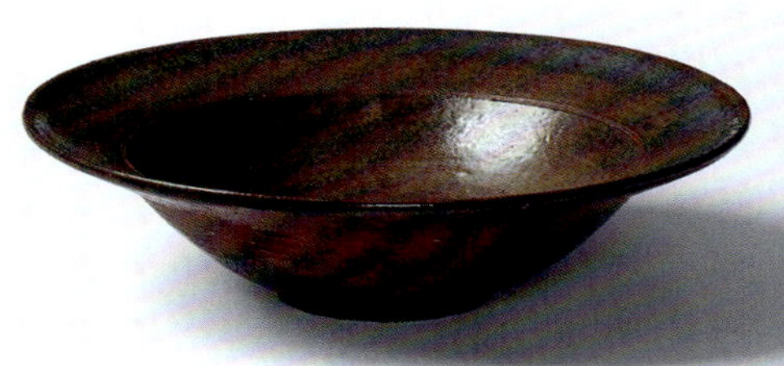

390 18/1990

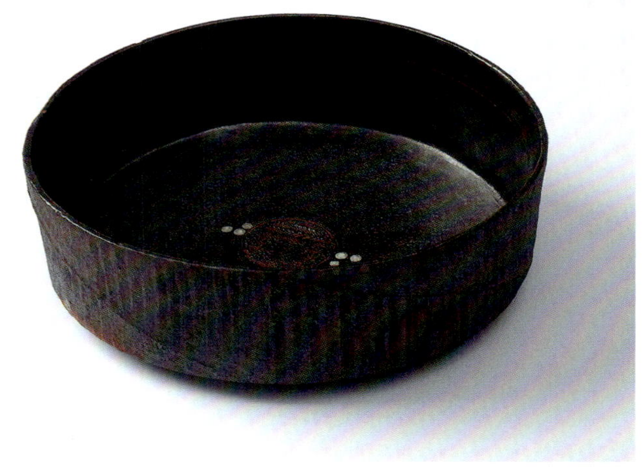

393 8/1992

Anne Lise Bruun Pedersen (ALBP) was a teacher for many years before she started to study Ceramics at Skolen for Brugskunst; she completed her studies in 1972 and then immediately set up her own studio workshop. Her favourite working method was raku technique, to which she dedicated herself, broadcasting its virtues not only through her own works, but also through publication of several instructive do-it-yourself books on ceramic techniques and raku, which were widely distributed (*Raku på dansk*, Borgens Forlag 1986; *Fra Ler til Potte – De ældste teknikker*, Aschehoug Dansk Forlag 1989). ALBP was also an active teacher, at the Kunsthåndværkerskolen in Kolding and elsewhere. Through years of consistent use of raku, and intense engagement with it and its historic and cultural origins in Japanese tea-culture, ALBP achieved a personal approach to the technique and a form of expression that was based on clear stable shapes and refined ceramic effects in interplay between dark and light slip combined with transparent frit glazes. For decoration she tended, in her later works, to use motifs and simple indications of colour which may perhaps relate to her Greenlandic-Danish background. This is expressed in several of her works in the museum's collection, perhaps especially in two whitish pieces with slip and decoration **(392,394)**. There are nine works by ALBP in the collection; two of them were acquired in connection with her participation in exhibitions in the museum. The earliest is the lidded pot from 1981, with a circular abstract decoration and sgrafitto in the dark surface of the slip **(388)**; it came from the exhibition '*Væv og Raku*' (Weaving and Raku), held in 1982 together with another Danish raku-master, Inger Rokkjær and the weaver Dorthe Sigsgaard. From another of the museum's exhibitions, in 2002, a bowl by ALBP, with black slip, clear glazing and sgrafitto decoration was acquired – a 'classic' type of object from her production **(395)**. After establishing her own studio workshop in 1973 ALBP rapidly became involved in exhibitions in *Håndarbejdets Fremme*, *Kunstnernes Efterårsudstilling* and

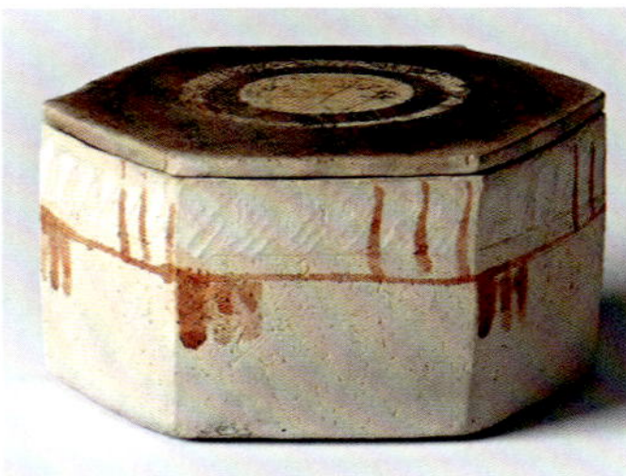

392 20a-b/1990

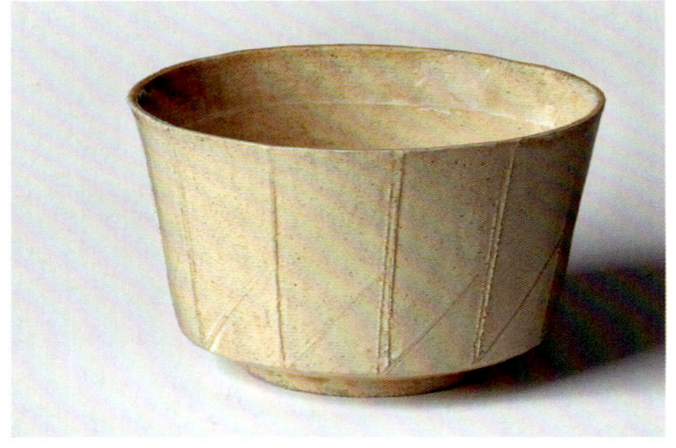

391 19/1990

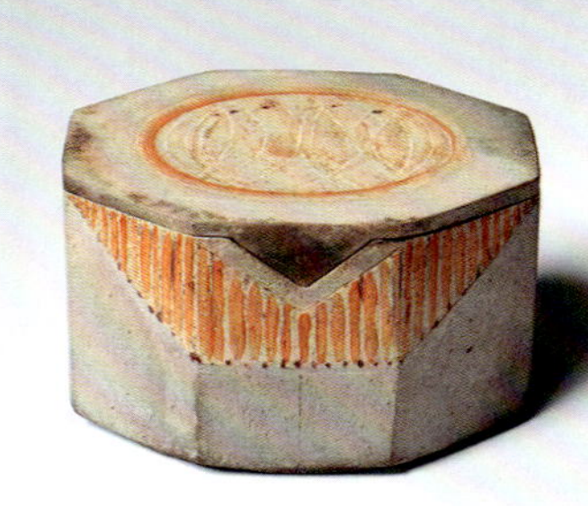

396 417a-b/2008

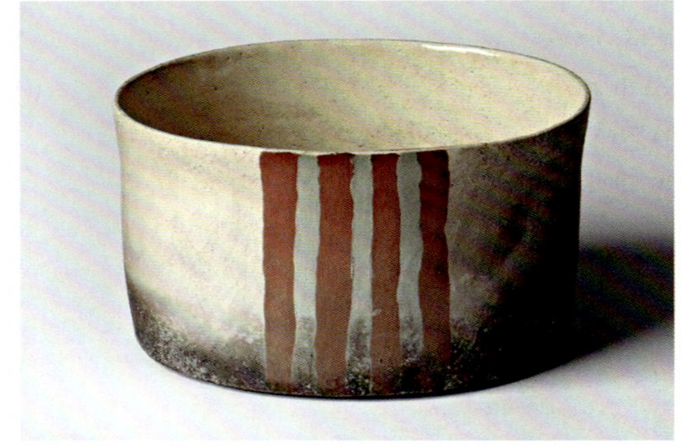

394 36/1994

Charlottenborg, as well as at *Den Permanente* and *Illums Bolighus*; she was also represented in the exhibition '*Danish Ceramic Design*' in the USA in 1982. See: Gelfer-Jørgensen, M., 2013

388. Lidded pot, 1981

Earthenware, clear and lustre glaze; thrown, modelled, sgrafitto, slip, raku.

395 78/2002

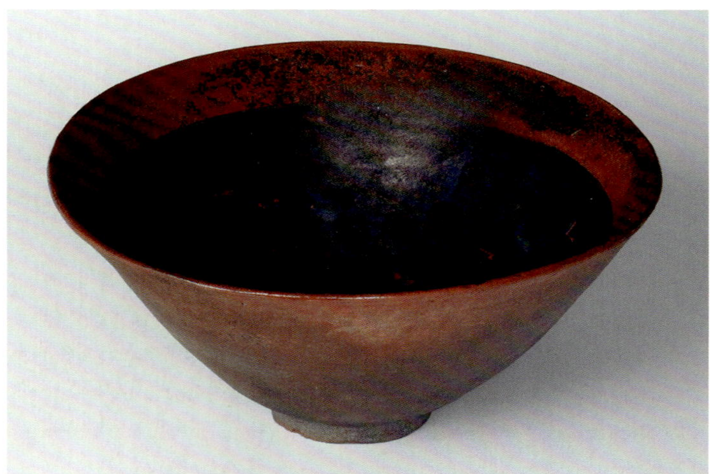

H 18.2 x Diam 8.7. Mark: 'AB' inscribed on base. Mus.no. 47a-b/1981
ACQUISITION: *Væv og raku – væveren Dorthe Sigsgaard og keramikerne Anne Lise Bruun Petersen og Inger Rokkjær*, 1982, Kunstindustrimuseet. Donation from *Kunstindustrimuseets 50-års Jubilæumslegat*

389. Bowl, 1984

Earthenware, clear- and lustre- glazed; thrown, modelled, black slip, sgrafitto, raku. H 13 x Diam 13.6. Mark: 'AB' inscribed on base. Mus.no. 115/1984
ACQUISITION: Donation from *Finansieringsinstituttet for Industri og Håndværk*, on its 25th anniversary. See: *Brændpunkter*, 1990. Dybdahl, L., 1997

390. Dish, c.1989

Earthenware, clear glazed; thrown, shaped, slip, decorated, raku.
H 8 x Diam 27. Mark: 'AB' inscribed on base. Mus.no. 18/1990
ACQUISITION: Galleri Trap, Korsør. Donation from *Benny Dessaus Mindelegat*

391. Bowl, c.1989

Earthenware, glazed; thrown, shaped, white slip, sgrafitto, raku.
H 10 x Diam 16.8. Mark: 'AB' inscribed on base. Mus.no. 19/1990
ACQUISITION: Galleri Trap, Korsør. Donation from *Benny Dessaus Mindelegat*

392. Box, 6-sided, c.1989

Earthenware, glazed; thrown, shaped, white slip, decorated, raku.

H 7 x Diam 11. Mark: 'AB' inscribed on base. Mus.no. 20a-b/1990

ACQUISITION: Galleri Trap, Korsør. Donation from *Benny Dessaus Mindelegat*

393. Bowl, c.1991

Earthenware, clear-glazed; thrown, shaped, black slip, decorated, raku.

H 7.5 x Diam 20.5. Mark: 'AB' inscribed on base. Mus.no. 8/1992

ACQUISITION: Donation from *Justitsråd J. F. Møllmanns Legatfond*

394. Bowl, 1994

Earthenware, glazed; thrown, shaped, white slip, decorated, raku.

H 7 x Diam 12.2. Mark: none. Mus.no. 36/1994.

ACQUISITION: Donation from *Ny Carlsberg Museumslegat* and *Bodil Hallers Mindelegat*

395. Bowl, 2002

Earthenware, clear- and lustre- glazed; thrown, black slip, sgrafitto, raku.

H 11.5 x Diam 24.5. Mark: 'AB' inscribed on base. Mus.no. 78/2002

ACQUISITION: *Ler og lange baner*, 2002, Kunstindustrimuseet

396. Herring bowl with lid, octagonal, 1990s

Earthenware, glazed; thrown, shaped, white slip, decoration, raku.

H 9 x Diam 13.3. Mark: none. Mus.no. 417a-b/2008.

ACQUISITION: Donation from the estate of Ambassador Niels Christian Tillisch, Copenhagen

PEDERSEN, ESTHER ELISABETH 1957 –

Ceramic designer

1984-88 Skolen for Brugskunst, Ceramic Design and Glass

1988-95 Workshop shared with Bente Elbæk

1996-2004 Workshop with Karen Salicath and Hanne Bertelsen, Cph.

2004- Own studio workshop and shop, Brønshøj, Copenhagen www.esther-elisabeth.dk

The spring 2003 exhibition held by *Danske Kunsthåndværkere*, the Danish Crafts and Design Association, had the theme 'Ellipse', and for the exhibition, in 'Officinet', Bredgade 66, Copenhagen, Esther Elisabeth Pedersen (EEP) contributed a white porcelain ellipse-shaped dish, with studs, which the museum acquired **(397)**. In 1993 EEP participated in the innovative exhibition entitled '*Keramikkens Underskov*' (The undergrowth of ceramics), which was held in the Round Tower in Copenhagen and in Ridehuset, Aarhus, and gave young ceramicists a platform to draw attention to new trends in ceramics. From her studio combined with a shop EEP has for many years produced a fine range of functional objects distinguished by assured design and conscious work with colours, both pastel nuances and clear mellow colours. Her products are sold throughout the whole country through selected stockists.

397. Dish, 2003. *Ellipse*

Porcelain, feldspar-glazed; cast, relief, fired at 1280°. H 1.6 x L 33 x W 11.3. Mark: Labelled 'Designed and made by Esther Elisabeth Pedersen Copenhagen'. Mus.no. 323/2003. ACQUISITION: *Ellipse*, 2003, Danske Kunsthåndværkere. Donation from *Kunstindustrimuseets Venner*

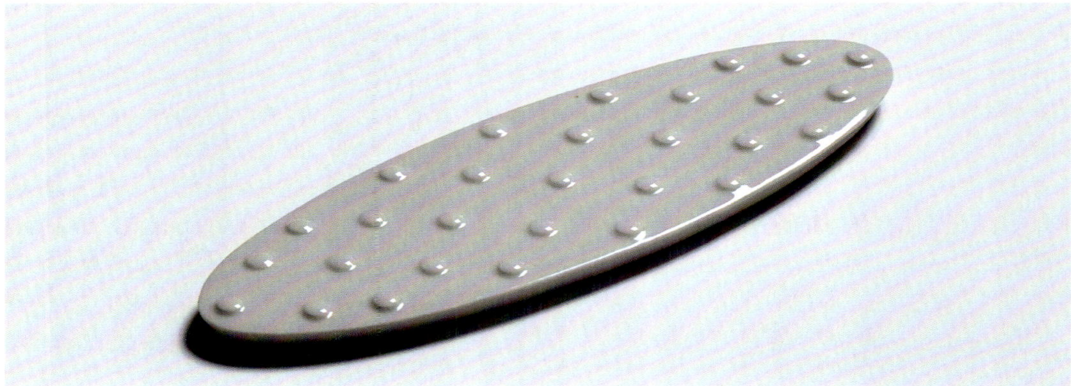

397 323/2003

PEDERSEN, TURI HEISSELBERG 1965 –

Ceramicist

1986-90	Kunsthåndværkerskolen in Kolding, Ceramic Design
1991-92	Grønland Keramisk Industri, Egernsund, Jutland, product developer
1993-	Shared workshop, Copenhagen; 2010- with Lone Skov Madsen
1996-2000	Udstillingssted for Ny Keramik, Copenhagen, co-founder and -owner
1994-07	Designskolen Kolding, teacher
2008-12	Danmarks Designskole, external examiner
	www.turiheisselberg.dk

Turi Heisselberg Pedersen (THP) is an exponent of the new trends in Danish ceramics brought in by the generation from the 1960s, and has played an important role in various projects aiming at promoting professional debate among ceramicists and at publicising new ceramics in the wider world. Alongside this activity she has taught for many years, held solo exhibitions and participated in a large number of group exhibitions in Denmark and elsewhere. Her work is represented in several museums and collections.

THP has continually created works in distinct designs, typically with matte textures that harmonise with the ceramic form; her works display to best advantage in groups of objects and have with justification been associated with those of the Italian painter Giorgio Morandi (1890-1964), who throughout his life painted still lifes with pots, bottles and jugs in penetrating studies of shapes, textures, light and shade. As in the calm, consciously-spaced depictions in those paintings, THP's works create the same kind of deliberate space around themselves – an inviolate zone of calm and reflection.

A significant step in the breaking away of the 60s generation from the domination of the older 'canonized' ceramicists was the holding of the exhibition in 1993 entitled '*Keramikkens Underskov*', with the subtitle 'Current ceramics by young ceramicists', in which 34 ceramicists took part in an exhibition in the Round Tower in Copenhagen and subsequently in Ridehuset in Aarhus. THP was among the organisers, and she was also a co-founder and -owner of the 'Udstillingssted for Ny Keramik' (exhibition space for new ceramics) in Kompagnistræde, Copenhagen, where an impressive number of exhibitions – 31 in all – were held in the four-year period of its existence, from 1996 to 2000. In 1999 THP herself exhibited a fine collection of diverse pots built up around combining the basic shapes of the cone and the ellipse; she has also held an exhibition with Karin Schou entitled '*Den dybe tallerken igen*' (The deep plate again), focusing on meals and associated table services. (See: *Udstillingssted for Ny Keramik*, 2009). The nucleus of ceramicists from 'Udstillingssted for Ny Keramik' joined together again in 2003 in the group *New Danish Ceramics*, which first showed its colours in a powerful exhibition in the museum, in which the exhibiting artists demonstrated on a grand scale the diversity and quality of their work.

THP exhibited in the museum again in 2009 in close partnership with Lone Skov Madsen, this time with an unusual curatorial angle – an exhibition concept created by the two ceramicists in dialogue with the museum's collections. With free access to select objects from those collections as inspiration for new works of their own, and by exhibiting this dialogue in the museum's rooms, a double exchange of values took place: the artists found new developments in the form and scale of their work, and the museum objects were given renewed vigour and a different significance through this fertilization. It was an ambitious and demanding project for the ceramicists, and inspiring for the museum. *Statens Kunstfond* awarded a prize to this ambitious exhibition. (See: *Time Out*, Exhibition catalogue, 2009).

In the museum's collection there are two works by THP from 2001, with contrasting shapes and undecorated matte stone-like surfaces, which despite their differences evidently relate to each other and create an intervening space / interplay between their forms **(398-399)**. Both works were acquired in Galleri Nørby at the exhibition held jointly in that year by THP and Lone Skov Madsen, in which THP convincingly displayed a large still life of many modelled cone-shaped pots with finely-judged nuances in the subtle choices of colour.
THP has through the years taken part in many Danish and

398 158/2001

399 159/2001

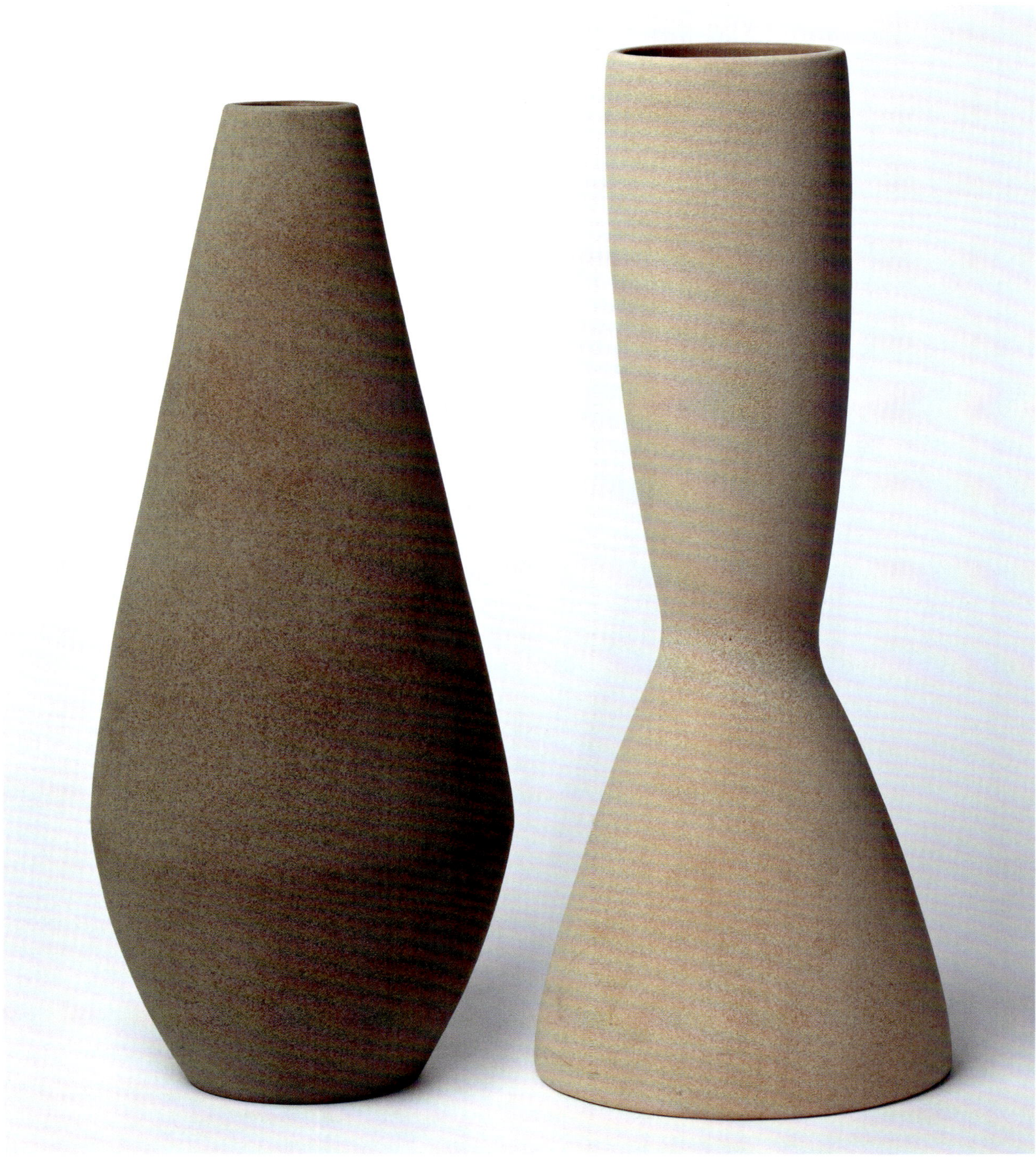

international exhibitions, and has received a number of bursaries and prizes, including *Annie og Otto Johs. Detlefs' Keramikpris* in 2016.

398. Vase, 2001

Stoneware, zinc-glazed; modelled, sinter slip, fired at 1260°. H 52 x Diam 20.

Mark: 'TH' painted on base. Mus.no. 158/2001

ACQUISITION: Galleri Nørby. Donation from *Kunstindustrimuseets Venner*

399. Vase, 2001

Stoneware, zinc-glazed; modelled, sinter slip, fired at 1260°. H 55 x Diam 21.

Mark: 'TH' painted on base. Mus.no. 159/2001

ACQUISITION: Galleri Nørby. Donation from *Kunstindustrimuseets Venner*

PETERSEN, GERD HIORT 1937 –

Ceramicist

1954-56 Apprentice with Michael Andersen & Søn, Bornholm
1956-57 Akademie für Angewandte Kunst, Vienna
1960-61 Søholm Keramikfabrik, Bornholm
1958-59, 1962-65 Kunsthåndværkerskolen
1965-73 The Royal Porcelain Factory, employed as artist
1973- Studio workshop shared with Hans Munck Andersen, Bornholm
www.gerdoghans.dk

Gerd Hiort Petersen (GHP) was born on Bornholm and trained as a ceramicist in the Bornholm factories of Michael Andersen & Søn and Søholm, with an intervening period spent on a study- and workshop-visit to Vienna. The next step was a course at the Kunsthåndværkerskolen and then employment as an artist in the Royal Porcelain Factory, where because of her artistry and her interpersonal skills she was chosen as head of the Stoneware Cellar, a position GHP had no interest in for the long term, but she continued as an artist in the workshop (see: Lautrup-Larsen, L., 2007, p. 251).

GHP exhibited several times with personal success under the auspices of the porcelain factory, and in 1972 she took part, along with Hans Munck Andersen, Bodil and Richard Manz, Hans and Birgitte Börjesson, Ursula Munch-Petersen, Marie Hjorth and Anne-Marie Trolle (married name Oxmond) in the epoch-making and experimental exhibition mounted in Den Permanente. It was named '*At være keramiker*' (Being a ceramicist), and raised existential issues about the legitimacy of being and living as a ceramicist in a plastic age, and about the need to be in contact with the surrounding world, which one was in a sense working for.

In 1973 GHP moved back to Bornholm with Hans Munck Andersen, ceramicist and later her husband, and they established a shared studio workshop in Rø. Technically and artistically they were fully equipped with experience and knowledge from their years at the factory, and in an impressively short time they built up the new workshop and set in motion a professional and ambitious exhibition-programme with an international perspective. This gave them recognition in the form of many prizes and bursaries both in Denmark and around the world, but particularly in the Nordic countries and in Germany and the Netherlands, where their work is well-represented in public institutions and private collections. From 1982 to 2006 GHP completed eight ceramic projects for church decorations in various areas of Denmark, and these contribute to projecting her image as an artist who has succeeded in giving form and expression, and thus significance, to the vital life content that for many people is embodied in nature and in faith.

There is a strong continuity in GHP's *oeuvre*, which follows two main – seemingly parallel – directions, one of them based on stoneware and the sculptural idiom, and the other based on porcelain and graphic art. In the matter of decoration, however, the two tracks cross.

GHP's works are free sculptural forms; this is also true of the bowls and pots that she throws in porcelain paste, decorates with scoring and/or brush painting with clay colours, using clear and/or coloured glazes and in some cases paints with gold, platinum or lustre and then fires for a third time at a lower temperature. In the museum's collection this type of work is well-represented with four works from the 1980s. The earliest is from 1982, a bowl that floats on a little circular base. The exterior decoration is divided into six fields with inscribed and inlaid lines and narrow strips of platinum **(401)**. The pot from 1984 **(406)** is decorated with hatched /scored line patterns in grey/black shades with a thin red-brown line that divides the corpus horizontally, while the two works from 1989 have bolder colouring. The two bowls float, like the earliest one, on a little circular base and are of very similar shape, but different decoration. One has the poetic title

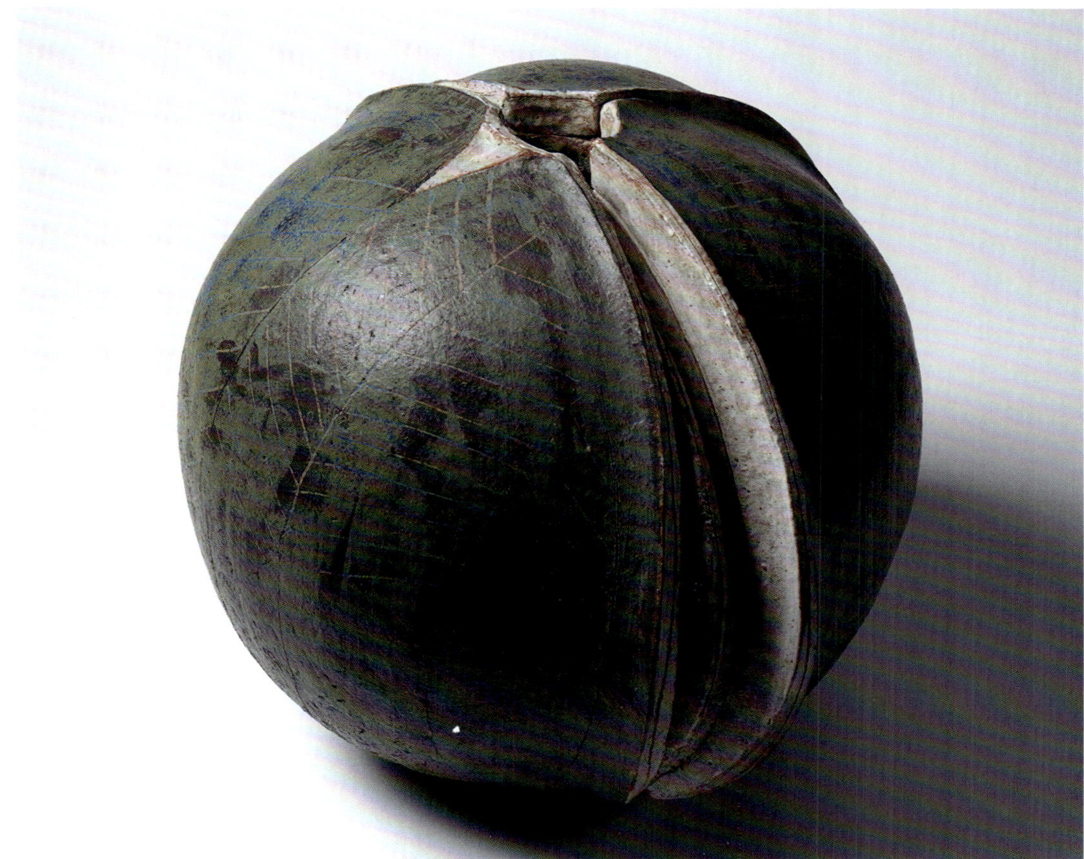

400 98/1978

Jomfrustrand nat (Virgin Beach night – the name of a beach southwest of Dueodde on Bornholm) and is in dark blue and brown colours with scored light decoration **(404)**, while the other is as light as day and is clear-glazed with dark blue and pale yellow painted fields with hatching that is similar to the earlier works **(403)**. Strength of inspiration taken from natural landscapes provides the fundamental harmony in GHP's stoneware works, which are fierce and expressive and in close emotional consonance with the grand, wild and romantic landscapes of Bornholm. The basic material is Bornholm stoneware clay, mixed with chamotte from Rabækkeværket, also on Bornholm. Thick clay slabs are shaped on a mould and structured with a saw-blade or some other tool, spread with slip and beaten out with a stone. Then they are decorated with coloured slip, patterns are scored in and the work is glazed, often partially, with clear or coloured glazes. The museum has two works of this type, a bowl-shaped *Klippeskål* (Rock bowl) from 1989 **(402)**, which is like a picture of a valley enclosed by crags, and a smaller square dish from 1997 **(405)** which looks as if it has been carved out of a landscape. The museum's earliest piece by GHP is from 1977, with the title *Frø* (Seed), a stoneware sculpture with a matte ash glaze and a spherical corpus with a small opening near the top that forms a little irregular hole, while four lines cut down from it into the corpus **(400)**. This early and powerful work was acquired at the exhibition '*Farver og strukturer*' in the museum in 1978, which firmly established the position of GHP and Hans Munck Andersen as strong new artists in the rich ceramic milieu and history of Bornholm.

In 2010 Denmark's Ceramic Museum (now CLAY) held a distinguished retrospective exhibition of 40 years of work by GHP and Hans Munck Andersen in their artistic tandem. See: *Keramisk Stoflighed*, Danmarks Keramikmuseum, 2010. Gelfer-Jørgensen, M., 2013, p. 303

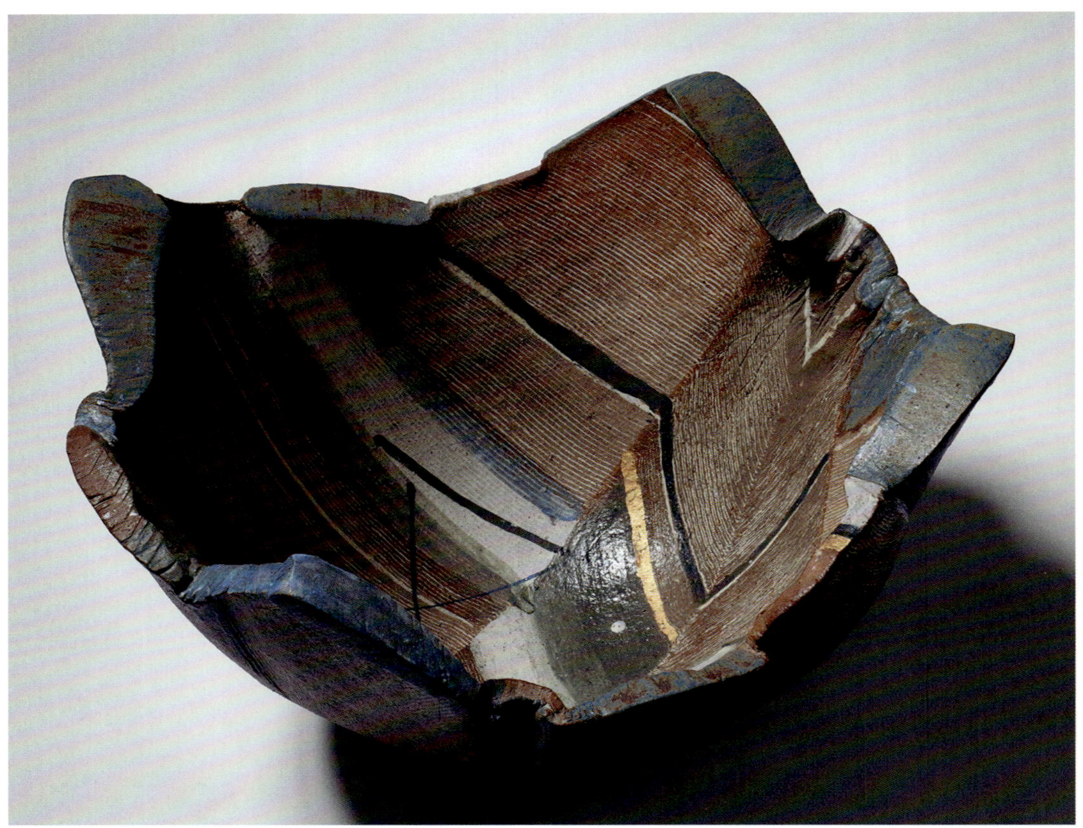

402 153/1989

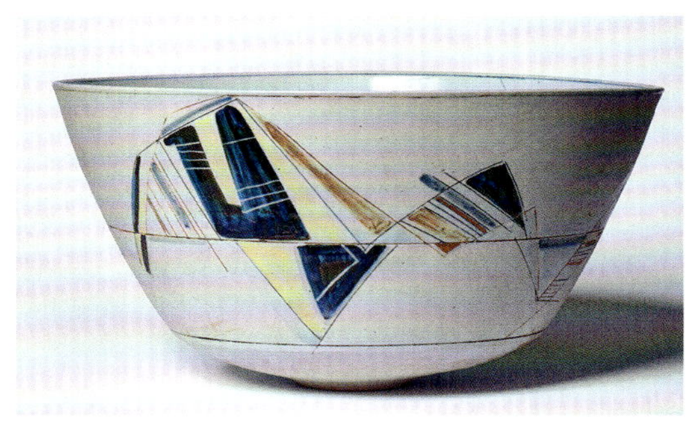
403 262/1989

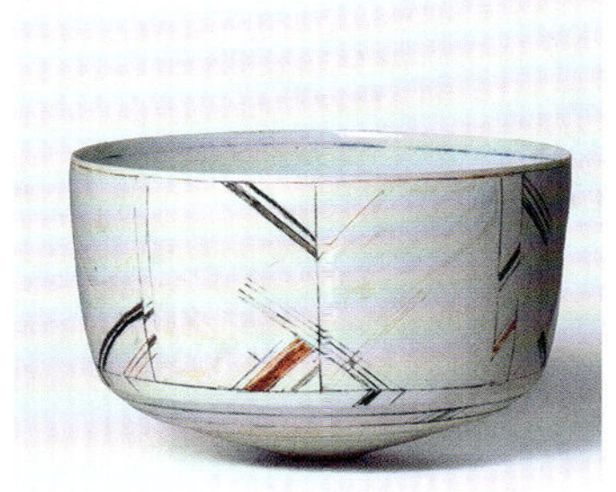
401 62/1982

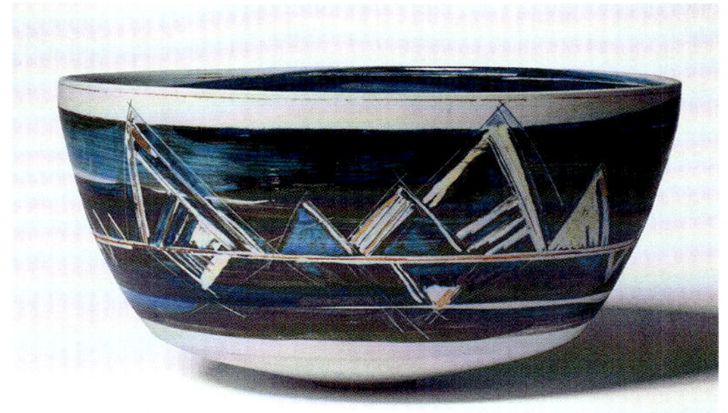
404 142/1990

400. Sculpture, 1977. *Frø* (Seed)
Stoneware, feldspar- and ash-glazed; modelled, fired at 1300°. H 38. Mark: 'GHP' painted on base. Mus.no. 98/1978. ACQUISITION: *Farver og strukturer*, 1978, Kunstindustrimuseet. Donation from *Det Thomsenske Legat og Statens 50-års Jubilæumslegat*. See: *Brændpunkter*, 1990

401. Bowl, 1982
Porcelain, feldspar-glazed, platinum; scored and inlaid decoration. H 13.5 x Diam 21.5. Mark: 'GHP' painted on base. Mus.no. 62/1982 ACQUISITION: *Efterårsudstillingen*, 1982, Charlottenborg. Donation from *Kunstindustrimuseets Venner.* See: *Brændpunkter*, 1990

402. Bowl, 1989. *Klippeskål* (Rock bowl)
Stoneware, feldspar- and ash- glazed; modelled, sgrafitto, fired at 1300°. H 38 x W 63. Mark: none. Mus.no. 153/1989
ACQUISITION: Donation from *Kunstindustrimuseets Venner*

403. Bowl, 1989
Porcelain, feldspar-glazed, silver; thrown, sgrafitto, painted. H 24.5 x Diam 42. Mark: 'GHP' painted on base. Mus.no. 262/1989
ACQUISITION: Donation from William Hull, USA

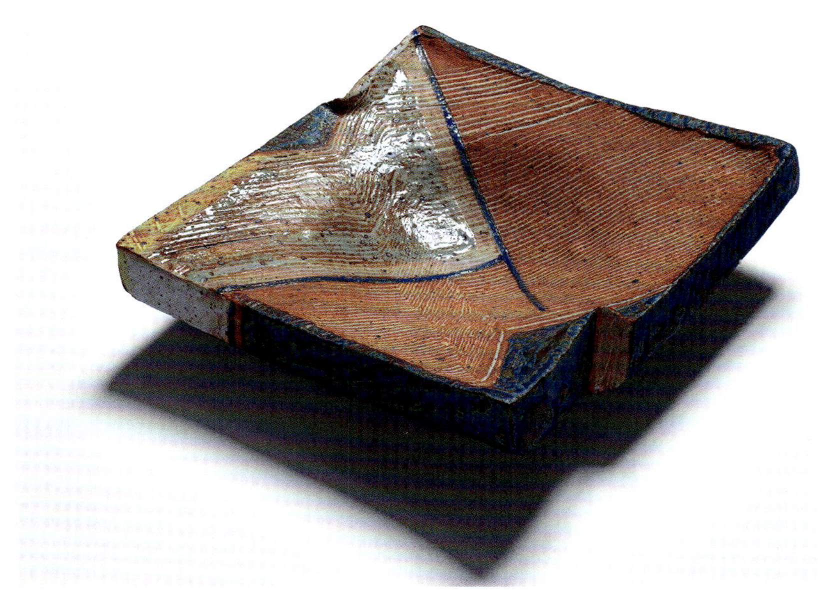
405 84/1997

404. Bowl, 1989. ***Jomfrustrand nat*** (Virgin Beach night**)**
Porcelain, ash- and feldspar-glazed, silver; thrown, sgrafitto. H 21.5 x Diam 36.5. Mark: 'GHP' painted on base. Mus.no. 142/1990. ACQUISITION: Gerd Hiort Petersen. Donation from *Kunstindustrimuseets Venner*

405. Dish, 1997
Stoneware, ash- and feldspar-glazed; modelled, brush-painted, sgrafitto. H 8.5 x W 27.5. Mark: 'GHP' painted on base. Mus.no. 84/1997. ACQUISITION: Galleri Nørby, Copenhagen. Donation from *Ausa Regitze Tillys Legat*

406. Pot, 1984
Porcelain, feldspar-glazed; thrown, sgrafitto. H 31 x Diam 27. Mark: 'GHP' painted on base. Mus.no. D 1651
ACQUISITION: On deposit from *Statens Kunstfond*, 1987

406 D 1651

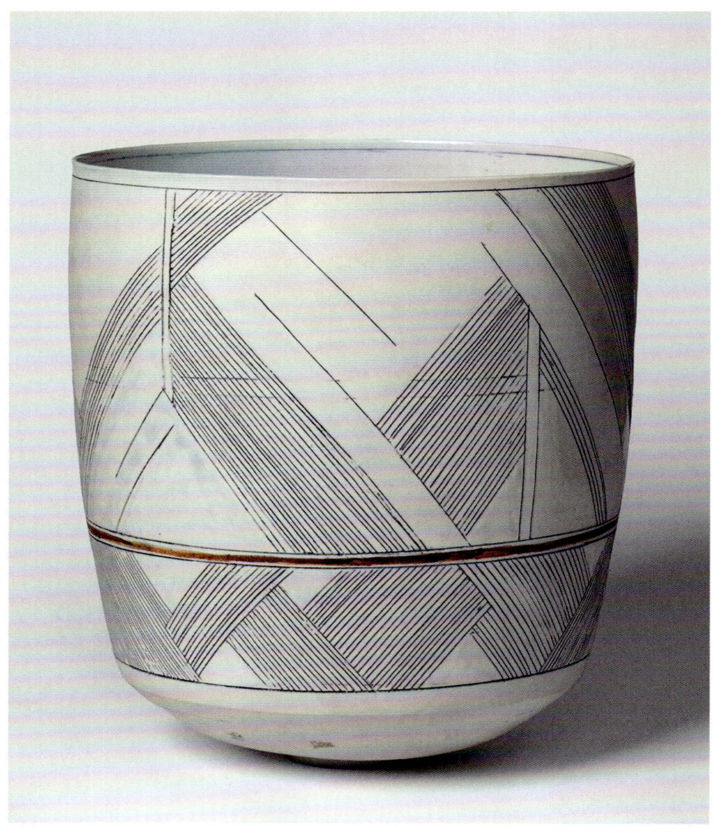

PETERSEN, LENE ADLER 1944 –

Painter

1964-66	Det Jyske Kunstakademi, Painting and Drawing
1968-69	The Royal Danish Academy of Fine Arts
1972-1979	EKS-Skolens Trykkeri ApS, co -founder and -owner
1985	Skolen for Brugskunst, teacher

Throughout the 1970s Lene Adler Petersen (LAP) worked with experimental techniques and tested out materials; she was active in Eks-skolen and became a co-founder and co-owner of Eks-skolen's printing firm, and together with her partner Bjørn Nørgaard she carried out a number of ground-breaking provocative happenings. In the 1970s LAP was also engaged in feminist-inspired and radical political art with collective exhibitions and publications, etc. She took part in the largest-scale collective manifestation of these trends in pictorial art, in Charlottenborg's women's exhibition in 1975; the idealistic basis of the exhibition is clearly evident in the statement of its purpose: 'To do away with mutual competition, to let the pictures grow out of openness and confidence has been our primary goal'. (See: Hellen Lassen, *Elleve unge kunstnere*, Sophienholm 1978).

After years of engagement in collective contexts, in 1974 LAP had her first solo exhibition, in Daner Galleriet, Copenhagen, which was established by the art collector John Hunov and was run by him from 1972 to 1976. In around 1980 LAP began to work with clay in an experimental process which in the following years, and up to the mid 1980s, came to encompass several large ceramic commissions and a number of small sculptures; the museum has a small collection of five of these works from 1982 to 85.

With the pot as departure-point LAP was at that time exploring diverse issues such as spatial effects and materials, including form, glazes and colour; she modelled some pots herself and had others thrown following her drawings, and she demonstrated that this initially traditional form could have unimagined potential in an artist's hands. It is the case, both with commissioned work and with individual pieces, that LAP is involved in the whole process, which is driven by

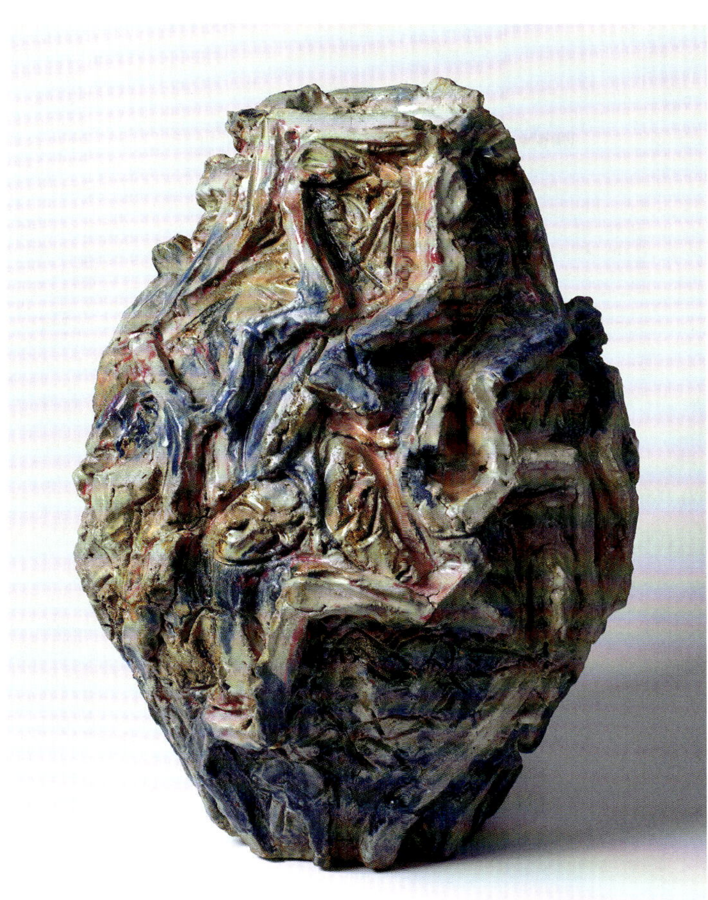

407 39/1983

an experimental approach to finding solutions; she is engaged in the craftwork aspects and in the cooperation with the workshops. (See: Claus Hagedorn-Olsen *(ed.) 'Komedien eller Den Guddommelige'*. Horsens Kunstmuseum, 1986).

An example of these pots, from 1982-83, is to be found in the museum's collection; it is expressionistically modelled with deep relief effects and running glazes in different colours, and is white-glazed on the inside **(407)**. The pot was made at NEES Fællesværksted (cooperative workshop) at Holstebro, set up in 1980 by a group including Esben Lyngsaa Madsen, (who moved in 1984 to Tommerup Teglværk); it has since then been a centre for the creation of major ceramic commissioned works and monuments, etc., primarily by pictorial artists. Both the museum's pot and two smaller sculptures from the early 1980s are influenced by neo-expressionism, which broke through internationally around the time that LAP was in New York in 1982. From 1983 there is the sculpture entitled *Elefanttemplet* (The elephant temple), a little construction work that is supported by six low unglazed pillars and that unceremoniously develops upwards in a spiral movement to terminate in a little yellow spire **(408)**. A couple of years later, from 1985, there is the sculpture *Monument for min mor* (Monument for my mother), which consists of two parts: a pillar-supported doorway with a rounded arch as its upper section, and leaning up against that there is a staircase/support with a curved slab which rises upwards like a ramp **(409)**. These three works were all acquired at a solo exhibition for LAP in Galleri Specta, Aarhus, in 1986, as was a dish from a series of 12 dishes entitled *Fade til Dickens* (Dishes for Dickens) from 1985, this one with the title *Mund, Mr. M'Choakumchild* **(410)**. From the same series in 2010 the museum acquired *Peachen, Cecilia Jupe* **(411)**, and those two plates were in fact the artist's contribution to

408 40/1983

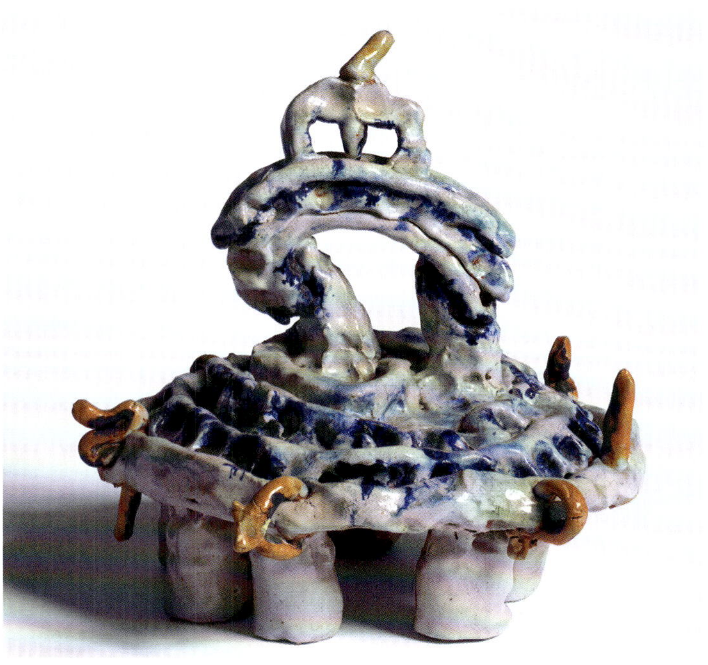

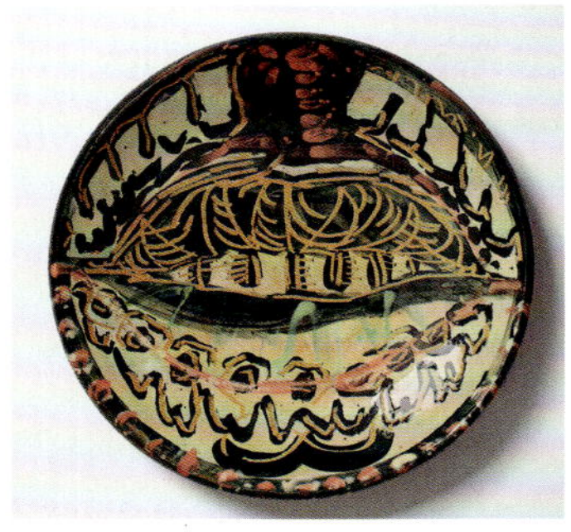

410 67/1986

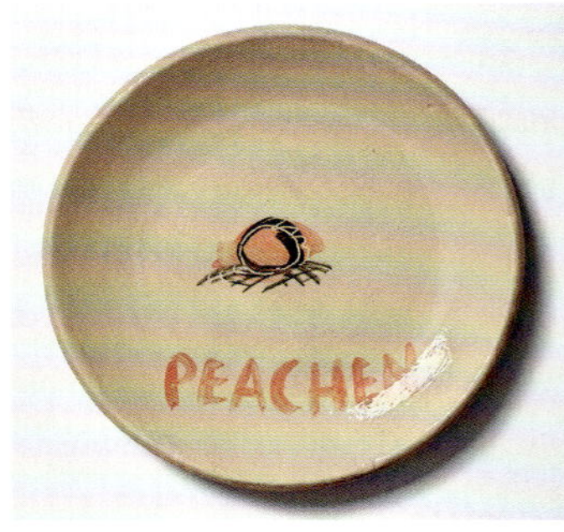

411 103/2010

'*Biennale des Friedens, Kunsthaus und Kunstverein*' in Hamburg, in 1985. In this series of works LAP experimented with slip, while the motifs are inspired by characters in Charles Dickens' novel *Hard Times*.

407. Pot, 1982-83
Stoneware, glazed; modelled, relief, brush-painted, fired at 1200°. Made at NEES Fællesværksted. H 53 x Diam 39.5. Mark: Dedication 'NF 8' painted on base. Mus.no. 39/1983
ACQUISITION: *Lene Adler Petersen – fade til Dickens*, 1986, Galleri Specta, Aarhus. Donation from *Kunstindustrimuseets 50-års Jubilæumslegat*

408. Sculpture, 1982-83. ***Elefanttempel*** (Elephant temple)
Stoneware, glazed; modelled, brush-painted, fired at 1200°. Made at NEES Fællesværksted. H 25.5 x Diam 24. Mark: none. Mus.no. 40/1983.
ACQUISITION: *Lene Adler Petersen – fade til Dickens*, 1986, Galleri Specta, Aarhus. Donation from *Kunstindustrimuseets 50-års Jubilæumslegat*.
See: Dybdahl. L., 1997

409. Sculpture, 1985. ***Monument for min mor*** (Monument for my mother)
Raku clay, glazed; modelled, brush-painted, reduction raku-fired at 900°. Made at Tommerup Teglværksted. H 21.5 x W 16 x D 23. Mark: 'LAP' painted on base. Mus.no. 68/1986. ACQUISITION: *Lene Adler Petersen – fade til Dickens*, 1986, Galleri Specta, Aarhus. Donation from *Kunstindustrimuseets Venner*

410. Dish, 1985. (From the series ***Fade til Dickens) Mund, Mr. M'Choakumchild*** (Mouth, Mr. M'Choakumchild)
Earthenware, clear-glazed; thrown, slip, engraved, brush-painted, fired at 900°. Made at Skolen for Brugskunst. H 8.2 x Diam 52. Mark: Dedication 'Lis 85' inscribed on base. Mus.no. 67/1986. ACQUISITION: *Lene Adler Petersen – fade til Dickens*, 1986, Galleri Specta, Aarhus. Donation from *Kunstindustrimuseets Venner*. See: *Brændpunkter*, 1990

411. Dish, 1985. (From the series ***Fade til Dickens) Peachen, Cecilia Jupe***
Earthenware, clear-glazed; thrown, slip, brush-painted motif. H 6.5 x Diam 52. Mark: 'LAP 1985 HM Lene Adler Petersen' painted on base. Mus.no. 103/2010. ACQUISITION: Lene Adler Petersen

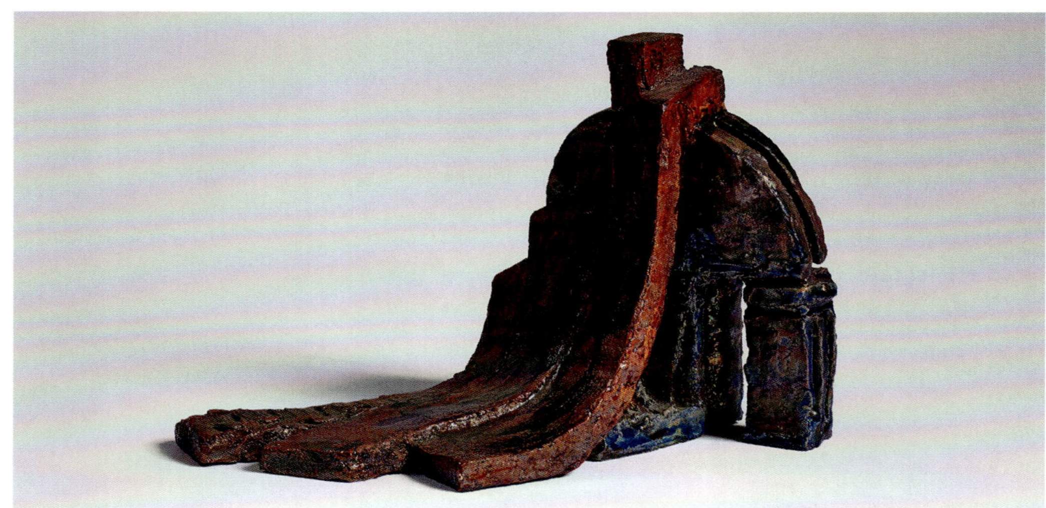

409 68/1986

POULSEN, BJØRN 1959 –

Sculptor

1978-81 Art College, Lolland
1981-88 The Royal Danish Academy of Fine Arts
1987-94 Holbæk Kunsthøjskole, guest teacher
1990-95 Danmarks Designskole, guest teacher
1992-94 Århus Kunstakademi, teacher
www.bjornpoulsen.dk

Bjørn Poulsen (BP) is a versatile and very productive artist; since completing his studies at the Academy of Fine Arts he has held an extensive series of solo exhibitions and carried out 15 commissions for art works in public spaces and buildings in many areas of Denmark. In the course of his career as an artist BP has created sculptures in all kinds of materials, such as bronze, stone, steel, wood and plastic,ery and in many works he has used 'ready-mades', as can be seen in the strongly expressive and moving *Strange Fruits* exhibited in Charlottenborg in 1999, in which a corporeal violence and pain is expressed in suspended 'bodies' of exploded and destroyed furniture-parts and textiles bound together with ring-clamps. Bulky inflated tractor tubes are the main material in another work named *Limbo* from 2003, inducing the same impression of pent-up power as imparted by the museum's sculptural vase.

412 120/2009

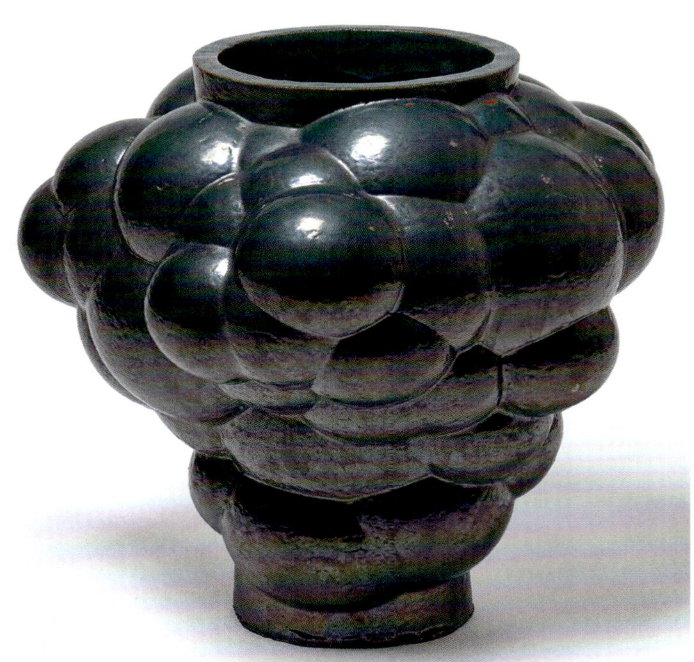

At the beginning of the 1990s BP was invited by the firm of Kähler Keramik to make a proposal for functional ceramic objects that could form a basis for production. One of the results was an impressive large blue-glazed bowl with round dents and bulges, as if cut out for holding oranges. The museum's sculptural vase from 2002 is another result of cooperation with Kähler Keramik; it is a vigorous organic structure somewhere between a machine-like construction and a bundle of muscles, and yet based on the form of a vase **(412)**. The sculpture is a fine addition to the museum's collection of works made by Danish pictorial artists.

BP has continued to use ceramic material, now in cooperation with Tommerup Ceramic Workshop, where in 2003 he made several glazed sculptures of the same type as the museum's work, and in 2007 he created the 6-metre-tall monumental *Vejviseren* (Signpost), an ambiguous work made in glazed stoneware in bright colours, set up outside the town hall in Vissenbjerg, West Funen.

See: *Longing for a Space Travel*, Bjørn Poulsen – selected sculptures 1994-2008. Copenhagen, 2008

412. Sculpture in the form of a vase, 2002

Stoneware, glazed; shaped, cast in a plaster mould. Made at Kähler Keramik, Næstved. H 55 x Diam 55. Mark: 'HAK' inscribed on base. Mus.no. 120/2009
ACQUISITION: Donation from *Ny Carlsbergfondet* 2009

POULSEN, CHRISTIAN 1911-1991

Ceramicist

1930-33 Kunsthåndværkerskolen, Copenhagen; teacher 1963
1933-34, 1940-45 Danmarks Tekniske Højskole, volunteer
1935 The Royal Porcelain Factory, volunteer
1938- Own workshop, Kolding
1938-39 École des Arts Décoratifs, Paris, student in the Sculpture Department
1940-44 Skolen for Boligindretning, Copenhagen, teacher
1945 Danmarks Tekniske Højskole, experiments with ceramic material and glazes
1946 Bing & Grøndahl's Porcelain Factory, stoneware (unique works), volunteer
1946 Own workshop, Lyngby
1954 Study visit, France
1961- Member of Den Frie Udstilling, Copenhagen
1987 Retrospective exhibition, Kunstmuseet Trapholt, Kolding
www.kid.dk/weilbach

In 1964 Christian Poulsen (CP) held a solo exhibition in the museum, with a total of 63 works, and this achievement did not go unnoticed. Merete Bodelsen, an expert on Danish stoneware, reviewed the exhibition and wrote an insightful article about the exhibits which concluded with a characterisation of CP as one of the major figures of Danish ceramics in the 20th century.

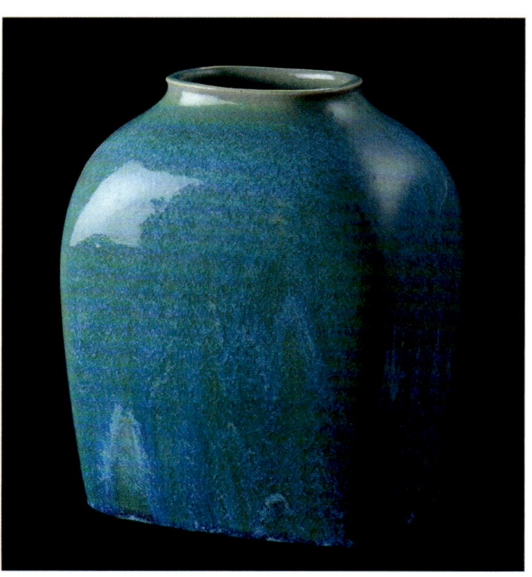

414 58/1956

> *Here we are confronted with something very rare: a ceramicist with a painter's eye and a sculptor's hands – but one who never forgets that he is first and foremost a craftsman. (Dansk Kunsthåndværk, 37, 2/1964-65, pp. 33-39).*

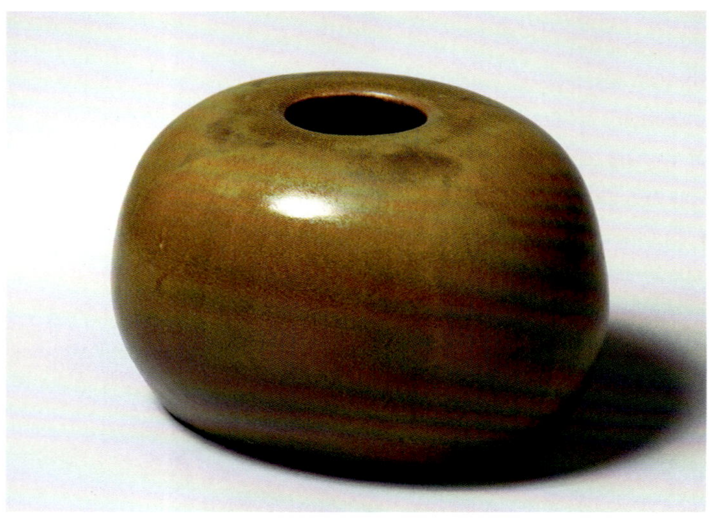

415 611/1962

To this characterization Merete Bodelsen could have added that CP was also a poet; in 1945 he published a collection of his poems entitled '*Den fremmede*' (The stranger), with illustrations by Richard Mortensen. As a writer he had a considerable wing-span. He attended the legendary first Ceramics class at the Kunsthåndværkerskolen, and was taught in the museum's Stensal, along with e.g. Richard Mortensen, Ejler Bille, Sonja Ferlov and the Hjorth sisters from the Hjorth Factory in Rønne (Gertrud Vasegaard and Lisbet Munch-Petersen). They were all engrossed in the new trends in European art, and in an article for the *Festschrift* for Lisbet Munch-Petersen in 1989 CP wrote about the experience of opening up to art that he gained from this group, and about their lifelong friendship. In the same volume CP writes about the Danish '*Kunsthåndværkerskoler*' and the teaching in the early years. (Poulsen, C. *På sporet efter den tabte tid*, in: *Gudinden fra Holkadalen – Lisbet Munch-Petersen*, Bornholms Kunstmuseum, 1989, pp. 37-45).

After a few years with earthenware, stoneware became CP's central area of work and research, focusing on studies of form; he supplemented his earlier education with studies at the École des Arts Décoratifs in Paris, in the Sculpture department, and at Danmarks Tekniske Højskole (Denmark's Technical University) for chemical studies and experiments with the production of glazes. Major efforts were made in the following years to develop both clay and glazes and to examine the connection between form and colour; these experiments with the textural possibilities of clay took place after 1946 in CP's stoneware workshop in Lyngby, and the results were displayed in Den Permanente and in Haandarbejdets Fremme, in Copenhagen, in the form of a number of unglazed works. It became clear that what CP wanted to achieve was quite different from the perfect stoneware that was cultivated in the porcelain factories and at the Saxbo works. CP's early stoneware was an abrupt departure from an aesthetic that had held sway since the end of the 19th century, and which had in part arisen out of inspiration from East Asian stoneware and from the French stoneware masters whose works had been prized, and bought e.g. by the museum, at the World Exhibitions around the year 1900.

In the course of the 1950s it became clear that CP had worked his way towards a significant artistic form of expression, in which a stable powerful design idiom and a new palette of luminous colourful glazes combined to form a higher unity. The basic forms were the traditional bowls, vases and pots, but in CP's hands they became abstract expressionistic sculptural forms. Through CP's strength of artistic will, the development of both clay and glazes was driven forward so that the products of his efforts emerged with an expressive and textural power that has no parallels in any other ceramic art in 20th century Danish stoneware.

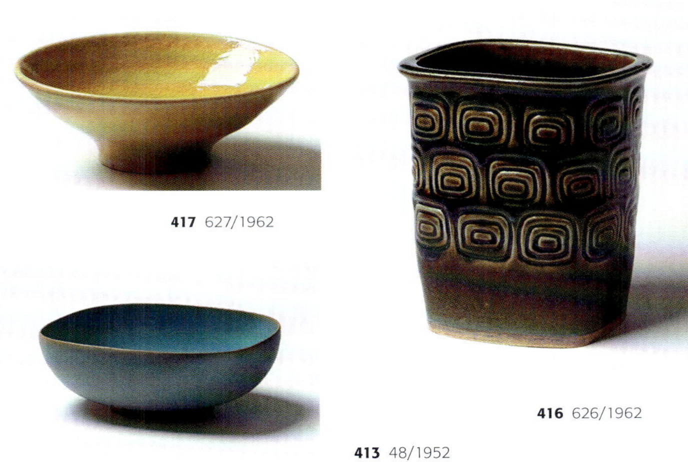

417 627/1962

416 626/1962

413 48/1952

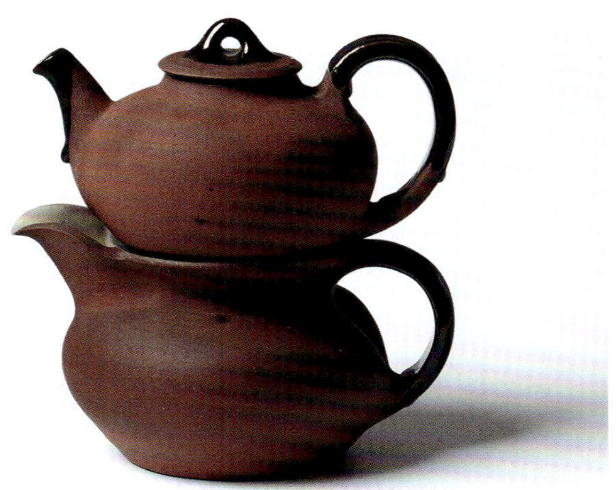

420 344a-c/1993

The museum's collection contains 11 works by CP, all of them made at the Lyngby workshop. Seven of them can be dated to around 1960; the earliest is a bowl from 1951 with a fine clair-de lune glaze **(413)**. From 1952 there is an example of functional art for domestic use, a handsome teapot with a hot water jug, unglazed on the outer side with black shiny glaze inside and on the spout and handle **(420)**; a similar but not identical set is in Trapholt Kunstmuseum. At Dansk Kunsthåndværk's '*Efterårsudtilling*' in 1956 the museum acquired a vase with a special crackle glaze that seems to be the result of two firings, with a pale bluish glaze over a greenish one **(414)**.

Three of the works are dated to 1961 and were acquired by the museum from CP in the same year; like the above works they were in the collection prior to CP's solo exhibition in the museum in 1964. The form of the exhibition was built up by CP himself using porous concrete slabs as stands for the ceramic exhibits. This was an uncompromising choice which clearly threw focus on his view of the ceramic works as art and not as elements of an interior. Also on display were several new examples of CP's rich palette of glazes with saturated colours, such as a new intense yellow uranium glaze used

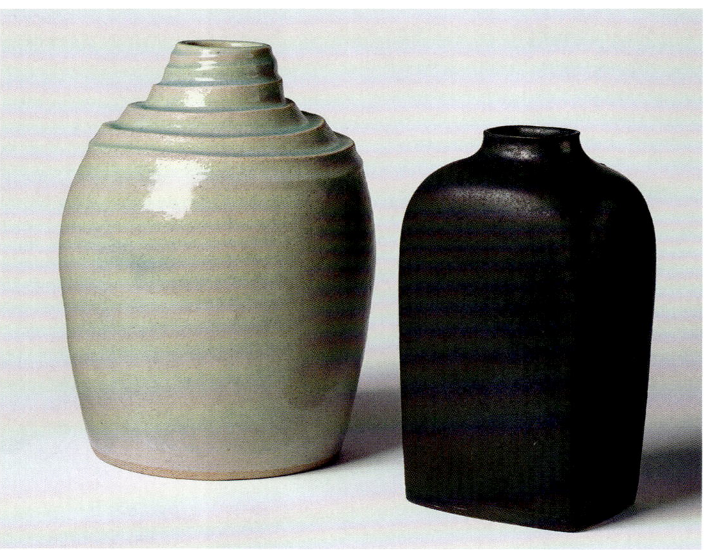

418 18/1964 **423** 137/1999

on the museum's bowl **(417)**, and a pale whitish-green celadon glaze, here on an egg-shaped pot that is topped with a screw-thread on which the glaze has collected and takes on a deeper colour. This fine work was acquired by the museum at the exhibition in 1964 **(418)**. From c.1975 there is a splendid work, a large bell-shaped vase with a deep green, shiny crackle glaze **(419)**. An unusual vase with a decoration of three rows of incised rectangles, repeating the rectangular shape of the vase itself (626/1962), was acquired directly from CP, and in 1999 the museum received a gift of three works, including a well-shaped vase with a black semi-matte glaze that was also a feature of some of the works displayed in 1964 **(423)**.

As an extension of his studio ceramics CP also carried out several ceramic commissions, including the large fountain at Hørecentralen in Fredericia. CP undertook several major journeys and was strongly interested in other cultures and in international cooperation; this led to involvement in the World Crafts Council, where he became the Danish representative. He wrote an informative account in 1967 of his experience of participating and observing in that capacity. CP was appointed artistic consultant for the state of Sikkim in 1972-73, and in 1974 he helped to arrange that the '*Tantra*' exhibition came to Denmark, to the Louisiana Museum of Modern Art and that '*Kunst fra Himalaya*' came to Sophienholm in 1976. Through his participation in a number of international exhibitions of Danish design throughout the 1950s and 60s CP contributed to forming those events, and his works are represented in museums in the Nordic region and in the rest of Europe. At the retrospective exhibition held at Trapholt Kunstmuseum in Kolding in 1987 there were 147 works on display, providing a unique insight into this artist's purposeful research into ceramic materials (see: Andersen, S.J., 1987). CP played an important role in the craft world in his lifetime and was a strong voice both within Denmark and beyond. He became a member of Den Frie Udstilling, Copenhagen, in 1962, and was awarded the Art Academy's Eckersberg Medal in 1970. Through his work and his clear vision of ceramics as an artistic manifestation his influence was instrumental for the next generation of ceramicists in setting ceramics free from the functional mantra.

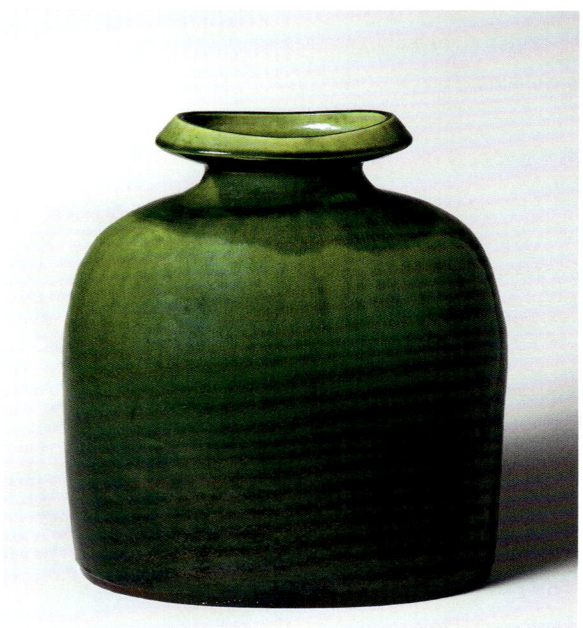

419 231/1992

413. Bowl, 1951

Stoneware, clair de lune glaze; thrown, shaped, fired at 1240°. H 6 x W 15.5. Mark: 'Chr. P. inscribed on base. Mus.no. 48/1952

ACQUISITION: Christian Poulsen. *Dansk Kunsthåndværks Forårsudstilling*, 1951. Donation from *Benny Dessaus Mindelegat*

414. Pot, 1956

Stoneware, crystal- and crackle- glazed; thrown, shaped, fired at 1240°. H 25.8 x W 16. Mark: 'Chr.-P. Danmark' inscribed on base. Mus.no. 58/1956

ACQUISITION: *Dansk Kunsthåndværks Efterårsudstilling*, Charlottenborg. Donation from *Statens 50-års Jubilæumslegat*. See: *Brændpunkter*, 1990. Dybdahl, L., 1997

415. Pot, 1961

Stoneware, crackle-glazed; thrown, modelled, fired at 1240°. H 20 x W 30. Mark: 'Chr.-P' inscribed on base. Mus.no. 611/1962. ACQUISITION: *Forårsudstillingen*, 1962, Den Frie, Copenhagen. Donation from *Benny Dessaus Mindelegat*

416. Vase, 1961

Stoneware, glazed; modelled, inscribed decoration, fired at 1240°. H 15.7 x W 13.4. Mark: 'Chr.-P' inscribed on base. Mus.no. 626/1962.

ACQUISITION: Christian Poulsen. Donation from *Benny Dessaus Mindelegat*. See: *Brændpunkter*, 1990

417. Bowl, 1961

Stoneware, crackle- and alkali-glazed; thrown, modelled, fired at 1250°. H 6.8 x Diam 18. Mark: 'Chr.-P' inscribed on base. Mus.no. 627/1962

ACQUISITION: Christian Poulsen. Donation from *Benny Dessaus Mindelegat*. See: *Brændpunkter*, 1990

418. Vase, 1964

Stoneware, crackle- and celadon- glazed; modelled, egg shaped with diminishing spiral motif on the shoulder and neck. Fired at 1240°. H 33. Mark: 'CHR-P' inscribed on base. Mus.no. 18/1964

ACQUISITION: *Danske kunsthåndværkere VII*, exhibition of the work of Mogens and Ea Koch and Christian Poulsen, Kunstindustrimuseet, 1964. Donation from *Kunsthåndværkets 50-års Jubilæumslegat*. See: Dybdahl, L., 1997

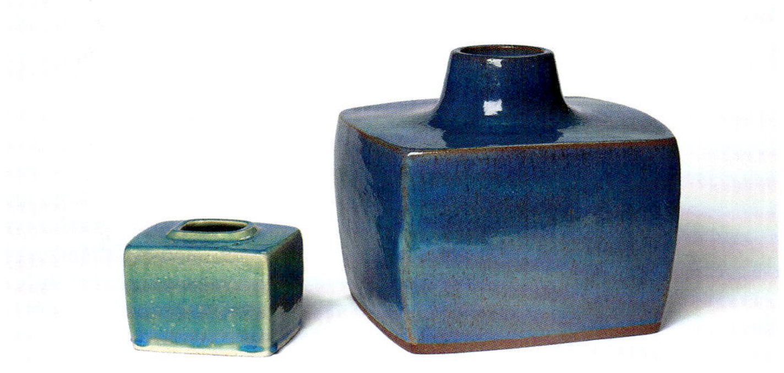

421 135/1999 **422** 136/1999

419. Vase, c.1975

Stoneware, crackle-glazed; thrown, modelled, fired at 1240°. H 42 x Diam 40. Mark: 'CHR-P' inscribed on base. Mus.no. 231/1992. ACQUISITION: Henning Hansted. Donation from *Kunstindustrimuseets Venner*. Exhibited at Trapholt Kunstmuseum, Kolding, 1987. See: Andersen, S. J., 1987, p. 36

420. Teapot with hot water jug, 1952

Stoneware, part glazed, part unglazed; thrown, modelled, fired at 1240°. H 18.5. Mark: 'CHR-P' inscribed on base. Mus.no. 344a-c/1993

ACQUISITION: Antique Moderne, Bagsværd. Donation from *Ny Carlsbergfondet*. See: Hiort, E., 1955

421. Pot, date unknown

Stoneware, crackle-glazed; modelled, fired at 1240°. H 13 x W 13.5. Mark: 'CHR-P' inscribed on base. Mus.no. 135/1999

ACQUISITION: Donation from Bank Director C.B. Andersen, Copenhagen

422. Pot, date unknown

Stoneware, crackle-glazed; modelled, fired at 1240°. H 30 x Diam 26. Mark: 'CHR-P' inscribed on base. Mus.no. 136/1999

ACQUISITION: Donation from Bank Director C.B. Andersen, Copenhagen

423. Pot, date unknown

Stoneware, glazed; thrown, modelled, slip, fired at 1250°. H 28 x W 15 x Diam 13. Mark: 'CHR-P DANMARK' inscribed on base. Mus.no. 137/1999

ACQUISITION: Donation from Bank Director C. B. Andersen, Copenhagen

POULSEN, METTE AUGUSTINUS 1945 –

Ceramicist

1966-70 Det Jyske Kunstakademi
1971- Own studio workshop, Risskov, Århus
www.mette-augustinus-poulsen.dk

Mette Augustinus Poulsen (MAP) studied Painting, Drawing and Ceramics at Det Jyske Kunstakademi, with Birthe Weggerby and Gutte Eriksen as ceramics teachers. MAP's first exhibition was '*Kunstnernes Efterårsudstilling*' in 1971, and in the same year she set up her own studio workshop, which she has used ever since. She has also invested her energy in joint projects, for instance as co-editor of the publication *Kunsthåndværkere i Århus Amt*, 1988, and as co-organiser of the exhibition '*Dansk Keramik 1991*' in Århus Kunstbygning.

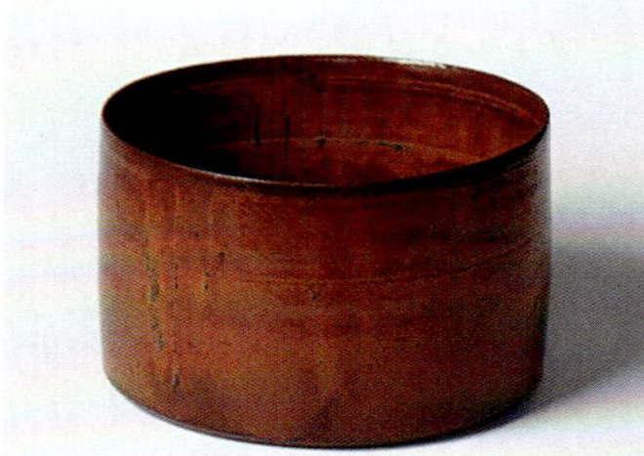

424 109/1983

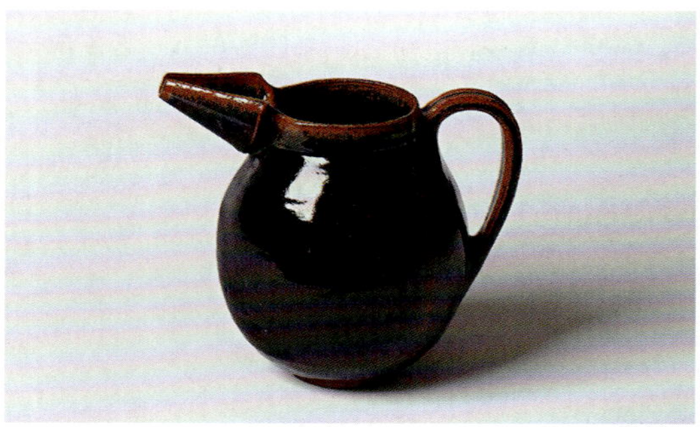

425 120/1988

MAP did not take long to find her own form of ceramic expression in terms of shape, the container, and in terms of material, the sandy red clay from the Esbjerg region, Jutland, which can be fired at high temperatures. She has also worked with slip glazes containing iron and tin oxides and ash, often in brown/reddish or pale/whitish colour ranges. The works are decorated with a simple line ornament incised in the slip, as the finishing touch to the overall lines. MAP has very consciously and with great empathy and quality sought to continue the rich tradition of hand-thrown unique functional objects that require special craftwork skill and sensitivity, and she takes inspiration from town, harbour, nature and coopers' products.

The museum's collection contains four works by MAP from 1980/90; one of them is a jug with well-shaped details and fine black iron glazing **(425)**, while the others are bowl- or pot-shaped. A fifth work, from 1990, is a delicate little pot, with whitish tin/straw-ash glaze and lines in black clay-colour, which was shown in the exhibition '*Dansk Keramik 1991*' **(426)**. Through the years MAP has taken part in many exhibitions in Denmark and elsewhere, and her works are represented in museums and both public and private collections in Denmark,

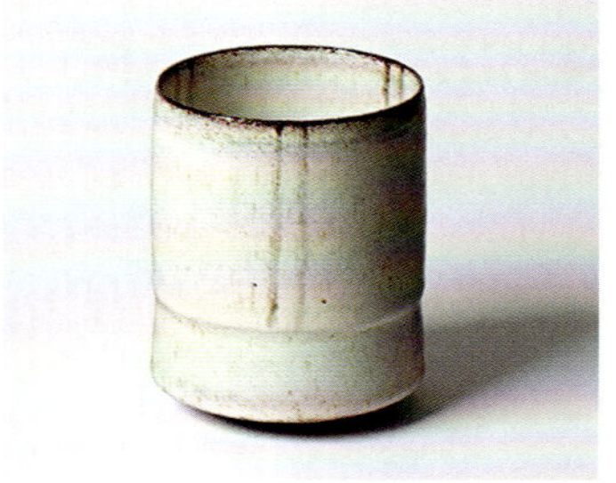

426 9/1992

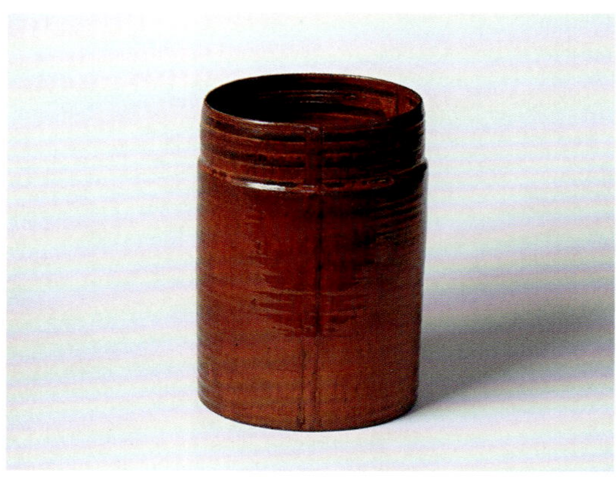

427 D 1685

Europe, the USA and Japan; she has also received bursaries and honorary awards.

424. Bowl, 1982

Earthenware, borax-glazed; thrown, scored, fired at 1160°. H 14 x Diam 22. Mark: 'MAP' inscribed on base. Mus.no. 109/1983

ACQUISITION: Donation from *Ny Carlsberg Museumslegat*. See: Dybdahl, L., 1997

425. Jug, 1988

Earthenware, borax-glazed; thrown, reduction-fired at 1160°. H 19.5. Mark: 'MAP' inscribed on base. Mus.no. 120/1988

ACQUISITION: Aabenraa Museum, 1988. Donation from *Kgl. Brand*. See: *Brændpunkter*, 1990

426. Pot, 1990

Earthenware, tin- and ash-glazed; thrown, scored with black clay-colour under the glaze, reduction-fired at 1160°. H 14.5 x Diam 11. Mark: 'MAP' inscribed on base. Mus.no. 9/1992

ACQUISITION: Exhibited in *Dansk Keramik 1991*. Donation from *Justitsråd J.F. Møllmanns Legatfond*

427. Pot, 1988

Earthenware, borax-glazed; thrown, scored, reduction-fired at 1160°. H 23,6 x Diam 16. Mark: 'MAP' inscribed on base. Mus.no. D 1685

ACQUISITION: Aabenraa Museum. Deposited by *Statens Kunstfond*, 1989

POULSEN, TUE 1939 –

Ceramicist, painter

1959-61 Kunsthåndværkerskolen

1963- Own studio workshop, Fårevejle, W Sealand
www.tuekeramik.dk

Tue Poulsen (TP) studied at Kunsthåndværkerskolen and has had his own workshop combined with an exhibition area since 1963. TP creates unique ceramic works and sculptures, and through the years he has completed a large number of ceramic commissions for churches and for both private and public buildings. Together with architect Johan Otto von Spreckelsen TP took part in architectural competitions in the 1960s, resulting in a 1st prize in *Statens Kunstfond's* town planning competition in 1967. In the 1970s TP designed the table-service MAREN for the firm of Eslau; it was produced in Esbern Johan Larsen's oven-proof and self-glazing brown material and was so successful that in the 1980s, when white became fashionable, it was made in porcelain under the name MILLE. TP later designed and produced the THILDE series in white bone china in his own workshop.

In the museum's collection there is a dish by TP from 1960, made while he was still at Kunsthåndværkerskolen; it is a well-executed piece of work characteristic of the 1960s **(428)**.

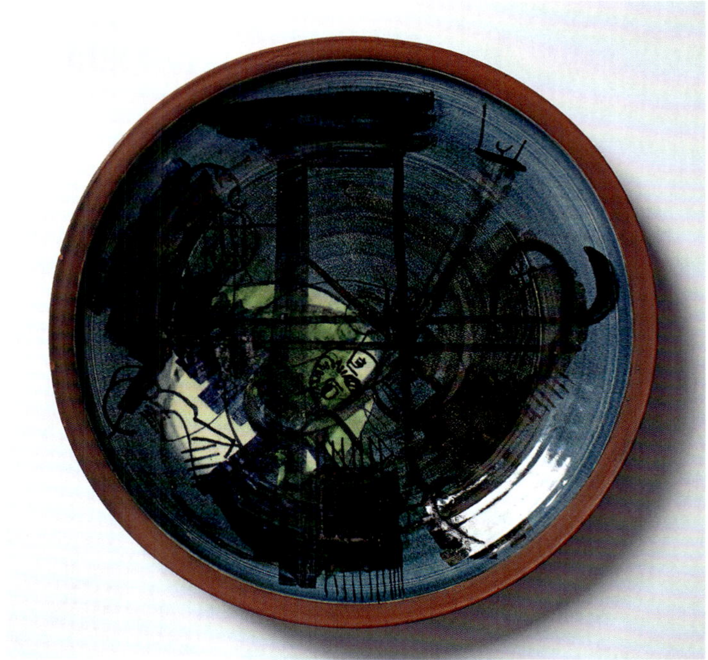

428 39/2010

428. Dish, 1960

Earthenware, glazed; thrown, painted with abstract decoration. H 8 x Diam 52. Mark: 'Tue 60' inscribed on base. Mus.no. 39/2010

ACQUISITION: Tue Poulsen

RANSLET, ARNE 1931 –

Ceramicist, sculptor

1951-54 The Royal Danish Academy of Fine Arts, School of Ceramics

1954-

c.1990 Own studio workshop with Tulla Ranslet, Bornholm; lives in Spain 1988-

www.arne-ranslet.com

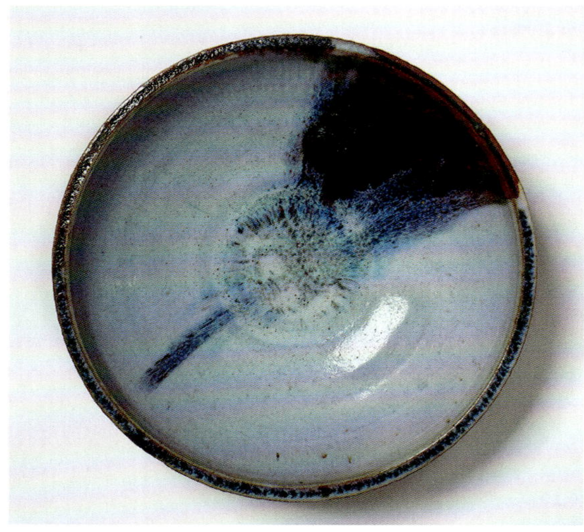

429 39/2067

Arne Ranslet (AR) opted for ceramics at an early stage in his studies and was already a trained thrower when he began attending the Art Academy's Ceramic department. From 1954 AR settled in Bornholm with his wife, Tulla Blomberg. For some years from 1958 AR was attached to the ceramics factory of Søholm, as a designer and technical adviser on development of glazes. Until around 1970 AR threw bowls, dishes and vases in coarse Bornholm stoneware clay, which he reduction-fired at 1400° in a large oil-fired kiln he had made himself, and he glazed what he made in a novel fluid style using poured, dripped and running glazing techniques.

AR soon established an intense programme of exhibition activities, particularly in Sweden and Germany, and won international prizes from as early as the mid 1950s. His ceramic works have been acquired by leading museums and private collectors, and he has also carried out a number of ceramic commissions. From the 1970s AR has increasingly worked sculpturally both in ceramics and later in bronze.
In 1967 the museum acquired a dish made by AR which is representative of his work in that period.**(429)**. See: Serena, L., 2004

429. Dish, 1967

Stoneware, feldspar- and tenmoku- glazed; thrown, reduction-fired at 1400°. Diam 37. Mark: 'AR' painted on base. Mus.no. 39/1967

ACQUISITION: Bosjökloster, 1967, Sweden. Donation from *Kunstindustrimuseets 50-års Jubilæumslegat*. See: Dybdahl, L., 1997

RASMUSSEN, PEDER I 1929-64

Ceramicist

Autodidact

1950- Own studio workshop, Baldersbrønde, Hedehusene, Sealand

1959-64 attached to Bing & Grøndahl, Copenhagen

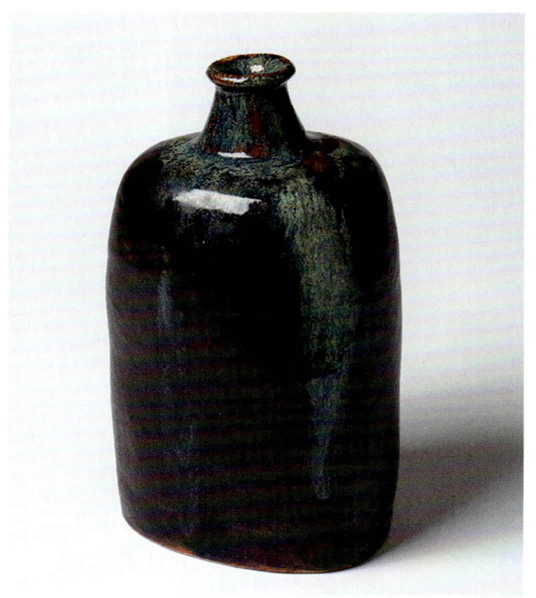

430 21/1959

There can be a particular aura about artists who 'die young', and this applies in the case of ceramicist Peder Rasmussen (PR), who died at the age of only 35. He had already made a name for himself, however, as a major talent among the younger ceramicists working with stoneware, and had won recognition from the highest authorities on the subject, Merete Bodelsen (*Bodelsen, M.*, 1960) and ceramicist Christian Poulsen (*Keramisk Nytårsstatus*, Dansk Kunsthåndværk 1956, p. 198). In 1958 PR was awarded *Chr. Grauballes Mindelegat*, a bursary which was allocated by Den Permanente to a promising craftsman. PR was self-taught and achieved impressive results with stoneware in a short time by independent study, *inter alia* of Bernard Leach's *A Potters Book*; he made his own alkali and ash glazes from locally available natural materials. He had his own workshop on a farm in Baldersbrønde, and he exhibited in Den Permanente, Copenhagen, from 1948 onwards and throughout the 1950s at the exhibitions held in Denmark and elsewhere by Landsforeningen Dansk Kunsthåndværk (the National Association of Danish Crafts).

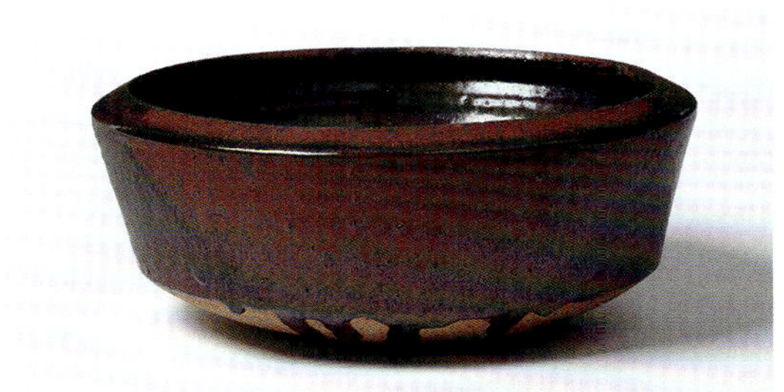

431 10/1960

From an early experiment with small-scale sculptures PR began to work, after developing his stoneware technique, with robust, strongly designed and clearly delineated shapes that were thrown and modelled before being glazed. It is the interplay between fabric and glaze that makes PR's works so exceptional, and in that there is common ground between his work and that of Christian Poulsen.

The museum has three works by PR, the earliest a bottle-shaped vase **(430)** with a distinctive play of colours in the part-shiny, part-matte glaze. From 1959 there is a bowl with red/brown running glaze **(431)**, which was acquired at the exhibition '*Stentøj*' in 1960 in the museum, and finally there is the strongly-shaped jug from c.1962 with black-brown shiny glaze inside and on the upper part of the jug, while the base and parts of the sides are clear-glazed with a distinct marking of the underlying fabric **(432)**. Through studying independently PR managed to acquire knowledge of ceramic techniques in a short period of time, and he achieved a distinctive design idiom with considerable textural quality both in his unique functional products and in his ceramic sculptures and reliefs. From 1959 until his early death he was employed by the firm of Bing & Grøndahl.

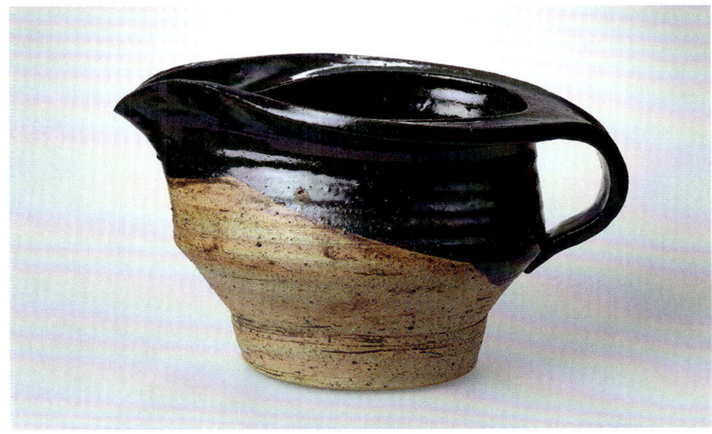

432 5/1965

430. Vase, bottle-shaped, 1958

Stoneware, ash- and iron- glazed; thrown, shaped, painted. H 24.5.
Mark: 'PR 58 DANMARK' on base. Mus.no. 21/1959
ACQUISITION: Den Permanente, Copenhagen. Donation from *Kunsthåndværkets Jubilæumslegat*. See: Dybdahl, L., 1997

431. Bowl, 1959

Stoneware, glazed, partly unglazed; thrown, shaped. H 12 x Diam 30.
Mark: 'Peder Rasmussen, Danmark' on base. Mus.no. 10/1960
ACQUISITION: *Stentøj*, 1960, Kunstindustrimuseet. Donation from *Statens 50-års Jubilæumslegat*

432. Jug, 1962

Stoneware, feldspar-glazed; thrown, modelled. H 15 x W 25.
Mark: 'Peder Rasmussen' inscribed on base. Mus.no. 5/1965
ACQUISITION: Asger Fischer. Donation from *Statens 50-års Jubilæumslegat*

RASMUSSEN, PEDER 2 1948 –

Ceramicist, author

1966-70	Kähler Keramik, Næstved, trained as a potter
1970-71	Accademia di Belle Arti, Instituto Statale per la Porcellana, Florence
1972-	Studio workshop, Copenhagen, shared with Karen Bennicke; from 1974- Bregentved, Sealand
1983-98	Kunsthåndværkerskolen in Kolding, guest teacher
1991-95	Danmarks Designskole, guest teacher
1998	Statens Kunstfonds honorary lifelong stipend
	www. pederrasmussen.dk

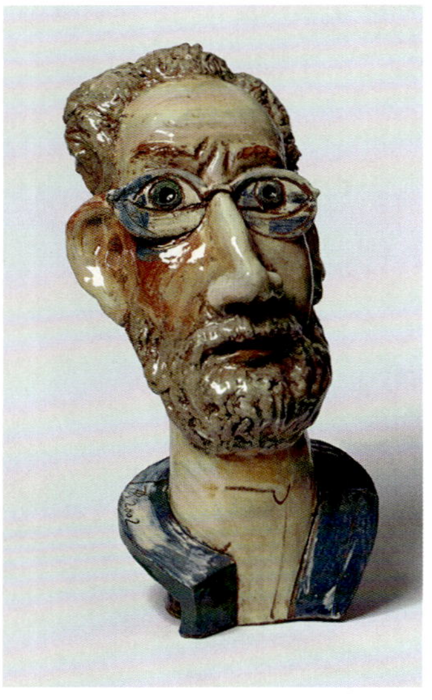

440 44/2010

Peder Rasmussen (PR) is a significantly skilful ceramicist and one of the pioneers of the new wave of Danish design and craftwork that broke through from the end of the 1970s in the wake of international post-modernism. PR has followed his own path throughout a long career and has managed to combine extensive ceramic activity with teaching at the design schools in Kolding and Copenhagen as well as with an impressive output as a writer on ceramics. PR trained as a potter at the important ceramic firm of Kähler Keramik in Næstved (1839-1974), and he has written knowledgeably and sympathetically about the firm's rich artistic and craft universe in *Kählers Værk* and in *Reistrup-Udsmykninger og keramik* (Rasmussen, P.,2002; Rasmussen, P., 2006). In 2002 PR also curated the lavish exhibition '*Kähler 1839-1969*' in the museum. The ballast acquired at Kähler's and the ceramic cultural heritage in general have always been a constant presence in PR's work, along with openness to contemporary art; through the years PR has written innumerable articles, catalogue texts and contributions about current conditions nationally and internationally in the field of ceramics and has worked actively for solidarity between generations of older and younger ceramicists.

PR has run his own studio workshop, shared with his wife, ceramicist Karen Bennicke, from 1972 onwards. Since they moved to Bregentved, near Haslev, in 1974, they have had a combined workshop, home and showroom and have also maintained an extensive scale of exhibition activity in Denmark and beyond. They have together been in several exhibition cooperatives, including *MULTI MUD*, which existed from 1979 to 1985 (apart from themselves it included Heidi and Aage Birck, Gunnar Palander and Lene Regius), and had a major breakthrough in connection with the 1983 exhibition at the Ny Carlsberg Glyptotek in Copenhagen, where they showed works inspired by the Glyptotek's collections. As the group's name indicates, its aim was to show the diversity of ceramics and to exhibit internationally. The number of exhibitions over the years was ambitious and exceptionally intense, with travels to Germany, Austria and the Scandinavian countries.

433 29/1985

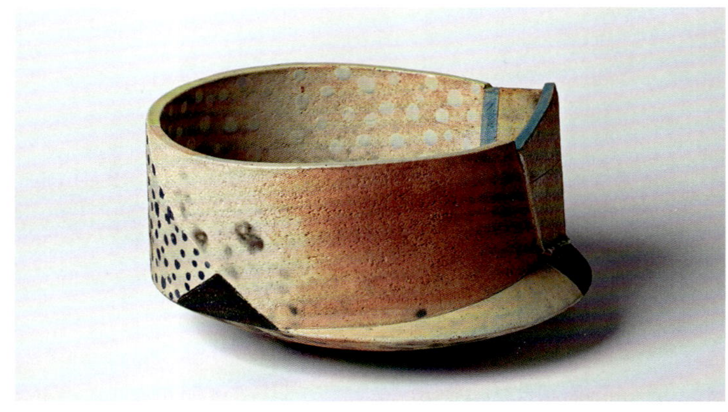

Another exhibition cooperative with international aims was set up in 2005 under the name *END* (with participants from England: Alison Britton, Richard Slee, Martin Smith; Norway: Marit Tingleff; Denmark: Karen Bennicke, Martin Bodilsen Kaldahl, Peder Rasmussen). The first exhibition took place in the museum in 2007.

PR's *oeuvre* as a ceramicist can be divided into different sections which are partly marked out by changes in technique. In the first years he mainly produced functional ceramics made of earthenware, but that chapter came to an end conclusively in 1976, when the desire to find a free ceramic mode of expression became dominant, both in PR's work and in Karen Bennicke's. PR made, for instance, a series of pictorial vases in stoneware with Pop-art motifs, including, of particular note, *Familievase* (Family vase) from 1983 (in Fyns Kunstmuseum), which is a paraphrase of the artist J.F. Willumsen's work of the same name from 1891 and at the same time an act of homage to an artist who was a source of inspiration.

From the beginning of the 1980s and in the following decade PR worked with the raku technique – not as it is used in Oriental traditions, but instead taking inspiration from the abstract expressionism of e.g. the American ceramic artist Peter Voulkos, and creating during this period a whole series of very fine works with natural-lyrical associations to curves and lines in the landscape. PR himself explained that he became tired of stoneware, but in the raku-technique and the different working process he had found textural possibilities that in time also made room for new pictorial motifs and different styles of ornamentation.

In the museum's collection there are three works from the mid 1980s that are all raku-fired. The earliest is the modernistic bowl from 1984 **(433)**, which is built up with slab technique and has a decoration of polka dots; it is clearly very different from the two following works, which express a strong sense of nature, which also finds expression in PR's abstract paintings from this time. In some notes from 1985-86 PR writes:

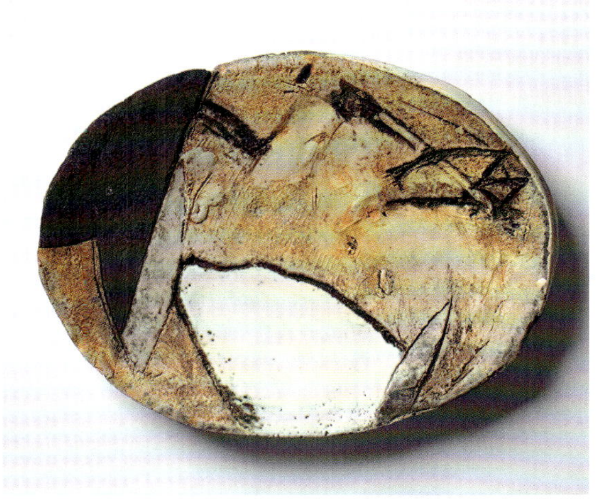

435 177/1988

For me, ceramic art is the artist working together with nature - with the mineralogical processes known from it - in order to create another kind of nature - in his own image. But of course there are things you can't do in clay and that is, I suppose, the reason why painting was invented... (Peder Rasmussen, Ceramics and Paintings 1986. Multi Mud 1986).

434 69/1986

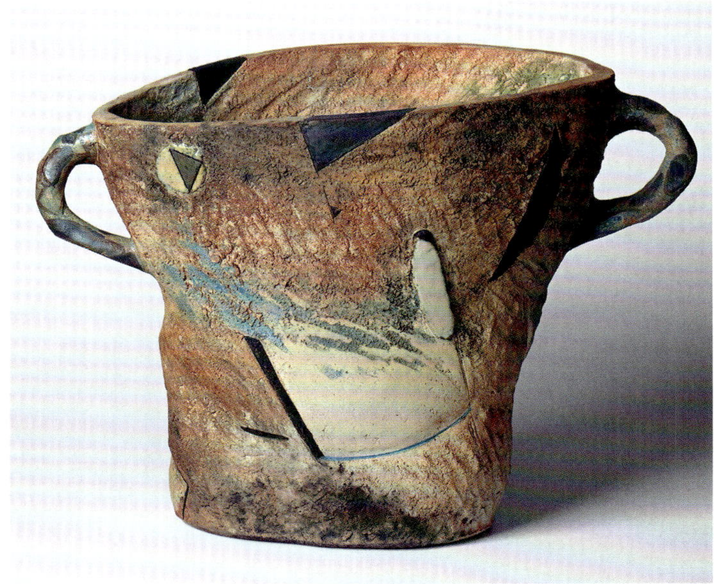

The titles of PR's works from this period refer directly to landscape and nature, as in the case of the museum's vase from 1986, called *Forår* (Spring) **(434)**. The other work is an oval dish from 1988, for which PR has used clay in the way a painter uses his canvas **(435)**.

Pictorial and decorative elements are present during the whole of PR's career, and they break through strongly towards the end of the raku period to become dominant at the beginning of the 1990s. This happened at the same time that PR turned back to the old pottery technique of slip and lead-glazed earthenware. The museum has two early modelled works from this period, a tall slim vase **(436)** and a jug-shaped creation **(439)**, both decorated with an ornament that PR uses frequently, a mesh with nodes joined by lines into a network where the knots are both held together and kept apart from each other in a dynamic movement that encircles the form. There are new developments in terms of design also: the sculptural element is strengthened, as can be seen in the work *Figur ved et tilfælde* (Accidental figure) from 1996, where even the title gives expression to the artist's undogmatic approach to his work **(437)**. Pleasure in decorative play with colours, shapes and materials radiates out of this work, which was first shown in Ribe Kunstmuseum in 1996.

The increased focus on narrative pictures and ornamentation had an effect on the shapes of PR's works, which had to provide the optimal conditions for painting. In 2004-05 this led to an ambitious project involving some 15 so-called *Spherical vases* of considerable size, around 50 cm tall and wide, and decorated with figurative stories and situations. PR has drawn and painted all his life, sketching and preserving impressions, ideas and experiences, and on the spherical vases these depicted memories were given free rein. PR used these 'floating' globes to explore the human figure in all possible and impossible movements, contortions and enterprises, and he experimented with a profusion of spatial compositions. He depicts people in free fall through life, but borne up by the artist's humour and empathy. The museum's work has the title *Oversætterne* (The translators) and shows people wildly hunting or fleeing from letters of the alphabet (language), which whirl around the universe **(438)**.

The spherical vases were shown together in 2006 at Holstebro Kunstmuseum.

The next phase of PR's work that is represented in the museum's collection consists of three-dimensional figures that are no longer confined to the surfaces of basic ceramic shapes, but now exist in

437 202/1997

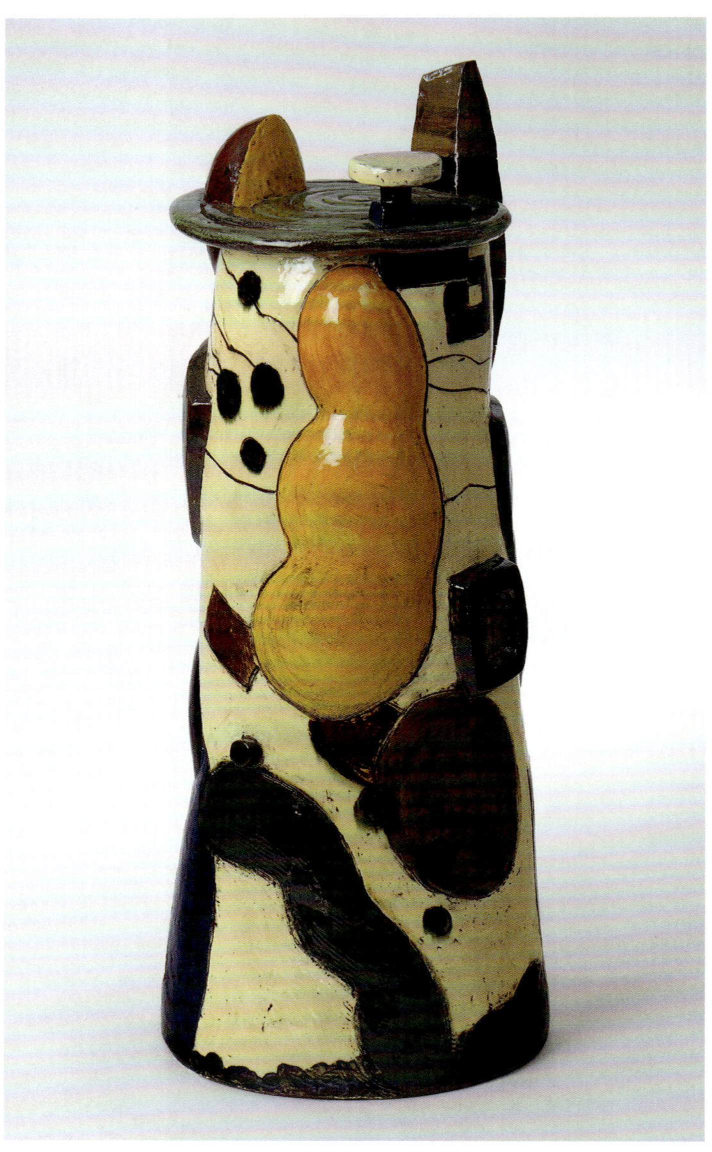

free, open space and narrate stories from the artist's universe. From 2002 there is a self-portrait with the expressive and slightly troubled/humorous title *Panik før lukketid* (Panic before closing time) **(440)**.

In the figure-composition *Ballade på parnasset* (Trouble on Parnassus), from 2006 **(441)**, one finds the artist's caustic opinion of the fight between competing branches of the arts to gain the best place in the Parnassus of the Gods, and the work is at the same time a comment on the public quarrelling around the 'Culture Canon' put forward by the Danish Minister of Culture, published in January 2006.

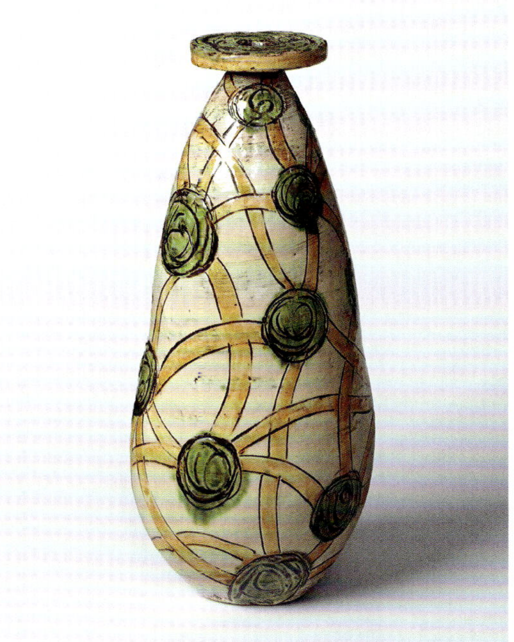

436 6/1994

The latest figure in the museum's collection provides a fine rounding off of the poetic and richly narrative world that PR conjures up through his figures, in this case *Vandringsmanden* (The traveller) from 2010, showing a young man or boy on his way into the woods with his rucksack and his faithful companion, the dog **(442)**. They are moving on top of a base of letters that form the word SKOV (wood), but it is the abstract and sculptural potential of the letters that is in focus. The whole scene emits a sense of harmony and expectation between the two, who have each found their own peg to stand on. The traveller is one of PR's favourite motifs, one with ancestors in Romanticism, but in this figure without undertones of threat and symbolism, only pure pleasure in nature.

All of PR's magical, unruly, lively world full of observations and debate was set out on display in the exhibition '*Det glaserede teater*' (The glazed theatre), in Koldinghus in 2009; this was a retrospective enterprise with both older and newer works, including two pots a metre tall, entitled *Det glaserede teater* and *Skyggeteater*, in earthenware with slip and glaze, black/white, echoing Thorvald Bindesbøll, who was also a ceramic idol for PR.

Works by PR are represented in leading Nordic and European museums and collections, and PR has made an important contribution through many professional assignments and honorary offices, most recently as chairman of the Danish Arts Foundation's Committee on Crafts and Design 2011-13.
See: Dybdal, L., 1997; Rasmussen, P., 2002; Rasmussen, P., 2006.

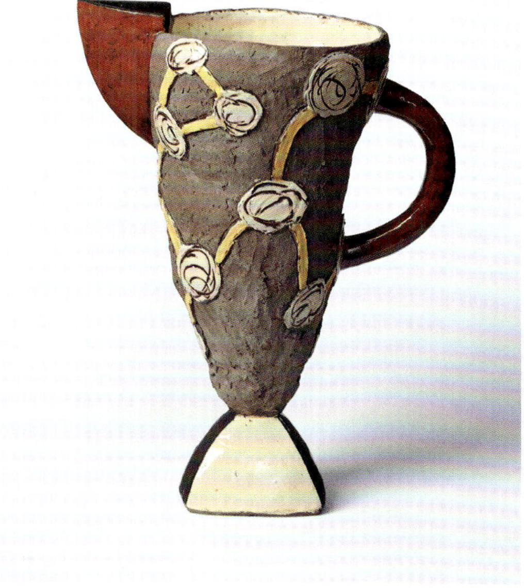

439 419/2008

433. Bowl, 1984

Stoneware, over-glazed; slab-technique, raku-fired at 1020°. H 11.5 x W 21.3. Mark: 'PR 84' painted on base. Mus.no. 29/1985

ACQUISITION: *De danske*, 1985, Kulturhuset, Stockholm. Donation from *Ny Carlsberg Mindelegat*. See: *De danske,* 1984. *Brændpunkter*, 1990. Dybdahl, L., 1997

434. Vase, 1986. *Forår* (Spring)

Stoneware, oxide-glazed; modelled, inlaid decoration, raku-fired at 1020°. H 32 x W 44. Mark: 'PR 86' painted on base. Mus.no. 69/1986. ACQUISITION: Køge Skitsesamling, 1986. Donation from *Kunstindustrimuseets Venner*

435. Dish, 1988

Faience, tin- and over- glazed; modelled, scored, brush-painted, raku-fired at 1020°. H 4 x W 35 x L 27. Mark: 'PR 1988' painted on base. Mus.no. 177/1988

ACQUISITION: Peder Rasmussen. Donation from *Kunstindustrimuseets 50-års Jubilæumslegat*

436. Vase, 1993

Earthenware, lead-glazed; thrown, modelled, slip, sgrafitto, glaze-decorated, fired at 1020°. H 34. Mark: 'PR 93' painted on base. Mus.no. 6/1994

ACQUISITION: *Ler*, Trapholt, 1994

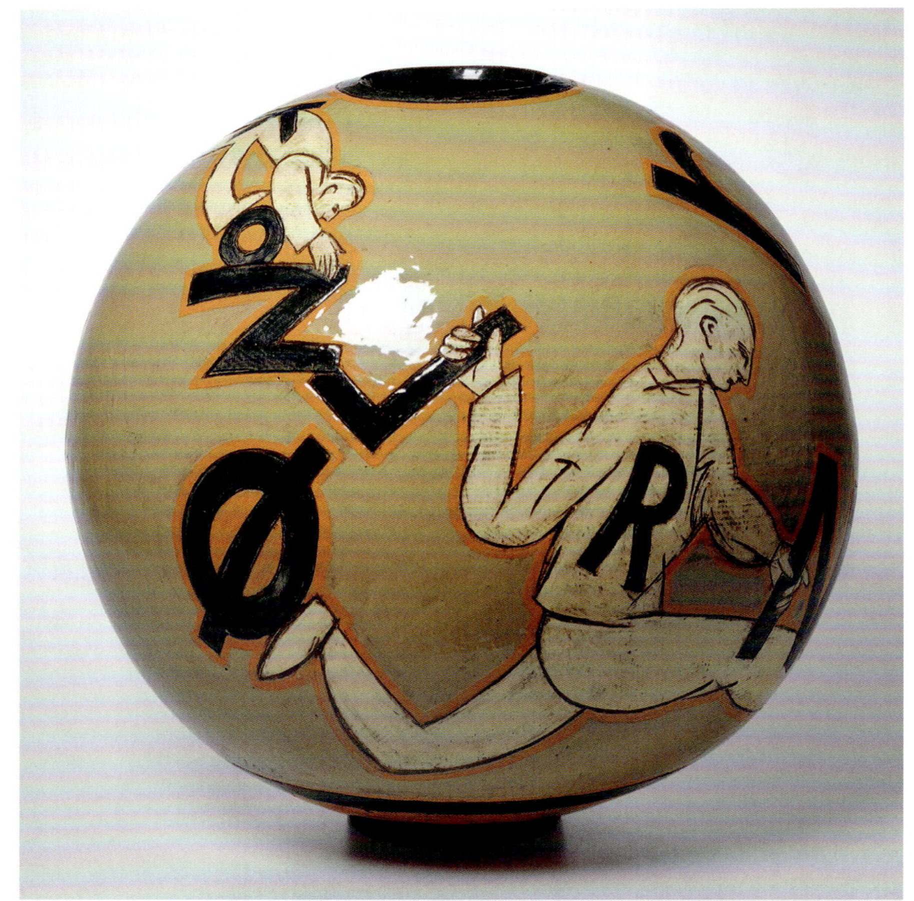

438 84/2006

437. Figure, 1996. ***Figur ved et tilfælde*** (Accidental figure)
Earthenware, lead-glazed; modelled, slip, relief, brush-painted, sgrafitto, fired at 1200°. H 89 x Diam 35. Mark: none. Mus.no. 202/1997
ACQUISITION: *Dansk Keramik 1850-1997*, Sophienholm. Donation from *Poul og Hildur Kongo Pedersens Mindelegat*. See: Dybdahl, L., 1997

438. Spherical vase, 2005. *Oversætterne (The translators)*
Earthenware, lead-glazed; cast, slip, brush-painted, sgrafitto, decorated, fired at 1200°. H 52 x Diam 54. Mark: 'PR 2005' (monogram) on the rim of the base. Mus.no. 84/2006.
ACQUISITION: Donation from *Højesteretssagfører C.L. Davids Legat for Slægt og Venner*

439. Jug, 1994
Earthenware, glazed; modelled, slip, applied and glazed decoration. H 37.2. Mark: 'PR 1994 FEB'. Mus.no. 419/2008
ACQUISITION: Donation from estate of Ambassador Niels Christian Tillisch, Copenhagen

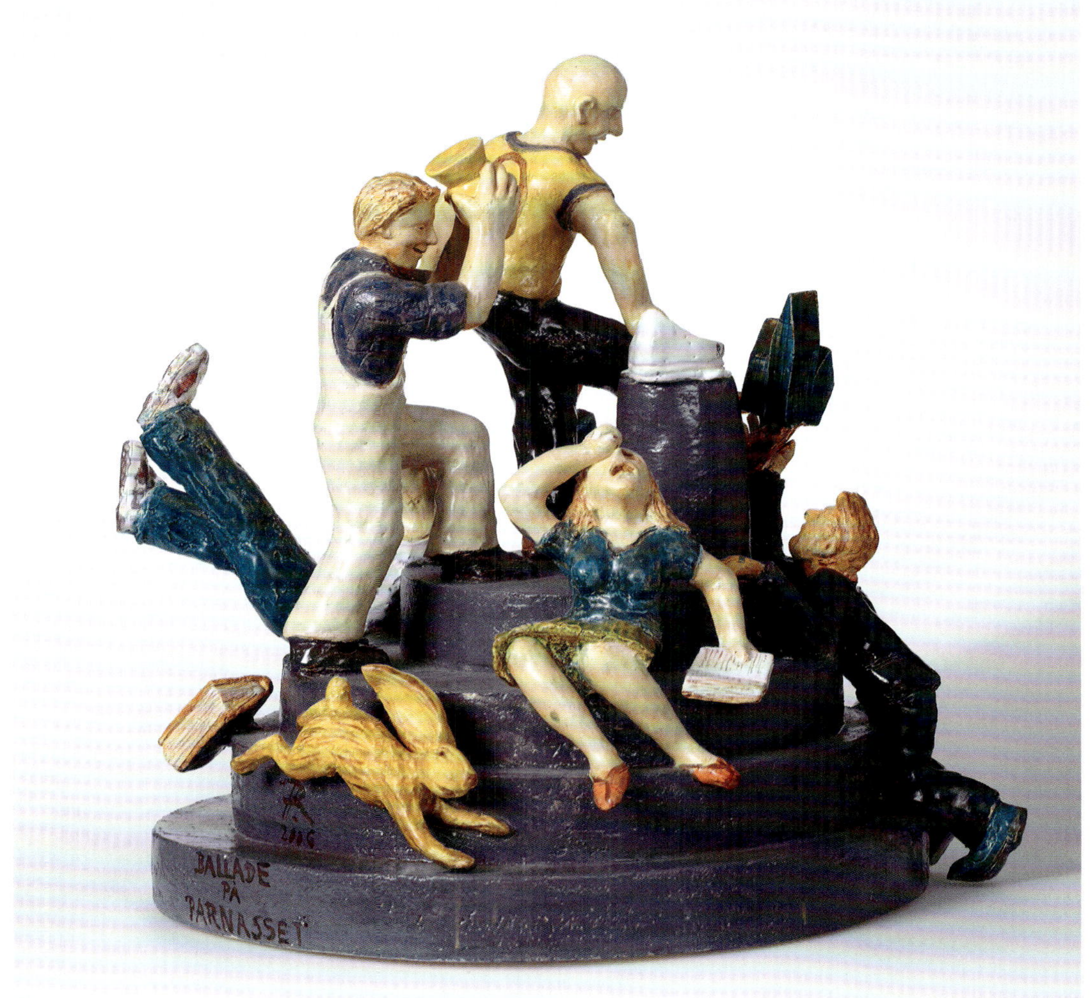

441 120/2010

440. Figure, 2006. *Ballade på parnasset* (Trouble on Parnassus)
Faience, glazed; modelled, brush-painted. H 40 x Diam 37. Mark: 'PR 2006'.
Mus.no. 120/2010
ACQUISITION: Donation from Birgit Petersson, Frederiksberg

441. Self-portrait, 2002. *Panik før lukketid* (Panic before closing time)
Earthenware, glazed; modelled, slip. H 38. Mark: PR 2002' on side. Mus.no. 44/2010. ACQUISITION: *Statens Kunstfond*

442. Figure, 2010. *Vandringsmanden* (The traveller)
Earthenware, glazed, 2 wooden sticks; modelled, slip, brush-painted. H 54.5. Mark: 'PR 10'. Mus.no. 50/2011. ACQUISITION: Donation from *Sølvsmed Kay Bojesen og hustru Erna Bojesens Mindelegat*

442 50/2011

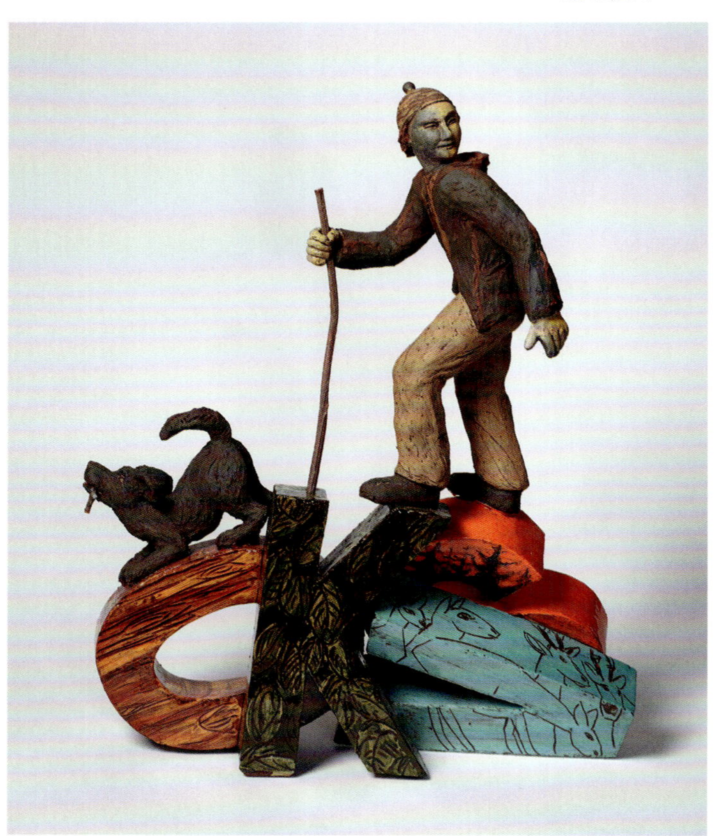

REGIUS, LENE 1940 –

Ceramicist

1958-60	Workshop trainee with Lillemor Clement and Inger Folmer Larsen; Eslau Keramik; Tue Poulsen
1962-65	Kunsthåndværkerskolen
1965-67	Ceramic workshop, Archaeological Research Centre, Lejre, Sealand
1967-	Own studio workshop; 1988- shared with Per Weiss, Lejre www.regius.dk

Lene Regius (LR) has created a strongly personal and ornamental pictorial idiom in her ceramic works, which take inspiration both from past civilisations and from present-day strip cartoon culture. LR studied at Skolen for Brugskunst and has been on study visits to Greece, Indonesia and Japan.

On LR's often large pots in vivid colours there are teeming hordes of symbols, pictures, ornaments, writing, prints, masks, trolls and beings that bear witness to the artist's connection with the modernist breakthrough in art which, in around 1950, led to the creation of the Cobra movement. In 1952 Asger Jorn wrote about his view of the role of the artist: '... I think that the task of the artist is to find a way in to the general human truths, to reach out beyond a local jargon to find a common human language' (translated from '*Ny Dansk Kunsthistorie*', 1995, vol. 8, p. 65). It would seem that this is exactly the task that LR has taken upon herself, and through her distinctive works with their rich pictorial form of expression and ceramic qualities she creates a surplus of energy and experiences that becomes transmitted to the beholder.

LR belonged to the exhibition group *MULTI MUD* (1979-85); the group's purpose was to show the public the new trends in Danish ceramics and the diversity of forms of expression to which clay could lend itself, and to work for reaching a larger public internationally. In addition to LR the members of the group were Karen Bennicke, Heidi and Aage Birck, Gunnar Palander and Peder Rasmussen. In the group's many exhibitions between 1979 and 1985 LR showed works in precoloured porcelain mosaic (Japanese *neriage*) with motifs from travels e.g. to Mediterranean countries. Other works were decorated with the artist's photographs, for instance from Egypt, transferred to the ceramic surface with silk-screen printing technique, while for others a stamped pattern was used.

The museum has one work by LR from 1991, shaped like an oblong shield (hence the work's title, *Masai shield*), with the surface completely covered with scored and painted decoration. It is a distinguished example of how LR integrates elements from her universal fund of images and ornaments into a powerful and fruitful cohesive form of expression **(443)**.

LR has exhibited her work in many contexts and has carried out some ten commissioned ceramic works in Denmark; she is represented in museums in the Nordic countries and in the rest of Europe.

443. Dish-shape, 1991. *Masai-skjold* (Masai shield)
Stoneware, alkali-glazed; modelled, incised, slip, painted using horn, relief, fired at 1200°. H 6.5 x L 74. Mark: 'R. 91' painted on base. Mus.no. 123/1992
ACQUISITION: Lene Regius

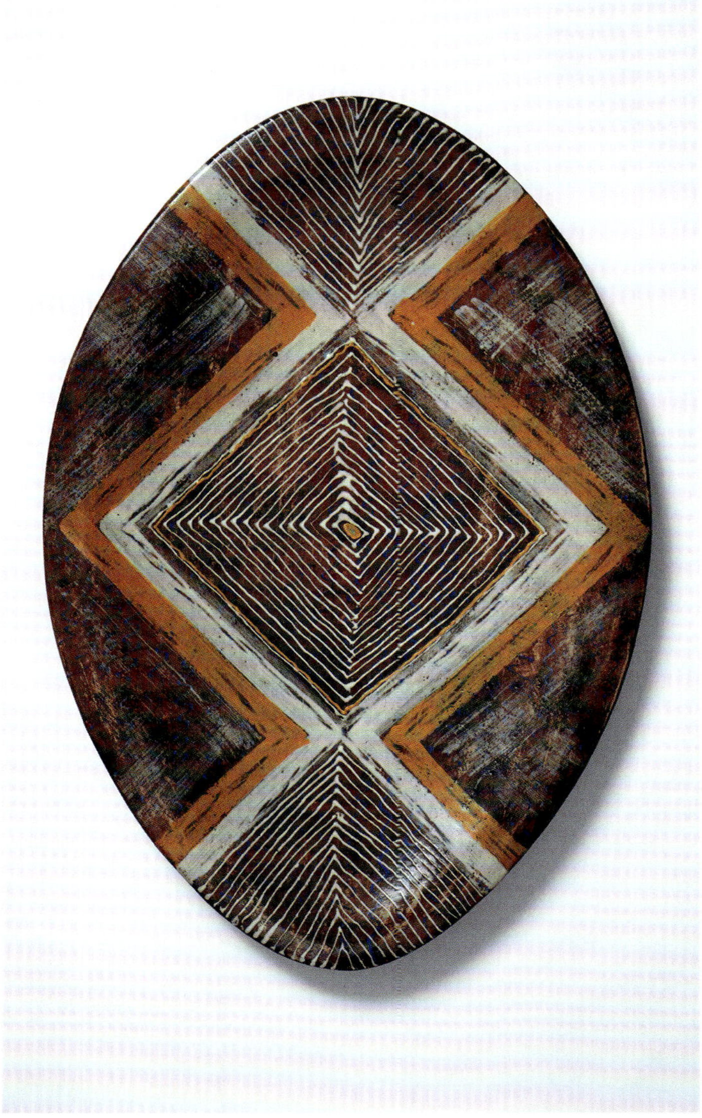

443 123/1992

REIFF, ERIK 1923 – 2006

Ceramicist

1946-47	Kähler Keramik, Næstved; 1948 Alf Magnussen, Norway
1949-50	Sèvres, Paris
1949-57	Bing & Grøndahl, employed as artist
1950-	c.1960 Own studio workshop, Copenhagen
1960	Qualified as a teacher
1963-74	Holbæk Teacher Training College, teacher
1960-85	Own studio workshop, Butterupgård, Holbæk
1975-77	Knabstrup Keramiske Teglværk, artistic manager
1977-84	Attached to the Royal Porcelain Factory, employed from 1979
1992- 2006	Galleri Reiff, Butterupgård

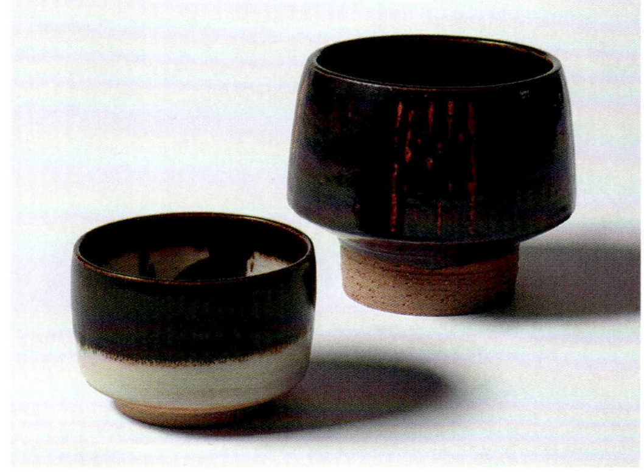

445 12/1960

444 11/1960

Erik Reiff (ER) had many talents; he began as a poet and painter and became a particularly gifted ceramicist, an autodidact but with training experience at e.g. Kähler's in Næstved and Sèvres in Paris. In 1949 he was brought in by Aksel Rode, artistic consultant for Bing & Grøndahl, to the factory's experimental department, where after 3-4 years of improving his skills he had his product series *Den Blå Serie* (the Blue Series), accepted for production. It consisted of tea caddies, vases, pots and bowls in porcelain with under-glaze painting in blue. In the years up to 1957 ER made many hundreds of 'one-off' pieces, and his blue painting in particular became a signature type for him. From an early age he had taken an interest in decoration from the Viking Age and in Persian and Chinese ceramics.

The well-balanced, classical shapes that were typical of ER's work, and of Danish ceramics in the Danish Design period in general, and the refined conjunction between form and stylised leaf and flower patterns in his works, gave them significant prominence in production both at Bing & Grøndahl and later at the Royal Porcelain Factory. Through his work for the factories ER's ceramics were exhibited in the context of international events for the firms and led to several solo exhibitions for ER in the 1960s and 70s, at e.g. Foyles' Art Gallery, London, and Tiffany, N.Y., with sales to e.g. the Victoria and Albert Museum in London and Boymans-van Beuningen in Rotterdam; ER also took

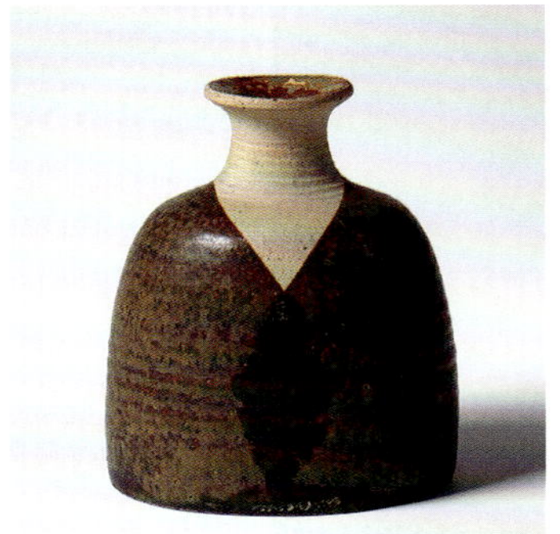

446 15/1972

447 214/1974

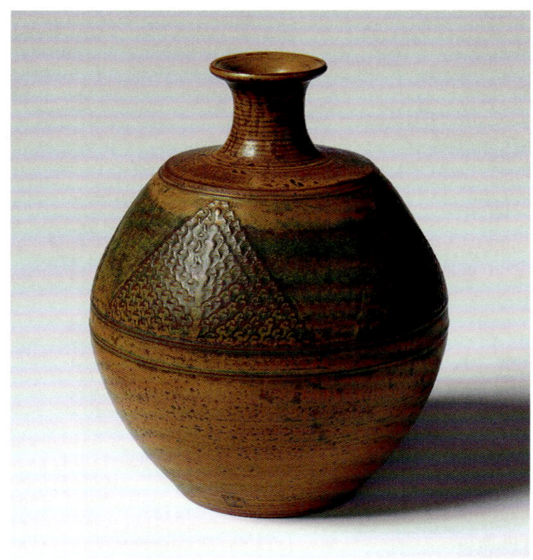

part in numerous group exhibitions in Denmark and elsewhere. Tasked by the Royal Porcelain Factory to work on a new hand-painted service to succeed the '*musselmalede*' or Blue Fluted service, ER wanted to have the individual pieces designed by the ceramicist and designer Niels Refsgaard (born 1934). The result was the '*Noblesse*' service from 1982, with ER's blue-painted stylised leaf and branch motif. In the context of the fusion of the two porcelain factories in 1983/84 the service did not reach the position it had been expected to achieve, and ER chose to leave Royal Copenhagen in 1984 to return to his own workshop at Butterupgård. Serious illness intervened shortly after, however and obstructed ER in his ceramic activities, but he resumed painting and set up Galleri Reiff, from where he sold many hundreds of his own works that he had retrieved from Royal Copenhagen.

The museum has seven works by ER from 1953-84, representing different stages of his ceramics; of them seven were made at his own workshop, while a tall cylindrical pot with brownish under-glaze painting from 1983 is from the Royal Porcelain Factory **(450)**. From 1959 and 1960 there are two smaller stoneware pots, partially glazed and more experimental in shape and glaze **(444-445)**, possibly inspired by a study visit to England at the end of the 1950s, when he met Bernard Leach and thus came into contact with Japanese ceramic culture. Interest in East Asiatic ceramics and calligraphy was something he shared with the skilled ceramicist Anne Marie Harrison, who had a workshop in Holbæk which ER evidently used. The museum has an interesting vase from 1974 which ER indicated was made in Harrison's workshop, and which was acquired by the museum at a joint exhibition that year at Butterupgård. The vase has an incised Celtic ornament and is glazed with Chinese tea-dust glaze **(447)**. Finally mention should be made of two works from 1984-85 made of porcelain in ER's workshop, with blue under-glaze painting providing a chance to appreciate the fine spiral movement of the branch and leaf motif on the body **(448-449)**.

ER completed a large number of ceramic commissions around Denmark, and also published collections of his poems, texts for radio cabarets, etc. (See: Løndahl I.: *Erik Reiff – Skår fra en pottemagers liv*, 1995). See: Dybdahl, L., 1997; Lautrup-Larsen, L., 2007.

448 54/1985 **449** 155/1985

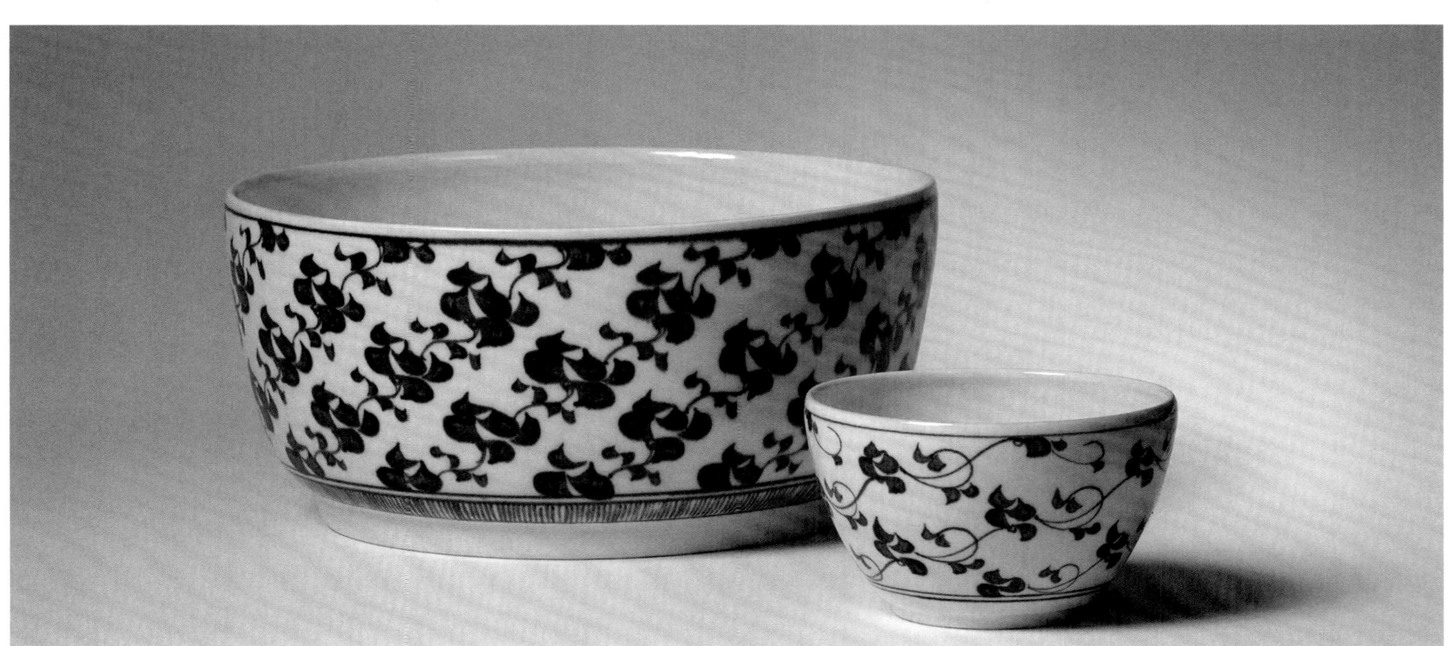

444. Bowl, 1960

Stoneware, partially glazed and unglazed; thrown. H 6 x Diam 9. Mark: 'ER' incised on base with a rectangular stamp. Mus.no. 11/1960

ACQUISITION: Erik Reiff. Donation from *Statens 50-års Jubilæumslegat*

445. Bowl, 1959

Stoneware, partially glazed, unglazed; thrown, decorated with glaze. H 11 x Diam 10.5. Mark: Rectangular stamp with 'ER' on base. Mus.no. 12/1960

ACQUISITION: Erik Reiff. Donation from *Statens 50-års Jubilæumslegat*

446. Jar, 1971

Earthenware, glazed; thrown, decorated with glaze. H 15. Mark: Rectangular stamp with 'ER' on base. Mus.no. 15/1972

ACQUISITION: *Erik Reiff og Bodil Bødtker*, 1972, Landsforeningen dansk Brugskunst og Design. Donation from *Statens 50-års Jubilæumslegat*. See: *Brændpunkter*, 1990

447. Pot, 1974

Stoneware, tea-dust glaze; thrown, incised decoration, glazed. Mark: 'ER' stamped above the foot. H 28.5. Mus.no. 214/1974

ACQUISITION: *Anne Marie Harrison, Erik og Tove Reiff*, 1974, Butterupgård. Donation from *Kunstindustrimuseets 50-års Jubilæumslegat*

448. Bowl, 1985

Porcelain, glazed; thrown, under-glaze painted, glazed. H 13.5 x Diam 28. Mark: 'ER 85 Denmark' painted on base with a rectangular stamp. Mus.no. 154/1985

ACQUISITION: Erik Reiff. Donation from *Statens 50-års Jubilæumslegat*

449. Bowl, 1984

Porcelain, glazed; thrown, under-glaze painted. H 8.5 x Diam 13.2. Mark: 'ER 84' painted on base. Mus.no. 155/1985

ACQUISITION: Erik Reiff. Donation from *Statens 50-års Jubilæumslegat*. See: *Brændpunkter*, 1990

450. Pot, 1983

Stoneware, glazed; thrown, under-glaze painted. H 36 x Diam 21. Mark: 'ER 83' and 3 waves painted on base. Mus.no. 164/1997

ACQUISITION: Galleri Reiff, Butterupgård. Donation from *Ausa Regitze Tillys Legat*

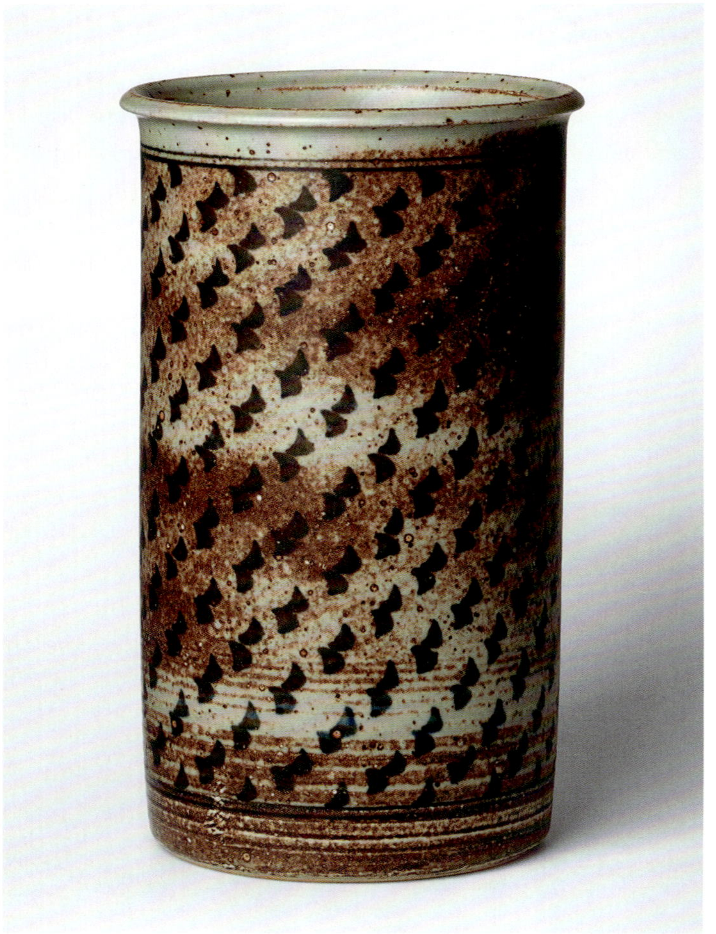

450 164/1997

REUMERT, JANE 1942 – 2016

Ceramicist

1960-64 Kunsthåndværkerskolen

1964- Strandstræde Keramik, workshop and shop shared with Beate Andersen and Gunhild Aaberg, Copenhagen

1972-82 Den Permanente and Eslau Keramik, freelance industrial designer

1986 Skolen for Brugskunst, guest teacher

1993-2003 Workshop, Svaneke

2004- Own studio workshop, Rådvad
www.strandstraedekeramik.dk

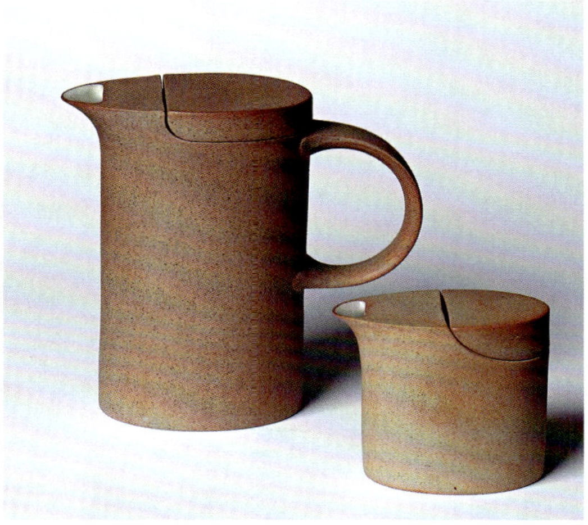

451 24a-b/1975

Jane Reumert (JR) holds a distinguished position in Danish and international ceramics, because of her work, throughout a 50-year career, to develop in terms of materials and artistry, with results that bear witness to her creativity and the high quality of her intellectual input and craft skills. Her search for something simple, something logical and above all something integrated with nature led to a number of peak achievements in a production that logically made way for a process of continual testing-out of methods, techniques and materials, and was sustained by a sensient, recollecting and abstract passion for nature. Through the museum's 12 works by JR this development can be followed, in general categories, from the functional objects and unique stoneware bowls of the 1970s to the transparent shell- and bowl-shapes in porcelain from the 1980s and on to the 1990s and the convincing use, in the following years, of salt-glazed fibre porcelain. Her work with reinforced glass fibre resulted in 1993 in a new type of product, called by the artist *Keramiske metamorfoser* (Ceramic metamorphoses) – gigantic transparent floating bowls of polyester/glass fibre with inlaid collages of paper, textiles, net and writing.

JR studied at Kunsthåndværkerskolen while Richard Kjærgaard was head of department, and she was therefore guided towards stoneware and functional ceramics, teaching of method and creation of design idioms. After completing her studies in 1964, with her class-mates Beate Andersen and Gunhild Aaberg she set up the shared workshop in Strandstræde, Copenhagen, which still exists today, and there JR made several series of functional stoneware products. Jugs had a special place in the work of the early years, when JR found success with a geometric, minimalistic and functional treatment of shape, as can be seen in the museum's example of the tall jug and cream-jug, each with an oval cross-section, flat top and cut-in lid **(451)**. In 1977 *Strandstræde Keramik* held an exhibition in the museum, and it was there that the museum acquired the modelled bowl with the spiral movement and zircon glaze sprayed on in varying thicknesses **(452)**.

Among the motifs from nature that JR worked with is the dragonfly,

452 30/1977

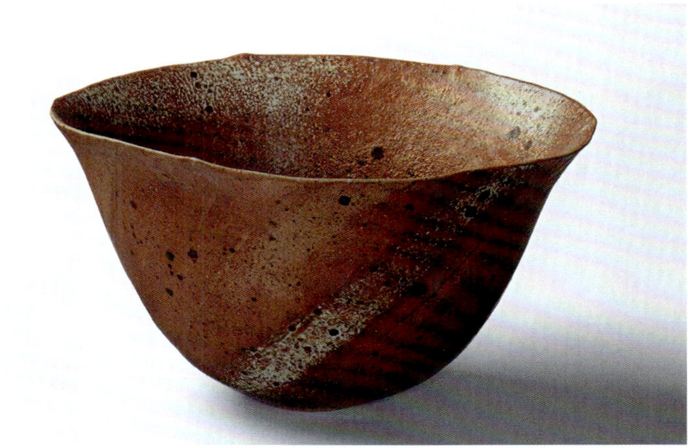

which is also to be found in works by e.g. Gertrud and Myre Vasegaard. In JR's work it appears on a porcelain bowl from 1973 (see: *Transparens*, 2003, p. 47) and on a stoneware bowl from 1980 in the museum, on which the insects are incised and impressed into the wet clay (138/1999). From 1984 there is a robust oval pot decorated with Native American inspired ornamentation, made of coarse stoneware with diverse means of decoration **(453)**.

The many years spent researching into materials and consciously seeking artistic solutions opened the way to the works which will always be synonymous with JR: the eggshell-thin floating 'shells' in which the fusion of form and decoration seems to arise from nature itself.

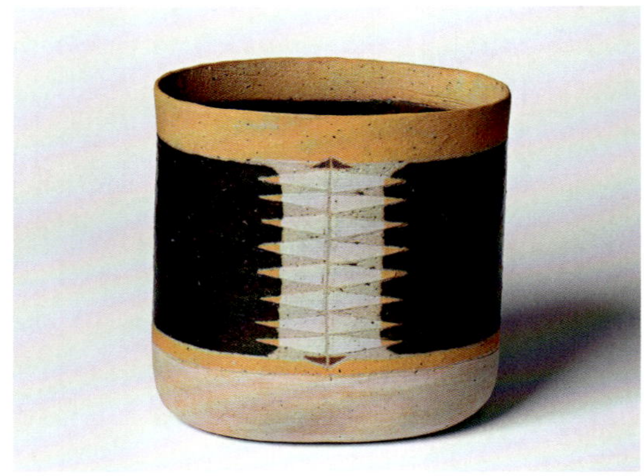

453 28/1985

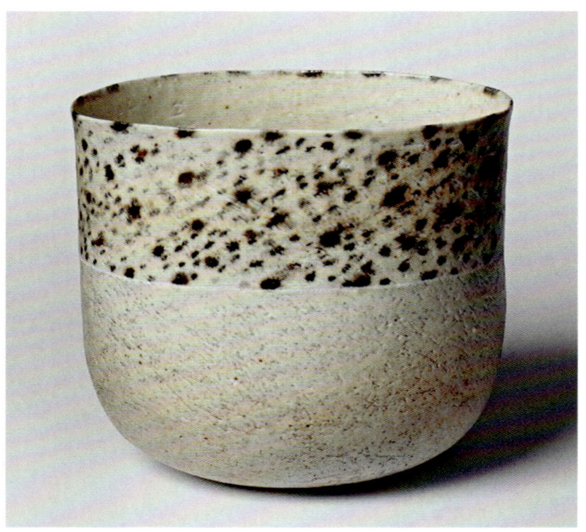

456 4/1995

Production of the shells, based on modelling on a mould, was carried out by JR in a large quantity throughout the 1990s, with different forms of decoration taken from the animal and plant kingdoms, from water and sea and beach; they are represented in the museum's collection **(454)**.

In JR's search for lightness and transparency the glass fibre technique suddenly came into the picture; here were the qualities she had been looking for – malleability, transparency and structure, with potential

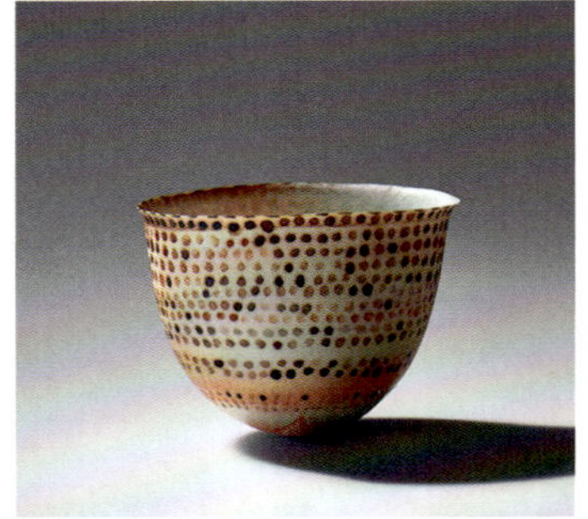

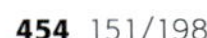

454 151/1989

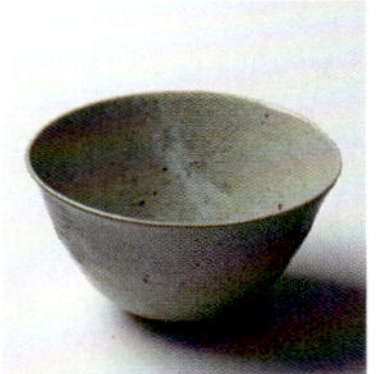

459 138/1999

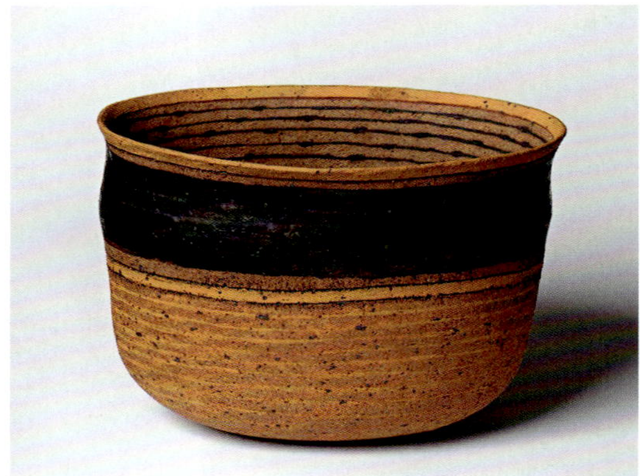

455 14/1990

for casting into the material collages of paper, net, textiles, colours and calligraphy, after which the material could be shaped over individual clay vessels. The first works entitled Keramiske *Metamorfoser* were presented at an exhibition in Nikolaj Church, Copenhagen, in 1993, and displayed a graphic strength in JR's decoration to which the titles in themselves bore witness: *Arabic Music, Writing, Bayeux, Visby* and

Typographic Paraphrase. The museum did not manage to acquire any of these works on that occasion, but when JR decided, in spite of the demanding process, to create 3 new metamorphoses in connection with the exhibition '*Keramiske Veje*' in 2009, the museum was able to secure for the collection the work entitled *Xian*, decorated with calligraphy, which was a field JR had studied and practised through a number of years **(462)**.

From the mid 1990s a new epoch began in JR's work when use of the salt kiln in connection with glazing and firing of fibre-porcelain opened the way for new developments resulting in ultra-thin transparent nature-inspired works, carried out in her own technique with

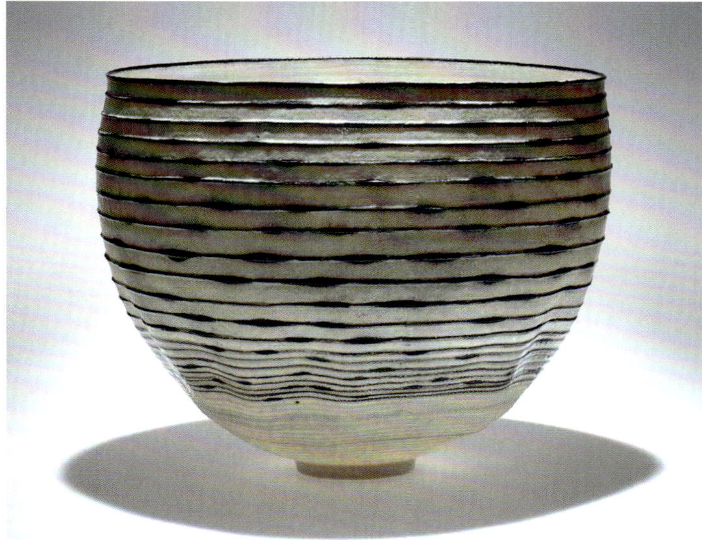

457 92/1997

assistance from the ceramicists Anne and Peter Stougaard, Bornholm. In the museum's collection there are three glass fibre porcelain works from the 1990s, very different in structure, surface treatment and decoration; the titles are indicative of the motifs, e.g. *Seashell* **(457)**, *Large nest* **(460)**, and a third work which has a complex jagged structure, entitled *Feather galaxy* **(458)**.

In 1994 JR was the first winner of the prestigious prize for craftwork and design entitled '*Torsten och Wanja Söderbergs Nordiska Designpris*', and in that context the museum acquired a fine oval hand-constructed porcelain pot with feather drawing **(456)**. The most recent work in the collection is from 2005 and has the title *Flamme* (Flame); it was fired suspended in the wood-fired soda kiln at the International Ceramic Research Center in Skælskør, and is a dramatic work that looks as if it would have been doomed to go up in flames if the fire had not been stopped at the very last minute **(461)**. The work can be seen as a metaphor for JR's courage in going to the outer edge in testing out ceramic material.

JR was a member of the exhibition group *Keramiske Veje*, and exhibited in Denmark and abroad in leading museums and institutions where her work is represented; she also received innumerable prizes and bursaries throughout her career. In 2003 she was awarded the Art Academy's Thorvald Bindesbøll medal.

See: *Transparency. Jane Reumert, Studio Ceramist*. Ed. Kim Dirckinck-Holmfeld, The Danish Architectural Press, Copenhagen 2003

461 203/2006

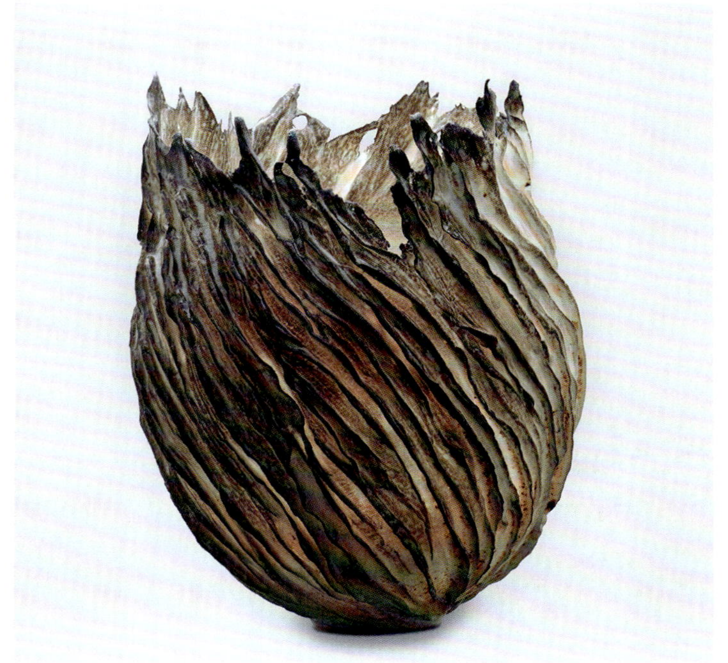

451. Jug and cream-jug, 1975. ***Høj kande med hank og flødekande***
(Tall jug with handle and cream-jug)
Stoneware, iron oxide, zircon-glazed, partially unglazed; cast, interior spray-glazed, fired at 1300°. a: H 17.6; b: H 9. Mark: 'Jane 75' inscribed on base. Mus.no. 24a-b/1975
ACQUISITION: Jane Reumert. Donation from *Kunstindustrimuseets Venner*

452. Bowl, 1977. ***Skål med spiral bevægelse***
(Bowl with spiral movement)
Stoneware, zircon-glazed; shaped over a mould, modelled, fired at 1300°. H 14.5 x Diam 26. Mark: 'Jane 77' inscribed on base. Mus.no. 30/1977
ACQUISITION: *Strandstræde Keramik*, 1977, Kunstindustrimuseet.
See: Dybdahl, L., 1997. *Brændpunkter*, 1990. *Transparens,* 2003. *Strandstræde keramik,* 2004

453. Pot, 1984
Stoneware, glazed; modelled, decorated, slip, sprayed, brush-painted, fired at 1300°. H 15.5 x Diam 13.5. Mark: 'Jane 84' on base. Mus.no. 28/1985
See: *De danske*, 1984

460 118/2000

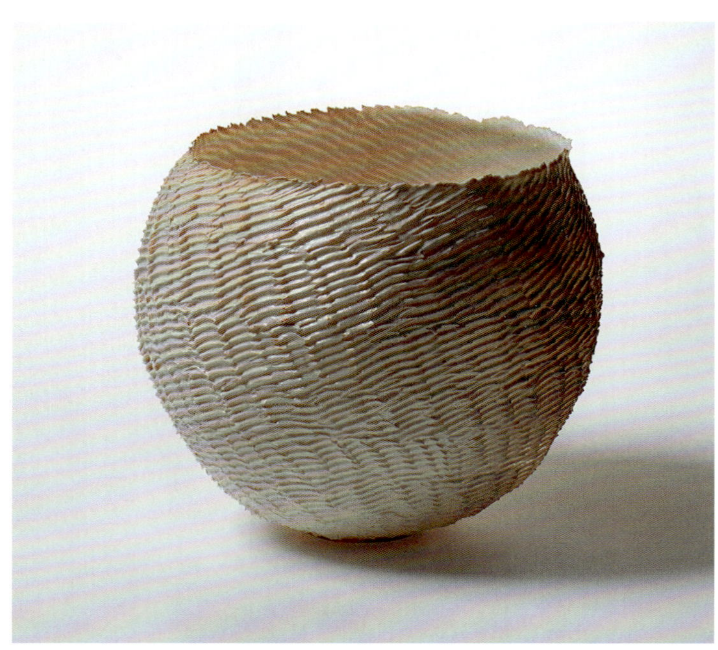

454. Bowl, 1989. ***Skal med prikker*** (Shell with dots)
Porcelain, zircon-glazed; own technique, brush-painted, fired at 1300°. H 10.5 x Diam 8. Mark: 'Jane 89'. Mus.no. 151/1989. ACQUISITION: *Keramiske Veje,* 1989. Donation from *Kunstindustrimuseets Venner*

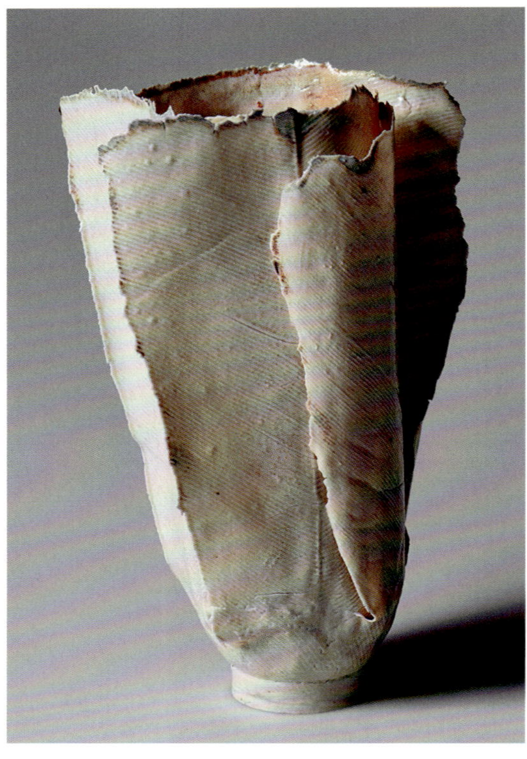

458 93/1997

455. Bowl, 1987
Stoneware, mortar clay, iron-oxide glazed, partially unglazed; modelled, porcelain slip, brush-painted. H 14 x W 17.5. Mark: none. Mus.no. 14/1990
ACQUISITION: Strandstræde Keramik. Donation from *Ny Carlsberg Museumslegat*. See: *Brændpunkter*, 1990

456. Pot, 1992. ***Krukke med fjertegning*** (Pot with feather drawing)
Porcelain, zircon-glazed; modelled, brush-painted, sprayed, fired at 1300°. H 20.7 x W 20. Mark: 'JANE 92' inscribed on base. Mus.no. 4/1995
ACQUISITION: *Torsten och Wanja Söderbergs Nordiska Designpris*, 1994, Röhsska Konstslöjdmuseet. Donation from *Helge Jacobsens Mindelegat.*
See: *Transparens*, 2003

457. Bowl, 1997. *Havskål* (Sea bowl)
Porcelain, fibre glass, salt-glazed, black oxide; own technique, brush-painted, fired suspended in a salt kiln at 1300°. H 27.5 x Diam 30. Mark: 'JANE 97' inscribed on base. Mus.no. 92/1997
ACQUISITION: Galleri Nørby, Copenhagen. Donation from *Kunstindustri-museets Venner*. See: *Transparens*, 2003

458. Jagged shape, 1996. *Fjergalakse* (Feather galaxy)
Porcelain, fibre glass, salt-glazed, iron sulphate, kaolin; thrown, modelled, brush-painted, sprayed, fired suspended in a salt kiln at 1300°.
H 22.5 x Diam 15.5. Mark: 'Jane 96' inscribed on base. Mus.no. 93/1997
ACQUISITION: Galleri Nørby, 1997, Copenhagen. Donation from *Kunstindustri-museets Venner*. See: *Transparens*, 2003

459. Bowl, 1980. *Skål med guldsmede* (Bowl with dragon-fly)
Porcelain, feldspar-glazed, iron oxide; thrown, decorated, porcelain slip, scored and printed motif, fired at 1300°. H 11.6 x Diam 20. Mark: 'JANE 80' inscribed on base. Mus.no. 138/1999
ACQUISITION: Donation from Bank Director C.B. Andersen, Copenhagen

460. Pot, 2000. *Stor rede* (Large nest)
Porcelain, fibre glass, salt-glazed, gold leaf; own technique, fired suspended in a salt kiln at 1300°. H 24 x Diam 20. Mark: 'JANE 2000' inscribed on base. Mus.no. 118/2000
ACQUISITION: Galleri Nørby, Copenhagen. Donation from *Kunstindustri-museets Venner*

461. Pot, 2005. *Flamme* (Flame)
Porcelain, fibre glass, shino-glazed; own technique, slip, fired suspended in a wood-fired soda kiln at 1300°. H 28.5. Mark: 'JANE 05' inscribed on base. Mus.no. 203/2006. ACQUISITION: Galleri Nørby, 2006, Copenhagen

462. Fibre bowl, 2009. *Keramisk metamorfose – Xian Street*
(Ceramic metamorphosis -Xian Street)
Fibre glass, polyester; calligraphy. H 34 x Diam 78. Mus.no. 88/2010
ACQUISITION: *Keramiske Veje*, 2009

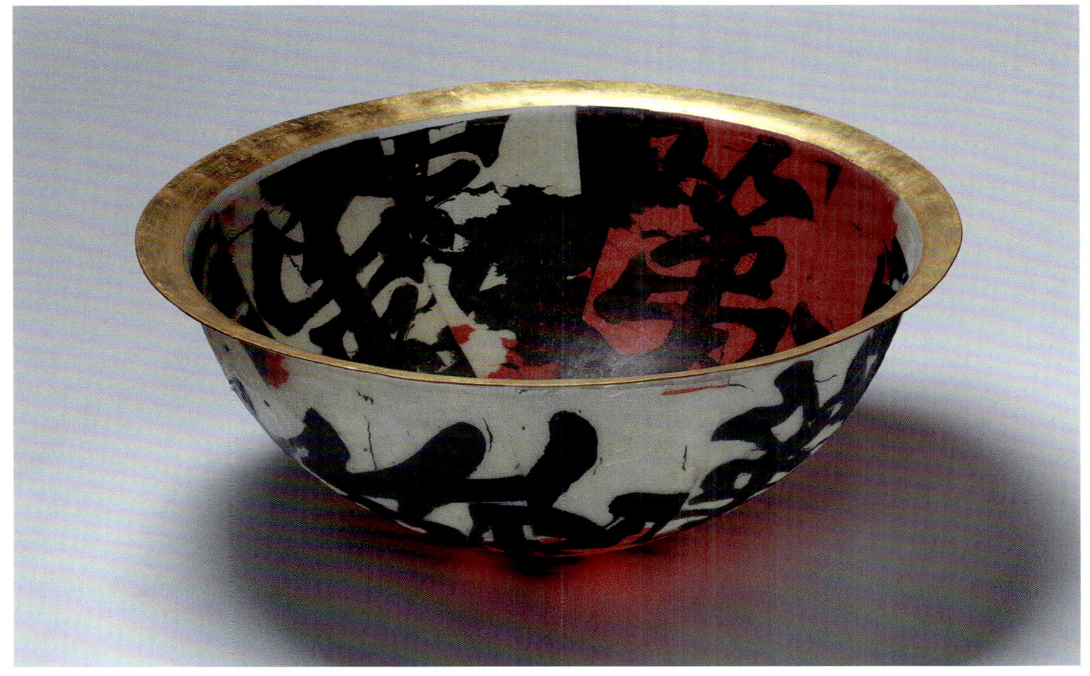

462 88/2010

ROKKJÆR, INGER 1934 – 2008

Ceramicist

1965-70	Det Jyske Kunstakademi
1971-	Own studio workshop, Hadsten, Jutland
1982-86	Det Jyske Kunstakademi, Ceramics teacher
2000	Shigaraki Cultural Ceramic Park, Japan, artist-in-residence

Inger Rokkjær (IR) began taking courses in Ceramics at a relatively late stage, but achieved a distinguished career both nationally and perhaps particularly internationally, as a celebrated artist in her field, which was raku ceramics. With a departure point in her own home, a former garden centre near Aarhus, she dug up clay from her own garden and treated it in a variety of ways, creating out of it an uncommonly perfected *oeuvre* based on a few strong shapes, often starting with cylinders, using a special wealth of colours.

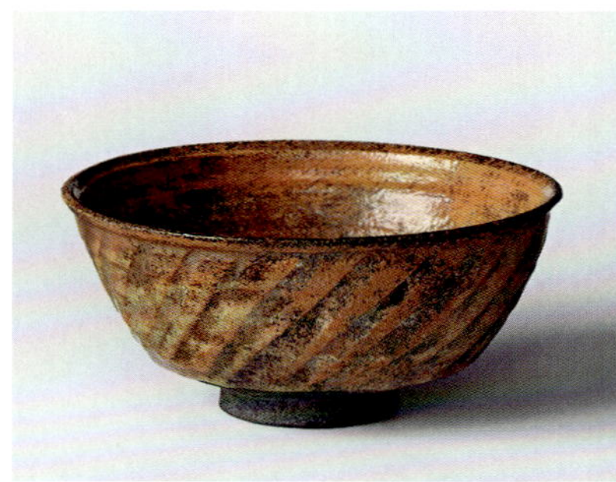

463 48/1981

Her works were appreciated, not least in the homeland of raku, Japan; she went there on several journeys and study visits, particularly in the 1990s, acquiring skills and a contact network, and she held several exhibitions around the country. Her work is represented in important Japanese collections and museums. IR shared her knowledge about raku in her role as leader of several seminars on the subject, including one in Oxford, England, and as a teacher from 1982 to 86 at Det Jyske Kunstakademi in Aarhus, where she herself had studied when Gutte Eriksen was head of the Ceramics department.

As a raku ceramicist IR developed her own method, which allowed her to achieve in her works a radiant calm and harmony – a balance

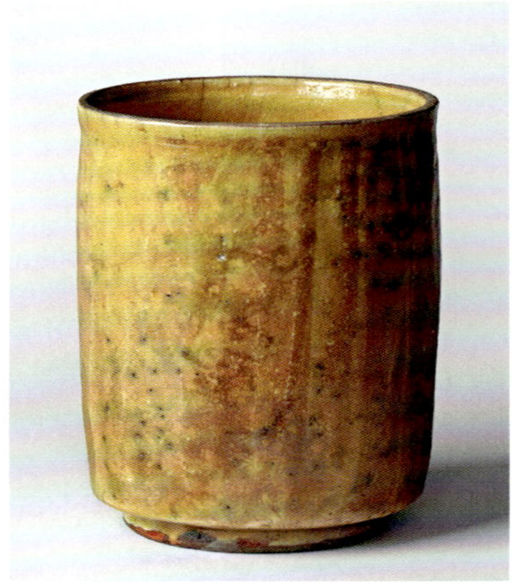

464 256/1990

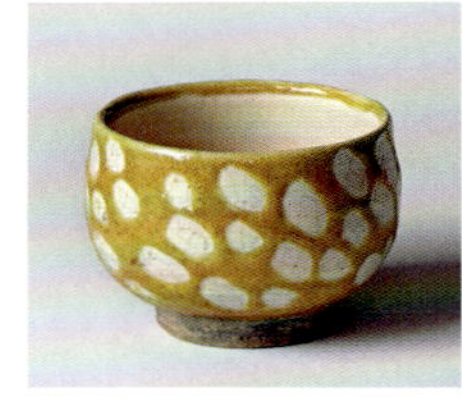

470 96/2010

between refined Japanese tradition and essentially Danish qualities, as described by an English authority on ceramics, David Whiting, in the catalogue '*Lågkrukker*', published for an exhibition in Galleri Nørby in 2004, on the occasion of IR's 70th birthday:

> *'These objects are inherently Danish. Earthenware is a traditional Jutland body still widely employed, and her pots are confidently Scandinavian in their economy. They have that particular understatement long associated with Danish functionalism.'*

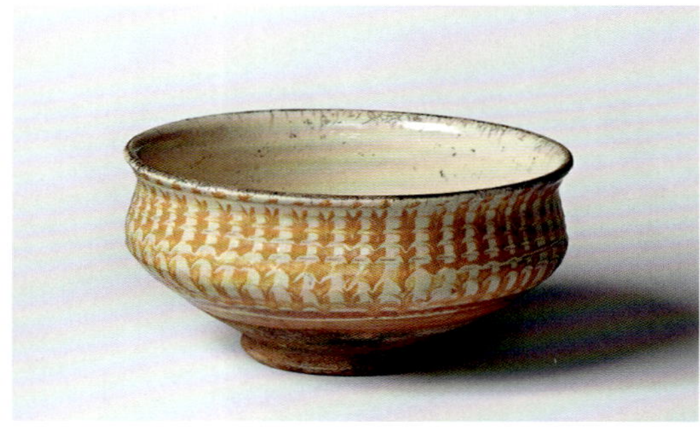

465 257/1990

Within the relatively few characteristic forms that IR used, she created a wealth of variations because of the luminous warm nuances of her glazes, in interplay with the structures of the surfaces with their diagonal hatching and relief effects. In combination with the controlled crackle effects of the glaze and the marks from firing this provides the very special 'karma' of these works.

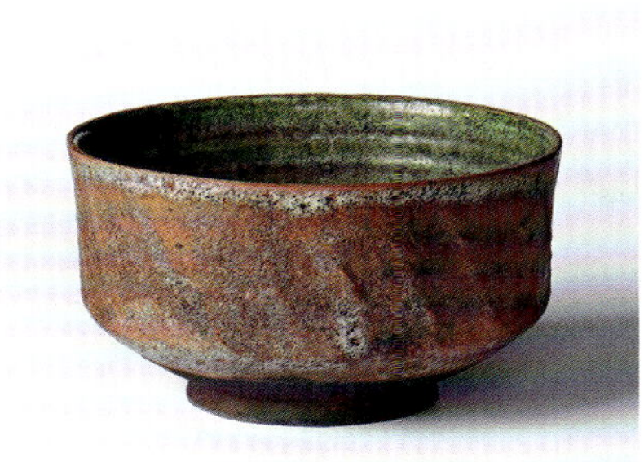

466 258/1990

463. Bowl, c.1980

Earthenware, transparent borax glaze; thrown, ochre slip, hatching, raku, fired at 980°. H 8.5 x Diam 16. Mark: 'IR' in a circle stamped on base. Mus.no. 48/1981

ACQUISITION: *'Væv og raku – væveren Dorthe Sigsgaard og keramikerne Anne Lise Bruun Petersen og Inger Rokkjær'*, 1981. Donation from *Statens 50-års Jubilæumslegat*. See: Dybdahl, L., 1997. *Brændpunkter*, 1990

In the museum's collection there are eight works by IR; the earliest of them is a bowl from 1980, acquired at the exhibition '*Væv og Raku*' (Weaving and Raku) held in 1981 in the museum **(463)**. IR provided a detail about this work in a letter to the museum in 1982: it was fired in clear frosty weather and cooled off in snow.

The museum acquired four works directly from the ceramicist, two of them from the 1980s and two from the 90s. The earliest is a bowl from 1984 which IR called a 'farmer's bowl', and which in fact has roots in popular ceramics both in form and in feathered decoration **(465)**. From 1990 there is a cylindrical vase with a warm yellow glaze, and such mellow yellow glaze colours are among IR's most characteristic works **(464)**. Among these four acquisitions there are none of the very fine lidded pots for which IR is rightly admired, but in 2008 the museum received as a donation a fine cylindrical bright red lidded pot with a pyramid-shaped lid and a relatively rare stamped decoration **(468)**.

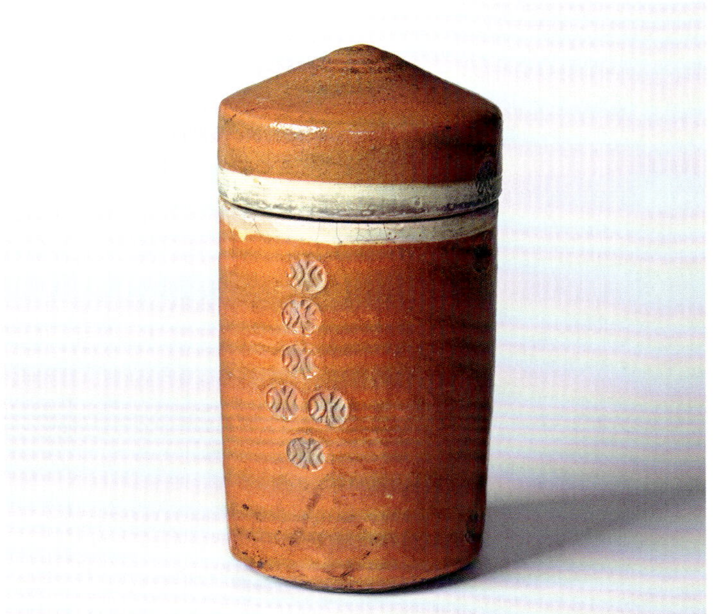

468 421/2008

467 259/1990

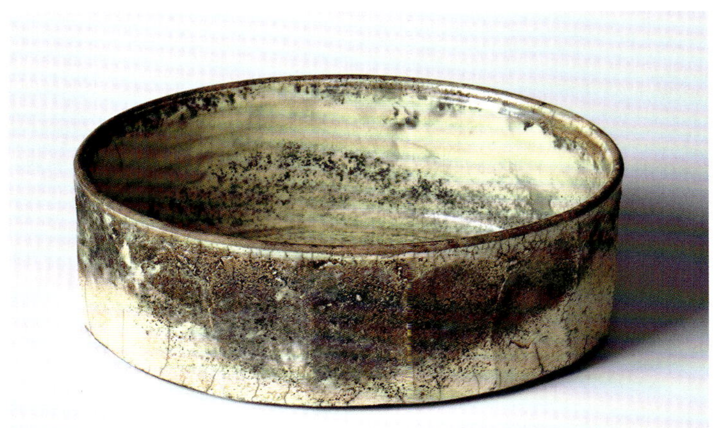

464. Vase, 1990.

Earthenware, transparent lead glaze; thrown, white slip, raku, fired at 980°. H 19.7 x Diam 13.8. Mark: 'IR' stamped in circle on base.

Mus.no. 256/1990

ACQUISITION: Inger Rokkjær. Donation from *Kunstindustrimuseets Venner*. See: Dybdahl, L., 1997

465. Bowl, 1984

Earthenware, transparent borax glaze; thrown, white and yellow slip, feather decorated, raku, fired at 980°. H 10.5 x Diam 19. Mark: none. Mus.no. 257/1990.

ACQUISITION: Inger Rokkjær. Donation from *Kunstindustrimuseets Venner*

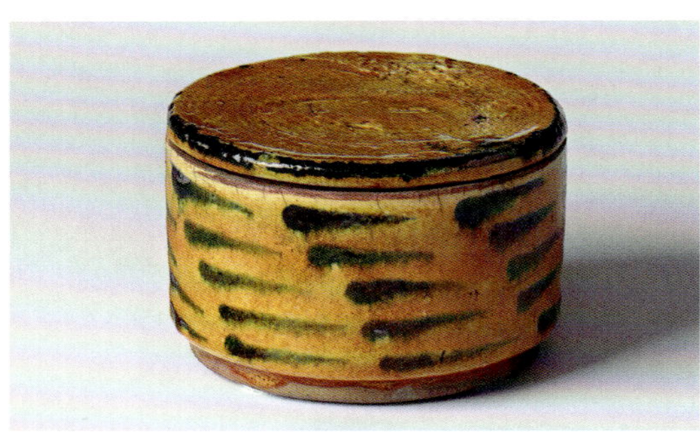

469 422/2008

466. Bowl, 1987

Earthenware, clear- and borax- glazed; thrown, white slip, carved relief, raku, fired at 980°. H 9.6 x Diam 15.5. Mark: 'IR' in circle stamped on base. Mus.no. 258/1990.
ACQUISITION: Inger Rokkjær. Donation from *Kunstindustrimuseets Venner*

467. Oval bowl, 1990

Earthenware, transparent-, lead- and frit- glazed; thrown, modelled, slip, faceted, raku, fired at 980°. H 8 x Diam 23. Mark: 'IR' in circle stamped on side. Mus.no. 259/1990
ACQUISITION: Inger Rokkjær. Donation from *Kunstindustrimuseets Venner*

468. Lidded pot, 1990s

Earthenware, glazed, partially unglazed; thrown, modelled, slip, stamped decoration, raku, fired at 980°. H 23.5 x Diam 12. Mark: 'IR' in circle stamped on base. Mus.no. 421/2008. ACQUISITION: Donation from estate of Ambassador Niels Christian Tillisch, Copenhagen, 2008

469. Lidded pot, 1990s

Earthenware, glazed, partially unglazed; thrown, shaped, slip, brush-painted, raku, fired at 980°. H 8 x Diam 12. Mark: 'IR' stamped on base. Mus.no. 422/2008. ACQUISITION: Donation from estate of Ambassador Niels Christian Tillisch, Copenhagen, 2008

470. Bowl, date unknown

Earthenware, glazed; thrown, shaped, slip, raku, fired at 980°. H 8 x Diam 10. Mark: 'IR' stamped on foot. Mus.no. 96/2010
ACQUISITION: Donation from Adam Grandjean, Copenhagen

RUHWALD, ANDERS 1974 –

Ceramicist

1997-2000	Glas og Keramikskolen, Bornholm
2003-2005	Royal College of Art, London, MA
2006-	Lecturer and instructor at universities and colleges in the USA and Europe
2006	Nova Scotia College of Art and Design, Canada, associate professor
2007	University of Colorado, Boulder, USA, instructor
2007-08	School of the Art Institute of Chicago, USA, associate professor
2008-	Cranbrook Academy of Art, USA, artist-in-residence, Head of the Ceramics Department
	www.ruhwald.net

With meteoric speed Anders Ruhwald (AR) has risen within 10 years to join the international elite of ceramic artists, as a result of the originality of his work and an extensive series of interesting exhibitions which are developing more and more into large multi-core installations/interventions either in his self-created surroundings or in existing interiors and buildings. Since 2008 AR has been attached to Cranbrook Academy of Art, Detroit, but he is also still active in Denmark.

AR studied ceramics on Bornholm, at the Glass and Ceramics School which is now part of the Art Academy's Design School. He then took an MA at the Royal College of Art, London, but by then he had already made himself a reputation in Denmark and won first prize at the Danish Biennale for Craft and Design 2002. The prize brought with it an invitation to exhibit in the museum, and that event took place in 2004 with the exhibition '*Tingenes tilstand/The State of Things*', in which AR displayed 14 works, most of them in organic forms made of earthenware, completely covered in glazes in synthetic colours. Seen in retrospect this exhibition prefigured a number of the themes that have characterised AR's later directions, and gave the Danish public the opportunity to experience for the first time on a large scale a new ceramic world, far from the familiar tradition.

Characteristically, the works in the exhibition were displayed without showcases or podiums, directly on the museum's floor or leaning in window niches, evoking an indefinable faint sense of connection with known things in the home – and yet not. To most of the visitors it became evident that they themselves had a role to play in this installation; it was not just a matter of finding out what the artist had intended to convey with the objects, but rather a question of absorbing them associatively into one's own environment and narratives, and reflecting on the world of things with which we surround ourselves. The museum acquired the work *Prototype rød* at this exhibition **(471)**.

AR describes himself as a ceramicist, and he expresses himself through clay, but he includes other materials as well in his works – e.g. wood, steel and glass. His works are sensuous, close to the materials and the techniques, with the ceramic works often carrying the impression of the hand's shaping of the clay, while others have perfectly smooth surfaces. The works remain fixed in an indefinable space between sculpture and design, at one and the same time simple in their shapes and colours and yet complicated and demanding of the observer; this is what makes them fascinating and significant in the present-day context. Strongly effective installations from recent years have found their way to diverse museums: for instance *You in between*, 2008, was acquired in its entirety by Nationalmuseet for Kunst, Arkitektur og Design, Oslo, and *Anders Ruhwald at Saarinen House*, 2013, is to be found at Cranbrook Art Museum; the permanent installation *Unit 1, 3583 Dubois St.*, is in Detroit, where AR has created a new base for dialogue with the surrounding world. AR's internet site provides detailed documentation of his exhibitions, publications and other achievements.

471. Object, 2004. *Prototype rød* (Prototype red**)**
Earthenware, frit- and lead- glazed, plexiglass; cast, modelled, pre-fired at 1000°, fired at 1085°. W 70. Mark: none. Mus.no. 364/2004
ACQUISITION: *Tingenes tilstand,* 2004, Kunstindustrimuseet. Donation from *Kunstindustrimuseets Venner*

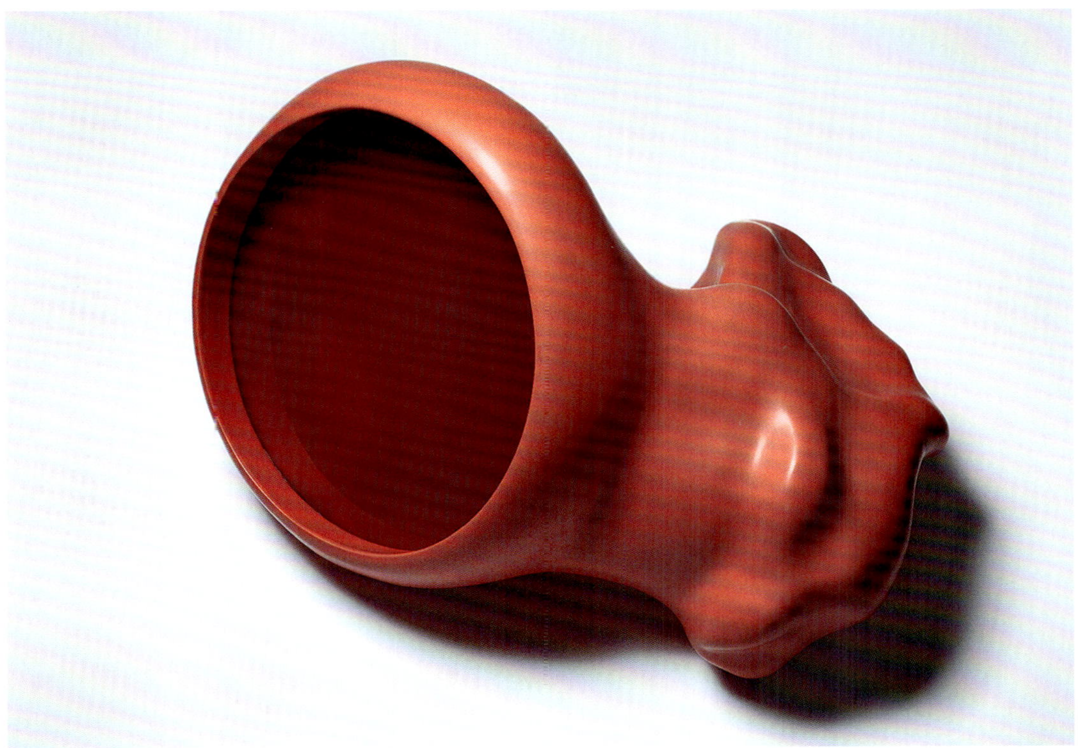

471 364/2004

RYTTER, VIBEKE 1967 –

Ceramicist, architect

1985-86	Glyptotekets Tegneskole
1986-90	Danmarks Designskole, Ceramics and Glass
1990-97	Own studio workshop, Lejre
1997-04	The Royal Danish Academy of Fine Arts, School of Architecture
2001-02	The Royal Danish Academy of Fine Arts, School of Sculpture
2006-	Own studio workshop, Copenhagen
2011-	Research project at the Art Academy's Architecture School and Technological Institute
	www.vibekerytter.dk

Vibeke Rytter (VR) has a broad educational background as both a ceramicist and architect, supplemented with a short study period in the Sculpture School of the Royal Academy of Fine Arts. On this basis VR has developed an artistic working method that arises from research into materials, media, space and architecture, all in constant interplay with ceramic material.

472 111/1995

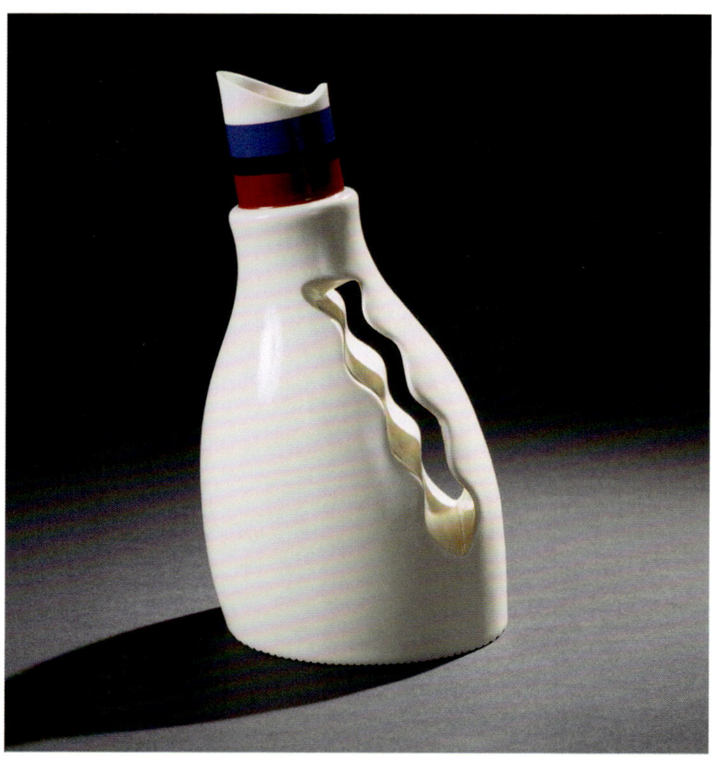

VR took part in exhibitions in the 1990s that marked the breakthrough of a new generation of Danish ceramicists – including '*Keramikkens Underskov*' in Copenhagen and Aarhus in 1993, where she exhibited expressionist earthenware works. In 1996/97 VR participated in the group exhibition '*Dyret i Leret*' at Marienlyst Slot, Elsinore and Vejen Kunstmuseum, with a modelled, naturalistic and politically focused work on animal welfare, made in porcelain and glazed with earthenware glazes.

From 1994 there is a work by VR entitled *Universalkande* (Universal jug) **(472)**, which the museum acquired in 1995 at the exhibition '*Dansk Design Aktuelt*' at Sophienholm. This cast functional jug, with its handle incorporated into the body, is far removed from the works mentioned above, and demonstrates VR's ability as a fine designer.

In 2014 and again in 2015 VR exhibited in Ann Linnemann Galleri, Copenhagen, showing works that explore the cross-field between space and object and using photographic printing on ceramic clay plaques in tableaux/stage-settings. These works take inspiration *inter alia* from images from the artist's study travels over many years. VR has been awarded a number of grants from e.g. *Nationalbankens Jubilæumsfond* in support of her research activities.

472. Jug, 1994. *Universalkande* (Universal jug)
Porcelain, feldspar-glazed; cast, thrown in a plaster mould, transfer, fired at 1240°. H 24.5 x Diam 13.5. Mark: none. Mus.no. 111/1995
ACQUISITION: Vibeke Rytter. Donation from *Bernhard Hirschsprungs Legat.*
See: *Den keramiske Kande*, Marienlyst Slot, 1994; *Dansk Design Aktuelt,* 1995

SCHMIDT, VIBEKE FONNESBERG 1967 –

Ceramicist

1988	Yoh Tanimoto, Japan, studies in Ceramics
1989-1994	Danmarks Designskole, Ceramic Conceptual Art
1993	Glasgow School of Art, Department of Ceramics
1994-97	Cooperative workshop with Jeanette List Amstrup, Hanne Bertelsen, Karen Salicath, Copenhagen
1997	Founded 'Fusion', cooperative workshop with Morten Løbner Espersen, Jeanette List Amstrup, Flemming Tvede Hansen
2002-2003	Hochschule Niederrhein, Krefeld, Germany
2011-	Own studio workshop, Hellerup www.vibekefonnesbergschmidt.dk

Vibeke Fonnesberg Schmidt (VFS) has a refined talent for materials and design, which she applies both in her ceramic works and in the types of work she has developed in recent years, involving wall-lighting, tables and product design in materials such as wood and plastic. In connection with the exhibition '*Dansk Keramik 1850-1997*' at Sophienholm in 1997, VFS was invited to take part with a new work which was acquired by the museum. The title of the work, Dobbelt *med trapez* (Double with trapezium) is an apt description of this work, which consists of two parts; the smaller part is trapezium-shaped and can be fitted into the large circular bowl with slightly sloping sides **(473)**. This work, in white porcelain slip, is thus assembled from basic geometric shapes, like other solutions found by VFS, who often starts with geometric constructions (deconstructions) and compositions which she manipulates and shapes so that contrasts and variations emerge. This method was demonstrated at an exhibition in 1999 in 'Udstillingssted for Ny Keramik', where VFS exhibited large cylinder-shaped pots cast in white porcelain with shiny and transparent glazes and finished using diverse techniques.

Variations in form and perception are also an element in other projects where VFS works with spatial compositions, e.g. open ellipses of porcelain or yellow semi-circular ceramic elements that if mounted on a wall-surface can create 'sunflowers'.

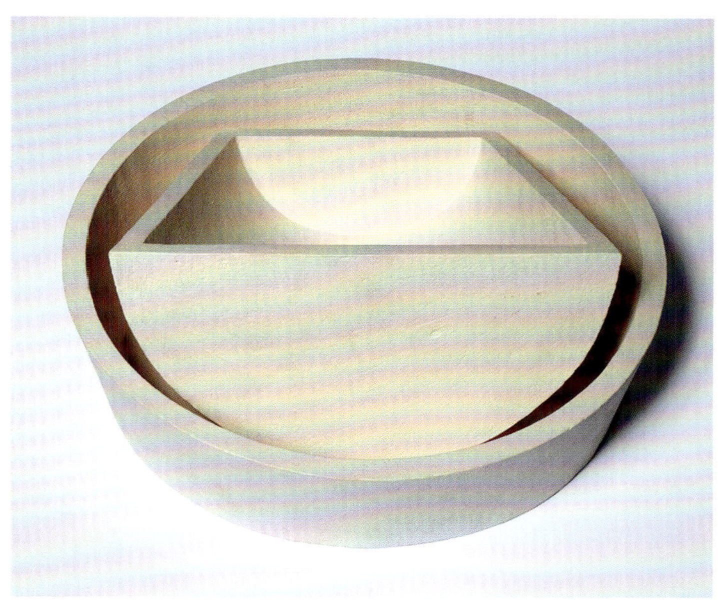

473 201a-b/1997

VFS has exhibited on an on-going basis in Denmark and elsewhere in Europe and has taken part in several of the Biennales for Danish Crafts and Design. She has been awarded prizes and grants and is represented in Danish museums and private collections.

473. Sculpture, 1997. ***Dobbelt med trapez*** (Double with trapezium)
Stoneware, unglazed; modelled, porcelain slip, fired at 1280°. H 22 x Diam 49.
Mark: Monogram inscribed on base. Mus.no. 201a-b/1997
ACQUISITION: *Dansk Keramik 1850-1997*, 1997, Sopienholm.
See: Dybdahl, L., 1997

SIESBYE, ALEV 1938 –

Ceramicist

1956-58	Art Academy, Istanbul, Sculpture; Füreya's ceramic workshop, Istanbul
1958-60	Ceramic factories in Höhr-Grenzhausen, Germany, production
1960-62	Eczacibasi ceramic factory, Istanbul
1963-68	Attached to the Royal Porcelain Factory as an artist
1969-87	Own studio workshop, Copenhagen
1975-90	Rosenthal, Selb, Bavaria, freelance designer
1984-	Royal Copenhagen, freelance designer
1987-	Own studio workshop, Paris

Alev Siesbye (AS) was born in Turkey, and studied sculpture and ceramics in Istanbul, but came to Denmark in 1962, attracted by Danish design ideals; in 1969 she set up her own studio workshop in Copenhagen, working there for almost 20 years before she moved it to Paris in 1987.

The many years during which AS lived and had her workshop in Copenhagen have resulted in her having a clear sense of attachment to Denmark, and this is recognised both from the Danish side and internationally; she is thus seen as having an important position in Danish ceramics from her breakthrough in the early 1970s onwards. Through the years AS has taken part in a number of Danish and international presentations of Danish/Nordic design. This is also the background for the three solo exhibitions of her work that have been held in the museum: the initial one in 1975, the comprehensive presentation in 1983, and most recently the major retrospective exhibition in 2002 – '*Alev Ebüzziya Siesbye – et keramisk univers 1964-2002*', looking back at

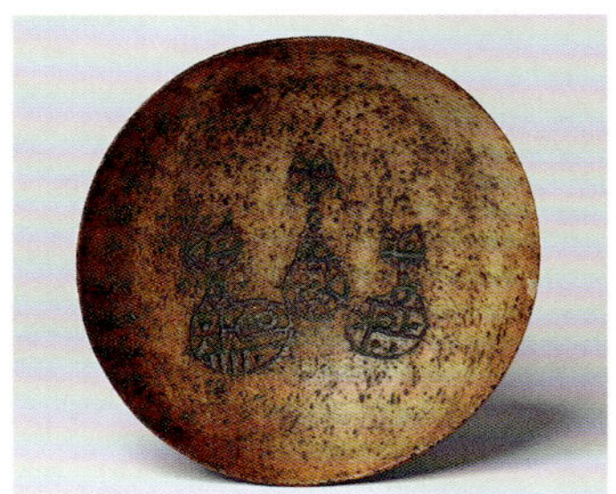

483 203/1994

the artist's ceramic career over almost 40 years. This exhibition was subsequently shown in Istanbul in the Turkish-Islamic Arts Museum. Through many years of conscious goal-directed efforts to achieve what one might call the ideal form, AS has created her personal and inter-

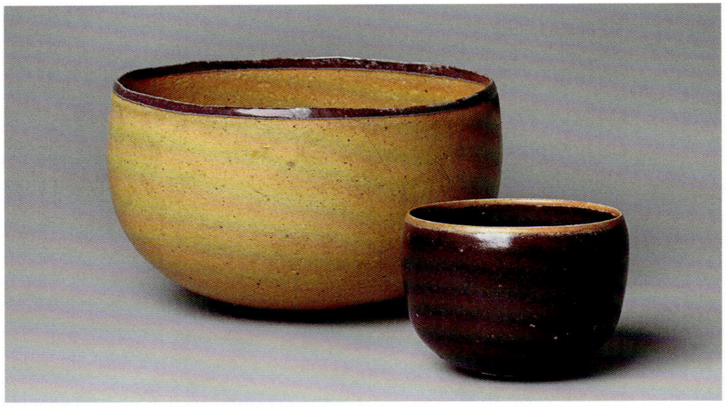

474 31/1973 **475** 32/1973

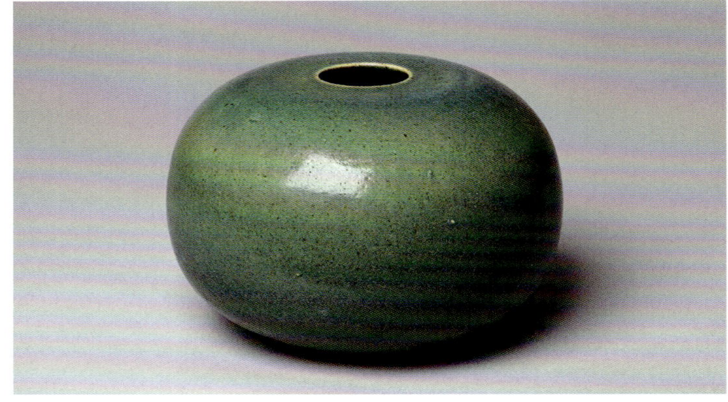

476 33/1973

nationally renowned archetypal work, the 'floating' vessel – bowls and pots that give an impression of weightlessness and have deservedly won a place in the art history of ceramics in the 20th century. The 'floating' expression was adopted for the artist's works at an early stage and the effect is achieved by minimising the area of the foot of the object and retracting it under the usually gently curved corpus. AS studied early sculpture at the Art Academy in Istanbul, and her fine mastery of form and equilibrium are distinguishing characteristics

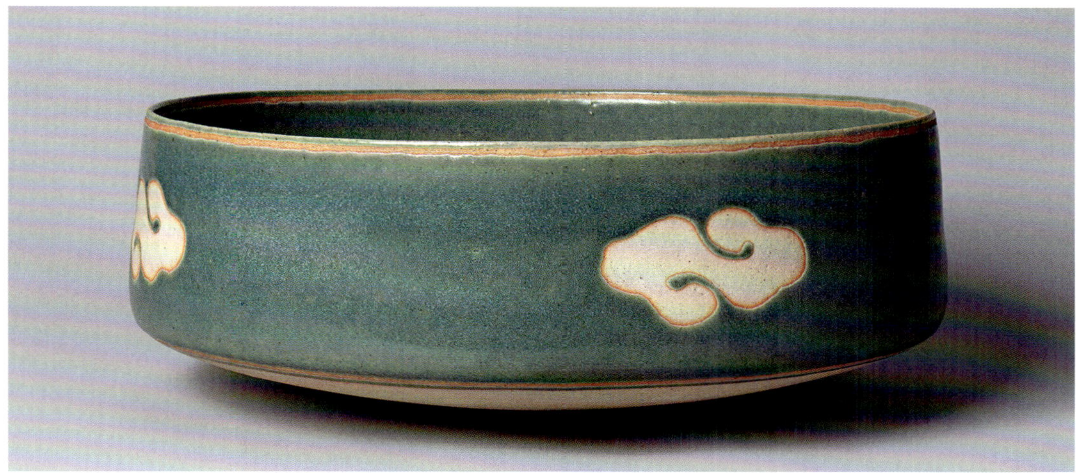

477 21/1975

of her works. Glazes make up a special chapter of their own in this artist's work, and it has been said that along with a few others she brought colour back into creative European stoneware in around 1970, possibly as a reaction to the strength of influence – on Danish studio ceramics as well – that emanated from the charismatic Bernard Leach through his 'Potter's Book', from 1940, with its colour range of mostly grey, tenmoku brown and blue glazes.

The museum's collection of works by AS consists of 17 acquisitions, spanning the period 1972-2001. The earliest is a little bowl, pressed out of a ball of clay and decorated with three little figures, made by AS in 1962/63 after she came to Denmark, while she was employed for a short time at Kähler's in Næstved, before she began working for the Royal Porcelain Factory (203/1994). From the museum's collection one can in fact gain an impression of the remarkable work with glazes that is characteristic of the whole *oeuvre*, from the early shiny warm red and greenish glazes that lie like a close-fitting layer on top of the clay **(474-477)** to the matte pastel-coloured ones from the early 1980s, which sink in and become one with the body **(478,481,484,490)**. There is a monumental beautifully shaped work from 1982-83 with a douce grey-blue matte glaze and masked-off striped decoration which was deposited in the museum by Statens Kunstfond in 1985 **(489)**.
In 2002 AS caused surprise by presenting examples of a novel shiny black glaze used on a series of large 'double bowls'(bowls within bowls), a form AS had previously worked with at the Royal Porcelain Factory. The museum acquired one of these new works, and it was included in the retrospective exhibition in 2002; it is the most recent work by AS in the collection **(488)**.

Throughout her whole career AS has also created works with ornamentation, and two frequently-used motifs are represented in the museum's collection. One of them, used from an early date, is the 'cloud' ornament **(477,486)**, and the other is the 'zigzag' pattern, which has preoccupied AS intermittently through her working years and is here seen on a fine bowl from 1979 **(485)**. From recent years there are several new works on which AS has developed a form of decoration with a white geometric pattern on a black background, and several pieces of this type were included in a large-scale solo exhibition in 2015 in connection with the opening of the Erimtan Museum of Art and Archaeology in Ankara. AS's work was there displayed together

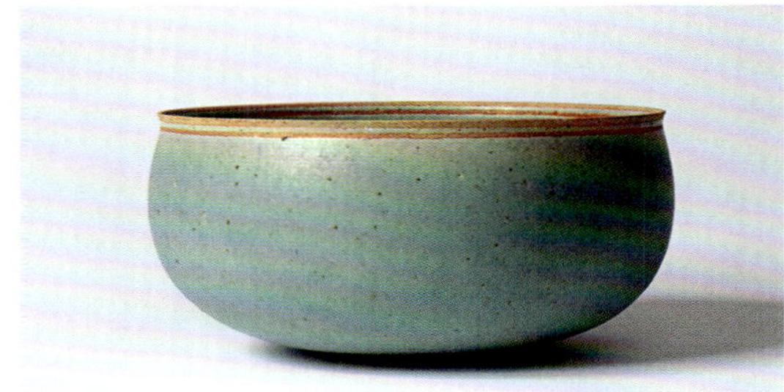

478 11/1981

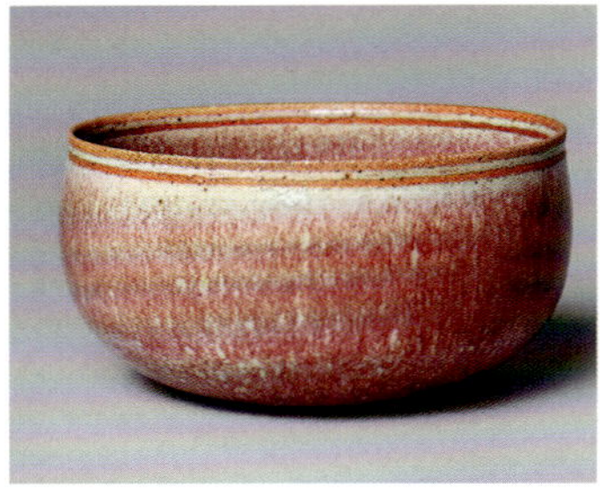

479 41/1981

482 52a-d/1993

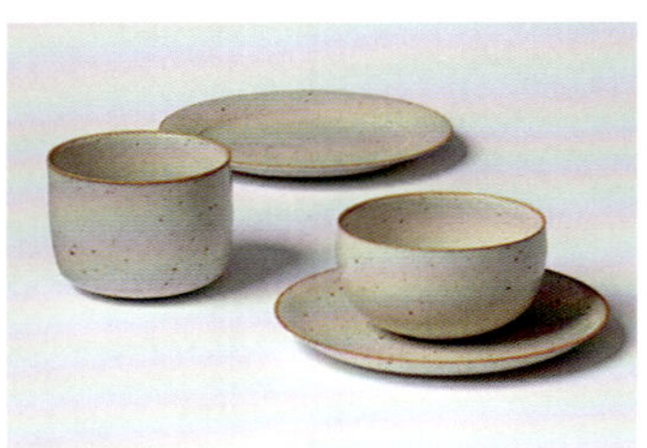

with masterpieces from Anatolia's prehistoric ceramic culture, and an impressive accompanying publication highlights a specific perspective on AS's works, stating that they 'fill the space with timeless stillness'. AS herself has remarked on the importance of memories for her work. Through the years AS has achieved international star status as a ceramic artist, and her prestigious solo exhibitions bear witness to this, as does the fact that she is represented in museums and private collections around the world, as well as the many distinctions and prizes she has received for her unique *oeuvre*, which is unparalleled in embracing inspiration and heritage from the rich cultures of the Near East at the same time as incorporating references to the Danish ceramic tradition.

See: *Alev Ebüzziya Siesbye-et keramisk univers 1964-2002*, Kunstindustrimuseet, 2002; Lautrup-Larsen, L, 2007; *Alev Ebüzziya Siesbye*, Istanbul, 2016, ISBN 978-605-86784-3-9.

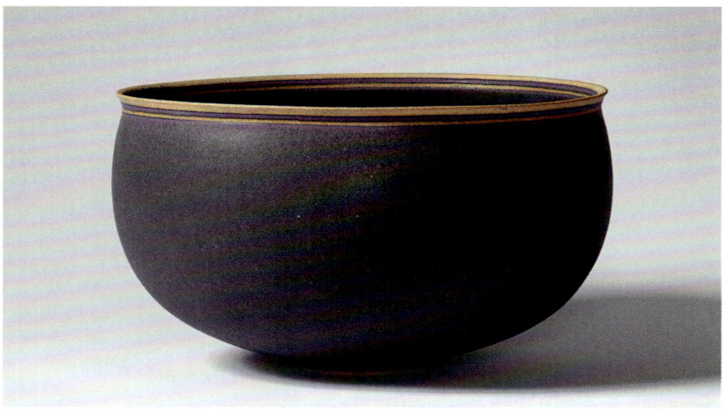

474. Bowl, 1972

Stoneware, talcum-glazed; modelled, fired at 1280°. H 15 x Diam 24.4. Mark: 'alev 1972' painted on base. Mus.no. 31/1973

ACQUISITION: *Alev Siesbye*, 1973, Lerchenborg Slot. Donation from *Kunstindustrimuseets 50-års Jubilæumslegat*. See: Dybdahl, L., 1997

475. Bowl, 1972-73

Stoneware, permatite-, and feldspar- glazed; modelled, fired at 1280°. H 9.1 x Diam 11.5. Mark: 'alev' painted on base. Mus.no. 32/1973.

ACQUISITION: *Alev Siesbye*, 1973, Lerchenborg Slot. Donation from *Kunstindustrimuseets 50-års Jubilæumslegat*

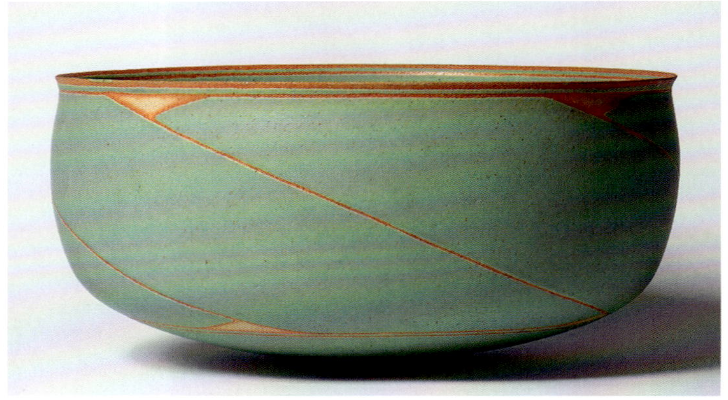

481 1/1988

476. Pot, 1972-73

Stoneware, permatite- and feldspar- glazed; modelled, sprayed, fired at 1280°. H 14.9 x Diam 22. Mark: 'alev' painted on base. Mus.no. 33/1973

ACQUISITION: *Alev Siesbye*, 1973, Lerchenborg Slot. Donation from *Kunstindustrimuseets 50-års Jubilæumslegat*

477. Basin, 1975

Stoneware, permatite and talcum- glazed, partially unglazed; modelled, masked-off cloud ornament, sprayed. H 16.6 x Diam 43.5. Mark: 'AS 75' painted on base. Mus.no. 21/1975

ACQUISITION: *Tekstil og Stoneware – Kim Naver og Alev Siesbye*, 1975, Kunstindustrimuseet. Donation from *Overretssagfører Odin Kaysers Legat*

480 53/1983

478. Bowl, 1981

Stoneware, glazed; modelled, sprayed. H 12.7 x Diam 23.2.
Mark: 'alev '81' inscribed on base. Mus.no. 11/1981
ACQUISITION: Alev Siesbye. Donation from *Benny Dessaus Mindelegat*

479. Bowl, 1979

Stoneware, permatite-glazed; modelled, sprayed. H 9 x Diam 16.6.
Mark: 'alev '79' inscribed on base. Mus.no. 41/1981
ACQUISITION: Alev Siesbye. *Statens 50-års Jubilæumslegat*

480. Basin, 1982-83

Stoneware, feldspar-glazed; modelled, sprayed, fired at 1280°. H 21 x Diam 36.5. Mark: 'S Alev 83' inscribed on base. Mus.no. 53/1983.
ACQUISITION: Alev Siesbye. Donation from *Overretssagfører Odin Kaysers Legat*

481. Basin, 1987

Stoneware, barium-glazed; modelled, masked-off decoration, fired at 1280°. H 18.5 x Diam 38.5. Mark: 'alev 87' inscribed on base. Mus.no. 1/1988
ACQUISITION: Artists' group *Grønningen*. Donation from *Nationalbankens Jubilæumsfond*. See: *Brændpunkter*, 1990. Dybdahl, L., 1997

482. Cup and saucer, mug with side-plate, 1976

Stoneware, iron stains, crackle-glazed; thrown. 4 trial pieces for the Royal Porcelain Factory. Diam 16 (a: side-plate), Diam 15 (b: saucer), H 7.7 x Diam 8.5 (c: coffee cup), H 6 x Diam 9 (d: tea cup). Mark: 'Alev 76'. Mus.no. 52a-d/1993

483. Bowl, 1963

Stoneware, glazed; modelled, sprayed, decorated, fired at 1280°. Diam 17.
Mark: 'Alev' inscribed on base. Mus.no. 203/1994
ACQUISITION: Donation from Herman J. Kähler, Næstved

484. Bowl, 1989

Stoneware, tin-glazed; modelled, sprayed. H 10 x Diam 17.5. Mark: 'Alev 89' inscribed on base. Mus.no. 132/1999
ACQUISITION: Donation from Bank Director C.B. Andersen, Copenhagen

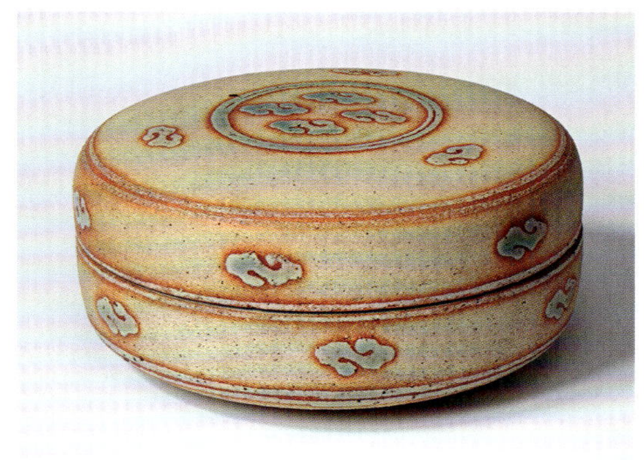

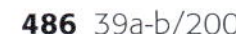

486 39a-b/2002

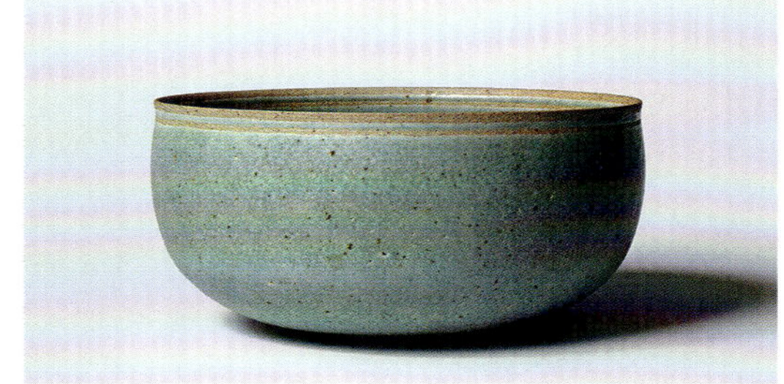

484 132/1999

485. Bowl, 1979

Stoneware, permatite-glazed; thrown, masked-off zigzag decoration, sprayed, fired at 1280°. H 10 x Diam 20. Mark: 'Alev '79' inscribed on base. Mus.no. 38/2002. ACQUISITION: Donation from *Statens Kunstfond*

485 38/2002

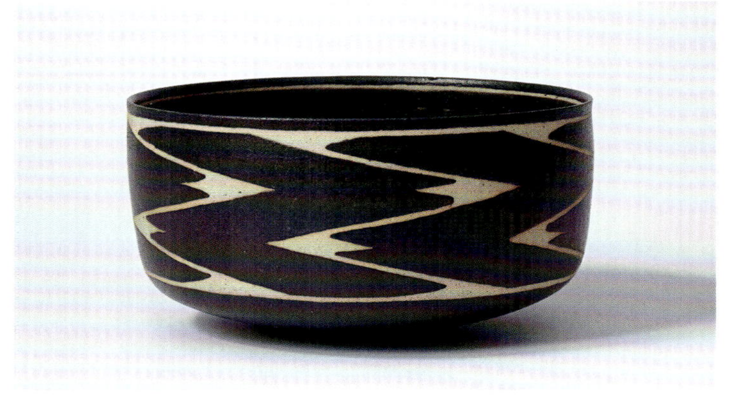

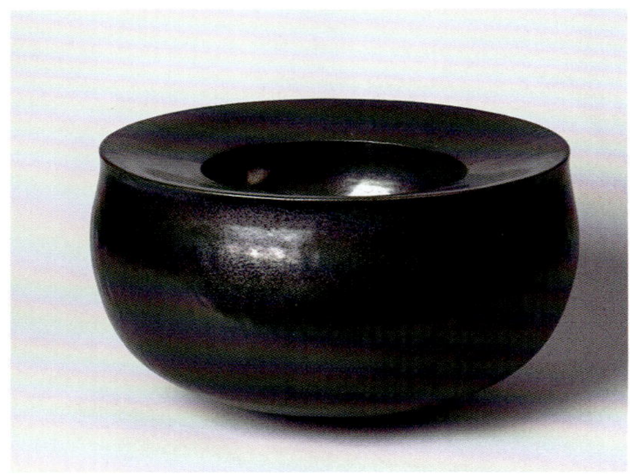

488 208/2003

486. Lidded bowl, 1974

Stoneware, feldspar-glazed, partly unglazed; modelled, glazed cloud ornaments, sprayed. H 9 x Diam 20. Mark: 'Alev 74' inscribed on base. Mus.no. 39a-b/2002. ACQUISITION: Donation from *Statens Kunstfon*

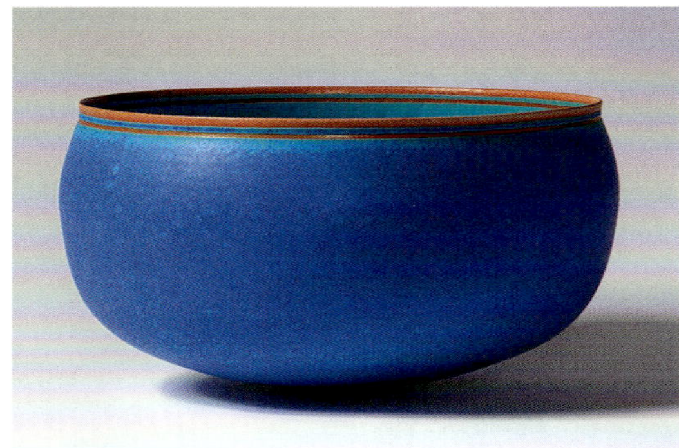

487 261/2002

487. Basin, 2001

Stoneware, glazed; modelled, sprayed, fired at 1280°. H 20.3 x Diam 34.8. Mark: 'Alev' inscribed on base. Mus.no. 261/2002

ACQUISITION: *Alev Ebüzziya Siesbye – et keramisk univers 1964-2002*, 2002, Kunstindustrimuseet. Donation from *Højesteretssagfører C.L. Davids Legat for Slægt og Venner*

488. Basin, 2001. ***Dobbeltskål*** **(Double bowl)**

Stoneware, feldspar-glazed; modelled, sprayed, fired at 1280°. H 24 x Diam 40. Mark: 'Alev 2001' inscribed on base. Mus.no. 208/2003. ACQUISITION: *Alev Ebüzziya Siesbye – et keramisk univers 1964-2002*, 2002, Kunstindustrimuseet

489. Basin, 1982-83

Stoneware, feldspar-glazed; modelled, masked-off and glaze-painted linear decoration, sprayed, fired at 1280°. H 42 x Diam 48.7. Mark: 'Alev' inscribed on base. Mus.no. D 1588. ACQUISITION: *Alev Siesbye Stentøj – Tine Jolander tæpper*, 1983, Kunstindustrimuseet. Deposited by *Statens Kunstfond*, 1985

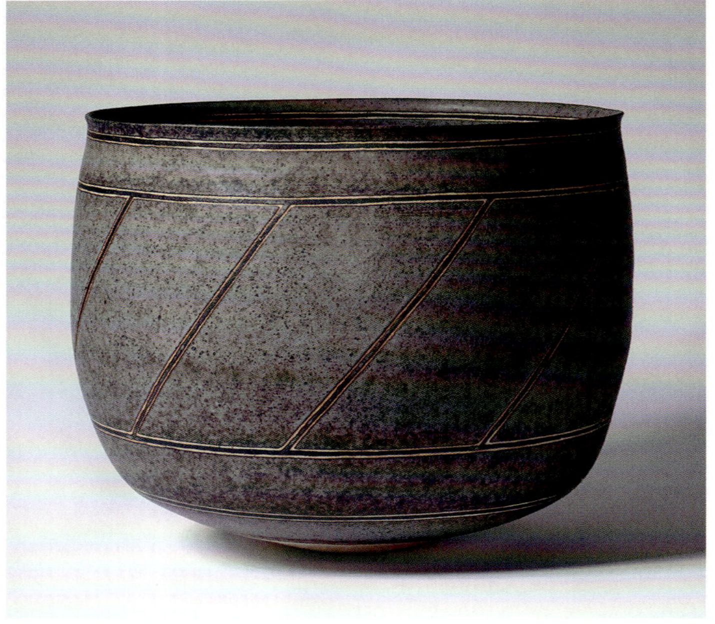

489 D 1588

490. Bowl, 1983

Stoneware, barium-glazed; modelled, sprayed. H 14.5 x Diam 21 4. Mark: 'S alev 83'. Mus.no. D 1589.

ACQUISITION: *Alev Siesbye Stentøj – Tine Jolander tæpper*, 1983, Kunstindustrimuseet. Deposited by *Statens Kunstfond*, 1985

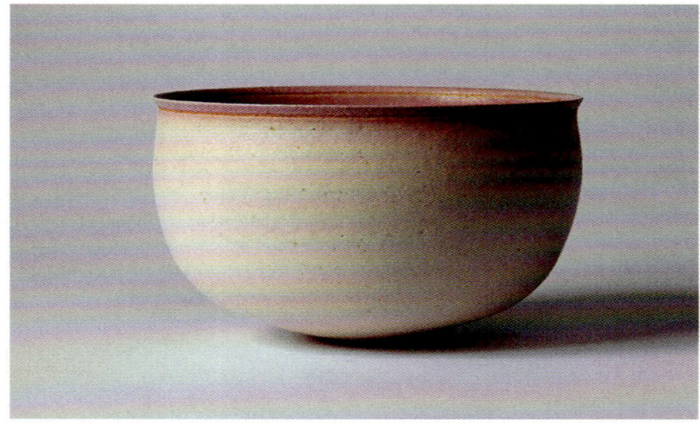

490 D 1589

BENTE SKJØTTGAARD 1961 –

Ceramicist

1982-86	Kunsthåndværkerskolen in Kolding; 1985 Bezalel Academy of Arts and Design, Jerusalem, exchange visit
1986-90	attached to Bing & Grøndahl and Royal Copenhagen, product development
1990-99	Cooperative workshop, Vesterbrogade 102, Copenhagen
1994-05	Designskolen Kolding and Danmarks Designskole, teacher
1999-	Own studio workshop with Ole Jensen, Copenhagen
1999-2000	Udstillingssted for Ny Keramik, Copenhagen, co-owner
2005-16	Danmarks Designskole, Ceramics, teacher
2012-14	Copenhagen Ceramics, exhibition venue, co -founder and -owner
	www.skjoettgaard.dk

Bente Skjøttgaard (BS) is now in mid-career as a ceramicist; she has demonstrated herself to be an artist with a wide span and a rare ability to work even on a monumental scale, supported by intensive research experience and a fearless experimental approach which has made it possible for her to carry through both sculptural works of barrier-breaking strength and a large-scale location-specific project *Spor* (Traces), at Hærvejen, 2010).

Before her definitive breakthrough in 2000 with the exhibition '*Glasurstykker*' (Glazed Items) in Galleri Nørby, BS had followed a career path like that of other Danish ceramicists before her, spending several years attached to one of the country's two major porcelain factories, in this case Bing & Grøndahl's department for product development, following on from her education as a ceramic designer at Designskolen in Kolding. With this background one could expect questions about e.g. mass-production v. handmade, use of reproduction methods, etc., to be of close interest. And they were raised for discussion at an exhibition in 1991, entitled *Never Compromise on Quality*, where BS, Signe Højmark, Ole Jensen and Tora Urup took part. The aim was to provide a method-study of reproduction as inspiration for design.

BS carried out other projects in the 1990s that were related to the design of products for functional use, for example a series with 'smoking requisites' – ashtrays, smoking trays, etc., made in a humorous satirical spirit in glazed stoneware and displayed at the exhibition '*Keramikkens underskov*' in 1993, where younger ceramicists displayed their desire to break away from the established Danish ceramic tradition. An ambitious project was *En Badeværelseshistorie* (A bathroom story) in 1995 in Galleri Nørby, together with Anne Tophøj and Tora Urup, where the aim was to give this typically industrial ceramic room a new treatment from a ceramic craftwork perspective, through

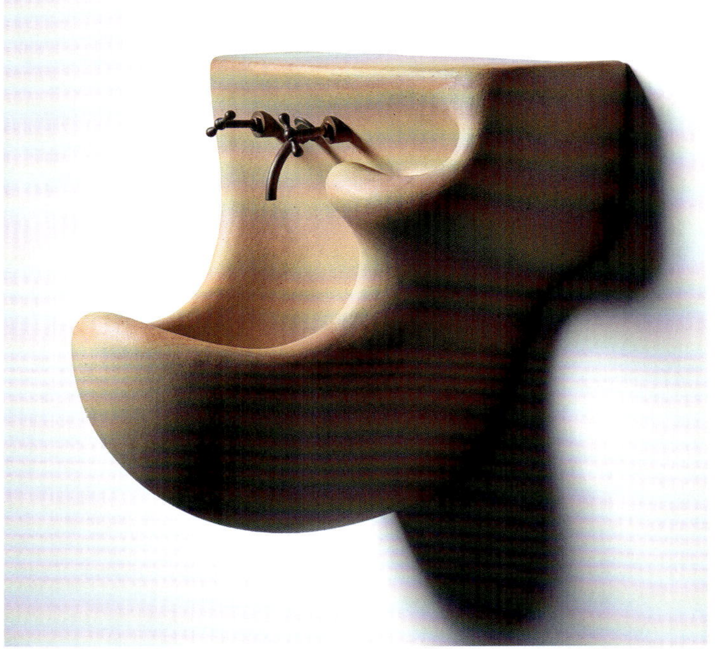

493 138/2009

proposals for new sensuous products. An offshoot of this was shown by BS in *Udstillingssted for ny keramik* in 1997 – including a handbasin with the basin, shelf and soap-dish shaped in a single organic and compact sculpture made of unglazed stoneware, pleasant to touch and easy to clean; the museum later acquired an example **(493)**.

There then followed, in 2000, the large-scale and impressive exhibition '*Glasurstykker*'*(Glazed Items)*, in which BS, as indicated by the title,

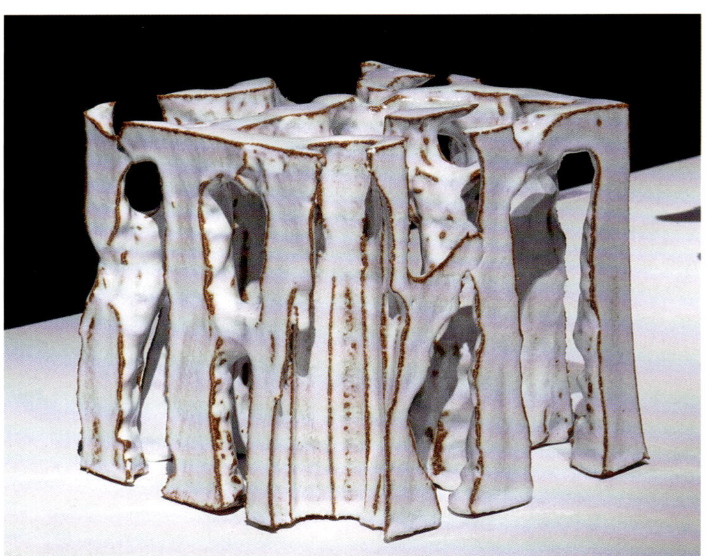

491 58/2004

concentrated on exploration of glazes and the interplay of glaze and clay. BS changed technique for the exhibition's many works, which despite the symmetrical common focus were not thrown but modelled, with a wide variety of shapes of stoneware pots, vases and bowls, creating diverse possibilities for the glazes to have free rein, collectively and layer by layer. Associations with the Art Nouveau period's stoneware pioneers come readily to mind, but the '*Glasurstykkerne*' moved the historical boundaries with their sumptuous mass and wealth of colour in the expressionist and nature-inspired glazes on their robustly modelled shapes, which BS has subsequently developed into an original *oeuvre*, with the ceramic glazes as an essential element.

With the exhibitions '*Glasurstykker*' (2000), '*Glasurstykker med forgreninger*' (Glazed Items with Ramifications)(2003), '*Mellemistid*' (Middle Ice Age)(2005), '*Elements in White*' (2008) and '*Cumulus Congestus*' (2014) as important milestones, BS has throughout the last 10 to 15 years BS has gradually forsaken the basic forms of functional ceramics - pots, dishes, and bowls – to work with increasingly strong sculptural, abstract and also nature-inspired idioms, often with reference to the earth, its vegetation and climate and the universe, including structurally complex modelled cloud formations. Nature's changing and eternally repeating circuits are the essential material that BS luxuriates in, and the means by which she creates intense images.

BS has been actively involved with the new Danish ceramicists' conscious drive to communicate with the public about their works, both in *Udstillingssted for ny keramik* and in *Copenhagen Ceramics*, and she is part of the exhibition group *New Danish Ceramics*, which was set up in 2003 and has exhibited, for instance, in the museum in 2004 with a convincing presentation of new works by the nine members of the group. There BS showed a number of works with the motif *Forgreninger* (Ramifications), i.e. developments of works from the exhibition at Holstebro Kunstmuseum the previous year, but now with a cropping of the organic ramifications into cubic-shaped sculptures. The museum acquired two works from the exhibition **(491-492)** and later the monumental hand-built and glazed work *Macro Cube* from 2011 **(494)**.

The glazes run like a red thread through the many years of intensive work that BS has achieved, and which for good reason determine her status, on both the Danish and the international ceramic scene. BS is an active participant in international exhibition life, has standing links with galleries in Paris and Brussels, and is represented with works in leading museums and collections, as well as having been awarded important prizes and distinctions. At the same time BS has constantly combined her artistic productivity with a significant amount of teaching at the design schools in Kolding and Copenhagen.

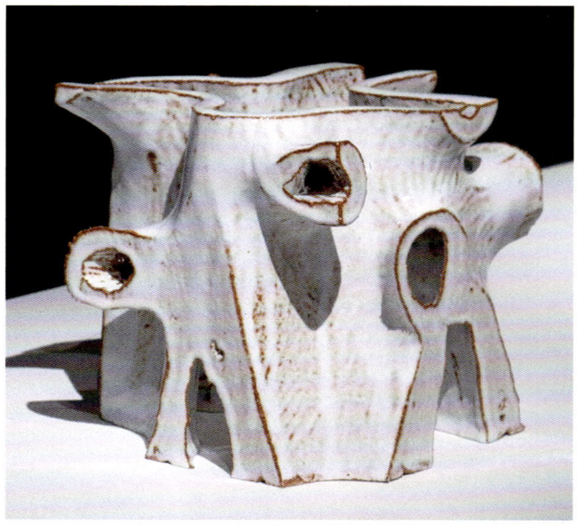

492 59/2004

491. Object, 2003. *Forgrening – hvid kube* (Ramification – white cube)
Stoneware, tin-glazed; modelled, fired at 1280°. H 22 x W 22 x D 22. Mark: 'BS' inscribed on base. Mus.no. 58/2004. ACQUISITION: *New Danish Ceramics*, 2003-2004, Kunstindustrimuseet. Donation from *Kunstindustrimuseets Venner*

492. Object, 2003. *Forgrening – hvid kube* (Ramification – white cube)
Stoneware, tin-glazed; modelled, fired at 1280°. H 22 x W 22 x D 22. Mark: 'BS' inscribed on base. Mus.no. 59/2004. ACQUISITION: *New Danish Ceramics*, 2003-2004, Kunstindustrimuseet. Donation from *Kunstindustrimuseets Venner*

493. Handbasin, 1997
Stoneware, unglazed, brass fittings; modelled. Mark: none. Mus.no. 138/2009 ACQUISITION: Bente Skjøttgaard. Exhibited in 1997 in *Udstillingssted for ny keramik*

494. Sculpture, 2011. *Macro Cube no 1101*
Stoneware, glazed; hand-built, fired at 1280°. H 47 x W 47. Mus.no. 160/2011 ACQUISITION: Donation from *Augustinusfonden*

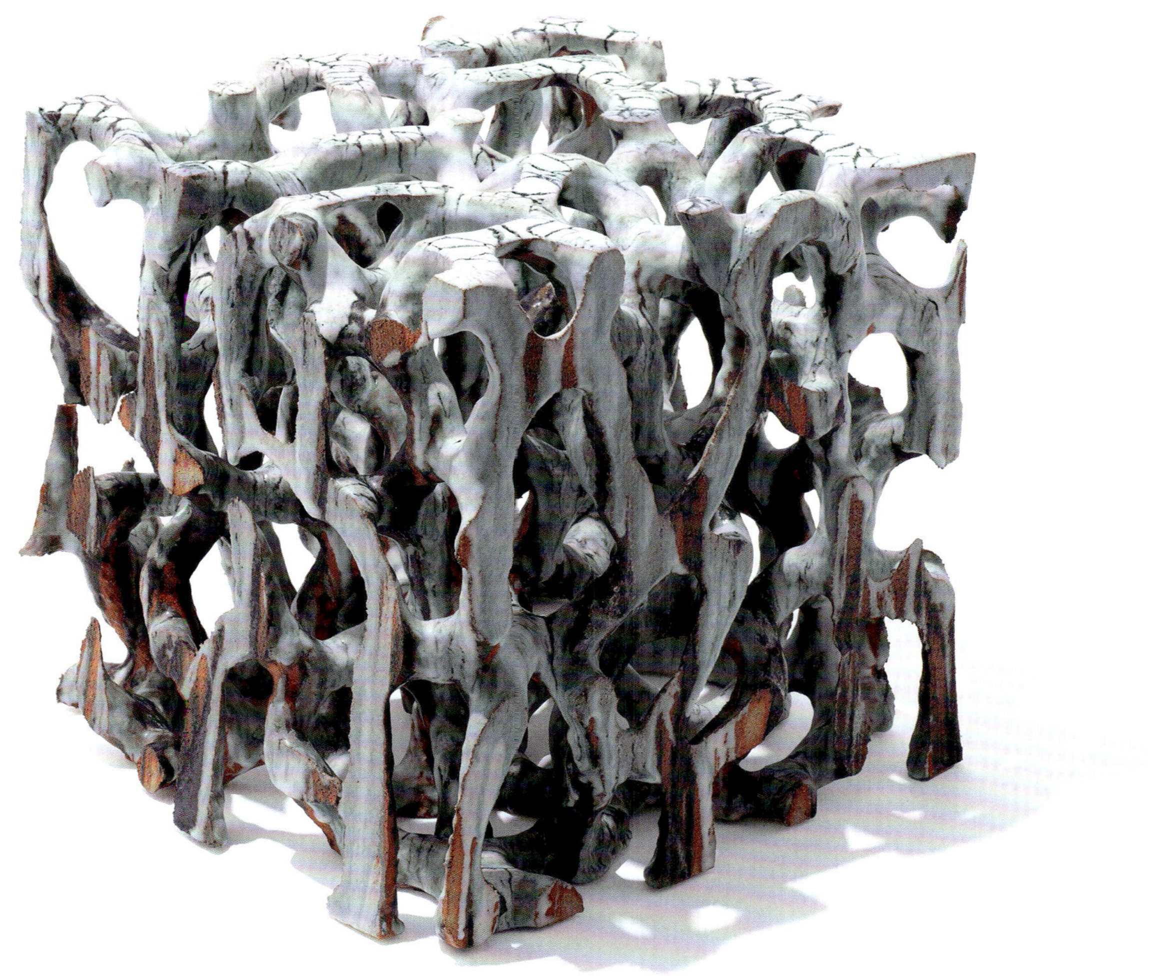

494 160/2011

SLOTH, KIRSTEN 1938 –

Ceramicist

1972-75 Det Jyske Kunstakademi

1976- Own studio workshop, Aarhus

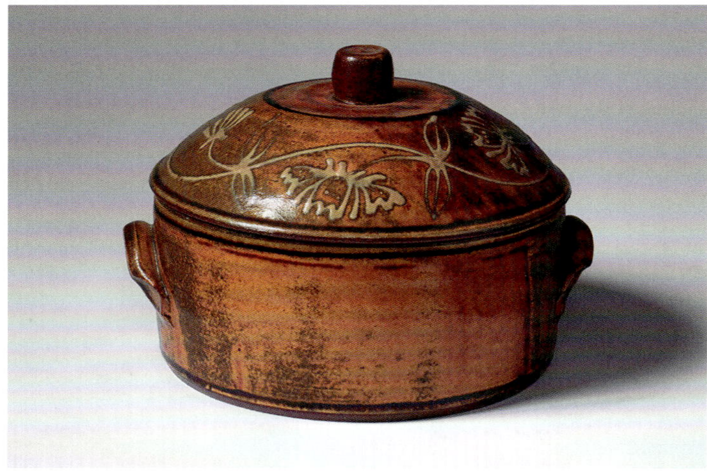

495 126a-b/1984

Kirsten Sloth (KS) studied at Det Jyske Kunstakademi with Gutte Eriksen and Gudrun Meedom Bæch among others as teachers of the Ceramics courses. She set up her own workshop in Aarhus in 1976 and has continued to work from there. KS has participated in many exhibitions, through the years, both in Denmark and elsewhere, and her works have been acquired by leading international museums in the Nordic countries, the USA and Europe. KS was represented in the US-initiated major exhibition '*Danish Ceramic Design*' held in the USA in 1981-82.

In 1987 the exhibition cooperative '*8 keramikere*' was set up, with the participation of several of the ceramicists who had attended Det Jyske Kunstakademi in the 1970s. Apart from KS the group included Lis Ehrenreich, Anne Fløche, Ulla Hansen, Kim Holm, Inger Rokkjær, Inge Trautner and Hans Vangsø, and by the time the group dissolved in 1996 12 exhibitions had been successfully held in Denmark, Sweden, Germany, the Netherlands and the UK, bringing recognition of the group's interpretation of the Danish ceramic tradition in an innovative and contemporary form of expression, incorporating inspiration e.g. from Japan, including the use of the raku technique.

KS has been preoccupied, over a span of many years, with the lidded pot as the basis for a rich variety of decorations; she uses diverse kinds of slip and glaze in attractive and warm nuances, often in striped patterns. Her works are made of red clay from southwest Jutland, which she throws and hard-fires. Apart from the lidded pots and boxes, often with flat lids, that are a recurring feature of her production, KS makes a number of other functional types of object, such as teapots, plates, bowls, etc. KS herself makes no distinction between art ceramics and functional ceramics.

In the museum's collection there are three works by KS. The earliest, from 1984, is a fine terrine with a rounded lid, a modelled handle and a decoration with a plant motif made using horn-painting **(495)**, while the two other works are cylinder-shaped, one a lidded container with striped decoration **(496)** and the other a monochrome lidded pot covered in a warm red iron glaze **(497)**.

497 232a-b/1990

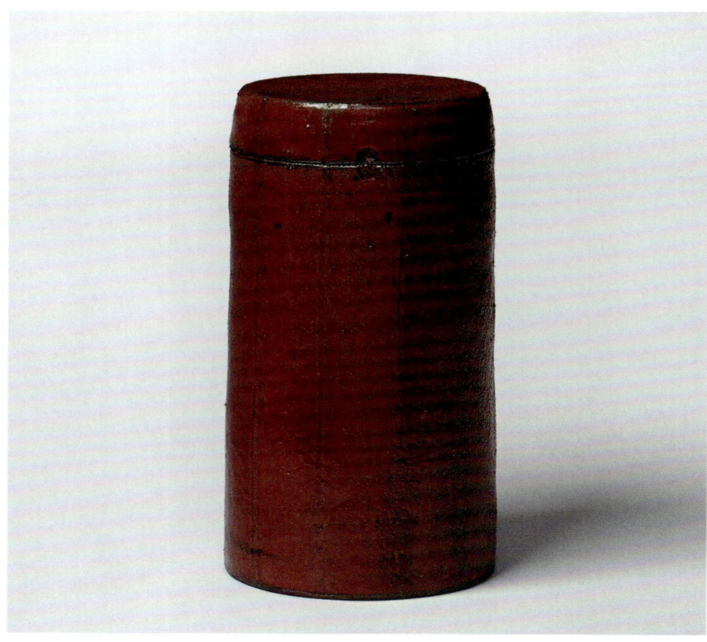

KS's work pursues at a high qualitative level the tradition of Danish studio ceramics that became widespread from the middle of the 20th century, and that has contributed to attracting international attention to Danish ceramic culture.

495. Lidded tureen, 1984

Earthenware, ochre-glazed; thrown, painted using horn, hard-fired at 1200°. H 17 x Diam 21.5. Mark: 'KS' impressed on base. Mus.no. 126a-b/1984
ACQUISITION: *Kunstnernes Påskeudstilling*, 1984, Århus Kunstbygning. Donation from *Foreningen for Industri og Håndværk ved Det jyske Kunstakademis 25-års jubilæum*

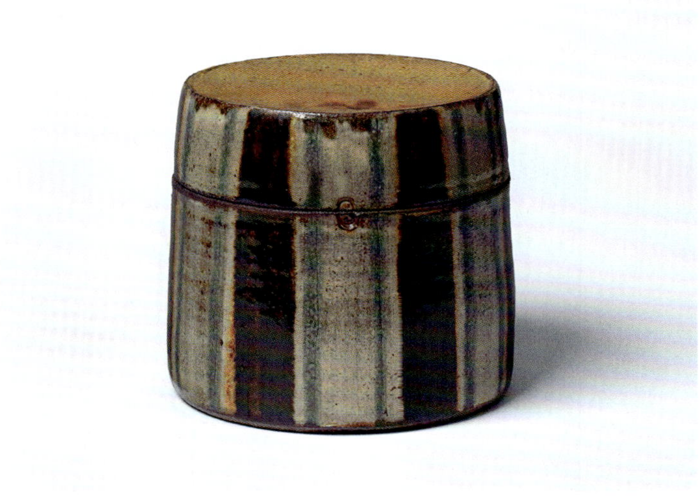

496 231a-b/1990

496. Lidded container, 1989

Earthenware, transparent iron glaze; thrown, slip, painted using horn, hard-fired at 1200°. H 14 x Diam 13.5. Mark: 'KS' impressed on base. Mus.no. 231a-b/1990.
ACQUISITION: Donation from *Kunstindustrimuseets Venner*

497. Lidded pot, 1990

Earthenware, iron-glazed; thrown, copper slip hard-fired at 1200°. H 21 x Diam 10. Mark: 'KS' impressed on base. Mus.no. 232a-b/1990
ACQUISITION: Donation from *Kunstindustrimuseets Venner*

SOUVENIX

SOUVENIX – a 'company' producing contextual souvenirs. Established in 1999 by Jobim A.M. Jochimsen and Anne Tophøj

JOCHIMSEN, JOBIM A.M. 1952 –

Painter

1972-79	Degree in Law, Copenhagen University
1985-89	The Royal Danish Academy of Fine Arts
1990-92	Carnegie Mellon University, USA, MFA and teacher
1994	Designskolen Kolding, guest teacher and consultant
1997-99	Designskolen Kolding, head of institute
2007	Danmarks Designskole, guest teacher
	www.jobim.dk

TOPHØJ, ANNE 1960 –

Ceramic designer, industrial designer

1984-89	Skolen for Brugskunst
1989-92	Own studio workshop with Lone Skov Madsen, Tora Urup and Vibeke Buciek, Copenhagen
1995-98	Studio workshop at Kulturfabrikken, Copenhagen
1998-2007	Designskolen Kolding, part-time teacher
1990-93	Pratt Institute, New York, Master of Industrial Design
1999-	Own studio workshop, Copenhagen
2006-	Danmarks Designskole, teacher
	www.atop.dk

In 2002/03 the firm *Souvenix* held an exhibition in Designstudiet in the museum. The people behind this untraditional firm, which still exists, are A.M. Jobim Jochimsen and Anne Tophøj, who are qualified in ceramics, painting, industrial design and law, and have specialised in conceptual projects in the interconnected area between craftwork, design and pictorial art. The duo broke through strongly by winning one of two first prizes in the Danish Biennale for Craftwork and Design 1999 with the project *Det sønderjyske kaffebord – uden kagekanon*

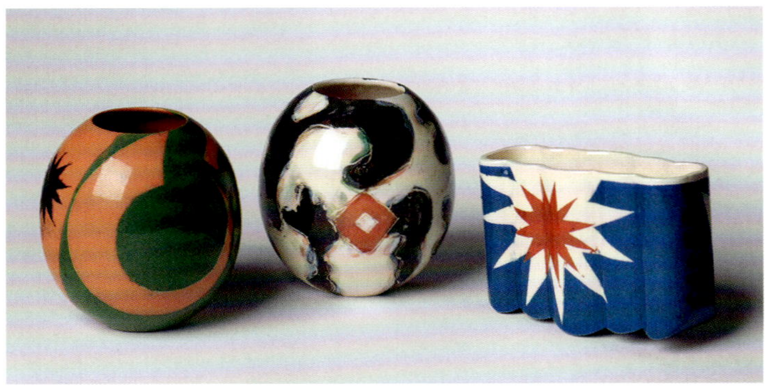

498 12a-c/2003

(The Southern Jutland Coffee Table – without the cake canon) which both provoked and delighted the public and set out new paths in Denmark for conceptual craftwork – paths that have since been trodden by many.

Souvenix began with the idea of producing souvenirs that would set focus on the particular character of a specific place or a special event, as an alternative to the globalised industrially produced souvenirs that can be bought all over the world. A souvenir should be something special, something in its own right, like one's own memories and quite individual. While the winning project at the Biennale gave gently ironical treatment to the traditional Southern Jutland 'cake buffet' and the national symbols it embodies, the departure-point for the exhibition in the museum was the study of 'Good Taste' through selected objects from the museum's collections that have the status of important pieces and classical objects, or which in some way were appealing and interesting. Out of the analysis of these works new souvenirs were created, pulling the past into the present with memories of design history style epochs, people, techniques, etc. The title of the exhibition was the subtle but humorous '*Skyggen af den gode smag*' (The shadow of good taste), and the exhibition's memory-laden souvenirs – like all Souvenix's projects – were grounded in functional objects connected with meals, so that they could form part of, and enrich, daily life. From this fine little manifestation the museum acquired three *Bøllevaser* (taking inspiration from the important Danish architect and ceramicist Thorvald Bindesbøll, 1846-1908) **(498)** and examples of dishes with inspiration from textiles, patterns and Japanese sword ornaments **(499)**. Anne Tophøj has in parallel created for herself an interesting career as a well-thought of and highly experimental ceramicist who exhibits, teaches and carries out research in the field of ceramics. In 2016 she was awarded *Annie og Otto Johs. Detlefs' Keramikpris.*

498. 3 Vases, 2002. *Bøllevaser*

Earthenware, glazed; slip, transfer technique, fired at 1040°. H 8.5 (a-b) x Diam 8.5; H 7.5 x L 10 x W 3 (c). Mark: 'SX02' painted on base. Mus.no. 12a-c/2003.
ACQUISITION: *Skyggen af den gode smag*, 2002, Kunstindustrimuseet

499. Three 'dishes', 2002. *Tekstiler, Snitmønster, Tsuba*

(Textiles, patterns, Tsuba)
Earthenware, transparent glaze (a-b), stoneware, oxide (c) ; impression of drawn thread embroidery, cast (a), millefiori technique (b), double cast, transferred silk print (c), fired at 1240° (a-b), 1040° (c). Diam 13.5 (a), L 9 x W 9 (b), Diam 12 (c). Mark: 'SX02' (a-b), 'Souvenix 2002 Platform' (c), painted. Mus.no. 13a-c/2003
ACQUISITION: *Skyggen af den gode smag*, 2002, Kunstindustrimuseet

499 13a-c/2003

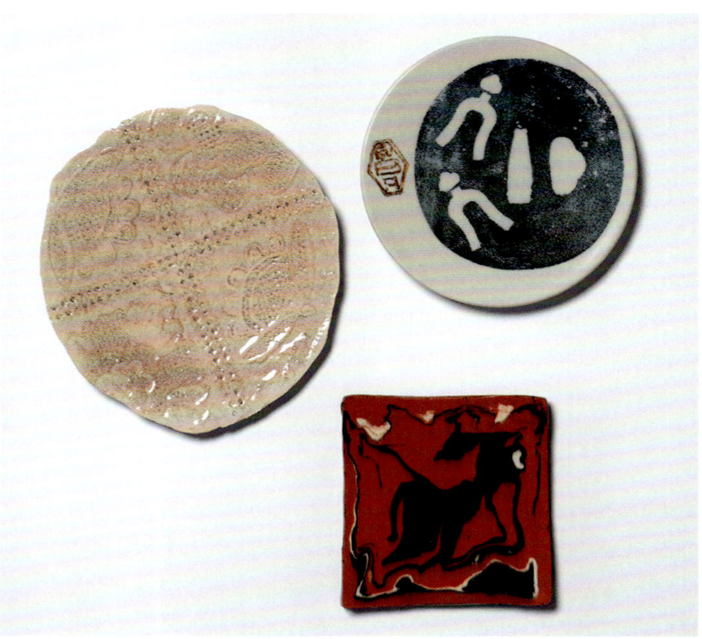

STEPHENSEN, SNORRE LÆSSØE 1943 –

Ceramicist, designer

1958-62	The Royal Porcelain Factory, trainee
1962-65	Kunsthåndværkerskolen
1965	Bing & Grøndahl, employed as artist
1965-	Own studio workshop
1966-68	Bijutsu Daigakku University, Kyoto, Ceramics department, visiting student; Tojiki Shikenjo, Ceramics Laboratory, volunteer
1968-70	Aarhus School of Architecture, research scholarship
1970-78	The Royal Porcelain Factory, designer, employed as artist
1984-91	Skolen for Brugskunst, Ceramic Design and Glass, Head of course
1991-97	Danmarks Designskole, Head of Institute for Ceramic Conceptual Art
1997-2004	Danmarks Designskole, Head of Institute for Product Design
2004-09	Danmarks Designskole, lecturer, senior researcher
2009-	Own studio workshop and design firm, Holmene, Elsinore www.stephensendesign.dk

Snorre Læssøe Stephensen (SLS) was born into an environment with significant architectural and design interests, in that his father was the internationally known architect Magnus Stephensen (1903-84), who in addition to his work on buildings had a successful career as a designer of furniture and of craft-made functional objects, including some, from 1956, in cooperation with the Royal Porcelain Factory. During a visit to the factory with his father in 1958 the fifteen-year-old SLS obtained an apprenticeship there, and his father also introduced him to Japanese arts and crafts, which later came to have decisive influence on his work; he went on several journeys to Japan, including a two-year study period in Kyoto. Interest in Japanese culture resulted in SLS and Magnus Stephensen jointly producing, in 1969, the handsome and perceptive book *Brugskunst fra Japan*. The book highlights Japanese dedication to skilled craftsmanship coupled with artistic ability, in a context where ethics and aesthetics are two sides of the same coin for the Japanese craftsman. The same can be said to characterize the

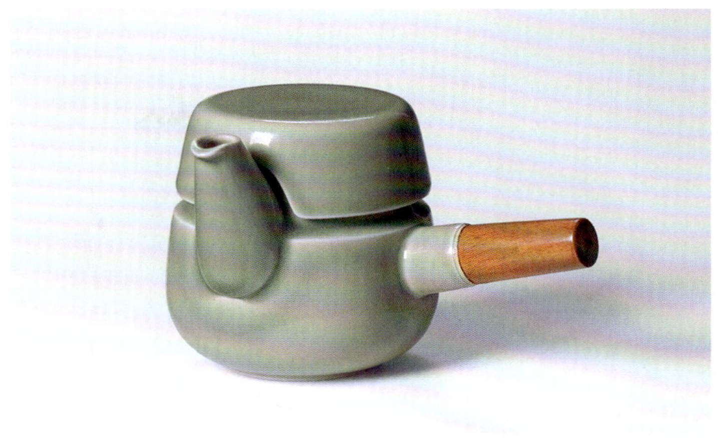

500 113a-b/1985

achievements that SLS has progressed through during the many years he has worked as ceramicist, designer and teacher, and in which he has championed the independence of craftsmanship and its importance in Danish culture.

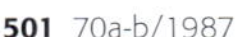

501 70a-b/1987

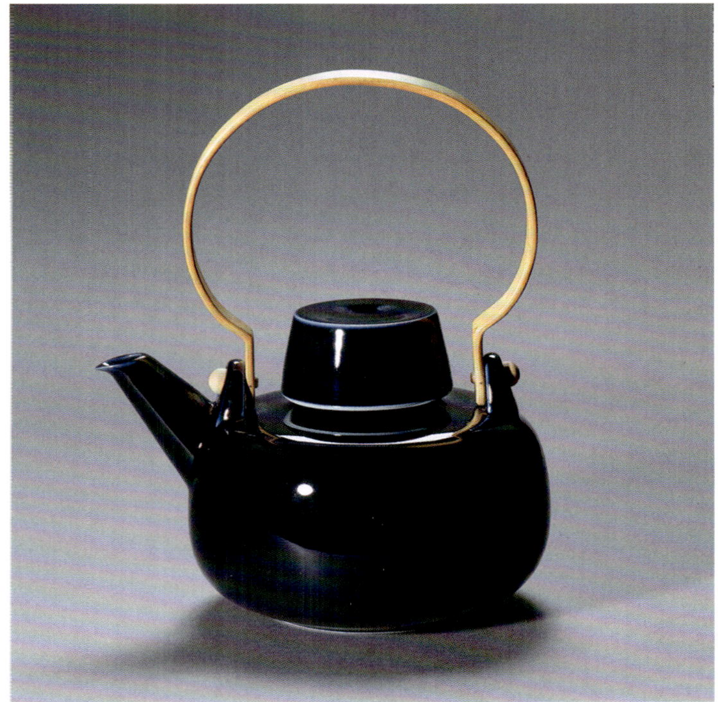

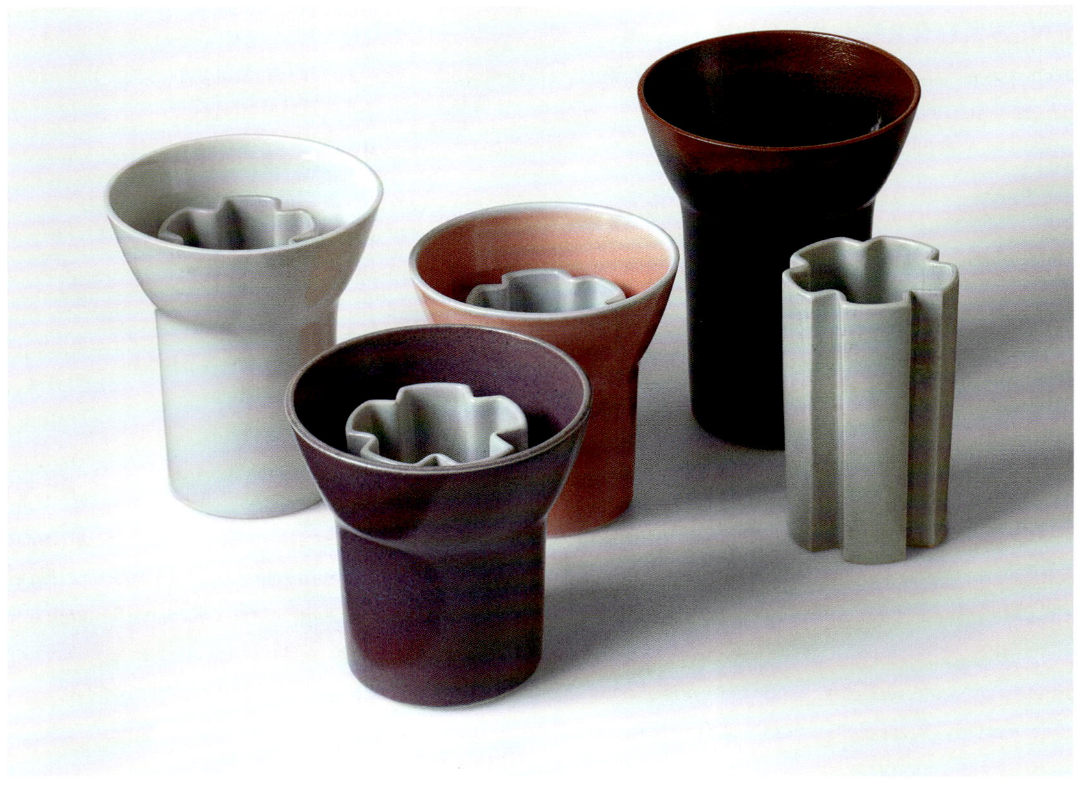

503 D 1585a-b **504** D 1591a-b **505** D 1592a-b **506** D 1593a-b

After studying in Japan SLS was attached to Aarhus School of Architecture as a research scholar in the department for building technology, with constructional ceramics as his special field. This area of research was pursued by SLS after he was employed in 1970 by the Royal Porcelain Factory and worked, among other things, with facade-cladding, with porcelain as a material. There were a number of experiments with production of elements in high-fired fire-proof concrete, for use in stoves and barbeques, but these were unfortunately not followed up by the factory. The same experimental and original approach to ceramic materials is to be found in the many good models for functional objects in stoneware that SLS developed for production, and also in his 'one-off' creative works, with which he successfully participated in the factory's exhibitions. In 1974 SLS had a solo exhibition under the auspices of the factory, and in the same year he was awarded a gold medal in Faenza, Italy, for a very distinctive glazed teapot **(501)**.

A new phase began in 1978, when SLS was employed as a teacher in Skolen for Brugskunst, later Danmarks Designskole; until he retired in 2009 he held leading positions there as Richard Kjærgaard's successor in Ceramic Design and Glass.

As head of the Institutes for Conceptual Art and for Product Design during a time of turbulence around the development of the new curriculum that was introduced in 1990, SLS was the spokesman for a revival of the experimental workshop:

> *If the concept of Danish Design for the moment seems to be stuck in a quagmire, this must be closely connected with the fact that craftwork in recent years has been given lower and lower priority... What we have forgotten is the idea of the WORKSHOP – the Danish development that is a tradition a century old and that through the 1950s and 60s brought us*

up to the forefront. The close cooperation between designer and producer – between workshop and small factory – the small series with the large effect. It is those fine mechanisms that we have to try to have recreated (Snorre Stephensen. In: Årsudstilling '90 91. Danmarks Designskole, Copenhagen 1991, p. 6).

The ideal of the importance of the workshop and the small unique series was brought by SLS himself to practical realisation through the years at the school, for instance in 1981 and 1984, through the exhibition project '*16 +*', in which a group of 16 of the teachers, with one or more guests, joined together to make functional objects based on a limited serial production. The highly praised exhibitions were held in the museum, the latter combined with the opportunity to eat and drink in the museum's garden, 'Grønnegården', where light meals were served using the ceramic pieces made for the purpose, in cooperation with the cooks Camilla Plum and Nanna Simonsen.

The Danish Arts Foundation (Statens Kunstfond) purchased objects at both these exhibitions and later deposited works by SLS in the museum. From 1981 the deposits consisted of four vases with inserts of thrown and glazed porcelain **(503-506)**, and from 1984 there were nine works in all, including jugs, a plate, bowls, an insulated cup and a teak tray with a base of formica **(507-512)**. In 1995 SLS won first prize in Statens Kunstfond's competition 'Ceramics for everyday use' (together with interior designer Bente Stephensen and architect Hannes Stephensen).

In his workshop SLS has through the years built up a successful little firm producing household objects of the same type as those in the museum's collection, made of very fine materials and with a high level of design quality and distinctive craftsmanship. Through his work as a teacher and institute leader SLS has been responsible for the education of several generations of craftworkers /designers, and through his own example as a researcher, communicator and ceramicist he has carried on a strong tradition in Danish craftsmanship, which he has publicized internationally as an adviser and through exhibitions in Denmark and internationally. See: Lautrup-Larsen, L., 2007, pp. 315 ff.; Gelfer-Jørgensen, M., 2013.

507 D 1653a-d **508** D 1654 **509** D 1655 **510** D 1656 **511** D 1657 **512** D 1658

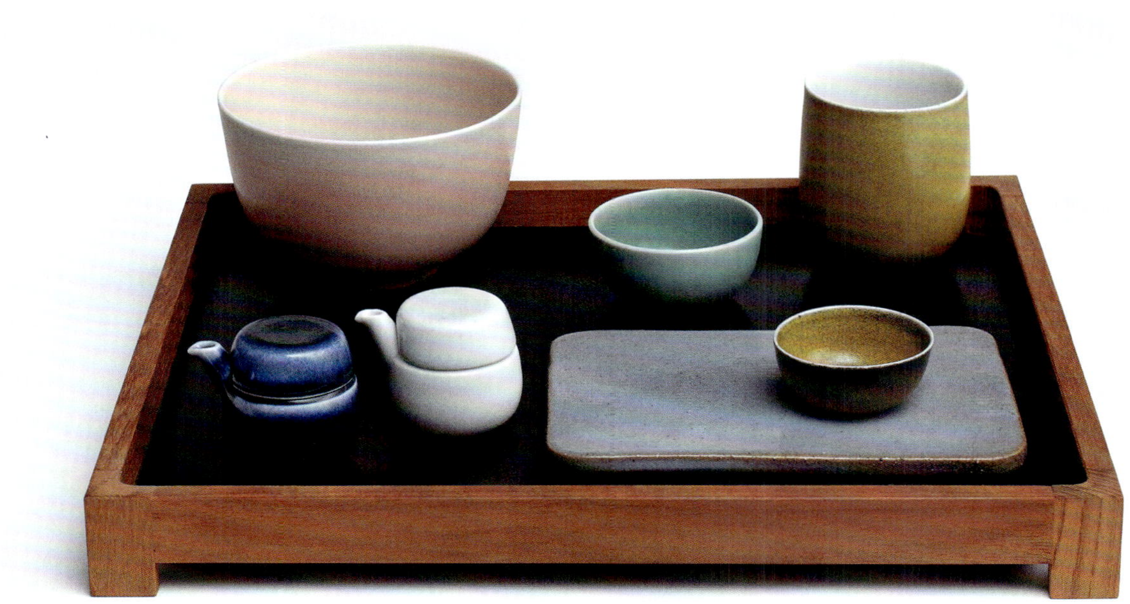

500. Teapot, 1985
Porcelain, celadon-glazed, beechwood; thrown, reduction-fired at 1300°. H 12 x W 19.5 x Diam 12. Mark: 'S' in a circle painted on base. Mus.no. 113a-b/1985.
ACQUISITION: Anonymous donation. See: *Brændpunkter*, 1990

501. Teapot, 1986 (original design from 1974)
Porcelain, feldspar-glazed, laminated ash and mahogany; cast, reduction-fired at 1400°. Handle made by furniture-maker Bente Stephensen.
H 18 x W 22.5 x Diam 19. Mark: none. Mus.no. 70a-b/1987
ACQUISITION: Snorre Stephensen. Donation from *Kunstindustrimuseets Venner*. See: Grandjean, B., 1983

502. Parts of service, 2002 (No photo)
Porcelain, glazed with covering layer of thin pigment-colour; thrown, cast, fired at 1270°. H 7.5-21.5. Mark: 'S' in a circle painted on base. Mus.no. 94a-f/2002
ACQUISITION: Galleri Nørby, Copenhagen. *Kunstindustrimuseets Venner*

503. Round vase with insert, 1980-81
Porcelain, celadon-glazed; thrown. H 14.5; insert H 10. Mark: 'S' in a circle painted on base. Mus.no. D 1585a-b. ACQUISITION: *16+*, 1981, Kunstindustrimuseet. Deposited by *Statens Kunstfond*, 1985

504. Double cone-shaped vase with insert, 1980-81
Porcelain, glazed; thrown. H 17. Mark: 'S' in a circle painted on base. Mus.no. D 1591a-b. ACQUISITION: *16+*, 1981, Kunstindustrimuseet. Deposited by *Statens Kunstfond*, 1985

505. Cone-shaped vase with insert, 1980-81
Porcelain, glazed; thrown. H 15; insert: H 10. Mark: 'S' in a circle painted on base. Mus.no. D 1592a-b. ACQUISITION: *16+*, 1981, Kunstindustrimuseet. Deposited by *Statens Kunstfond*, 1985

506. Cone-shaped vase with insert, 1980-81
Porcelain, glazed; thrown. H 21.5; insert: H 19. Mark: 'S' in a circle painted on base. Mus.no. D 1593a-b. ACQUISITION: *16+*, 1981, Kunstindustrimuseet. Deposited by *Statens Kunstfond,* 1985

507. Two jugs with lids and one bowl, 1984
Porcelain, uranium-glazed, transparent glaze with covering layer of thin pigment-colour; thrown, fired at 1270°. Mark: 'S' in a circle painted on base. Mus.no. D 1653a-d.
ACQUISITION: Deposited by *Statens Kunstfond*, 1987

508. Plate, 1984
Porcelain, ash-glazed, transparent glaze with covering layer of thin pigment-colour; fired at 1270°. W 13 x L 19. Mark: none. Mus.no. D 1654
ACQUISITION: Deposited by *Statens Kunstfond*, 1987

509. Bowl, 1984
Porcelain, alkali-glazed; thrown, fired at 1270°. Diam 7.5. Mark: none. Mus.no. D 1655.
ACQUISITION: Deposited by *Statens Kunstfond*, 1987

510. Insulated cup, 1984
Porcelain, uranium-glazed; thrown, fired at 1270°. H 7.5. Mark: none. Mus.no. D 1656.
ACQUISITION: *16+*, Kunstindustrimuseet, 1984. Deposited by *Statens Kunstfond*, 1987

511. Bowl, 1984
Porcelain, transparent glaze with covering layer of thin pigment-colour; thrown, fired at 1270°. H 9.5 x Diam 14. Mark: 'S' in a circle painted on base. Mus.no. D 1657.
ACQUISITION: Deposited by *Statens Kunstfond*, 1987

512. Tray, 1984
Teak, plastic (in cooperation with furniture-maker Sigurd Højland Olsen). L 34 x W 40. Mark: none. Mus.no. D 1658.
ACQUISITION: *16+*, Kunstindustrimuseet, 1984. Deposited by *Statens Kunstfond*, 1987

SØRENSEN, JØRGEN HAUGEN 1934 –

Sculptor

1949	Pottery apprenticeship with P. Ipsens Enke, ceramics firm, Copenhagen; brief period at Kunsthåndværkerskolen
1956-76	Member of exhibition group *Decembristerne,*
1979-89	Member of exhibition group *Grønningen*
1975-	Living in Italy
	www.haugen-sorensen.dk

Jørgen Haugen Sørensen (JHS) is one of Denmark's eminent and internationally-known sculptors, with a large number of works and public commissions among his accomplishments; with robust realism his works reflect a morbid world of dread, stupidity and gruesomeness, but also contrition and sympathy. Through the years the forms of expression of his works have changed from the expressive and organic to include geometric elements, and his use of materials has moved from bronze and marble to clay, textiles, fibre glass, aluminium and plastic.

Ceramics as a material has interested and inspired JHS ever since his childhood efforts at modelling and up to the moving and indelibly memorable commissioned work for Domhuset, the courthouse in Copenhagen, with five large modelled and white-glazed reliefs; it was begun in 2010 and inaugurated, together with two free-standing sculptures in travertine for the same courtroom, in 2014.

Experiments with clay led the young JHS to begin training in ceramics, at first at the firm of P. Ipsens Enke and then at

513 188/2005

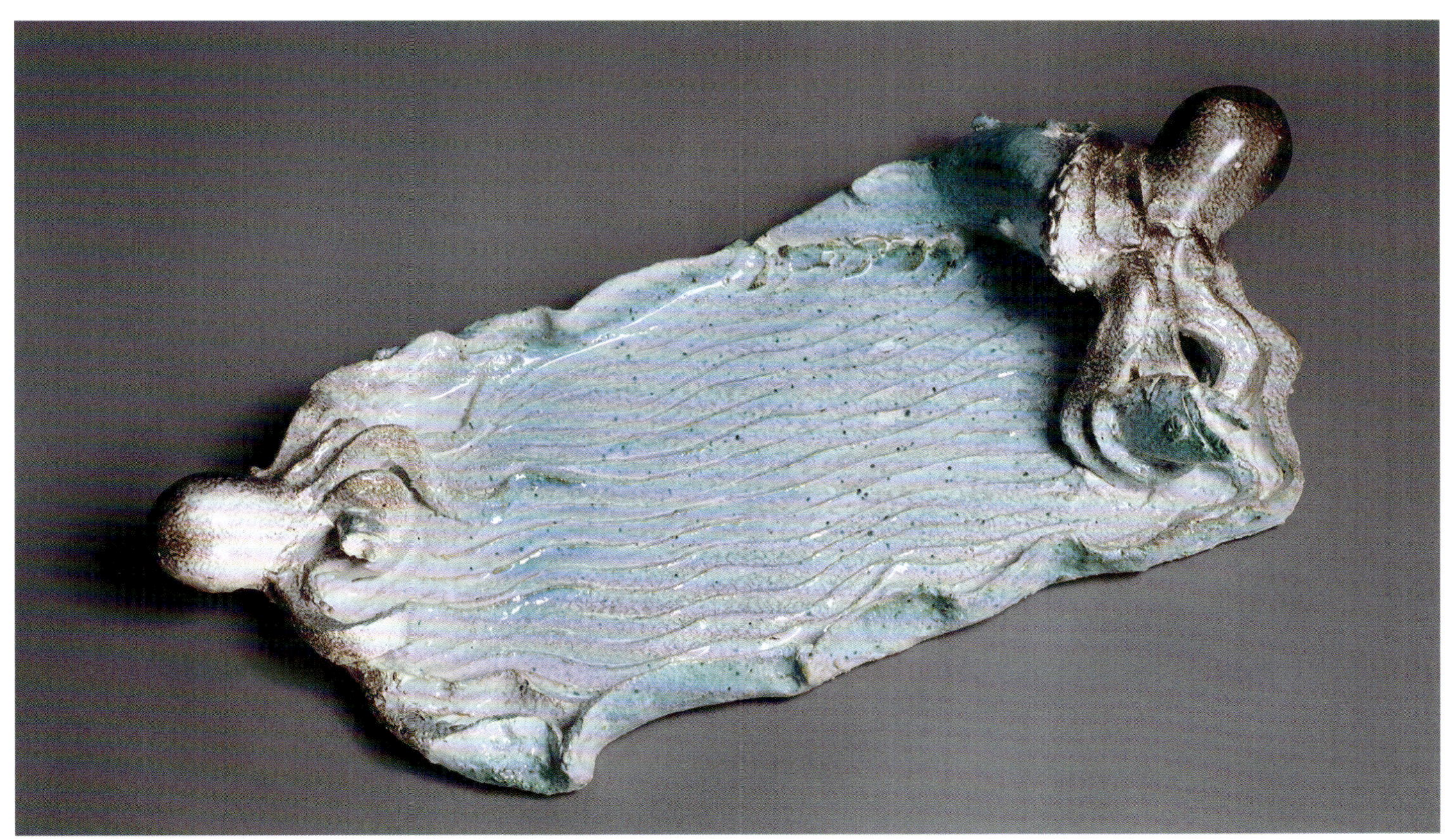

Kunsthåndværkerskolen, where he was a pupil of Christian Poulsen's, but then he broke this off and chose to become a sculptor. In around 1960 JHS won attention with a series of constructivist ceramic pipe-sculptures, which he produced at a well-known Bornholm industrial workplace, Rabækkeværket.

Since 1975 JHS has lived in Italy, mostly in Pietrasanta, attracted by the proximity to the town's bronze-casters and the nearby marble quarries, but from the mid 1990s JHS also resumed working with ceramics. In 2004/05 he made a series of modelled dishes in faience, and some of them were exhibited in the museum in 2005 with the title *Vi spiser – de æder* (We eat, they feed), a reference to the motifs on the dishes, with octopuses in the process of devouring fish. In that context the museum acquired one of the dishes **(513)**.

513. Sculpture, 2004/2005. *Havdyr* (Sea-creatures)
Faience; modelled, decorated. H 15 x W 75 x D 34. Mark: none. Mus.no. 188/2005. ACQUISITION: *Vi spiser – de* æder, 2005, Kunstindustrimuseet.

THING, INGER 1924 – 2014

Ceramicist

1944-47	Kunsthåndværkerskolen
1950	Studied sculpture with sculptor Henry Luckow-Nielsen
1950-70	Worked in ceramic workshops in Denmark and Sweden
1970-2001	Own studio workshop, Vedbæk, Sealand

Inger Thing (IT) studied Ceramics at Kunsthåndværkerskolen in the mid 1940s, but did not set up her own ceramic workshop until 1970, after some years of working as a designer of functional objects in glass and wood, and working in various ceramic workshops in Denmark and Sweden. In 1974 an exhibition of IT's work was held in the museum, and a sculptural vase was acquired there for the collection; it is thrown, with incised vertical grooves which conclude, at the top, in three modelled 'collars' **(514)**. In addition to this early work, in the course of the following years five further works by IT came into the collection, all bowls from the 1980s, which show different sides of this fine ceramicist's mastery of her material and the assured harmony between the thickness of the body, the simple defined shapes, the pale pastel glazes and the delicate ornamentation.

Another work was acquired at an exhibition in the museum in 1981 – a whitish glazed thrown bowl in porcelain; the rim, painted with iron glaze, runs elegantly down in relief over the little organic ornament that is recessed into the clay **(515)**. From 1984 there is a pale glazed thrown bowl that is modelled in a hexagonal optic form; this work was included in the major exhibition '*De Danske*', which was part of a Swedish initiative focusing on Danish culture in 1984-85 at Liljevalchs Konsthall and Kulturhuset in Stockholm, with a fine array of Danish art craftworkers, including 12 ceramicists and furniture architects. The hexagonal form is also found in the museum's most recent work by IT, from 1989, which has a thrown base and then has been modelled up with slanting sides **(519)**.

The most monumental work by IT in the museum's collection is a large sculptural bowl from 1983 in stoneware with a strongly retracted little standing surface. The lower part of the corpus is matte, glazed in dark grey, and above that there is a broad whitish glazed stripe that continues in the interior of the bowl. The horizontal division of the glazed decoration creates an impression of a double bowl **(518)**. The same retracted foot can be seen on a small stoneware bowl from 1982 with a pale glaze and the foot and rim outlined in brown. Inside the bowl is a circle-based decoration and on the outside there is a slightly impressed and painted motif that reflects the interest in calligraphy that engaged IT in the final years of her life **(516)**.

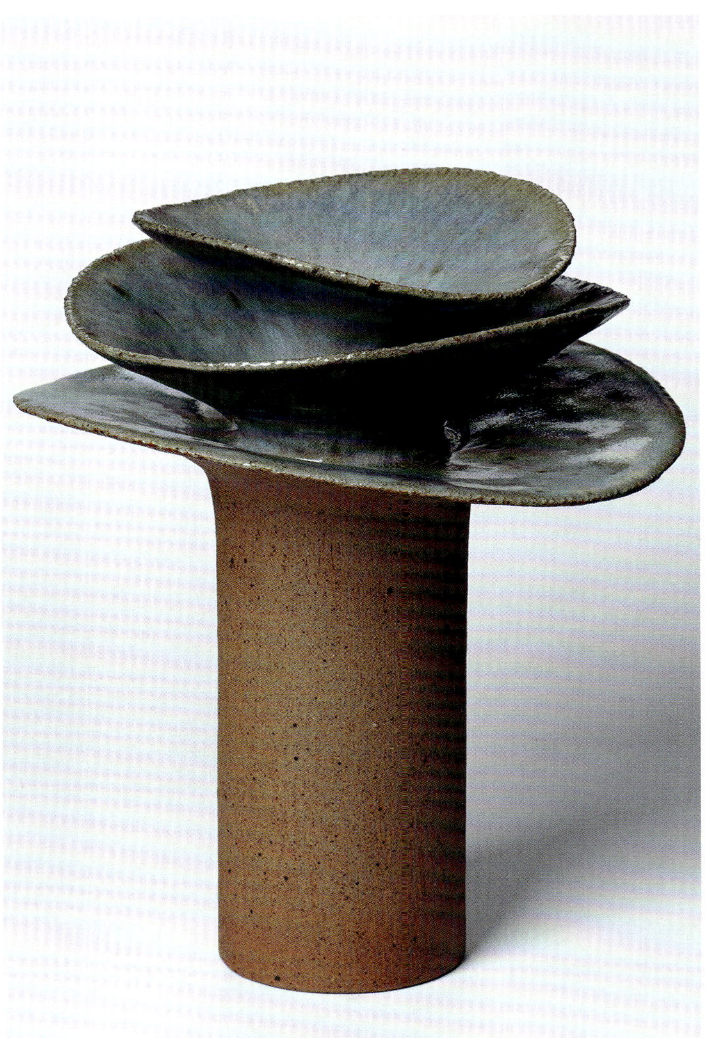

514 187/1974

IT herself, in the catalogue for '*De Danske*', wrote that ceramics for her meant working with form, throwing and modelling in such a way as to retain the movement in the form and be able to see the light catching in the different planes. For IT decoration had to support form, not distract from it, and the light-coloured glazes she used were intended to highlight the effect of lightness of the clay that she sought to bring out. The harmony in the *oeuvre* which IT has left behind her does full justice to her aspirations.

IT undertook several journeys to Japan and the USA, and won high regard from international connoisseurs of contemporary Danish ceramics. She took part in many exhibitions both in Denmark and abroad, including the first Danish group exhibition in the USA in 1981. Her works are represented in influential museums around the world.

514. Vase, 1973-74

Stoneware, ash-glazed; thrown, modelled, engraved, fired at 1280°. H 30.5. Mark: 'I Thing' inscribed on base. Mus.no. 187/1974

ACQUISITION: *Inger Thing – Stentøjsarbejder,* 1974, Kunstindustrimuseet. Donation from *Overretssagfører Odin Kaysers Legat*. See: Dybdahl, L., 1997

515. Bowl, 1980

Porcelain, iron- and feldspar- glazed; thrown, scraped, relief, fired at 1280°. H 11 x Diam 27.3. Mark: 'IT' stamped on the base in a circle with 80. Mus.no. 23/1981.

ACQUISITION: *Forårstoner – keramikeren Inger Thing og væveren Vibeke Gregers,* 1981, Kunstindustrimuseet. Donation from *Benny Dessaus Mindelegat*

516. Bowl, 1982

Porcelain, stoneware, glazed, partially unglazed; thrown, brush-painted, decoration. H 8.7 x Diam 15.8. Mark: 'IT' in a circle stamped on base. Mus.no. 59/1982

ACQUISITION: Galleriet, Kolding. Donation from *Benny Dessaus Mindelegat*

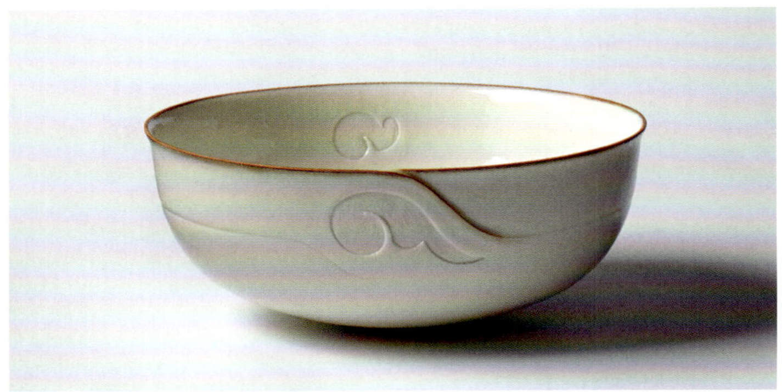

515 23/1981

517. Bowl, 1984

Porcelain, feldspar-glazed, partially unglazed; thrown, modelled, fired at 1280°.

H 15.5 x Diam 25.3. Mark: Stamped mark in circle on base.

Mus.no. 38/1985. ACQUISITION: *De danske*, 1985, Kulturhuset, Stockholm.

Donation from *Benny Dessaus Mindelegat*. See: *De danske*, 1984

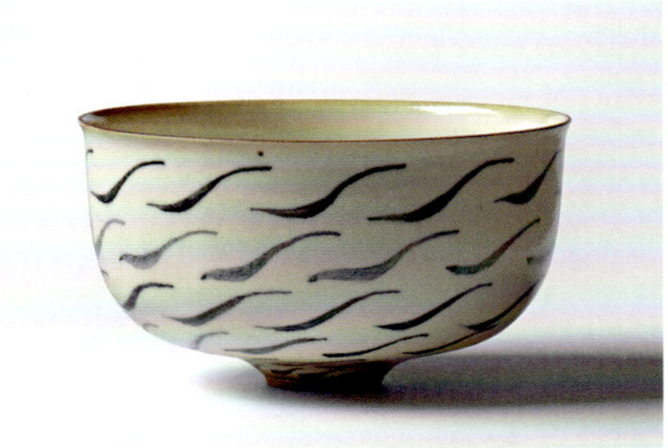

516 59/1982

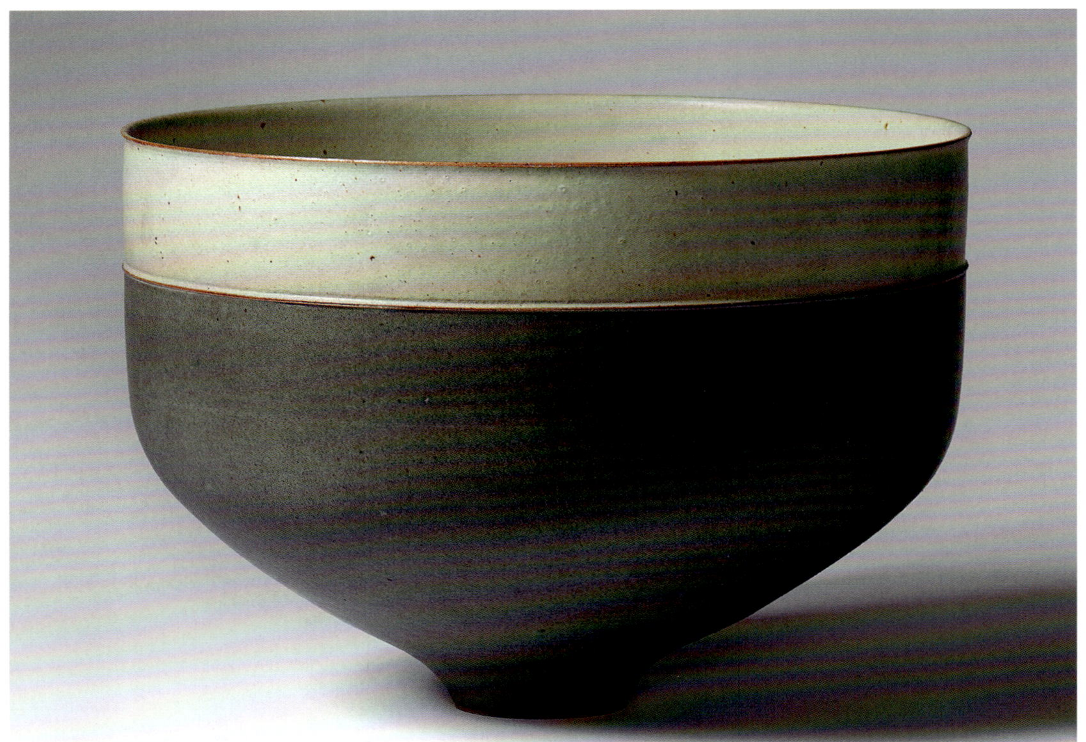

518 191/1985

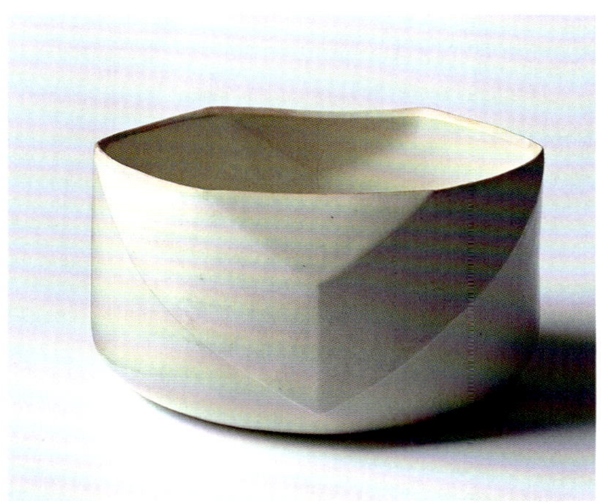

519 151/1990

518. Bowl, 1983

Stoneware, barium-glazed; thrown, fired at 1231°. H 29 x Diam 40.8. Mark: 'IT' in a circle with 65 inscribed on base. Mus.no. 191/1985. ACQUISITION: Court Gallery Copenhagen, 1985. Donation from *Thomas B. Thriges Fond*

519. Bowl, 1989

Porcelain, clear iron- and feldspar-glazed; thrown, modelled, fired at 1280°. H 10 x Diam 18. Mark: 'IT' in a circle stamped on base. Mus.no. 151/1990 ACQUISITION: Donation from *Kgl. Brand*. See: *Brændpunkter*, 1990

517 38/1985

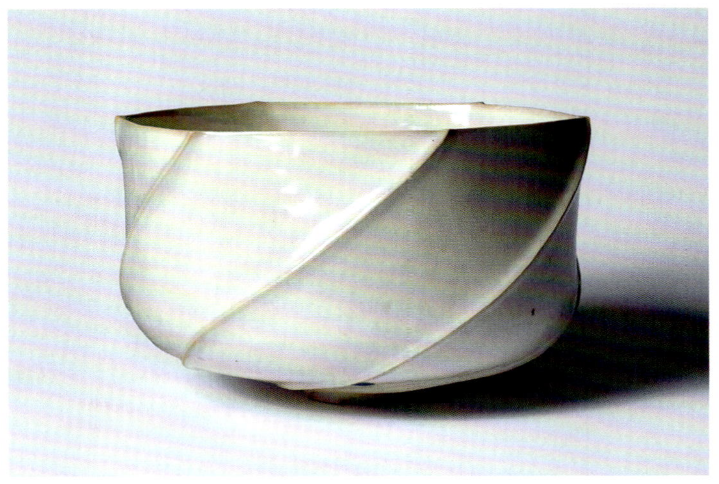

THOMSEN, SYS 1939 – 2000

Ceramicist, painter, author

1960-62	Skolen for Boligindretning (School of Interior Design)
1962-67	Interior Architect; worked for Illums Bolighus Drawing office, Cotil, C. Olesen
1966-90	Studies in Applied Art and Ceramics, Japan, over a total period of 9 years
1970-71	Waseda University, Tokyo
1972-75	Apprentice with ceramicist Yamamoto Genta, Kyushu.
1975-84	Copenhagen University, cand.phil. Japanese Language and Culture
1975-2000	Own studio workshop, Møn

Sys Thomsen (ST) was living proof of the inspiration from Japan that became so important for Danish art and design, in so many ways, from the middle of the 19th century, and which Mirjam Gelfer-Jørgensen has traced in her comprehensive work from 2013. The Danish ceramicists in particular, in the period from the 1950s onwards, became deeply interested in Japan's ceramic culture, as is evident from the biographies of many of the ceramicists included in the present catalogue, and as can be seen from their works in the museum's collection. But for ST the encounter with Japan's culture, way of life and people became life-changing both for her personally and for her work as a ceramicist.

The sources that tell us about the unusual and moving course of ST's life are chiefly the writing that she herself left behind, which makes it possible to follow her on her route into the eastern way of thinking and into Japanese culture, in which ethics, aesthetics and religion form the basis for a way of life that is built on traditions, on respect and trust, and in which craftwork is accredited with value and significance. ST was inspired by the philosopher and writer Yanagi Soetsu (1889-1961), who was intensely absorbed in folk art, and who took the initiative to found the Folk Art Museum in Tokyo in 1936, with the material he had collected on his many journeys around Japan as the starting-point. ST translated and published some of Yanagi's essays in the book '*Forunderlige skønhed – vandring i japansk hverdagskunst*' (1987) in connection with an exhibition held in the museum and elsewhere. ST was educated as an interior architect and went to Japan by chance in the first place; she was to spend a total of more than 9 years of her life there, in intermittent periods. There were 2,5 years as an apprentice, spent living as a family member with the well-known ceramicist Genta Yamamoto. In the publication *'Hverdagskvaler, Hverdagsglæder'* (1980) ST described this existential experience, which resulted in ceramics becoming the meaningful focus of her studies of Japanese culture and of her way of life after her return to Denmark in 1975, when she established her own studio workshop on the island of Møn. ST consolidated her experience and studies in Japan with study of the Japanese language and culture at Copenhagen University, taking her concluding examination in 1984.

For ST it was important to explain to a Danish public what she had found out about the values in Japanese culture, and this resulted in many years of lecturing activities for adult education classes as well as in a number of exhibitions, several of them in cooperation with the museum; important examples of her ceramic works were acquired for the museum's collection. The exhibitions were based on Japanese daily life, with subjects such as *'Japansk håndværk og legetøj'* (Japanese craftwork and toys) (1971), *'Nutidig japansk brugskunst'* (Present-day Japanese applied art) (1973), *'Drager, dukker, dyr'* (Dragons, dolls and animals) (1975/76), *'Dagens Ret'* (Dish of the day) (1983) and *'Japansk keramik'* (Japanese ceramics) (1991); many of them had associated publications, often published in the author's fine handwriting and illustrated with her own drawings. In the exhibition *'Dagens Ret'*, held in the museum in 1983) ST showed a large number of Japanese meals using wax imitation food from restaurants in Japan, collected by ST for this very successful exhibition, which became very popular and contributed to stimulating interest in Japanese culture and design; the collection is still in the museum today.

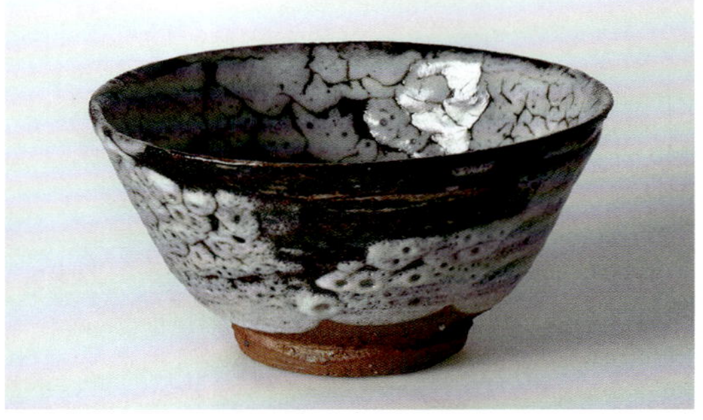

521 223/1984

522 79/1987

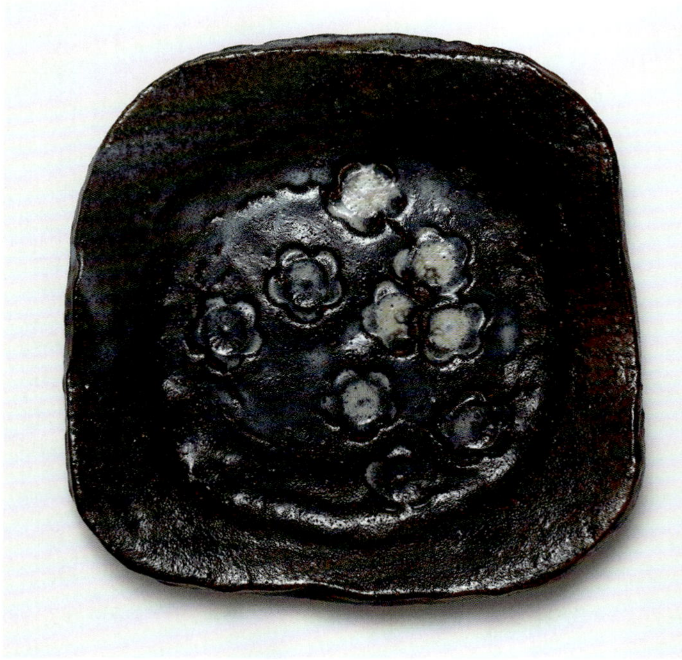

The museum's ceramic collection is in possession of seven works by ST, dating from 1983 to 1995 and representative of various types of her work; all of them were made in the workshop on Møn. ST built her own wood-fired kiln there, tested out a range of stoneware clays, and put into use the materials and techniques that she had learnt about in her apprenticeship and the many years in Japan. Her methods were experimental, involving stoneware with or without slip and ash glazes, and using a variety of forms of decoration, including Japanese stamps, as in the work entitled *Blommeblomst i klippe* (Plum flower in a rock) **(522)**. On another work from that time ST used burnt-on seaweed **(523)**, and on the most recent work, from the mid 1990s, the form and decoration were achieved by means of the imprint of a basket **(526)**. It is typical of the works that the clay plays a leading role and is often wholly or partly unglazed **(525)**. To Danish eyes there is a strongly Japanese influence in ST's work, but she herself laid stress on her attachment to the Danish ceramic tradition.

There is a potentially extensive future task to be carried out in analysing ST's work in the dual context provided by the course of her life and represented in her ceramic works; a large amount of background material was donated to the museum after her death, and would have to be supplemented with study of Japanese sources.

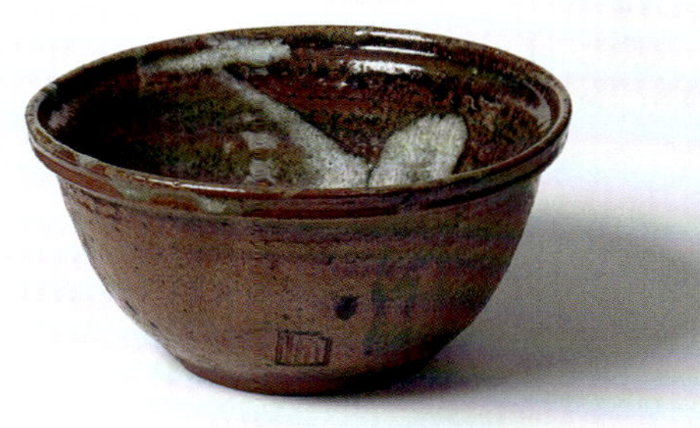

520 60/1983

See: Lilli Lehmann, *Sys Thomsen. Et forsøg på at belyse hendes keramiske arbejders forudsætning i mødet mellem japansk filosofi og form og vestens kultur*, unpublished dissertation, Copenhagen University, 1988, Designmuseum Danmarks Library; Gelfer-Jørgensen, M., 2013.

520. Bowl, 1983

Stoneware, glazed, partially unglazed; thrown, wood-fired at 1280°. H 11.7 x Diam 23. Mark: Stamped mark on base. Mus.no. 60/1983
ACQUISITION: Sys Thomsen. Donation from *Eenny Dessaus Mindelegat*. See: Gelfer-Jørgensen, M., 2013, p. 255

521. Bowl, 1983

Stoneware, glazed; thrown, wood-fired at 1280°. H 9.5 x Diam 17.5. Mark: Stamped mark on base. Mus.no. 223/1984. ACQUISITION: Sys Thomsen. Donation from *Benny Dessaus Mindelegat*. See: Sys Thomsen, *Dagens Ret*, Borgens Forlag, 1983, pp. 89-91. Published in connection with the exhibition with the same title and date in the museum. Gelfer-Jørgensen, M., 2013

522. Dish, 1986. *Blommeblomst i klippe* (Plum flower in rock)

Stoneware, barley-ash-glazed, several layers of glaze; modelled, stamped decoration, wood-fired at 1280°. H 2.5 x W 20. Mark: Stamped mark on base. Mus.no. 79/1987
ACQUISITION: Galleri Birkdam, 1987, Copenhagen. Donation from *Kunstindustrimuseets Venner*. See: Gelfer-Jørgensen, M., 2013, p. 257

523. Bowl, 1986. *Kinesisk drage* (Chinese Dragon)

Stoneware, glazed; burnt-on seaweed, wood-fired at 1280°. H 6 x Diam 19. Mark: Stamped mark on base. Mus.no. 80/1987
ACQUISITION: Galleri Birkdam, 1987, Copenhagen. Donation from *Kunstindustrimuseets Venner*. See: Gelfer-Jørgensen, M., 2013, p. 256

524. Pot, 1980s

Earthenware, glazed; thrown, oxidised, wood-fired with saggar technique, packed in seaweed, at 1280°. H 14.5 x W 7. Mark: Stamped mark on base. Mus.no. 6/1991
ACQUISITION: *Mit stentøjshus*, 2007, Kunstindustrimuseet. Donation from *Fonden af 26. maj 1978*

523 80/1987

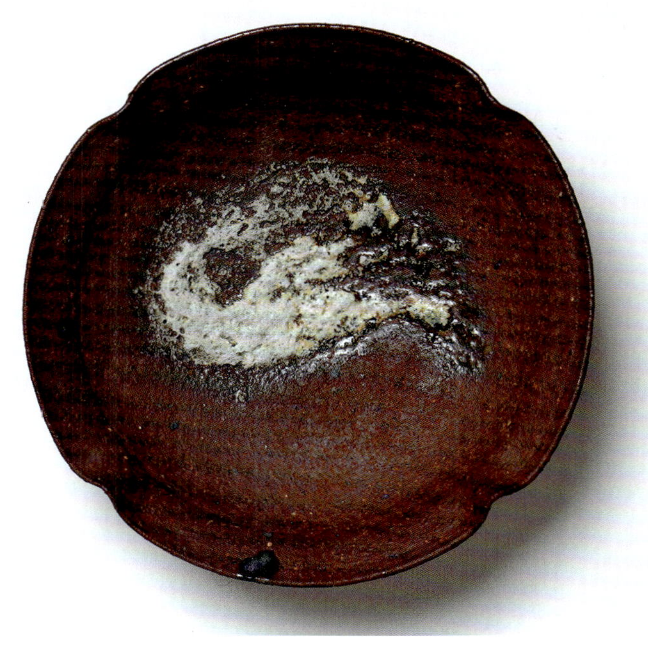

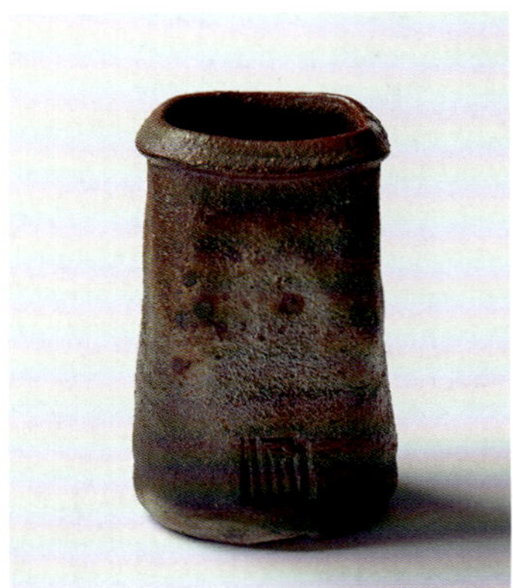

524 6/1991

526. Bowl on three legs, 1995

Stoneware, unglazed; modelled, shaped, imprint of basket, wood-fired at 1280°. H 12 x W 30.5. Mark: Stamped mark on side. Mus.no. 166/1995

ACQUISITION: Galleri Nørby, Copenhagen. Donation from ISS.

See: Dybdahl, L., 1997

525. Bowl, date unknown

Earthenware, unglazed; thrown, wood-fired at 1280°. H 10.5 x Diam 25.5. Mark: Stamped mark on base. Mus.no. 218/1994

ACQUISITION: Sys Thomsen, 1994

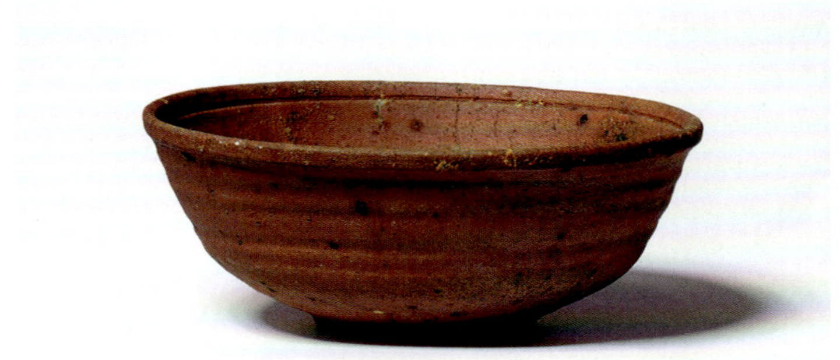

525 218/1994

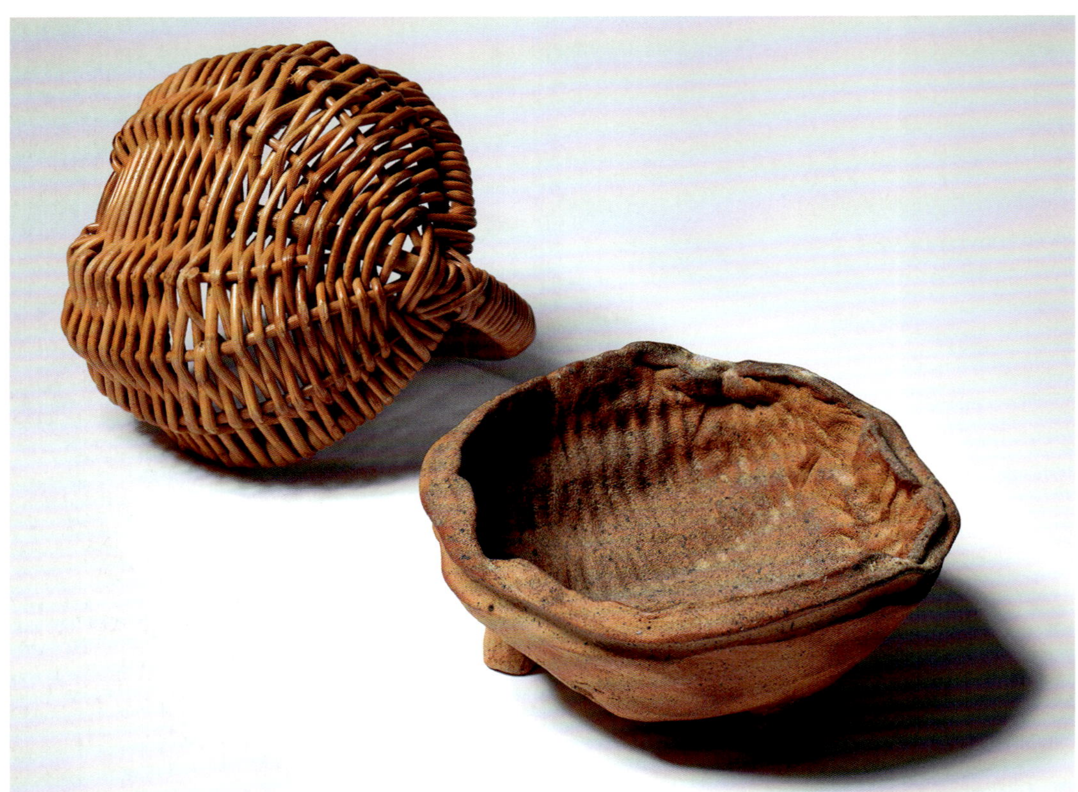

526 166/1995

TOPHØJ, ANNE see SOUVENIX p. 291

TYBJERG, PETER 1944 –

Ceramicist, sculptor
Autodidact

1959-64 Mechanic, Årslev Maskinfabrik
1966-96 Own studio workshop, Hindsholm, Kerteminde, Funen; 1996- Assens, Funen
1976-78 Committee member, Danish Crafts and Design Association
1981- Guest teacher at art schools, teacher training colleges, senior schools and colleges; lecturer on international studio ceramics
1987-90 Chairman of Guest Atelier, Hollufgård, Odense
1994-96 Co-founder, board chairman and manager of Grimmerhus Museum of Ceramic Art, Middelfart, Funen
1997 Co-founder of the ceramic group *Clay Today*
www.petertybjerg.dk

Peter Tybjerg (PT) has to be seen as one of the significant initiative-takers within Danish ceramics in the last decades of the 20th century. An international dimension was apparent in his work from an early stage, both in his ceramics and in his activities as a teacher and consultant for the development of ceramic materials and techniques.

PT became involved with ceramics through the development of kilns and potters' wheels for friends who were interested in ceramics. This, combined with seeing ceramics by Picasso on a journey to Antibes, in France, in 1964, provided inspiration to begin the work with sculptural ceramics that ended up in many years of extensive activities. The results can be seen in a large number of monumental commissioned works, mainly in ceramic materials, but also in bronze and other metals, testifying to PT's fruitful combination of great technical ability, creative artistic potential and lively interest in new initiatives and enterprises which have played a far-reaching role in strengthening the position of studio ceramics in Denmark. PT's major efforts towards the setting up of Denmark's International Museum of Ceramic Art (now CLAY) demonstrate the international outlook that has been characteristic of his exploits and achievements, which have included being employed at an Art & Craft Centre in South Africa, many journeys to different parts of the world for study purposes and to participate in symposiums and workshops, involvement in the World Craft Council and association with the *Clay Today* movement.

Among PT's commissioned works mention should be made of the huge stoneware relief from 1978, *Bjergkongens Hal* (The hall of the King of the Mountains) (300 x 1600 cm) for Mulernes Legatskole, Odense, and of the four-metre tall sculpture *Symbolæg* (Symbolic egg), also in stoneware, for the University of Southern Denmark, Odense, from 1993, which is covered with thousands of incised symbols and characters from cultures all over the world, displaying the spiritual and material inspiration taken by the artist from the universal cultural heritage that characterizes this and other works.

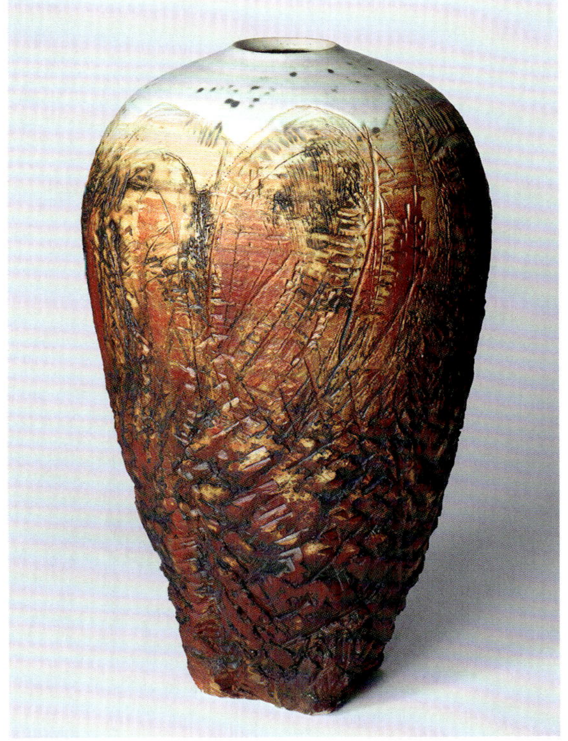

527 116/2009

Alongside these place-related commissioned works PT has maintained extensive exhibition activities in Denmark and abroad, with sculptural stoneware pots, glazed and with a great diversity of colours, structures, and surface incisions, often depicting abstract impressions of nature. The museum's work by PT belongs to a group of objects with a basic form that concludes with a finely-rounded dome-like top **(527)**. In 2004 PT was accorded the honour of a major retrospective exhibition, with associated catalogue, at Denmark's Museum of Ceramics, CLAY. See: Seisbøll, L., 1991; Dybdahl, L., 1997

527. Pot, 1990

Stoneware, metal oxides, glazed; modelled, scored. H 65. Mark: 'Peter Tybjerg 1990' painted on base. Mus.no. 116/2009
ACQUISITION: Donation from *Ny Carlsbergfondet*, 2009

VANGSGAARD, METTE 1968 –

Painter
1989-96 The Royal Danish Academy of Fine Arts
www.mettevangsgaard.com

The museum's collection includes works made by artists in ceramic material. During the whole period of its existence the museum has attached importance to continuing to add to the collection in this area, which has played a role in Danish ceramic history ever since Thorvald Bindesbøll at the beginning of the 1880s strolled out, with his painter friends, to Johan Wallmann's pottery in Utterslev, outside Copenhagen. Some 100 years later, in the 1980s, a new generation of painters became interested in the possibilities of clay, and this has continued, partly because the Academy still has a ceramics laboratory.
Mette Vangsgaard (MV) is one of the younger artists who have experimented with ceramic material; she studied painting but uses an impressively diverse range of materials and media in her works, combining figuratively modelled ceramic elements with oil painting and photographic prints. Works with these mixed components were most recently exhibited at the Marie Kirkegaard Gallery in 2016, in a series of works with childhood memories from the countryside as theme. MV's motif world grows out of modern life in the immediate vicinity, and she gives it expression in a poetic realistic form. The breaking down of nature in man-made present-day existence was the theme of a number of her ceramic works from the early years of this century which show different versions of small islands, with no signs of human life, but one or more naked trees, with glaze of a colour that suggests a catastrophic environmental condition. The museum acquired one of those works from 2005 **(528)**.

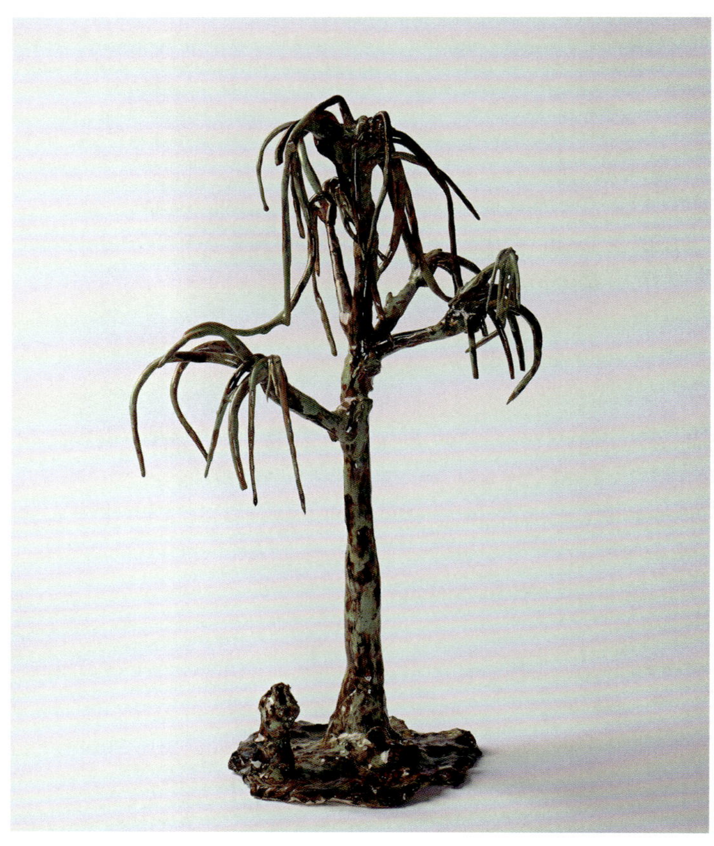

528 199/2005

528. Sculpture, 2005

Earthenware, glazed; modelled. H 47 x W 30 x D 20. Mark: none. Mus.no. 199/2005. ACQUISITION: *Imaginary Realities,* Galerie Mikael Andersen, Copenhagen, 2005.

VANGSØ, HANS 1950 –

Ceramicist

1972-76 Det Jyske Kunstakademi

1984- Own studio workshop with Anne Fløche, Knebel, Jutland
www.hansvangsoe.dk

Hans Vangsø (HV) first trained as a cabinet-maker and was then admitted to Det Jyske Kunstakademi and in the years 1972-76 completed his studies in Ceramics under the guidance of Gutte Eriksen, with whom he retained a close relationship. This education inspired his interest in the textures of ceramics and his sense of the importance of experimentation.

It is characteristic of HV's work that the ceramic process culminates in actual firing in which thick-flowing glazes on pots and dishes have salt and material with iron content added to them. Firing is often repeated 3 or 4 times before the artist is satisfied with the result. When one looks at the disrupted surfaces and the volcanic flow of the glazes it is hard to imagine that this dynamic eruptive effect is controlled, but after the artist's many years of research and tests in the workshop the results achieved are not accidental. For HV it is the textural in ceramics that is absolutely central, and he has made his mark as a ceramicist who succeeds in creating works in which clay and glaze, through masterly firing technique, become one entity which amazes with its strength and robustness of expression and wealth of textural structures.

HV is a highly respected ceramic artist on the international ceramic scene, possibly better known abroad than in Denmark. He has found strong inspiration from the Japanese and Far Eastern ceramic tradition, which he met through Gutte Eriksen, but later acquired personal knowledge of, through journeys and study visits to many parts of the world. At the same time HV unmistakably also has roots in Danish ceramics, with its pure lines and functional ideals from the 20th century.

The four works by HV in the museum's collection came from the 1990s to 2008 **(529-532)**. Their basic shapes are the simple pots typical of HV's work, all of stoneware, thrown and then cut and shaped into angular forms. The colours of the glazes range from pale white to pale green, blue, yellowish and brown. The latest work is from 2008 and is a tall slender pot-shape with a fine pale celadon glaze **(532)**.

HV has had his studio on Mols together with his wife and colleague Anne Fløche since 1984. They were both in the exhibition group *8 keramikere* (1987-96), whose members all had a connection with the Ceramics courses at Det Jyske Kunstakademi. HV exhibits internationally and has links to prestigious galleries in London, Stockholm, Paris and elsewhere.

529. Pot, 1990s

Stoneware, ash and clay-glazed; thrown, cut, fired at 1300°. H 21.8 x Diam 10.5. Mark: 'HV' in a circle impressed on base. Mus.no. 38/1994
ACQUISITION: Galleri Nørby, Copenhagen

529 38/1994

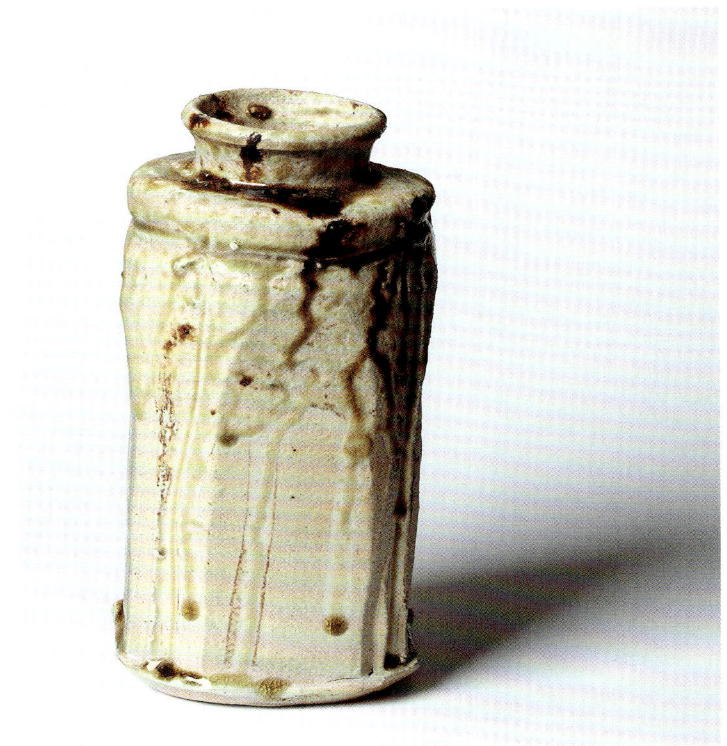

530. Pot, 1990s

Stoneware, glazed; thrown, modelled, hard-fired. H 14 x Diam 17. Mark: 'HV' in a circle impressed on base. Mus.no. 423/2008

ACQUISITION: Donation from estate of Ambassador Niels Christian Tillisch, Copenhagen

531. Pot, 2008

Stoneware, celadon-glazed; modelled. H 76.6 x W 20.5. Mark: 'HV' in a circle impressed on base. Mus.no. 13/2009.

ACQUISITION: Ann Linnemann Studie Galleri, Copenhagen

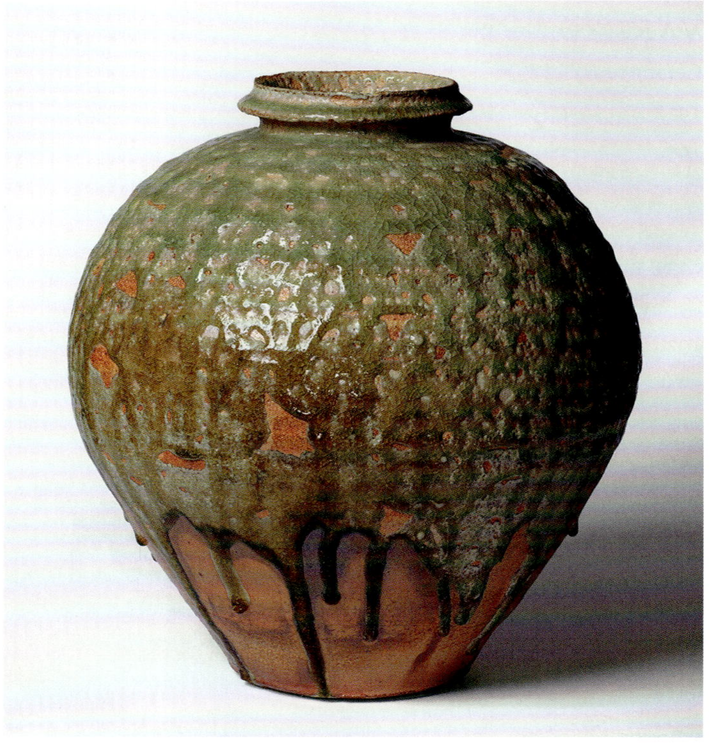

532 114/2009

532. Pot, 2003

Stoneware, running glaze; modelled. H 38 x Diam 34. Mark: 'HV' in a circle impressed on base. Mus.no. 114/2009.

ACQUISITION: Donation from *Ny Carlsbergfondet*

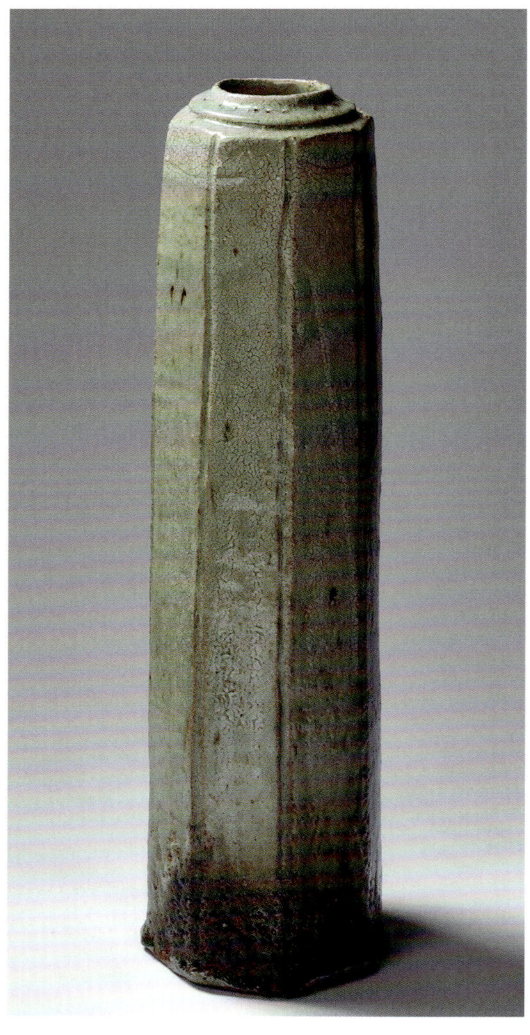

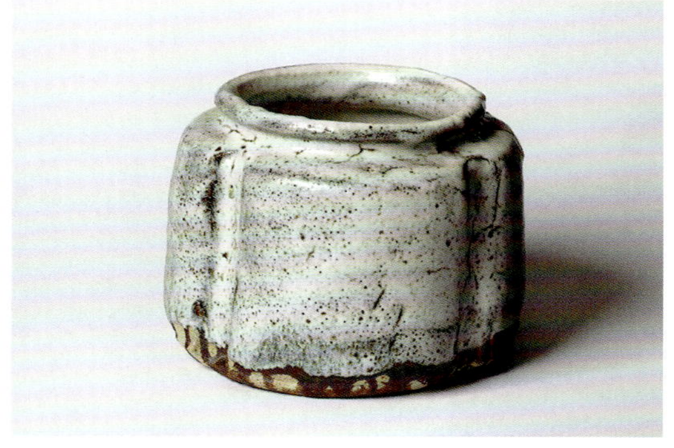

530 423/2008

531 13/2009

VASEGAARD, GERTRUD 1913 – 2007

Ceramicist

1927-29	Hjorths Fabrik, Rønne, Bornholm, workshop experience
1930-31	Kunsthåndværkerskolen
1932-33	Workshop experience in Copenhagen with Axel Salto and Bode Willumsen; potter Olga Jensen
1933-36	Workshop with Lisbet Munch-Petersen, Gudhjem, Bornholm
1938-48	Own studio workshop, Holkadalen, Bornholm
1949-59	Employed by Bing & Grøndahl
1959-68	Workshop with Aksel Rode and Myre Vasegaard, Frederiksberg
1969-2006	Studio workshop with Myre Vasegaard, Frederiksberg
1971	Awarded Statens Kunstfonds honorary lifelong stipend

Gertrud Vasegaard (GV) was the 20th century's leading Danish ceramicist whose lifework is recognised on the level of internationally celebrated ceramicists such as Lucie Rie. GV herself took no action to make herself known while she was alive. She worked with deep concentration throughout her life, and interruptions were not welcome. This intensity of focus on the ceramic material, the energy and nerve invested in it, can be felt very strongly when one stands in front of her works; they resonate and one is caught up in them as in all real art.

The admiration and recognition GV won from an early stage, first for her earthenware works and later for the unparalleled works in stoneware that she made right up to a few years before her death, can be seen from the museum's collection; with 40 works in all, GV is by far the best represented ceramicist. Many works have come to the museum as donations from foundations, from private persons and as deposits from *Statens Kunstfond*, but always in a context where the museum has in advance made an evaluation and accepted in principle; the many donations are also an expression of opinion in the external environment that these works should be protected by being acquired by the museum and should be preserved as an important part of the Danish ceramic cultural heritage. GV received many distinctions and awards in the course of her life; she participated in exhibitions and was a prominent artist-contributor to many of the international initiatives to promote Danish and Scandinavian design and crafts through the 1950s and 60s. She was awarded a gold medal at the Milan Triennale in 1957.

GV's life-pattern fell into several chapters, beginning with her childhood and early youth on Bornholm, where, as the third generation of the Hjorth ceramic dynasty, she naturally had clay in her hands and an artistic dimension in her living conditions. As a 17-year-old she extended her education by attending the newly established Kunsthåndværkerskole in Copenhagen, but left there after a couple of years to take up workshop experience with some of the best-known ceramicists at the time. The following year she went back to Bornholm. There for a time she shared a workshop with her sister, the ceramicist Lisbet Munch-Petersen, before she set up her own workshop in Holkadalen in 1938. From the 1930s there are three earthenware works in the museum's collection **(533, 543-544)**, and from the earthenware pieces of those years one can already trace links with GVs' later works: her sense of the coarse fabric, the simple forms, the glaze treatment and the incised decoration – all foreshadow the herringbone and braided patterns, the rhomboid motives, zigzag- and stepped lines that were to become an integrated part of GV's ceramic form of expression, developed to a masterly stage and diversified through the many years of her work. They set the standard and became almost synonymous with Danish ceramics seen from abroad.

At Kunsthåndværkerskolen GV met a number of artists, including Ejler Bille, Sonja Ferlov Mancoba, Harald Leth, Richard Mortensen and fellow ceramicist Christian Poulsen, who became an important influence in GV's artistic perspective and through whom she made many friends and contacts, e.g. association with Den Frie Udstilling, Copenhagen, although this was broken off by membership of the artists' group *Martsudstillingen* (1969-82). GV was widely-read and well-informed about contemporary art and the long and rich history of ceramics; Chinese ceramics were an important source of inspiration for her for a time, but she was above all an independent, hard-working and unique artist in her own right.

The war years and the period after that were difficult, with constricting material shortages, but through acquaintanceship with the chemically knowledgeable art historian Aksel Rode, artistic consultant at Bing & Grøndahl, GV was invited in the post-war years to work at the factory's artists' workshop, from 1949 until 1959 as a fulltime member of staff: in 1959 GV and her daughter Myre Vasegaard broke away from the factory and together set up a shared workshop with Aksel Rode (to whom GV was married 1961-73) in Allégade in the Frederiksberg district of Copenhagen.

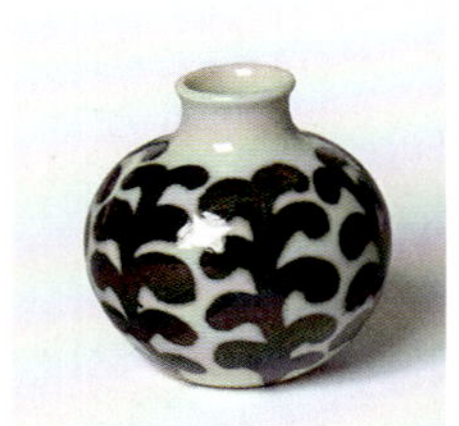
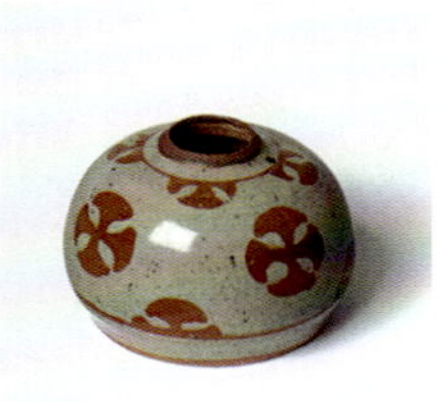

Donation samples from Bing & Grøndahl. Mus.no. 106/2011, 107/2011.

Donation from Mrs. Helle Lassen

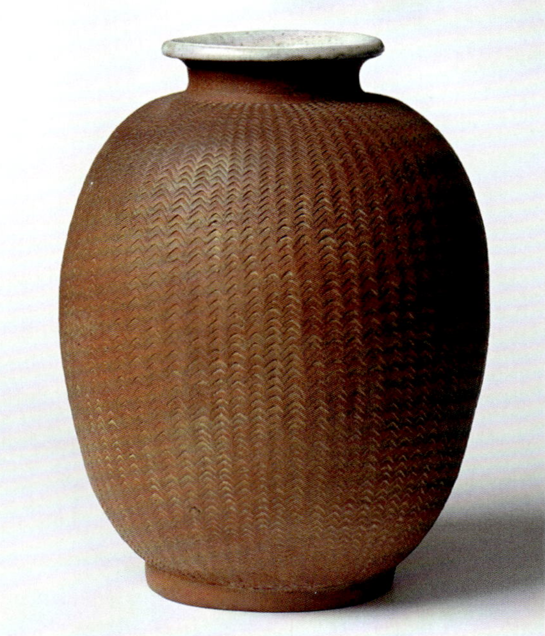

533 B2/1943

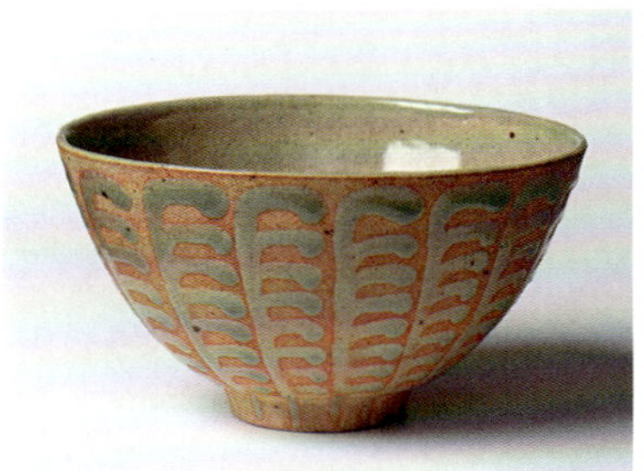

534 27/1947

The years at Bing & Grøndahl's porcelain factory meant that GV exchanged earthenware for stoneware, but she transferred her personal ceramic sensibility to the new material and contributed to a shift in the style of the factory's stoneware production, because among

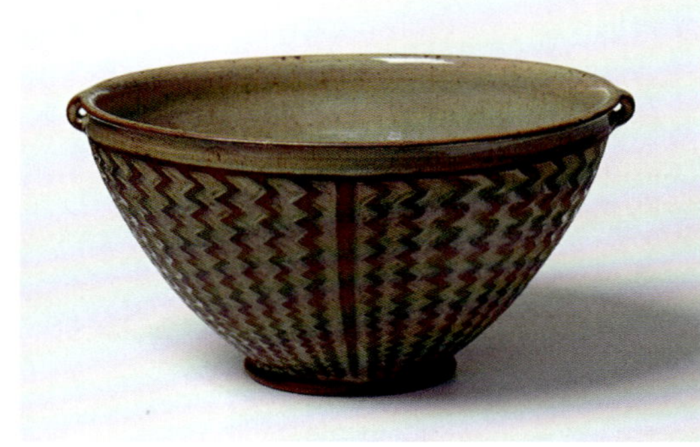

536 46/1952

other things she preferred clear, more glass-like glazes, through which the texture of the clay could be sensed. Her close cooperation with senior engineer Busch Jensen and with Aksel Rode led to intense work on development of the glazes that GV sought and that she herself contributed to producing. Among the many new glazes were the celadon types, but also e.g. a richly-coloured yellow uranium glaze **(535)**, oxblood glaze and various nuances of the grey-white glaze that is characteristic of many of the products from the workshop in Allégade.
From the beginning of the period at Bing & Grøndahl, from 1946-51, there are three works in the museum's collection that show examples of GV's ornamentation: a bowl with vertical decoration painted on the outside with celadon glaze on an unglazed body, with the inside glazed with the same glaze **(534)**; a monumental pot with seven rows of impressed ornaments (46/1952), and a bowl with a zigzag ornament

in relief **(538)**. Comparing these with GV's later works one can clearly see the simplification and refinement of the decoration that develops through time.

A particular chapter in the years at the factory was defined by GV's work with blue underglaze painting, when she achieved success in finding a perfect balance between the white and blue glazing. Examples of the blue painting are to be found in the museum's collection **(537,539,552,556,558)**; several of the works were connected with a decorative commission from Statens Kunstfond in 1966 for a well for Jonstrup Seminarium in Lyngby. GV's interest in blue painting was linked to her desire to develop a new blue-painted porcelain service, but after she left the factory in 1959 this was not realised until a later date, in cooperation with the Royal Porcelain Factory. The result was

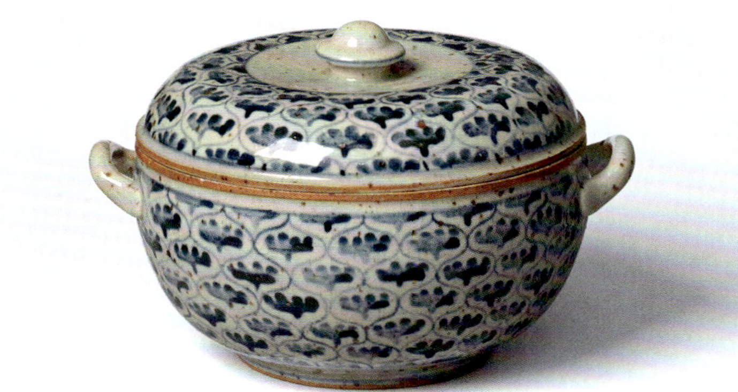

537 9/1953

the 'Gemina' service, decorated in blue underglaze painting (1962), and that was followed by two further services, the white 'Gemma' with stamped rhomboid ornaments (1962), and 'Capella', in stoneware (1975). It was the case for each service that Vasegaard herself threw the models in her own workshop. For Bing & Grøndahl GV created in 1956 the very lovely Chinese inspired pale glazed tea service with brown rims that was set in production in 1957. In 2006 that service was included in the Minister of Culture's Cultural Canon, in the category Design and Crafts. The museum has an example of this thoroughly

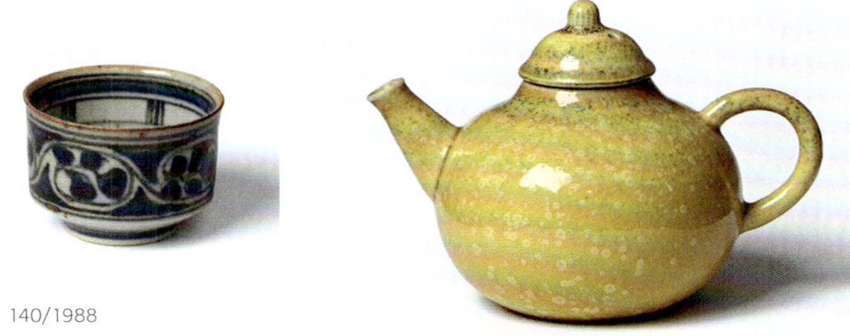

552 140/1988

535 28a-b/1947

worked-through and unique service, but it falls outside the remit of this catalogue; unfortunately all the services have gone out of production at Royal Copenhagen.

From 1969 and until their death, Myre Vasegaard in 2006 and Gertrud Vasegaard in 2007, they lived together, mother and daughter, and worked in the workshop in Frederiksberg in a constructive and meaningful partnership that made space for their very different ceramic forms of expression and development. In the museum's collection GV is more-or-less evenly represented through the decades, with six

539 8/1956

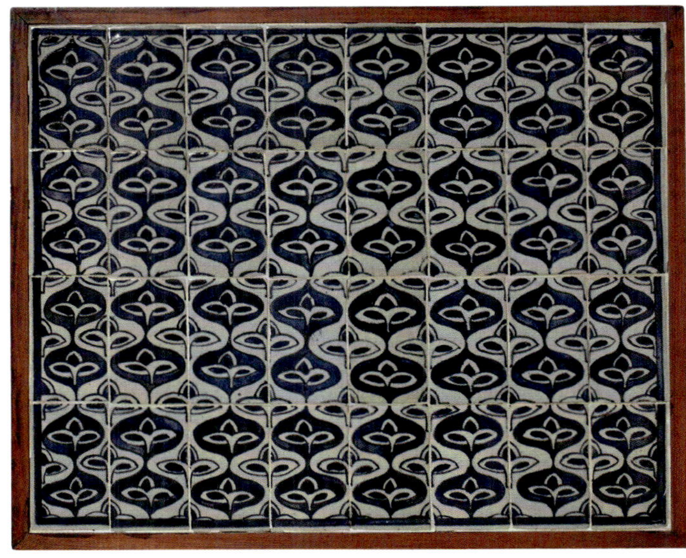

works from the 1960s, seven from the 70s, nine from the 80s and four from the 90s. The constantly present form is the container: basins, trays, pots, bowls, lidded dishes and lidded pots; virtually all stand directly on a base, often oval, as for instance in the case of the bowls with handles from the 1990s or the boxes and pots with flat lids and a variety of types of decoration. Technical details of each of the individual works can be found below, but a couple of GV's works ought to be highlighted here: two monumental masterpieces, large thrown basins, both from the 1970s, with greyish-white glaze and decoration in nuances of brown. The earlier one **(570)** is from 1972 and is cylindrical with triangular patterns between encircling lines; the other **(569)**, is from 1978 and is 16-sided, with a black-brown stepped pattern marking out the angles of the container in a calm rhythm. Throwing these large containers is an achievement in itself, but in spite of the format there is the same intensity and exquisite sense of the material as in the smaller works. The cylindrical basin was acquired by Statens Kunstfond at the first retrospective exhibition in the museum in 1984, arranged by the ceramic connoisseur and museum curator Vibeke Woldbye in cooperation with GV. In 2011 Holstebro Kunstmuseum held an extensive retrospective exhibition in cooperation with Professor Henning Jørgensen. Every single work by GV that is known today has met the test of passing through the needle's eye of GV's approval; she was remorseless in her self-criticism, and many works fell to the hammer. One can therefore be sure that the works which GV exhibited, in the many exhibitions she participated in, and which were disseminated from there to those who loved her works, collectors and museums, were approved of by the artist. A review of the museum's collection of GV's works shows eloquently that GV was not seeking perfection, but a kind of unity of ceramic expression, in which the interplay of body, glaze and decoration become truly vibrant form. See: Gertrud Vasegaard – keramiske arbejder 1930-1984, 1964; Jørgensen, H., 2011

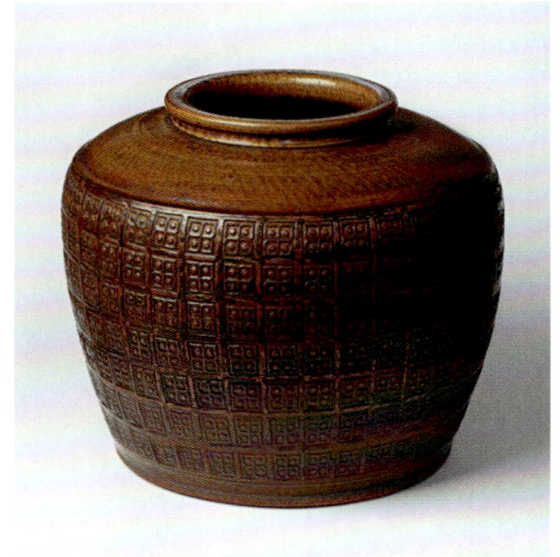

538 10/1953

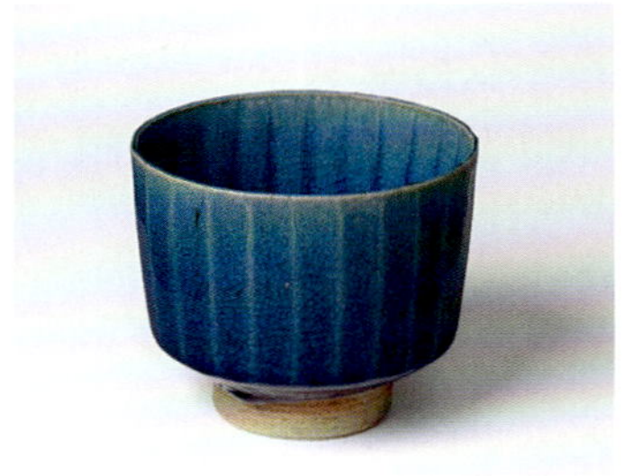

540 691/1962

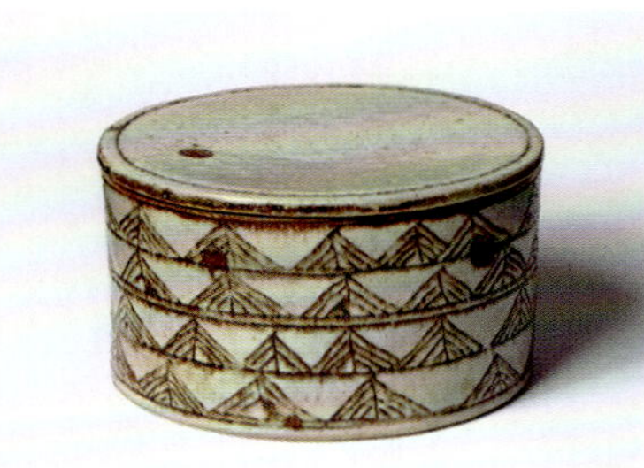

542 34/1969

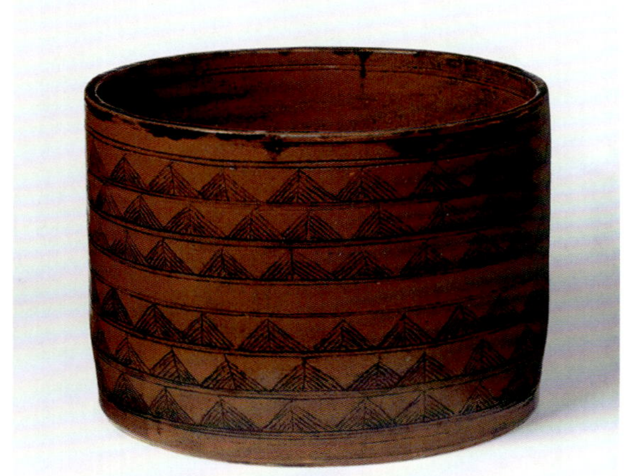

541 33/1969

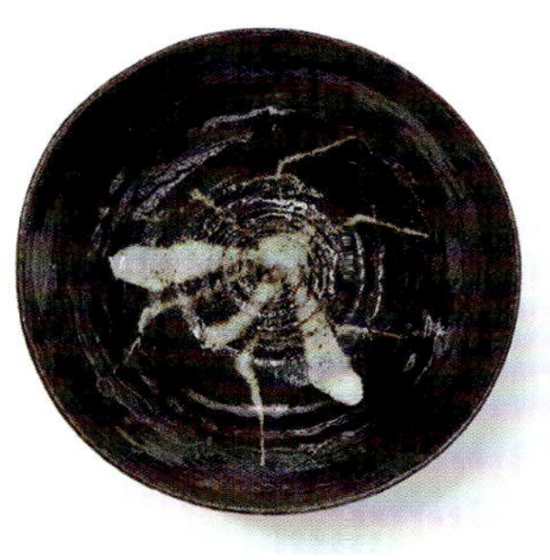

544 116/1969

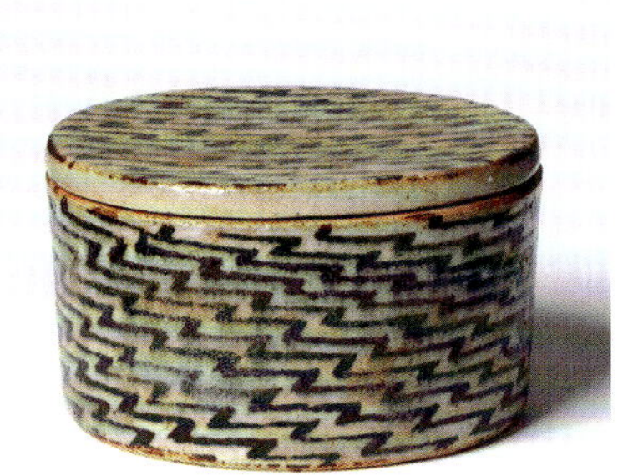

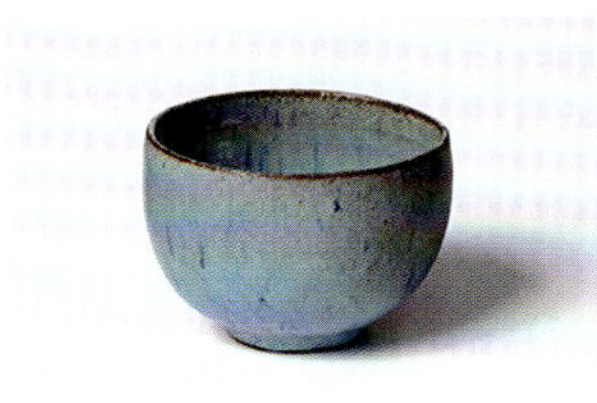

543 104/1969

546 18a-b/1980

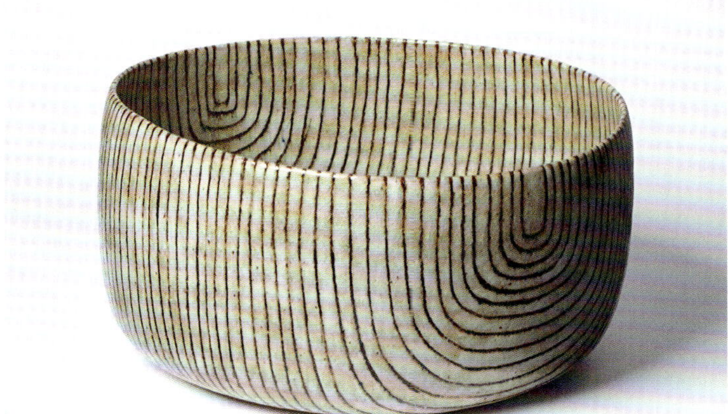

545 94/1978

533. Pot, 1937

Earthenware, glazed; sgrafitto. H 26.5 x Diam 19.7. Mark: 'GV NOV 1937' stamped on base. Mus.no. B2/1943

ACQUISITION: *Dansk kunsthåndværk*, 1943 Kunstindustrimuseet. Donation from *Ny Carlsbergfondet*

534. Bowl, 1946

Stoneware, celadon-glazed, partially unglazed; horn painting technique, glaze decoration. H 10.2 x Diam 19.5. Mark: 'GV' and B&G's mark stamped on base. Mus.no. 27/1947

ACQUISITION: Bing & Grøndahl, 1947. See: Lassen, E., 1947. Lassen, E., 1978

535. Teapot, 1946

Stoneware, uranium-glazed; thrown. H 12.5 x W 17.7. Mark: 'Gertrud Vasegaard B&G' written on base. Mus.no. 28a-b/1947

ACQUISITION: Bing & Grøndahl, 1947. See: Lassen, E., 1947. Lassen, E., 1978

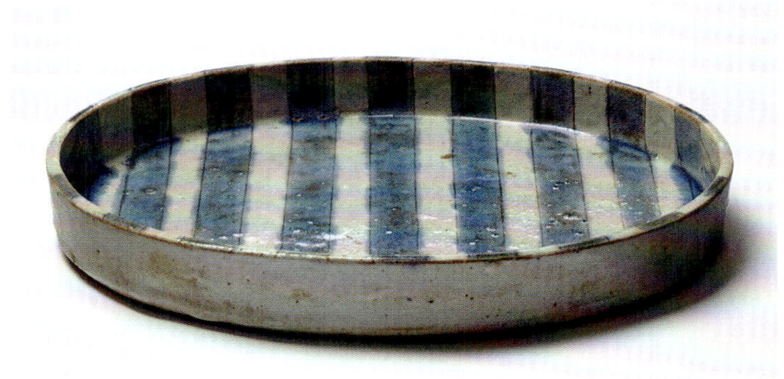

547 94/1983

536. Bowl, 1951

Stoneware, celadon-glazed, partially unglazed; relief, cut zig-zag decoration. H 17 x Diam 30. Mark: 'GV B&G' stamped on base. Mus.no. 46/1952

ACQUISITION: Bing & Grøndahl. Donation from *Benny Dessaus Mindelegat*. See: Lassen, E., 1978

537. Tureen, 1953

Stoneware, glazed; thrown, onion decoration. H 15 x Diam 20. Mark: 'GV B&G' painted on base. Mus.no. 9/1953. ACQUISITION: Bing & Grøndahl, 1953. Donation from *Benny Dessaus Mindelegat*. See: E. Lassen, 1978

538. Pot, 1950

Stoneware, glazed; stamped decoration. H 8.5 x W 15 x D 12.5. Mark: 'november 1950 GV' painted on base. Mus.no. 10/1953. ACQUISITION: Bing & Grøndahl's Jubilee exhibition, 1953. Donation from *Benny Dessaus Mindelegat*

539. Tile picture, 1956

Stoneware, glazed; decorated with onion and trifoliate motifs, 32 tiles mounted in a wooden frame. H 57.5 x W 47. Mark: indecipherable. Mus.no. 8/1956

ACQUISITION: *Unge danske kunsthåndværkere I*, 1956, Kunstindustrimuseet. Donation from *Kunstindustrimuseets 50-års Jubilæumslegat*.

See: Lassen, E., 1978

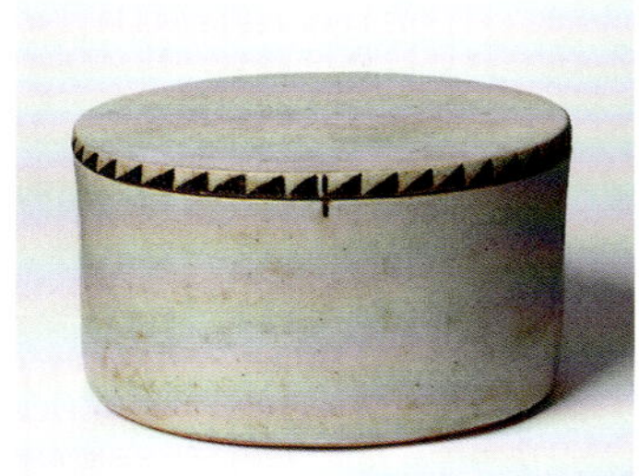

548 167/1984

540. Bowl, 1962

Stoneware, alkali-glazed; thrown, shaped. H 12. Mark: 'GV' stamped on base with Myre Vasegaard's monogram. Mus.no. 691/1962. ACQUISITION: *Nordisk keramik*, 1962, Lund Konsthal. Donation from *Benny Dessaus Mindelegat*

550 2/1988

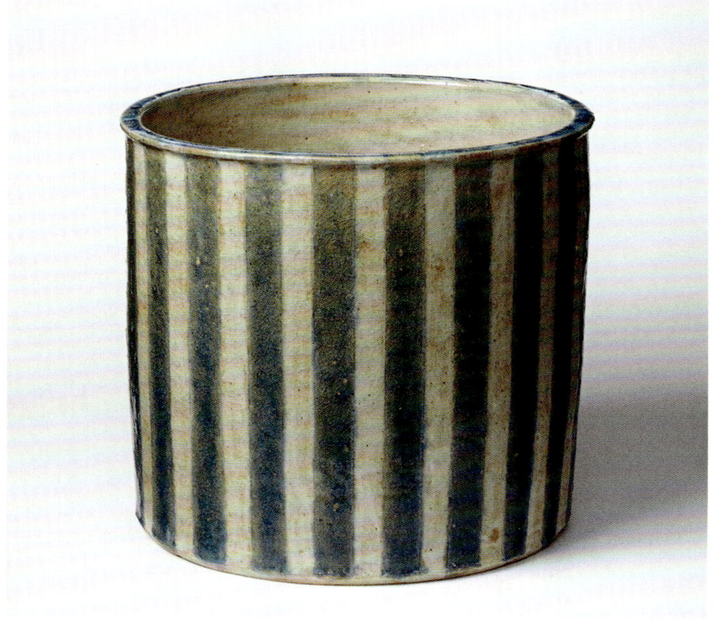

541. Basin, 1968

Stoneware, glazed; thrown, incised triangular decoration.

H 28 x Diam 39. Mark: 'GV' stamped on base. Mus.no. 33/1969

ACQUISITION: *Martsudstillingen*, 1969, Den Frie, Copenhagen. Donation from *Statens 50-års Jubilæumsgave*.

542. Lidded box, 1968

Stoneware, glazed; thrown, incised triangular decoration.

H 11 x Diam 19.3. Mark: 'GV M' stamped on base. Mus.no. 34/1969

ACQUISITION: *Martsudstillingen*, 1969, Den Frie, Copenhagen.

Donation from *Statens 50-års Jubilæumsgave*. See: Steen Møller, V., 1970

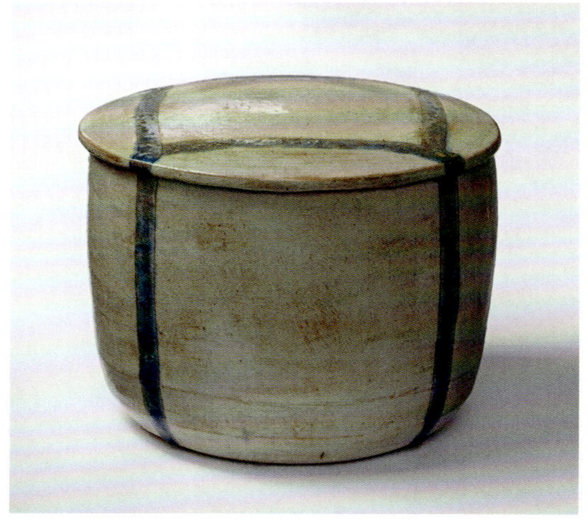

549 92a-b/1986

543. Beaker, 1940

Earthenware, glazed; thrown. H 6. Mark: 'GV' inscribed on base.

Mus.no. 104/1969

ACQUISITION: Director Christian V. Christensen's collection. Donation from *Den kongelige Porcelainsfabrik*

544. Bowl, 1939

Earthenware, glazed; slip, thrown, decorated with mosquito motif.

H 5 x Diam 12. Mark: 'GV' inscribed on base. Mus.no. 116/1969

ACQUISITION: Kuben, 1939, Copenhagen. See: *Brændpunkter*, 1990

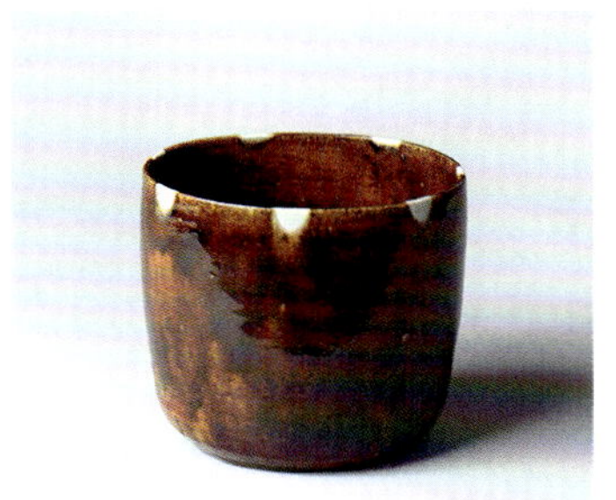

551 3/1988

553 122/1990

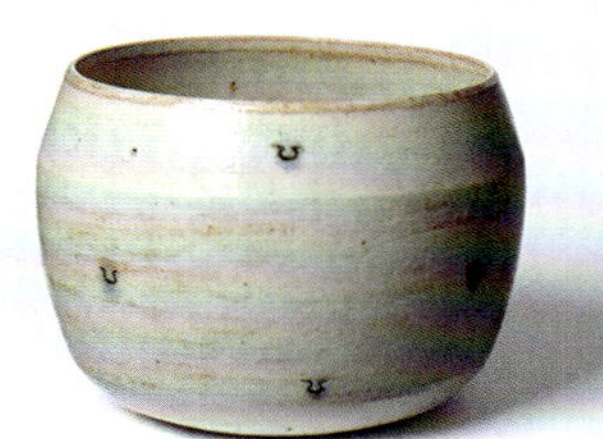

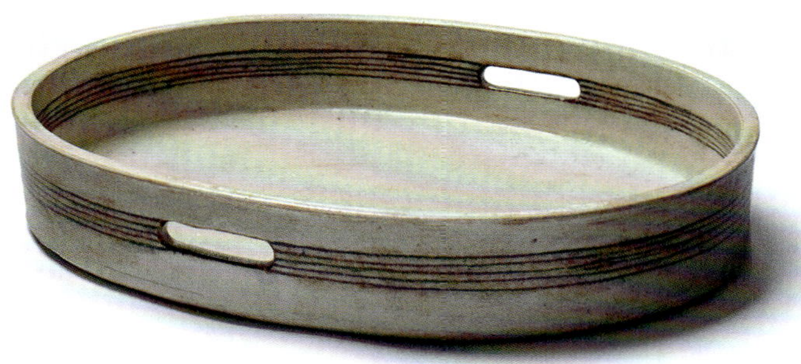

554 240/1990

545. Bowl, 1978

Stoneware, glazed; slip, line decoration. H 16.7 x Diam 34.5.
Mark: 'GV' inscribed on base. Mus.no. 94/1978
ACQUISITION: Clausens Kunsthandel, 1978, Copenhagen.
Donation from *Gutenberghus*

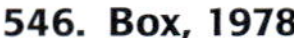

546. Box, 1978

Stoneware, glazed; thrown, step-decoration. H 7.2 x W 12.1.
Mark: 'GV' inscribed on base. Mus.no. 18a-b/1980
ACQUISITION: Gertrud Vasegaard.
Donation from *Statens 50-års Jubilæumslegat*

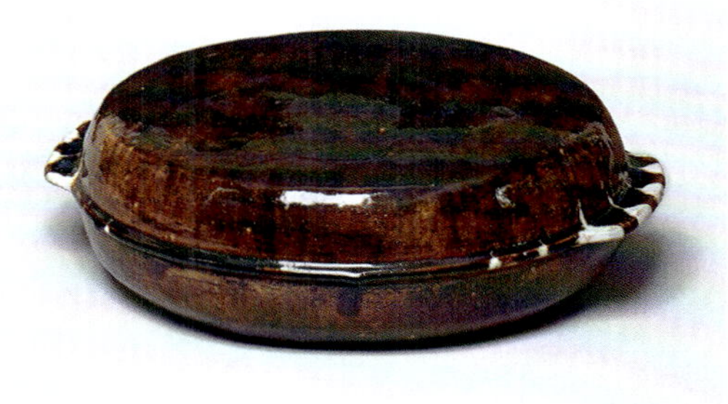

555 44a-b/1991

547. Dish, 1982

Stoneware, clear- and cobalt- glazed; slip, brush-painted, fired at 1320°.
H 5.5 x W 40.5. Mark: 'GV 1982' inscribed on base. Mus.no. 94/1983
ACQUISITION: Clausens Kunsthandel, 1983, Copenhagen.
Donation from *Ny Carlsberg Museumslegat*

560 310/1993

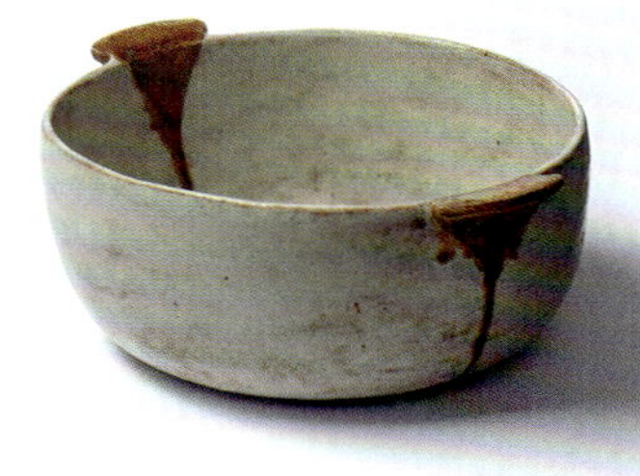

562 201/1995

557 206/1992

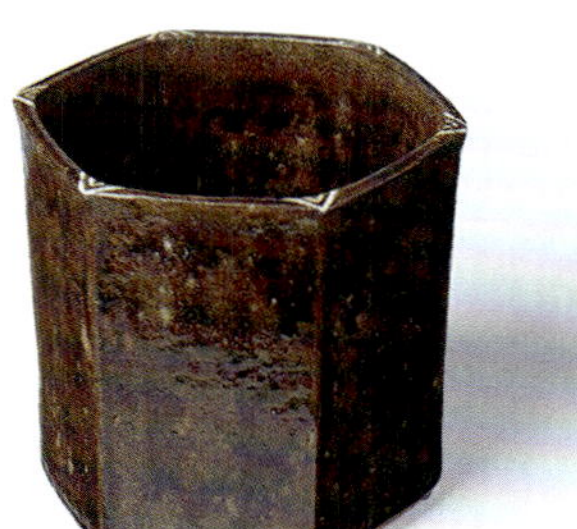

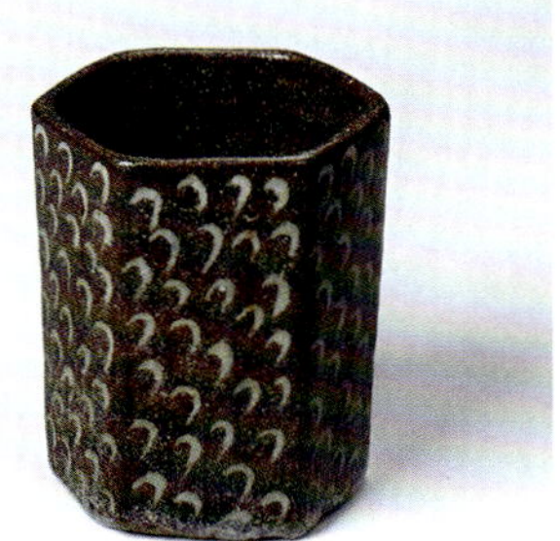

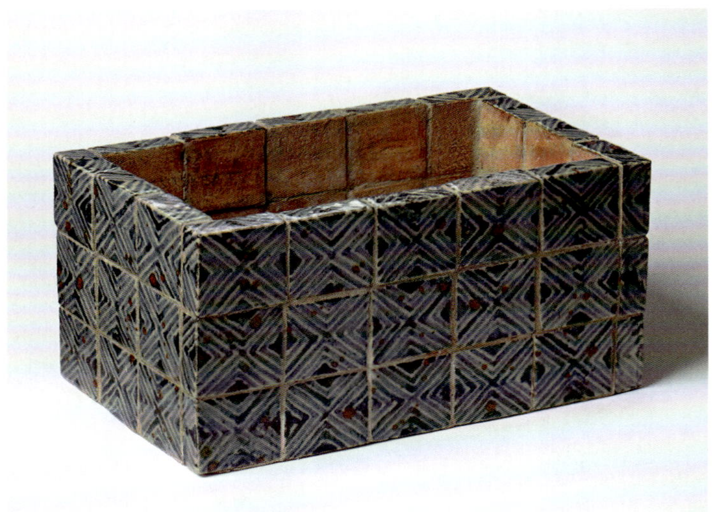

556 131/1992

548. Lidded box, 1984

Stoneware, glazed; thrown, decoration on lid. H 14.8 x W 24.7. Mark: 'GV 1984' inscribed on base. Mus.no. 167/1984. ACQUISITION: Gertrud Vasegaard. Donation from *Benny Dessaus Mindelegat*. See: *Brændpunkter*, 1990

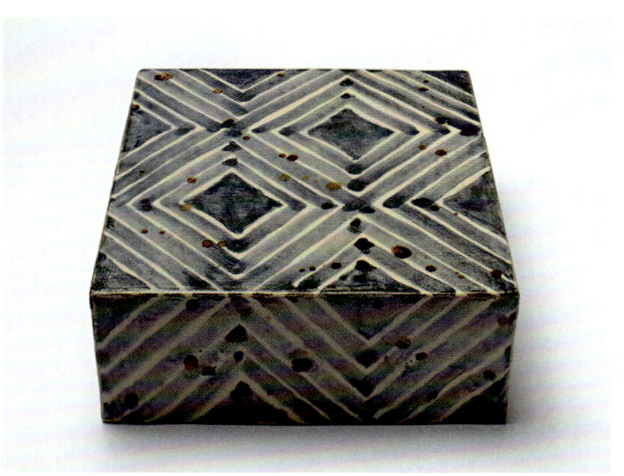

558 4/1993

549. Lidded pot, 1986

Stoneware, clear- and cobalt-glazed; thrown, striped decoration.
H 26.5 x Diam 33.5. Mark: 'GV' stamped on base. Mus.no. 92a-b/1986
ACQUISITION: Clausens Kunsthandel, 1986, Copenhagen. Donation from *C.L. Davids Legat af 1978*

550. Basin, 1987

Stoneware, clear- and cobalt-glazed; thrown, slip, brush-painted stripe decoration, fired at 1320°. H 34 x Diam 36. Mus.no. 2/1988
ACQUISITION: Den Frie, Copenhagen, 1988. Donation from *Nationalbankens Jubilæumsfond af 1968*. See: *Brændpunkter*, 1990. *From the Kilns of Denmark*, 2002

551. Pot, 1986

Stoneware, glazed; thrown, glaze-decoration. H 17 x Diam 19. Mark: 'GV 1986' inscribed on base. Mus.no. 3/1988
ACQUISITION: Den Frie, Copenhagen, 1988. Donation from *Nationalbankens Jubilæumsfond af 1968*

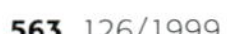

563 126/1999

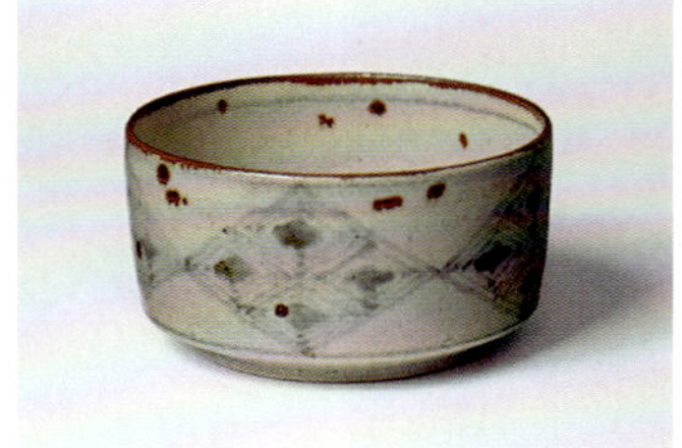

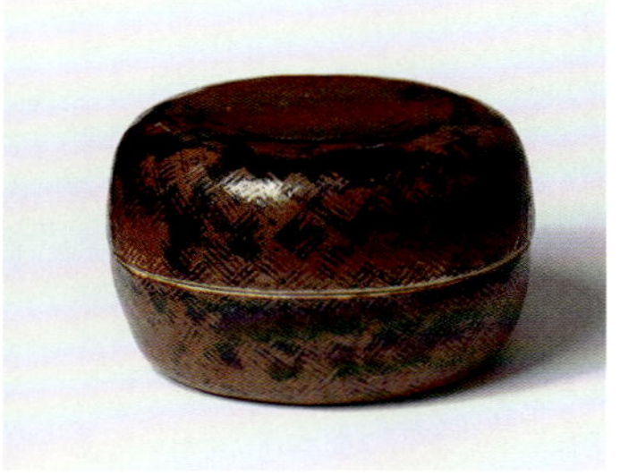

564 127a-b/1999

552. Cup, 1955

Stoneware, glazed; thrown, brush-painted, plant decoration. H 5.8 x Diam 7.8. Mark: 'GV B&G' inscribed on base. Mus.no. 140/1988
ACQUISITION: Donation from the estate of Rigmor Krarup
See: *Brændpunkter*, 1990

553. Bowl, 1989-90

Stoneware, glazed; thrown, dot-decoration. H 19.5 x Diam 23. Mark: 'GV 1988' inscribed on base. Mus.no. 122/1990. ACQUISITION: Den Frie, Copenhagen, 1990. Donation from *Benny Dessaus Mindelegat*

554. Tray, 1986-89

Stoneware, glazed; thrown, slip, decorated with stripes, integrated handles.
H 8.4 x W 46.8. Mark: 'GV' inscribed on base. Mus.no. 240/1990

ACQUISITION: Donation from *Poul og Hildur Pedersens Mindelegat ved Kunstindustrimuseets 100-års Jubilæum*

555. Lidded dish, 1991. *Skildpadde* (Tortoise)
Stoneware, glazed; thrown, shaped, glaze-decoration on handles. H 12.5 x Diam 35.5. Mark: 'EK 5' on base. Mus.no. 44a-b/1991

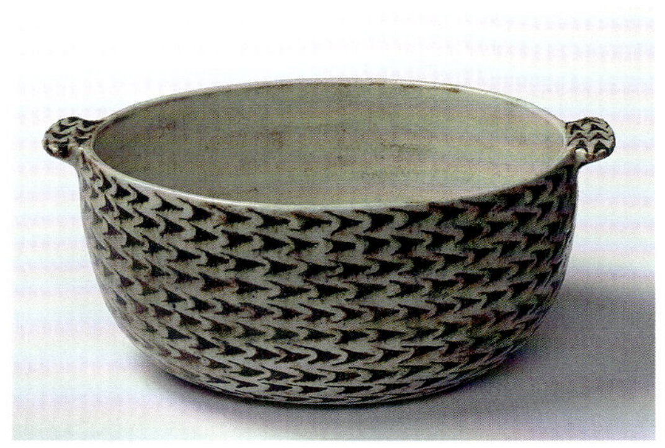

559 309/1993

ACQUISITION: Århus Kunstbygning, 1991. Donation from *Poul og Hildur Kingo Pedersens Mindelegat*

556. Model for well, 1967. (Preparation for commissioned work for Jonstrup Teachers' College)
Earthenware, glazed; assembled tiles, rhomboid decoration. H 18 x W 36. Mus. no. 131/1992. ACQUISITION: *Gertrud Vasegaard – keramiske arbejder 1930-1984*, 1984, Kunstindustrimuseet. Donation from Kristian Jacobsen.
See: *Gertrud Vasegaard – keramiske arbejder 1930-1984,* 1984

557. Beaker, 1982
Stoneware, glazed; thrown, shaped, brush-painted, halfmoon-decoration. H 11 x W 9.3. Mark: 'GV PRØVE RM 1982' stamped on base. Mus.no. 206/1992
ACQUISITION: Donation from Kirsten Hofgaard. See: *Gertrud Vasegaard – keramiske arbejder 1930-84*, 1984, Kunstindustrimuseet

558. Tile, 1967. (Preparation for commissioned work for Jonstrup Teachers' College)
Stoneware, glazed; decorated on two sides, rhomboid decoration. H 34 x W 31 x D 13. Mus.no. 4/1993.
ACQUISITION: Donation from *Den Weinbergske Familiefond*

559. Bowl, 1992. ***Øreskål*** (Bowl with handles)
Stoneware, glazed; thrown, shaped, arrowhead decoration. H 13.5 x W 32.3. Mark: 'GV 1993' stamped on base. Mus.no. 309/1993
ACQUISITION: Donation from *Ny Carlsbergfondet*

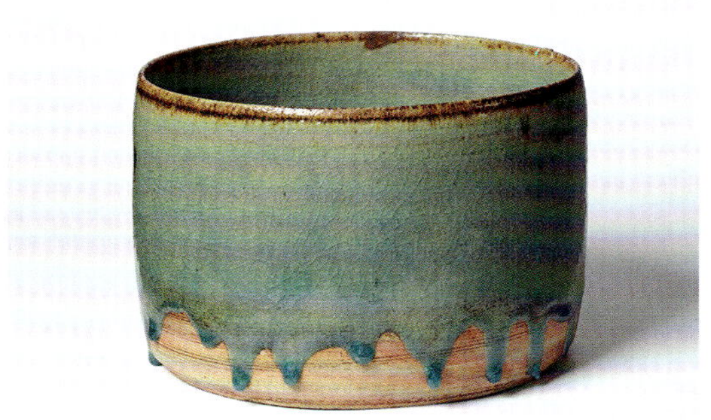

566 129/1999

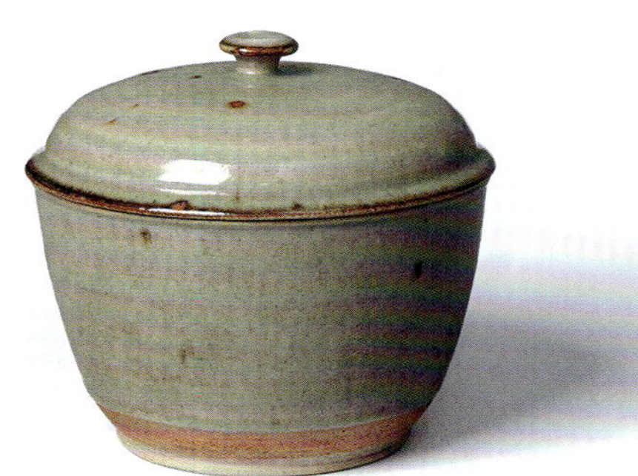

567 130a-b/1999

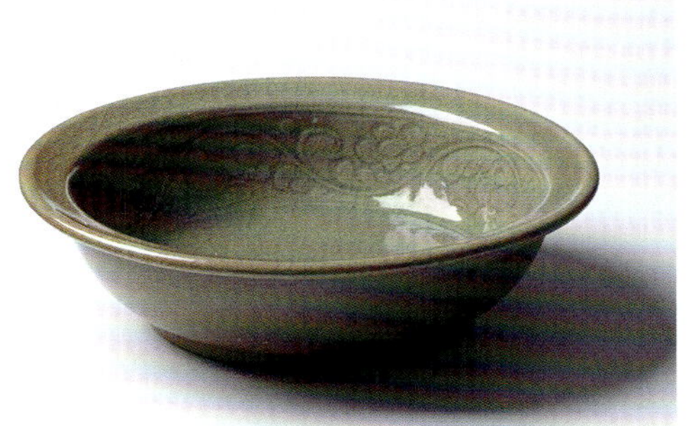

561 206/1994

560. Bowl, 1992. ***Øreskål*** **(Bowl with handles)**
Stoneware, glazed; thrown, shaped, glaze-decoration. H 11.4 x W 31.2. Mark: 'GV 1993' inscribed on base. Mus.no. 310/1993
ACQUISITION: Donation from *Ny Carlsbergfondet*

561. Bowl, 1982
Stoneware, crackle- and celadon- glazed; slip, thrown, fired at 1320°. Diam 30. Mark: 'Gertrud Vasegaard' inscribed on base. Mus.no. 206/1994
ACQUISITION: Jørgen L. Dalgaard, Copenhagen

562. 6-sided pot, 1993
Stoneware, glazed; thrown, modelled, glaze-decorated. H 27 x W 25. Mark: 'GV dec. 93' inscribed on base. Mus.no. 201/1995
ACQUISITION: Galleri Profilen, Aarhus. Donation from *Kunstindustrimuseets Jubilæums- og Mindelegater*

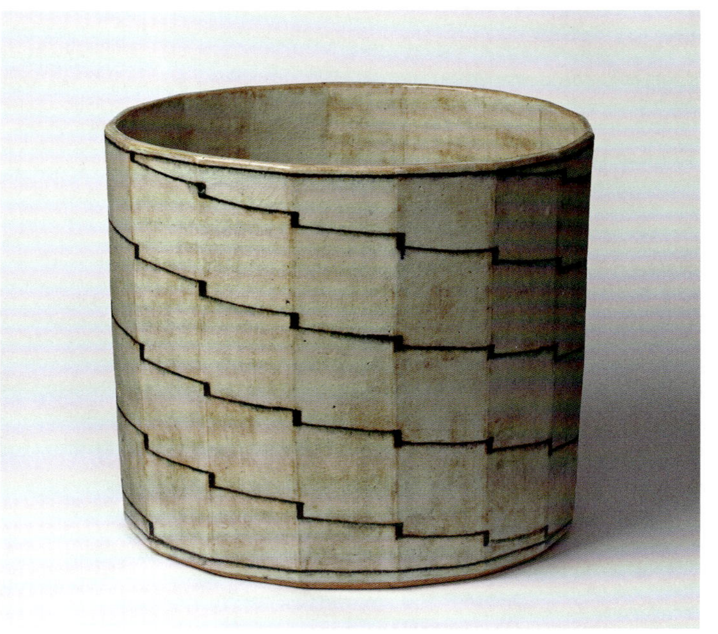

569 D 1551

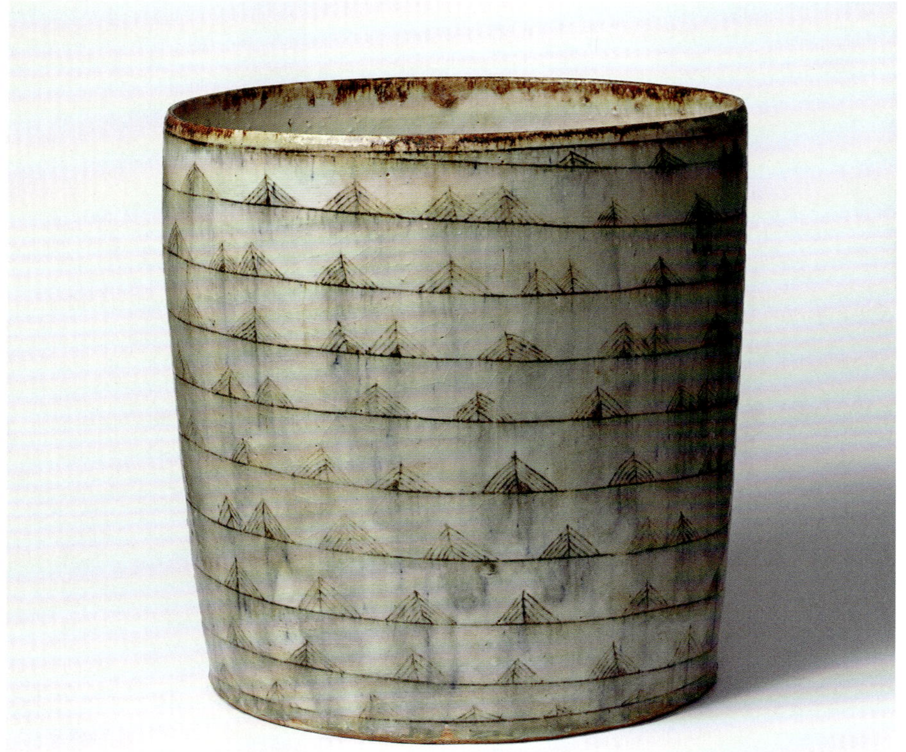

570 D 1577

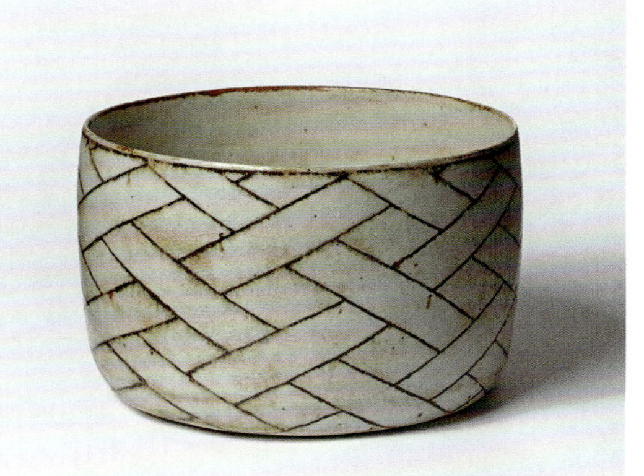

572 D 1701

563. Bowl, 1959-69

Stoneware, glazed; thrown, brush-painted, rhomboid decoration. H 8.5 x Diam 15. Mark: 'GV M' inscribed on base. Mus.no. 126/1999

ACQUISITION: Donation from Bank Director C. B. Andersen, Copenhagen

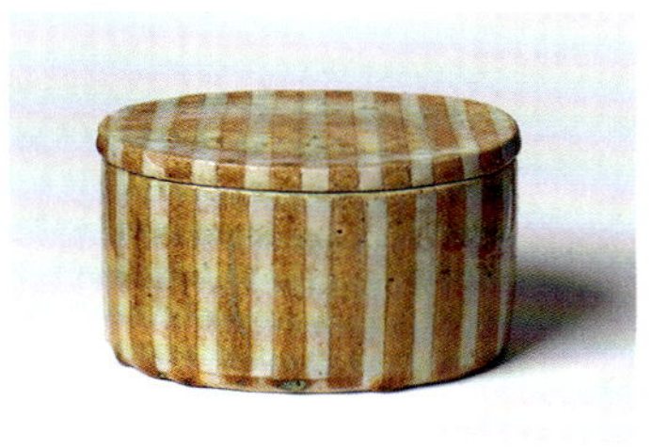

568 D 1544

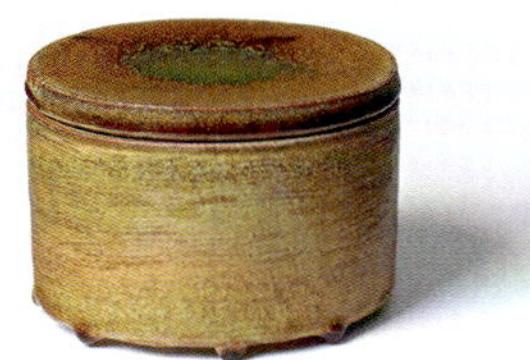

571 D 1594a-b

564. Lidded bowl, date unknown

Stoneware, glazed; thrown, incised basketwork pattern. H 10.5 x Diam 16.5. Mark: 'GV' stamped on base. Mus.no. 127a-b/1999

ACQUISITION: Donation from Bank Director C. B. Andersen, Copenhagen

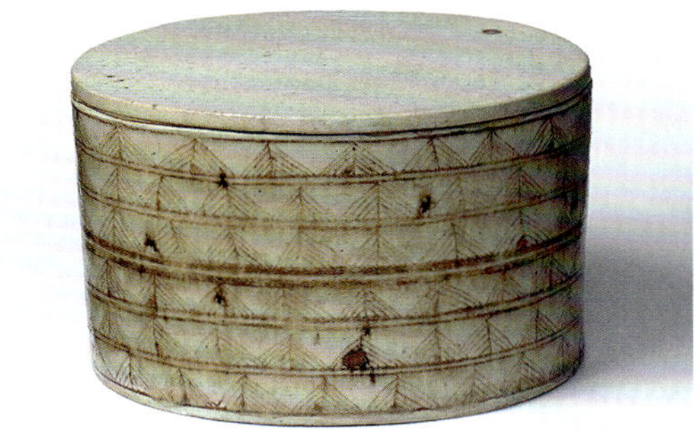

565 128a-b/1999

565. Lidded pot, date unknown

Stoneware, glazed; thrown, triangular decoration. H 18 x Diam 29.5. Mark: 'GV' stamped on base. Mus.no. 128a-b/1999

ACQUISITION: Donation from Bank Director C. B. Andersen, Copenhagen

566. Pot, 1968

Stoneware, thrown; running glaze over the body. H 17.3 x Diam 24. Mark: 'GV' inscribed on base. Mus.no. 129/1999

ACQUISITION: Donation from Bank Director C. B. Andersen, Copenhagen

567. Tureen with lid, date unknown

Stoneware, glazed, partially unglazed; thrown, decorated. H 21 x Diam 22. Mark: 'GV M' painted on base. Mus.no. 130a-b/1999

ACQUISITION: Donation from Bank Director C. B. Andersen, Copenhagen

568. Box, 1979

Stoneware, glazed; thrown, shaped, brush-painted, striped decoration. H 8.4 x W 14.8 x D 13.2. Mark: none. Mus.no. D 1544

ACQUISITION: *Martsudstillingen*, 1981, Den Frie, Copenhagen. Deposited by *Ny Carlsbergfondet*, 1981

569. 16-sided basin, 1978

Stoneware, glazed; thrown, shaped, black-brown step pattern. Mark: 'GV' inscribed on base. H 34 x Diam 37. Mus.no. D 1551

ACQUISITION: Deposited by *Statens Kunstfond*, 1982. See: Dybdahl, L., 1997

570. Basin, 1972

Stoneware, glazed; thrown, triangular decoration. H 38.5 x W 46. Mark: 'GV' inscribed on base. Mus.no. D 1577

ACQUISITION: Deposited by *Statens Kunstfond*, 1985. See: *Gertrud Vasegaard – keramiske arbejder 1930-1984,* 1984, Kunstindustrimuseet

571. Lidded box, 1970

Stoneware, glazed; thrown, glaze-decoration. H 9.5. Mark: 'GV' inscribed on base. Mus.no. D 1594a-b

ACQUISITION: Deposited by Statens Kunstfond, 1985. See: *Gertrud Vasegaard – keramiske arbejder 1930-1984,* 1984

572. Vessel, 1978

Stoneware, crackle-glazed; thrown, incised basketwork pattern. H 17.1 x Diam 25.9. Mark: 'GV' inscribed on base. Mus.no. D 1701. ACQUISITION: Deposited by *Statens Kunstfond*, 1989. See: *From the Kilns of Denmark,* 2002

VASEGAARD, MYRE 1936 – 2006

Ceramicist

1955	completed studies at Kunsthåndværkerskolen
1955-59	Kähler Keramik and Bing & Grøndahl, volunteer
1959-69	studio workshop with Gertrud Vasegaard and Aksel Rode, Frederiksberg
1969-2006	studio workshop with Gertrud Vasegaard, Frederiksberg

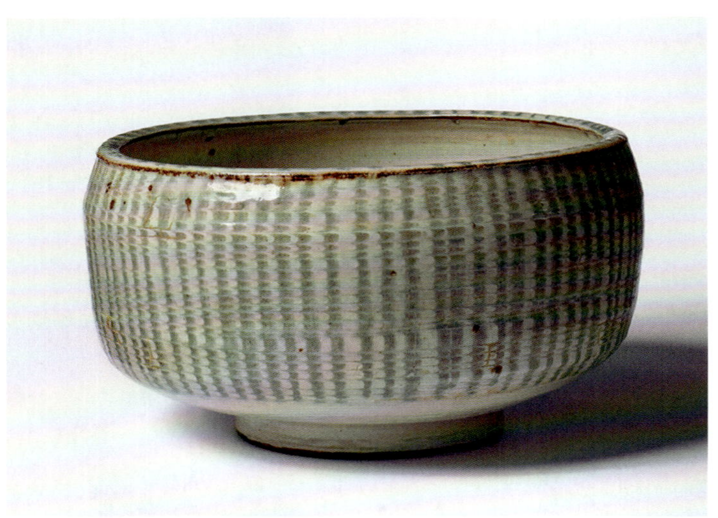

573 1/1968

As the daughter of Gertrud Vasegaard, and of the painter and graphic artist Sigurd Vasegaard, Myre Vasegaard (MV) was the fourth generation of the Hjorth ceramics dynasty fra Bornholm. She and her mother shared a workshop in Allégade in Frederiksberg from 1959 onwards, for the rest of her life. Having studied at Kunsthåndværkerskolen and subsequently spent time in Bing & Grøndahl's stoneware workshop, MV's chosen material was stoneware. She threw dishes, pots and vases, and then worked on them with glazing, inlaid pictorial motifs and decoration. Both Myre and Gertrud Vasegaard worked intensively with stoneware glazes, including the whitish-grey type they often used, which was a development of a type from the Bing & Grøndahl period, sometimes with a warmer nuance in MV's works, but there are also examples in the museum's collection of her use of strong red and blue glazes. In many works the motifs have been directly inlaid into the clay before glazing and firing. MV rapidly developed her own very personal and poetic form of expression as a ceramicist, taking nature as her chief source of inspiration, and using her distinct talent for drawing and painting to give life to the clay. Most of the museum's 17 works by MV have motifs from the animal and plant worlds, and the artist's sharp-eyed empathy with nature gives them an exceptionally vibrant appeal.

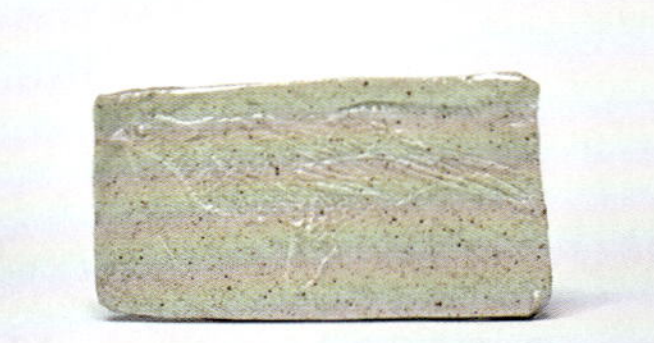

577 24/1977

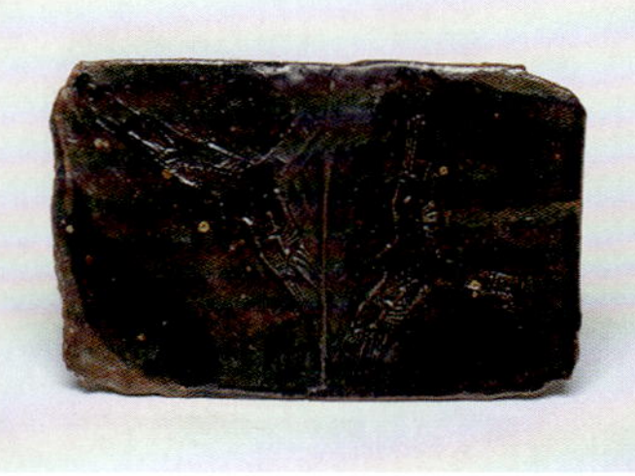

578 25/1977

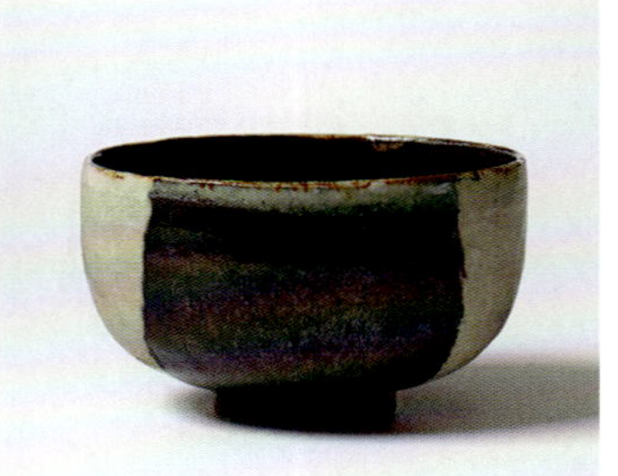

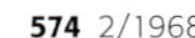

574 2/1968

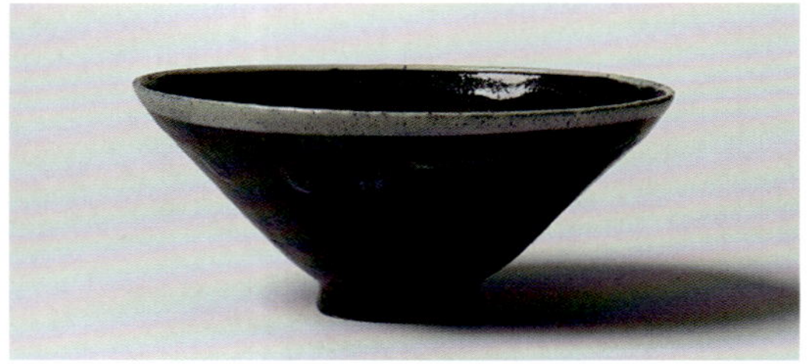

576 23/1977

Drama in the animal world is strongly depicted in a series of large dishes with birds of prey circling around – sometimes on a background of a bright cloudless sky, while other dishes are dominated by a menacing shadow in the form of a closeknit mesh of 'black rain' that seems to swallow up the birds and throw them off course. In an intense sensitive way the artist depicts this bird universe that rises freely above

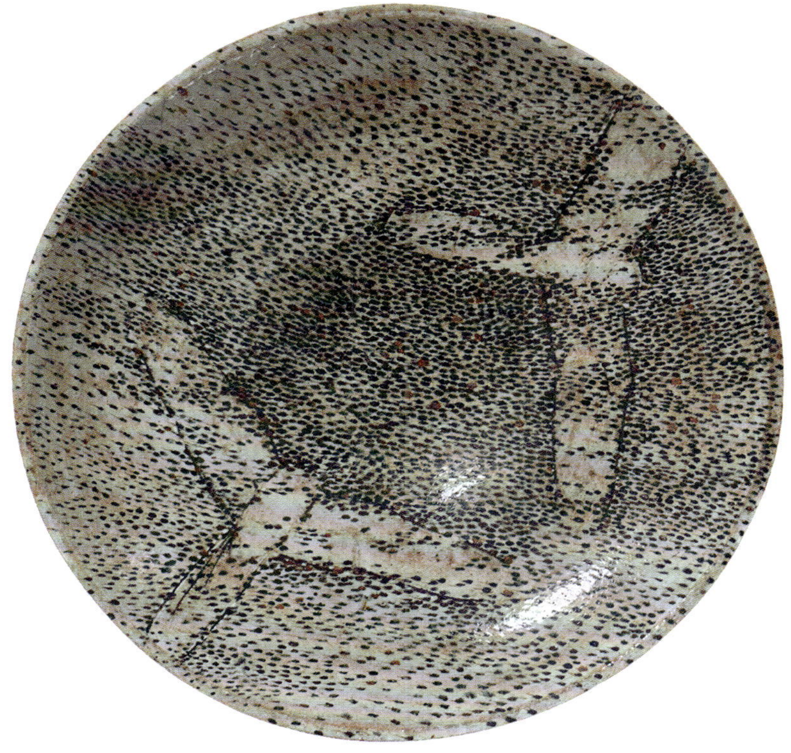

579 9/1981

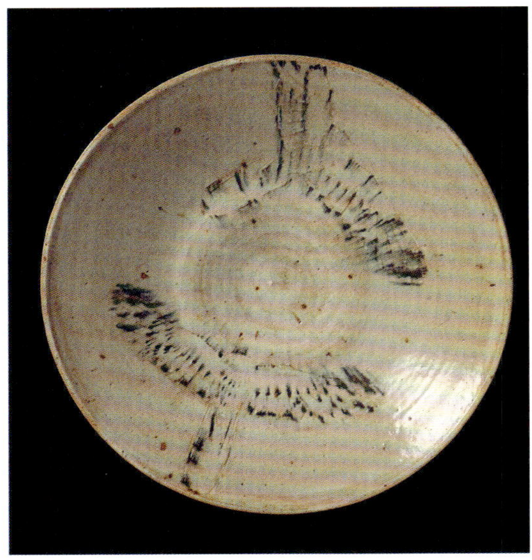

575 22/1977

humans. In the museum's collection there are two of these masterpieces that contain the essence of MV's artistic skill **(575,579)**. Another large dish is decorated superbly with a garfish **(582)**.

The museum's collection contains several works decorated with plants and insects; a particularly expressive example of the latter is the dish with dragonflies that are flying towards a bluish-black star-strewn night sky **(588)**. Seen as a whole MV's works show that it is not the form but the motifs and the ceramic texture that are the most important elements. The contours and the character of animals and plants are drawn with great empathy and sensitivity, as can be sensed in the uneven surfaces of the clay, the inlaid motifs, the colours and the glazing. But first and foremost it is the noble unity of the ceramic texture of her works that makes MV an outstanding ceramicist. In the 1950s

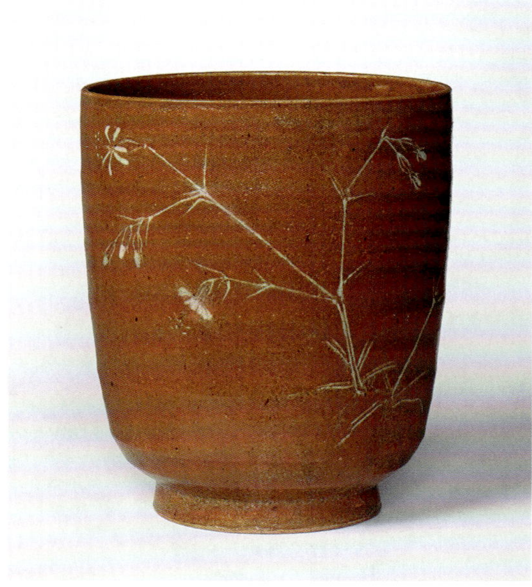

580 93/1986

and 60s MV took part in several official Danish exhibitions abroad, and her works are represented in influential museums with ceramic collections around the world.

573. Bowl, 1967

Stoneware, glazed; thrown, cow-horn technique, decorated. H 18.5 x Diam 33. Mark: 'MV' in a square on the base. Mus.no. 1/1968.
ACQUISITION: Galleri Birkdam, 2005, Copenhagen. Donation from *Kunstindustrimuseets 50-års Jubilæumslegat*

574. Bowl, 1967

Stoneware; slip with porcelain clay and bluish-black colour. H 8.5 x Diam 14. Mark: 'MV' in a square painted on the base. Mus.no. 2/1968
ACQUISITION: Clausens Kunsthandel, 2005, Copenhagen. Donation from *Kunstindustrimuseets Venners 50-års Jubilæumslegat*

575. Dish, 1975-77

Stoneware with chamotte, clear-glazed; slip with porcelain clay, incised/inlaid motif with 2 circling birds. H 12 x Diam 56. Mark: 'MV' in a square painted on base. Mus.no. 22/1977
ACQUISITION: Clausens Kunsthandel, 1977. Donation from *Overretssagfører Odin Kaysers Legat*. See: *Brændpunkter*, 1990. *Det danske Kunstindustrimuseums Virksomhed*, 1969-1982

576. Bowl, 1975-77

Stoneware, glazed; thrown, slip in blackish-blue colour. H 10 x Diam 23. Mark: 'MV' and 36 in a square painted on the base. Mus.no. 23/1977
ACQUISITION: Clausens Kunsthandel, 1977, Copenhagen. Donation from *Overretssagfører Odin Kaysers Legat*. See: *Brændpunkter*, 1990

577. Tile, 1975-77

Stoneware, clear-glazed; negative print of plaster-board with bird. H 6.5 x W 11.5. Mark: none. Mus.no. 24/1977
ACQUISITION: Clausens Kunsthandel, 1977, Copenhagen. Donation from *Overretssagfører Odin Kaysers Legat*

578. Tile, 1975-77

Stoneware, iron-glazed; negative print of plasterboard with two birds of prey. H 25.5 x W 17. Mark: none. Mus.no. 25/1977
ACQUISITION: Clausens Kunsthandel, 1977, Copenhagen. Donation from *Overretssagfører Odin Kaysers Legat*

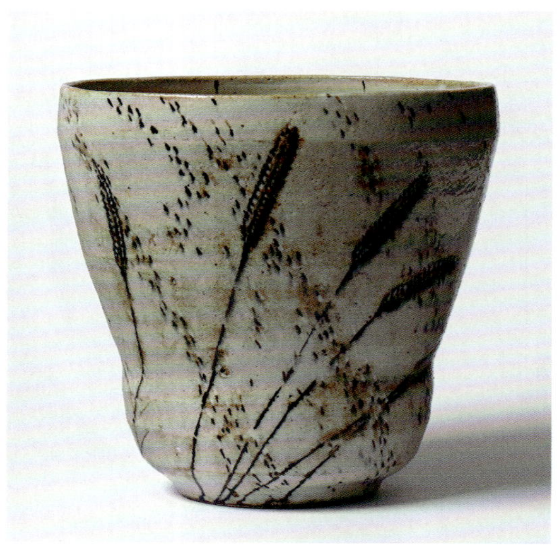

581 152/1990

579. Dish with kestrels, 1976

Stoneware, clear-glazed; thrown, slip with porcelain clay, incised motif with two circling birds of prey and a net of black dots, fired at 1300°. H 11.5 x Diam 58.6. Mark: 'MV' in a square painted on base. Mus.no. 9/1981. ACQUISITION: Clausens Kunsthandel, Copenhagen. Donation from *Ny Carlsbergfondet*

580. Tall bowl, 1986

Stoneware, earthenware, clear-glazed; thrown, brown slip with painted wormwood. H 32 x Diam 25.5. Mark: 'MV' in a square with 85 painted on base. Mus.no. 93/1986. ACQUISITION: Den Frie Udstilling, 1986. Donation from *Poul og Hildur Kingo Petersens Mindelegat*

581. Vase, 1989

Stoneware, glazed; thrown, slip, inlaid plant decoration. H 20 x Diam 20.5. Mus.no. 152/1990

ACQUISITION: Den Frie, Copenhagen, 1990. Donation from *Kunstindustrimuseets Venners 50-års Jubilæumslegat.* See: *Brændpunkter*, 1990

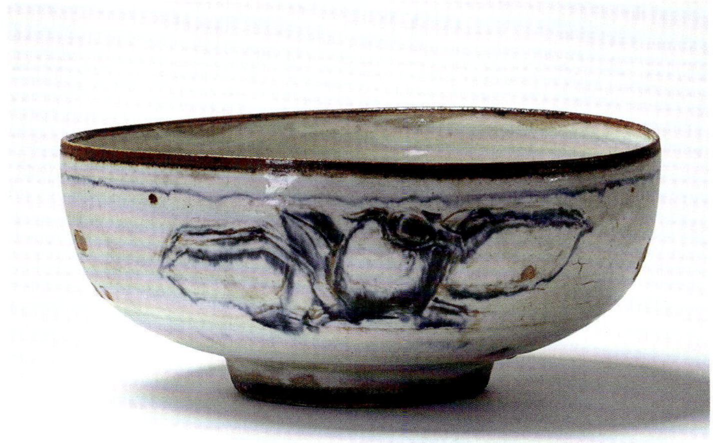

583 139/1999

582. Dish with garfish, 1991

Stoneware, glazed; thrown, slip with porcelain clay, inlaid black garfish. Diam 66.5 x H 10. Mark: 'MV' in a square painted on base. Mus.no. 7/1992

ACQUISITION: Donation from *Ellen og Knud Dalhoff Larsens Legat*

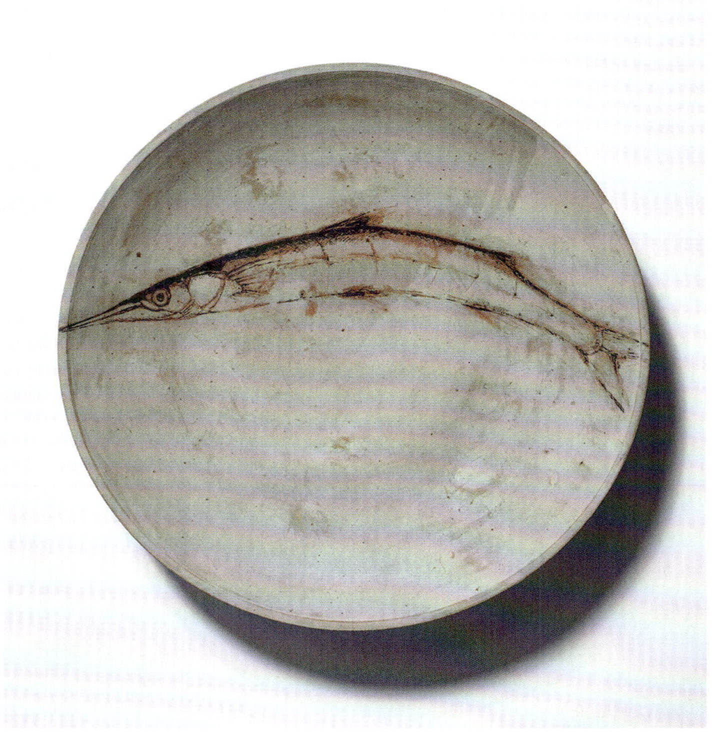

582 7/1992

583. Bowl, date unknown

Stoneware, glazed; thrown, decorated with brush-painted quince. H 14.2 x Diam 30.4. Mark: 'MV' in a square inscribed on base. Mus.no. 139/1999

ACQUISITION: Galleri Birkdam, Copenhagen. Donation from Bank Director C.B. Andersen, Copenhagen

584. Vase, date unknown

Stoneware, glazed; thrown, inlaid plant decoration. H 12.5 x Diam 7.3.

Mark: "MV' inscribed in a square on base. Mus.no. 301/2007

ACQUISITION: Donation from Dorris Kuyken-Schneider, Museum Boijmans van Beuningen, Rotterdam

585. Bowl, date unknown

Stoneware, glazed; thrown, simple colour-decoration. H 3.2 x Diam 11.3.

Mark: 'MOM MV' in a square painted on base. Mus.no. 316/2007

ACQUISITION: Donation from estate of Gertrud and Myre Vasegaard, 2007

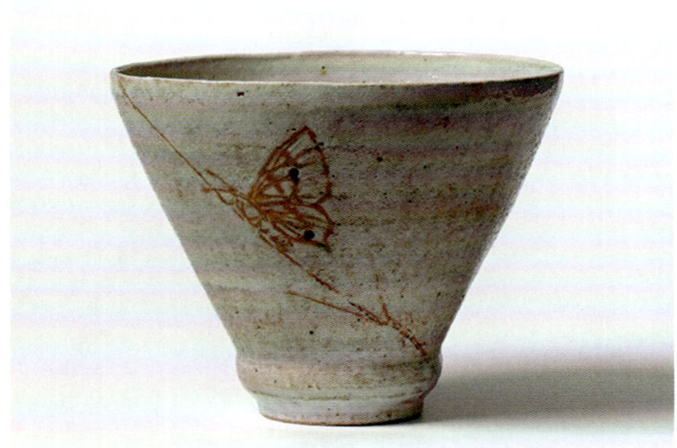
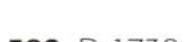

589 D 1730

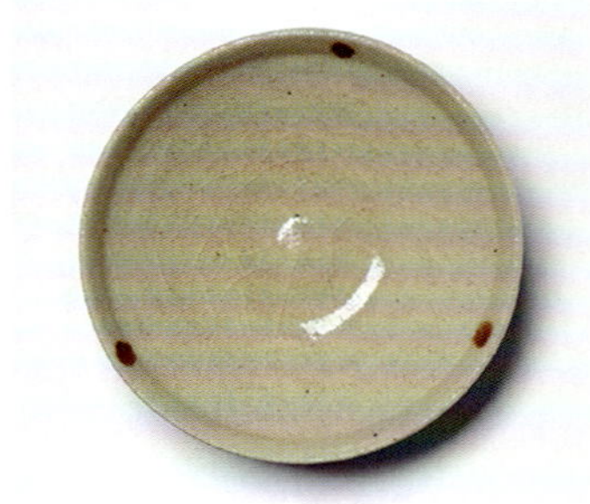

585 316/2007

584 301/2007

586. Teapot with sieve, date unknown

Porcelain, transparent glaze; thrown, shaped, used in the workshop in Allégade. a: H 15.2 x W 11.5 x D 25; b: H 3.5 x Diam 9.5; c: H 7.3 x Diam 12.3. Mark: none. Mus.no. 317a-c/2007
ACQUISITION: Donation from estate of Gertrud and Myre Vasegaard, 2007

587. Teapot with sieve, date unknown

Stoneware, transparent glaze; thrown, shaped, used in the workshop in Allégade. a: H 15.2 x W 11.5 x D 25; b: H 3.5 x Diam 9.5; c: H 7.3 x Diam 12.3. Mark: 'MV' in a square painted on base. Mus.no. 318a-c/2007
ACQUISITION: Donation from estate of Gertrud and Myre Vasegaard, 2007

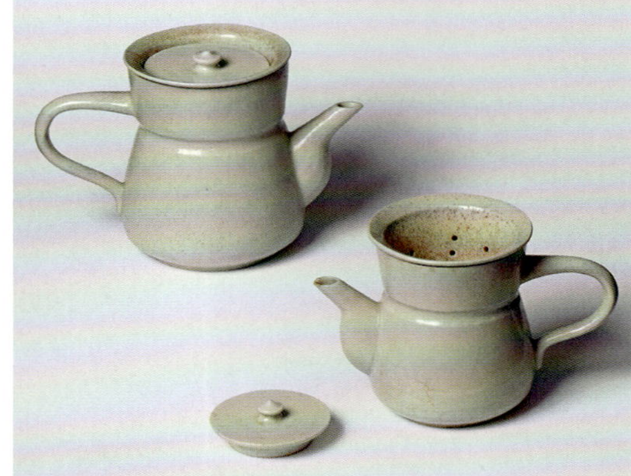

586 317a-c/2007

587 318a-c/2007

588 D 1587

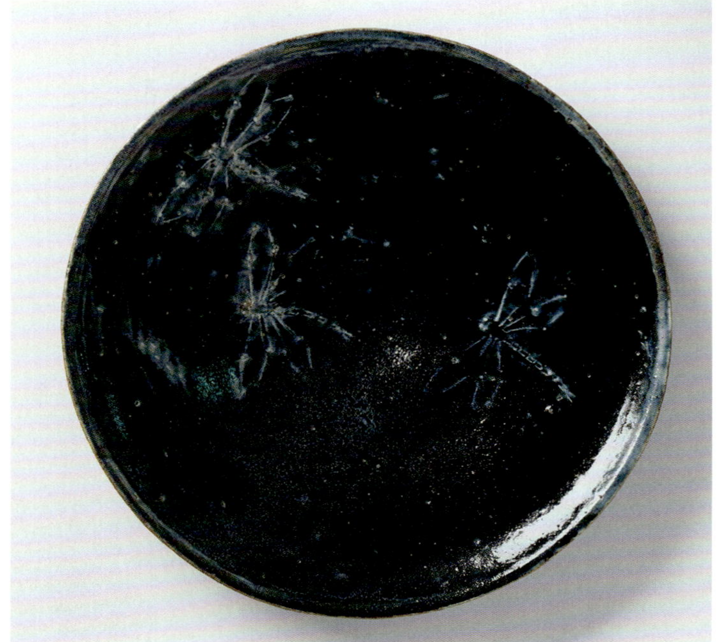

588. Dish with dragonflies, 1982-83

Stoneware, glazed; thrown, slip with blackish-blue colour and inlaid motif with dragonflies in white porcelain slip, fired at 1300°. H 9 x Diam 44. Mus.no. D 1587. ACQUISITION: Den Frie Udstillingsbygning. Deposited by *Statens Kunstfond*, 1985. See: Dybdahl, L., 1997

589. Bowl, 1994

Stoneware, glazed; thrown, slip, inlaid motif with butterfly. H 14.5. Mark: 'MV 94' incised on base. Mus.no. D 1730
ACQUISITION: Donated by *Ny Carlsbergfondet,* 1995

VEJLØ, CHARLOTTE 1967 –

Ceramic designer

1988-90 Aarhus University, Art History
1990-96 Danmarks Designskole, Ceramics and Glass; 1995-96 Institute for Ceramic Conceptual Art
1999-08 Own studio workshop and firm, Birkerød; Charlotte Vejlø Design, production in Germany
2008- Teacher, art-related subjects

After completing her studies at Danmarks Designskole in 1996, Charlotte Vejlø (CV) developed a project with the title *Et stel til det sanselige måltid* (A table-service for a sensory feast), consisting of a number of prototypes for components of a table service, all in the form of fine shell-shapes with the refined treatment of the materials as the connecting link. Vejlø herself described the project with the words: 'Forms that create variation and reciprocal connections. Contrast between the angled and the rounded. The glossy inner surface against the soft, wet-ground outer one. Functionalism is toned down in order to highlight symbolic and image-creating elements.'
The pleasing proportions of the service, the thin delicate body and soft monochrome colouring matched exactly the sophisticated fashionable taste of the time and it became instantly known and selected for inclusion in several official design initiatives such as *Designfondens* '*Exponent 97*' and Danish Crafts contribution to the *Tendence* Frankfurt International Fair 1999. In 2000 CV was awarded a 2-year start-up stipend from *Statens Kunstfond*, which also acquired parts of the table service made in CV's own workshop and presented them to the museum **(590-592)**. The success of the service led to a cooperative production arrangement until 2008 with a small German firm, to which CV delivered the moulds for the cast works. It is well-justified to describe this service as functional art of first-class quality.

590. 2 bowls, 1995-97. ***Et stel til det sanselige måltid***
(A table-service for a sensory feast)
Coloured porcelain, glazed, partially unglazed; modelled in a plaster mould, cast, water-ground on unglazed body, fired at 1280°. H 8.3 x W 18 x D 24.3. Mark: 'C. Vejlø' inscribed on base. Mus.no. 41a-b/2010
ACQUISITION: Donation from *Statens Kunstfond*

591. 3 bowls, 1995-97. ***Et stel til det sanselige måltid***
(A table-service for a sensory feast)
Coloured porcelain, unglazed; modelled in a plaster mould, cast, water-ground on unglazed body, fired at 1280°. H 6 x W 10.1 x D 17.5. Mark: 'C. Vejlø' inscribed on base. Mus.no. 42a-c/2010.
ACQUISITION: Donation from *Statens Kunstfond*

592. 7 cups and saucers, 1995-97. ***Mokkakopper – et stel til det sanselige måltid*** (Small coffee cups – a table-service for a sensory feast)
Porcelain, transparent glaze, iron glaze; cast, water-ground on unglazed body, fired at 1280°. Cups: H 5 x W 6.8 x D 7.3; saucers: H 2 x W 9.6 x D 11.3. Mark: 'C. Vejlø' inscribed on base. Mus.no. 43a-n/2010
ACQUISITION: Donation from *Statens Kunstfond*

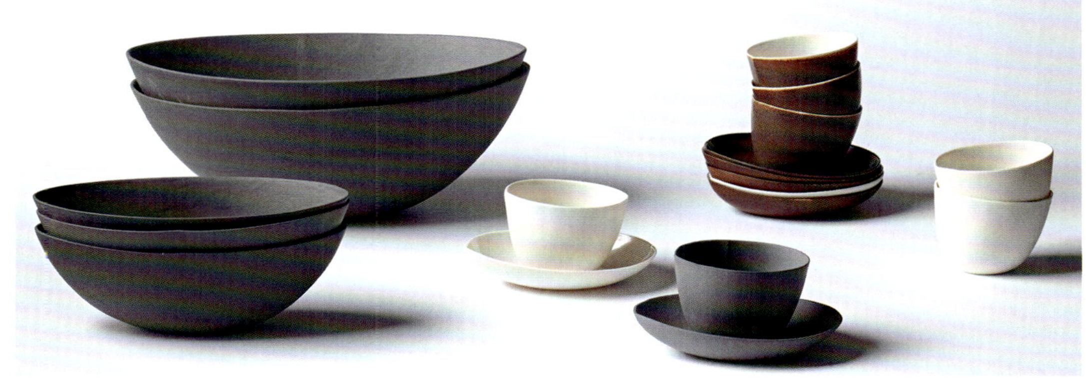

590 41a-b/2010
591 42a-c/2010
592 43a-n/2010

WEGGERBY, BIRTHE 1927 – 1982

Ceramicist, sculptor

1946-49	Kunsthåndværkerskolen
1949	Saxbo
1950-	Own studio workshop, Copenhagen
1959-62	Kunsthåndværkerskolen, teacher
1965-68	Det Jyske Kunstakademi, co-founder and teacher of Ceramics
1970-	Danmarks Lærerhøjskole, teacher

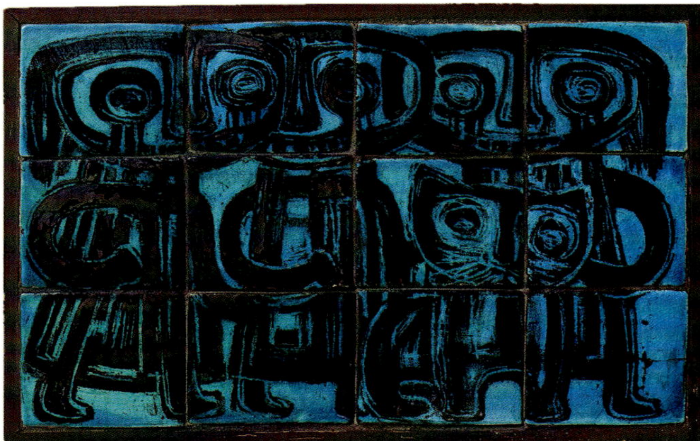

595 113/1958

'Functional art on the scaffold' was what Birthe Weggerby (BW) wrote as her programme statement in the catalogue for '*Kunstnernes Efterårsudstilling*' in 1958; she was a dedicated advocate of setting ceramics free. She lived up to this in her own works, in the many teaching posts she held, and through her involvement with the setting up of Det Jyske Kunstakademi, where she held leading positions from 1965 to 68 and taught the Ceramics course. Det Jyske Kunstakademi was for its first many years an art school for all branches of plastic creative art - painting, sculpture and graphics, and ceramics and weaving as well.

BW was involved in the postwar era's new artistic movements and used clay and glazes inspired by abstract painters and sculptors, chiefly those in the Cobra movement. Unlike the new generation of the ceramicists who emerged from Kunsthåndværkerskolen around 1960, with stoneware and later porcelain as their favoured materials, BW continued to work with the traditional earthenware with glazes and slip, and fantasized around the basic forms of homely ceramics – jugs, dishes and bowls. BW's ceramic works are unpretentious and vivacious, with energetic depictions and decoration.

In the museum's collection there are four early works from the years just after BW finished studying in Kunsthåndværkerskolen in 1949; they demonstrate the technical skills of the newly qualified practitioner, and show signs of a good grasp of an independent style of decoration. In the tile picture from 1957 **(595)** one can see a genuinely painterly motif with stylised people and animals, painted in black on a background of a turquoise alkali glaze – one which BW used

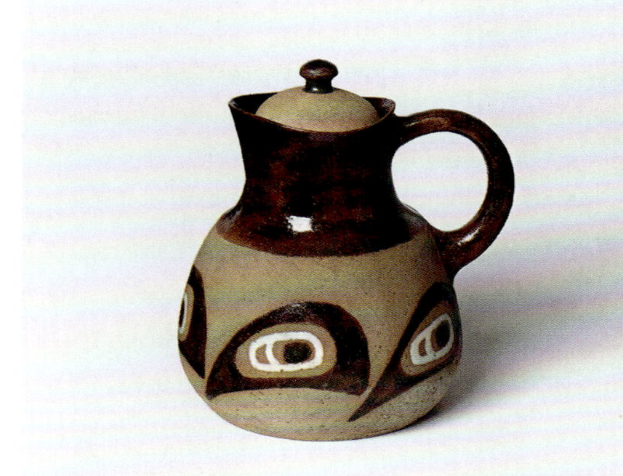

596 122a-b/1984

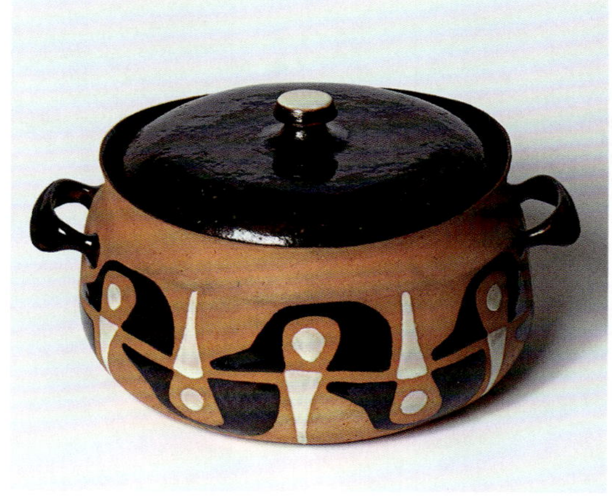

597 123a-b/1984

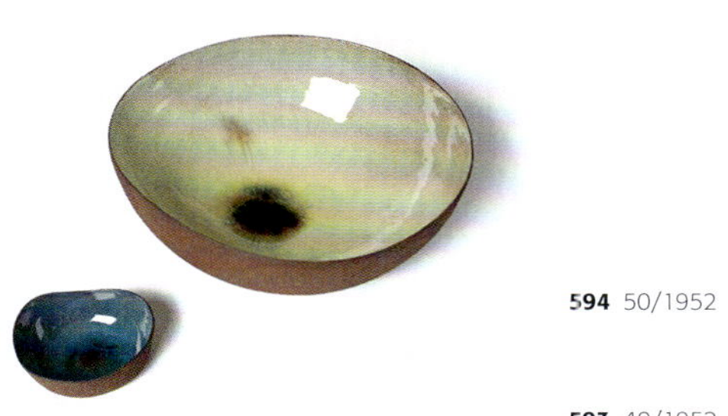

594 50/1952

593 49/1952

frequently. The latest work is a lidded pot from 1968, a fine work which shows the full development of her particular pictorial style **(598)**.

BW was a member of the Grønningen artist's group from 1961 onwards, and exhibited in Denmark and abroad, with several solo exhibitions in museums and galleries in Denmark. She completed commissions in the form of ceramic reliefs and pictures as well as a few pictorial tapestries on which she worked with the textile artists Benedikte and Jan Groth.

598 140a-b/1999

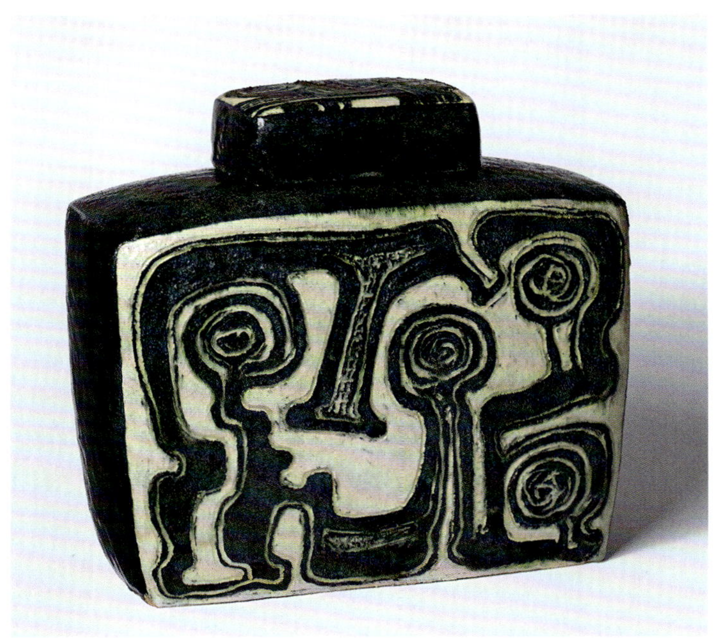

593. Bowl, 1951

Earthenware, glazed; thrown, decorated. H 3.5 x W 9 x D 8. Mark: 'BW' inscribed on base. Mus.no. 49/1952

ACQUISITION: Birthe Weggerby. Donation from *Benny Dessaus Mindelegat*

594. Bowl, 1951

Earthenware, glazed; thrown, decorated. H 8.5 x Diam 24. Mark: 'BW' inscribed on base. Mus.no. 50/1952

ACQUISITION: Birthe Weggerby. Donation from *Benny Dessaus Mindelegat*

595. Tile picture, 1957

Stoneware, alkali-glazed, wood; 12 decorated tiles mounted in a wooden frame. H 23.5 x W 36. Mark: 'Weggerby -57' painted on back. Mus.no. 113/1958

ACQUISITION: Den frie Udstilling 1958. Donation from *Fonden af 7. januar*

596. Lidded Jug, 1952

Earthenware, glazed; thrown, shaped, decorated. H 17.5 x Diam 13.5. Mark: 'BW -52' inscribed on base. Mus.no. 122a-b/1984

ACQUISITION: Donation from Pia Hartvig Jacobsen, daughter of the artist.

See: *Brændpunkter*, 1990

597. Lidded bowl, 1952

Earthenware; thrown, shaped, decorated. H 15 x Diam 23.5. Mark: 'BW -52' inscribed on base. Mus.no. 123a-b/1984

ACQUISITION: Donation from Pia Hartvig Jacobsen, daughter of the artist.

See: *Brændpunkter*, 1990

598. Lidded pot, 1968

Earthenware, stoneware, glazed; thrown, shaped, decorated. H 30 x W 30 x D 12.5. Mark: 'Weggerby -68' inscribed on base. Mus.no. 140a-b/1999

ACQUISITION: Donation from Bank Director C. B. Andersen, Copenhagen

WEISS, IVAN 1946 –

Ceramicist, designer

1962-66	The Royal Porcelain Factory, qualified over-glaze painter
1966-70	The Royal Porcelain Factory, assistant to Niels Thorsson
1970-72	workshop experience in Japan, ceramic apprenticeship
1972-2004	The Royal Porcelain Factory, employed as artist
2004-	Own studio workshop, Herfølge, Sealand

Danmarks Designskole, guest teacher

www.ivanweiss.dk

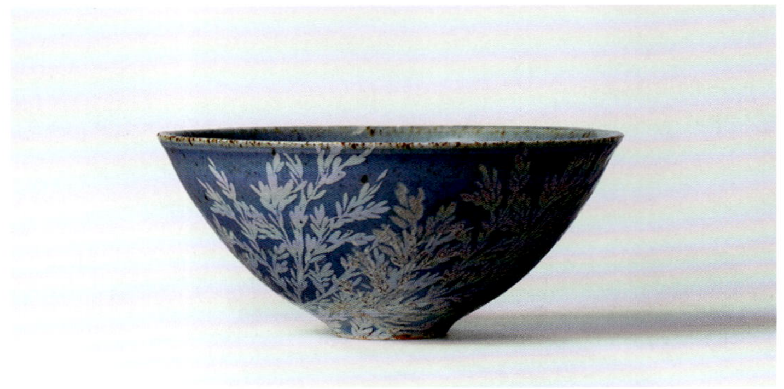

599 40/1979

Ivan Weiss (IW) began an apprenticeship in the Royal Porcelain Factory as a 16-year-old, completed his training as an over-glaze painter and remained in employment at the factory until 2004, when the time-honoured arrangement with fulltime employed artists came to an end. In the factory IW worked for several years as assistant to the renowned ceramicist and artistic leader Nils Thorsson (1898-1975), gaining comprehensive knowledge about work with ceramics both in terms of craft skills and artistic aspects. From an early age he showed distinct talent for decorative painting and he worked on many special projects for the factory, including the restauration of the Dipylon Gate on the Carlsberg Brewery site in 1990.

600 41a-b/1979

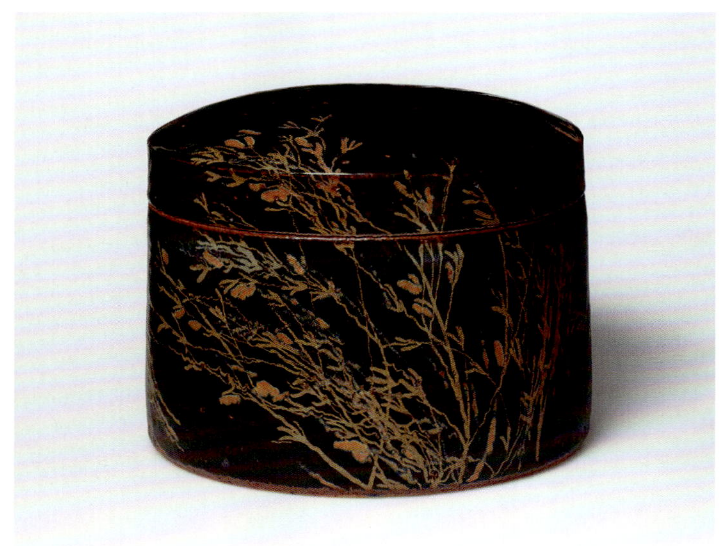

Like many ceramicists, IW became interested in Japanese ceramic art, and he spent a period of two years there; he was accepted in a workshop and learned from scratch how to throw and produce stoneware. On his return from Japan IW was employed fulltime in the Royal Porcelain Factory, where he developed into one of the factory's major stoneware artists, designing innumerable models for production as well as creating unique works right up to the time when the factory closed the stoneware cellar as a consequence of the fusion of the factory with Georg Jensen and Holmegaard in 1985. After that IW continued until 2004 with his artistic projects at the factory, but now working mainly with porcelain; since then he has had his own workshop and firm.

In 1979 IW was invited to hold a solo exhibition in the museum, and he exhibited nearly 200 unique works, particularly bowls, vases, lidded pots and boxes, the majority of them decorated with an impressive range of trees and plants that were specified in the list of exhibits: dwarf medlar, thuja, Siberian crab-apple tree, cypress, ficus benjamina and many others. The museum acquired two works from the exhibition, and they represent well IW's very early works. One is a bowl with *clair de lune* glaze decorated with thuja branches **(599)**, and the other is a cylindrical lidded pot with olivine glaze **(600)**. In both cases silk screen printing technique is used for transferring the artist's painted motifs – a technique that developed in the factory around 1960, inspired by Niels Thorsson's experiments and was then used in connection with faience production and also by the stoneware artists.

The next work by IW, out of a total of eight in the museum's collection, is dated to 1986 and was acquired from the factory's solo exhibition for IW in 1987. This shows another side of IW's work, a cylinder-shaped basin of coarse stoneware clay with chamotte and abstract decoration in the form of asymmetric white applied fields, transferred from paper using silk screen printing on the barium-glazed basin **(601)**. The museum has another work, a dish, in the same material and with an abstract painted pattern which IW has used on both small and monumental works, including screens and columns on a commissioned work for Forskningscentret Skov og Landskab, Frederiksberg, from 2011. Through the years IW completed several large-scale commissioned projects, for instance for the Carlsberg breweries.

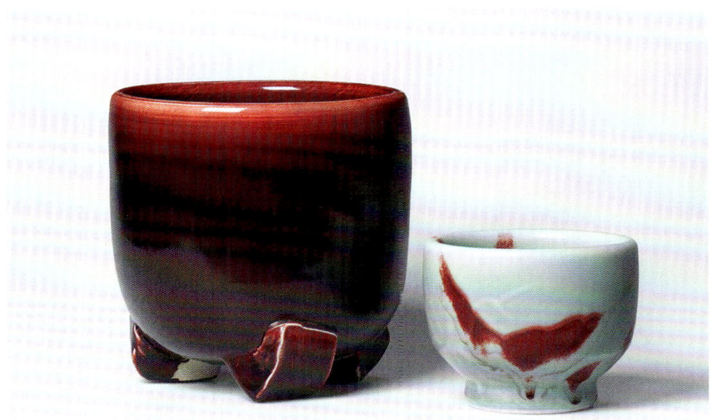

603 111/1999 **604** 112/1999

In a solo exhibition in the Royal Porcelain Factory in 1999 with the title '*Stentøj og Porcelain*' IW displayed a distinguished selection of unique works with a range of the classic glazes used by the factory; the museum was eager to have these represented in the collection, and in fact acquired three works: a pot on three legs with ox-blood glaze **(603)**, a little pot on a foot, entitled *Smeltevand* (melting water) with celadon-glazing and, over that, painted decoration with ox-blood glazing **(604)**, as well as a tray with four bowls of porcelain with calligraphic decoration, entitled *En hyldest til den blå underglasurfarve KOBOLT* (A salute to the blue underglaze colour COBALT)**(605)**.

Throughout his career IW has maintained extensive exhibiting activities both in connection with the factory and outside that framework, in Denmark and beyond, in influential museums in Japan, the Nordic countries and the rest of Europe, where his work is represented in collections. IW is justly valued and respected, not least for his decorative painting, which shows his mastery of both Danish nature-inspired decoration and Japanese calligraphy.
See: Lautrup-Larsen, L., 2007, pp. 319-22. Gelfer-Jørgensen, M., 2013, pp. 272, 295-97.

599. Bowl, 1979

Stoneware, feldspar-glaze, *clair de lune* glaze, shiny glaze; thrown, silk screen printed decoration, fired in a coal-fired kiln at 1360°. H 7.5 x Diam 16.
Mark: 'IW' with 3 wavy lines. Mus.no. 40/1979
ACQUISITION: *Ivan Weiss – keramiske arbejder i stentøj udført 1978-79 på Den kongelige Porcelainsfabrik*, Kunstindustrimuseet, 1979. Donation from *Overretssagfører Odin Kaysers Legat*

601 41/1987

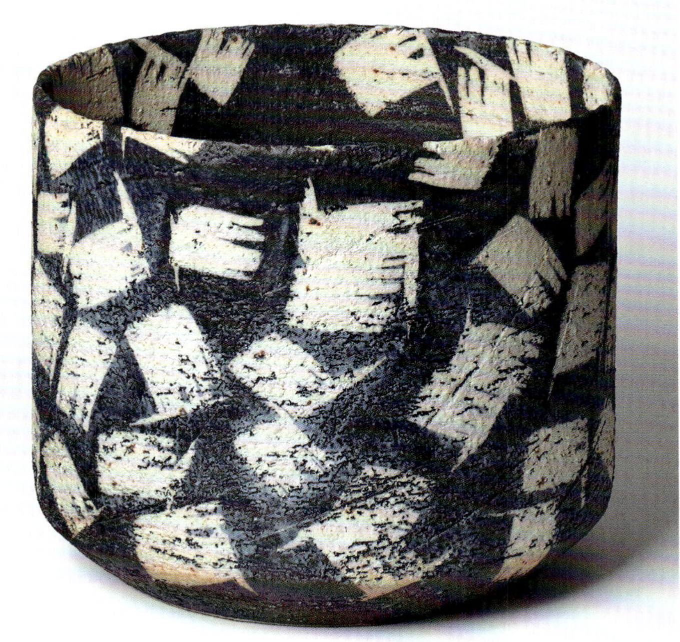

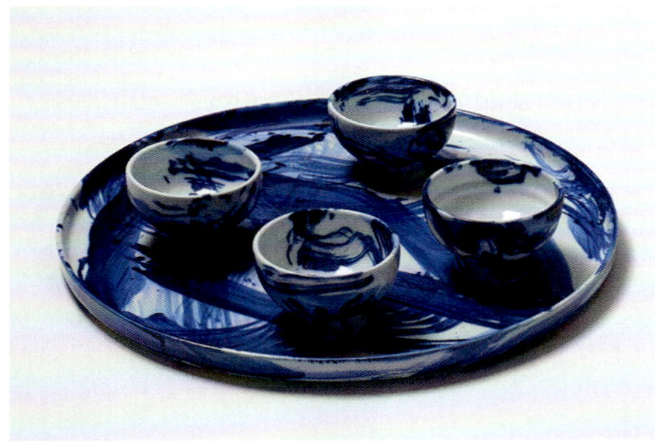

605 113a-e/1999

600. Lidded pot, 1979
Stoneware, feldspar- and olivine glazed, shiny glaze; thrown, silk screen print decoration, fired in coal-fired kiln at 1360°. H 23.5 x Diam 28. Mark: 'IW' inscribed on base with 3 wavy lines and Denmark. Mus.no. 41a-b/1979
ACQUISITION: *Ivan Weiss – keramiske arbejder i stentøj udført 1978-79 på Den kongelige Porcelainsfabrik*, Kunstindustrimuseet, 1979. Donation from *Overretssagfører Odin Kaysers Legat*.
See: Dybdahl, L., 1997. Gelfer-Jørgensen, M., 2013

601. Basin, 1986
Stoneware with chamotte, iron oxide, barium-glazed; thrown, silk screen print decoration, fired in a gas-fired kiln at 1380°. H 32 x Diam 36. Mark: 'Weiss' with 3 wavy lines painted on base. Mus.no. 41/1987
ACQUISITION: Ivan Weiss's solo exhibition, The Royal Porcelain Factory, 1987. Donation from *Nationalbankens Jubilæumsfond*. See: *Brændpunkter*, 1990

602. Bowl, 1979 (No photo)
Stoneware, feldspar-glazed, shiny glaze; thrown, silk screen print decoration, fired in coal-fired kiln at 1380°. H 8 x Diam 12. Mark: 'IW' and 3 wavy lines painted on base. Mus.no. 239/1994
ACQUISITION: Donation from Karl Mogensen, Frederiksberg

603. Pot, 1999
Stoneware, feldspar- and ox-blood-glazed; thrown, fired in coal-fired kiln at 1380°. H 20.5 x Diam 19. Mark: 'IW' inscribed on base. Mus.no. 111/1999
ACQUISITION: *Stentøj og Porcelain*, 1999, *Den kongelige Porcelainsfabrik*

604. Pot, 1999. *Smeltevand* (Melt water)
Stoneware, celadon-, ox-blood- and feldspar- glazed; thrown, decorated, fired in coal-fired kiln at 1380°. H 10 x Diam 13.5. Mark: 'IW' and 3 wavy lines inscribed on base. Mus.no. 112/1999
ACQUISITION: *Stentøj og Porcelain*, 1999, *Den kongelige Porcelainsfabrik*

605. Tray with 4 bowls, 1999. ***En hyldest til den blå underglasurfarve KOBOLT*** (A salute to the blue underglaze colour COBALT)
Porcelain, cobalt- and feldspar-glazed; thrown, brush-painted, calligraphy, fired in a gas-fired kiln at 1380°. a: H 3.5 x Diam 53; b: H 8 x Diam 12.5. Mark: 'IW' with 3 wavy lines painted on base (bowls). Mus.no. 113a-e/1999
ACQUISITION: *Stentøj og Porcelain*, 1999, *Den kongelige Porcelainsfabrik*

606. Dish, 1999
Stoneware, barium-glazed; thrown, brush-painted, fired in a gas-fired kiln at 1380°. H 7.5 x Diam 67.0. Mark: 'IW' with 3 wavy lines. Mus.no. 114/1999
ACQUISITION: *Stoneware og Porcelain*, 1999, *Den kongelige Porcelainsfabrik*

606 114/1999

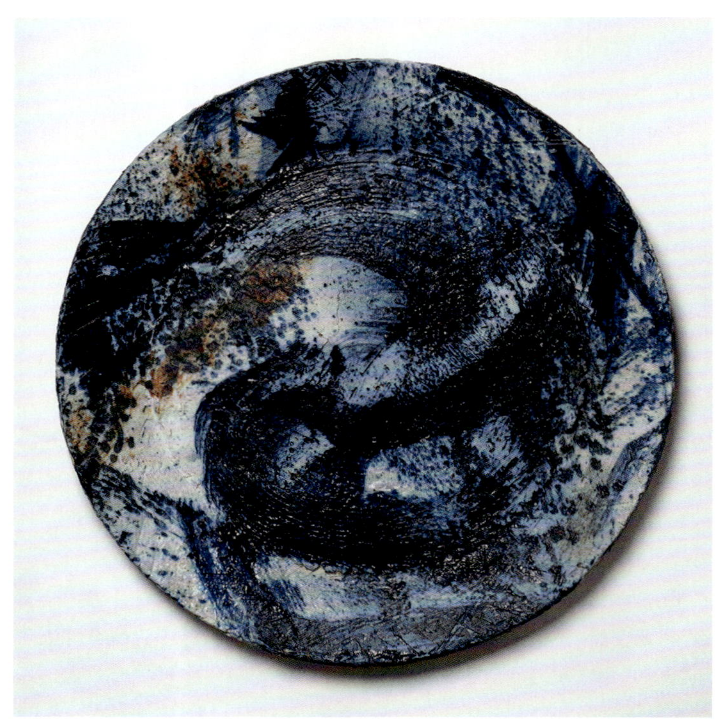

WEISS, PER 1953 –

Ceramicist

1971-77	Skolen for Brugskunst
1974-76	Pupil of ceramicist Taibi Yosiga, Japan
1977-79	Workshop experience as assistant to several ceramicists, Hagi, Japan
1979-86	Own workshop 'Weiss Gama', Hagi, Japan
1986	Own studio workshop, Frederiksværk
1988-	Own workshop shared with Lene Regius, Lejre, Sealand www.perweiss.dk

Ever since the mid 19th century, when the World Exhibitions provided a stage for exchange of artistic sources of inspiration, the ceramics tradition of Japan has had far-reaching influence on Danish ceramics, sometimes in circuitous ways, but more directly in the second half of the 20th century, through visits and study periods spent in Japanese workshops by Danish craftspeople, architects and designers. Per Weiss (PW) belongs to this group who sought out experience in Japan, prompted e.g. by Richard Kjærgaard's teaching at Skolen for Brugskunst; in the middle of his student years he travelled to Japan and spent two years there as an apprentice in his craft before returning to Denmark to finish his studies.

But PW was not finished with Japan. He returned there and settled for 10 years in Hagi, one of Japan's great traditional ceramics centres, where he eventually had his own workshop, until 1986. He became a reputed ceramicist in Japan, and was the first European to be accepted for '*Nitten*', the Japanese Academy's annual exhibition. The years of apprenticeship in Japan had a decisive influence on PW's whole approach to working with ceramics, not only technically, but also intellectually and in terms of attitude. The ideals of respect for tradition, and concentration on the refinement of the individual work, are deeply rooted in Japanese ceramics, and those ideals have been guiding principles for PW's work, so that his workshop activities have taken on the character of meditative immersion in the creation of the form and ornamentation of the work.

From the basis of a shared workshop with his colleague Lene Regius since 1988, Weiss has created for himself an international position, not least through the results of the last 10 years of technically and artistically demanding work with monumental thrown and decorated stoneware pots. In these works PW interprets the Japanese approach in interplay with inspiration from the gigantic pots that are known from the Minoan culture of Crete.

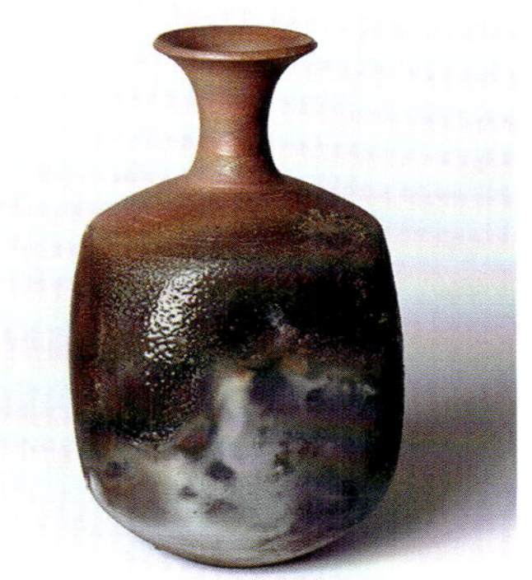

607 221/1989

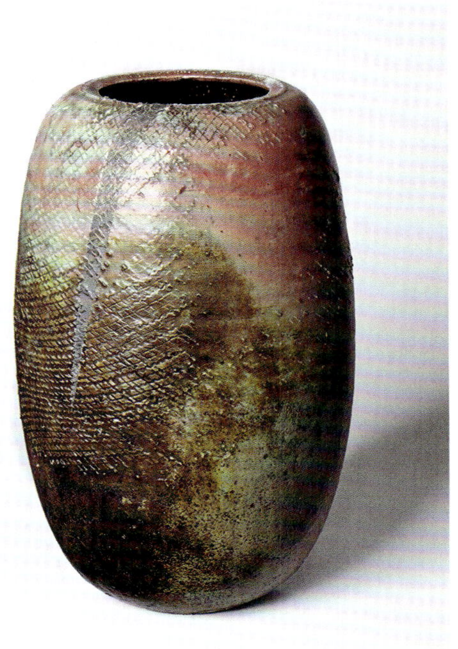

609 13/1990

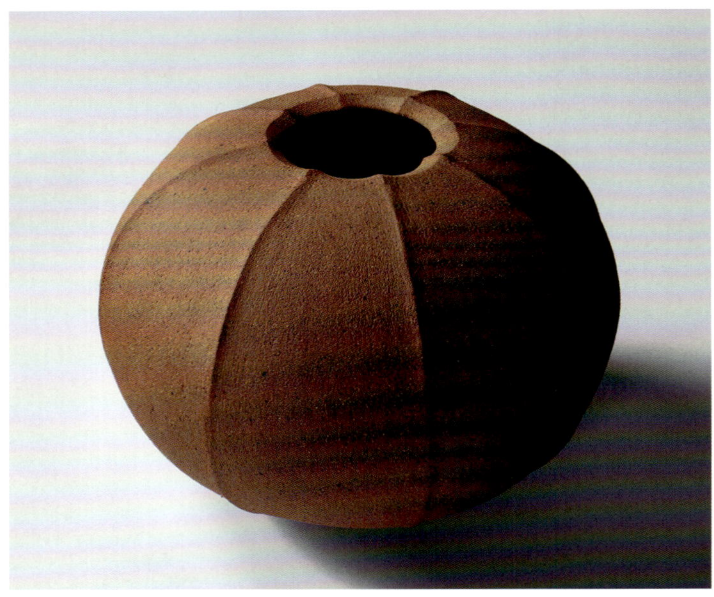

608 222/1989

In the museum's collection there is a fine example of such a pot. Its decoration consists of encircling horizontal wavy lines, worked in wax on a background of slip **(611)**. PW is also represented in the collection by four earlier works from the end of the 1980s **(607-608)** and the beginning of the 1990s **(609-610)**, which provide examples of several firing techniques, both high-fired raku-ceramics and muffle-kiln fired ceramics.

PW has taken part in many exhibitions around the world, both group exhibitions and solo exhibitions, and particularly in the 1990s he undertook alone or with Lene Regius a number of commissions for works for public buildings. PW is represented in leading ceramic museums in Denmark, Japan and Europe.
See: *Brændpunkter*, 1990; Seisbøll, L., 2007; Gelfer-Jørgensen, M., 2013.

607. Vase, 1989

Stoneware, unglazed; thrown, muffle-fired at 1300°. H 21. Mark: none. Mus.no. 221/1989
ACQUISITION: *Statens 50-års Jubilæumsgave*.
See: Gelfer-Jørgensen, M., 2013

608. Pot, 1988

Stoneware, unglazed; thrown, shaped, fired at 1300°. H 26. Mark: 'Per Weiss' inscribed (indistinctly) on base. Mus.no. 222/1989
ACQUISITION: *Statens 50-års Jubilæumsgave*

609. Pot, 1990

Earthenware, alkali-glazed; thrown, slip, scored, raku, hard-fired at 1200°. H 31.5 x Diam c. 15. Mark: Indecipherable signature inscribed on base, with '90'. Mus.no. 13/1990
ACQUISITION: Galleri SCAG, Copenhagen. Donation from *Benny Dessaus Mindelegat*. See: *Brændpunkter*, 1990. Gelfer-Jørgensen, M., 2013

610. Lidded pot, 1994

Stoneware, alkali-glazed; thrown, inscribed amoeba decoration, raku, hard-fired at 1200°. H 18.5 x Diam 13. Mark: none. Mus.no. 62a-b/1994
ACQUISITION: Per Weiss

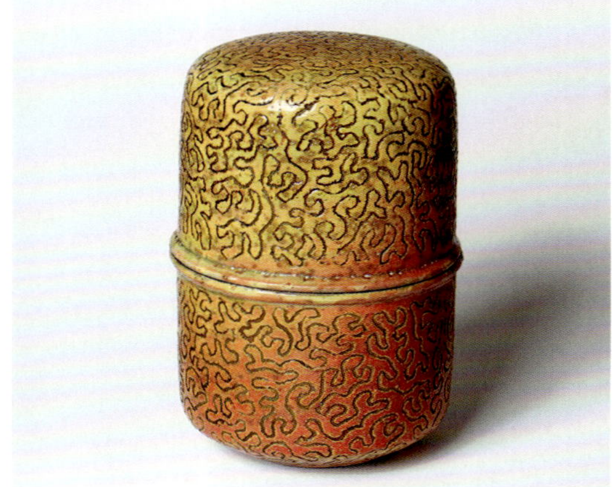

610 62a-b/1994

611. Pot, 2007. *Unika Krukke* **(Unique pot)**

Semi stoneware, borax-glazed; thrown in c. 12 sections, underlying sgrafitto made with saw-blade, black slip in sgrafitto, many thin layers of porcelain slip, pattern with flowing latex, cobalt and iron chloride, pre-fired, clear alkali glaze, fired at 1135°. H 123 x Diam 123. Mark: none. Mus.no. 388/2007
ACQUISITION: Jørgen L. Dalgaard, Copenhagen. Donation from *Højesterets-sagfører C.L. Davids Legat for Slægt og Venner*. See: Seisbøll, L., 2007. Fordybelse, 2007. Gelfer-Jørgensen, M., 2013.

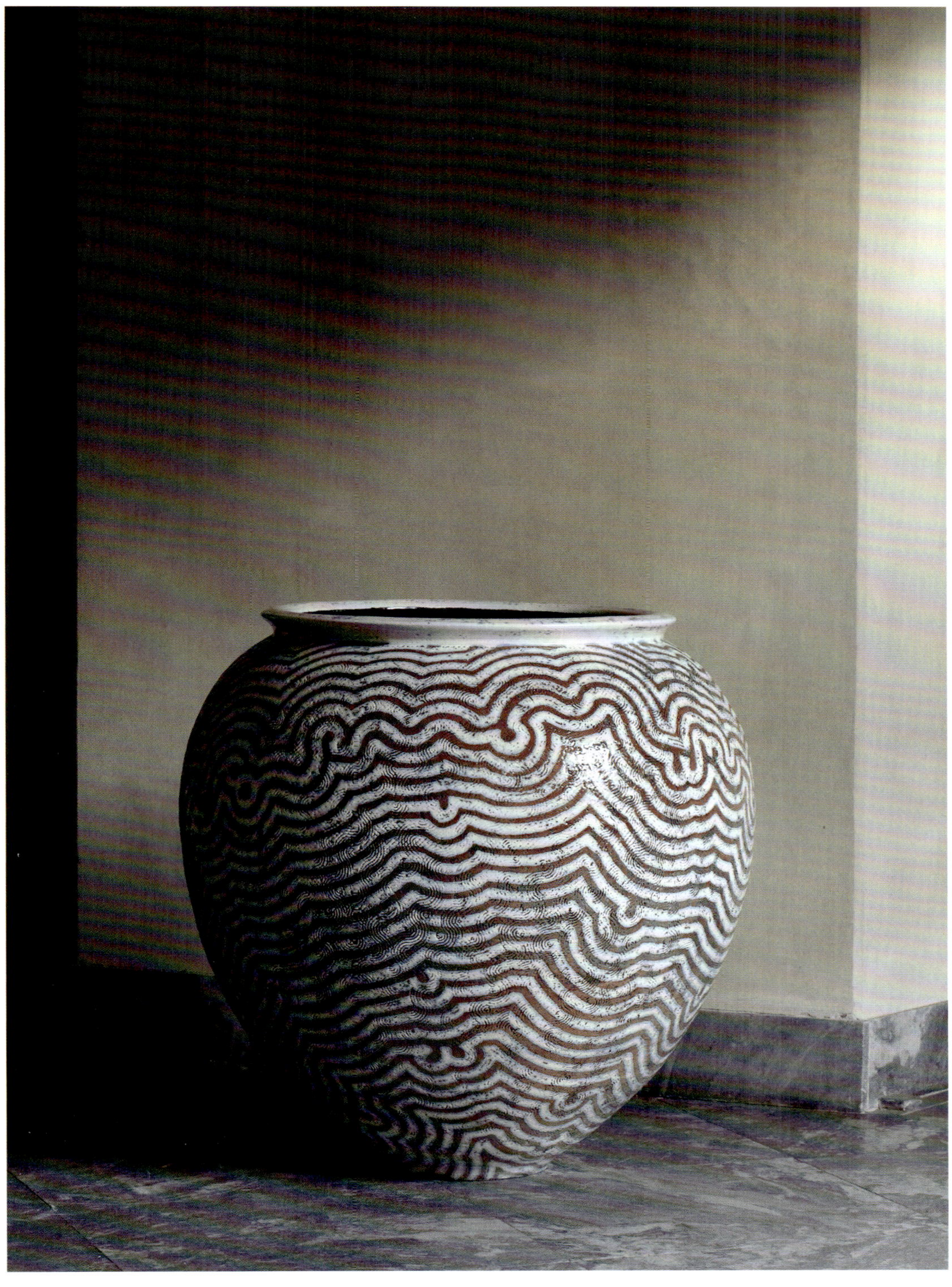

611 388/2007

WIINBLAD, BJØRN 1918 –2006

Ceramicist, graphic artist, painter, designer

1935	Apprentice in typography
1936-39	Teknisk Skole, Frederiksberg, typography
1940-43	The Royal Danish Academy of Fine Arts, Graphics
1946-56	Nymølle Keramiske Fabrik
1952-66	Own studio workshop, Lyngby
1957-	Rosenthal Porzellan AG, Germany, designer
1966-2006	'Det Blå Hus', Lyngby, studio/home

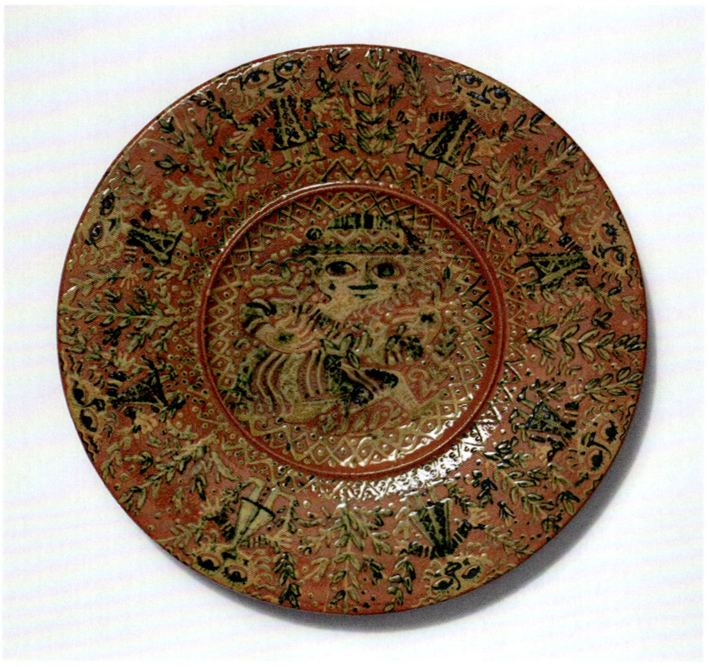

612 14/1947

Bjørn Wiinblad (BW) demonstrated what is often considered to be the greatest creative decorative talent in Denmark in the latter half of 20th century; he was both criticised and loved for his extraordinary images, his fantasy and the diversity of his work, within all genres of the time-honoured areas of applied art – ceramics, scenography, poster-art, glass, printed fabrics, tapestries and patterns for embroidery. For BW the departure point was graphic art, which he had studied both in qualifying as a typographer and at the Academy of Fine Arts, but

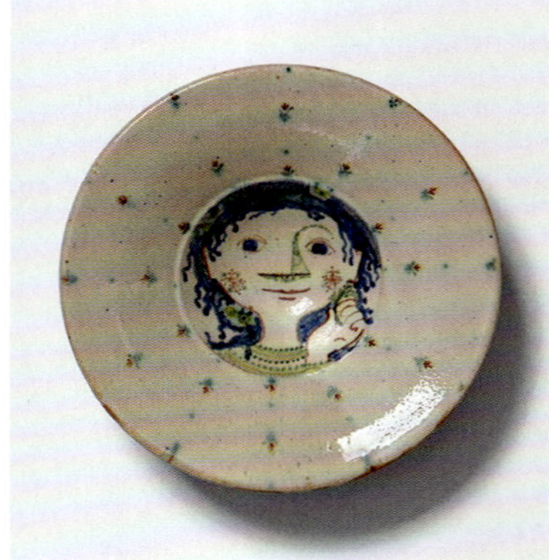

613 61/1978

his career then took a different direction, and through his incontestable and inexhaustible talent for ornamentation he created illustrations that opened up a world of beauty and joy like the oriental '1001 Nights'. His style of drawing remained recognisable throughout his whole life and this was, for better or worse, the basis for the growth of his international image and production, which developed in workshops and commercial firms in Denmark, Germany, Japan, USA and Portugal.

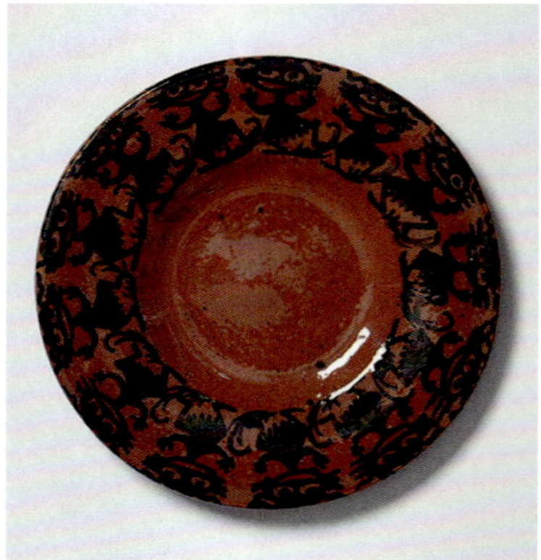

614 62/1978

From the beginning BW's ceramic work was linked to the potter's traditional way of working: earthenware, decorated with painting using horn in slip colours, and brush-painting on tin glaze as the central techniques. But he was also open to new methods, and in the end this resulted in mass-production of his designs on the basis of good long-lasting cooperation with several important producers. The first of those was Nymølle Keramiske Fabrik, for whom he designed products in the years 1946-56, with a view, for example, to reproduction of his motifs via copperplate printing onto faience. He was enthusiastic about this technique – 'I loved to sit with the finest pen possible and draw tiny little details' (*'Bjørn Wiinblad, Arbejder gennem 40 år'*; catalogue p. 12, Kunstindustrimuseet, 1981). He was baffled by his fellow-artists' criticism of working for the purpose of reproduction, which they called prostitution. BW himself explained his motivation for doing this as being his eagerness to express himself in a new way, adapted to what was for him a new technique.

The production from Nymølle led in 1957 to an approach from Philip Rosenthal, from the major German Rosenthal factories, and subsequently to a close cooperation, which lasted for all of BW's life, and provided the context in which he designed everything from large porcelain table services to small items for daily use.

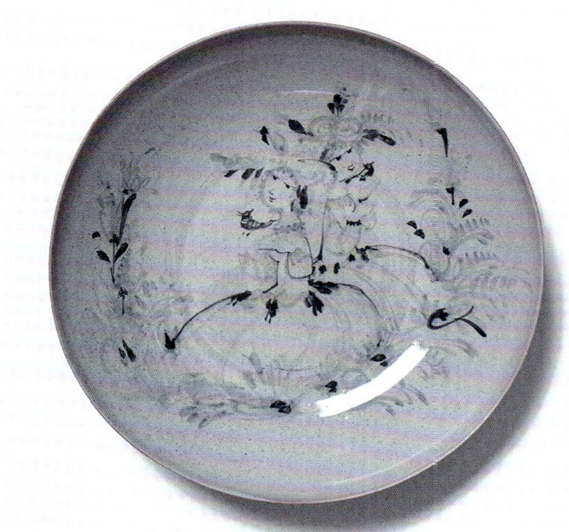

615 51/1981

BW set up his own workshop in 1952, with several employees, and in 1966 he moved the workshop to 'Det Blå Hus' (The Blue House), where he also established his famously hospitable home with his large art collection, including ceramics from many cultures and epochs. He also had a smaller collection of contemporary Danish studio ceramics, which he had acquired from diverse exhibitions. He wrote about his

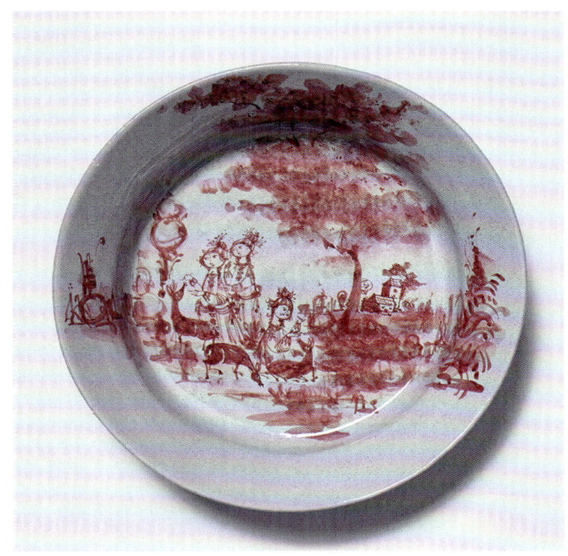

616 52/1981

relationship to these ceramic pieces in the catalogue to the exhibition in the museum in 1981 in the following words (p. 19): 'I admire the people who can create things with the quality of great simplicity, like Gutte (Eriksen), like Alev (Siesbye), like Tapio (Wirkkala) – but as for me, I could never express myself so simply'.

BW said of himself that he was self-taught as a ceramicist, and the fact is that he could neither throw pots nor compose glazes, but he could decorate. Originally it was horn-painting that aroused his interest, and in the museum's collection it is only works from his early working years that are represented – five works from the second half of the 1940s, and six from the 1950s. BW himself donated seven pieces to the museum in connection with the retrospective exhibition in 1981. Together they give an engaging picture of the young BW experimenting with horn-painted earthenware **(612,614)** and there are several charming little figure-compositions painted with brush directly on lead glaze, including an example of the many Christmas presents he made in the early years to delight family and friends **(617)**. The largest work **(620)** is made of blue clay with tin glaze, decorated with pictorial sensitivity in the configuring of the poetic and dreaming female figure who seems to grow together with the surrounding features from nature.

At the present time work is underway to open up Wiinblad's 'Det Blå Hus' to the public and to resume actual production of his designs. There are indications that a new wave of popularity is on its way for BW's fantasy-filled and delicately graceful decorative idiom.

See: *Bjørn Wiinblad. Lyst og livsværk. An oeuvre of Joy and Delight.* Ed. by Majbritt Løland & Pia Wirnfeldt. Danmarks Keramikmuseum Grimmerhus. Middelfart 2012

612. Dish, 1946
Earthenware, lead-glazed; thrown, slip, horn- and brush-painted, fired at 960°. Diam 56.5. Mark: 'Bjørn Wiinblad -46' on base. Mus.no. 14/1947
ACQUISITION: Den Permanente, 1946, Copenhagen. See: *Brændpunkter*, 1990. Dybdahl, L., 1997

613. Bowl, 1946
Earthenware, lead-glazed; thrown, fired at 970°. H 6.5 x Diam 22.8.
Mark: 'Bjørn Wiinblad -46' painted on base. Mus.no. 61/1978
ACQUISITION: Anker Nørregaard. Donation from *Helge Jacobsens Legat*

614. Plate, 1946
Earthenware, glazed; thrown, brush-painted, fired at 960°. H 1.8 x Diam 16.
Mark: 'Bjørn Wiinblad – 46' painted on base. Mus.no. 62/1978
ACQUISITION: Anker Nørregaard. Donation from *Helge Jacobsens Legat*.
See: *Brændpunkter*, 1990

615. Dish, 1961
Blue clay, tin-glazed; thrown, fired at 970°. H 9.4 x Diam 41.5.
Mark: 'Bjørn Wiinblad 61 S 77 Danmark' painted on base.
Mus.no. 51/1981
ACQUISITION: Donation from Bjørn Wiinblad

616. Dish, 1957
Blue clay, tin-glazed; thrown, fired at 970°. H 9.5 x Diam 39.
Mark: 'Bjørn Wiinblad 57 selvportræt med nummerskilt 21 Danmark' painted on base. Mus.no. 52/1981
ACQUISITION: Donation from Bjørn Wiinblad

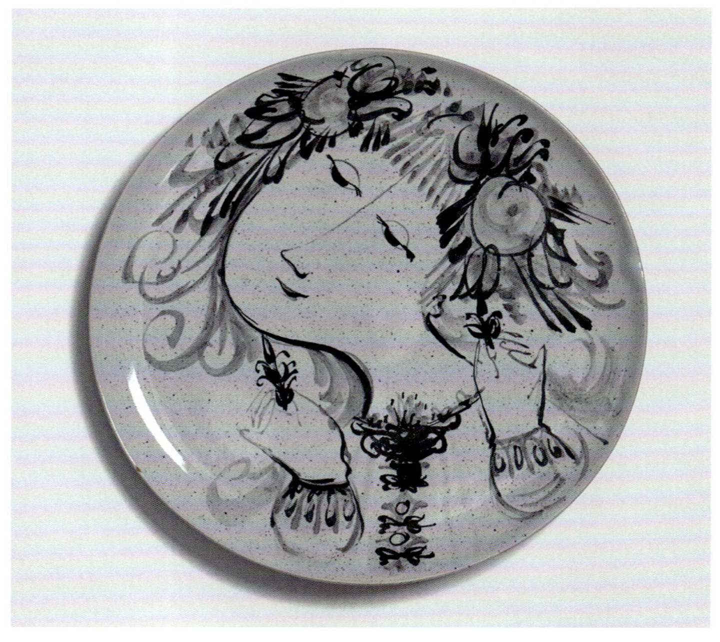

618 54/1981

617. Bowl, 1948
Blue clay, earthenware, tin-glazed; brush-painted, fired at 970°. H 6.8 x W 21.
Mark: 'Bjørn Wiinblad -48 Danmark dedikation' painted on base.
Mus.no. 53/1981. ACQUISITION: Donation from Bjørn Wiinblad

618. Dish, 1954
Blue clay, tin-glazed; brush-painted, fired at 970°. H 2.6 x Diam 20.3.
Mark: 'Bjørn Wiinblad 54 [self-portrait] 370 Danmark' painted on base. Mus.no. 54/1981. ACQUISITION: Donation from Bjørn Wiinblad

617 53/1981

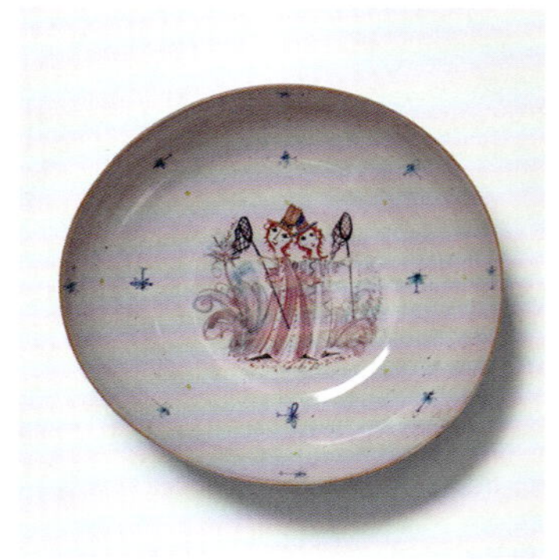

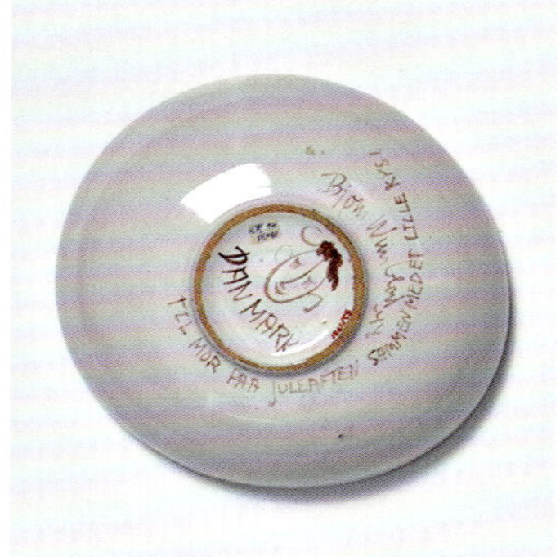

619. Bowl, 1949 (no photo)

Blue clay, tin-glazed; brush-painted, fired at 970°. H 4.6 x Diam 7.2.

Mark: 'Bjørn Wiinblad 49 Danmark' painted around the base.

Mus.no. 55/198.

ACQUISITION: Donation from Bjørn Wiinblad

620. Dish, 1952

Blue clay. tin-glazed; brush-painted, fired at 970°. Diam 57.5.

Mark: 'Bjørn Wiinblad Danmark [self-portrait] 52' painted on base.

Mus.no. 137/1998. ACQUISITION: Antik Birkehuset, Nykøbing Sjælland.

Donation from Kunstindustrimuseet, Oslo

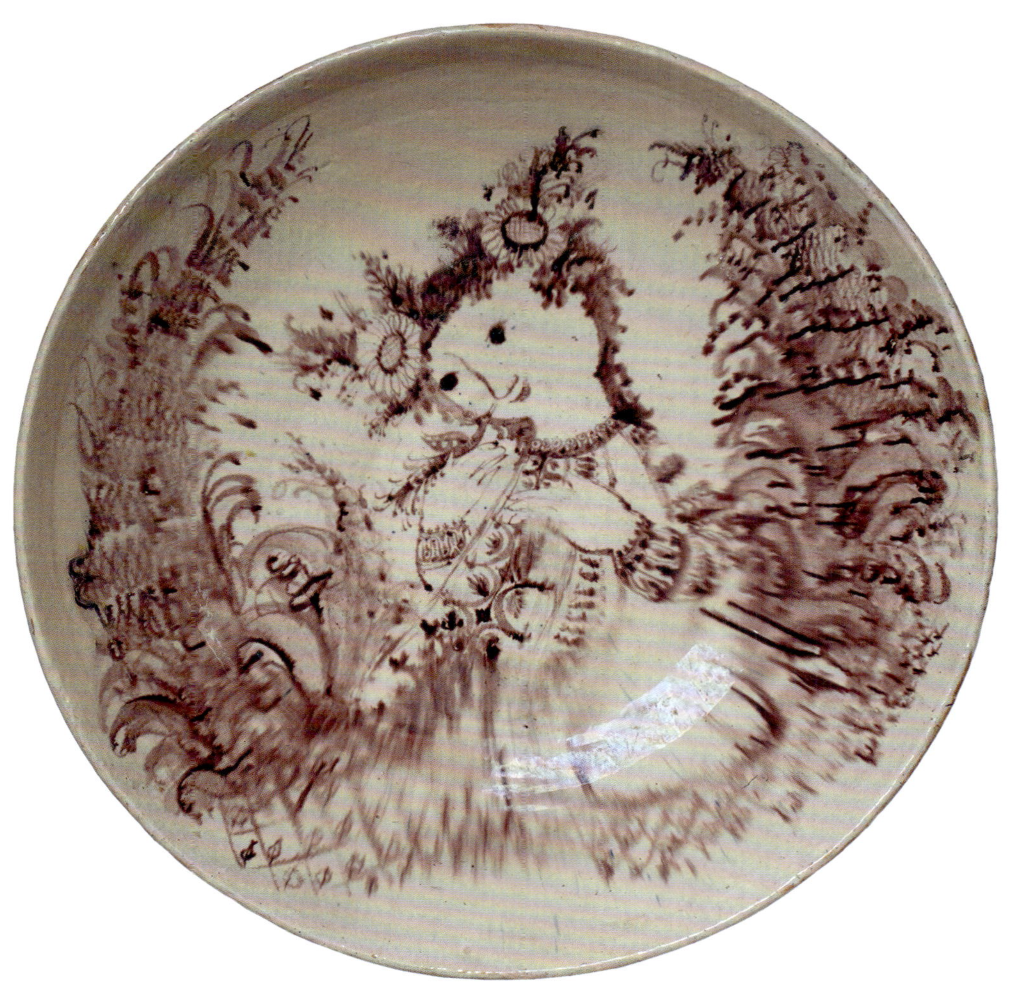

620 137/1998

ØRSTED, METTE MARIE 1952 –

Ceramicist

1973-77	Skolen for Brugskunst, Ceramics and Glass
1984-1986	Billedskolen, Jagtvej, Copenhagen
1988-1996	Danmarks Designskole, guest teacher
1990-	Own studio workshop, Copenhagen
1993-94	Danmarks Designskole, tutor
	www.mettemarieoersted.dk

The interplay of form and function has engaged Danish ceramicists through many generations, and it is also the red thread running through the ceramic works of Mette Marie Ørsted (MMØ). She has an ingrained sense of clay, and she has clung to red clay as few have, in her generation, as a recurring basis for her work. At the same time she has experimented with mixing in diverse fibrous materials to give the clay character and porosity, and she has also worked with porcelain. For her work with *terra sigillata* in the decoration of a series of large vessels in high-fired earthenware MMØ was awarded the Biennale prize at the first Danish Ceramics Triennale at Trapholt in 1994.

In September 2005 in her solo exhibition '*Kander klippet med en saks*' (Jugs cut with scissors) in Galleri Nørby, MMØ showed new aspects of her talent, but once again based on her fascination with the jug, which she has cultivated since qualifying from Skolen for Brugskunst in 1977. The theme of this exhibition was not functional use of the objects, however, but toying with completely new forms inspired by historic jugs from diverse sources – daily work in the workshop, ordinary housekeeping, and industrial uses: oil cans, jerry-cans and kettles, to name a few examples. The materials and techniques developed by MMØ through the years were here used in a new language which with striking effect characterised the jugs and their relations with an older workshop culture. The material texture of the objects is remarkable, with the unglazed red body on the outer side, where one can see all the joins, while the inner surfaces are white, tin-glazed, bringing to mind the many enamelled household objects that were earlier in use everywhere in society.

This striking exhibition, in which materials and form of expression together made up a higher unity, placing the objects in a conceptual zone, was followed up by MMØ with her exhibition '*Keramisk Konkretion*' in Galleri Ann Linnemann in 2013, in which she explored architectural space in interplay with ceramic spatial forms, cutting out and then re-assembling ceramic structures.

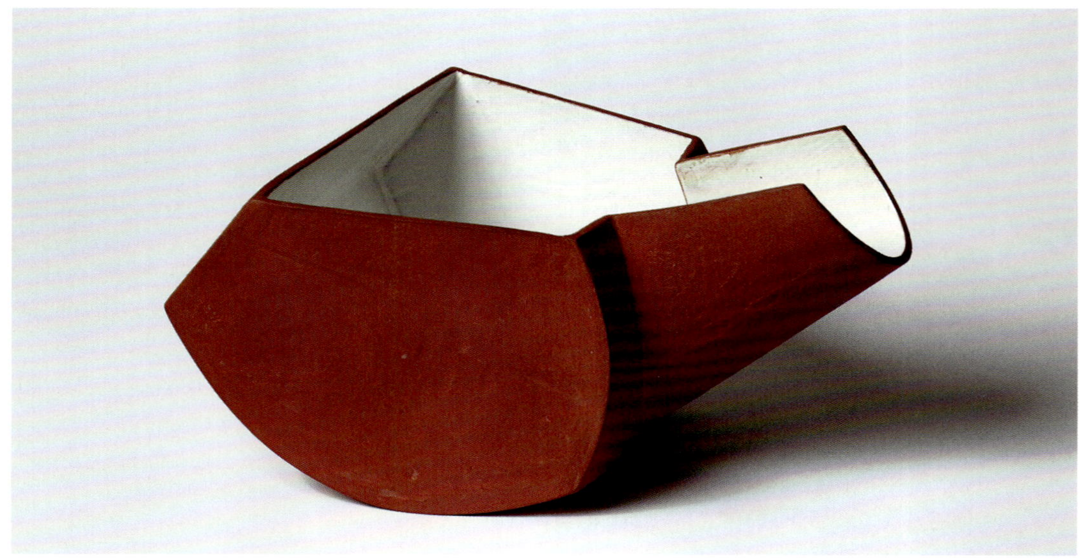

621 330/2007

In the museum's collection there is a fine representative work that is a continuation of the breakthrough exhibition in 2005. The title of the work is *Kanonkande* **(621)** and it was made for the Craft and Design Biennale at Trapholt in 2007. The museum's later work from 2010, *Sandbund* **(622)**, has a distinctive repeated pattern that is seen as though through a water surface.

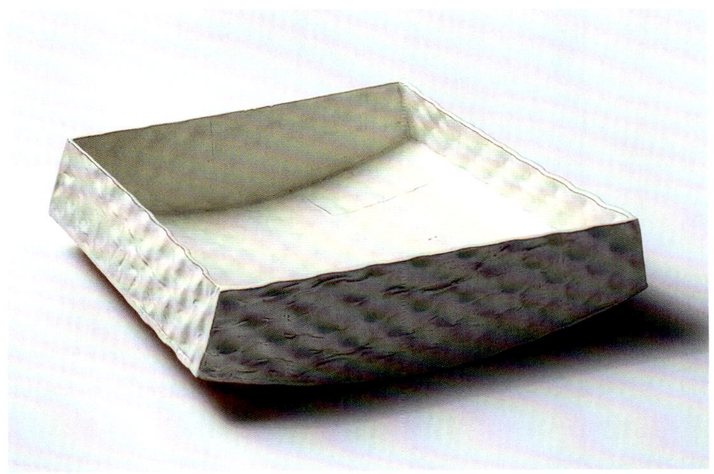

622 101/2011

621. Jug, 2007. *Kanonkande* (Cannon-jug)

Faience, paper-fibre, tin-glazed; assembled slabs, fired at 1140°. H 32 x W 24 x D 17. Mark: none. Mus.no. 330/2007

ACQUISITION: Galleri Nørby, Copenhagen

622. Dish, 2010. *Sandbund* (Seabed)

Earthenware, glazed; slab technique, stamped decoration, fired at 1140°. H 10 x W 36. Mark: 'Mette Marie Ørsted 2010' inscribed on base. Mus.no. 101/2011

ACQUISITION: *Verden på et fad – undersøgelser i ler*, 2011, Kunst og Kulturcenter, Gammelgaard

AABERG, GUNHILD 1939 –

Ceramicist, designer

1959-64	Kunsthåndværkerskolen, Ceramics
1964-	Strandstræde Keramik, shop and workshop shared with Jane Reumert and Beate Andersen
1976-79	The Royal Porcelain Factory, freelance designer
	Det Jyske Kunstakademi and Danmarks Designskole, guest teacher
1999-	Awarded Statens Kunstfond's honorary lifelong stipend
	www.gunhildaaberg.dk
	www.strandstraedekeramik.dk

Gunhild Aaberg (GAA) creates ceramic works with a pronounced sense of the monumental, displayed in their design, in the robustness of the materials and in the choice of colour, with nuances of black and white dominating. For GAA it is the experience of the textural and the references integral to the work that are decisive. A constantly recurring source of inspiration is her upbringing in a harbour and sailing milieu; the physicality of raw building-structures and the many tools and objects one finds around a working harbour have influenced her attitude to ceramic expression, resulting in an approach in which perfection of detail is not allowed to overshadow the effect of the whole.

GAA works almost exclusively with stoneware clay, to which she adds sand or chamotte to lend character and expressiveness, and as decoration she uses matte slip and only occasionally glaze with shine. Her works are modelled and finished with hammering and scraping tools.

The firm basis for GAA's long and distinguished career is the workshop *Strandstræde Keramik*, which she established together with Jane Reumert and Beate Andersen after they finished studying at Kunsthåndværkerskolen in 1964. These three very different ceramicists have together maintained this institution in Danish ceramics throughout more than 40 years, and they are all members of the exhibition group *Keramiske Veje*, which celebrated its 30th anniversary in 2015.

In the museum's collection GAA is represented with six works, from the 1970s to 2004. The earliest work, from 1977, is a fine dish in grey clay with porcelain slip and clear glaze on the inner surface, on which three stylized petals are inscribed **(623)**. From the 1990s there are two works; one of them, from '*Keramiske Veje*' fro 1997, is a sculpture with the title *Stregkode – pind med rum* (Bar-code – stick with compartments), an elongated lidded box, which is a recurrent motif in GAA's work, in which the lidded pot with a concealed space inside is to be found in many versions, the inner space always containing a surprise **(625)**. This motif can be found recurring in three further works. The earliest, from 1985 **(630)**, is a typical example, developed by GAA at the beginning of the 1980s, with two identical counter-posed shapes, one sitting on top of the other, while the lidded pot from 1999 entitled *The Wall* is of a different nature, consisting of a firm regular-sided little sculpture with a rounded lid and a decoration with an X shape on the front as a salute to all things maritime (105 a-b/1999). A very special 'lidded pot' is the sculpture *Form med hæl og låg* (Shape with heel and lid) acquired from '*Keramiske Veje 2004*', an armadillo-like shape modelled from vertical strips or bands, with the upper surfaces covered in slip and with rubbed-in glaze **(627)**.

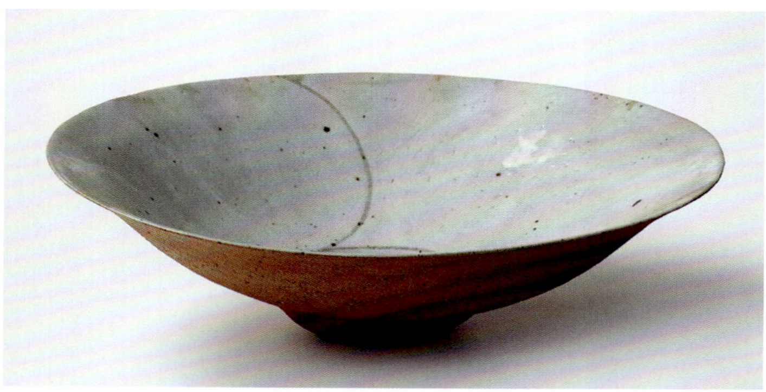

623 31/1977

In 2010 the museum received from Statens Kunstfond a monumental and significant work consisting of *Kæmpeparabol* (Giant satellite dish) **(628)**, along with *Part of Circle* **(629)**, with the theme of communication; the latter work was included in a solo exhibition for GAA in Galleri Nørby in 1999, and it was there exhibited with a large photostat as background showing the Grandfey-viaduct in Fribourg, Switzerland.

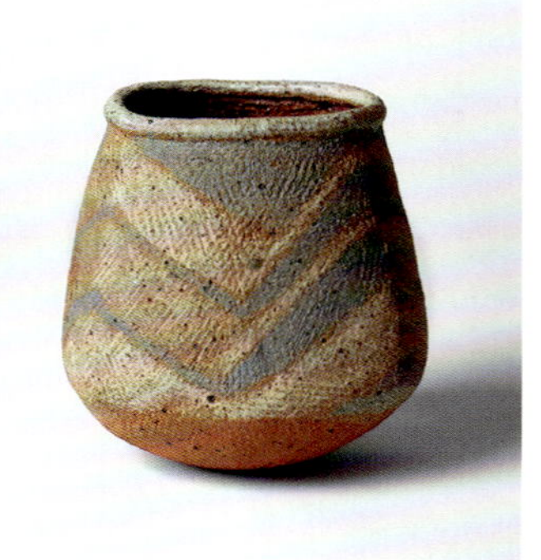

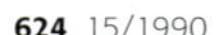

624 15/1990

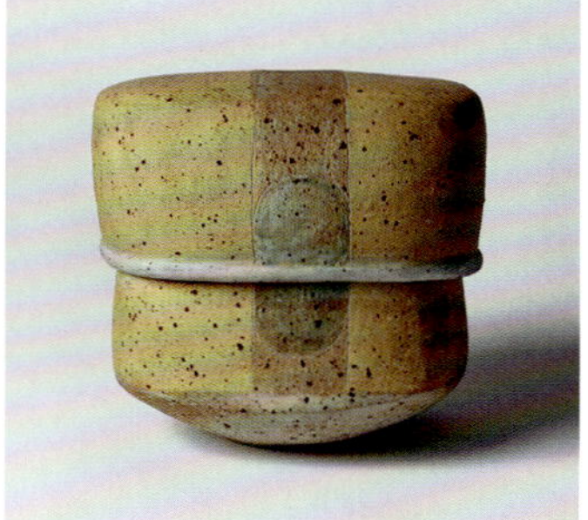

630 D 1660a-b

At the anniversary exhibition held by '*Keramiske Veje*' at Sophienholm in 2015, GAA exhibited a conceptual work with the title *To byer* (Two cities), shaped like an installation above two conurbations, *Metropolis* and *Den måske ikke-eksisterende by* (The perhaps non-existent city), consisting of many ceramic shapes in closely-packed formations, reflecting two very different town structures, societies and atmospheres. The work is a clear expression of GAA's continuing interest in the spatial – here an issue of forms of city space and structures with concealed entrances and spaces. The installation shows great potential for new layers of significance finding expression in GAA's ceramic art.

As a widely recognised ceramic artist GAA has an extensive exhibition history in the USA, Europe and the Nordic region, and is represented in a number of Danish museums and prestigious international museums and institutions. In 1999 she was awarded Statens Kunstfond's honorary lifelong stipend.

623. Dish, 1977

Stoneware, porcelain, transparent glaze; thrown, slip, sgrafitto, brush-painted, fired at 1300°. H 13 x Diam 43. Mus.no. 31/1977

ACQUISITION: *Strandstræde keramik*, 1977, Kunstindustrimuseet. Donation from *Overretssagfører Odin Kaysers Legat*. See: *Brændpunkter*, 1990

624. Vase, 1990
Stoneware; modelled, slip, inscribed, brush-painted, fired at 1300°. H 15.5.
Mark: 'GUNHILD' inscribed on base. Mus.no. 15/1990
ACQUISITION: *Strandstræde Keramik*, Copenhagen. Donation from *Ny Carlsberg Museumslegat*. See: *Brændpunkter*, 1990

625. Sculpture, 1997. ***Stregkode – pind med rum***
(Bar-code –stick with compartments)
Stoneware; modelled, cut, slip, brush-painted fired at 1300°. a: H 6 x L 73;
b: H 5.5 x L 78. Mark: 'GUNHILD' painted on base. Mus.no. 217a-b/1997
ACQUISITION: *Keramiske Veje,* 1997, Den Frie, Copenhagen

626. Lidded pot, 1999. ***The Wall***
Stoneware; modelled, slip, brush-painted, fired at 1300°. H 28 x W 25.5.
Mark: none. Mus.no. 105a-b/1999
ACQUISITION: *Gunhild Aaberg*, 1999, Galleri Nørby, Copenhagen

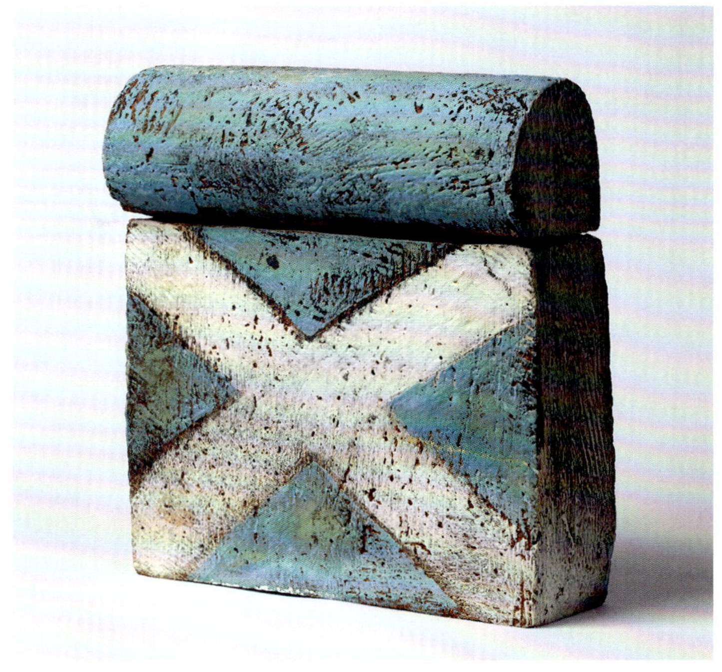
626 105a-b/1999

627. Sculpture, 2004. ***Form med hæl og låg*** (Shape with heel and lid)
Stoneware, rubbed-in glaze; slip, brush-painted, reduction-fired at 1300-1290°.
H 51 x L 65. Mark: none. Mus.no. 313/2004
ACQUISITION: Donation from *Annie & Otto Johs. Detlefs' Almennyttige Fond* (OJD)

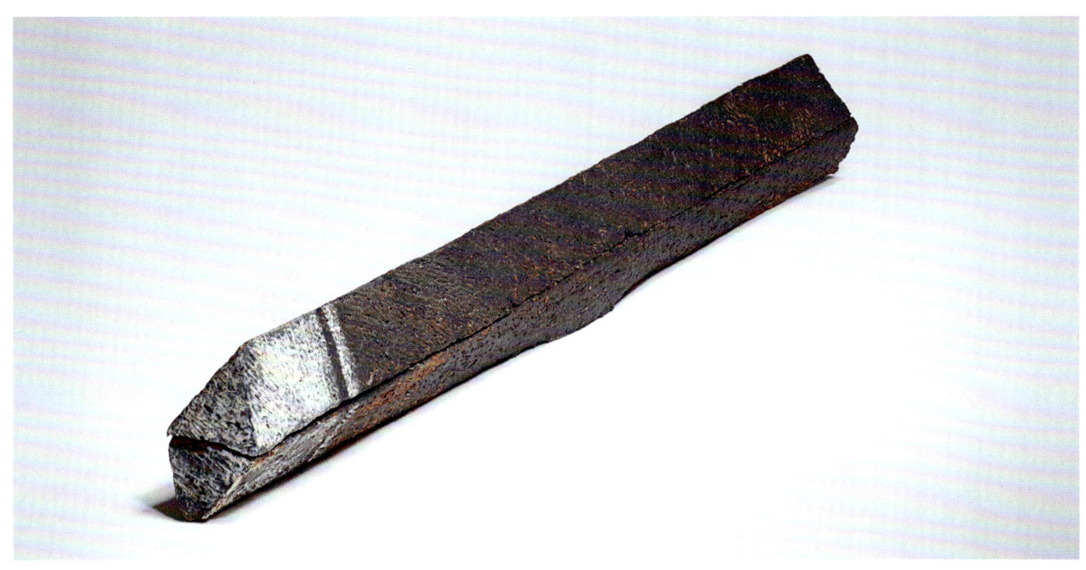
625 217a-b/1997

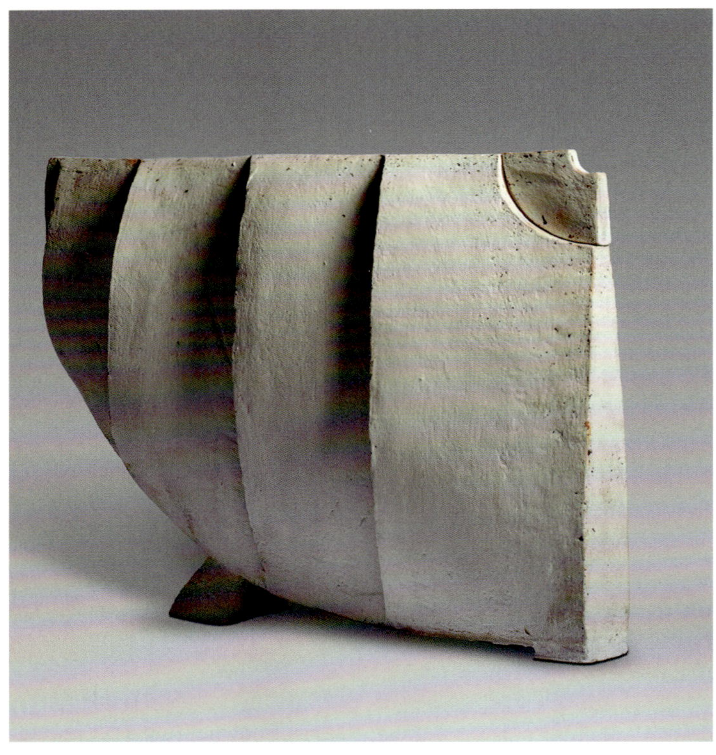

627 313/2004

628 51/2010 629 52a-b/2010

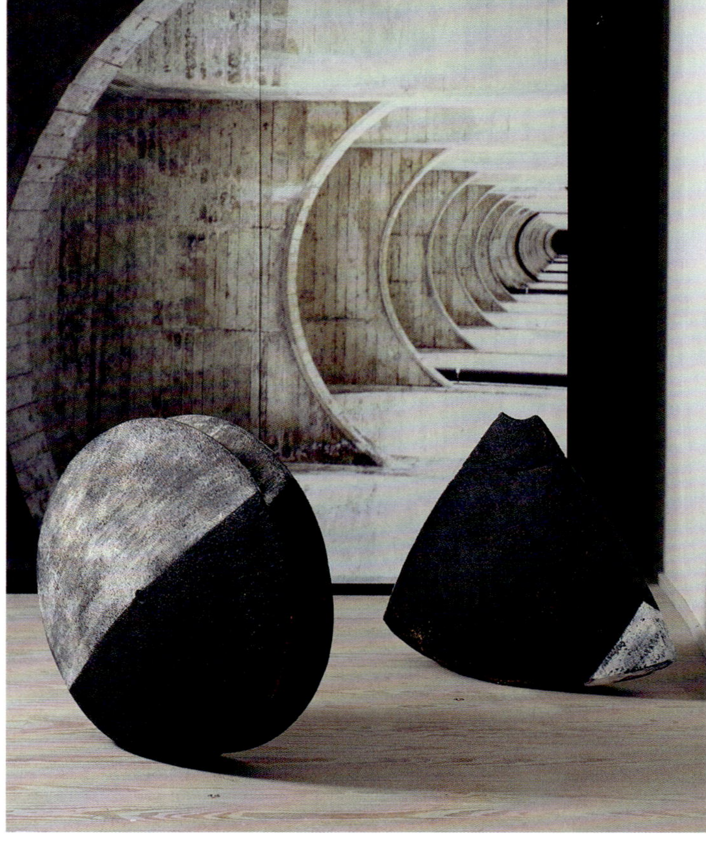

628. Sculpture, 1999. *Kæmpeparabol* (Giant satellite dish)
Stoneware clay with gravel; modelled, black and white slip. Diam 78 x D 19.
Mark: none. Mus.no. 51/2010
ACQUISITION: Solo exhibition, Galleri Nørby, 1999. Donation from *Statens Kunstfond*

629. Sculpture, 1999. *Part of Circle*
Stoneware with gravel; modelled, black and white slip. H (with lid) 72.5 x W 88 x D 5.5. Mark: none. Mus.no. 52a-b/2010
ACQUISITION: Solo exhibition, Galleri Nørby, 1999. Donation from *Statens Kunstfond*

630. Lidded pot, 1985
Stoneware; modelled, slip, brush-painted, fired at 1300°. H 14 x W 15 x D 15.
Mark: 'GUNHILD' inscribed on base. Mus.no. D 1660a-b
ACQUISITION: Deposited by *Statens Kunstfond*, 1987

ÅBERG, BARBRO 1958 –

Ceramicist

1979-82	Art Education, Clackamas Community College, Oregon City, USA
1983	Pupil of ceramicist Susan Steinman, Berkley, USA
1984-85	Art School, Uppsala, Sweden
1984-88	Kunsthåndværkerskolen in Kolding, Ceramics and Glass
2002	Guldagergaard, International Ceramic Research Center, guest artist
	Lecturer and teacher in Design and Ceramics- colleges in Europe, USA and Japan
1988-99	Cooperative workshop, Århus
1999-	Own studio workshop, Ry, Jutland www.barbroaaberg.dk

From an early stage of her work Barbro Åberg (BÅ) found a personal form of ceramic expression, and this is recognizable even though in terms of shape and colour her works show diversity of approach to the material. In general one senses a unity of direction of current in the works, which appear to build on structures taken from natural forms, e.g. fossils, geological formations, tissues and cells. There is an insistence on close examination of surfaces and on exploration of layers, which brings to mind the research methods of archaeologists and geologists, but in BÅ's case this is converted into artistic creation. At the same time the works contain associations with anthropological materials from earlier times, cult objects and symbols.

The ideas behind the works and their form of expression are closely linked in their material realisation, developed through years of experimentation and research into ceramic materials, which BÅ became fascinated with during her study years at Kunsthåndværkerskolen in Kolding. To be able to model the open structures that are a feature of many of her works makes special demands of the clay, which BÅ herself mixes, using pipe clay with perlite and paper-fibre, which adds strength to the clay for the modelling process.

In the museum's two works by BÅ it is in fact this clay blend that has been used. The sculptures are shaped upside down on a plaster mould

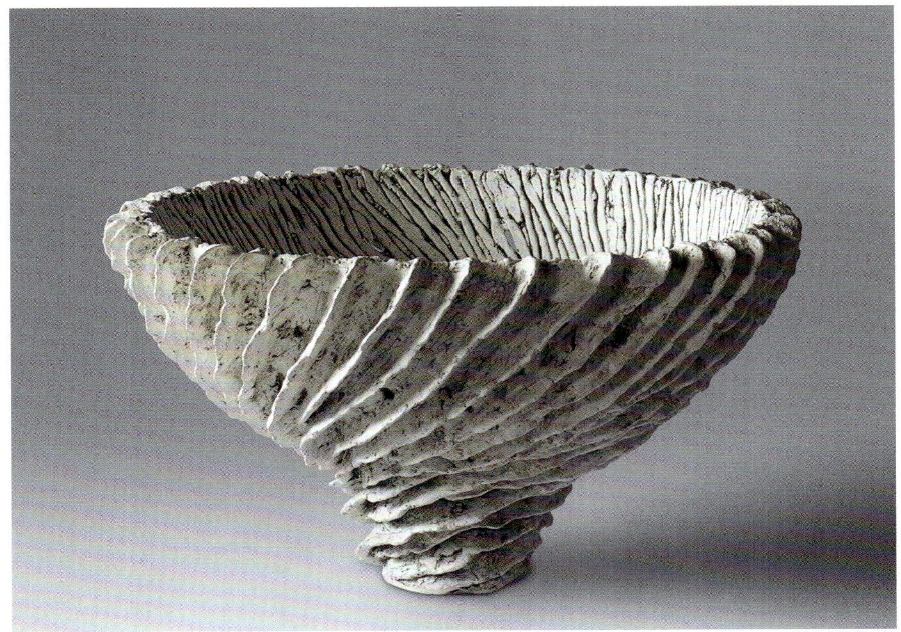

632 110/2009

which is then turned over so that the modelling can be completed from above. Both works were displayed in Galleri Nørby in 2005 in the exhibition '*Tanker om tid*' (Thoughts about time), and represent two idioms in BÅ's work at that time: one, with the title *Feather Boat* **(631)** is built up like basket-work with contours associated with a ship, while the other is a large spiral bowl **(632)**.

BÅ belongs among the internationally placed ceramic artists with a sound foundation of links to prestigious galleries in Paris, USA and the UK; she has also been represented at the major art fairs SOFA and Collect and at important exhibitions in Denmark and abroad.
See: Barbro Åberg, '*Erindring og Erkendelse / Recollection and Recognition*', Danmarks Keramikmuseum – Grimmerhus (CLAY), 2011

631. Sculpture, 2005. *Feather Boat II*
Pipe clay with perlite and paper-fibre, *terra sigillata*, prepared stains; modelled on a plaster mould, brushes, sponge, fired on clay plates with supports at 1140°. H 45 x W 70 x D 20. Mark: 'BA' inscribed and painted on side. Mus.no. 179/2005. ACQUISITION: *Tanker om tid*, 2005, Galleri Nørby, Copenhagen. See: *From the Kilns of Denmark,* 2002

632. Sculpture, 2004. *Stor spiralskål* (Large spiral bowl)
Pipe clay with perlite, oxides, *terra sigillata*, prepared stains; modelled on a plaster mould, fired at 1150°. H 24 x Diam 41. Mark: '2004' with an indecipherable name inscribed on base. Mus.no. 110/2009
ACQUISITION: *Tanker om tid,* 2005, Galleri Nørby, Copenhagen. Donation from *Ny Carlsbergfondet*

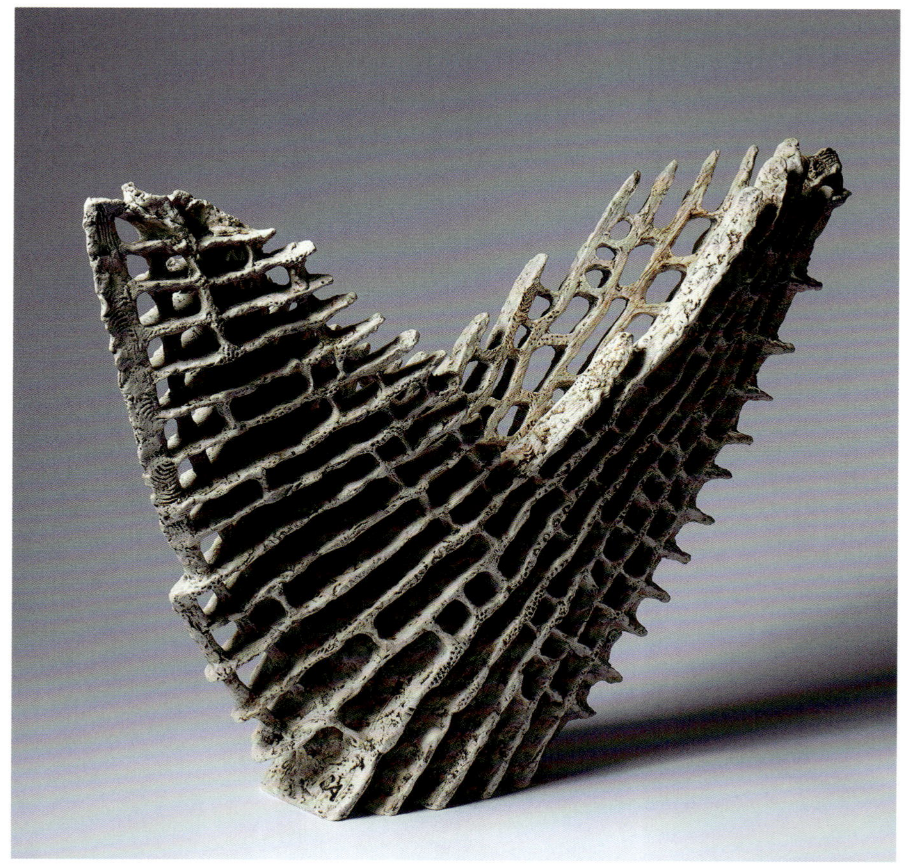

631 179/2005

APPENDICES

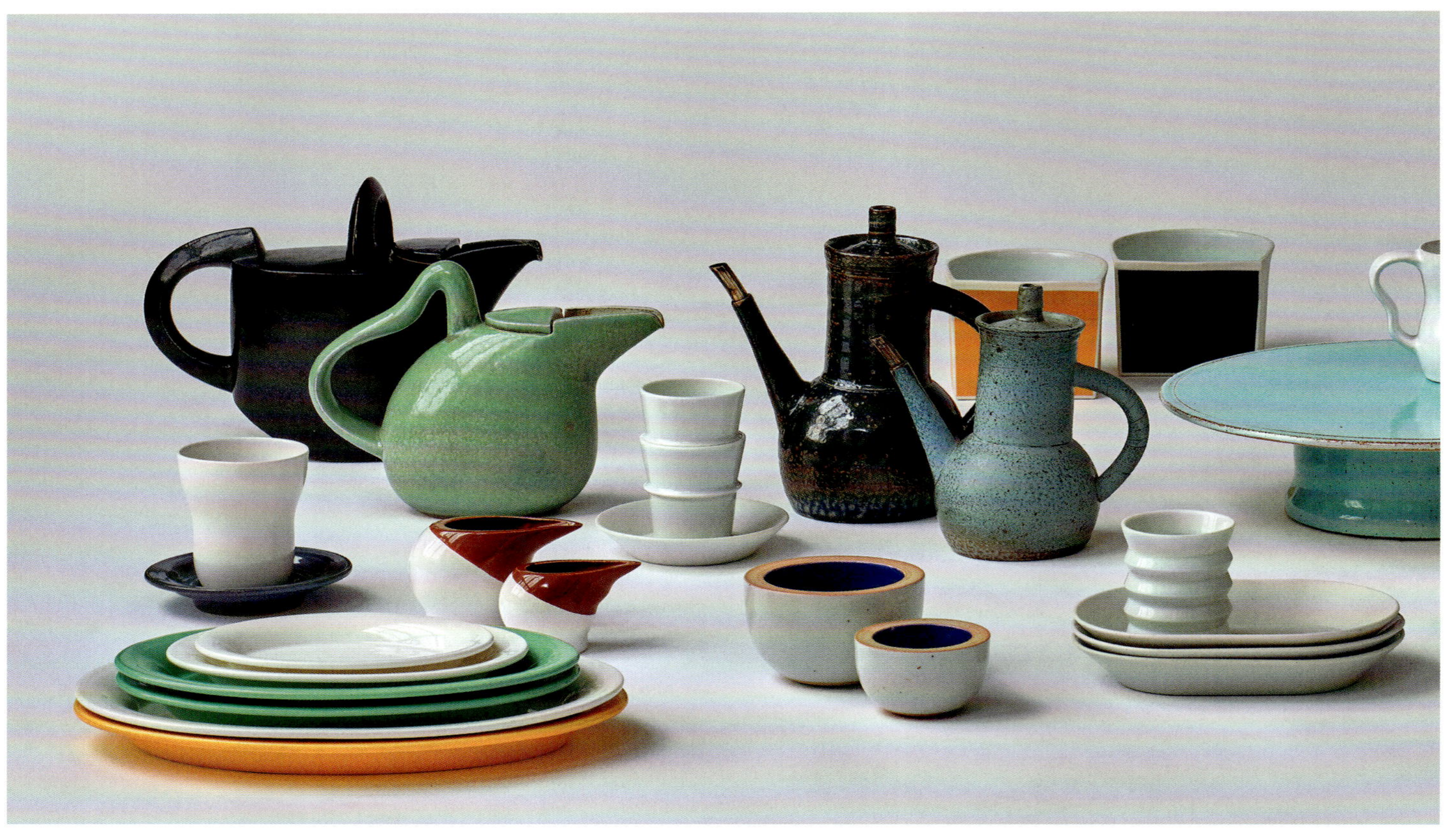

The 'Lark' table service (Lærkestellet)

In the early 1990s a unique ceramic project was embarked on: the creation of a table service named *Lærkestellet* – the Lark service. This was in a sense an extension of the type of production engaged in by the many small workshops of the post-war period, but it developed in a remarkable direction in the last decade of the 20th century, when many ceramicists had abandoned production of functional objects in favour of unique sculptural works. The creation of the Lark service was in essence an idealistic action with the purpose of focusing the attention of the surrounding world on studio ceramics and on the pleasure that can be gained from using fine tableware distinguished by good design and craftsmanship to enhance the experience of mealtimes and everyday life.

This present catalogue of the museum's collection of studio ceramics from 1950 to 2010 does not include industrially produced ceramic table services, even though several such services from this period were created by ceramicists discussed in the catalogue, working in collaboration with the Danish porcelain factories.[1] But *Lærkestellet* is an exceptional case and belongs to the highest degree among the works included in this catalogue. The many individual pieces that combine to form the service were made in many small series by a selected group of ceramicists in their own studio workshops – ceramicists who are all represented in the museum's collection by unique works as well as their contribution to the Lark service.

The initiative to carry through the vision of producing a different kind of table service came from Louise Lerche-Lerchenborg, a warm

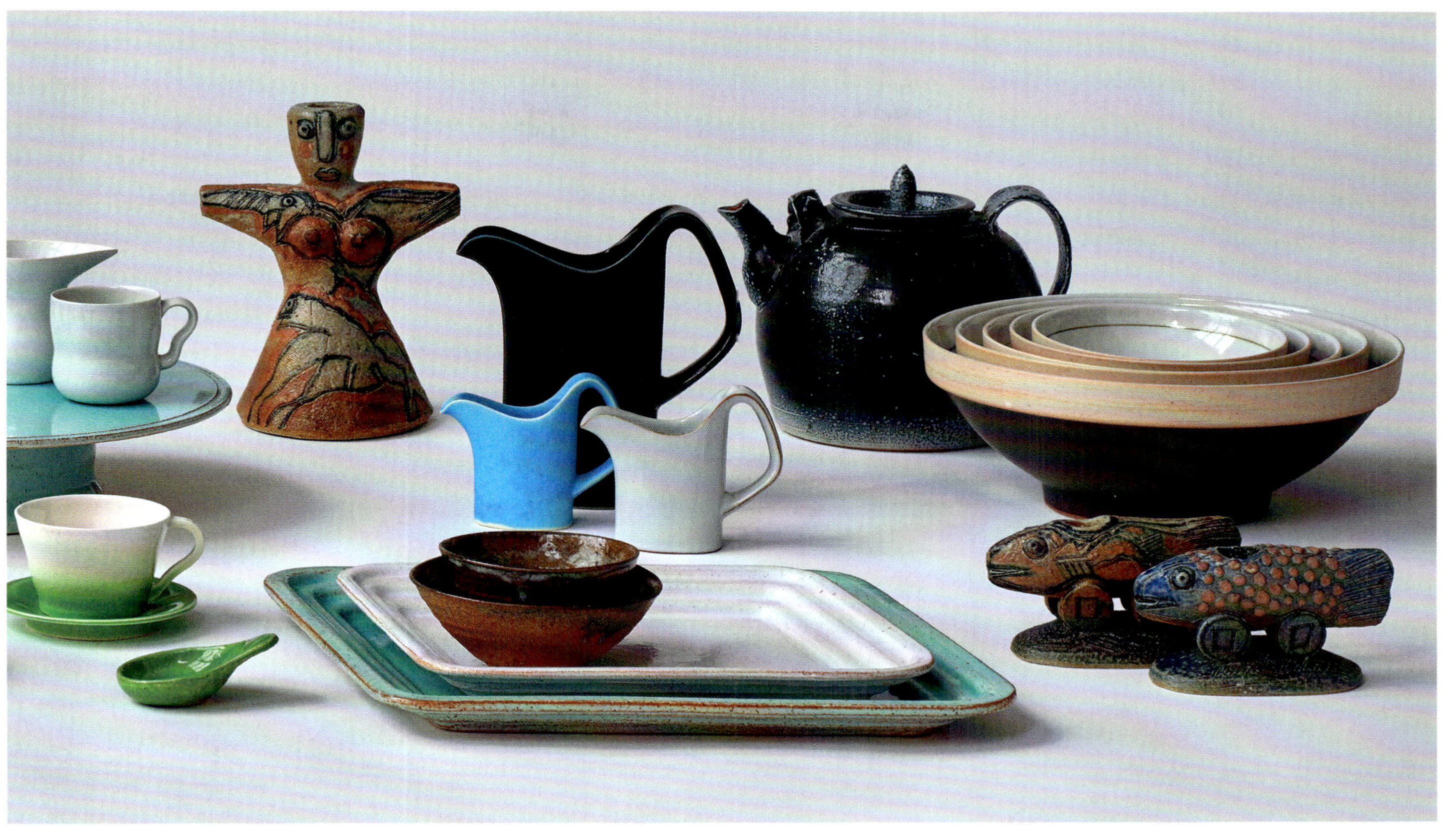

and enthusiastic supporter of craftwork and not least ceramics, which she has cultivated in a variety of ways through many years, including holding exhibitions in the manor house of Lerchenborg on Sealand. The idea was described by Louise Lerche-Lerchenborg in the publication *Lærkestellet*, from 1997:

> *'The Lark service was created in 1994 as an expression of the wish to inspire, encourage and develop Danish functional ceramics, particularly studio ceramics. Throughout my life I have been fascinated by ceramics and I have for instance, organized a number of ceramic exhibitions; this has given me the opportunity through some 30 years, to follow the work of many ceramicists. The textures of ceramic expression, the depth of a glaze or the sweep of a bold line are what I see as virtually the breath of the artist. The intense pleasure in the experience of using ceramics in daily life is something I have felt I had to try to communicate to many others'.*

As a result of cooperation with a number of ceramicists these thoughts led to the plan to create a table service consisting of individual pieces made by different ceramicists, either as newly developed elements or as evolved versions of objects from their existing studio production. The group of participating ceramicists, almost all of them, with only a few exceptions, born around 1940, consisted of Beate Andersen, Birgitte and Hans Börjeson, Bente Hansen, Sten Lykke Madsen, Bodil and Richard Manz, Ursula Munch-Petersen and Sys Thomsen. Those particularly involved in the whole development process and the subsequent production phase were Ursula Munch-Petersen, Sten Lykke Madsen, Sys Thomsen, Bodil Manz and Richard Manz.

Thanks to unquenchable enthusiasm and great skill Louise Lerche-Lerchenborg successfully secured the essential economic basis for the project, obtaining support both from official Ministry of Culture resources and from foundations, in particular the New Carlsberg Foundation.

The Lark service came to have 34 components (see photo of collected display on pp. 344-345), glazed and made in porcelain or stoneware and including everything from little salt dishes to double-armed candle-sticks and several different types of cups, saucers, plates, bowls, serving dishes, jugs and plant-pots. All the pieces were marked with a lark symbol designed by Sten Lykke Madsen and with the ceramicists' individual signatures. The variations in expression, design, glaze and colour reflect the individuality of the participants and can be seen as extensions of their previous work with functional ceramics. But the range of variation does not prevent the pieces from also functioning as a whole when they are experienced in use as a table service. The strong sensory and functional characteristics of the ceramic pieces set off food to best advantage, in a festive way – qualities given high priority by the initiative-takers. The individual pieces in the service can also easily be used in many other contexts and have been much in demand.

The Lark service was produced for 100 persons and in the years 1994 to 1997 it was offered to museums and cultural institutions during limited periods for use in their cafés and restaurants. It was also included in several of the craft events and displays at the time, for instance during Copenhagen's European Capital of Culture year in 1996, and in the exhibitions *Unika* and *Duplika.*

Until 1997 the Lark service was owned by an independent institution, *Den selvejende institution Keramikbanken af 1994*, administered by Louise Lerche-Lerchenborg with assistance from architect John Vedel-Rieper, but in 1997 those involved in that institution decided to dissolve it. This took place in conjunction with the transfer of the Lark service to the museum for use in the museum's café. Before the transfer four other complete services were assembled as donations: one to the museum's own collection, one to Bornholms Kunstmuseum, one to Danmarks Keramikmuseum Grimmerhus (CLAY), in Middelfart, and one to Kunstmuseet Trapholt in Kolding. The Lark service is thus to be found in the collections of four public museums, where it bears witness to a unique initiative and to the participating ceramicists' passion for their work with objects for functional use – a legacy of their education and early workshop experience in the 1960s.

A hoped-for continuation of the Lark service under the auspices of the museum turned out to run into several problems, including economic obstacles, since what was planned was now a matter of a running operation rather than a development project. In brief, it was not possible to obtain the funds necessary for further orders to be commissioned from the ceramicists, nor to proceed to inclusion of new pieces. Moreover, it proved to be the case that many pieces of the service could not withstand intensive use, with frequent machine washing and handling by staff in situations of pressure in the museum's popular café. By 2012 it became necessary to replace the café's tableware.

For the museum and its visitors the years with the Lark service were an enriching experience of Danish studio ceramics, involving the pleasure of not just seeing, but also being able to touch and use the tableware in warm and appropriately evocative surroundings. The generosity that the service radiated communicated itself to the café's customers. The Lark service was and is distinguished functional art, according equal weight to function and to art.

See: *Lærkestellet. Den selvejende institution Keramikbanken af 1997 og Kunstindustrimuseet, København 1997.* Nielsen, T.: *Ursula Munch-Petersen,* Copenhagen 2004, pp. 164-169.
Gelfer-Jørgensen, M.: *Influences from Japan in Danish Art and Design 1870-2010*, Copenhagen 2013, pp. 258-260.

In the museum's collection the Lark service is registered under two main numbers: Mus.nos. 96/1997 and 97/1997, while a third number, 351/1997, covers several 'trial pieces' of slightly later date which were intended to be produced in a subsequent phase, and which therefore are not included in the original service. In the spirit of the project all the components of the Lark service and the trial pieces are included in a photograph of a collected display here in this catalogue.

Mus.no. 96/1997 a-å refers to:

Richard Manz:

bowls (a-e), cake plate (f, v), mugs (g-h, v-y), saucer (x)

(a) H 12.9 x Diam 33.9; Mark: 'Manz' inscribed on base with stamped lark symbol;
(b) H 11.1 x Diam 28.8; Mark: 'Manz' inscribed on base with stamped lark symbol;
(c) H 9.2 x Diam 25; Mark: 'Manz' inscribed on base with stamped lark symbol;
(d) H 8.2 x Diam 21.2; Mark: 'Manz' inscribed on base with stamped lark symbol;
(e) H 7.2 x Diam 18; Mark: 'Manz' inscribed on base with stamped lark symbol;
(f) H 3 x W 21; Mark: 'Manz' underglaze-painted on the base with stamped lark symbol;
(g) H 8 x Diam 7.2; Mark: 'R. Manz' underglaze-painted on the base with stamped lark symbol;
(h) H 7.7 x Diam 7.1; Mark: 'MANZ' underglaze-painted on base with stamped lark symbol;
(v) H 3 x L 21.3; Mark: 'Manz' underglaze-painted on the base with stamped lark symbol;
(x) H 2.7 x Diam 13.2; 'Manz' underglaze-painted on the base with stamped lark symbol;
(v-y); H 7.7 x Diam 7.2; Mark: 'RM' (monogram) underglaze-painted on base with stamped lark symbol (indistinct);

Ursula Munch-Petersen:

rhomboid dishes (i-j), cake dish (k)

(i) W 36 x L 44; Mark: stamped bear figure and URSULA in a square, with lark symbol, on base;
(j) W 28 x L 37.3; Mark: stamped bear figure and URSULA in a square, with lark symbol, on base;
(k) H 9.2 x Diam 96.7; Mark: stamped bear figure and URSULA in a square, with lark symbol, on base;

Bodil Manz:

pot-holders (l-n), sugar bowl (o), salt dish (p)

(l-n) H 10 x W 14; Mark: 'BODIL MANZ' underglaze-painted on base, with BMBM in square mark and stamped lark symbol;
(o) H 6.9 x Diam 11.2; Mark: 'MANZ' inscribed on base with stamped lark symbol;
(p) H 4.9 x Diam 8.2; Mark: 'MANZ' inscribed on base with stamped lark symbol;

Sys Thomsen:

dessert bowl (q)

(q) H 6.6 x Diam 12.7; Mark: 'Th' (Sys Thomsen's monogram) stamped on base with a lark symbol low on the outer side of the bowl;

Beate Andersen:

cream jugs (r-t), milk jug (u)

(r) H 11.2 x W 13.3; Mark: 'B' (for Beate Andersen) painted on base with stamped lark symbol;
(s) H 11.3 x W 13.9; Mark: 'B' (for Beate Andersen) painted on base with stamped lark symbol;
(t) H 11.9 x W 14; Mark: 'B' (for Beate Andersen) painted on base with stamped lark symbol;
(u) H 22 x W 20.5; Mark: 'B' (for Beate Andersen) painted on base with stamped lark symbol;

Ursula Munch-Petersen:

mug (z), saucer (æ), cream jugs (ø-å)

(z) H 10.2 x Diam 8.5; Mark: stamped bear figure and URSULA on base with lark symbol (indistinct);
(æ) Diam 13.3; Mark: 'UM-P' inscribed on base with stamped lark symbol;
(ø) H 5.5 x W 9; Mark: stamped bear figure on base with URSULA and lark symbol.
(å) H 7 x W 11.5; Mark: stamped bear figure on base with URSULA and lark symbol.

Mus.no. 97/1997 a-n refers to:

Birgitte and Hans Börjeson:

teapot (a-b), two coffee pots (e-h)

(a-b) H 21.4 x W 26.5; Mark: 'FULDBY' impressed below the lower handle-join, with a lark symbol;
(e-f) H 22.2 x W 21.5; Mark: stamped lark symbol below the handle;
(g-h) H 18.8 x W 18.7; Mark: 'FULDBY' impressed below the lower handle-join, with a lark symbol;

Bente Hansen:

teapot (c-d), teapot (l-m)

(c-d) H 21 x W 29.2; Mark: 'BH' (monogram) and '94' painted on base with a stamped lark symbol below the lower handle-join;
(l-m) H 18.8 x W 25; Mark: 'BH' (monogram) and'94' painted on base with a stamped lark symbol;

Sten Lykke Madsen:

two small candle-holders (i-j), large candle-holder (k)

(i) H 9.6 x W 16; Mark: 'STEN 94' in a wavy mark inscribed on base with a stamped lark symbol;
(j) H 9.5 x W 16; Mark: 'STEN 94' in a wavy mark inscribed on base with a stamped lark symbol;
(k) H 25.7 x W 19.8; Mark: 'STEN 1994' in a wavy mark with a stamped lark symbol;

Sys Thomsen:

salad bowl (n)

(n) H 6.2 x W 15.2; (n) Mark: 'Th' (Sys Thomsen's monogram) impressed low on the outer side with a lark symbol.

Mus.no. 351/1997 a-g refers to:

Bente Hansen:

cup (a)

(a) H 7.8 x W 10.7; Mark: 'BH' (monogram) and '98' stamped on base under glaze, with lark symbol;

Ursula Munch-Petersen:

cup and saucer (b-c), scoop (d), pentagonal bowl (e), rhomboid bowl (f), cream-jug (g)

(b) H 7 x W 12.7; Mark: 'FORM II, UM-P' inscribed on base;
(c) Diam 13.5; Mark: 'UM-P 2001' inscribed on base;
(d) H 4.5 x W 10.3; Mark: 'UM-P' inscribed low on the side with stamped lark symbol.
(e) H 3.3 x W 7.5; Mark: 'UM-P' inscribed low on the side with stamped lark symbol.
(f) H 2.2 x W 9.3.; Mark: 'UM-P' inscribed low on the side with stamped lark symbol.

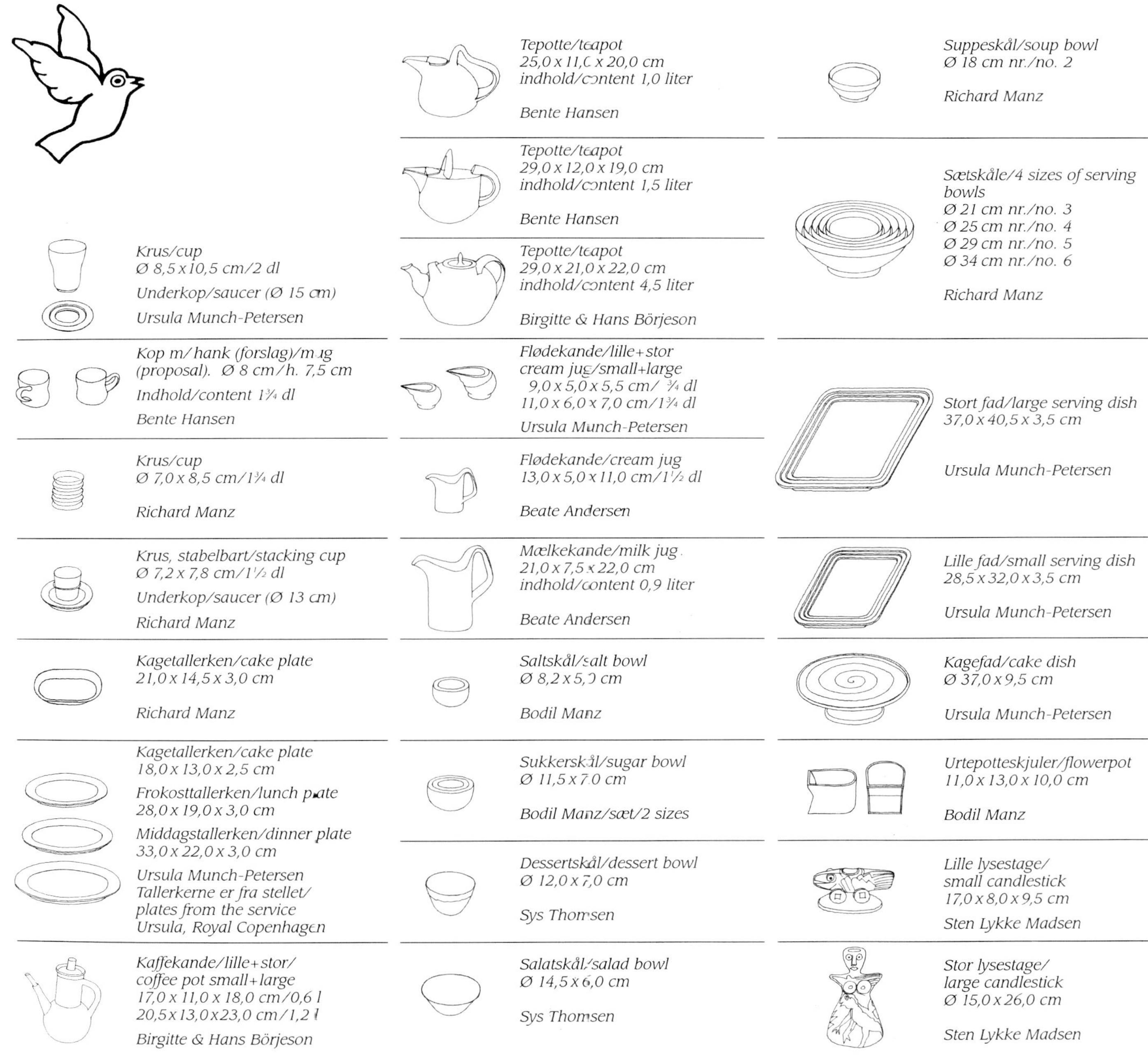

Krus/cup
Ø 8,5 x 10,5 cm/2 dl
Underkop/saucer (Ø 15 cm)
Ursula Munch-Petersen

Kop m/ hank (forslag)/mug
(proposal). Ø 8 cm/h. 7,5 cm
Indhold/content 1¾ dl
Bente Hansen

Krus/cup
Ø 7,0 x 8,5 cm/1¾ dl
Richard Manz

Krus, stabelbart/stacking cup
Ø 7,2 x 7,8 cm/1½ dl
Underkop/saucer (Ø 13 cm)
Richard Manz

Kagetallerken/cake plate
21,0 x 14,5 x 3,0 cm
Richard Manz

Kagetallerken/cake plate
18,0 x 13,0 x 2,5 cm
Frokosttallerken/lunch plate
28,0 x 19,0 x 3,0 cm
Middagstallerken/dinner plate
33,0 x 22,0 x 3,0 cm
Ursula Munch-Petersen
Tallerkerne er fra stellet/
plates from the service
Ursula, Royal Copenhagen

Kaffekande/lille+stor/
coffee pot small+large
17,0 x 11,0 x 18,0 cm/0,6 l
20,5 x 13,0 x 23,0 cm/1,2 l
Birgitte & Hans Börjeson

Tepotte/teapot
25,0 x 11,0 x 20,0 cm
indhold/content 1,0 liter
Bente Hansen

Tepotte/teapot
29,0 x 12,0 x 19,0 cm
indhold/content 1,5 liter
Bente Hansen

Tepotte/teapot
29,0 x 21,0 x 22,0 cm
indhold/content 4,5 liter
Birgitte & Hans Börjeson

Flødekande/lille+stor
cream jug/small+large
9,0 x 5,0 x 5,5 cm/ ¾ dl
11,0 x 6,0 x 7,0 cm/1¾ dl
Ursula Munch-Petersen

Flødekande/cream jug
13,0 x 5,0 x 11,0 cm/1½ dl
Beate Andersen

Mælkekande/milk jug
21,0 x 7,5 x 22,0 cm
indhold/content 0,9 liter
Beate Andersen

Saltskål/salt bowl
Ø 8,2 x 5,0 cm
Bodil Manz

Sukkerskål/sugar bowl
Ø 11,5 x 7,0 cm
Bodil Manz/sæt/2 sizes

Dessertskål/dessert bowl
Ø 12,0 x 7,0 cm
Sys Thomsen

Salatskål/salad bowl
Ø 14,5 x 6,0 cm
Sys Thomsen

Suppeskål/soup bowl
Ø 18 cm nr./no. 2
Richard Manz

Sætskåle/4 sizes of serving bowls
Ø 21 cm nr./no. 3
Ø 25 cm nr./no. 4
Ø 29 cm nr./no. 5
Ø 34 cm nr./no. 6
Richard Manz

Stort fad/large serving dish
37,0 x 40,5 x 3,5 cm
Ursula Munch-Petersen

Lille fad/small serving dish
28,5 x 32,0 x 3,5 cm
Ursula Munch-Petersen

Kagefad/cake dish
Ø 37,0 x 9,5 cm
Ursula Munch-Petersen

Urtepotteskjuler/flowerpot
11,0 x 13,0 x 10,0 cm
Bodil Manz

Lille lysestage/
small candlestick
17,0 x 8,0 x 9,5 cm
Sten Lykke Madsen

Stor lysestage/
large candlestick
Ø 15,0 x 26,0 cm
Sten Lykke Madsen

Illustration from the publication *Lærkestellet,* 1997, by John Vedel-Rieper.

Glossary of terms used in ceramics

Blue clay A malleable type of clay, that is commonly found in Denmark. After firing the clay becomes pale yellow/whitish in colour.

Body Term used for the pre-fired or completely fired clay substance.

Ceramics General term for clay that has undergone the ceramic process, i.e. has been fired at such a high temperature that the chemically bound water has been driven out of the material, and it has become indissoluble in water. The term "ceramics" covers e.g. earthenware, faience, stoneware and porcelain. Forms of the material are in rapid development, however, and are today being used in car motors, artificial ski slopes, knives etc. Space shuttles have ceramic insulation to prevent them burning up in the atmosphere.

Chamotte Clay that is fired at a high temperature, crushed and ground and then added to malleable clay to give it greater strength, porosity and texture. Chamotte can have a variety of granule-sizes or be ground down to 'flour'.

Clay General term for a large number of combinations of mineral materials. Clay can be fine-grained or coarse-grained. If it is fine-grained it has great plasticity, contains a lot of water and loses volume when it is dried or fired, with a high risk of cracking in the process. If it is coarse-grained, it has correspondingly less plasticity, contains less water and loses less volume. As a rule it is not a question of a choice between extremes. Clay is today made up of combinations of different types, designed for specific purposes.

Drying The water content of the clay is driven out, either by natural drying or in a drying kiln. The latter method allows the drying process to be controlled, for instance with a view to avoiding cracking.

Earthenware Ceramics fired at a low temperature (under c. 1050°). The term 'earthenware' covers both low-fired raku (c. 600°) and high-fired earthenware (1050°-1100°). Earthenware is porous and typically made of red or blue clay. It is often given a layer of slip on the surface.

Faience Is often classified as earthenware. There are many different types of faience, and it is not defined in exactly the same way in Italian, British, Dutch or German faience traditions. Faience differs technically from other types of earthenware in that the first firing (pre-firing) takes place at a higher temperature (c.1250°) than the subsequent glaze-firing (c.1100°). The name comes from the Italian ceramics-producing town of Faenza.

Glaze A mixture of different crystalline minerals which, when subjected to a melting process and subsequent cooling, creates a glass-like non-crystalline covering layer over a ceramic object. Depending on the composition of the glaze and the amount of lead, feldspar, quartz or coloured oxides it contains, the result may be matte, shiny, concealing, transparent or coloured. Glaze is related to glass.

Glaze-firing The last firing, in which, after pre-firing and glazing, the clay material is fired at the melting temperature of the glaze.

Horn-painted Decorated using cow horn or a similar tool.

Lead compounds general term for glazes in which the main fluxing agent is red lead oxide, which is extremely poisonous.

Leather-hard At a certain point during drying, clay reaches a stable stage in which it is still sufficiently moist to be worked on with a knife, scraper etc. The term 'leather-hard' is used of this stage.

Majolica Term of Italian origin used for a particular type of earthenware which was thought to have come from Majorca (hence the name). Majolica is white tin-glazed earthenware with polychrome over-glaze decoration. The term is sometimes used as an equivalent for faience, but it is not necessarily the same.

Oxides Metal oxides of e.g. iron, copper, manganese, cobalt, chrome etc. can be used to colour glaze and slip, or for over- and under-glaze decoration.

Porcelain Can be defined roughly as white vitrified and translucent pottery. It is usually fired at a high temperature, like stoneware, so that the clay particles melt together and become impervious to water without being distorted.

Porosity The capacity of clay to absorb water.

Pre-firing The first firing, which often serves to give the clay material a certain strength and porosity, so that the body is able to absorb the glaze. Pre-firing can be omitted, but is normally used because non-fired objects are difficult to handle for further processing.

Raku A form of firing in which the clay is fired at a very low temperature. Unlike ordinary ceramics fired at low temperature, Raku is taken directly out of the hot kiln, which is often constructed outdoors particularly for raku firing. The hot ceramic object is then placed in a closed container with flammable material, causing 'reduction', i.e. reduced access of oxygen. The special chemical compounds can result in relatively dark charred-looking surfaces.

Red clay The most common type of Danish clay, known, for example, from red brick, tiles and plant pots. The clay is suitable for raku-firing, and it can take on a particularly attractive colour when local reduction technique is used.

Reduction Form of firing in which the access of oxygen is restricted.

Salt-glazing One of the oldest known techniques used in Europe for making glazed stoneware. Used since the 16th century for mass-production of domestic objects in stoneware. Used by many Danish studio ceramicists.

Sgrafitto A technique of decoration in which a ceramic object is covered in slip and then some of the slip is scratched or scraped off again, so that the underlying surface becomes visible, creating decorative motifs.

Slip A thin paste of clay that may be coloured with oxides or dyes. Used either as decoration on the raw clay object or to cover it entirely. Slip can be applied with brush or horn, or by dipping.

Stoneware Ceramics made with stoneware clay, fired at a high temperature, vitrified, coloured or white, and non-translucent. This term covers a wide range of different types of clay. Common to almost all of them is a high content of kaolin and aluminium, which makes it possible to fire stoneware at high temperatures. Stoneware and porcelain overlap to a certain degree; both come from China / Korea, where in the past no distinction was made between them. Many of the earliest Chinese porcelain wares could be defined as stoneware.

Terracotta Italian term meaning "fired earth", used of fired unglazed earthenware.

Tin glaze Generic term for basic glazes which as a result of the addition of 5-10% tin oxide can form a white covering surface. Tin-glazed objects are well-suited to over-glaze decoration.

Under- and **over-glaze paint** These largely self-explanatory terms refer to paint products, usually bought ready to use, that can be applied as decoration either under or over the glaze.

Vitrification The process that occurs when clay is fired at a high temperature, so that the moisture in it evaporates and the other constituents melt together.

The Danish version of this glossary is an edited version of the one published in Keramisk Kunst, 1991, by Lise Seisbøll, used in the present context with the kind permission of the author.

Ceramic exhibitions in Designmuseum Danmark 1950 – 2010

1950 Danish Crafts and Design Association's Spring Exhibition *(Dansk Kunsthaandværks forårsudstilling)*
1951 Henning Seidelin – retrospective exhibition
1951 Danish Crafts and Design Association's Spring Exhibition *(Dansk Kunsthaandværks forårsudstilling)*
1952 Danish Crafts and Design Association's Spring Exhibition *(Dansk Kunsthaandværks forårsudstilling)*
1953 Bing & Grøndahl's Jubilee exhibition
1953 Danish Crafts and Design Association's Spring Exhibition *(Dansk Kunsthaandværks forårsudstilling)*
1953 *Saxbo – 25 years of stoneware / *Stentøj gennem 25 år*
1954 Axel Salto – solo exhibition
1955 *Asger Jorn – Ceramic works
1956 Young Danish Craftworkers / *Unge Danske Kunsthaandværkere*
1959 *Clay- weaving- wood / *Ler-Væv-Træ* – Adam Fischer, Lis Ahlmann, Børge Mogensen
1960 Stoneware / *Stentøj* – Nils Thorsson, Nils J. Kähler, Georg Hetting, Erik Reiff, Peder Rasmussen
1960 Ceramic tiles / *Keramiske fliser* - Else Fischer-Hansen
1962 Danish table services – before and now / *Danske Spisestel – før og nu*
1964 Stoneware – Christian Poulsen
1965 Modern Craftwork / *Moderne Kunsthåndværk 1915 – 1965*
1968 Form 68
1969 Nina Koppel & Erik Magnussen
1971 Stoneware - Erik Nyholm
1972 A Dutch ceramicist exhibits new works / *En hollandsk keramiker viser nye arbejder* – Sonja Landweer, Netherlands
1973 *Works in Porcelain / *Arbejder af porcelæn* – Kurt and Gerda Spurey, Austria
1973 Stoneware / *Stentøj/arkigrafi* – Lise Honoré and Steen Estvad
1973 A potter and his workshop / *En pottemager og hans værksted* – David Leach, England
1973 Stoneware from Norway / *Stentøj fra Norge* – Erik Ploen, Norway
1973 Ceramic Building Blocks– Glenys Barton, England
1973 Fire and clay / *Ild og ler* – works in stoneware – Ryozo Miki, Japan
1973 Stoneware - Bo Kristiansen
1974 Ceramics and drawings - Jens Thirslund
1974 *Kunsthåndværkergruppen* (Danish Crafts Group) – ceramics and textiles
1974 * Works in stoneware / *Stentøjsarbejder* – Inger Thing
1974 Retrospective exhibition – Gunnar Nylund, Sweden
1974 Stoneware sculptures / *Stentøjsskulpturer* – Carlos Carlé (Argentina/Italy)
1974 Stoneware - Emi Fuzii, Japan
1974 *Europäische Keramik zur Zeit des Jugendstils*, Hetjens Museum, Düsseldorf
1974 Summer in the museum's Stensal – Danish Crafts & Design Association / *Foreningen Dansk Kunsthåndværk og Industriel Design*
1974 * Stoneware, Lotte Glob
1975 Textiles and stoneware / *Textil og stentøj* – Kim Naver and Alev Siesbye
1975 Ceramic works - Dorothy Kazemi, Lebanon
1975 Ceramic pictures - Kirsten Christensen
1975 Blue Fluted China – 200 years of the Royal Porcelain Factory / *Musselmønstret – Den kongelige Porcelainsfabrik 200 år*
1975 Stoneware and textiles / *Stentøj og tekstil* – Inge Skov-Nielsen and Villy Olsen
1975 100 ceramic things / *100 Keramiske Ting* – Arne L. Hansen
1976 Glaze and Shape / *Glasur og Form* – Edith Sonne Bruun
1976 Project 75 –Ten ceramicists exhibit models for serial production / *Ti keramikere viser forarbejder til serieproduktioner*
1977 * Stoneware and textiles - Else Kamp Jensen and Synnøve Vedel
1977 Commercial ceramics and textiles from Southeast Asia / *Handelskeramik og Textiler fra Sydøstasien*
1977 New works in stoneware/ *Ny arbejder i stentøj* – Erik Nyholm

1977 ∗ *Strandstræde Keramik* – Beate Andersen, Jane Reumert, Gunhild Aaberg

1977 L. Hjort – A ceramic firm in Rønne / *En keramisk virksomhed i Rønne*

1977 ∗ Danish Crafts and Design / *Danske kunsthåndværkere*

1977 Modern Danish Crafts

1977 Variations in porcelain / *Variation i porcelæ* – Bodil and Richard Manz

1977 Johan van Loon – works made in 1977 at the Royal Porcelain Factory / *Arbejder udført 1977 på Den kongelige Porcelains-fabrik*

1977 Stoneware and printed fabric / *Stentøj og stoftryk* – Nathalie Krebs and Marie Gudme Leth

1978 Stoneware and textile pictures / *Stentøj og stofbilleder* — Merete Bloch and Nina Ferlov

1978 The snail with its house on its back wants to take a walk / *Sneglen med hus på ryggen vil vandre* – Dorthe Møller

1978 Decoration and Function / *Pryd og Nytte* – Bing & Grøndahls Jubilee exhibition

1978 ∗ Colours and Structures – stoneware and porcelain / *Farver og Strukturer - Stentøj og porcelæn* – Hans Munck Andersen and Gerd Hiort Petersen

1979 ∗ Works made at the Royal Porcelain Factory 1978-79 / *Arbejder udført 1978-79 på Den kongelige Porcelainsfabrik* – Ivan Weiss

1979 Transformation / *Forvandling* – Jette Arendal Winther and Lone Høyer Hansen

1979 Ceramics and Glass / *Keramik og glas* – Hiroaki Morino, Japan, and Finn Lynggaard

1980 Lis Ahlmanns legat (Bursary award exhibition) – Myre Vasegaard

1980 Ceramic Works / *Keramiske arbejder* – Lone Munkegaard

1980 Modern Australian Ceramics / *Moderne australsk keramik*

1981 ∗ Spring Notes / *Forårstoner* – Inger Thing and weaver Vibeke Gregers

1981 Ceramics in space / *Keramik i rum* – Karen Park, Ulla Viotti, Francesca Lindh

1981 Bjørn Wiinblad – 40 years of work / *Arbejder gennem 40 år*

1981 ∗Weaving and Raku – Dorthe Sigsgaard, Anne Lise Bruun Pedersen, Inger Rokkjær

1981 16+ two – Crafts and graphics / *Brugskunst og grafik*

1981 A German ceramicist in Japan / *En tysk keramiker i Japan* – Gerd Knäpper, Germany

1982 *Kunsthåndværkerrådets årspris* (Craft Council's Annual Prize-winner's Exhibition) – Gerd Hiort Petersen

1983 ∗ Pots, jugs, vessels / *Krukker, kander, kar* - Malene Müllertz

1983 Dish of the Day – about using a plate / *Dagens ret – om at bruge en tallerken* –Sys Thomsen

1983 Alev Siesbye - Stoneware / Tine Jolander – carpets...quilts... wall-hangings?

1983 Nature's poetry – new ceramic works / *Naturens poesi-nye keramiske arbejder* – Tove Anderberg

1984 Gertrud Vasegaard – Retrospective exhibition

1984 Arnold Krog and the Royal Porcelain Factory

1984 16+ three – Café and ceramics in Grønnegården

1986 Small services / *Små stel* – from the Royal Porcelain Factory

1986 *Kunsthåndværkerrådets årspris* (Craft Council's Annual Prize-winner's Exhibition) – Ursula Munch-Petersen

1987 ∗ Five Facets – new Danish craftwork/ *Fem facetter – nyt dansk kunsthåndværk*

1989 ∗ Jutland summer / *Jysk sommer*

1989 Burning moment / *Det brændende nu* – Axel Salto

1989 Lisbeth Munch-Petersen at 80

1990 Firing point – Danish ceramics 1890-1990 *Brændpunkter – dansk keramik*

1990 Kay Bojesens Mindelegat (Prize exhibition) - Bodil and Richard Manz

1991 Kay Bojesens Mindelegat (Prize exhibition) - Ursula Munch-Petersen

1991 My stoneware house and other pots with and without lids / *Mit stentøjshus og andre krukker med og uden låg* – Sys Thomsen

1992 *Jyllands Postens Kunstpris 1991* (Art prize exhibition) – Gerd Hiort Petersen

1992 Danish Ceramics' new roads to industry – new focus points / *Dansk keramiks veje til industrien – nye brændpunkter*

1994 * A Faithful Copy – seven fantastic fantasies around objects from the museum's collection / *En tro kopi – syv fantastiske fantasier over objekter fra museets samling*
1995 Three ceramicists – Karen Bennicke, Bente Hansen and Peder Rasmussen
1995 20 years of raku – Anne Lise Bruun Pedersen
1996 Unika – *Dansk kunsthåndværk* 1996
1996 The Lark table service / *Lærkestellet*
1997 *Kay Bojesens Mindelegat* (Prize exhibition) - Ole Jensen
1997 Danish Ceramics 1947-97 – from the museum's collections / *Dansk keramik 1947-1997 – fra Kunstindustrimuseets samlinger*
1997 * New Ceramic Boxes / *Nye keramiske æsker* – Malene Müllertz
1997 * New Ceramic Works / *Nye keramiske arbejder* – Julie Høm
1997 Danish Biennale for Craft and Design – Prize-winners' exhibition – Maiken Charlotte Bang & Flemming Tvede Hansen
1997 Thorvald Bindesbøll – a Danish pioneer
1999 Bodil and Richard Manz – Form-Transform 1966 -1999
1999 Ceramics and stone / *Keramik og sten* – Inge-Lise Koefoed
2000 Danish Porcelain 1775 -2000: Jubilee exhibition for Royal Scandinavia
2000 Asger Jorn and COBRA ceramics
2001 Danish Studio Ceramics / *Dansk værkstedskeramik* – from the museum's collections
2001 Contents/Void – Bente Hansen and Ole Palsby
2001 Kähler Ceramics 1839 -1969
2001 Clay in long strips / *Ler i lange baner* – Anne Lise Bruun Pedersen and Torill Galsøe
2002 * Alev Ebüzziya Siesbye – a ceramic universe 1964-2002 – retrospective exhibition
2002 The Shadow of Good Taste / *Skyggen af den gode smag* – Souvenix, by Anne Tophøj and Jobim A.M. Jochimsen
2003 Jane Reumert 1965-2003 – retrospective exhibition
2003 *New Danish Ceramics – Anne Tophøj, Bente Skjøttgaard, Flemming Tvede Hansen, Gitte Jungersen, Lone Skov Madsen, Michael Geertsen, Morten Løbner Espersen, Steen Ipsen and Turi Heisselberg Pedersen
2003 Memory – ten table services for dolls / *Ti dukkestel*
2004 There's Joy in Repetition – Helle Hove
2004 The Georg Jensen Prize – Ursula Munch-Petersen
2005 * New ceramic works – Jørgen Haugen Sørensen
2005 * Fuld form Fulby 1963-2005 – Birgitte and Hans Börjeson
2006 in reality...Danish Biennale for Craft and Design – Prize-winners' exhibition – Louise Hindsgavl and Mette Saabye
2007 * Network / *Netværk* – New ceramic works – Malene Müllertz
2007 END – 7 ceramicists from England, Norway and Denmark – Karen Bennicke, Martin Bodilsen Kaldahl, Alison Britton, Peder Rasmussen, Richard Slee, Martin Smith, Marit Tingleff
2007 Ceramics and design / *Keramik og design* – Ib Georg Jensen
2008 *Bodil Manz – retrospective exhibition
2008 New works - Gitte Jungersen
2008 Digital tools in the ceramic process / *Digitale redskaber i den keramiske proces* – Martin Bodilsen Kaldahl
2009 Time Out – Turi Heisselberg Pedersen and Lone Skov Madsen in dialogue with the museum's collections
2010 From China to Europe / *Fra Kina til Europa* – the secret of porcelain

* Where exhibition titles are marked with * , this indicates that the museum acquired works from them that are included in this catalogue.

Select bibliography

Abrahamsen, Lars (ed.): *Bornholmsk værkstedskeramik gennem 100 år.* Thisted, 2007

Adamson, Glenn: *The craft reader.* Oxford, 2010

Alev Ebüzziya Siesbye. Istanbul, 2016, ISBN 978-605-86784-3-9

Andersen, Johs. and Viggo Sten Møller: *Keramik. Keramisk teknik - keramisk kunst.* Copenhagen, 1946

Andersen, Sven Jørn and Eva Bræmer-Jensen (eds): *Den danske keramiktriennale.* Kolding, 1994, 1997 and 2002

Andersen, Troels (ed.): *Asger Jorn – Keramik* (dansk/tysk). Silkeborg, 1991

Bennicke, Karen (ed.): *Spatial Destabilization.* Copenhagen, 2016

Bloxham, Gerd: *Oversigt over dansk studiolertøj i perioden 1930-1960.* Eksamensopgave Københavns Universitet, 1990

Bloxham, Gerd: *Studiolertøj i tre årtier,* - in: Brændpunkter i dansk keramik 1890-1990. Copenhagen, 1990

Bloxham, Gerd: *Richard Kjærgaard. A modernist in Danish ceramics,* - in: Scandinavian Journal of Design History, vol.4, 1994, pp. 81-107. Copenhagen, 1994

Bloxham Zettersten, Gerd: *Perspective on Danish studio ceramics,* - in: Wendy Tarlow Kaplan & Hope Barkan: From the kilns of Denmark. Copenhagen, 2002, pp. 21-44

Bloxham Zettersten, Gerd and Arvid Honoré: *Strandstræde keramik - værkstedsfællesskab i 40 år.* Copenhagen, 2004

Bodelsen, Merete: *Stentøj fra Danmark,* - in: Dansk Kunsthåndværk, 25th year, no. 7. Copenhagen, 1952

Bodelsen, Merete: *Tradition og stilskifte i dansk stentøj,* - in: Porslin, nos. 5-6, 1960

Bornholms Museum: *L. Hjorth – keramik gennem 150 år.* Rønne, 2006

Britton, Alison: *The backstory,*- in: END. (Exhibition catalogue). Kunstindustrimuseet, Copenhagen, 2007

Britton, Alison: *Seing things.* London, 2012

Bruun, Nanna and Bodil Busk Laursen (eds): *Keramikeren Bodil Manz/ The Ceramist Bodil Manz.* Copenhagen, 2009

Burkard, Lene (ed.): *Mønstring : mellem arabesk og objekt / Patterns : between object and arabesque.* Odense, 2001

Christensen, Charlotte: *...at give af et godt Hjerte og et glad Sind.* Kunstindustrimuseets Venner 1910-2010. Copenhagen, 2010

Christiansen, Anne (ed.): *Fynske kunsthåndværkere, vol. II: Keramiske gæster.* Odense, 1995

Clark, Garth: *Shifting paradigms in contemporary ceramics: The Garth Clark and Mark Del Vecchio collection.* New Haven, 2012

Clark, Garth: *Ceramic millennium : Critical writings on ceramic history, theory, and art.* Halifax, 2006

Cooper, Emmanuel: *A history of world pottery.* London, 1988

Cooper, Emmanuel: *Contemporary ceramics.* London, 2009

Copenhagen Ceramics: *Copenhagen Ceramics.* Copenhagen, 2016

Damsbo, Mads og Louise Birch Sørensen (eds): *The Magic of Clay – Ceramics in Contemperary Art* (Danish/English). (Exhibition catalogue) Gl. Holtegaard. Copenhagen, 2011

Dannesboe, Kirsten (ed.): *Brændpunkter i dansk keramik 1890-1990.* Kunstindustrimuseet, Copenhagen, 1990

Dansk Kunsthåndværkerleksikon I-II. Copenhagen, 1979

De danske: Konsthantverk till livs, bruk och glädje. (Exhibition catalogue) Stockholm, 1984

Dirckinck-Holmfeld, Kim (ed.): *Transparency: The Ceramicist Jane Reumert.* Copenhagen, 2003

Domine Hansen, Claus: *Håndbog i studiokeramik: teori og teknik.* Vejle, 2003

Dormer, Peter: *The new ceramics: trends and traditions.* London, 1986

Dybdahl, Lars: *Det brændende nu: Axel Salto.* Kunstindustrimuseet, Copenhagen, 1989

Dybdahl, Lars: *Dansk keramik 1850-1945.* (Exhibition catalogue) Sophienholm, Lyngby, 1997

Dybdahl, Lars: *Keramisk polyfoni,* - in: *Peder Rasmussen : Album – retrospektiv keramik 1973-1998.* Næstved, 1998, pp. 3-20

Ertberg, Marianne: *Fransk art nouveau keramik i Danmark : fra Kunstindustrimuseets og John Hunovs samlinger / French art nouveau ceramics in Denmark : from the Museum of Decorative Art's and John Hunov's collections.* Vejen, 1999

Gelfer-Jørgensen, Mirjam: *Dansk kunsthåndværk fra 1850 til vor tid.* Copenhagen, 1982

Gelfer-Jørgensen, Mirjam: *Influences from Japan in Danish Art and Design 1870-2010.* Copenhagen, 2013

Gelfer-Jørgensen, Mirjam: *Pietro Krohn - Danmarks kunstneriske puls.* Copenhagen, 2014

Groom, Simon: *A secret history of clay.* London, 2004

Gutte Eriksen 50 års keramiske arbejder. (Exhibition catalogue) Copenhagen, 1987

Hagedorn-Olsen, Claus (ed.): *Komedien eller den Guddommelige : Bjørn Nørgård : en keramisk udsmykning på Horsens Rådhus.* Horsens, 1986

Hanaor, Ziggy: *Breaking the mould: new approaches to ceramics.* London, 2007

Hannover, Emil: *Det danske Kunstindustrimuseum I de første 25 Aar 1895-1920.* Copenhagen, 1920

Hannover, Emil: *Et Par Principper for Kunstindustrimuseets Erhvervelser af moderne danske Arbejder.* Skønvirke 1916, pp. 133-136

Hedebo, Lars: *Bjørn Wiinblad – en livskunstner.* Copenhagen, 2016

Hiort, Esbjørn: *Modern Danish ceramics.* New York, 1955

Hull, William: *Danish ceramic design.* (Exhibition catalogue). Pennsylvania, 1981

Jakobsen, Gunnar: *Dansk keramisk bibliografi.* (Danish/English/German). Copenhagen, 2014

Jydske krukker på Trapholt. (Exhibition catalogue). Kolding, 1991

Jørgensen, Henning: *Gertrud Vasegaard.* (English summary). Holstebro, 2011

Kaplan, Wendy Tarlow and Hope Barkan (eds): *From the kilns of Denmark – contemporary Danish ceramics.* Copenhagen, 2002

Karlsen, Arne and Anker Tiedemann: *Dansk brugskunst.* Copenhagen, 1960

Keramikkens underskov: aktuel keramik af yngre keramikere. (Exhibition catalogue). Copenhagen, 1993

Kjærgaard, Richard: *Scrapbog.* [without pagination], [1949-2003]

Kjærulf Møller, Lars (ed.): *Lisbet Munch-Petersen – gudinden fra Holkadalen.* Bornholm, 1989

Krogh, Leila: *Kunst i rummet – monumentaludsmykning i Danmark 1964-1988.* Copenhagen, 1989

Kuyken-Schneider, Dorris U.: *Deense keramiek Museum Boymans-van Beuningen verzameld 1970-1995 / Danish Ceramics Boymans-van Beuningen Museum collected 1970-1995.* Rotterdam, 1995

Lassen, Erik: *Keramik.* Copenhagen, 1968

Laursen, Bodil Busk (ed.): *Thorvald Bindesbøll – en dansk pioner.* Kunstindustrimuseet. Copenhagen, 1996

Laursen, Bodil Busk and Steen Nottelmann (eds): *Royal Danish Porcelain 1775-2000* . Copenhagen, 2000

Laursen, Bodil Busk: *Værkhistorie – The story of her works,* - in: *Keramikeren / The Ceramist Bodil Manz.* Copenhagen, 2008, pp. 9-75

Laursen, Bodil Busk: *Richard Manz – Keramiker, kunstner, menneske / Richard Manz – Ceramicist, artist, human being,* - in: *Keramikeren/ the ceramist Richard Manz.* Copenhagen, 2015, pp. 25-80

Lautrup-Larsen, Leif: *Stentøj: Den kongelige Porcelainsfabrik.* Copenhagen, 2007

Leach, Bernard: *A potter's book.* London, 1940

Lehmann-Brockhaus, Ursula: *Asger Jorn i Italien – værker i keramik, bronze og marmor 1954-1972.* Silkeborg, 2007

Lerche-Lerchenborg, Louise and John Vedel-Rieper (eds): *Lærkestellet.* Copenhagen, 1997

Lynggaard, Finn: *Keramisk håndbog.* Copenhagen, 1972

Løland, Majbritt & Pia Wirnfeldt (eds): *Bjørn Wiinblad. Lyst og livsværk. / An oeuvre of joy and delight.* Middelfart, 2012

MacNaughton, Mary Davis: *Clay's tectonic shift 1956-1968 : John Mason, Ken Price, Peter Voulkos.* Claremont, 2012

Manz, Cecilie (ed.): *Keramikeren: the ceramist Richard Manz.* (Danish/English). Copenhagen, 2015

Mazanti, Louise: *Superobjekter – en teori for nutidigt, konceptuelt kunsthåndværk.* Ph.D. Danmarks Designskole, 2006

McFadden, David Revere: *Scandinavian modern design 1880-1980.* New York, 1982

Munch-Petersen, Ursula: *Lerformning.* Copenhagen, 1982

Munch-Petersen, Ursula: *Easier said than done: craft, design and industry in the year 2001,* - in: Scandinavian Journal of Design History, vol. 12, pp. 48-57. Copenhagen, 2002

New Danish Ceramics: *New Danish Ceramics.* (Exhibition catalogue Danish/English). Copenhagen, [2003]

Nielsen, Teresa: *Gutte Eriksen.* Vejen, 2001

Nielsen, Teresa: *Ursula Munch-Petersen.* Copenhagen, 2004

Nielsen, Teresa: *Keramik i lange baner.* Vejen, 2009

Nyholm, Erik: *Keramikkens veje – artikler om keramik og kunst.* Silkeborg, 1986

Opie, Jennifer Hawkins: *Scandinavian ceramics & glass in the twentieth century.* London, 1989

Pedersen, Anne Lise Bruun: *Fra ler til potte. De ældste keramiske teknikker som inspiration i dag.* Copenhagen 1989

Poulsen, Christian: *Kunsthåndværkernes Verdensråd / World Crafts Council.* Copenhagen, 1967

Rasmussen, Peder: *Familie på træben: om J.F. Willumsens "Familievasen".* Copenhagen, 2016

Rasmussen, Peder: *Kählers værk.* Copenhagen, 2002

Rasmussen, Peder: *Keramisk kunst på Kählers Værksted 1993-2003.* Næstved, 2003

Seisbøll, Lise (ed.): *Britisk keramik / British Ceramics.2000.dk.* (Danish/English). Copenhagen, 2000

Seisbøll, Lise (ed.): *Fra ler til keramik.* Middelfart, 2002

Seisbøll, Lise: *Keramisk kunst – dansk kunstnerkeramik gennem 100 år.* Copenhagen, 1991

Seisbøll, Lise (ed.): *Til kunst skal du brændes / To Art be thou burnt. Keramisk kunst fra Tommerup 1985-1998 / Ceramic art from Tommerup 1985-1998.* Copenhagen, 1998

Serena, Lars: *Bornholmsk værkstedskeramik.* Rønne, 2004

Sieck, Frederik: *Dansk Kunsthåndværk og Kunstindustri 1931-1981 – belyst gennem glimt af Den Permanentes historie.* Copenhagen, 1981

Strandstræde keramik – værkstedsfællesskab i 40 år. Copenhagen, 2004

Tolstrup, Lisbeth: *Resumé 1966-1999 : Heidi Guthmann Birck, Aage Birck : skulptur, unika.* Copenhagen, 1999

Tvermoes, Michael (ed.): *Spillets regler. En bog om Helge Bertram.* Copenhagen, 1994

Veiteberg, Jorunn and Erik Steffensen: *Udstillingssted for ny keramik.* Copenhagen, 2002

Veiteberg, Jorunn: *Kunsthandverk – frå tause ting til talande objekt.* Oslo, 2005

Veiteberg, Jorunn (ed..): *Ting Tang Trash – Upcycling in Contemporary Ceramics.* Norway by HBO, 2011

Waal, Edmund de: *20th century ceramics.* London, 2003

Waal, Edmund de: *Bernard Leach.* London, 2003

Waal, Edmund de: *The pot book.* London, 2011

Watson, Oliver: *Studio pottery : twentieth century British ceramics in the Victoria and Albert Museum collection.* Oxford, 1990

Woldbye, Vibeke: *Gertrud Vasegaard – keramiske arbejder 1930-1984.* (Summary in English). (Exhibition catalogue). Kunstindustrimuseet. Copenhagen, 1984

Woldbye, Vibeke (ed.): *Alev Ebüzziya Siesbye – et keramisk univers 1964-2002.* (Exhibition catalogue). Kunstindustrimuseet. Copenhagen, 2002

Århus Kunstforening af 1847: *Dansk Keramik 1991: arbejder fra 22 værksteder.* Århus, 1991

This publication was made possible by a donation from the New Carlsberg Foundation on the occasion of its 100th anniversary in 2002

English translation: Joan F. Davidson

Photo of catalogue no. 1 – 632: Photographer Pernille Klemp

Other photographers:
Ole Akhøj: Catalogue no. 38, 320 og 322
Erik Brahl: Catalogue no. 321 og 323l

Layout: Design Factory Aps.
Typography: Proforma and Formata
Repro and printing: Narayana Press
Paper: Invercote 350g og Mat dobbeltbestrøget 130g

ISBN 978-87-90786-62-5

Front cover: Bente Hansen. Cat.no. 184. Mus.no. 305/2004
Indset detail: Malene Müllertz. Cat.nr. 375. Mus.no. 30/2002
Back cover: Gertrud Vasegaard. Cat.nr. 537. Mus.no. 9/1953